# Dodge Pick-ups Automotive Repair Manual

## by Jeff Killingsworth and John H Haynes

Member of the Guild of Motoring Writers

### Models covered:

Dodge Full-size Pick-ups

1994 through 2008 - 1500/2500/3500 models

*Does not include information specific to SRT-10 models*

Haynes Group Limited    (30042-6AA19)
Sparkford Nr Yeovil
Somerset BA22 7JJ England

ABCDE
FGHIJ
KLMNO
3

Haynes North America, Inc.
2801 Townsgate Road, Suite 340
Thousand Oaks, CA 91361 USA

www.haynes.com

## Acknowledgements

We are grateful to the Chrysler Corporation for providing technical information and certain illustrations. Special thanks to Bill Bunce, diesel technician at Crown Dodge of Ventura, CA. Technical writers who contributed to this project include Rob Maddox, Mike Stubblefield, Jay Storer, John Wegmann and Larry Warren. Some wiring diagrams originated exclusively for Haynes North America, Inc. by Solution Builders.

---

© **Haynes North America, Inc.  2005, 2008, 2018**
With permission from Haynes Group Limited

---

**A book in the Haynes Automotive Repair Manual Series**

---

**Printed in India**

---

---

**ISBN-13: 978-1-62092-287-3**
**ISBN-10: 1-62092-287-8**

---

**Library of Congress Catalog Card Number: 2018945180**

---

## Disclaimer

There are risks associated with automotive repairs. The ability to make repairs depends on individual skill, experience and proper tools. Individuals should act with due care, and acknowledge and assume the risk of making automotive repairs. While every attempt is made to ensure that the information in this manual is correct, no liability can be accepted by the authors or publishers for loss, damage or injury caused by any errors in, or omissions from, the information given.

---

# Contents

Haynes photographer, mechanic and author with 1995 Dodge Ram pickup

Haynes mechanic and photographer with a 2003 Dodge Ram pickup

# About this manual

## Its purpose

The purpose of this manual is to provide comprehensive, useful and accessible automotive repair information, to help you get the best value from your vehicle. It can do so in several ways. It can help you decide what work must be done, even if you choose to have it done by a dealer service department or a repair shop; it provides information and procedures for routine maintenance and servicing; and it offers diagnostic and repair procedures to follow when trouble occurs.

We hope you use the manual to tackle the work yourself. For many simpler jobs, doing it yourself may be quicker than arranging an appointment to get the vehicle into a shop and making the trips to leave it and pick it up. More importantly, a lot of money can be saved by avoiding the expense the shop must pass on to you to cover its labor and overhead costs. An added benefit is the sense of satisfaction and accomplishment that you feel after doing the job yourself. However, this manual is not a substitute for a professional certified technician or mechanic. There are risks associated with automotive repairs. The ability to make repairs on a vehicle depends on individual skill, experience and proper tools. Individuals should act with due care, and acknowledge and assume the risk of performing automotive repairs.

## Using the manual

The manual is divided into Chapters. Each Chapter is divided into numbered Sections, which are headed in bold type between horizontal lines. Each Section consists of consecutively numbered paragraphs.

The reference numbers used in illustration captions pinpoint the pertinent Section and the Step within that Section. That is, illustration 3.2 means the illustration refers to Section 3 and Step (or paragraph) 2 within that Section.

Procedures, once described in the text, are not normally repeated. When it's necessary to refer to another Chapter, the reference will be given as Chapter and Section number. Cross references given without use of the word "Chapter" apply to Sections and/or paragraphs in the same Chapter. For example, "see Section 8" means in the same Chapter. References to the left or right side of the vehicle assume you are sitting in the driver's seat, facing forward.

This repair manual is produced by a third party and is not associated with an individual car manufacturer. If there is any doubt or discrepancy between this manual and the owner's manual or the factory service manual, please refer to factory service manual or seek assistance from a professional certified technician or mechanic. Even though we have prepared this manual with extreme care, neither the publisher nor the author can accept responsibility for any errors in, or omissions from, the information given.

**NOTE**

A **Note** provides information necessary to properly complete a procedure or information which will make the procedure easier to understand.

**CAUTION**

A **Caution** provides a special procedure or special steps which must be taken while completing the procedure where the Caution is found. Not heeding a Caution can result in damage to the assembly being worked on.

**WARNING**

A **Warning** provides a special procedure or special steps which must be taken while completing the procedure where the Warning is found. Not heeding a Warning can result in personal injury.

# Introduction

Dodge Ram pick-ups are available in standard and quad-cab body styles. All cabs are single welded unit construction and bolted to the frame. Ram pick-ups are available in short-bed and long-bed models. All models are available in two-wheel drive (2WD) and four-wheel drive (4WD) versions.

Powertrain options include a 5.9L or 6.7L inline six-cylinder diesel engine; 3.7L or 3.9L V6 gasoline engine; 4.7L, 5.2L, 5.7L ("Hemi") or 5.9L V8 gasoline engine; 8.0L V10 gasoline engines. Transmissions used are either a three-speed, four-speed or six speed automatic, five-speed manual or six-speed manual.

Chassis layout is conventional, with the engine mounted at the front and the power being transmitted through either the manual or automatic transmission to a driveshaft and solid rear axle. On 4WD models a transfer case also transmits power to the front axle by way of a driveshaft.

2001 and earlier 1500 models/2002 and earlier 2500 and 3500 models: The front suspension on light duty 2WD models features an independent coil spring, upper and lower A-arm type front suspension, while 4WD and heavy duty 2WD models use coil springs and a solid rear axle located by four links. All models have a solid axle and leaf springs at the rear.

2002 and later 1500 models/2003 and later 2500 and 3500 models: The front suspension on 2WD models features an independent coil spring, upper and lower A-arm type front suspension, while heavy duty 4WD models use coil springs and a solid axle located by four links. Light-duty 4WD models with independent front suspension use torsion bars. All models have a solid axle and leaf springs at the rear.

All models are equipped with power assisted brakes. 2001 and earlier 1500 models and 2002 and earlier 2500/3500 models have front disc brakes and rear drum brakes. 2002 and later 1500 models and 2003 and later 2500/3500 models have front disc brakes and rear drum brakes. A Rear Wheel Anti-Lock (RWAL) braking system is standard; a four-wheel Anti-lock Braking System (ABS) is used on some models.

# Vehicle identification numbers

1    Modifications are a continuing and unpublicized process in vehicle manufacturing. Since spare parts manuals and lists are compiled on a numerical basis, the individual vehicle numbers are essential to correctly identify the component required.

## Vehicle Identification Number (VIN)

2    This very important identification number is stamped on a plate attached to the left side of the dashboard just inside the windshield on the driver's side of the vehicle (see illustration). The VIN also appears on the Vehicle Certificate of Title and Registration. It contains information such as where and when the vehi-

cle was manufactured, the model year and the body style.

## VIN year and engine codes

3    Two particularly important pieces of information located in the VIN are the model year and engine code. Counting from the left, the engine code is the eighth digit and the model year code is the 10th digit.

On the models covered by this manual the engine codes are:

K............... 3.7L V6
X............... 3.9L V6
N............... 4.7L V8
Y ............... 5.2L V8
D............... 5.7L V8
6 ............... 5.9L inline 6-cylinder diesel
C............... 5.9L inline 6 cylinder
                diesel H.O.(high-output)
Z ............... 5.9L V8
5 ............... 5.9L V8 heavy duty
7 ............... 5.9L inline 6-cylinder diesel,
                H.O. (high-output)
A............... 6.7L inline 6-cylinder diesel
W.............. 8.0L V10

On the models covered by this manual the model year codes are:

R............... 1994
S............... 1995
T ............... 1996
V ............... 1997
W.............. 1998
X............... 1999

Y............... 2000
1 ............... 2001
2 ............... 2002
3 ............... 2003
4 ............... 2004
5 ............... 2005
6 ............... 2006
7 ............... 2007
8 ............... 2008

## Equipment identification plate

4    This plate is located on the inside of the hood. It contains valuable information concerning the production of the vehicle as well as information on all production or special equipment.

## Safety Certification label

5    The Safety Certification label is affixed to the end of the left front door (see illustration), or to the door pillar. The plate contains the name of the manufacturer, the month and year of production, the Gross Vehicle Weight Rating (GVWR) and the safety certification statement. This label also contains the paint code. It is especially useful for matching the color and type of paint during repair work.

## Engine identification number

6    The engine ID number on gasoline engines is located on either the left or right side of the engine block, on a machined pad near the engine mount (see illustration). On diesel engines, the engine data plate is located on the left (driver's) side of the engine in front of the fuel injection pump.

3.2 The VIN is visible from the outside of the vehicle, through the driver's side of the windshield

3.5 Typical Safety Certification label

3.6 On Hemi engines the identification number is located on a pad near the right side engine mount

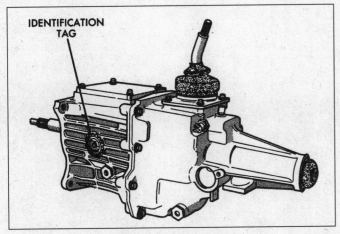

3.7a Typical manual transmission identification number location

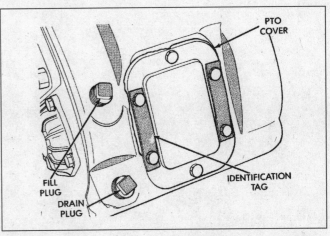

3.7b On NV-4500 transmissions the identification tag is attached to the PTO cover

## Transmission identification number

7    The ID number on manual transmissions is located on the left side of the case **(see illustrations)**. On automatic transmissions, the number is stamped on the left side of the transmission case above the oil pan flange **(see illustration)**.

## Transfer case identification number

8    The transfer case identification plate is attached to the rear side of the case **(see illustration)**.

## Axle identification numbers

9    On both front and rear axles the identification number is located on a tag attached to the differential cover **(see illustration)**.

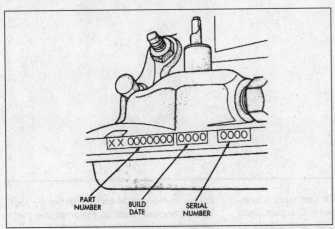

3.7c Automatic transmission identification number pad location - early models

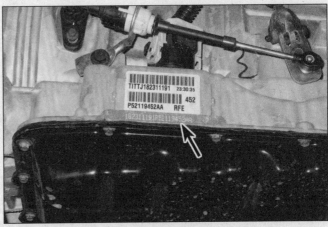

3.7d Automatic transmission identification number location - later models

3.8 Typical transfer case identification tag location

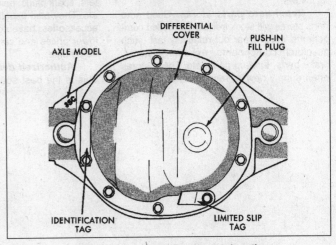

3.9 Typical axle identification tag location

# Buying parts

Replacement parts are available from many sources, which generally fall into one of two categories - authorized dealer parts departments and independent retail auto parts stores. Our advice concerning these parts is as follows:

*Retail auto parts stores:* Good auto parts stores will stock frequently needed components which wear out relatively fast, such as clutch components, exhaust systems, brake parts, tune-up parts, etc. These stores often supply new or reconditioned parts on an exchange basis, which can save a considerable amount of money. Discount auto parts stores are often very good places to buy materials and parts needed for general vehicle maintenance such as oil, grease, filters, spark plugs, belts, touch-up paint, bulbs, etc. They also usually sell tools and general accessories, have convenient hours, charge lower prices and can often be found not far from home.

*Authorized dealer parts department:* This is the best source for parts which are unique to the vehicle and not generally available elsewhere (such as major engine parts, transmission parts, trim pieces, etc.).

*Warranty information:* If the vehicle is still covered under warranty, be sure that any replacement parts purchased - regardless of the source - do not invalidate the warranty!

To be sure of obtaining the correct parts, have engine and chassis numbers available and, if possible, take the old parts along for positive identification.

# Maintenance techniques, tools and working facilities

## Maintenance techniques

There are a number of techniques involved in maintenance and repair that will be referred to throughout this manual. Application of these techniques will enable the home mechanic to be more efficient, better organized and capable of performing the various tasks properly, which will ensure that the repair job is thorough and complete.

## Fasteners

Fasteners are nuts, bolts, studs and screws used to hold two or more parts together. There are a few things to keep in mind when working with fasteners. Almost all of them use a locking device of some type, either a lockwasher, locknut, locking tab or thread adhesive. All threaded fasteners should be clean and straight, with undamaged threads and undamaged corners on the hex head where the wrench fits. Develop the habit of replacing all damaged nuts and bolts with new ones. Special locknuts with nylon or fiber inserts can only be used once. If they are removed, they lose their locking ability and must be replaced with new ones.

Rusted nuts and bolts should be treated with a penetrating fluid to ease removal and prevent breakage. Some mechanics use turpentine in a spout-type oil can, which works quite well. After applying the rust penetrant, let it work for a few minutes before trying to loosen the nut or bolt. Badly rusted fasteners may have to be chiseled or sawed off or removed with a special nut breaker, available at tool stores.

If a bolt or stud breaks off in an assembly, it can be drilled and removed with a special tool commonly available for this purpose. Most automotive machine shops can perform this task, as well as other repair procedures, such as the repair of threaded holes that have been stripped out.

Flat washers and lockwashers, when removed from an assembly, should always be replaced exactly as removed. Replace any damaged washers with new ones. Never use a lockwasher on any soft metal surface (such as aluminum), thin sheet metal or plastic.

## Fastener sizes

For a number of reasons, automobile manufacturers are making wider and wider use of metric fasteners. Therefore, it is important to be able to tell the difference between standard (sometimes called U.S. or SAE) and metric hardware, since they cannot be interchanged.

All bolts, whether standard or metric, are sized according to diameter, thread pitch and length. For example, a standard 1/2 - 13 x 1 bolt is 1/2 inch in diameter, has 13 threads per inch and is 1 inch long. An M12 - 1.75 x 25 metric bolt is 12 mm in diameter, has a thread pitch of 1.75 mm (the distance between threads) and is 25 mm long. The two bolts are nearly identical, and easily confused, but they are not interchangeable.

In addition to the differences in diameter, thread pitch and length, metric and standard bolts can also be distinguished by examining the bolt heads. To begin with, the distance across the flats on a standard bolt head is measured in inches, while the same dimension on a metric bolt is sized in millimeters (the same is true for nuts). As a result, a standard wrench should not be used on a metric bolt and a metric wrench should not be used on a standard bolt. Also, most standard bolts have slashes radiating out from the center of the head to denote the grade or strength of the bolt, which is an indication of the amount of torque that can be applied to it. The greater the number of slashes, the greater the strength of the bolt. Grades 0 through 5 are commonly used on automobiles. Metric bolts have a property class (grade) number, rather than a slash, molded into their heads to indicate bolt strength. In this case, the higher the number, the stronger the bolt. Property class numbers 8.8, 9.8 and 10.9 are commonly used on automobiles.

Strength markings can also be used to distinguish standard hex nuts from metric hex nuts. Many standard nuts have dots stamped into one side, while metric nuts are marked with a number. The greater the number of

dots, or the higher the number, the greater the strength of the nut.

Metric studs are also marked on their ends according to property class (grade). Larger studs are numbered (the same as metric bolts), while smaller studs carry a geometric code to denote grade.

It should be noted that many fasteners, especially Grades 0 through 2, have no distinguishing marks on them. When such is the case, the only way to determine whether it is standard or metric is to measure the thread pitch or compare it to a known fastener of the same size.

Standard fasteners are often referred to as SAE, as opposed to metric. However, it should be noted that SAE technically refers to a non-metric fine thread fastener only. Coarse thread non-metric fasteners are referred to as USS sizes.

Since fasteners of the same size (both standard and metric) may have different

strength ratings, be sure to reinstall any bolts, studs or nuts removed from your vehicle in their original locations. Also, when replacing a fastener with a new one, make sure that the new one has a strength rating equal to or greater than the original.

## Tightening sequences and procedures

Most threaded fasteners should be tightened to a specific torque value (torque is the twisting force applied to a threaded component such as a nut or bolt). Overtightening the fastener can weaken it and cause it to break, while undertightening can cause it to eventually come loose. Bolts, screws and studs, depending on the material they are made of and their thread diameters, have specific torque values, many of which are noted in the Specifications at the beginning of each Chapter. Be sure to follow the torque recommen-

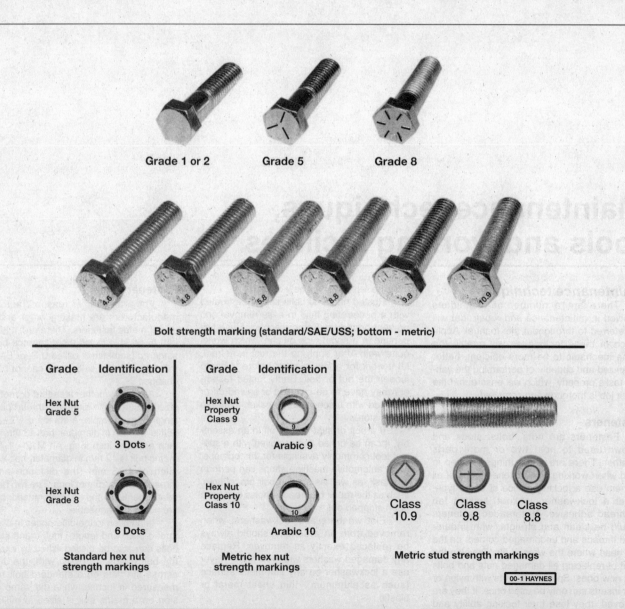

Bolt strength marking (standard/SAE/USS; bottom - metric)

| Grade | Identification |
|---|---|
| Hex Nut Grade 5 | 3 Dots |
| Hex Nut Grade 8 | 6 Dots |

**Standard hex nut strength markings**

| Grade | Identification |
|---|---|
| Hex Nut Property Class 9 | Arabic 9 |
| Hex Nut Property Class 10 | Arabic 10 |

**Metric hex nut strength markings**

Class 10.9          Class 9.8          Class 8.8

**Metric stud strength markings**

00-1 HAYNES

dations closely. For fasteners not assigned a specific torque, a general torque value chart is presented here as a guide. These torque values are for dry (unlubricated) fasteners threaded into steel or cast iron (not aluminum). As was previously mentioned, the size and grade of a fastener determine the amount of torque that can safely be applied to it. The figures listed here are approximate for Grade 2 and Grade 3 fasteners. Higher grades can tolerate higher torque values.

Fasteners laid out in a pattern, such as cylinder head bolts, oil pan bolts, differential cover bolts, etc., must be loosened or tightened in sequence to avoid warping the component. This sequence will normally be shown in the appropriate Chapter. If a specific pattern is not given, the following procedures can be used to prevent warping.

Initially, the bolts or nuts should be assembled finger-tight only. Next, they should be tightened one full turn each, in a criss-cross or diagonal pattern. After each one has been tightened one full turn, return to the first one and tighten them all one-half turn, following the same pattern. Finally, tighten each of them one-quarter turn at a time until each fastener has been tightened to the proper torque. To loosen and remove the fasteners, the procedure would be reversed.

| Metric thread sizes | Ft-lbs | Nm |
|---|---|---|
| M-6 | 6 to 9 | 9 to 12 |
| M-8 | 14 to 21 | 19 to 28 |
| M-10 | 28 to 40 | 38 to 54 |
| M-12 | 50 to 71 | 68 to 96 |
| M-14 | 80 to 140 | 109 to 154 |

| Pipe thread sizes | | |
|---|---|---|
| 1/8 | 5 to 8 | 7 to 10 |
| 1/4 | 12 to 18 | 17 to 24 |
| 3/8 | 22 to 33 | 30 to 44 |
| 1/2 | 25 to 35 | 34 to 47 |

| U.S. thread sizes | | |
|---|---|---|
| 1/4 - 20 | 6 to 9 | 9 to 12 |
| 5/16 - 18 | 12 to 18 | 17 to 24 |
| 5/16 - 24 | 14 to 20 | 19 to 27 |
| 3/8 - 16 | 22 to 32 | 30 to 43 |
| 3/8 - 24 | 27 to 38 | 37 to 51 |
| 7/16 - 14 | 40 to 55 | 55 to 74 |
| 7/16 - 20 | 40 to 60 | 55 to 81 |
| 1/2 - 13 | 55 to 80 | 75 to 108 |

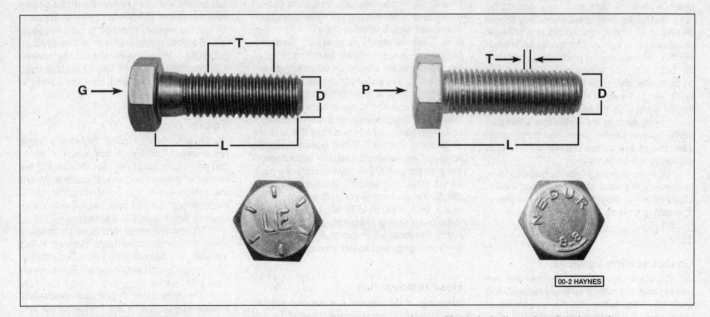

00-2 HAYNES

**Standard (SAE and USS) bolt dimensions/grade marks**

G   Grade marks (bolt strength)
L   Length (in inches)
T   Thread pitch (number of threads per inch)
D   Nominal diameter (in inches)

**Metric bolt dimensions/grade marks**

P   Property class (bolt strength)
L   Length (in millimeters)
T   Thread pitch (distance between threads in millimeters)
D   Diameter

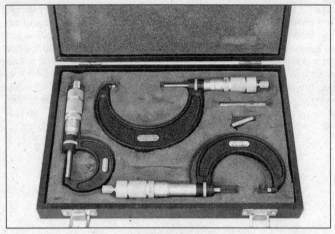

**Micrometer set**

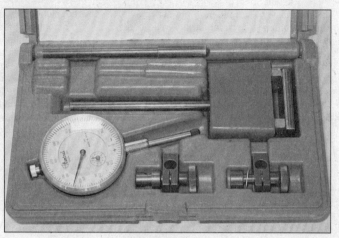

**Dial indicator set**

## Component disassembly

Component disassembly should be done with care and purpose to help ensure that the parts go back together properly. Always keep track of the sequence in which parts are removed. Make note of special characteristics or marks on parts that can be installed more than one way, such as a grooved thrust washer on a shaft. It is a good idea to lay the disassembled parts out on a clean surface in the order that they were removed. It may also be helpful to make sketches or take instant photos of components before removal.

When removing fasteners from a component, keep track of their locations. Sometimes threading a bolt back in a part, or putting the washers and nut back on a stud, can prevent mix-ups later. If nuts and bolts cannot be returned to their original locations, they should be kept in a compartmented box or a series of small boxes. A cupcake or muffin tin is ideal for this purpose, since each cavity can hold the bolts and nuts from a particular area (i.e. oil pan bolts, valve cover bolts, engine mount bolts, etc.). A pan of this type is especially helpful when working on assemblies with very small parts, such as the carburetor, alternator, valve train or interior dash and trim pieces. The cavities can be marked with paint or tape to identify the contents.

Whenever wiring looms, harnesses or connectors are separated, it is a good idea to identify the two halves with numbered pieces of masking tape so they can be easily reconnected.

## Gasket sealing surfaces

Throughout any vehicle, gaskets are used to seal the mating surfaces between two parts and keep lubricants, fluids, vacuum or pressure contained in an assembly.

Many times these gaskets are coated with a liquid or paste-type gasket sealing compound before assembly. Age, heat and pressure can sometimes cause the two parts to stick together so tightly that they are very difficult to separate. Often, the assembly can be loosened by striking it with a soft-face hammer near the mating surfaces. A regular hammer can be used if a block of wood is placed between the hammer and the part. Do not hammer on cast parts or parts that could be easily damaged. With any particularly stubborn part, always recheck to make sure that every fastener has been removed.

Avoid using a screwdriver or bar to pry apart an assembly, as they can easily mar the gasket sealing surfaces of the parts, which must remain smooth. If prying is absolutely necessary, use an old broom handle, but keep in mind that extra clean up will be necessary if the wood splinters.

After the parts are separated, the old gasket must be carefully scraped off and the gasket surfaces cleaned. Stubborn gasket material can be soaked with rust penetrant or treated with a special chemical to soften it so it can be easily scraped off. **Caution:** *Never use gasket removal solutions or caustic chemicals on plastic or other composite components.* A scraper can be fashioned from a piece of copper tubing by flattening and sharpening one end. Copper is recommended because it is usually softer than the surfaces to be scraped, which reduces the chance of gouging the part. Some gaskets can be removed with a wire brush, but regardless of the method used, the mating surfaces must be left clean and smooth. If for some reason the gasket surface is gouged, then a gasket sealer thick enough to fill scratches will have to be used during reassembly of the components. For most applications, a non-drying (or semi-drying) gasket sealer should be used.

## Hose removal tips

**Warning:** *If the vehicle is equipped with air conditioning, do not disconnect any of the A/C hoses without first having the system depressurized by a dealer service department or a service station.*

Hose removal precautions closely parallel gasket removal precautions. Avoid scratching or gouging the surface that the hose mates against or the connection may leak. This is especially true for radiator hoses. Because of various chemical reactions, the rubber in hoses can bond itself to the metal spigot that the hose fits over. To remove a hose, first loosen the hose clamps that secure it to the spigot. Then, with slip-joint pliers, grab the hose at the clamp and rotate it around the spigot. Work it back and forth until it is completely free, then pull it off. Silicone or other lubricants will ease removal if they can be applied between the hose and the outside of the spigot. Apply the same lubricant to the inside of the hose and the outside of the spigot to simplify installation.

As a last resort (and if the hose is to be replaced with a new one anyway), the rubber can be slit with a knife and the hose peeled from the spigot. If this must be done, be careful that the metal connection is not damaged.

If a hose clamp is broken or damaged, do not reuse it. Wire-type clamps usually weaken with age, so it is a good idea to replace them with screw-type clamps whenever a hose is removed.

## Tools

A selection of good tools is a basic requirement for anyone who plans to maintain and repair his or her own vehicle. For the owner who has few tools, the initial investment might seem high, but when compared to the spiraling costs of professional auto maintenance and repair, it is a wise one.

To help the owner decide which tools are needed to perform the tasks detailed in this manual, the following tool lists are offered: *Maintenance and minor repair, Repair/overhaul* and *Special*.

The newcomer to practical mechanics should start off with the *maintenance and minor repair* tool kit, which is adequate for the simpler jobs performed on a vehicle. Then, as confidence and experience grow, the owner can tackle more difficult tasks, buying additional tools as they are needed. Eventually the basic kit will be expanded into the *repair and overhaul* tool set. Over a period of time, the

Dial caliper

Hand-operated vacuum pump

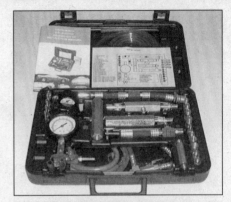

Fuel pressure gauge set

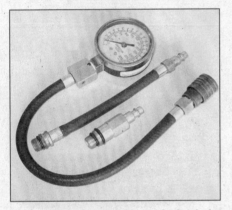

Compression gauge with spark plug hole adapter

Damper/steering wheel puller

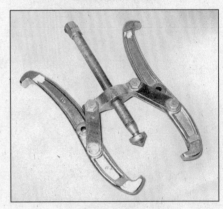

General purpose puller

Hydraulic lifter removal tool

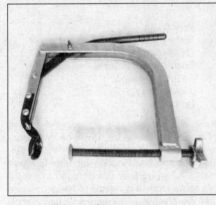

Valve spring compressor

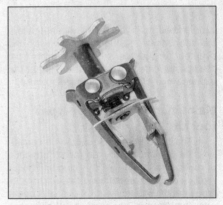

Valve spring compressor

Ridge reamer

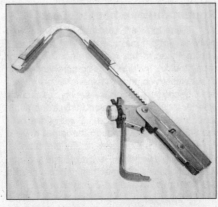

Piston ring groove cleaning tool

Ring removal/installation tool

Ring compressor

Cylinder hone

Brake hold-down spring tool

Torque angle gauge

Clutch plate alignment tool

Tap and die set

experienced do-it-yourselfer will assemble a tool set complete enough for most repair and overhaul procedures and will add tools from the special category when it is felt that the expense is justified by the frequency of use.

## Maintenance and minor repair tool kit

The tools in this list should be considered the minimum required for performance of routine maintenance, servicing and minor repair work. We recommend the purchase of combination wrenches (box-end and open-end combined in one wrench). While more expensive than open end wrenches, they offer the advantages of both types of wrench.

*Combination wrench set (1/4-inch to 1 inch or 6 mm to 19 mm)*
*Adjustable wrench, 8 inch*
*Spark plug wrench with rubber insert*
*Spark plug gap adjusting tool*
*Feeler gauge set*
*Brake bleeder wrench*
*Standard screwdriver (5/16-inch x 6 inch)*
*Phillips screwdriver (No. 2 x 6 inch)*
*Combination pliers - 6 inch*
*Hacksaw and assortment of blades*
*Tire pressure gauge*
*Grease gun*
*Oil can*
*Fine emery cloth*

*Wire brush*
*Battery post and cable cleaning tool*
*Oil filter wrench*
*Funnel (medium size)*
*Safety goggles*
*Jackstands (2)*
*Drain pan*

**Note:** *If basic tune-ups are going to be part of routine maintenance, it will be necessary to purchase a good quality stroboscopic timing light and combination tachometer/dwell meter. Although they are included in the list of special tools, it is mentioned here because they are absolutely necessary for tuning most vehicles properly.*

## Repair and overhaul tool set

These tools are essential for anyone who plans to perform major repairs and are in addition to those in the maintenance and minor repair tool kit. Included is a comprehensive set of sockets which, though expensive, are invaluable because of their versatility, especially when various extensions and drives are available. We recommend the 1/2-inch drive over the 3/8-inch drive. Although the larger drive is bulky and more expensive, it has the capacity of accepting a very wide range of large sockets. Ideally, however, the mechanic should have a 3/8-inch drive set and a 1/2-inch drive set.

*Socket set(s)*
*Reversible ratchet*

*Extension - 10 inch*
*Universal joint*
*Torque wrench (same size drive as sockets)*
*Ball peen hammer - 8 ounce*
*Soft-face hammer (plastic/rubber)*
*Standard screwdriver (1/4-inch x 6 inch)*
*Standard screwdriver (stubby - 5/16-inch)*
*Phillips screwdriver (No. 3 x 8 inch)*
*Phillips screwdriver (stubby - No. 2)*
*Pliers - vise grip*
*Pliers - lineman's*
*Pliers - needle nose*
*Pliers - snap-ring (internal and external)*
*Cold chisel - 1/2-inch*
*Scribe*
*Scraper (made from flattened copper tubing)*
*Centerpunch*
*Pin punches (1/16, 1/8, 3/16-inch)*
*Steel rule/straightedge - 12 inch*
*Allen wrench set (1/8 to 3/8-inch or 4 mm to 10 mm)*
*A selection of files*
*Wire brush (large)*
*Jackstands (second set)*
*Jack (scissor or hydraulic type)*

**Note:** *Another tool which is often useful is an electric drill with a chuck capacity of 3/8-inch and a set of good quality drill bits.*

## Special tools

The tools in this list include those which are not used regularly, are expensive to buy, or which need to be used in accordance with their manufacturer's instructions. Unless these tools will be used frequently, it is not very economical to purchase many of them. A consideration would be to split the cost and use between yourself and a friend or friends. In addition, most of these tools can be obtained from a tool rental shop on a temporary basis.

This list primarily contains only those tools and instruments widely available to the public, and not those special tools produced by the vehicle manufacturer for distribution to dealer service departments. Occasionally, references to the manufacturer's special tools are included in the text of this manual. Generally, an alternative method of doing the job without the special tool is offered. However, sometimes there is no alternative to their use. Where this is the case, and the tool cannot be purchased or borrowed, the work should be turned over to the dealer service department or an automotive repair shop.

*Valve spring compressor*
*Piston ring groove cleaning tool*
*Piston ring compressor*
*Piston ring installation tool*
*Cylinder compression gauge*
*Cylinder ridge reamer*
*Cylinder surfacing hone*
*Cylinder bore gauge*
*Micrometers and/or dial calipers*
*Hydraulic lifter removal tool*
*Balljoint separator*
*Universal-type puller*
*Impact screwdriver*
*Dial indicator set*
*Stroboscopic timing light (inductive pick-up)*
*Hand operated vacuum/pressure pump*
*Tachometer/dwell meter*
*Universal electrical multimeter*
*Cable hoist*
*Brake spring removal and installation tools*
*Floor jack*

## Buying tools

For the do-it-yourselfer who is just starting to get involved in vehicle maintenance and repair, there are a number of options available when purchasing tools. If maintenance and minor repair is the extent of the work to be done, the purchase of individual tools is satisfactory. If, on the other hand, extensive work is planned, it would be a good idea to purchase a modest tool set from one of the large retail chain stores. A set can usually be bought at a substantial savings over the individual tool prices, and they often come with a tool box. As additional tools are needed, add-on sets, individual tools and a larger tool box can be purchased to expand the tool selection. Building a tool set gradually allows the cost of the tools to be spread over a longer period of time and gives the mechanic the freedom to choose only those tools that will actually be used.

Tool stores will often be the only source of some of the special tools that are needed, but regardless of where tools are bought, try to avoid cheap ones, especially when buying screwdrivers and sockets, because they won't last very long. The expense involved in replacing cheap tools will eventually be greater than the initial cost of quality tools.

## Care and maintenance of tools

Good tools are expensive, so it makes sense to treat them with respect. Keep them clean and in usable condition and store them properly when not in use. Always wipe off any dirt, grease or metal chips before putting them away. Never leave tools lying around in the work area. Upon completion of a job, always check closely under the hood for tools that may have been left there so they won't get lost during a test drive.

Some tools, such as screwdrivers, pliers, wrenches and sockets, can be hung on a panel mounted on the garage or workshop wall, while others should be kept in a tool box or tray. Measuring instruments, gauges, meters, etc. must be carefully stored where they cannot be damaged by weather or impact from other tools.

When tools are used with care and stored properly, they will last a very long time. Even with the best of care, though, tools will wear out if used frequently. When a tool is damaged or worn out, replace it. Subsequent jobs will be safer and more enjoyable if you do.

## *How to repair damaged threads*

Sometimes, the internal threads of a nut or bolt hole can become stripped, usually from overtightening. Stripping threads is an all-too-common occurrence, especially when working with aluminum parts, because aluminum is so soft that it easily strips out.

Usually, external or internal threads are only partially stripped. After they've been cleaned up with a tap or die, they'll still work. Sometimes, however, threads are badly damaged. When this happens, you've got three choices:

1) *Drill and tap the hole to the next suitable oversize and install a larger diameter bolt, screw or stud.*
2) *Drill and tap the hole to accept a threaded plug, then drill and tap the plug to the original screw size. You can also buy a plug already threaded to the original size. Then you simply drill a hole to the specified size, then run the threaded plug into the hole with a bolt and jam nut. Once the plug is fully seated, remove the jam nut and bolt.*
3) *The third method uses a patented thread repair kit like Heli-Coil or Slimsert. These easy-to-use kits are designed to repair damaged threads in straight-through holes and blind holes. Both are available as kits which can handle a variety of sizes and thread patterns. Drill the hole, then tap it with the special included tap. Install the Heli-Coil and the hole is back to its original diameter and thread pitch.*

Regardless of which method you use, be sure to proceed calmly and carefully. A little impatience or carelessness during one of these relatively simple procedures can ruin your whole day's work and cost you a bundle if you wreck an expensive part.

## *Working facilities*

Not to be overlooked when discussing tools is the workshop. If anything more than routine maintenance is to be carried out, some sort of suitable work area is essential.

It is understood, and appreciated, that many home mechanics do not have a good workshop or garage available, and end up removing an engine or doing major repairs outside. It is recommended, however, that the overhaul or repair be completed under the cover of a roof.

A clean, flat workbench or table of comfortable working height is an absolute necessity. The workbench should be equipped with a vise that has a jaw opening of at least four inches.

As mentioned previously, some clean, dry storage space is also required for tools, as well as the lubricants, fluids, cleaning solvents, etc. which soon become necessary.

Sometimes waste oil and fluids, drained from the engine or cooling system during normal maintenance or repairs, present a disposal problem. To avoid pouring them on the ground or into a sewage system, pour the used fluids into large containers, seal them with caps and take them to an authorized disposal site or recycling center. Plastic jugs, such as old antifreeze containers, are ideal for this purpose.

Always keep a supply of old newspapers and clean rags available. Old towels are excellent for mopping up spills. Many mechanics use rolls of paper towels for most work because they are readily available and disposable. To help keep the area under the vehicle clean, a large cardboard box can be cut open and flattened to protect the garage or shop floor.

Whenever working over a painted surface, such as when leaning over a fender to service something under the hood, always cover it with an old blanket or bedspread to protect the finish. Vinyl covered pads, made especially for this purpose, are available at auto parts stores.

# Jacking and towing

## Jacking

1    The jack supplied with the vehicle should only be used for raising the vehicle when changing a tire or placing jackstands under the frame. NEVER work under the vehicle or start the engine when the vehicle supported only by a jack.

2    The vehicle should be parked on level ground with the wheels blocked, the parking brake applied and the transmission in Park (automatic) or Reverse (manual). If the vehicle is parked alongside the roadway, or in any other hazardous situation, turn on the emergency hazard flashers. If a tire is to be changed, loosen the lug nuts one-half turn before raising off the ground.

3    Place the jack under the vehicle in the indicated positions (see illustrations). Operate the jack with a slow, smooth motion until the wheel is raised off the ground. Remove the lug nuts, pull off the wheel, install the spare and thread the lug nuts back on with the beveled or flanged side facing in. Tighten the lug nuts snugly, lower the vehicle until some weight is on the wheel, tighten them com-

pletely in a criss-cross pattern and remove the jack. On models with dual rear wheels, it is important that the lug nuts are clean and properly lubricated. Put two drops of oil at the point where the flange portion of the nut assembly attaches to the nut itself. This will ensure consistent torque readings. Note that some spare tires are designed for temporary use only - don't exceed the recommended speed, mileage or other restriction instructions accompanying the spare.

## Towing

4    Equipment specifically designed for towing should be used and attached to the main structural members of the vehicle. Optional tow hooks may be attached to the frame at both ends of the vehicle; they are intended for emergency use only, such as rescuing a stranded vehicle. Do not use the tow hooks for highway towing. Stand clear when using tow straps or chains, as they could break and cause serious injury.

5    Safety is a major consideration when towing and all applicable state and local laws

must be obeyed. In addition to a tow bar, a safety chain must be used for all towing.

6    Two-wheel drive vehicles with an automatic transmission may be towed with four wheels on the ground for a distance of 15 miles or less, as long as the speed doesn't exceed 30 mph. If the vehicle has to be towed more than 15 miles, place the rear wheels on a towing dolly.

7    Four-wheel drive vehicles should be towed on a flatbed or with all four wheels off the ground to avoid damage to the transfer case.

8    Vehicles equipped with the NV-021 PTO adapter must be towed with the transfer case and transmission in Neutral with the rear wheels off the ground to avoid drivetrain damage.

9    If any vehicle is to be towed with the front wheels on the ground and the rear wheels raised, the ignition key must be turned to the OFF position to unlock the steering column and a steering wheel clamping device designed for towing must be used or damage to the steering column lock may occur.

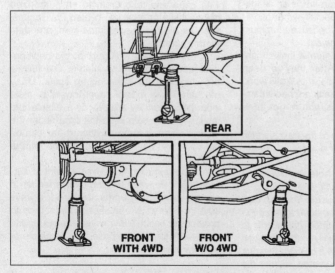

7.3a Front and rear jacking points
(2001 and earlier 1500 models/2002 and earlier 2500
and 3500 models)

7.3b Front jacking point (all 2002 and later 1500 2WD and
4WD models)

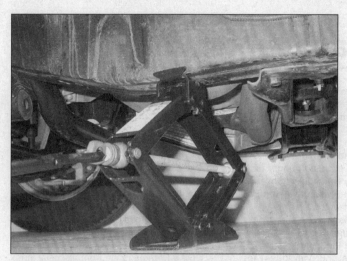

**7.3c Front jacking point, 2003 and later 2500/3500 2WD models - on 2500/3500 4WD models, the jack head must be placed under the front axle tube, nearest the wheel to be changed**

**7.3d Rear jacking point (2002 and later 1500 models/2003 and later 2500 and 3500 models)**

# Booster battery (jump) starting

1    Observe these precautions when using a booster battery to start a vehicle:

a) *Before connecting the booster battery, make sure the ignition switch is in the Off position.*

b) *Turn off the lights, heater and other electrical loads.*

c) *Your eyes should be shielded. Safety goggles are a good idea.*

d) *Make sure the booster battery is the same voltage as the dead one in the vehicle.*

e) *The two vehicles MUST NOT TOUCH each other!*

f) *Make sure the transaxle is in Neutral (manual) or Park (automatic).*

g) *If the booster battery is not a maintenance-free type, remove the vent caps and lay a cloth over the vent holes.*

2    Connect the red jumper cable to the positive (+) terminals of each battery (see illustration).
**Note:** *On diesel models, the connections must be made to the left (driver's side) battery.*

3    Connect one end of the black jumper cable to the negative (-) terminal of the booster battery. The other end of this cable should be connected to a good ground on the vehicle to be started, such as a bolt or bracket on the body.

4    Start the engine using the booster battery, then, with the engine running at idle speed, disconnect the jumper cables in the reverse order of connection.

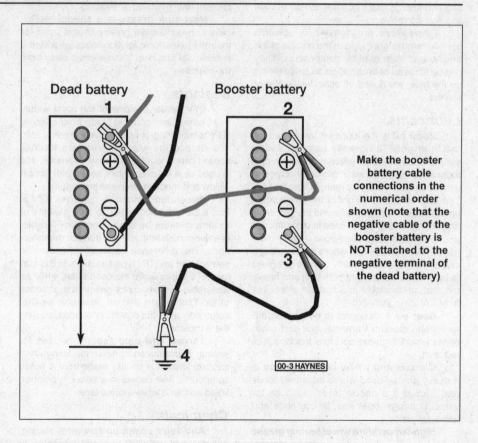

Dead battery    Booster battery

Make the booster battery cable connections in the numerical order shown (note that the negative cable of the booster battery is NOT attached to the negative terminal of the dead battery)

00-3 HAYNES

# Automotive chemicals and lubricants

A number of automotive chemicals and lubricants are available for use during vehicle maintenance and repair. They include a wide variety of products ranging from cleaning solvents and degreasers to lubricants and protective sprays for rubber, plastic and vinyl.

## Cleaners

**Carburetor cleaner and choke cleaner** is a strong solvent for gum, varnish and carbon. Most carburetor cleaners leave a dry-type lubricant film which will not harden or gum up. Because of this film it is not recommended for use on electrical components.

**Brake system cleaner** is used to remove brake dust, grease and brake fluid from the brake system, where clean surfaces are absolutely necessary. It leaves no residue and often eliminates brake squeal caused by contaminants.

**Electrical cleaner** removes oxidation, corrosion and carbon deposits from electrical contacts, restoring full current flow. It can also be used to clean spark plugs, carburetor jets, voltage regulators and other parts where an oil-free surface is desired.

**Demoisturants** remove water and moisture from electrical components such as alternators, voltage regulators, electrical connectors and fuse blocks. They are non-conductive and non-corrosive.

**Degreasers** are heavy-duty solvents used to remove grease from the outside of the engine and from chassis components. They can be sprayed or brushed on and, depending on the type, are rinsed off either with water or solvent.

## Lubricants

**Motor oil** is the lubricant formulated for use in engines. It normally contains a wide variety of additives to prevent corrosion and reduce foaming and wear. Motor oil comes in various weights (viscosity ratings) from 0 to 50. The recommended weight of the oil depends on the season, temperature and the demands on the engine. Light oil is used in cold climates and under light load conditions. Heavy oil is used in hot climates and where high loads are encountered. Multi-viscosity oils are designed to have characteristics of both light and heavy oils and are available in a number of weights from 0W-20 to 20W-50.

**Gear oil** is designed to be used in differentials, manual transmissions and other areas where high-temperature lubrication is required.

**Chassis and wheel bearing grease** is a heavy grease used where increased loads and friction are encountered, such as for wheel bearings, balljoints, tie-rod ends and universal joints.

**High-temperature wheel bearing grease** is designed to withstand the extreme temperatures encountered by wheel bearings in disc brake equipped vehicles. It usually contains molybdenum disulfide (moly), which is a dry-type lubricant.

**White grease** is a heavy grease for metal-to-metal applications where water is a problem. White grease stays soft under both low and high temperatures (usually from -100 to +190-degrees F), and will not wash off or dilute in the presence of water.

**Assembly lube** is a special extreme pressure lubricant, usually containing moly, used to lubricate high-load parts (such as main and rod bearings and cam lobes) for initial start-up of a new engine. The assembly lube lubricates the parts without being squeezed out or washed away until the engine oiling system begins to function.

**Silicone lubricants** are used to protect rubber, plastic, vinyl and nylon parts.

**Graphite lubricants** are used where oils cannot be used due to contamination problems, such as in locks. The dry graphite will lubricate metal parts while remaining uncontaminated by dirt, water, oil or acids. It is electrically conductive and will not foul electrical contacts in locks such as the ignition switch.

**Moly penetrants** loosen and lubricate frozen, rusted and corroded fasteners and prevent future rusting or freezing.

**Heat-sink grease** is a special electrically non-conductive grease that is used for mounting electronic ignition modules where it is essential that heat is transferred away from the module.

## Sealants

**RTV sealant** is one of the most widely used gasket compounds. Made from silicone, RTV is air curing, it seals, bonds, waterproofs, fills surface irregularities, remains flexible, doesn't shrink, is relatively easy to remove, and is used as a supplementary sealer with almost all low and medium temperature gaskets.

**Anaerobic sealant** is much like RTV in that it can be used either to seal gaskets or to form gaskets by itself. It remains flexible, is solvent resistant and fills surface imperfections. The difference between an anaerobic sealant and an RTV-type sealant is in the curing. RTV cures when exposed to air, while an anaerobic sealant cures only in the absence of air. This means that an anaerobic sealant cures only after the assembly of parts, sealing them together.

**Thread and pipe sealant** is used for sealing hydraulic and pneumatic fittings and vacuum lines. It is usually made from a Teflon compound, and comes in a spray, a paint-on liquid and as a wrap-around tape.

## Chemicals

**Anti-seize compound** prevents seizing, galling, cold welding, rust and corrosion in fasteners. High-temperature anti-seize, usually made with copper and graphite lubricants, is used for exhaust system and exhaust manifold bolts.

**Anaerobic locking compounds** are used to keep fasteners from vibrating or working loose and cure only after installation, in the absence of air. Medium strength locking compound is used for small nuts, bolts and screws that may be removed later. High-strength locking compound is for large nuts, bolts and studs which aren't removed on a regular basis.

**Oil additives** range from viscosity index improvers to chemical treatments that claim to reduce internal engine friction. It should be noted that most oil manufacturers caution against using additives with their oils.

**Gas additives** perform several functions, depending on their chemical makeup. They usually contain solvents that help dissolve gum and varnish that build up on carburetor, fuel injection and intake parts. They also serve to break down carbon deposits that form on the inside surfaces of the combustion chambers. Some additives contain upper cylinder lubricants for valves and piston rings, and others contain chemicals to remove condensation from the gas tank.

## Miscellaneous

**Brake fluid** is specially formulated hydraulic fluid that can withstand the heat and pressure encountered in brake systems. Care must be taken so this fluid does not come in contact with painted surfaces or plastics. An opened container should always be resealed to prevent contamination by water or dirt.

**Weatherstrip adhesive** is used to bond weatherstripping around doors, windows and trunk lids. It is sometimes used to attach trim pieces.

**Undercoating** is a petroleum-based, tar-like substance that is designed to protect metal surfaces on the underside of the vehicle from corrosion. It also acts as a sound-deadening agent by insulating the bottom of the vehicle.

**Waxes and polishes** are used to help protect painted and plated surfaces from the weather. Different types of paint may require the use of different types of wax and polish. Some polishes utilize a chemical or abrasive cleaner to help remove the top layer of oxidized (dull) paint on older vehicles. In recent years many non-wax polishes that contain a wide variety of chemicals such as polymers and silicones have been introduced. These non-wax polishes are usually easier to apply and last longer than conventional waxes and polishes.

# Conversion factors

### Length (distance)
| | | | | | |
|---|---|---|---|---|---|
| Inches (in) | X | 25.4 | = Millimeters (mm) | X 0.0394 | = Inches (in) |
| Feet (ft) | X | 0.305 | = Meters (m) | X 3.281 | = Feet (ft) |
| Miles | X | 1.609 | = Kilometers (km) | X 0.621 | = Miles |

### Volume (capacity)
| | | | | | |
|---|---|---|---|---|---|
| Cubic inches (cu in; in³) | X | 16.387 | = Cubic centimeters (cc; cm³) | X 0.061 | = Cubic inches (cu in; in³) |
| Imperial pints (Imp pt) | X | 0.568 | = Liters (l) | X 1.76 | = Imperial pints (Imp pt) |
| Imperial quarts (Imp qt) | X | 1.137 | = Liters (l) | X 0.88 | = Imperial quarts (Imp qt) |
| Imperial quarts (Imp qt) | X | 1.201 | = US quarts (US qt) | X 0.833 | = Imperial quarts (Imp qt) |
| US quarts (US qt) | X | 0.946 | = Liters (l) | X 1.057 | = US quarts (US qt) |
| Imperial gallons (Imp gal) | X | 4.546 | = Liters (l) | X 0.22 | = Imperial gallons (Imp gal) |
| Imperial gallons (Imp gal) | X | 1.201 | = US gallons (US gal) | X 0.833 | = Imperial gallons (Imp gal) |
| US gallons (US gal) | X | 3.785 | = Liters (l) | X 0.264 | = US gallons (US gal) |

### Mass (weight)
| | | | | | |
|---|---|---|---|---|---|
| Ounces (oz) | X | 28.35 | = Grams (g) | X 0.035 | = Ounces (oz) |
| Pounds (lb) | X | 0.454 | = Kilograms (kg) | X 2.205 | = Pounds (lb) |

### Force
| | | | | | |
|---|---|---|---|---|---|
| Ounces-force (ozf; oz) | X | 0.278 | = Newtons (N) | X 3.6 | = Ounces-force (ozf; oz) |
| Pounds-force (lbf; lb) | X | 4.448 | = Newtons (N) | X 0.225 | = Pounds-force (lbf; lb) |
| Newtons (N) | X | 0.1 | = Kilograms-force (kgf; kg) | X 9.81 | = Newtons (N) |

### Pressure
| | | | | | |
|---|---|---|---|---|---|
| Pounds-force per square inch (psi; lbf/in²; lb/in²) | X | 0.070 | = Kilograms-force per square centimeter (kgf/cm²; kg/cm²) | X 14.223 | = Pounds-force per square inch (psi; lbf/in²; lb/in²) |
| Pounds-force per square inch (psi; lbf/in²; lb/in²) | X | 0.068 | = Atmospheres (atm) | X 14.696 | = Pounds-force per square inch (psi; lbf/in²; lb/in²) |
| Pounds-force per square inch (psi; lbf/in²; lb/in²) | X | 0.069 | = Bars | X 14.5 | = Pounds-force per square inch (psi; lbf/in²; lb/in²) |
| Pounds-force per square inch (psi; lbf/in²; lb/in²) | X | 6.895 | = Kilopascals (kPa) | X 0.145 | = Pounds-force per square inch (psi; lbf/in²; lb/in²) |
| Kilopascals (kPa) | X | 0.01 | = Kilograms-force per square centimeter (kgf/cm²; kg/cm²) | X 98.1 | = Kilopascals (kPa) |

### Torque (moment of force)
| | | | | | |
|---|---|---|---|---|---|
| Pounds-force inches (lbf in; lb in) | X | 1.152 | = Kilograms-force centimeter (kgf cm; kg cm) | X 0.868 | = Pounds-force inches (lbf in; lb in) |
| Pounds-force inches (lbf in; lb in) | X | 0.113 | = Newton meters (Nm) | X 8.85 | = Pounds-force inches (lbf in; lb in) |
| Pounds-force inches (lbf in; lb in) | X | 0.083 | = Pounds-force feet (lbf ft; lb ft) | X 12 | = Pounds-force inches (lbf in; lb in) |
| Pounds-force feet (lbf ft; lb ft) | X | 0.138 | = Kilograms-force meters (kgf m; kg m) | X 7.233 | = Pounds-force feet (lbf ft; lb ft) |
| Pounds-force feet (lbf ft; lb ft) | X | 1.356 | = Newton meters (Nm) | X 0.738 | = Pounds-force feet (lbf ft; lb ft) |
| Newton meters (Nm) | X | 0.102 | = Kilograms-force meters (kgf m; kg m) | X 9.804 | = Newton meters (Nm) |

### Vacuum
| | | | | | |
|---|---|---|---|---|---|
| Inches mercury (in. Hg) | X | 3.377 | = Kilopascals (kPa) | X 0.2961 | = Inches mercury |
| Inches mercury (in. Hg) | X | 25.4 | = Millimeters mercury (mm Hg) | X 0.0394 | = Inches mercury |

### Power
| | | | | | |
|---|---|---|---|---|---|
| Horsepower (hp) | X | 745.7 | = Watts (W) | X 0.0013 | = Horsepower (hp) |

### Velocity (speed)
| | | | | | |
|---|---|---|---|---|---|
| Miles per hour (miles/hr; mph) | X | 1.609 | = Kilometers per hour (km/hr; kph) | X 0.621 | = Miles per hour (miles/hr; mph) |

### Fuel consumption*
| | | | | | |
|---|---|---|---|---|---|
| Miles per gallon, Imperial (mpg) | X | 0.354 | = Kilometers per liter (km/l) | X 2.825 | = Miles per gallon, Imperial (mpg) |
| Miles per gallon, US (mpg) | X | 0.425 | = Kilometers per liter (km/l) | X 2.352 | = Miles per gallon, US (mpg) |

### Temperature
Degrees Fahrenheit = (°C x 1.8) + 32        Degrees Celsius (Degrees Centigrade; °C) = (°F - 32) x 0.56

*It is common practice to convert from miles per gallon (mpg) to liters/100 kilometers (l/100km), where mpg (Imperial) x l/100 km = 282 and mpg (US) x l/100 km = 235

## DECIMALS to MILLIMETERS

| Decimal | mm | Decimal | mm |
|---|---|---|---|
| 0.001 | 0.0254 | 0.500 | 12.7000 |
| 0.002 | 0.0508 | 0.510 | 12.9540 |
| 0.003 | 0.0762 | 0.520 | 13.2080 |
| 0.004 | 0.1016 | 0.530 | 13.4620 |
| 0.005 | 0.1270 | 0.540 | 13.7160 |
| 0.006 | 0.1524 | 0.550 | 13.9700 |
| 0.007 | 0.1778 | 0.560 | 14.2240 |
| 0.008 | 0.2032 | 0.570 | 14.4780 |
| 0.009 | 0.2286 | 0.580 | 14.7320 |
| | | 0.590 | 14.9860 |
| 0.010 | 0.2540 | | |
| 0.020 | 0.5080 | | |
| 0.030 | 0.7620 | | |
| 0.040 | 1.0160 | 0.600 | 15.2400 |
| 0.050 | 1.2700 | 0.610 | 15.4940 |
| 0.060 | 1.5240 | 0.620 | 15.7480 |
| 0.070 | 1.7780 | 0.630 | 16.0020 |
| 0.080 | 2.0320 | 0.640 | 16.2560 |
| 0.090 | 2.2860 | 0.650 | 16.5100 |
| | | 0.660 | 16.7640 |
| 0.100 | 2.5400 | 0.670 | 17.0180 |
| 0.110 | 2.7940 | 0.680 | 17.2720 |
| 0.120 | 3.0480 | 0.690 | 17.5260 |
| 0.130 | 3.3020 | | |
| 0.140 | 3.5560 | | |
| 0.150 | 3.8100 | | |
| 0.160 | 4.0640 | 0.700 | 17.7800 |
| 0.170 | 4.3180 | 0.710 | 18.0340 |
| 0.180 | 4.5720 | 0.720 | 18.2880 |
| 0.190 | 4.8260 | 0.730 | 18.5420 |
| | | 0.740 | 18.7960 |
| 0.200 | 5.0800 | 0.750 | 19.0500 |
| 0.210 | 5.3340 | 0.760 | 19.3040 |
| 0.220 | 5.5880 | 0.770 | 19.5580 |
| 0.230 | 5.8420 | 0.780 | 19.8120 |
| 0.240 | 6.0960 | 0.790 | 20.0660 |
| 0.250 | 6.3500 | | |
| 0.260 | 6.6040 | | |
| 0.270 | 6.8580 | 0.800 | 20.3200 |
| 0.280 | 7.1120 | 0.810 | 20.5740 |
| 0.290 | 7.3660 | 0.820 | 21.8280 |
| | | 0.830 | 21.0820 |
| 0.300 | 7.6200 | 0.840 | 21.3360 |
| 0.310 | 7.8740 | 0.850 | 21.5900 |
| 0.320 | 8.1280 | 0.860 | 21.8440 |
| 0.330 | 8.3820 | 0.870 | 22.0980 |
| 0.340 | 8.6360 | 0.880 | 22.3520 |
| 0.350 | 8.8900 | 0.890 | 22.6060 |
| 0.360 | 9.1440 | | |
| 0.370 | 9.3980 | | |
| 0.380 | 9.6520 | | |
| 0.390 | 9.9060 | | |
| | | 0.900 | 22.8600 |
| 0.400 | 10.1600 | 0.910 | 23.1140 |
| 0.410 | 10.4140 | 0.920 | 23.3680 |
| 0.420 | 10.6680 | 0.930 | 23.6220 |
| 0.430 | 10.9220 | 0.940 | 23.8760 |
| 0.440 | 11.1760 | 0.950 | 24.1300 |
| 0.450 | 11.4300 | 0.960 | 24.3840 |
| 0.460 | 11.6840 | 0.970 | 24.6380 |
| 0.470 | 11.9380 | 0.980 | 24.8920 |
| 0.480 | 12.1920 | 0.990 | 25.1460 |
| 0.490 | 12.4460 | 1.000 | 25.4000 |

## FRACTIONS to DECIMALS to MILLIMETERS

| Fraction | Decimal | mm | Fraction | Decimal | mm |
|---|---|---|---|---|---|
| 1/64 | 0.0156 | 0.3969 | 33/64 | 0.5156 | 13.0969 |
| 1/32 | 0.0312 | 0.7938 | 17/32 | 0.5312 | 13.4938 |
| 3/64 | 0.0469 | 1.1906 | 35/64 | 0.5469 | 13.8906 |
| 1/16 | 0.0625 | 1.5875 | 9/16 | 0.5625 | 14.2875 |
| 5/64 | 0.0781 | 1.9844 | 37/64 | 0.5781 | 14.6844 |
| 3/32 | 0.0938 | 2.3812 | 19/32 | 0.5938 | 15.0812 |
| 7/64 | 0.1094 | 2.7781 | 39/64 | 0.6094 | 15.4781 |
| 1/8 | 0.1250 | 3.1750 | 5/8 | 0.6250 | 15.8750 |
| 9/64 | 0.1406 | 3.5719 | 41/64 | 0.6406 | 16.2719 |
| 5/32 | 0.1562 | 3.9688 | 21/32 | 0.6562 | 16.6688 |
| 11/64 | 0.1719 | 4.3656 | 43/64 | 0.6719 | 17.0656 |
| 3/16 | 0.1875 | 4.7625 | 11/16 | 0.6875 | 17.4625 |
| 13/64 | 0.2031 | 5.1594 | 45/64 | 0.7031 | 17.8594 |
| 7/32 | 0.2188 | 5.5562 | 23/32 | 0.7188 | 18.2562 |
| 15/64 | 0.2344 | 5.9531 | 47/64 | 0.7344 | 18.6531 |
| 1/4 | 0.2500 | 6.3500 | 3/4 | 0.7500 | 19.0500 |
| 17/64 | 0.2656 | 6.7469 | 49/64 | 0.7656 | 19.4469 |
| 9/32 | 0.2812 | 7.1438 | 25/32 | 0.7812 | 19.8438 |
| 19/64 | 0.2969 | 7.5406 | 51/64 | 0.7969 | 20.2406 |
| 5/16 | 0.3125 | 7.9375 | 13/16 | 0.8125 | 20.6375 |
| 21/64 | 0.3281 | 8.3344 | 53/64 | 0.8281 | 21.0344 |
| 11/32 | 0.3438 | 8.7312 | 27/32 | 0.8438 | 21.4312 |
| 23/64 | 0.3594 | 9.1281 | 55/64 | 0.8594 | 21.8281 |
| 3/8 | 0.3750 | 9.5250 | 7/8 | 0.8750 | 22.2250 |
| 25/64 | 0.3906 | 9.9219 | 57/64 | 0.8906 | 22.6219 |
| 13/32 | 0.4062 | 10.3188 | 29/32 | 0.9062 | 23.0188 |
| 27/64 | 0.4219 | 10.7156 | 59/64 | 0.9219 | 23.4156 |
| 7/16 | 0.4375 | 11.1125 | 15/16 | 0.9375 | 23.8125 |
| 29/64 | 0.4531 | 11.5094 | 61/64 | 0.9531 | 24.2094 |
| 15/32 | 0.4688 | 11.9062 | 31/32 | 0.9688 | 24.6062 |
| 31/64 | 0.4844 | 12.3031 | 63/64 | 0.9844 | 25.0031 |
| 1/2 | 0.5000 | 12.7000 | 1 | 1.0000 | 25.4000 |

# Safety first!

Regardless of how enthusiastic you may be about getting on with the job at hand, take the time to ensure that your safety is not jeopardized. A moment's lack of attention can result in an accident, as can failure to observe certain simple safety precautions. The possibility of an accident will always exist, and the following points should not be considered a comprehensive list of all dangers. Rather, they are intended to make you aware of the risks and to encourage a safety conscious approach to all work you carry out on your vehicle.

## Essential DOs and DON'Ts

**DON'T** rely on a jack when working under the vehicle. Always use approved jackstands to support the weight of the vehicle and place them under the recommended lift or support points.

**DON'T** attempt to loosen extremely tight fasteners (i.e. wheel lug nuts) while the vehicle is on a jack - it may fall.

**DON'T** start the engine without first making sure that the transmission is in Neutral (or Park where applicable) and the parking brake is set.

**DON'T** remove the radiator cap from a hot cooling system - let it cool or cover it with a cloth and release the pressure gradually.

**DON'T** attempt to drain the engine oil until you are sure it has cooled to the point that it will not burn you.

**DON'T** touch any part of the engine or exhaust system until it has cooled sufficiently to avoid burns.

**DON'T** siphon toxic liquids such as gasoline, antifreeze and brake fluid by mouth, or allow them to remain on your skin.

**DON'T** inhale brake lining dust - it is potentially hazardous (see *Asbestos* below).

**DON'T** allow spilled oil or grease to remain on the floor - wipe it up before someone slips on it.

**DON'T** use loose fitting wrenches or other tools which may slip and cause injury.

**DON'T** push on wrenches when loosening or tightening nuts or bolts. Always try to pull the wrench toward you. If the situation calls for pushing the wrench away, push with an open hand to avoid scraped knuckles if the wrench should slip.

**DON'T** attempt to lift a heavy component alone - get someone to help you.

**DON'T** rush or take unsafe shortcuts to finish a job.

**DON'T** allow children or animals in or around the vehicle while you are working on it.

**DO** wear eye protection when using power tools such as a drill, sander, bench grinder, etc. and when working under a vehicle.

**DO** keep loose clothing and long hair well out of the way of moving parts.

**DO** make sure that any hoist used has a safe working load rating adequate for the job.

**DO** get someone to check on you periodically when working alone on a vehicle.

**DO** carry out work in a logical sequence and make sure that everything is correctly assembled and tightened.

**DO** keep chemicals and fluids tightly capped and out of the reach of children and pets.

**DO** remember that your vehicle's safety affects that of yourself and others. If in doubt on any point, get professional advice.

## Steering, suspension and brakes

These systems are essential to driving safety, so make sure you have a qualified shop or individual check your work. Also, compressed suspension springs can cause injury if released suddenly - be sure to use a spring compressor.

## Airbags

Airbags are explosive devices that can **CAUSE** injury if they deploy while you're working on the vehicle. Follow the manufacturer's instructions to disable the airbag whenever you're working in the vicinity of airbag components.

## Asbestos

Certain friction, insulating, sealing, and other products - such as brake linings, brake bands, clutch linings, torque converters, gaskets, etc. - may contain asbestos or other hazardous friction material. Extreme care must be taken to avoid inhalation of dust from such products, since it is hazardous to health. If in doubt, assume that they do contain asbestos.

## Fire

Remember at all times that gasoline is highly flammable. Never smoke or have any kind of open flame around when working on a vehicle. But the risk does not end there. A spark caused by an electrical short circuit, by two metal surfaces contacting each other, or even by static electricity built up in your body under certain conditions, can ignite gasoline vapors, which in a confined space are highly explosive. Do not, under any circumstances, use gasoline for cleaning parts. Use an approved safety solvent.

Always disconnect the battery ground (-) cable at the battery before working on any part of the fuel system or electrical system. Never risk spilling fuel on a hot engine or exhaust component. It is strongly recommended that a fire extinguisher suitable for use on fuel and electrical fires be kept handy in the garage or workshop at all times. Never try to extinguish a fuel or electrical fire with water.

## Fumes

Certain fumes are highly toxic and can quickly cause unconsciousness and even death if inhaled to any extent. Gasoline vapor falls into this category, as do the vapors from some cleaning solvents. Any draining or pouring of such volatile fluids should be done in a well ventilated area.

When using cleaning fluids and solvents, read the instructions on the container carefully. Never use materials from unmarked containers.

Never run the engine in an enclosed space, such as a garage. Exhaust fumes contain carbon monoxide, which is extremely poisonous. If you need to run the engine, always do so in the open air, or at least have the rear of the vehicle outside the work area.

## The battery

Never create a spark or allow a bare light bulb near a battery. They normally give off a certain amount of hydrogen gas, which is highly explosive.

Always disconnect the battery ground (-) cable at the battery before working on the fuel or electrical systems.

If possible, loosen the filler caps or cover when charging the battery from an external source (this does not apply to sealed or maintenance-free batteries). Do not charge at an excessive rate or the battery may burst.

Take care when adding water to a non maintenance-free battery and when carrying a battery. The electrolyte, even when diluted, is very corrosive and should not be allowed to contact clothing or skin.

Always wear eye protection when cleaning the battery to prevent the caustic deposits from entering your eyes.

## Household current

When using an electric power tool, inspection light, etc., which operates on household current, always make sure that the tool is correctly connected to its plug and that, where necessary, it is properly grounded. Do not use such items in damp conditions and, again, do not create a spark or apply excessive heat in the vicinity of fuel or fuel vapor.

## Secondary ignition system voltage

A severe electric shock can result from touching certain parts of the ignition system (such as the spark plug wires) when the engine is running or being cranked, particularly if components are damp or the insulation is defective. In the case of an electronic ignition system, the secondary system voltage is much higher and could prove fatal.

## Hydrofluoric acid

This extremely corrosive acid is formed when certain types of synthetic rubber, found in some O-rings, oil seals, fuel hoses, etc. are exposed to temperatures above 750-degrees F (400-degrees C). The rubber changes into a charred or sticky substance containing the acid. *Once formed, the acid remains dangerous for years. If it gets onto the skin, it may be necessary to amputate the limb concerned.*

When dealing with a vehicle which has suffered a fire, or with components salvaged from such a vehicle, wear protective gloves and discard them after use.

# Troubleshooting

## Contents

This section provides an easy reference guide to the more common problems which may occur during the operation of your vehicle. These problems and possible causes are grouped under various components or systems; i.e., Engine, Cooling System, etc., and also refer to the Chapter and/or Section which deals with the problem.

Remember that successful troubleshooting is not a mysterious black art practiced only by professional mechanics. It's simply the result of a bit of knowledge combined with an intelligent, systematic approach to the problem. Always work by a process of elimination, starting with the simplest solution and working through to the most complex - and never overlook the obvious. Anyone can forget to fill the gas tank or leave the lights on overnight, so don't assume that you are above such oversights.

Finally, always get clear in your mind why a problem has occurred and take steps to ensure that it doesn't happen again. If the electrical system fails because of a poor connection, check all other connections in the system to make sure that they don't fail as well. If a particular fuse continues to blow, find out why - don't just go on replacing fuses. Remember, failure of a small component can often be indicative of potential failure or incorrect functioning of a more important component or system.

## Engine

### 1 Engine will not rotate when attempting to start

1  Battery terminal connections loose or corroded. Check the cable terminals at the battery. Tighten the cable or remove corrosion as necessary.
2  Battery discharged or faulty. If the cable connections are clean and tight on the battery posts, turn the key to the On position and switch on the headlights and/or windshield wipers. If they fail to function, the battery is discharged.
3  Automatic transmission not completely engaged in Park or Neutral or clutch pedal not completely depressed.
4  Broken, loose or disconnected wiring in the starting circuit. Inspect all wiring and connectors at the battery, starter solenoid and ignition switch.
5  Starter motor pinion jammed in flywheel ring gear. If manual transmission, place transmission in gear and rock the vehicle to manually turn the engine. Remove starter and inspect pinion and flywheel (Chapter 5).
6  Starter solenoid faulty (Chapter 5).
7  Starter motor faulty (Chapter 5).
8  Ignition switch faulty (Chapter 12).

### 2 Engine rotates but will not start

1  Fuel tank empty, fuel filter plugged or fuel line restricted.
2  Fault in the fuel injection system (Chapter 4A).
3  Battery discharged (engine rotates slowly). Check the operation of electrical components as described in the previous Section.
4  Battery terminal connections loose or corroded (see previous Section).
5  Fuel pump faulty (Chapter 4A).
6  Excessive moisture on, or damage to, ignition components (see Chapter 5).
7  Worn, faulty or incorrectly gapped spark plugs (Chapter 1).
8  Broken, loose or disconnected wiring in the starting circuit (see previous Section).
9  Broken, loose or disconnected wires at the ignition coil (Chapter 5).
10  Broken, loose or disconnected wires at the fuel shutdown solenoid (diesel) (Chapter 4A).
11  Air in the fuel system or defective fuel injection pump or injector (diesel) (Chapter 4A).
12  Contaminated fuel.

### 3 Starter motor operates without rotating engine

1  Starter pinion sticking. Remove the starter (Chapter 5) and inspect.
2  Starter pinion or flywheel teeth worn or broken. Remove the flywheel/driveplate access cover and inspect.

### 4 Engine hard to start when cold

1  Battery discharged or low. Check as described in Chapter 1.
2  Fault in the fuel or electrical systems (Chapters 4A, 4B and 5).
3  Fault in the intake manifold heater or fuel heater systems (diesel) (Chapter 4A).
4  Air in the fuel system or defective fuel injection pump or injector (diesel) (Chapter 4A).

### 5 Engine hard to start when hot

1  Air filter clogged (Chapter 1).
2  Fault in the fuel or electrical systems (Chapters 4A, 4B and 5).
3  Fuel not reaching the injectors (see Chapter 4A).
4  Air in the fuel system or defective fuel injection pump or injector (diesel) (Chapter 4A).
5  Low cylinder compression (Chapter 2A).

### 6 Starter motor noisy or excessively rough in engagement

1  Pinion or flywheel gear teeth worn or broken. Remove the cover at the rear of the engine (if equipped) and inspect.
2  Starter motor mounting bolts loose or missing.

### 7 Engine starts but stops immediately

1  Loose or faulty electrical connections at distributor, coil or alternator.
2  Fault in the fuel or electrical systems (Chapters 4A, 4B and 5).
3  Vacuum leak at the gasket surfaces of the intake manifold or throttle body. Make sure all mounting bolts/nuts are tightened securely and all vacuum hoses connected to the manifold are positioned properly and in good condition.
4  Restricted intake or exhaust systems (Chapter 4A)
5  Fault in the fuel heater system (diesel) (Chapter 4A).
6  Air in the fuel system or defective fuel injection pump or injector (diesel) (Chapter 4A).
7  Contaminated fuel.

### 8 Engine lopes while idling or idles erratically

1  Vacuum leakage. Check the mounting bolts/nuts at the throttle body and intake manifold for tightness. Make sure all vacuum hoses are connected and in good condition. Use a stethoscope or a length of fuel hose held against your ear to listen for vacuum leaks while the engine is running. A hissing sound will be heard. A soapy water solution will also detect leaks.
2  Fault in the fuel or electrical systems (Chapter 4A and 5).
3  Plugged PCV valve or hose (see Chapter 1 and 6).
4  Air filter clogged (Chapter 1).
5  Fuel pump not delivering sufficient fuel to the fuel injectors (see Chapter 4A).
6  Leaking head gasket. Perform a compression check (Chapter 2A).
7  Camshaft lobes worn (Chapter 2A).
8  Air in the fuel system or defective fuel injection pump or injector (diesel) (Chapter 4A).

## 9  Engine misses at idle speed

1   Spark plugs worn, fouled or not gapped properly (Chapter 1).
2   Fault in the fuel or electrical systems (Chapter 4A and 5).
3   Faulty spark plug wires (Chapter 1).
4   Vacuum leaks at intake or hose connections.
5   Uneven or low cylinder compression. Check compression as described in Chapter 2A.
6   Air in the fuel system or defective fuel injection pump or injector (diesel) (Chapter 4A).

## 10  Engine misses throughout driving speed range

1   Fuel filter clogged and/or impurities in the fuel system (Chapter 1).
2   Faulty or incorrectly gapped spark plugs (Chapter 1).
3   Fault in the fuel or electrical systems (Chapter 4A and 5).
4   Defective spark plug wires (Chapter 1).
5   Faulty emissions system components (Chapter 6).
6   Low or uneven cylinder compression pressures. Remove the spark plugs and test the compression with a gauge (Chapter 2A).
7   Weak or faulty ignition system (Chapter 5).
8   Vacuum leaks at the throttle body, intake manifold or vacuum hoses.
9   Air in the fuel system or defective fuel injection pump or injector (diesel) (Chapter 4A).

## 11  Engine stalls

1   Idle speed incorrect. Refer to the VECI label.
2   Fuel filter clogged and/or water and impurities in the fuel system (Chapter 1).
3   Fault in the fuel system or sensors (Chapters 4A, 4B and 6).
4   Faulty emissions system components (Chapter 6).
5   Faulty or incorrectly gapped spark plugs (Chapter 1). Also check the spark plug wires.
6   Vacuum leak at the throttle body, intake manifold or vacuum hoses.
7   Air in the fuel system or defective fuel injection pump or injector (diesel) (Chapter 4A).

## 12  Engine lacks power

1   Fault in the fuel or electrical systems (Chapter 4A and 5).
2   Faulty or incorrectly gapped spark plugs (Chapter 1).
3   Faulty coil (Chapter 5).

4   Brakes binding (Chapter 1).
5   Automatic transmission fluid level incorrect (Chapter 1).
6   Clutch slipping (Chapter 8).
7   Fuel filter clogged and/or impurities in the fuel system (Chapter 1).
8   Emissions control system not functioning properly (Chapter 6).
9   Use of substandard fuel. Fill the tank with the proper fuel.
10  Low or uneven cylinder compression pressures. Test with a compression tester, which will detect leaking valves and/or a blown head gasket (Chapter 2A).
11  Air in the fuel system or defective fuel injection pump or injector (diesel) (Chapter 4A).
12  Defective turbocharger or wastegate (diesel) (Chapter 4A).
13  Restriction in the intake or exhaust system (Chapter 4A).

## 13  Engine backfires

1   Emissions system not functioning properly (Chapter 6).
2   Fault in the fuel or electrical systems (Chapter 4A and 5).
3   Faulty secondary ignition system (cracked spark plug insulator or faulty plug wires) (Chapter 1 and 5).
4   Vacuum leak at the throttle body, intake manifold or vacuum hoses.
5   Valves sticking (Chapter 2A).
6   Crossed plug wires (Chapter 1).

## 14  Pinging or knocking engine sounds during acceleration or uphill

1   Incorrect grade of fuel. Fill the tank with fuel of the proper octane rating.
2   Fault in the fuel or electrical systems (Chapter 4A and 5).
3   Improper spark plugs. Check the plug type against the VECI label located in the engine compartment. Also check the plugs and wires for damage (Chapter 1).
4   Faulty emissions system (Chapter 6).
5   Vacuum leak.

## 15  Engine continues to run after switching off

1   Idle speed too high (Chapter 4A).
2   Fault in the fuel or electrical systems (Chapters 4A, 4B and 5).
3   Excessive engine operating temperature. Probable causes of this are a low coolant level (see Chapter 3), malfunctioning thermostat, clogged radiator or faulty water pump (see Chapter 1).
4   Defective fuel injection pump relay.

## Engine electrical system

## 16  Battery will not hold a charge

1   Alternator drivebelt defective or not adjusted properly (Chapter 1).
2   Electrolyte level low or battery discharged (Chapter 1).
3   Battery terminals loose or corroded (Chapter 1).
4   Alternator not charging properly (Chapter 5).
5   Loose, broken or faulty wiring in the charging circuit (Chapter 5).
6   Wiring or component problem causing a continuous drain on the battery (refer to Chapter 12 and the Wiring Diagrams).
7   Battery defective internally.

## 17  Ignition light fails to go out

1   Fault in the alternator or charging circuit (Chapter 5).
2   Alternator drivebelt defective or not properly adjusted (Chapter 1).

## 18  Ignition light fails to come on when key is turned on

1   Instrument cluster warning light bulb defective (Chapter 12).
2   Alternator faulty (Chapter 5).
3   Fault in the instrument cluster printed circuit, dashboard wiring or bulb holder (Chapter 12).

## Fuel system

## 19  Excessive fuel consumption

1   Dirty or clogged air filter element (Chapter 1).
2   Emissions system not functioning properly (Chapter 6).
3   Fault in the fuel or electrical systems (Chapter 4A and 5).
4   Low tire pressure or incorrect tire size (Chapter 1).
5   Restricted exhaust system (Chapter 4A).

## 20  Fuel leakage and/or fuel odor

1   Leak in a fuel feed line (Chapter 4A).
2   Tank overfilled.
3   Evaporative emissions system canister clogged (Chapter 6).
4   Vapor leaks from system lines (Chapter 4A).

## Cooling system

### 21 Overheating

1    Insufficient coolant in the system (Chapter 1).
2    Water pump drivebelt defective or not adjusted properly (Chapter 1).
3    Radiator core blocked or radiator grille dirty and restricted (see Chapter 3).
4    Thermostat faulty (Chapter 3).
5    Fan blades broken or cracked (Chapter 3).
6    Cooling system pressure cap not maintaining proper pressure (Chapter 3).

### 22 Overcooling

1    Thermostat faulty (Chapter 3).
2    Inaccurate temperature gauge.

### 23 External coolant leakage

1    Deteriorated or damaged hoses or loose clamps. Replace hoses and/or tighten the clamps at the hose connections (Chapter 1).
2    Water pump seals defective. If this is the case, water will drip from the weep hole in the water pump body (Chapter 3).
3    Leakage from the radiator core or side tank(s) (Chapter 3).
4    Coolant drain plug(s) leaking (Chapter 2A).

### 24 Internal coolant leakage

**Note:** *Internal coolant leaks can usually be detected by examining the oil. Check the dipstick and inside of the valve cover for water deposits and an oil consistency like that of a milkshake.*
1    Leaking cylinder head gasket. Have the cooling system pressure tested.
2    Cracked cylinder bore or cylinder head. Dismantle the engine and inspect (Chapter 2A).
3    Leaking intake manifold gasket (gasoline engines).

### 25 Coolant loss

1    Too much coolant in the system (Chapter 1).
2    Coolant boiling away due to overheating (see Chapter 1 Section 15).
3    External or internal leakage (see Sections 23 and 24).
4    Faulty pressure cap (Chapter 3).

### 26 Poor coolant circulation

1    Inoperative water pump. A quick test is to pinch the top radiator hose closed with your hand while the engine is idling, then let it loose. You should feel the surge of coolant if the pump is working properly (see Chapter 1).
2    Restriction in the cooling system. Drain, flush and refill the system (Chapter 1). If necessary, remove the radiator (Chapter 3) and have it reverse flushed.
3    Water pump drivebelt defective or not adjusted properly (Chapter 1).
4    Thermostat sticking (Chapter 3).
5    Drivebelt incorrectly routed, causing the pump to turn backwards (Chapter 1).

## Clutch

### 27 Fails to release (pedal pressed to the floor - shift lever does not move freely in and out of Reverse)

1    Leak in the clutch hydraulic system. Check the master cylinder, slave cylinder and lines (Chapters 1 and 8).
2    Clutch plate warped or damaged (Chapter 8).

### 28 Clutch slips (engine speed increases with no increase in vehicle speed)

1    Clutch plate oil soaked or lining worn. Remove clutch (Chapter 8) and inspect.
2    Clutch plate not seated (Chapter 8).
3    Pressure plate worn (Chapter 8).
4    Weak diaphragm springs (Chapter 8).
5    Clutch plate overheated. Allow to cool.

### 29 Grabbing (chattering) as clutch is engaged

1    Oil on clutch plate lining. Remove (Chapter 8) and inspect. Correct any leakage source.
2    Worn or loose engine or transmission mounts. These units move slightly when the clutch is released. Inspect the mounts and bolts (Chapter 2A).
3    Worn splines on clutch plate hub. Remove the clutch components (Chapter 8) and inspect.
4    Warped pressure plate or flywheel. Remove the clutch components and inspect.

### 30 Squeal or rumble with clutch fully engaged (pedal released)

 Release bearing binding on transmission bearing retainer. Remove clutch components (Chapter 8) and check bearing. Remove any burrs or nicks; clean and relubricate bearing retainer before installing.

### 31 Squeal or rumble with clutch fully disengaged (pedal depressed)

1    Worn, defective or broken release bearing (Chapter 8).
2    Worn or broken pressure plate springs (or diaphragm fingers) (Chapter 8).

### 32 Clutch pedal stays on floor when disengaged

1    Linkage or release bearing binding. Inspect the linkage or remove the clutch components as necessary.
2    Make sure proper pedal stop (bumper) is installed.

## Manual transmission

### 33 Noisy in Neutral with engine running

1    Input shaft bearing worn.
2    Damaged main drive gear bearing.
3    Worn countershaft bearings.
4    Worn or damaged countershaft endplay shims.

### 34 Noisy in all gears

1    Any of the above causes, and/or:
2    Insufficient lubricant (see the checking procedures in Chapter 1).

### 35 Noisy in one particular gear

1    Worn, damaged or chipped gear teeth for that particular gear.
2    Worn or damaged synchronizer for that particular gear.

### 36 Slips out of high gear

1    Transmission loose on clutch housing.
2    Internal transmission problem (Chapter 7A).

### 37 Difficulty in engaging gears

1  Clutch not releasing completely (see clutch adjustment in Chapter 1).
2  Loose, damaged or out-of-adjustment shift linkage. Make a thorough inspection, replacing parts as necessary (Chapter 7A).

### 38 Oil leakage

1  Excessive amount of lubricant in the transmission (see Chapter 1 for correct checking procedures). Drain lubricant as required.
2  Transmission oil seal or speedometer oil seal in need of replacement (Chapter 7A).
**Note:** *All of the following references are in Chapter 7A, unless noted.*

## Automatic transmission

### 39 General shift mechanism problems

**Note:** *Due to the complexity of the automatic transmission, it's difficult for the home mechanic to properly diagnose and service this component. For problems other than the following, the vehicle should be taken to a dealer service department or a transmission shop.*
1  Chapter 7B deals with checking and adjusting the shift linkage on automatic transmissions. Common problems which may be attributed to poorly adjusted linkage are:
  a) *Engine starting in gears other than Park or Neutral.*
  b) *Indicator on shifter pointing to a gear other than the one actually being selected.*
  c) *Vehicle moves when in Park.*
2  Refer to Chapter 7B to adjust the linkage.

### 40 Transmission will not downshift with accelerator pedal pressed to the floor

Throttle valve (TV) cable misadjusted (if equipped).

### 41 Transmission slips, shifts rough, is noisy or has no drive in forward or reverse gears

1  There are many probable causes for the above problems, but the home mechanic should be concerned with only one possibility - fluid level.
2  Before taking the vehicle to a repair shop, check the level and condition of the fluid as described in Chapter 1. Correct fluid level

as necessary or change the fluid and filter if needed. If the problem persists, have a professional diagnose the probable cause.

### 42 Fluid leakage

1  Automatic transmission fluid is a deep red color. Fluid leaks should not be confused with engine oil, which can easily be blown by air flow to the transmission.
2  To pinpoint a leak, first remove all built-up dirt and grime from around the transmission. Degreasing agents and/or steam cleaning will achieve this. With the underside clean, drive the vehicle at low speeds so air flow will not blow the leak far from its source. Raise the vehicle and determine where the leak is coming from. Common areas of leakage are:
  a) *Pan: Tighten the mounting bolts and/ or replace the pan gasket as necessary (see Chapter 7A).*
  b) *Filler pipe: Replace the rubber seal where the pipe enters the transmission case.*
  c) *Transmission oil lines: Tighten the connectors where the lines enter the transmission case and/or replace the lines.*
  d) *Vent pipe: Transmission overfilled and/or water in fluid (see checking procedures, Chapter 1).*
  e) *Speedometer connector: Replace the O-ring where the speedometer sensor enters the transmission case (Chapter 7A).*
**Note:** *All of the following references are in Chapter 7B, unless noted.*
**Note:** *Due to the complexity of the automatic transmission, it's difficult for the home mechanic to properly diagnose and service this component. For problems other than the following, the vehicle should be taken to a dealer service department or a transmission shop.*

## Transfer case

### 43 Transfer case is difficult to shift into the desired range

1  Speed may be too great to permit engagement. Stop the vehicle and shift into the desired range.
2  Shift linkage loose, bent or binding. Check the linkage for damage or wear and replace or lubricate as necessary (Chapter 7C).
3  If the vehicle has been driven on a paved surface for some time, the driveline torque can make shifting difficult. Stop and shift into two-wheel drive on paved or hard surfaces.
4  Insufficient or incorrect grade of lubricant. Drain and refill the transfer case with the specified lubricant. (Chapter 1).
5  Worn or damaged internal components. Disassembly and overhaul of the transfer case may be necessary (Chapter 7C).

### 44 Transfer case noisy in all gears

Insufficient or incorrect grade of lubricant. Drain and refill (Chapter 1).

### 45 Noisy or jumps out of four-wheel drive Low range

1  Transfer case not fully engaged. Stop the vehicle, shift into Neutral and then engage 4L.
2  Shift linkage loose, worn or binding. Tighten, repair or lubricate linkage as necessary.
3  Shift fork cracked, inserts worn or fork binding on the rail. Disassemble and repair as necessary (Chapter 7C).

### 46 Lubricant leaks from the vent or output shaft seals

1  Transfer case is overfilled. Drain to the proper level (Chapter 1).
2  Vent is clogged or jammed closed. Clear or replace the vent.
3  Output shaft seal incorrectly installed or damaged. Replace the seal and check contact surfaces for nicks and scoring.

## Driveshaft

### 47 Oil leak at seal end of driveshaft

Defective transmission or transfer case oil seal. See Chapter 7A for replacement procedures. While this is done, check the splined yoke for burrs or a rough condition which may be damaging the seal. Burrs can be removed with crocus cloth or a fine whetstone.

### 48 Knock or clunk when the transmission is under initial load (just after transmission is put into gear)

1  Loose or disconnected rear suspension components. Check all mounting bolts, nuts and bushings (see Chapter 10).
2  Loose driveshaft bolts. Inspect all bolts and nuts and tighten them to the specified torque.
3  Worn or damaged universal joint bearings. Check for wear (see Chapter 8).

### 49 Metallic grinding sound consistent with vehicle speed.

Pronounced wear in the universal joint bearings. Check as described in Chapter 8.

## 50  Vibration

**Note:** *Before assuming that the driveshaft is at fault, make sure the tires are perfectly balanced and perform the following test.*

1  Install a tachometer inside the vehicle to monitor engine speed as the vehicle is driven. Drive the vehicle and note the engine speed at which the vibration (roughness) is most pronounced. Now shift the transmission to a different gear and bring the engine speed to the same point.
2  If the vibration occurs at the same engine speed (rpm) regardless of which gear the transmission is in, the driveshaft is NOT at fault since the driveshaft speed varies.
3  If the vibration decreases or is eliminated when the transmission is in a different gear at the same engine speed, refer to the following probable causes.
4  Bent or dented driveshaft. Inspect and replace as necessary (see Chapter 8).
5  Undercoating or built-up dirt, etc. on the driveshaft. Clean the shaft thoroughly and recheck.
6  Worn universal joint bearings. Remove and inspect (see Chapter 8).
7  Driveshaft and/or companion flange out of balance. Check for missing weights on the shaft. Remove the driveshaft (see Chapter 8) and reinstall 180-degrees from original position, then retest. Have the driveshaft professionally balanced if the problem persists.

## Axles

## 51  Noise

1  Road noise. No corrective procedures available.
2  Tire noise. Inspect tires and check tire pressures (Chapter 1).
3  Rear wheel bearings loose, worn or damaged (Chapter 8).

## 52  Vibration

See probable causes under Driveshaft. Proceed under the guidelines listed for the driveshaft. If the problem persists, check the rear wheel bearings by raising the rear of the vehicle and spinning the rear wheels by hand. Listen for evidence of rough (noisy) bearings. Remove and inspect (see Chapter 8).

## 53  Oil leakage

1  Pinion seal damaged (see Chapter 8).
2  Axleshaft oil seals damaged (see Chapter 8).
3  Differential inspection cover leaking. Tighten the bolts or replace the gasket as required (Chapters 1 and 8).

## Brakes

## 54  Vehicle pulls to one side during braking

**Note:** *Before assuming that a brake problem exists, make sure that the tires are in good condition and inflated properly (see Chapter 1), that the front end alignment is correct and that the vehicle is not loaded with weight in an unequal manner.*

1  Defective, damaged or oil contaminated disc brake pads on one side. Inspect as described in Chapter 9.
2  Excessive wear of pad material or disc on one side. Inspect and correct as necessary.
3  Loose or disconnected front suspension components. Inspect and tighten all bolts to the specified torque (Chapter 10).
4  Defective caliper assembly. Remove the caliper and inspect for a stuck piston or other damage (Chapter 9).
5  Inadequate lubrication of front brake caliper slide rails. Remove caliper and lubricate slide rails (Chapter 9).

## 55  Noise (high-pitched squeal with the brakes applied)

1  Disc brake pads worn out. The noise comes from the wear sensor rubbing against the disc (does not apply to all vehicles) or the actual pad backing plate itself if the material is completely worn away. Replace the pads with new ones immediately (Chapter 9). If the pad material has worn completely away, the brake discs should be inspected for damage as described in Chapter 9.
2  Missing or damaged brake pad insulators. Replace pad insulators (see Chapter 9).
3  Linings contaminated with dirt or grease. Replace pads.
4  Incorrect linings. Replace with correct linings.

## 56  Excessive brake pedal travel

1  Partial brake system failure. Inspect the entire system (Chapter 9) and correct as required.
2  Insufficient fluid in the master cylinder. Check (Chapter 9), add fluid and bleed the system if necessary (Chapter 1).

## 57  Brake pedal feels spongy when depressed

1  Air in the hydraulic lines. Bleed the brake system (Chapter 9).
2  Faulty flexible hoses. Inspect all system hoses and lines. Replace parts as necessary.

3  Master cylinder mounting bolts/nuts loose.
4  Master cylinder defective (Chapter 9).

## 58  Excessive effort required to stop vehicle

1  Power brake booster or vacuum pump (diesel models) not operating properly (Chapter 9).
2  Excessively worn pads. Inspect and replace if necessary (Chapter 9).
3  One or more caliper pistons seized or sticking. Inspect and replace as required (Chapter 9).
4  Brake pads contaminated with oil or grease. Inspect and replace as required (Chapter 9).
5  New pads installed and not yet seated. It will take a while for the new material to seat against the disc.

## 59  Pedal travels to the floor with little resistance

1  Little or no fluid in the master cylinder reservoir caused by leaking caliper piston(s), loose, damaged or disconnected brake lines. Inspect the entire system and correct as necessary.
2  Worn master cylinder seals (Chapter 9).

## 60  Brake pedal pulsates during brake application

1  Caliper improperly installed. Remove and inspect (Chapter 9).
2  Disc defective. Remove (Chapter 9) and check for excessive lateral runout and parallelism. Have the disc resurfaced or replace it with a new one.
**Note:** *Before assuming that a brake problem exists, make sure that the tires are in good condition and inflated properly (see Chapter 1), that the front end alignment is correct and that the vehicle is not loaded with weight in an unequal manner.*

## Suspension and steering systems

## 61  Vehicle pulls to one side

1  Tire pressures uneven (Chapter 1).
2  Defective tire (Chapter 1).
3  Excessive wear in suspension or steering components (Chapter 10).
4  Front end in need of alignment.
5  Front brakes dragging. Inspect the brakes as described in Chapter 9.

## 62 Shimmy, shake or vibration

1   Tire or wheel out-of-balance or out-of-round. Have professionally balanced.
2   Loose, worn or out-of-adjustment front wheel bearings (Chapter 1).
3   Shock absorbers and/or suspension components worn or damaged (Chapter 10).

## 63 Excessive pitching and/or rolling around corners or during braking

1   Defective shock absorbers. Replace as a set (Chapter 10).
2   Broken or weak springs and/or suspension components. Inspect as described in Chapter 10.

## 64 Excessively stiff steering

1   Lack of fluid in power steering fluid reservoir (Chapter 1).
2   Incorrect tire pressures (Chapter 1).
3   Lack of lubrication at steering joints (see Chapter 1).
4   Front end out of alignment.
5   Power steering pump faulty (see Chapter 10).

## 65 Excessive play in steering

1   Loose or worn front wheel bearings (Chapters 1 and 10).
2   Excessive wear in suspension or steering components (Chapter 10).
3   Steering gearbox damaged or out of adjustment (Chapter 10).

## 66 Lack of power assistance

1   Steering pump drivebelt faulty or not adjusted properly (Chapter 1).
2   Fluid level low (Chapter 1).
3   Hoses or lines restricted. Inspect and replace parts as necessary.
4   Air in power steering system. Bleed the system (Chapter 10).

## 67 Excessive tire wear (not specific to one area)

1   Incorrect tire pressures (Chapter 1).
2   Tires out-of-balance. Have professionally balanced.
3   Wheels damaged. Inspect and replace as necessary.
4   Suspension or steering components excessively worn (Chapter 10).

## 68 Excessive tire wear on outside edge

1   Inflation pressures incorrect (Chapter 1).
2   Excessive speed in turns.
3   Front end alignment incorrect. Have professionally aligned.
4   Suspension arm bent (Chapter 10).

## 69 Excessive tire wear on inside edge

1   Inflation pressures incorrect (Chapter 1).
2   Front end alignment incorrect. Have professionally aligned.
3   Loose or damaged steering components (Chapter 10).

## 70 Tire tread worn in one place

1   Tires out-of-balance.
2   Damaged or buckled wheel. Inspect and replace if necessary.
3   Defective tire (Chapter 1).

# Chapter 1
# Tune-up and routine maintenance

## Contents

## Specifications

### Recommended lubricants and fluids

**Note:** *Listed here are manufacturer recommendations at the time this manual was written. Manufacturers occasionally upgrade their fluid and lubricant specifications, so check with your local auto parts store for current recommendations.*

Engine oil type
- Gasoline engine ... API "Certified for gasoline engines"
- Diesel engine ... API multi-grade and low sulfated ash limit engine oil

Engine oil viscosity
- 3.7L V6 engine ... 5W-30
- 4.7L V8 engine ... 5W-30
- 5.7L V8 engine (2004 and earlier) ... 5W-30
- 5.7L V8 engine (2005) ... 5W-20
- 5.9L V8 ... 10W-30
- V10 engine ... 10W-30
- Diesel engine
  - 2002 and earlier models
    - Above 10-degrees F ... 15W-40
    - Below 10-degrees F
      - With block heater ... 10W-30 synthetic
      - Without block heater ... 5W-30 synthetic
  - 2003 through 2007 models
    - Above 0-degrees F ... 15W-40
    - Below 0-degrees F ... 5W-40 synthetic
  - 2008 models ... 15W-40

Automatic transmission fluid type
    2000 and earlier models...................................................... Mopar ATF Plus 3, type 7176 (or equivalent meeting this specification)
    2001 and later models......................................................... Mopar type ATF+4, type 9602 or equivalent
Manual transmission lubricant type
    NV3500/NV5600 ................................................................. Mopar manual transmission lubricant part no. 4761526 or equivalent
    NV4500 ................................................................................ Mopar synthetic 75W-85 manual transmission lubricant or equivalent
    G238/G56............................................................................. Mopar type ATF+4 or equivalent
Transfer case lubricant type
    2002 and earlier models...................................................... DEXRON III automatic transmission fluid
    2003 and later models......................................................... Mopar type ATF+4 or equivalent
Coolant .......................................................................................... 50/50 mixture of Mopar 5 year/100,000 mile Formula antifreeze/coolant
                                                                                                     with HOAT (Hybrid Organic Additive Technology) and water

**Note:** *Most models are filled with a 50/50 mixture of Mopar® 5 year/100,000 mile coolant that shouldn't be mixed with other coolants. Some early model diesel engines are filled with a 50/50 mixture of ethylene glycol-based antifreeze and water. Refer to the owner's manual for your vehicle to determine what type coolant you have. Always refill with the correct coolant.*

## Differential lubricant type

Front axle
    2001 and earlier 1500 models/2002 and
        earlier 2500 and 3500 models ......................................... SAE 80W-90 GL-5 gear lubricant
    2002 and later 1500 models/2003 and
        later 2500 and 3500 models ............................................ SAE 75W-90 GL-5 gear lubricant
Rear axle
    2001 and earlier 1500 models/2002 and
        earlier 2500 and 3500 models ......................................... SAE 90W GL-5 gear lubricant
    2002
        1500 model .................................................................... SAE 75W-90 GL-5 gear lubricant*
        2500/3500 models......................................................... SAE 75W-90 GL-5 gear lubricant**
    2003 and later
        1500 model .................................................................... Mopar® Synthetic gear lubricant SAE 75W-140***
        2500/3500 models......................................................... Mopar® Synthetic gear lubricant SAE 75W-90
Brake fluid type.............................................................................. DOT 3 brake fluid
Power steering fluid ....................................................................... Mopar® type ATF+4 or equivalent
Chassis grease type........................................................................ NLGI no. 2 EP chassis grease

## Capacities****

Cooling system
    2001 and earlier models
        V6 and V8 engines ........................................................ Up to 20.0 quarts
        V10 engine...................................................................... 24.0 quarts
        Diesel engine.................................................................. 26.0 quarts
    2002 models
        3.7L V6 engine................................................................ 16.2 quarts
        4.7L V8 engine................................................................ 16.2 quarts
        5.9L V8 (1500 models) ................................................... 16.3 quarts
        5.9L V8 (2500/3500 models) .......................................... 20 quarts
        V10 engine...................................................................... 26 quarts
        5.9L diesel engine.......................................................... 24 quarts
    2003 and later models
        3.7L V6 engine................................................................ 17 quarts
        4.7L V8 engine................................................................ 17 quarts
        5.7L V8 engine................................................................ 18.7 quarts
        5.9L V8 (gasoline engine) .............................................. 18.7 quarts
        V10 engine...................................................................... 24.2 quarts
        5.9L diesel engine.......................................................... 28 quarts
        6.7L diesel engine.......................................................... 22.6 quarts

\* *Limited-slip rear axles add 5 oz. of Mopar limited slip additive or equivalent, to the specified lubricant.*
\** *Limited-slip rear axles add Mopar limited slip additive or equivalent, to the specified lubricant:*
    *(Model 60) 2WD add 5 oz.*
    *(Model 60) 4WD add 6 oz.*
    *(Model 70/80) 2WD add 7 oz.*
    *(Model 70) 4WD add 8 oz.*
    *(Model 80) 4WD add 10 oz.*
\*** *Limited-slip rear axles add 4 oz. of Mopar limited slip additive or equivalent, to the specified lubricant.*

\**** *All capacities approximate. Add as necessary to bring to the appropriate levels.*

## Capacities**** (continued)

Engine oil (with filter change)

| | |
|---|---|
| 3.7L V6 engine | 5 quarts |
| 3.9L V6 engine | 4 quarts |
| 4.7L V8 engine | 6 quarts |
| 5.7L V8 engine | 7 quarts |
| 5.2L and 5.9L V8 (gasoline engine) | 5 quarts |
| V10 engine | 7 quarts |
| 5.9L diesel engine | 11 quarts |
| 6.7L diesel engine | 11.4 quarts |

Automatic transmission (drain and refill)

| | |
|---|---|
| 2002 and earlier models (all) | 4.0 quarts |
| **2003 and later models** | |
| 42RLE | 4.0 quarts |
| **45RFE/545RFE/68RFE** | |
| 2WD | 5.5 quarts |
| 4WD | 6.5 quarts |
| 46RE/47RE/48RE | 4.0 quarts |
| AS68RC | 7.2 quarts |

**Note:** *The best way to determine the amount of fluid to add during a routine fluid change is to measure the amount drained. It is important not to overfill the transmission. After draining the transmission, begin the refilling procedure by initially adding 1-1/2 quarts, then adding 1/2-pint at a time until the level is correct on the dipstick.*

Manual transmission

| | |
|---|---|
| NV3500 (2WD) | 2.4 quarts |
| NV3500 (4WD) | 2.1 quarts |
| NV4500 | 4 quarts |
| NV5600 | 4.8 quarts |
| G56 | 6 quarts |

Transfer case

| | |
|---|---|
| NV231 HD | 1.25 quarts |
| NV241 | 2.3 quarts |
| NV241 GENII | 1.7 quarts |
| NV241 HD | 3.25 quarts |
| NV241 HD w/PTO | 4.5 quarts |
| NV243/NV244 GENII | 1.7 quarts |
| NV271/NV273 | 2 quarts |

Front axle

| | |
|---|---|
| **2002** | |
| 1500 model | 1.75 quarts |
| 2500/3500 models | 4.25 quarts |
| **2003 and later** | |
| 1500 model | 1.75 quarts |
| 2500/3500 models | 2.37 quarts |

Rear axle

| | |
|---|---|
| **2001 and earlier** | |
| 9-1/4 inch | 2.4 quarts |
| Dana 60 | 3.15 to 3.65 quarts |
| Dana 70 | 3.5 to 3.9 quarts |
| Dana 80 | 3.4 to 5.05 quarts |
| **2002** | |
| 1500 model | 2.45 quarts |
| **2500/3500 models** | |
| 248-RBI (Model 60) 2WD | 2.95 quarts |
| 248-RBI (Model 60) 4WD | 3.4 quarts |
| 267-RBI (Model 70) 2WD | 3.25 quarts |
| 267-RBI (Model 70) 4WD | 3.6 quarts |
| 286-RBI (Model 80) 2WD | 3.15 quarts |
| 286-RBI (Model 80) 4WD | 4.74 quarts |
| **2003 and later** | |
| 1500 model | 2.45 quarts |
| **2500/3500** | |
| 10 1/2 inch axle | 2.65 quarts |
| 11 1/2 inch axle | 3.81 quarts |

*****All capacities approximate. Add as necessary to bring to the appropriate levels.*

## Ignition system

Spark plug type
- 3.7L V6 engine ................................................... NGK ZFR6F-11G
- 3.9L V6 engine ................................................... Champion RC12YC or equivalent
- 4.7L V8 engine ................................................... Champion RC12MCC4
- 5.7L V8 engine ................................................... Champion - RE14MCC4
- 2002 and earlier 5.2L and 5.9L V8 engine ................ Champion RC12YC or equivalent
- 2003 and later 5.9L V8 engine ............................. Champion RC12LC4
- 1995 and earlier 8.0L V10 engine ......................... Champion RC9MC4 or equivalent
- 1996 and later 8.0L V10 engine ........................... Champion QC9MC4 or equivalent

Spark plug gap
- 3.7L V6 engine ................................................... 0.042 inch
- 3.9L V6 engine ................................................... 0.035 inch
- 4.7L V8 engine ................................................... 0.040 inch
- 5.7L V8 engine ................................................... 0.045 inch
- 2002 and earlier 5.2L and 5.9L V8 engine ................ 0.035 inch
- 2003 and later 5.9L V8 engine ............................. 0.040 inch
- 8.0L V10 engine ................................................. 0.045 inch

Firing order
- V6 engines ....................................................... 1-6-5-4-3-2
- V8 engines ....................................................... 1-8-4-3-6-5-7-2
- V10 engine ....................................................... 1-10-9-4-3-6-5-8-7-2

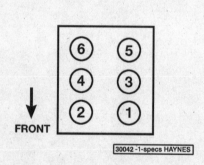

**3.7L V6 engine cylinder locations**

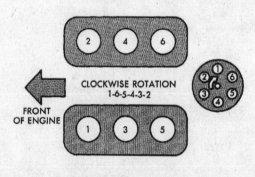

**3.9L V6 engine cylinder locations and distributor rotation diagram**

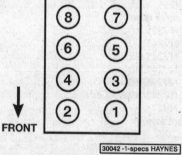

**4.7L and 5.7L (Hemi) V8 engine cylinder locations**

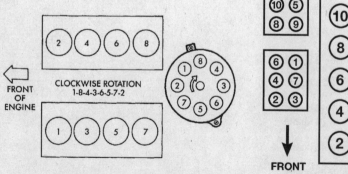

**5.2L and 5.9L V8 engine cylinder location and distributor rotation diagram**

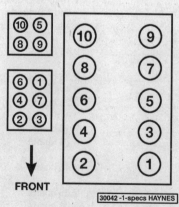

**8.0L V10 engine cylinder and coil terminal location diagram**

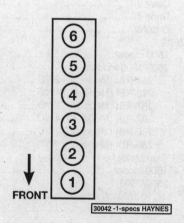

**Diesel engine cylinder locations**

## General
Valve clearance - diesel engines (cold)
    1998 and earlier models
        Intake................................................................ 0.010 inch
        Exhaust............................................................ 0.020 inch
    1999 and later models
        Intake................................................................ 0.006 to 0.015 inch
        Exhaust............................................................ 0.015 to 0.030 inch

## Brakes
Disc brake pad lining thickness (minimum) ............................................. 1/8 inch
Parking brake shoe lining thickness (minimum) ..................................... 1/16 inch

## Automatic transmission band adjustment
Front band
    1994 models (all).................................................. Tighten to 72 in-lbs, back off 2-1/2 turns
    1995 models
        42RH............................................................. Tighten to 72 in-lbs, back off 2-1/4 turns
        46RH............................................................. Tighten to 72 in-lbs, back off 2-7/8 turns
        47RH............................................................. Tighten to 72 in-lbs, back off 1-7/8 turns
    1996 and 1997 models......................................... Tighten to 72 in-lbs, back off 2-7/8 turns
    1998 and later models
        46RE transmission........................................ Tighten to 72 in-lbs, back off 2-7/8 turns
        47RE transmission........................................ Tighten to 72 in-lbs, back off 1-7/8 turns
        48RE transmission........................................ Tighten to 72 in-lbs, back off 1-3/4 turns
Rear band
    1994 models
        32/42RH........................................................ Tighten to 72 in-lbs, back off 4 turns
        36/37/46/47RH.............................................. Tighten to 72 in-lbs, back off 2 turns
    1995 models
        42RH............................................................. Tighten to 72 in-lbs, back off 4 turns
        46RH............................................................. Tighten to 72 in-lbs, back off 2 turns
        47RH............................................................. Tighten to 72 in-lbs, back off 3 turns
    1996 and 1997 models......................................... Tighten to 72 in-lbs, back off 2 turns
    1998 and later models
        46RE transmission........................................ Tighten to 72 in-lbs, back off 2 turns
        47RE transmission........................................ Tighten to 72 in-lbs, back off 3 turns
        48RE transmission........................................ Tighten to 72 in-lbs, back off 3 turns

## Torque specifications
**Ft-lbs** (unless otherwise indicated)

**Note:** *One foot-pound (ft-lb) of torque is equivalent to 12 inch-pounds (in-lbs) of torque. Torque values below approximately 15 ft-lbs are expressed in inch-pounds, because most foot-pound torque wrenches are not accurate at these smaller values.*

Automatic transmission band adjusting screw locknut
    Front band............................................................ 30
    Rear band ............................................................ 25
Automatic transmission pan bolts
    2001 and earlier models...................................... 156 in-lbs
    2002 and later models
        46RE/47RE transmissions............................ 156 in-lbs
        45RFE/545RFE transmissions ..................... 105 in-lbs
        47RE transmission........................................ 125 in-lbs
        48RE transmission........................................ 120 in-lbs
        68RFE transmission ..................................... 105 in-lbs
        AS68RC transmission................................... 62 in-lbs
        46RE/47RE/48RE transmissions................. 125 in-lbs
        454RFE/545RFE transmissions ................... 105 in-lbs
Engine oil pan drain plug
    Gasoline engines ................................................ 25
    Diesel engines
        1997 and earlier .......................................... 60
        1998 through 2001........................................ 44
        2002 and later.............................................. 37
Fuel filter cap (diesel)................................................ 25
Fuel line-to-injection pump banjo fitting bolt ............. 18
Manual transmission drain/fill plug
    NV3500 ............................................................... 14 to 20
    NV4500 ............................................................... 25 to 35
    NV5600 ............................................................... 22
    G56 ..................................................................... 42

## Torque specifications (continued)                  Ft-lbs (unless otherwise indicated)

**Note:** *One foot-pound (ft-lb) of torque is equivalent to 12 inch-pounds (in-lbs) of torque. Torque values below approximately 15 ft-lbs are expressed in inch-pounds, because most foot-pound torque wrenches are not accurate at these smaller values.*

Spark plugs
    3.9L V6, 5.2L V8, 5.9L V8 and 8.0L V10 engines ............................ 30
    3.7L V6 and 4.7L V8 engines .......................................................... 20
    5.7L V8 (Hemi) engine ................................................................... 156 in-lbs
Wheel lug nuts
    2002 and earlier 5 stud wheel ....................................................... 95
    2004 and earlier
        1500/2500 models or 8 stud single wheel ................................. 135
        3500 models or 8 stud dual wheel ............................................ 145
    2005 and later
        1500 models .............................................................................. 135
        2500 models .............................................................................. 145
        3500 models .............................................................................. 155
2WD (sealed) hub bearing nut (2001 and earlier 1500 models/2002 and earlier 2500 and 3500 models
    1500 models ................................................................................. 185
    2500/3500 models ........................................................................ 280

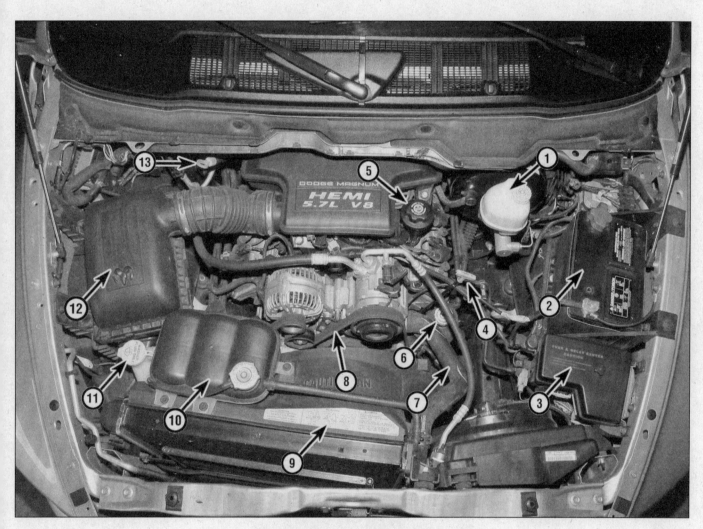

**5.7L V8 (Hemi) engine compartment layout**

| | | | | | |
|---|---|---|---|---|---|
| 1 | Brake fluid reservoir | 6 | Power steering fluid reservoir | 10 | Coolant expansion tank |
| 2 | Battery | 7 | Upper radiator hose | 11 | Windshield washer fluid reservoir |
| 3 | Underhood fuse/relay block | 8 | Drivebelt | 12 | Air filter housing |
| 4 | Engine oil dipstick | 9 | Drivebelt routing decal | 13 | Automatic transmission fluid dipstick |
| 5 | Engine oil filler cap | | | | |

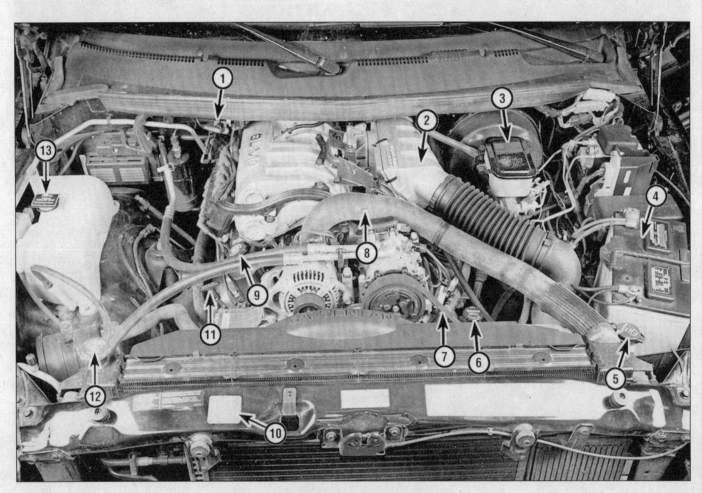

**V10 engine compartment layout**

| | | | | | | |
|---|---|---|---|---|---|---|
| 1 | Automatic transmission fluid dipstick | 6 | Power steering fluid reservoir | 10 | Drivebelt routing decal |
| 2 | Air filter housing | 7 | Drivebelt | 11 | Engine oil dipstick |
| 3 | Brake fluid reservoir | 8 | Upper radiator hose | 12 | Radiator cap |
| 4 | Battery | 9 | Engine oil filler cap | 13 | Coolant reservoir |
| 5 | Windshield washer fluid reservoir | | | | |

**5.9L diesel engine compartment layout (2003 and later models shown, earlier models similar)**

| | | | | | |
|---|---|---|---|---|---|
| *1* | *Brake fluid reservoir* | *6* | *Clutch fluid reservoir* | *10* | *Windshield washer fluid reservoir* |
| *2* | *Battery* | *7* | *Coolant reservoir* | *11* | *Upper radiator hose* |
| *3* | *Underhood fuse/relay block* | *8* | *Air filter housing* | *12* | *Power steering fluid reservoir* |
| *4* | *Engine oil dipstick* | *9* | *Radiator cap* | | *(not visible in this photo)* |
| *5* | *Engine oil filler cap* | | | | |

**Typical underside components (5.7L [Hemi] V8 shown, others similar)**

| | | | | |
|---|---|---|---|---|
| 1 | Lower radiator hose | | 4 | Engine oil drain plug |
| 2 | Drivebelt | | 5 | Automatic transmission fluid pan |
| 3 | Engine oil filter | | | |

Typical engine compartment underside components (early diesel engine shown, others similar)

| | | | | | |
|---|---|---|---|---|---|
| 1 | Idler arm grease fitting | 4 | Balljoint | 7 | Engine oil pan drain plug |
| 2 | Engine oil filter | 5 | Fuel filter drain location | 8 | Exhaust system |
| 3 | Tie-rod end | 6 | Transmission | | |

**Typical rear underside components**

| | | | |
|---|---|---|---|
| 1 | Shock absorber | 4 | Fuel tank |
| 2 | Disc brake caliper | 5 | Differential check/fill plug |
| 3 | Brake hose | | |

# 1 Maintenance schedule

The maintenance intervals in this manual are provided with the assumption that you, not the dealer, will be doing the work. These are the minimum maintenance intervals recommended by the factory for vehicles that are driven daily. If you wish to keep your vehicle in peak condition at all times, you may wish to perform some of these procedures even more often. Because frequent maintenance enhances the efficiency, performance and resale value of your car, we encourage you to do so. If you drive in dusty areas, tow a trailer, idle or drive at low speeds for extended periods or drive for short distances (less than four miles) in below freezing temperatures, shorter intervals are also recommended.

When your vehicle is new, it should be serviced by a factory authorized dealer service department to protect the factory warranty. In many cases, the initial maintenance check is done at no cost to the owner.

## Every 250 miles or weekly, whichever comes first

Check the engine oil level (see Section 4)
Check the engine coolant level (see Section 4)
Check the brake fluid level (see Section 4)
Check the power steering fluid level (see Section 4)
Check the windshield washer fluid level (see Section 4)
Check the automatic transmission fluid level (see Section 4)
Check the tires and tire pressures (see Section 5)
Check the operation of all lights
Check the horn operation

## Every month, regardless of mileage

Drain the fuel filter of water (diesel engine) (see Section 6)
Check the air filter (diesel engine) (see Section 7)

## Every 3,000 miles or 3 months, whichever comes first

*All items listed above, plus:*
Check the manual transmission fluid level (see Section 4)
Change the engine oil and filter (see Section 8)

## Every 6,000 miles or 6 months, whichever comes first

*All items listed above, plus:*
Check the wiper blade condition (see Section 9)
Check and clean the battery and terminals (see Section 10)
Rotate the tires (see Section 11)
Check the seatbelts (see Section 12)
Check the steering linkage (2500/3500 4WD models) (see Section 13)
Inspect underhood hoses (see Section 14)
Check the cooling system hoses and connections for leaks and damage (see Section 15)
Check the brake hoses (see Section 16)
Check the suspension, steering components and driveaxle boots (see Section 17)
Check the exhaust pipes and hangers (see Section 18)

## Every 12,000 miles

Change the differential lubricant on 3500 diesel models or any model operated under the conditions described as "severe" (*) at the end of this schedule (Section 38)

## Every 15,000 miles or 12 months, whichever comes first

*All items listed above, plus:*
Check the brake system (see Section 19)*
Check the drivebelts and replace if necessary (see Section 20)
Check the fuel system hoses and connections for leaks and damage (see Section 21)
Replace the fuel filter (diesel engine) (see Section 22)
Check the water pump (diesel engine) (see Section 23)
Check the manual transmission lubricant level (see Section 24)
Check the transfer case lubricant level (see Section 24)
Check the differential lubricant level (Section 24)

## Every 24,000 miles

Check and adjust if necessary, the valve clearances (diesel engine, 1998 and earlier models) (see Section 25)

## Every 30,000 miles or 24 months, whichever comes first

*All items listed above, plus:*
Check the condition of the front wheel bearings (see Section 26)
Repack and adjust the front wheel bearings (1999 and earlier 2WD models) (see Section 26)
Check the condition of the cooling fan hub (diesel engine) (see Section 27)
Check the condition of the vibration damper (diesel engine) (see Section 28)
Change the brake fluid (see Section 29)
Replace the air filter element (gasoline engines) (see Section 30)
Replace the spark plugs (see Section 31)
Check the spark plug wires, distributor cap and rotor (see Section 33)
Check the ignition coil(s) (see Section 32)

## Every 60,000 miles or 48 months, whichever comes first

*All items listed above, plus:*
Replace the spark plug wires (5.9L gasoline engine)
   (see Section 33)
Check and replace, if necessary, the PCV valve
   (see Section 34)
Replace the crankcase breather filter (2007 and later models)
   (see Chapter 6)

## Every 60 months (regardless of mileage)

Service the cooling system (drain, flush and refill)
   (see Section 37)

## Every 72,000 miles

Change the manual transmission lubricant (see Section 38)
Change the transfer case lubricant (see Section 38)
Change the differential lubricant (see Section 38)

## Every 90,000 miles or 72 months, whichever comes first

Change the power steering fluid and flush the system
   (see Section 39)

## Every 100,000 miles

Change the automatic transmission fluid and filter
   (Section 35)**
Adjust the automatic transmission bands
   (46RE, 47RE and 48RE transmissions) (see Section 36)

## Every 150,000 miles

Check and adjust if necessary, the valve clearances
   (diesel engine, 1999 and later models)
   (see Section 25)***

*\*This item is affected by "severe" operating conditions as described below. If your vehicle is operated under "severe" conditions, perform all maintenance indicated with an asterisk (\*) at 3000 mile/3 month intervals (unless otherwise specified in the schedule). Severe conditions are indicated if you mainly operate your vehicle under one or more of the following conditions:*
   Operating in dusty areas
   Towing a trailer
   Idling for extended periods and/or low speed operation
   Operating in extended temperatures below freezing
     (32-degrees F/0-degrees C)

*\*\*If operated under one or more of the following conditions, change the or automatic transmission fluid every 30,000 miles:*
   In heavy city traffic where the outside temperature regularly
     reaches 90-degrees F (32-degrees C) or higher
   In hilly or mountainous terrain
   Frequent towing of a trailer

*\*\*\*If operated under one or more of the following conditions, check and, if necessary adjust the valve clearances every 135,000 miles:*
   Frequent short trips (less than five miles)
   Driving in dusty conditions
   Frequent towing of a trailer
   Prolonged periods of idling
   Prolonged high-speed driving (more than 50-percent of the time)
     during hot weather (temperatures over 90-degrees F)

---

## 2   Introduction

1    This Chapter is designed to help the home mechanic maintain the Dodge Ram pickup truck with the goals of maximum performance, economy, safety and reliability in mind.

2    Included is a master maintenance schedule, followed by procedures dealing specifically with each item on the schedule. Visual checks, adjustments, component replacement and other helpful items are included. Refer to the accompanying illustrations of the engine compartment and the underside of the vehicle for the locations of various components.

3    Servicing your vehicle in accordance with the mileage/time maintenance schedule and the step-by-step procedures will result in a planned maintenance program that should produce a long and reliable service life.

Keep in mind that it's a comprehensive plan, so maintaining some items but not others at the specified intervals will not produce the same results.

4    As you service your vehicle, you will discover that many of the procedures can - and should - be grouped together because of the nature of the particular procedure you're performing or because of the close proximity of two otherwise unrelated components to one another.

5    For example, if the vehicle is raised for chassis lubrication, you should inspect the exhaust, suspension, steering and fuel systems while you're under the vehicle. When you're rotating the tires, it makes good sense to check the brakes since the wheels are already removed. Finally, let's suppose you have to borrow or rent a torque wrench. Even if you only need it to tighten the spark plugs, you might as well check the torque of as many

critical fasteners as time allows.

6    The first step in this maintenance program is to prepare yourself before the actual work begins. Read through all the procedures you're planning to do, then gather up all the parts and tools needed. If it looks like you might run into problems during a particular job, seek advice from a mechanic or an experienced do-it-yourselfer.

### Owner's manual and VECI label information

7    Your vehicle owner's manual was written for your year and model and contains very specific information on component locations, specifications, fuse ratings, part numbers, etc. The owner's manual is an important resource for the do-it-yourselfer to have; if one was not supplied with your vehicle, it can generally be ordered from a dealer parts department.

8    Among other important information, the

Vehicle Emissions Control Information (VECI) label contains specifications and procedures for applicable tune-up adjustments and, in some instances, spark plugs. The information on this label is the exact maintenance data recommended by the manufacturer. This data often varies by intended operating altitude, local emissions regulations, month of manufacture, etc.

9    This Chapter contains procedural details, safety information and more ambitious maintenance intervals than you might find in manufacturer's literature. However, you may also find procedures or specifications in your owner's manual or VECI label that differ with what's printed here. In these cases, the owner's manual or VECI label can be considered correct, since it is specific to your particular vehicle.

## 3    Tune-up general information

1    The term tune-up is used in this manual to represent a combination of individual operations rather than one specific procedure.
2    If, from the time the vehicle is new, the routine maintenance schedule is followed closely and frequent checks are made of fluid levels and high wear items, as suggested throughout this manual, the engine will be kept in relatively good running condition and the need for additional work will be minimized.
3    More likely than not, however, there will be times when the engine is running poorly due to lack of regular maintenance. This is even more likely if a used vehicle, which has not received regular and frequent maintenance checks, is purchased. In such cases, an engine tune-up will be needed outside of the regular routine maintenance intervals.
4    The first step in any tune-up or diagnostic procedure to help correct a poor running engine is a cylinder compression check. A compression check (see Chapter 2E)

will help determine the condition of internal engine components and should be used as a guide for tune-up and repair procedures. If, for instance, a compression check indicates serious internal engine wear, a conventional tune-up will not improve the performance of the engine and would be a waste of time and money. Because of its importance, the compression check should be done by someone with the right equipment and the knowledge to use it properly.
5    The following procedures are those most often needed to bring a generally poor running engine back into a proper state of tune.

## Minor tune-up

Check all engine-related fluids (Section 4)
Check the air filter (diesel engine)
    (Section 7)
Clean, inspect and test the battery
    (Section 10)
Check all underhood hoses (Section 14)
Check the cooling system (Section 15)

## Major tune-up

Check the drivebelt (Section 20)
Replace the PCV valve (Section 34)
Replace the air filter (Section 7 or
    Section 30)
Replace the spark plugs (Section 31)
Replace the distributor cap and rotor
    (Section 33)
Check the charging system (Chapter 5)

## 4    Fluid level checks (every 250 miles or weekly)

1    Fluids are an essential part of the lubrication, cooling, brake and windshield washer systems. Because the fluids gradually become depleted and/or contaminated during normal operation of the vehicle, they must be periodically replenished. See *Recommended lubricants and fluids* at the beginning of this Chapter before adding fluid to any of the fol-

lowing components.
**Note:** *The vehicle must be on level ground when fluid levels are checked.*

## Engine oil

2    The oil level is checked with a dipstick, which is located on the side of the engine (see illustration). The dipstick extends through a metal tube down into the oil pan.
3    The oil level should be checked before the vehicle has been driven, or about 5 minutes after the engine has been shut off. If the oil is checked immediately after driving the vehicle, some of the oil will remain in the upper part of the engine, resulting in an inaccurate reading on the dipstick.
4    Pull the dipstick out of the tube and wipe all the oil from the end with a clean rag or paper towel. Insert the clean dipstick all the way back into the tube and pull it out again. Note the oil at the end of the dipstick. At its highest point, the level should be between the ADD and FULL marks on the dipstick (see illustration).
5    On gasoline engines it takes one quart of oil to raise the level from the ADD mark to the FULL mark on the dipstick. Do not allow the level to drop below the ADD mark or oil starvation may cause engine damage. Conversely, overfilling the engine (adding oil above the FULL mark) may cause oil fouled spark plugs, oil leaks or oil seal failures. On diesel engines, it takes two quarts of oil to raise the level from the ADD to the FULL mark on the dipstick. Maintaining the oil level above the FULL mark can cause excessive oil consumption.
6    To add oil, remove the filler cap (see illustration). After adding oil, wait a few minutes to allow the level to stabilize, then pull out the dipstick and check the level again. Add more oil if required. Install the filler cap and tighten it by hand only.
7    Checking the oil level is an important preventive maintenance step. A consistently low oil level indicates oil leakage through damaged seals, defective gaskets or past worn

**4.2 Engine oil dipstick location on most models**

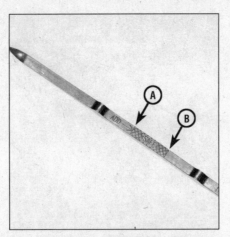

**4.4 On gasoline models, it takes about one quart of oil to raise the level from ADD mark (A) to the FULL mark (B). On diesel models it takes about two quarts**

**4.6 Engine oil filler cap location (5.7L V8 shown, others similar)**

rings or valve guides. If the oil looks milky in color or has water droplets in it, the cylinder head gasket(s) may be blown or the head(s) or block may be cracked. The engine should be checked immediately. The condition of the oil should also be checked. Whenever you check the oil level, slide your thumb and index finger up the dipstick before wiping off the oil. If you see small dirt or metal particles clinging to the dipstick, the oil should be changed (see Section 8). Some later models are equipped with an engine oil change reminder system. This system will alert you by displaying "Oil Change Required" on the EVIC (Electronic Vehicle Information Center) when it is time to change your engine oil.

### Engine coolant

**Warning:** *Do not allow antifreeze to come in contact with your skin or painted surfaces of the vehicle. Flush contaminated areas immediately with plenty of water. Don't store new coolant or leave old coolant lying around where it's accessible to children or pets - they're attracted by its sweet smell. Ingestion of even a small amount of coolant can be fatal! Wipe up garage floor and drip pan spills immediately. Keep antifreeze containers covered and repair cooling system leaks as soon as they're noticed.*

8    All vehicles covered by this manual are equipped with a pressurized coolant recovery system. A plastic coolant reservoir or expansion tank is located either on the fan shroud or in the right side of the engine compartment.

**Warning:** *Do not remove the pressure cap or expansion tank cap to check the coolant level when the engine is warm!*

9    The coolant level in the tank should be checked regularly. The level in the tank varies with the temperature of the engine.

On models with an expansion tank, when the engine is cold, the coolant level should be at the COLD FILL RANGE mark on the expansion tank. If it isn't, remove the cap from the tank and add a 50/50 mixture of ethylene gly-

col based antifreeze and water (see illustration).

On models equipped with a coolant reservoir, start the engine. Once the engine has warmed up, let the engine idle and check the coolant level in the reservoir. The level should be between the marks (see illustration). If it isn't, allow the engine to cool, then remove the cap from the reservoir tank and add a 50/50 mixture of ethylene glycol based antifreeze and water.

10    Drive the vehicle and recheck the coolant level. If only a small amount of coolant is required to bring the system up to the proper level, water can be used. However, repeated additions of water will dilute the antifreeze and water solution. In order to maintain the proper ratio of antifreeze and water, always top up the coolant level with the correct mixture. Don't use rust inhibitors or additives. An empty plastic milk jug or bleach bottle makes an excellent container for mixing coolant.

11    If the coolant level drops consistently, there may be a leak in the system. Inspect the radiator, hoses, filler cap, drain plugs and water pump (see Section 15). If no leaks are noted, have the pressure cap or expansion tank cap pressure tested by a service station.

12    If you have to remove the pressure cap or expansion tank cap, wait until the engine has cooled completely, then wrap a thick cloth around the cap and turn it to the first stop. If coolant or steam escapes, or if you hear a hissing noise, let the engine cool down longer, then remove the cap.

13    Check the condition of the coolant as well. It should be relatively clear. If it's brown or rust colored, the system should be drained, flushed and refilled. Even if the coolant appears to be normal, the corrosion inhibitors wear out, so it must be replaced at the specified intervals.

### Brake and clutch fluid

14    The brake master cylinder is located in the driver's side of the engine compartment,

near the firewall. The hydraulic clutch master cylinder used on manual transmission vehicles is sealed at the factory and requires replacement if leaks develop.

15    To check the fluid level of the brake master cylinder, simply look at the MAX and MIN marks on the reservoir (see illustration). The level should be within the specified distance from the maximum fill line.

16    If the level is low, wipe the top of the reservoir cover with a clean rag to prevent contamination of the brake system before lifting the cover.

17    Add only the specified brake fluid to the brake reservoir (refer to *Recommended lubricants and fluids* at the front of this Chapter or to your owner's manual). Mixing different types of brake fluid can damage the system. Fill the brake master cylinder reservoir only to the MAX line.

**Warning:** *Use caution when filling either reservoir - brake fluid can harm your eyes and damage painted surfaces. Do not use brake fluid that is more than one year old or has been left open. Brake fluid absorbs moisture from the air. Excess moisture can cause a dangerous loss of braking.*

18    While the reservoir cap is removed, inspect the master cylinder reservoir for contamination. If deposits, dirt particles or water droplets are present, the system should be drained and refilled.

19    After filling the reservoir to the proper level, make sure the lid is properly seated to prevent fluid leakage and/or system pressure loss.

20    The fluid in the brake master cylinder will drop slightly as the brake pads at each wheel wear down during normal operation. If the master cylinder requires repeated replenishing to keep it at the proper level, this is an indication of leakage in the brake system, which should be corrected immediately. If the brake system shows an indication of leakage check all brake lines and connections, along with the calipers and booster (see Section 19

**4.9a When the engine is cold, the engine coolant level should be within the COLD FILL RANGE (models with an expansion tank)**

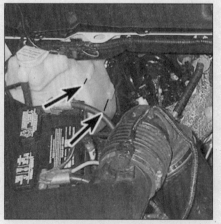

**4.9b Coolant level marks (models with a coolant reservoir; this one's a diesel)**

**4.15 Never let the brake fluid level drop below the MIN mark**

for more information). If the hydraulic clutch system shows an indication of leakage check all clutch lines and connections, along with the clutch release cylinder (see Chapter 8 for more information).

21   If, upon checking the brake master cylinder fluid level, you discover the reservoir empty or nearly empty, the system should be bled (see Chapter 9).

### Power steering fluid

22   Check the power steering fluid level periodically to avoid steering system problems, such as damage to the pump.

**Caution:** *DO NOT hold the steering wheel against either stop (extreme left or right turn) for more than five seconds. If you do, the power steering pump could be damaged.*

23   The power steering reservoir, located at the left side of the engine compartment (see illustration).

24   For the check, the front wheels should be pointed straight ahead and the engine should be off.

25   Use a clean rag to wipe off the reservoir cap and the area around the cap. This will help prevent any foreign matter from entering the reservoir during the check.

26   Twist off the cap and check the temperature of the fluid at the end of the dipstick with your finger.

27   Wipe off the fluid with a clean rag, reinsert the dipstick, then withdraw it and read the fluid level. The fluid should be at the proper level, depending on whether it was checked hot or cold (see illustration). Never allow the fluid level to drop below the lower mark on the dipstick.

28   If additional fluid is required, pour the specified type directly into the reservoir, using a funnel to prevent spills.

29   If the reservoir requires frequent fluid additions, all power steering hoses, hose connections, steering gear and the power steering pump should be carefully checked for leaks.

### Windshield washer fluid

30   Fluid for the windshield washer system is stored in a plastic reservoir located in the engine compartment, either in the left or right-front corner (see illustration).

31   In milder climates, plain water can be used in the reservoir, but it should be kept no more than 2/3 full to allow for expansion if the water freezes. In colder climates, use windshield washer system antifreeze, available at any auto parts store, to lower the freezing point of the fluid. Mix the antifreeze with water in accordance with the manufacturer's directions on the container.

**Caution:** *Do not use cooling system antifreeze - it will damage the vehicle's paint.*

### Automatic transmission

32   The automatic transmission fluid level should be carefully maintained. Low fluid level can lead to slipping or loss of drive, while overfilling can cause foaming and loss of fluid.

33   With the parking brake set, start the engine, then move the shift lever through all the gear ranges, ending in Neutral. The fluid level must be checked with the vehicle level and the engine running at idle.

**Note:** *Incorrect fluid level readings will result if the vehicle has just been driven at high speeds for an extended period, in hot weather in city traffic, or if it has been pulling a trailer. If any of these conditions apply, wait until the fluid has cooled (about 30 minutes).*

### Models with a dipstick

34   With the transmission at normal operating temperature, remove the dipstick from the filler tube. The dipstick is located at the rear of the engine compartment on the passenger's side (see illustration).

**Note:** *Normal operating temperature is after a few minutes of engine operation or after 15 miles of driving.*

35   Wipe the fluid from the dipstick with a clean rag and push it back into the filler tube until the cap seats.

36   Pull the dipstick out again and note the fluid level.

37   At normal operating temperature, the

**4.23 The power steering fluid reservoir is located on the left side of the engine (5.7L V8 engine shown, others similar)**

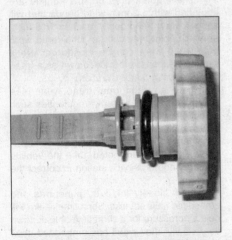

**4.27 With the engine cold, the fluid level should be at the FULL COLD mark**

**4.30 Windshield washer fluid reservoir location (5.7L V8 shown, others similar)**

**4.34 The automatic transmission dipstick is located at the rear of the engine compartment**

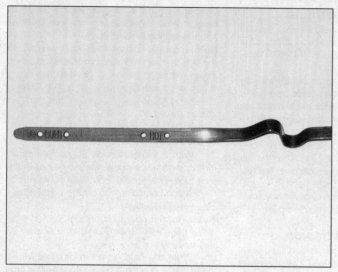

4.37 Check the fluid with the transmission at normal operating temperature - the level should be in the HOT range

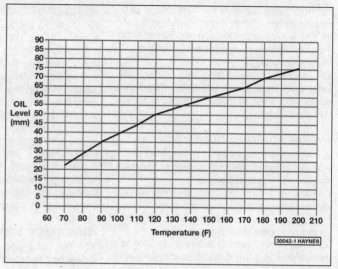

4.45 68RFE transmission fluid level-to-temperature indexing chart

fluid level should be between the two upper reference holes (HOT) (see illustration). On 5.9L diesel engine models, if the fluid is warm, the level should be between the two holes. If it's hot, the level should be in the area marked OK (crosshatched area). If additional fluid is required, add it directly into the tube using a funnel. Add the fluid a little at a time and keep checking the level until it's correct.

**Note:** *Wait at least two minutes before rechecking the fluid level allowing the fluid to fully drain into the transmission.*

### Models without a dipstick (some 68RFE transmissions)

**Note:** *Some 68RFE transmissions require the use of a scan tool to check transmission fluid temperature and special tool no. 9336 (or a homemade equivalent) to measure the fluid level. If you do not have both tools to make*

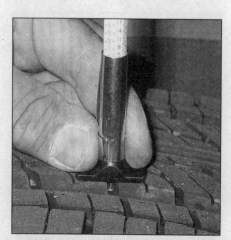

5.2 A tire tread depth indicator should be used to monitor tire wear - they are available at auto parts stores and service stations and cost very little

*the proper temperature-to-fluid level comparisons, we do not recommend attempting this procedure.*

38    Make sure the vehicle is parked on a level area.

**Warning:** *Be sure to set the parking brake and block the front wheels to prevent the vehicle from moving when the engine is running.*

39    Apply the parking brake, start the engine and allow it to idle for a minute, then move the shift lever through each gear position, ending in Park or Neutral.

40    Special fluid dipstick tool no. 9336 will be required to check the fluid level. An alternative to this tool can be fabricated from a straightened-out coat hanger long enough to be inserted into the dipstick tube opening and contact the fluid pan.

41    Allow the transmission to warm up, waiting at least two minutes, then remove the fluid filler tube cap.

42    With the engine warmed up and running, check the transmission fluid temperature with a scan tool.

**Note:** *To obtain an accurate fluid temperature reading, the shifter must be placed in Drive or Reverse. When the temperature reading is obtained, place the shifter back into Park.*

43    Insert the tool into the filler tube until the tip of the tool contacts the fluid pan. Then pull it out and measure the fluid level (from the bottom of the tool). It may be necessary to repeat this several times to get an accurate reading.

44    Compare the reading on the dipstick tool with the fluid temperature reading on the scan tool.

45    Match the two readings with the fluid level chart (see illustration) to make sure the fluid level is correct

46    Add or remove transmission fluid as necessary, then recheck the fluid level and install the dipstick tube cap.

### All models

47    The condition of the fluid should also be checked along with the level. If the fluid at the end of the dipstick is a dark reddish-brown color, or if it smells burned, it should be changed. If you are in doubt about the condition of the fluid, purchase some new fluid and compare the two for color and smell.

## 5    Tire and tire pressure checks (every 250 miles or weekly)

1    Periodic inspection of the tires may spare you the inconvenience of being stranded with a flat tire. It can also provide you with vital information regarding possible problems in the steering and suspension systems before major damage occurs.

2    The original tires on this vehicle are equipped with 1/2-inch wide bands that will appear when tread depth reaches 1/16-inch, at which point they can be considered worn out. Tread wear can be monitored with a simple, inexpensive device known as a tread depth indicator (see illustration).

3    Note any abnormal tread wear (see illustration). Tread pattern irregularities such as cupping, flat spots and more wear on one side than the other are indications of front end alignment and/or balance problems. If any of these conditions are noted, take the vehicle to a tire shop or service station to correct the problem.

4    Look closely for cuts, punctures and embedded nails or tacks. Sometimes a tire will hold air pressure for a short time or leak down very slowly after a nail has embedded itself in the tread. If a slow leak persists, check the valve stem core to make sure it is tight (see illustration). Examine the tread for an object that may have embedded itself in the tire or

**UNDERINFLATION**

**CUPPING**

Cupping may be caused by:
- Underinflation and/or mechanical irregularities such as out-of-balance condition of wheel and/or tire, and bent or damaged wheel.
- Loose or worn steering tie-rod or steering idler arm.
- Loose, damaged or worn front suspension parts.

**OVERINFLATION**

**INCORRECT TOE-IN OR EXTREME CAMBER**

**FEATHERING DUE TO MISALIGNMENT**

**5.3 This chart will help you determine the condition of your tires, the probable cause(s) of abnormal wear and the corrective action necessary**

for a plug that may have begun to leak (radial tire punctures are repaired with a plug that is installed in a puncture). If a puncture is suspected, it can be easily verified by spraying a solution of soapy water onto the puncture area (see illustration). The soapy solution will bubble if there is a leak. Unless the puncture is unusually large, a tire shop or service station can usually repair the tire.

5    Carefully inspect the inner sidewall of each tire for evidence of brake fluid leakage. If you see any, inspect the brakes immediately.

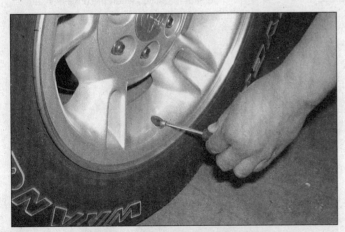

**5.4a If a tire loses air on a steady basis, check the valve core first to make sure it's snug (special inexpensive wrenches are commonly available at auto parts stores)**

**5.4b If the valve core is tight, raise the corner of the vehicle with the low tire and spray a soapy water solution onto the tread as the tire is turned slowly - slow leaks will cause small bubbles to appear**

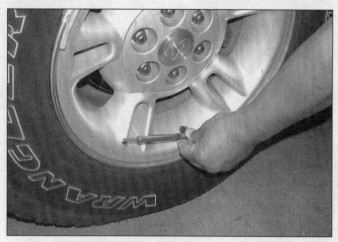

5.8 To extend the life of your tires, check the air pressure at least once a week with an accurate gauge (don't forget the spare!)

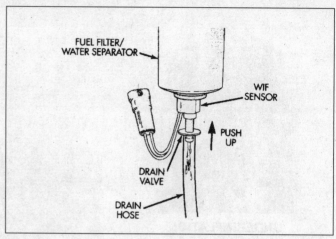

6.3a Push up on the valve to drain out the water that has collected in the fuel filter/water separator (1996 and earlier models)

6    Correct air pressure adds miles to the life span of the tires, improves mileage and enhances overall ride quality. Tire pressure cannot be accurately estimated by looking at a tire, especially if it's a radial. A tire pressure gauge is essential. Keep an accurate gauge in the glove compartment. The pressure gauges attached to the nozzles of air hoses at gas stations are often inaccurate.

7    Always check tire pressure when the tires are cold. Cold, in this case, means the vehicle has not been driven over a mile in the three hours preceding a tire pressure check. A pressure rise of four to eight pounds is not uncommon once the tires are warm.

8    Unscrew the valve cap protruding from the wheel or hubcap and push the gauge firmly onto the valve stem (see illustration). Note the reading on the gauge and compare the figure to the recommended tire pressure shown on the tire placard on the driver's side door. Be sure to reinstall the valve cap to keep dirt and moisture out of the valve stem mechanism. Check all four tires and, if necessary, add enough air to bring them up to the recommended pressure.

9    Don't forget to keep the spare tire inflated to the specified pressure (refer to the pressure molded into the tire sidewall).

## 6    Fuel filter draining (diesel engine) (every month, regardless of mileage)

1    The diesel engine fuel filter incorporates a water separator that removes and traps water in the fuel. This water must be drained from the filter at the specified intervals or when the Water In Fuel (WIF) light is on.

2    Place a small container under the filter drain tube (diesel fuel can damage asphalt paving).

3    With the engine off, push the drain valve handle outward and allow the accumulated water to drain out (see illustrations). Repeat the procedure until clean fuel flows from the filter drain, then place the drain valve handle in the closed position.

4    Remove the container and dispose of the fuel/water mixture properly.

5    If more than a couple of ounces had to be drained to remove any accumulated water, the fuel system may have to be primed in order for the engine to start. Refer to Chapter 4B for the priming procedure.

## 7    Air filter check and replacement (diesel engine) (every month, regardless of mileage)

### Check

1    Since the supply of air is crucial to the operation of a diesel engine, these models have an air restriction gauge built into the air filter housing to monitor the condition of the filter element. This gauge should be checked periodically to determine if the element is restricted with dirt (see illustration).

2    The gauge has a yellow disc inside a graduated scale that remains at the highest point of restriction when the engine is shut off.

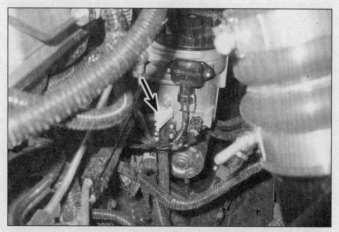

6.3b Rotate the drain valve handle to the DRAIN position to drain accumulated water from the fuel filter canister/water separator (1997 and later models)

7.1 When the yellow disc drops into the red zone on the graduated scale, the air filter element must be replaced with a new one

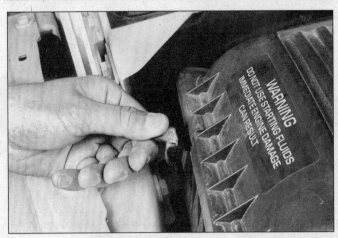

**7.4a Detach the air filter housing clips...**

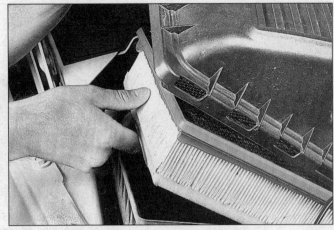

**7.4b ... then raise the cover and lift the filter element out - early models shown, later models similar**

With the engine off, check the position of the disc to see if it moved to within the red zone. If it has, replace the air filter element.

## Replacement

3    The air filter is located inside the air filter housing mounted in the right side of the engine compartment.

4    Detach the clips securing the housing cover, then separate the housing halves and lift the filter out (see illustrations).

5    Wipe out the inside of the air filter housing with a clean rag.

6    Place the new filter in the air filter housing. Make sure it seats properly, seat the two halves together and secure them with the clips.

7    After installation, press the button on the top of the gauge to reset it.

---

## 8    Engine oil and filter change (every 3000 miles or 3 months)

---

1    Frequent oil changes are the best preventive maintenance the home mechanic can give the engine, because aging oil becomes diluted and contaminated, which leads to premature engine wear.

2    Make sure you have all the necessary tools before you begin this procedure (see illustration). You should also have plenty of rags or newspapers handy for mopping up any spills.

3    Access to the underside of the vehicle is greatly improved if the vehicle can be lifted on a hoist, driven onto ramps or supported by jackstands.

**Warning:** *Do not work under a vehicle which is supported only by a bumper, hydraulic or scissors-type jack.*

4    If this is your first oil change, get under the vehicle and familiarize yourself with the locations of the oil drain plug and the oil filter. The engine and exhaust components will be warm during the actual work, so try to anticipate any potential problems before the engine

and accessories are hot.

5    Park the vehicle on a level spot. Start the engine and allow it to reach its normal operating temperature. Warm oil and sludge will flow out more easily. Turn off the engine when it's

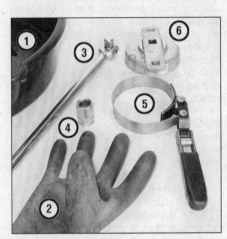

**8.2 These tools are required when changing the engine oil and filter**

*1    Drain pan - It should be fairly shallow in depth, but wide to prevent spills*

*2    Rubber gloves - When removing the drain plug and filter, you will get oil on your hands (the gloves will prevent burns)*

*3    Breaker bar - Sometimes the oil drain plug is tight, and a long breaker bar is needed to loosen it*

*4    Socket – To be used with the breaker bar or a ratchet (must be the correct size to fit the drain plug - six-point preferred)*

*5    Filter wrench - This is a metal band-type wrench, which requires clearance around the filter to be effective*

*6    Filter wrench - This type fits on the bottom of the filter and can be turned with a ratchet or breaker bar (different-size wrenches are available for different types of filters)*

warmed up. Remove the filler cap from the valve cover.

6    Raise the vehicle and support it securely on jackstands.

7    Being careful not to touch the hot exhaust components, place the drain pan under the drain plug in the bottom of the pan and remove the plug (see illustration). You may want to wear gloves while unscrewing the plug the final few turns if the engine is hot.

8    Allow the old oil to drain into the pan. It may be necessary to move the pan farther under the engine as the oil flow slows to a trickle. Inspect the old oil for the presence of metal shavings and chips.

9    After all the oil has drained, wipe off the drain plug with a clean rag. Even minute metal particles clinging to the plug would immediately contaminate the new oil.

10    Clean the area around the drain plug opening, reinstall the plug and tighten it securely, but do not strip the threads.

11    Move the drain pan into position under the oil filter.

**8.7 Use a proper size box-end wrench or socket to remove the oil drain plug and avoid rounding it off**

8.12 Use an oil filter wrench to remove the filter

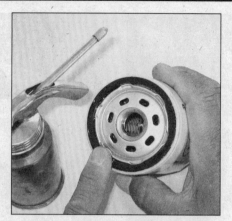

8.14 Lubricate the oil filter gasket with clean engine oil before installing the filter on the engine

9.5a To release the blade holder, push the release lever . . .

9.5b . . . and pull the wiper blade in the direction of the arrow to separate it from the arm

12   Loosen the oil filter (see illustration) by turning it counterclockwise with an oil filter wrench. Once the filter is loose, use your hands to unscrew it from the block. Keep the open end pointing up to prevent the oil inside the filter from spilling out.

**Warning:** *The exhaust system may still be hot, so be careful.*

13   With a clean rag, wipe off the mounting surface on the block. If a residue of old oil is allowed to remain, it will smoke when the block is heated up. Also make sure that none of the old gasket remains stuck to the mounting surface. It can be removed with a scraper if necessary.

14   Compare the old filter with the new one to make sure they are the same type. Smear some clean engine oil on the rubber gasket of the new filter (see illustration).

15   Attach the new filter to the engine, following the tightening directions printed on the filter canister or packing box. Most filter manufacturers recommend against using a filter wrench due to the possibility of overtightening and damaging the seal.

16   Remove all tools, rags, etc., from under the vehicle, being careful not to spill the oil in the drain pan, then lower the vehicle.

17   Add new oil to the engine through the oil filler cap in the valve cover. Use a funnel, if

necessary, to prevent oil from spilling onto the top of the engine. Pour three quarts of fresh oil into the engine. Wait a few minutes to allow the oil to drain into the pan, then check the level on the oil dipstick (see Section 4). If the oil level is at or near the FULL mark on the dipstick, install the filler cap hand tight, start the engine and allow the new oil to circulate.

18   Allow the engine to run for about a minute. While the engine is running, look under the vehicle and check for leaks at the oil pan drain plug and around the oil filter. If either is leaking, stop the engine and tighten the plug or filter.

19   Wait a few minutes to allow the oil to trickle down into the pan, then recheck the level on the dipstick and, if necessary, add enough oil to bring the level to the FULL mark.

20   During the first few trips after an oil change, make it a point to check frequently for leaks and proper oil level.

21   The old oil drained from the engine cannot be reused in its present state and should be disposed of. Check with your local auto parts store, disposal facility or environmental agency to see if they will accept the oil for recycling. After the oil has cooled it can be drained into a container (capped plastic jugs, topped bottles, milk cartons, etc.) for transport to one of these disposal sites. Don't dispose of the oil by pouring it on the ground or down a drain!

## Resetting the Oil Change Required light

22   Some later models have an "Oil Change Required" light. After completing your scheduled oil change, it will be necessary to reset the light.

23   Without starting the engine, turn the key to the On position.

24   Slowly depress the accelerator pedal to the floor three times within 10 seconds.

25   Turn the key to the Off/Lock position.

26   Start the engine and verify on the EVIC (Electronic Vehicle Information Center) that the "Oil Change Required" indicator message

is no longer illuminated. Repeat the steps above if the "Oil Change Required" indicator message still appears.

## 9   Windshield wiper blade inspection and replacement (every 6000 miles or 6 months)

1   The windshield wiper and blade assembly should be inspected periodically for damage, loose components and cracked or worn blade elements.

2   Road film can build up on the wiper blades and affect their efficiency, so they should be washed regularly with a mild detergent solution.

3   The action of the wiping mechanism can loosen bolts, nuts and fasteners, so they should be checked and tightened, as necessary, at the same time the wiper blades are checked.

4   If the wiper blade elements are cracked, worn or warped, or no longer clean adequately, they should be replaced with new ones.

5   Lift the arm assembly away from the glass for clearance, press the release lever, then slide the wiper blade assembly out of the hook at the end of the arm (see illustrations).

6   Attach the new wiper to the arm. Connection can be confirmed by an audible click.

## 10   Battery check, maintenance and charging (every 6000 miles or 6 months)

**Warning:** *Certain precautions must be followed when checking and servicing the battery. Hydrogen gas, which is highly flammable, is always present in the battery cells, so keep lighted tobacco and all other open flames and sparks away from the battery. The electrolyte inside the battery is actually diluted sulfuric acid, which will cause injury if splashed on your skin or in your eyes. It will also ruin*

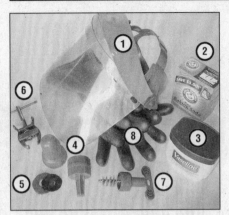

**10.1 Tools and materials required for battery maintenance**

1   *Face shield/safety goggles - When removing corrosion with a brush, the acidic particles can easily fly up into your eyes*
2   *Baking soda - A solution of baking soda and water can be used to neutralize corrosion*
3   *Petroleum jelly - A layer of this on the battery posts will help prevent corrosion*
4   *Battery post/cable cleaner - This wire brush cleaning tool will remove all traces of corrosion from the battery posts and cable clamps*
5   *Treated felt washers - Placing one of these on each post, directly under the cable clamps, will help prevent corrosion*
6   *Puller - Sometimes the cable clamps are very difficult to pull off the posts, even after the nut/bolt has been completely loosened. This tool pulls the clamp straight up and off the post without damage*
7   *Battery post/cable cleaner - Here is another cleaning tool which is a slightly different version of Number 4 above, but it does the same thing*
8   *Rubber gloves - Another safety item to consider when servicing the battery; remember that's acid inside the battery!*

*clothes and painted surfaces. When removing the battery cables, always detach the negative cable first and hook it up last!*

1   A routine preventive maintenance program for the battery in your vehicle is the only way to ensure quick and reliable starts. But before performing any battery maintenance, make sure that you have the proper equipment necessary to work safely around the battery (see illustration).
2   There are also several precautions that should be taken whenever battery maintenance is performed. Before servicing the battery, always turn the engine and all accessories off and disconnect the cable from the negative terminal of the battery

**10.6a Battery terminal corrosion usually appears as light, fluffy powder**

**10.7a When cleaning the cable clamps, all corrosion must be removed**

(see Chapter 5, Section 1).
3   The battery produces hydrogen gas, which is both flammable and explosive. Never create a spark, smoke or light a match around the battery. Always charge the battery in a ventilated area.
4   Electrolyte contains poisonous and corrosive sulfuric acid. Do not allow it to get in your eyes, on your skin or your clothes. Never ingest it. Wear protective safety glasses when working near the battery. Keep children away from the battery.
5   Note the external condition of the battery. If the positive terminal and cable clamp on your vehicle's battery is equipped with a rubber protector, make sure that it's not torn or damaged. It should completely cover the terminal. Look for any corroded or loose connections, cracks in the case or cover or loose hold-down clamps. Also check the entire length of each cable for cracks and frayed conductors.
6   If corrosion, which looks like white, fluffy deposits (see illustration) is evident, particu-

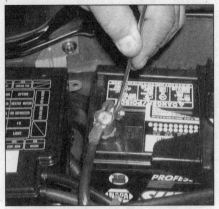

**10.6b Removing a cable from the battery post with a wrench - sometimes a pair of special battery pliers are required for this procedure if corrosion has caused deterioration of the nut hex (always remove the ground (-) cable first and hook it up last!)**

**10.7b Regardless of the type of tool used to clean the battery posts, a clean, shiny surface should be the result**

larly around the terminals, the battery should be removed for cleaning. Loosen the cable clamp bolts with a wrench, being careful to remove the ground cable first, and slide them off the terminals (see illustration). Then disconnect the hold-down clamp bolt and nut, remove the clamp and lift the battery from the engine compartment.
7   Clean the cable clamps thoroughly with a battery brush or a terminal cleaner and a solution of warm water and baking soda (see illustration). Wash the terminals and the top of the battery case with the same solution but make sure that the solution doesn't get into the battery. When cleaning the cables, terminals and battery top, wear safety goggles and rubber gloves to prevent any solution from coming in contact with your eyes or hands. Wear old clothes too - even diluted, sulfuric acid splashed onto clothes will burn holes in them. If the terminals have been extensively corroded, clean them up with a terminal cleaner (see illustration). Thoroughly wash all cleaned areas with plain water.

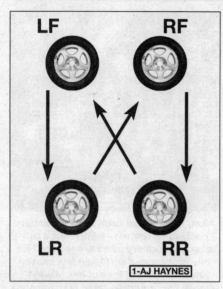

**11.2a The recommended four-tire rotation pattern**

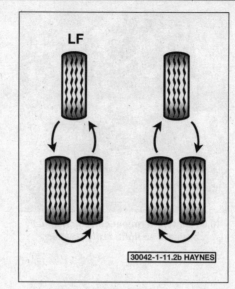

**11.2b Six-tire rotation pattern for models with dual rear wheels**

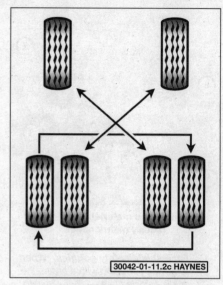

**11.2c Alternate six-tire rotation pattern for models with dual rear wheels**

8    Make sure that the battery tray is in good condition and the hold-down clamp fasteners are tight. If the battery is removed from the tray, make sure no parts remain in the bottom of the tray when the battery is reinstalled. When reinstalling the hold-down clamp bolts, do not overtighten them.

9    Information on removing and installing the battery can be found in Chapter 5. If you disconnected the cable(s) from the negative and/or positive battery terminals, see Chapter 5, Section 1. Information on jump starting can be found at the front of this manual. For more detailed battery checking procedures, refer to the *Haynes Automotive Electrical Manual.*

### Cleaning

10    Corrosion on the hold-down components, battery case and surrounding areas can be removed with a solution of water and baking soda. Thoroughly rinse all cleaned areas with plain water.

11    Any metal parts of the vehicle damaged by corrosion should be covered with a zinc-based primer, then painted.

### Charging

**Warning:** *When batteries are being charged, hydrogen gas, which is very explosive and flammable, is produced. Do not smoke or allow open flames near a charging or a recently charged battery. Wear eye protection when near the battery during charging. Also, make sure the charger is unplugged before connecting or disconnecting the battery from the charger.*

12    Slow-rate charging is the best way to restore a battery that's discharged to the point where it will not start the engine. It's also a good way to maintain the battery charge in a vehicle that's only driven a few miles between starts. Maintaining the battery charge is particularly important in the winter when the bat-

tery must work harder to start the engine and electrical accessories that drain the battery are in greater use.

13    It's best to use a one- or two-amp battery charger (sometimes called a "trickle" charger). They are the safest and put the least strain on the battery. They are also the least expensive. For a faster charge, you can use a higher amperage charger, but don't use one rated more than 1/10th the amp/hour rating of the battery. Rapid boost charges that claim to restore the power of the battery in one to two hours are hardest on the battery and can damage batteries not in good condition. This type of charging should only be used in emergency situations.

14    The average time necessary to charge a battery should be listed in the instructions that come with the charger. As a general rule, a trickle charger will charge a battery in 12 to 16 hours.

### 11    Tire rotation (every 6000 miles or 6 months)

1    The tires should be rotated at the specified intervals and whenever uneven wear is noticed.

2    Refer to the accompanying illustrations for the preferred tire rotation pattern.

**Note:** *If the front tires are different than the rear tires, rotate the tires from side-to-side only. Additionally, the tires on 3500 models with dual rear wheels are directional; when rotating (or installing the spare) the tires may have to be remounted so they rotate in the proper direction.*

3    Refer to the information in *Jacking and towing* at the front of this manual for the proper procedures to follow when raising the vehicle and changing a tire. If the brakes are to be checked, don't apply the parking brake

as stated. Make sure the tires are blocked to prevent the vehicle from rolling as it's raised.

4    Preferably, the entire vehicle should be raised at the same time. This can be done on a hoist or by jacking up each corner and then lowering the vehicle onto jackstands placed under the frame rails. Always use four jackstands and make sure the vehicle is safely supported.

5    After rotation, check and adjust the tire pressures as necessary. Tighten the lug nuts to the torque listed in this Chapter's Specifications.

### 12    Seat belt check (every 6000 miles or 6 months)

1    Check seat belts, buckles, latch plates and guide loops for obvious damage and signs of wear.

2    Where the seat belt receptacle bolts to the floor of the vehicle, check that the bolts are secure.

3    See if the seat belt reminder light comes on when the key is turned to the Run or Start position.

### 13    Steering linkage lubrication (2500/3500 4WD models) (every 6000 miles or 6 months)

1    The tie-rod ends on models equipped with lubrication fittings can be lubricated with a standard grease gun through the fitting at the bottom of the tie-rod end (see illustration).

2    When using a grease gun, pump the gun only a couple of times, or just enough to make the tie-rod end boot swell a little bit. If you overdo it, you could damage the boot.

**13.1 Wipe the dirt from the grease fitting before pushing the grease gun nozzle onto the fitting**

## 14  Underhood hose check and replacement (every 6000 miles or 6 months)

### General

**Caution:** *Replacement of air conditioning hoses must be left to a dealer service department or air conditioning shop that has the equipment to depressurize the system safely and recover the refrigerant. Never remove air conditioning components or hoses until the system has been depressurized.*

1    High temperatures in the engine compartment can cause the deterioration of the rubber and plastic hoses used for engine, accessory and emission systems operation. Periodic inspection should be made for cracks, loose clamps, material hardening and leaks. Information specific to the cooling system hoses can be found in Section 15.

2    Some, but not all, hoses are secured to their fittings with clamps. Where clamps are used, check to be sure they haven't lost their tension, allowing the hose to leak. If clamps aren't used, make sure the hose has not expanded and/or hardened where it slips over the fitting, allowing it to leak.

### Vacuum hoses

3    It's quite common for vacuum hoses, especially those in the emissions system, to be color-coded or identified by colored stripes molded into them. Various systems require hoses with different wall thickness, collapse resistance and temperature resistance. When replacing hoses, be sure the new ones are made of the same material.

4    Often the only effective way to check a hose is to remove it completely from the vehicle. If more than one hose is removed, be sure to label the hoses and fittings to ensure correct installation.

5    When checking vacuum hoses, be sure to include any plastic T-fittings in the check. Inspect the fittings for cracks and the hose where it fits over the fitting for distortion, which

**Check for a chafed area that could fail prematurely.**

**Check for a soft area indicating the hose has deteriorated inside.**

**Overtightening the clamp on a hardened hose will damage the hose and cause a leak.**

**Check each hose for swelling and oil-soaked ends. Cracks and breaks can be located by squeezing the hose.**

**15.4 Hoses, like drivebelts, have a habit of failing at the worst possible time - to prevent the inconvenience of a blown radiator or heater hose, inspect them carefully as shown here**

could cause leakage.

6    A small piece of vacuum hose (1/4-inch inside diameter) can be used as a stethoscope to detect vacuum leaks. Hold one end of the hose to your ear and probe around vacuum hoses and fittings, listening for the "hissing" sound characteristic of a vacuum leak. **Warning:** *When probing with the vacuum hose stethoscope, be very careful not to come into contact with moving engine components such as the drivebelt, cooling fan, etc.*

### Fuel hose

**Warning:** *There are certain precautions that must be taken when inspecting or servicing fuel system components. Work in a well-ventilated area and do not allow open flames (cigarettes, appliances, etc.) or bare light bulbs near the work area. Mop up any spills immediately and do not store fuel soaked rags where they could ignite. The fuel system is under high pressure, so if any fuel lines are to be disconnected, the pressure in the system must be relieved first*

(see Chapter 4A for more information).

7    Check all rubber fuel lines for deterioration and chafing. Check especially for cracks in areas where the hose bends and just before fittings, such as where a hose attaches to the fuel filter.

8    High quality fuel line, made specifically for high-pressure fuel injection systems, must be used for fuel line replacement. Never, under any circumstances, use unreinforced vacuum line, clear plastic tubing or water hose for fuel lines.

9    Spring-type clamps are commonly used on fuel lines. These clamps often lose their tension over a period of time, and can be "sprung" during removal. Replace all spring-type clamps with screw clamps whenever a hose is replaced.

### Metal lines

10    Sections of metal line are routed along the frame, between the fuel tank and the engine. Check carefully to be sure the line has not been bent or crimped and that cracks have not started in the line.

11    If a section of metal fuel line must be replaced, only seamless steel tubing should be used, since copper and aluminum tubing don't have the strength necessary to withstand normal engine vibration.

12    Check the metal brake lines where they enter the master cylinder and brake proportioning unit for cracks in the lines or loose fittings. Any sign of brake fluid leakage calls for an immediate and thorough inspection of the brake system.

## 15  Cooling system check (every 6000 miles or 6 months)

1    Many major engine failures can be attributed to a faulty cooling system. If the vehicle is equipped with an automatic transmission, the cooling system also cools the transmission fluid and thus plays an important role in prolonging transmission life.

2    The cooling system should be checked with the engine cold. Do this before the vehicle is driven for the day or after it has been shut off for at least three hours.

3    Remove the cooling system pressure cap and thoroughly clean the cap, inside and out, with clean water. Also clean the filler neck on the radiator. All traces of corrosion should be removed. The coolant inside the radiator should be relatively transparent. If it is rust-colored, the system should be drained, flushed and refilled (see Section 37). If the coolant level is not up to the top, add additional anti-freeze/coolant mixture (see Section 4).

4    Carefully check the large upper and lower radiator hoses along with the smaller diameter heater hoses that run from the engine to the firewall. Inspect each hose along its entire length, replacing any hose that is cracked, swollen or shows signs of deterioration. Cracks may become more apparent if the hose is squeezed (see illustration). Regard-

**17.6 Check for signs of fluid leakage at this point on shock absorbers (rear shock shown)**

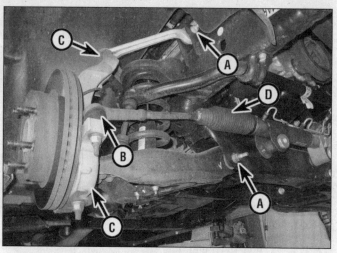

**17.9 Examine the mounting points for the upper and lower control arms on the front suspension (A), the tie-rod ends (B), the balljoints (C), and the steering gear boots (D)**

**17.11 With the steering wheel in the locked position and the vehicle raised, grasp the front tire as shown and try to move it back-and-forth - if any play is noted, check the steering gear mounts and tie-rod ends for looseness**

less of condition, it's a good idea to replace hoses with new ones every two years.

5      Make sure all hose connections are tight. A leak in the cooling system will usually show up as white or rust-colored deposits on the areas adjoining the leak. If wire-type clamps are used at the ends of the hoses, it may be a good idea to replace them with more secure screw-type clamps.

6      Use compressed air or a soft brush to remove bugs, leaves, etc., from the front of the radiator or air conditioning condenser. Be careful not to damage the delicate cooling fins or cut yourself on them.

7      Every other inspection, or at the first indication of cooling system problems, have the cap and system pressure tested. If you don't have a pressure tester, most repair shops will do this for a minimal charge.

## 16   Brake hose check (every 6000 miles or 6 months)

1      With the vehicle raised and supported securely on jackstands, the rubber hoses which connect the steel brake lines with the front and rear brake assemblies should be inspected for cracks, chafing of the outer cover, leaks, blisters and other damage. These are important and vulnerable parts of the brake system and inspection should be complete. A light and mirror will be helpful for a thorough check. If a hose exhibits any of the above conditions, replace it with a new one (see Chapter 9).

## 17   Suspension, steering and driveaxle boot check (every 6000 miles or 6 months)

**Note:** *The steering linkage and suspension components should be checked periodically. Worn or damaged suspension and steering linkage components can result in excessive and abnormal tire wear, poor ride quality and vehicle handling and reduced fuel economy. For detailed illustrations of the steering and suspension components, refer to Chapter 10.*

### Shock absorber check

1      Park the vehicle on level ground, turn the engine off and set the parking brake. Check the tire pressures.

2      Push down at one corner of the vehicle, then release it while noting the movement of the body. It should stop moving and come to rest in a level position within one or two bounces.

3      If the vehicle continues to move up-and-down or if it fails to return to its original position, a worn or weak shock absorber is prob-

ably the reason.

4      Repeat the above check at each of the three remaining corners of the vehicle.

5      Raise the vehicle and support it securely on jackstands.

6      Check the shock absorbers for evidence of fluid leakage (see illustration). A light film of fluid is no cause for concern. Make sure that any fluid noted is from the shocks and not from some other source. If leakage is noted, replace the shocks as a set.

7      Check the shocks to be sure that they are securely mounted and undamaged. Check the upper mounts for damage and wear. If damage or wear is noted, replace the shocks as a set (front or rear).

8      If the shocks must be replaced, refer to Chapter 10 for the procedure.

### Steering and suspension check

9      Visually inspect the steering and suspension components (front and rear) for damage and distortion. Look for damaged seals, boots and bushings and leaks of any kind. Examine the bushings where the control arms meet the chassis (see illustration).

10      Clean the lower end of the steering knuckle. Have an assistant grasp the lower edge of the tire and move the wheel in-and-out while you look for movement at the steering knuckle-to-control arm balljoint. If there is any movement the suspension balljoint(s) must be replaced.

11      Grasp each front tire at the front and rear edges, push in at the front, pull out at the rear and feel for play in the steering system components. If any freeplay is noted, check the idler arm and the tie-rod ends for looseness (see illustration).

12      Additional steering and suspension system information and illustrations can be found in Chapter 10.

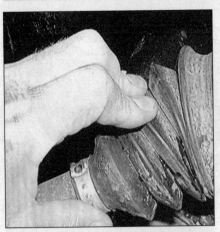

**17.14 Inspect the inner and outer driveaxle boots for loose clamps, cracks or signs of leaking lubricant**

**18.2a Inspect the muffler (A) for signs of deterioration, and all hangers (B)**

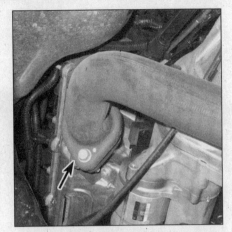

**18.2b Inspect all flanged joints (arrow indicates pipe-to-manifold joint) for signs of exhaust gas leakage**

### Driveaxle boot check (4WD models with independent front suspension)

13   The driveaxle boots are very important because they prevent dirt, water and foreign material from entering and damaging the constant velocity (CV) joints. Oil and grease can cause the boot material to deteriorate prematurely, so it's a good idea to wash the boots with soap and water. Because it constantly pivots back and forth following the steering action of the front hub, the outer CV boot wears out sooner and should be inspected regularly.

14   Inspect the boots for tears and cracks as well as loose clamps (see illustration). If there is any evidence of cracks or leaking lubricant, they must be replaced as described in Chapter 8.

### 18   Exhaust system check (every 6000 miles or 6 months)

1   With the engine cold (at least three hours after the vehicle has been driven), check the complete exhaust system from the manifold to the end of the tailpipe. Be careful around the catalytic converter, which may be hot even after three hours. The inspection should be done with the vehicle on a hoist to permit unrestricted access. If a hoist isn't available, raise the vehicle and support it securely on jackstands.

2   Check the exhaust pipes and connections for signs of leakage and/or corrosion indicating a potential failure. Make sure that all brackets and hangers are in good condition and tight (see illustrations).

3   Inspect the underside of the body for holes, corrosion, open seams, etc., which may allow exhaust gasses to enter the passenger's compartment. Seal all body openings with silicone sealant or body putty.

4   Rattles and other noises can often be traced to the exhaust system, especially the

**19.7a With the wheel off, check the thickness of the inner pad through the inspection hole (front disc shown, rear disc caliper similar)**

hangers, mounts and heat shields. Try to move the pipes, mufflers and catalytic converter. If the components can come in contact with the body or suspension parts, secure the exhaust system with new brackets and hangers

### 19   Brake system check (every 15,000 miles or 12 months)

**Warning:** *The dust created by the brake system is harmful to your health. Never blow it out with compressed air and don't inhale any of it. An approved filtering mask should be worn when working on the brakes. Do not, under any circumstances, use petroleum-based solvents to clean brake parts. Use brake system cleaner only!*

**Note:** *For detailed photographs of the brake system, refer to Chapter 9.*

1   In addition to the specified intervals, the brakes should be inspected every time the wheels are removed or whenever a defect is suspected.

2   Any of the following symptoms could indicate a potential brake system defect: The

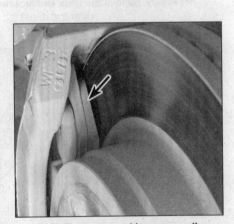

**19.7b The outer pad is more easily checked at the edge of the caliper**

vehicle pulls to one side when the brake pedal is depressed; the brakes make squealing or dragging noises when applied; brake pedal travel is excessive; the pedal pulsates; or brake fluid leaks, usually onto the inside of the tire or wheel.

3   Loosen the wheel lug nuts.

4   Raise the vehicle and place it securely on jackstands.

5   Remove the wheels (see Jacking and towing at the front of this book, or your owner's manual, if necessary).

### Disc brakes

6   There are two pads (an outer and an inner) in each caliper. The pads are visible with the wheels removed.

7   Check the pad thickness by looking at each end of the caliper and through the inspection window in the caliper body (see illustrations). If the lining material is less than the thickness listed in this Chapter's Specifications, replace the pads.

**Note:** *Keep in mind that the lining material is riveted or bonded to a metal backing plate and the metal portion is not included in this measurement.*

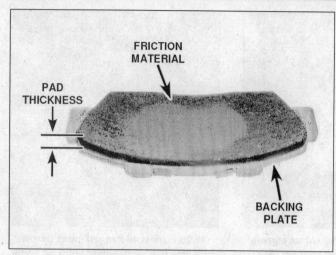

**19.9 If a more precise measurement of pad thickness is necessary, remove the pads and measure the remaining friction material**

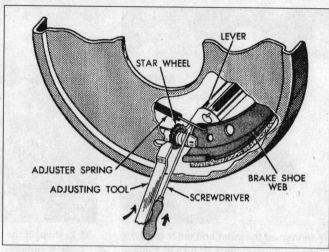

**19.14 Use a thin screwdriver to push the lever away, then use an adjusting tool or another screwdriver to back off the star wheel**

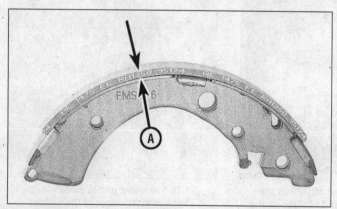

**19.16 If the lining is bonded to the brake shoe, measure the lining thickness from the outer surface to the metal shoe, as shown here; if the lining is riveted to the shoe, measure from the lining outer surface to the rivet head**

**19.18 To check for wheel cylinder leakage, use a small screwdriver to pry the boot away from the cylinder**

8    If it is difficult to determine the exact thickness of the remaining pad material by the above method, or if you are at all concerned about the condition of the pads, remove the caliper(s), then remove the pads from the calipers for further inspection (refer to Chapter 9).

9    Once the pads are removed from the calipers, clean them with brake cleaner and re-measure them with a ruler or a vernier caliper (see illustration).

10   Measure the disc thickness with a micrometer to make sure that it still has service life remaining. If any disc is thinner than the specified minimum thickness, replace it (refer to Chapter 9). Even if the disc has service life remaining, check its condition. Look for scoring, gouging and burned spots. If these conditions exist, remove the disc and have it resurfaced (see Chapter 9).

11   Before installing the wheels, check all brake lines and hoses for damage, wear, deformation, cracks, corrosion, leakage, bends and twists, particularly in the vicinity of the rubber hoses at the calipers. Check the clamps

for tightness and the connections for leakage. Make sure that all hoses and lines are clear of sharp edges, moving parts and the exhaust system. If any of the above conditions are noted, repair, reroute or replace the lines and/or fittings as necessary (see Chapter 9).

### Drum brakes

12   Remove the drum by pulling it off the axle and brake assembly. If this proves difficult, make sure the parking brake is released, then squirt penetrating oil around the center hub areas. Allow the oil to soak in and try to pull the drum off again.

13   If the drum still cannot be pulled off, the parking brake lever will have to be lifted slightly off its stop. This is done by first removing the small plug from the backing plate.

14   With the plug removed, insert a thin screwdriver and lift the adjusting lever off the star wheel, then use an adjusting tool or screwdriver to back off the star wheel several turns (see illustration). This will move the brake shoes away from the drum. If the drum

still won't pull off, tap around its inner circumference with a soft-faced hammer.

15   With the drum removed, do not touch any brake dust (see the Warning at the beginning of this Section).

16   Note the thickness of the lining material on both the front and rear brake shoes. If the material has worn away to within 1/16-inch of the recessed rivets or metal backing, the shoes should be replaced (see illustration). The shoes should also be replaced if they're cracked, glazed (shiny surface) or contaminated with brake fluid.

17   Make sure that all the brake assembly springs are connected and in good condition.

18   Check the brake components for any signs of fluid leakage. Carefully pry back the rubber cups on the wheel cylinders located at the top of the brake shoes (see illustration). Any leakage is an indication that the wheel cylinders should be overhauled immediately (see Chapter 9). Also check brake hoses and connections for signs of leakage.

19   Wipe the inside of the drum with a clean

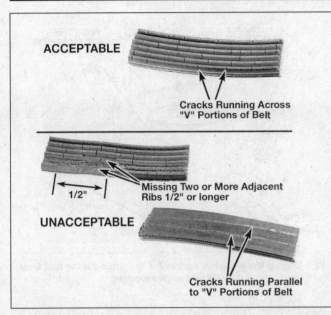

ACCEPTABLE

Cracks Running Across
"V" Portions of Belt

1/2"

Missing Two or More Adjacent
Ribs 1/2" or longer

UNACCEPTABLE

Cracks Running Parallel
to "V" Portions of Belt

20.4 Here are some of the more common problems associated
with drivebelts (check the belts very carefully to prevent an
untimely breakdown)

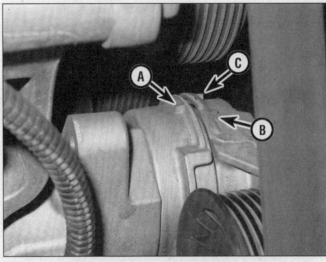

20.5 Belt wear indicator marks are located on the tensioner body -
when the belt reaches the maximum wear mark it must
be replaced

A   Stationary mark
B   When the belt is new, this mark will be near the stationary mark
C   When this mark reaches the stationary mark, the belt is worn out

rag and brake system cleaner. Again, be careful not to breathe the dangerous asbestos dust.

20   Check the inside of the drum for cracks, score marks, deep scratches and hard spots, which will appear as small discolorations. If these imperfections cannot be removed with fine emery cloth, the drums must be taken to an automotive machine shop for resurfacing.

21   If after the inspection process all parts are in good working condition, reinstall the brake drum.

22   Install the wheels and lower the vehicle.

### Brake booster check

23   Sit in the driver's seat and perform the following sequence of tests.

24   With the brake fully depressed, start the engine - the pedal should move down a little when the engine starts.

25   With the engine running, depress the brake pedal several times - the travel distance should not change.

26   Depress the brake, stop the engine and hold the pedal in for about 30 seconds - the pedal should neither sink nor rise.

27   Restart the engine, run it for about a minute and turn it off. Then firmly depress the brake several times - the pedal travel should decrease with each application.

28   If your brakes do not operate as described, the brake booster has failed. Refer to Chapter 9 for the replacement procedure.

### Parking brake

29   One method of checking the parking brake is to park the vehicle on a steep hill with the parking brake set and the transmission in Neutral (be sure to stay in the vehicle for this

check!). If the parking brake cannot prevent the vehicle from rolling, it's in need of adjustment (see Chapter 9).

### 20   Drivebelt check and replacement (every 15,000 miles or 12 months)

1   The drivebelt is located at the front of the engine and plays an important role in the overall operation of the vehicle and its components. Due to its function and material make-up, the drivebelt is prone to failure after a period of time and should be inspected and adjusted periodically to prevent major engine damage.

2   The vehicles covered by this manual are equipped with a single self-adjusting serpentine drivebelt, which is used to drive all of the accessory components such as the alternator, power steering pump, water pump and air conditioning compressor.

### Inspection

3   With the engine off, open the hood and locate the drivebelt at the front of the engine. Using your fingers (and a flashlight, if necessary), move along the belts checking for cracks and separation of the belt plies. Also check for fraying and glazing, which gives the belt a shiny appearance. Both sides of each belt should be inspected, which means you will have to twist the belt to check the underside.

4   Check the ribs on the underside of the belt. They should all be the same depth, with none of the surface uneven (see illustration).

5   The tension of the belt is automatically adjusted by the belt tensioner and does not

20.6 Rotate the tensioner arm to relieve
belt tension

require any adjustments. Drivebelt wear can be checked visually by inspecting the wear indicator marks located on the side of the tensioner body. Locate the belt tensioner at the front of the engine, then find the tensioner operating marks (see illustration). If the indicator mark is outside the operating range, the belt should be replaced.

### Replacement

6   To replace the belt, rotate the tensioner to relieve the tension on the belt (see illustration). Some models have a square hole in the tensioner arm that will accept a breaker bar or ratchet. On other models, place a wrench on the tensioner pulley bolt.

7   Remove the belt from the auxiliary components and carefully release the tensioner.

**20.8 The routing schematic for the serpentine belt is usually found on the fan shroud**

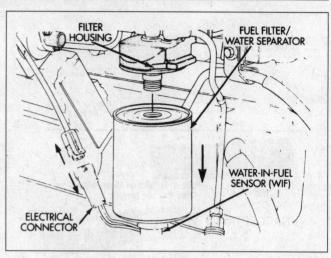

**22.3 Unplug the electrical connector and unscrew the fuel filter (1996 and earlier models)**

8    Route the new belt over the various pulleys, again rotating the tensioner to allow the belt to be installed, then release the belt tensioner. Make sure the belt fits properly into the pulley grooves - it must be completely engaged. Most models have a drivebelt routing decal on the upper radiator panel to help during drivebelt installation (see illustration).

## 21   Fuel system check (every 15,000 miles or 12 months)

**Warning:** *Gasoline and diesel fuels are flammable, so take extra precautions when you work on any part of the fuel system. Don't smoke or allow open flames or bare light bulbs near the work area, and don't work in a garage where a gas-type appliance (such as a water heater or clothes dryer) is present. Since fuel is carcinogenic, wear fuel-resistant gloves when there's a possibility of being exposed to fuel, and, if you spill any fuel on your skin, rinse it off immediately with soap and water. Mop up any spills immediately and do not store fuel-soaked rags where they could ignite. When you perform any kind of work on the fuel system, wear safety glasses and have a Class B type fire extinguisher on hand. The fuel system is under constant pressure, so, before any lines are disconnected, the fuel system pressure must be relieved (see Chapter 4A).*

1    If you smell fuel while driving or after the vehicle has been sitting in the sun, inspect the fuel system immediately.
2    Remove the fuel filler cap and inspect it for damage and corrosion. The gasket should have an unbroken sealing imprint. If the gasket is damaged or corroded, install a new cap.
3    Inspect the fuel feed line for cracks. Make sure that the connections between the fuel lines and the fuel injection system and between the fuel lines and the in-line fuel filter are tight.

**Warning:** *Your vehicle is fuel injected, so you must relieve the fuel system pressure before servicing fuel system components. The fuel system pressure relief procedure is outlined in Chapter 4A.*
4    Since some components of the fuel system - the fuel tank and part of the fuel feed and return lines, for example - are underneath the vehicle, they can be inspected more easily with the vehicle raised on a hoist. If that's not possible, raise the vehicle and support it on jackstands.
5    With the vehicle raised and safely supported, inspect the fuel tank and filler neck for punctures, cracks and other damage. The connection between the filler neck and the tank is particularly critical. Sometimes a rubber filler neck will leak because of loose clamps or deteriorated rubber. Inspect all fuel tank mounting brackets and straps to be sure that the tank is securely attached to the vehicle.
**Warning:** *Do not, under any circumstances, try to repair a fuel tank (except rubber components). A welding torch or any open flame can easily cause fuel vapors inside the tank to explode.*
6    Carefully check all rubber hoses and metal lines leading away from the fuel tank. Check for loose connections, deteriorated hoses, crimped lines and other damage. Repair or replace damaged sections as necessary (see Chapter 4A or Chapter 4B).

## 22   Fuel filter replacement and system bleeding (diesel engine) (every 15,000 miles or 12 months)

**Warning:** *Diesel fuel is flammable, so take extra precautions when you work on any part of the fuel system. Don't smoke or allow open flames or bare light bulbs near the work area, and don't work in a garage where a gas-type appliance (such as a water heater or clothes*

dryer) is present. Since fuel is carcinogenic, wear fuel-resistant gloves when there's a possibility of being exposed to fuel, and, if you spill any fuel on your skin, rinse it off immediately with soap and water. Mop up any spills immediately and do not store fuel-soaked rags where they could ignite. When you perform any kind of work on the fuel system, wear safety glasses and have a Class B type fire extinguisher on hand.
1    At the specified intervals, the fuel filter element (which incorporates a water separator) should be replaced with a new one.

## *Replacement*
### 1994 through 1996 models
2    Drain any water from the filter (see Section 6).
3    Unplug the Water In Filter (WIF) sensor, detach the drain tube, then unscrew the filter canister from the housing (see illustration). An oil filter wrench may be helpful in loosening the filter.
4    Unscrew the WIF sensor from the old filter and install it on the new one (see illustration).
5    Remove the O-ring seal from the housing and discard it (see illustration).
6    Carefully clean the filter housing contact area and WIF sensor probes.
7    Fill the new filter with clean fuel.
**Note:** *If the filter isn't filled with fuel, air could be trapped in the system and cause rough running.*
8    Install a new O-ring seal in the filter housing.
9    Lubricate the contact surface of the new filter with clean engine oil.
10    Apply a light coat of clean oil to the rubber gasket on the new filter.
11    Attach the new filter to the housing and tighten it one half turn by hand only. Don't use a filter wrench due to the possibility of over-tightening and damage to the seal.
12    Plug in the WIF electrical connector and install the hose on the drain valve.

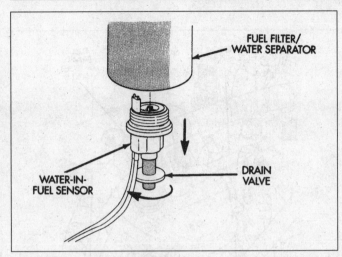

22.4 Remove the WIF sensor by unscrewing it from the fuel filter assembly (1996 and earlier models)

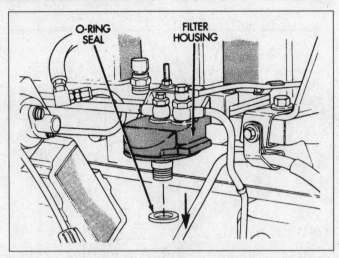

22.5 Be sure to remove the old O-ring seal from the filter housing and replace it with a new one

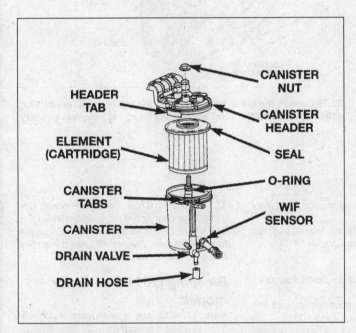

22.15a Exploded view of the fuel filter/water separator canister (1997 and 1998 models)

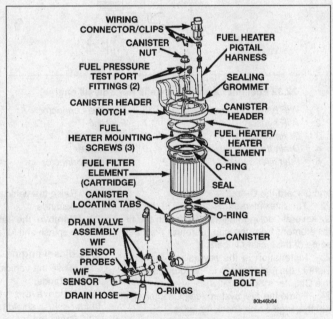

22.15b An exploded view of the fuel filter/water separator (1999 models)

### 1997 through 1999 models

13   Drain the contents of the fuel filter canister into a container by pushing the drain valve handle to the DRAIN position (see illustration 6.3b), and then close the drain valve handle when the canister is completely drained.

14   Detach the drain hose from the drain valve, then unplug the Water-In-Fuel electrical connector.

15   Unscrew the filter canister nut from the top of the canister header (see illustrations). Separate the canister from the header and remove the center O-ring.

16   Remove the filter element from the canister. Look down into the canister and check the probes of the Water-In-Fuel sensor. If they are dirty, clean them or replace the sensor as

necessary. Also clean out the inside of the canister.

17   Install a new O-ring on the canister stud, then install the new filter in the canister.

18   Fill the canister with clean diesel fuel. Also lubricate the seals with fuel.

19   Position the canister onto the header, aligning the locating tabs on the canister with the tab on the header. Install the canister nut, tightening it to a torque of 120 in-lbs.

### 2000 and later models

#### 5.9L diesel engines

20   Unscrew and remove the fuel filter cap from the top of the fuel filter housing (see illustration).

21   Remove the O-ring from the filter cap

22.20 To unscrew the cap, put a socket on the hex lug at the center of the cap. Do NOT try to loosen the cap at its outer edge

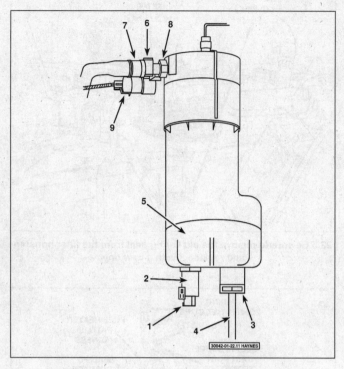

**22.32 Fuel filter assembly details (6.7L diesel engine)**

| | | | |
|---|---|---|---|
| 1 | WIF harness connector | 6 | Fuel line connector |
| 2 | WIF sensor | 7 | Fuel line |
| 3 | Drain valve | 8 | Filter screen |
| 4 | Drain tube | 9 | Fuel heater |
| 5 | Fuel filter canister | | element connector |

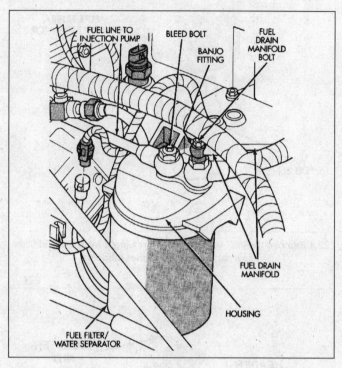

**22.39 Loosen the bleed bolt located in the top of the filter housing (1994 through 1996 model shown, 1997 and 1998 models similar)**

and discard the O-ring.

22    The filter element is secured to the cap by several "locking fingers." To detach the filter element from the cap, carefully pry back some of the locking fingers.

23    Installation is the reverse of removal. Tighten the fuel filter cap to the torque listed in this Chapter's Specifications.

24    Prime the fuel system (see Chapter 4B), run the engine and check for leaks.

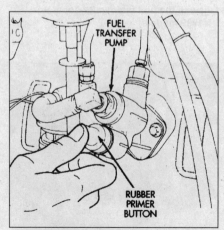

**22.40 Continue to press the rubber primer button on the fuel transfer pump until bubble-free fuel comes out of the bleed bolt (1994 through 1998 models)**

25    Raise the vehicle and support it securely on jackstands.

26    Remove the left front wheel and the fender splash shield (see Chapter 11).

**6.7L diesel engines**

27    Raise the vehicle and support it securely on jackstands.

28    Remove the left front wheel and the fender splash shield (see Chapter 11).

29    Drain the water and fuel contaminants (see Section 6).

30    Disconnect the Water In Fuel (WIF) harness connector.

31    Disconnect the drain hose from the drain valve.

32    Use an oil filter wrench to rotate the bottom portion (canister filter) from the fuel filter assembly (see illustration).

33    Spin the fuel filter by hand from the fuel filter/canister assembly and set it aside.

34    Remove the secondary fuel filter screen from the fuel filter assembly. Release the quick-connect fuel line fitting from the filter assembly. Refer to Chapter 4A for detailed information on fuel line disconnection procedures.

35    Unscrew the line fitting from the fuel filter assembly and remove the fuel line along with the O-ring and filter screen.

36    Clean the fuel filter screen and replace the O-ring with a new one.

37    Installation is the reverse of removal. Use a new filter cartridge in the fuel filter assembly and a new O-ring in the fuel line. Prime the fuel system (see Chapter 4B), run the engine and check for leaks.

## Bleeding (2001 and earlier models)

**Note:** On 2002 and later models, a different priming method is used (see Chapter 4B).

### 1994 through 1998 models

38    Should some air enter the system during the above procedure, it can be bled out through the filter housing bleed bolt.

39    With the engine off and cold, loosen the bleed bolt on the top of the filter housing (see illustration).

40    Pump the rubber primer button on the fuel transfer pump until clean, bubble free fuel issues from the bleed bolt, then tighten the bolt securely (see illustration).

### 1999 through 2001 models

41    Loosen - but don't remove - the banjo bolt that attaches the fuel supply line to the fuel injection pump (see illustrations). Wrap the fitting in a shop towel to catch any excess fuel.

42    Turn the ignition key to the Crank position and then quickly, before the engine starts, release the key to the On position. In

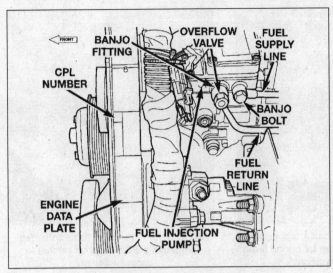

**22.41a Fuel supply line banjo bolt (1999 models)**

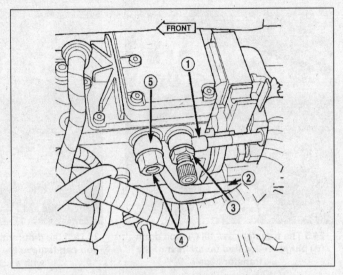

**22.41b Fuel supply line banjo/test port fitting
(2000 and 2001 models)**

| | | | |
|---|---|---|---|
| 1 | Fuel supply line banjo fitting | 4 | Overflow valve |
| 2 | Fuel return line | 5 | Fuel return line banjo fitting |
| 3 | Test port fitting | | |

this mode, the transfer pump will operate for about 25 seconds. Watch for fuel leaking out at the loosened fuel supply line banjo bolt. If fuel is not present after 25 seconds, repeat this step until fuel is leaking out at the banjo fitting.

43  Tighten the banjo fitting to the torque listed in this Chapter's Specifications.

44  Try to start the engine. If the engine does start, it might run erratically and noisily for a few minutes. This is normal. If the fuel tank has been allowed to run dry, if the injection pump has been replaced or if the vehicle hasn't been operated for awhile, the engine might not start. If it doesn't, proceed to the next Step.

45  Repeat the previous air bleeding procedure using the transfer pump. Make sure that there is fuel at the fuel supply line banjo fitting before proceeding.

46  Crank the engine for 30 seconds at a time, to allow any air trapped in the injection pump to vent out the drain manifold. The engine might start during cranking, and then run erratically and noisily. This is normal.

47  If the engine still doesn't start, bleed the excess air from the high-pressure fuel lines by cracking the fittings at cylinders 3, 4 and 5. **Warning:** *The injection pump supplies fuel to the injectors at extremely high pressure. At this pressure, fuel can penetrate human skin and cause personal injury. When bleeding high-pressure fuel lines, wear safety goggles and suitable protective clothing to protect yourself from contact with fuel spray.*

48  Continue to bleed the injectors until the engine runs smoothly. This might take a few minutes. Then tighten the injector fuel line fittings securely.

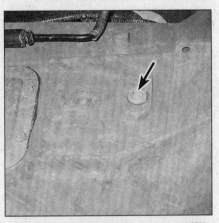

**24.1 The manual transmission check/fill plug is located on the side of the case**

### 23  Water pump check (diesel engine) (every 15,000 miles or 12 months)

1  A failure in the water pump can cause serious engine damage due to overheating.

2  There are several ways to check the operation of the water pump while it's installed on the engine. If the pump is defective, it should be replaced with a new or rebuilt unit.

3  Water pumps are equipped with weep or vent holes. If a failure occurs in the pump seal, coolant will leak from the hole. In most cases you'll need a flashlight to find the hole on the water pump from underneath to check for leaks or blockage.

4  If the water pump shaft bearings fail there may be a howling sound at the front of

the engine while it's running. Shaft wear can be felt if the water pump pulley is rocked up and down. Don't mistake drivebelt slippage, which causes a squealing sound, for water pump bearing failure.

5  It is possible for a water pump to be bad, even if it doesn't howl or leak water. Sometimes the fins on the back of the impeller can corrode away until the pump is no longer effective. The only way to check for this is to remove the pump for examination (see Chapter 3).

### 24  Manual transmission, transfer case and differential lubricant level check (every 15,000 miles or 12 months)

### *Manual transmission*

1  The manual transmission has a filler plug which must be removed to check the lubricant level (see illustration). If the vehicle is raised to gain access to the plug, be sure to support it safely on jackstands - DO NOT crawl under a vehicle that is supported only by a jack! Be sure the vehicle is level or the check may be inaccurate.

2  Using the appropriate wrench, unscrew the plug from the transmission.

3  Use your little finger to reach inside the housing to feel the lubricant level. The level should be at or near the bottom of the plug hole. If it isn't, add the recommended lubricant through the plug hole with a syringe or squeeze bottle.

4  Install and tighten the plug. Check for leaks after the first few miles of driving.

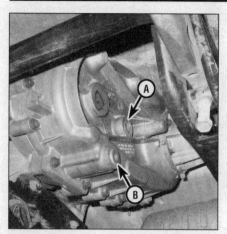

**24.5 The transfer case fill (A) and drain (B) plugs are located on the rear of the transfer case**

**24.7a If the differential has a rubber plug, you can remove the plug by prying it out with a screwdriver**

**24.7b If the differential has a threaded plug, use a 3/8-inch drive ratchet to unscrew the plug**

### Transfer case (4WD models)

5    The transfer case lubricant level is checked by removing the fill plug (see illustration).

6    After removing the plug, reach inside the hole. The lubricant level should be just at the bottom of the hole. If not, add the appropriate lubricant through the opening.

### Differential

7    The differential lubricant level is checked by removing a filler plug from the differential cover (see illustrations). If the vehicle is raised to gain access to the plug, be sure to support it safely on jackstands - DO NOT crawl under a vehicle that is supported only by a jack! Be sure the vehicle is level or the check may be inaccurate.

8    With the differential cold, remove the fill plug. The lubricant should be level with the bottom of the fill plug hole.

9    If the level is low, add the recommended lubricant through the filler plug hole with a pump, syringe or squeeze bottle.

10   Install the plug and check for leaks after the first few miles of driving.

### 25   Valve clearance check and adjustment (see Maintenance Schedule for service intervals)

1    Make sure the engine is cold before beginning this procedure (below 140-degrees F).

2    Refer to Chapter 2D and remove the valve cover, then use the "barring" tool (and, on 1998 and earlier models, the timing pin) to position the number one piston at TDC on the compression stroke (see Chapter 2D, Section 3). On 1998 and earlier models, disengage the timing pin after locating TDC.

3    With the crankshaft at number one TDC, measure the clearance of the indicated valves (see illustration). Insert a feeler gauge of the specified thickness listed in this Chapter's Specifications, between the valve stem tip and the rocker arm. The feeler gauge should slip between the valve stem tip and rocker arm with a slight amount of drag.

4    If the clearance is incorrect (too loose or too tight), loosen the locknut and turn the adjusting screw slowly until you can feel a slight drag on the feeler gauge as you withdraw it from between the valve stem tip and the rocker arm (see illustration).

5    Once the clearance is adjusted, hold the adjusting screw with a screwdriver (to keep it from turning) and tighten the locknut to the torque listed in this Chapter's Specifications. Recheck the clearance to make sure it hasn't changed after tightening the locknut.

6    Make a mark on the crankshaft pulley and an adjacent mark on the front cover. Rotate the crankshaft one complete revolution (360-degrees) and realign the marks (make sure the timing pin is removed before rotating the crankshaft). Check the clearance of the remaining valves (see illustration).

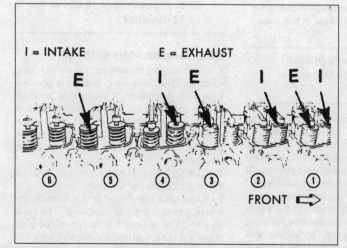

**25.3 With the no. 1 piston at TDC on the compression stroke, check and adjust the clearance of the indicated valves (12-valve model shown, 24-valve model similar)**

**25.4 Loosen the locknut and turn the adjusting screw until the feeler gauge slips between the valve stem tip and rocker arm with a slight amount of drag**

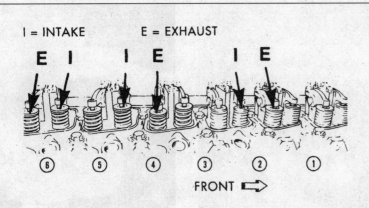

**25.6 Rotate the crankshaft 360-degrees from no. 1 TDC, then check and adjust the clearance of the indicated valves (12-valve model shown, 24-valve model similar)**

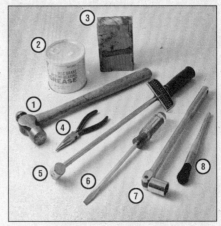

**26.1 Tools and materials needed for front wheel bearing maintenance**

7    If necessary, repeat the adjustment procedure described in Steps 3, 4 and 5 until all the valves are adjusted to specifications.
8    Install the valve covers.

## 26  Front wheel bearing check (every 30,000 miles or 24 months)

**Note:** *On 2000 and later 2WD models, the hub and bearing assembly is a sealed unit and is not serviceable or adjustable. The hub nut is not reusable if removed.*

### 1999 and earlier 2WD models

1    In most cases the front wheel bearings will not need servicing until the brake pads are changed. However, the bearings should be checked whenever the front of the vehicle is raised for any reason. Several items, including a torque wrench and special grease, are required for this procedure (see illustration).
2    With the vehicle securely supported on jackstands, spin each wheel and check for noise, rolling resistance and freeplay.
3    Grasp the top of each tire with one hand and the bottom with the other. Move the wheel in-and-out on the spindle. If there's any noticeable movement, the bearings should be checked and then repacked with grease or replaced if necessary.
4    Remove the wheel.
5    Remove the brake caliper (see Chapter 9) and hang it out of the way on a piece of wire. A wood block can be slid between the brake pads to keep them separated, if necessary.
6    Remove the dust cap using large pliers or by prying it out of the hub using a hammer and chisel (see illustration).
7    Straighten the bent ends of the cotter pin, then pull the cotter pin out of the nut lock (see illustration). Discard the cotter pin and use a new one during reassembly.
8    Remove the nut lock, nut and washer from the end of the spindle (see illustration).
9    Pull the hub/disc assembly out slightly, then push it back into its original position. This

1    *Hammer - A common hammer will do just fine*
2    *Grease - High-temperature grease that is formulated for front wheel bearings should be used*
3    *Wood block - If you have a scrap piece of 2x4, it can be used to drive the new seal into the hub*
4    *Needle-nose pliers - Used to straighten and remove the cotter pin in the spindle*
5    *Torque wrench - This is very important in this procedure; if the bearing is too tight, the wheel won't turn freely - if it's too loose, the wheel will "wobble" on the spindle. Either way, it could mean extensive damage*
6    *Screwdriver - Used to remove the seal from the hub (a long screwdriver is preferred)*
7    *Socket/breaker bar - Needed to loosen the nut on the spindle if it's extremely tight*
8    *Brush - Together with some clean solvent, this will be used to remove old grease from the hub and spindle*

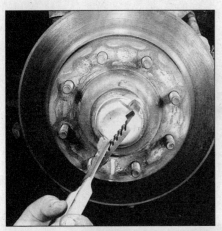

**26.6 You may be able to use large pliers to grasp the grease cap securely and work it out of the hub - if it's stuck, you'll have to use a hammer and chisel to detach it**

**26.7 Remove the cotter pin**

**26.8 Remove the nut lock and nut**

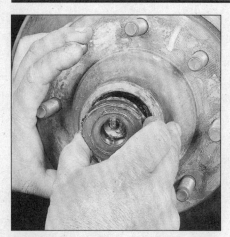

**26.9 Pull the hub out to dislodge the outer wheel bearing and washer**

**26.10 Reinstall the hub nut, then grasp the hub securely and pull out sharply to dislodge the inner bearing and seal against the back of the nut**

**26.12 Slide the inner bearing and seal assembly off the spindle**

should force the outer bearing off the spindle enough so it can be removed (see illustration).

10    Temporarily reinstall the hub/disc assembly and spindle nut. Dislodge the inner bearing and seal by grasping the assembly and pulling out sharply (see illustration).

11    Once the bearing and seal are free, remove the hub/disc assembly from the spindle.

12    Remove the inner wheel bearing and seal from the spindle, noting how the seal is installed (see illustration).

13    Use solvent to remove all traces of the old grease from the bearings, hub and spindle. A small brush may prove helpful; however make sure no bristles from the brush embed themselves inside the bearing rollers. Allow the parts to air dry.

14    Carefully inspect the bearings for cracks, heat discoloration, worn rollers, etc. Check the bearing races inside the hub for wear and damage. If the bearing races are defective, the hubs should be taken to a machine shop with the facilities to remove the old races and press new ones in. Note that the bearings and races come as matched sets and old bearings should never be installed on new races.

15    Use high-temperature front wheel bearing grease to pack the bearings. Work the grease completely into the bearings, forcing it between the rollers, cone and cage from the back side (see illustration).

16    Apply a thin coat of grease to the spindle at the outer bearing seat, inner bearing seat, shoulder and seal seat.

17    Put a small quantity of grease inboard of each bearing race inside the hub. Using your finger, form a dam at these points to provide extra grease availability and to keep thinned grease from flowing out of the bearing.

18    Place the grease-packed inner bearing into the rear of the hub and put a little more grease outboard of the bearing.

19    Place a new seal over the inner bearing and tap the seal evenly into place with a hammer and blunt punch until it's flush with the hub (see illustration).

20    Carefully place the hub assembly onto the spindle and push the grease-packed outer bearing into position.

21    Install the washer and spindle nut. Tighten the nut only slightly (no more than 12 ft-lbs of torque).

22    Spin the hub in a forward direction while tightening the spindle nut to approximately 20 ft-lbs to seat the bearings and remove any grease or burrs which could cause excessive bearing play later (see illustration).

23    Loosen the spindle nut 1/4-turn, then using your hand (not a wrench of any kind), tighten the nut until it's snug. Install the nut lock and a new cotter pin through the hole in the spindle and the slots in the nut lock. If the nut lock slots don't line up, remove the nut lock and turn it slightly until they do.

**26.15 Work the grease completely into the bearing rollers - if you don't like getting greasy, special bearing packing tools that work with a common grease gun are available inexpensively from auto parts stores**

**26.19 Use a block of wood and a hammer to tap the inner bearing seal evenly into the hub**

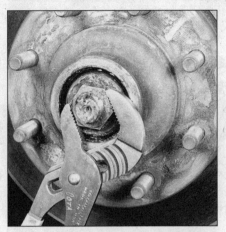

**26.22 Seat the bearings by spinning the hub while tightening the hub nut**

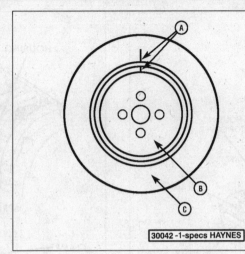

**28.3 Vibration damper details**

A   The index lines should be no more than 1/16 inch out of alignment
B   Damper hub
C   Damper

24   Bend the ends of the cotter pin until they're flat against the nut. Cut off any extra length which could interfere with the dust cap.
25   Install the dust cap, tapping it into place with a hammer.
26   Place the brake caliper near the rotor and carefully remove the wood spacer. Install the caliper (see Chapter 9).
27   Install the wheel on the hub and tighten the lug nuts to the torque listed in this Chapter's Specifications.
28   Grasp the top and bottom of the tire and check the bearings in the manner described earlier in this Section.
29   Lower the vehicle.

### 2000 and later models

30   Front wheel bearings are incorporated into the front hub, and are serviced as a unit.
31   Because the hub/bearing assembly is "lifetime-lubricated," there is no need for periodic lubrication. They should, however, be checked at regular intervals for wear.
32   Raise the vehicle and suitably support the front end with jackstands. Grasp the tire/wheel at the top and bottom and rock them to check for noticeable play.
33   If any amount of play is felt, refer to Chapter 9 and remove the wheel, brake caliper and brake disc.
34   Rock just the hub itself on the spindle. If any play is felt, the hub/bearing assembly should be replaced. Refer to Chapter 10 for hub/bearing replacement.

### 27   Cooling fan hub check (diesel engine) (every 30,000 miles or 24 months)

1   Disconnect the cables from the negative battery terminals (see Chapter 5, Section 1), then rock the fan back and forth by hand to

check for excessive bearing play.
2   With the engine cold (and not running), turn the fan blades by hand. The fan should turn freely.
3   Visually inspect for substantial fluid leakage from the clutch assembly. If problems are noted, replace the clutch assembly.
4   With the engine completely warmed up, turn off the ignition switch and disconnect the negative battery cable from the battery. Turn the fan by hand. Some drag should be evident. If the fan turns easily, replace the fan clutch (see Chapter 3).

### 28   Vibration damper check (diesel engine) (every 30,000 miles or 24 months)

1   Disconnect the cables from the negative battery terminals (see Chapter 5, Section 1).
2   If you can't see the index lines on the vibration damper, remove the damper (see Chapter 2D, Section 8).
3   Check to see if the damper index lines are within specification (see illustration). Also, check between the damper and damper hub to see if the rubber is cracked, separated or missing segments which would indicate a need for replacement.
4   See Chapter 2D, Section 8, for the replacement procedure. Be sure to tighten the damper mounting bolts to the torque listed in the Chapter 2A Specifications

### 29   Brake fluid change (every 30,000 miles or 24 months)

**Warning:** *Brake fluid can harm your eyes and damage painted surfaces, so use extreme caution when handling or pouring it. Do not use brake fluid that has been standing open*

*or is more than one year old. Brake fluid absorbs moisture from the air. Excess moisture can cause a dangerous loss of braking effectiveness.*
1   At the specified intervals, the brake fluid should be drained and replaced. Since the brake fluid may drip or splash when pouring it, place plenty of rags around the master cylinder to protect any surrounding painted surfaces.
2   Before beginning work, purchase the specified brake fluid (see *Recommended lubricants and fluids* at the beginning of this Chapter).
3   Remove the cap from the master cylinder reservoir.
4   Using a hand suction pump or similar device, withdraw the fluid from the master cylinder reservoir.
5   Add new fluid to the master cylinder until it rises to the base of the filler neck.
6   Bleed the brake system as described in Chapter 9 at all four brakes until new and uncontaminated fluid is expelled from the bleeder screw. Be sure to maintain the fluid level in the master cylinder as you perform the bleeding process. If you allow the master cylinder to run dry, air will enter the system.
7   Refill the master cylinder with fluid and check the operation of the brakes. The pedal should feel solid when depressed, with no sponginess.
**Warning:** *Do not operate the vehicle if you are in doubt about the effectiveness of the brake system.*

### 30   Air filter replacement (gasoline engines) (every 30,000 miles or 24 months)

1   At the specified intervals, the air filter element should be replaced with a new one.

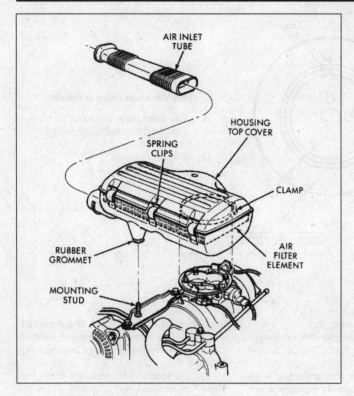

30.3 V6 and V8 engine air filter housing details

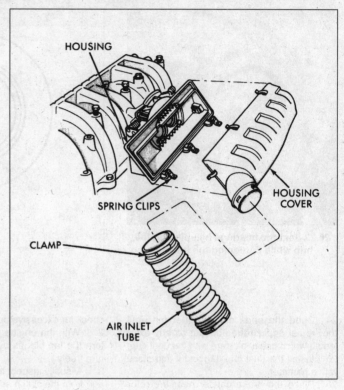

30.9 V10 engine air filter housing details

### 2001 and earlier 1500 models/2002 and earlier 2500 and 3500 models

#### V6 and V8 engines

2    The filter housing is located on top of the throttle body.

3    Remove the air inlet tube, loosen the housing to throttle body clamp screw, then lift the assembly up and off the mounting stud (see illustration). On some models it will be necessary to detach the air pump hose from the air filter.

4    Detach the spring clips and rotate the housing cover rearward, then lift the air filter element out of the housing. Wipe out the inside of the air filter housing with a clean rag.

5    While the housing is off, be careful not to drop anything down into the throttle body.

6    Place the new filter element in the air filter housing. Make sure it seats properly in the bottom of the housing.

7    Installation is the reverse of removal.

#### V10 engine

8    The filter is mounted on the side of the throttle body.

9    Use adjustable pliers to loosen the clamps and remove the air inlet tube, detach the spring clips and rotate the housing cover off, then lift the air filter element out of the housing (see illustration). Wipe out the inside of the air filter housing with a clean rag.

10    While the housing cover is off, be careful not to drop anything down into the throttle body.

11    Place the new filter element in the air filter housing. Make sure it seats properly in the bottom of the housing.

12    Installation is the reverse of removal.

### 2002 and later 1500 models/2003 and later 2500 and 3500 models

13    On all models, the air filter is housed in a black plastic box mounted on the inner fenderwell on the right side of the engine compartment.

14    Detach the spring clips and pull the housing cover up, then lift the air filter element out of the housing (see illustrations). Wipe out the inside of the air filter housing with a clean rag.

15    While the cover is off, be careful not to drop anything down into the air filter housing.

16    Place the new filter element in the air filter housing. Make sure it seats properly in the groove of the housing.

17    Installation is the reverse of removal.

30.14a Release the spring clips and lift the air filter housing cover

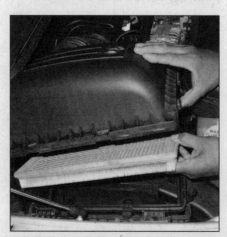

30.14b Remove the air filter element from the housing

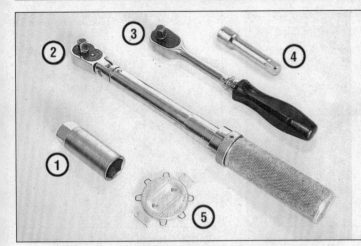

**31.2 Tools required for changing spark plugs**

1   **Spark plug socket** - This will have special padding inside to protect the spark plug's porcelain insulator
2   **Torque wrench** - Although not mandatory, using this tool is the best way to ensure the plugs are tightened properly
3   **Ratchet** - Standard hand tool to fit the spark plug socket
4   **Extension** - Depending on model and accessories, you may need special extensions and universal joints to reach one or more of the plugs
5   **Spark plug gap gauge** - This gauge for checking the gap comes in a variety of styles. Make sure the gap for your engine is included

## 31   Spark plug replacement (gasoline engines) (every 30,000 miles or 24 months)

1   The spark plugs are threaded into the cylinder heads.

2   In most cases, the tools necessary for spark plug replacement include a spark plug socket which fits onto a ratchet (spark plug sockets are padded inside to prevent damage to the porcelain insulators on the new plugs), various extensions and a gap gauge to check and adjust the gaps on the new plugs (see illustration). A special plug wire removal tool is available for separating the wire boots from the spark plugs, but it isn't absolutely necessary. A torque wrench should be used to tighten the new plugs.

3   The best approach when replacing the spark plugs is to purchase the new ones in advance, adjust them to the proper gap and replace them one at a time. When buying the new spark plugs, be sure to obtain the correct plug type for your particular engine. This information can be found on the Emission Control Information label located under the hood, in the factory owner's manual and the Specifications at the front of this Chapter. If differ-ences exist between the plug specified on the emissions label and in the owner's manual, assume that the emissions label is correct.

4   Allow the engine to cool completely before attempting to remove any of the plugs. While you're waiting for the engine to cool, check the new plugs for defects and adjust the gaps.

5   The gap is checked by inserting the proper-thickness gauge between the electrodes at the tip of the plug (see illustration). The gap between the electrodes should be the same as the one specified on the Emissions Control Information label or in this Chapter's Specifications. The gauge should just slide between the electrodes with a slight amount of drag. If the gap is incorrect, use the adjuster on the gauge body to bend the curved side electrode slightly until the proper gap is obtained (see illustration). If the side electrode is not exactly over the center electrode, bend it with the adjuster until it is. Check for cracks in the porcelain insulator (if any are found, the plug should not be used).

6   Some engines are equipped with individual ignition coils which must be removed first to access the spark plugs (see illustration). On engines equipped with spark plug wires, with the engine cool, remove the spark plug wire from one spark plug. Pull only on the boot at the end of the wire - do not pull on the wire (see illustration).

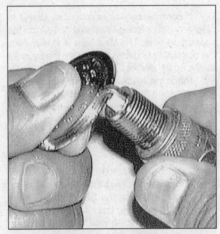

**31.5a Using a tapered thickness gauge to check the spark plug gap - slide the thin side into the gap and turn it until the gauge just fills the gap, then read the thickness on the gauge - do not force the tool into the gap or use the tapered portion to widen a gap**

**31.5b To change the gap, bend the side electrode only, using the adjuster hole in the tool, and be very careful not to crack or chip the porcelain insulator surrounding the center electrode**

**31.6a On models with individual ignition coils, remove the mounting bolts and the individual coil(s) to access the spark plug(s) (one type shown, others similar)**

**31.6b Hemi engines have spark plug(s) located under spark plug wire(s) in addition to the individual ignition coils**

**31.8 Use a socket and extension to unscrew the spark plugs**

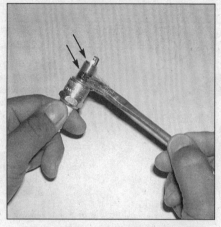

**31.10a Apply a thin film of anti-seize compound to the spark plug threads to prevent damage to the cylinder head**

**31.10b A length of snug-fitting rubber hose will save time and prevent damaged threads when installing the spark plugs**

7    If compressed air is available, use it to blow any dirt or foreign material away from the spark plug hole. The idea here is to eliminate the possibility of debris falling into the cylinder as the spark plug is removed.

8    Place the spark plug socket over the plug and remove it from the engine by turning it in a counterclockwise direction (see illustration).

9    Compare the spark plug with the chart on the inside back cover of this manual to get an indication of the general running condition of the engine.

10    Apply a small amount of anti-seize compound to the spark plug threads (see illustration). Thread one of the new plugs into the hole until you can no longer turn it with your fingers, then tighten it with a torque wrench (if available) or the ratchet. It's a good idea to slip a short length of rubber hose over the end of the plug to use as a tool to thread it into place (see illustration). The hose will grip the plug well enough to turn it, but will start to slip if the plug begins to cross-thread in the hole - this will prevent damaged threads and the accompanying repair costs.

11    On engines with individual ignition coils, before pushing the ignition coil onto the end of the plug, inspect the ignition coil following the procedures outlined in Section 32. On engines with spark plug wires, inspect the plug wire following the procedures outlined in Section 33.

12    Repeat the procedure for the remaining spark plugs.

## 32   Ignition coil check

1    Clean the coils with a dampened cloth and dry them thoroughly.

2    Inspect each coil for cracks, damage and carbon tracking. Make sure the coil fits securely onto the spark plug. If damage exists, replace the coil.

## 33   Spark plug wires and distributor cap and rotor check and replacement (every 60,000 miles or 48 months)

**Note:** *5.7L Hemi engines are equipped with a distributorless ignition system. The spark plug wires are connected directly to the ignition coils. The distributors used on the 5.2L and 5.9L V8 gasoline engines are mounted at the rear of the block.*

1    The spark plug wires should be checked whenever new spark plugs are installed.

2    Begin this procedure by making a visual check of the spark plug wires while the engine is running. In a darkened garage (make sure there is adequate ventilation) start the engine and observe each plug wire. Be careful not to come into contact with any moving engine parts. If there is a break in the wire, you will see arcing or a small spark at the damaged area. If arcing is noticed, make a note to obtain new wires, then allow the engine to cool and check the distributor cap and rotor.

3    The spark plug wires should be inspected one at a time to prevent mixing up the order, which is essential for proper engine operation. Each original plug wire should be numbered to help identify its location. If the number is illegible, a piece of tape can be marked with the correct number and wrapped around the plug wire.

4    Disconnect the plug wire from the spark plug. A removal tool can be used for this purpose or you can grasp the rubber boot, twist the boot half a turn and pull the boot free. Do not pull on the wire itself.

5    Check inside the boot for corrosion, which will look like a white crusty powder.

6    Push the wire and boot back onto the end of the spark plug. It should fit tightly onto the end of the plug. If it doesn't, remove the wire and use pliers to carefully crimp the metal connector inside the wire boot until the fit is snug.

7    Using a clean rag, wipe the entire length of the wire to remove built-up dirt and grease. Once the wire is clean, check for burns, cracks and other damage. Do not bend the wire sharply, because the conductor might break.

8    Remove the rubber boot and disconnect the wire from the distributor or coil. Again, pull only on the rubber boot. Check for corrosion and a tight fit. Replace the wire in the distributor or coil.

9    Inspect the remaining spark plug wires, making sure that each one is securely fastened at the distributor or coil and spark plug when the check is complete.

10    If new spark plug wires are required, purchase a set for your specific engine model. Remove and replace the wires one at a time to avoid mix-ups in the firing order.

11    Detach the distributor cap (if equipped) by loosening the cap retaining screws. Look inside it for cracks, carbon tracks and worn, burned or loose contacts (see illustration).

12    Pull the rotor off the distributor shaft and examine it for cracks and carbon tracks (see illustration). Replace the cap and rotor if any damage or defects are noted.

13    When installing a new cap, remove the wires from the old cap one at a time and attach them to the new cap in the exact same location.

**Note:** *If an accidental mix-up occurs, refer to the firing order Specifications at the beginning of this Chapter.*

## 34   Positive Crankcase Ventilation (PCV) valve check and replacement (every 60,000 miles or 48 months)

**Note:** *This section applies to the 3.7L V6, 4.7L V8, 5.2L V8 and 5.9L V8 gasoline engines only.*

**Note:** *For additional information on the PCV system refer to Chapter 6.*

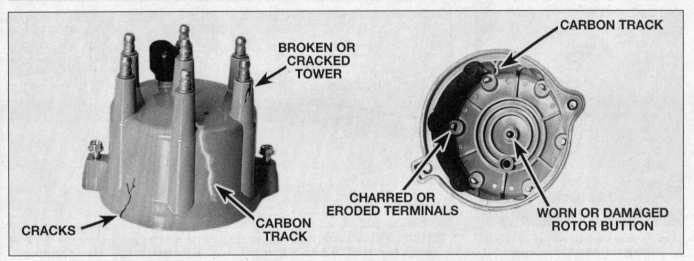

**33.11 Shown here are some of the common defects to look for when inspecting the distributor cap (if in doubt about its condition, install a new one)**

1    The PCV valve is located in the neck of the oil filler tube on 3.7L V6 and 4.7L V8 engines (see illustration). On 5.2L and 5.9L gasoline engines, the PCV valve is located in the valve cover.

2    With the engine idling at normal operating temperature, remove the PCV valve. If you're working on a 5.2L or 5.9L gasoline engine, pull the PCV from the valve cover.

3    Place your finger over the valve opening. If there's no vacuum at the valve, check for a plugged hose, manifold port, or the valve itself. Replace any plugged or deteriorated hoses.

4    Turn off the engine and shake the PCV valve, listening for a rattle. If the valve doesn't rattle, replace it with a new one.

5    To replace the valve, pull it from the end of the hose, noting its installed position.

6    When purchasing a replacement PCV valve, make sure it's for your particular vehicle and engine size. Compare the old valve with the new one to make sure they're the same.

7    Push the valve into the end of the hose

until it's seated.

8    Inspect the rubber grommet for damage and hardening. Replace it with a new one if necessary.

9    Install the PCV valve and hose securely into position.

## 35  Automatic transmission fluid and filter change (every 100,000 miles)

**Note:** *1997 and earlier models may have a shorter fluid change interval, every 24 months or 24,000 miles. Check your owner's manual to verify the interval changing time and mileage under the maintenance section.*

1    At the specified intervals, the transmission fluid should be drained and replaced. Since the fluid will remain hot long after driving, perform this procedure only after the engine has cooled down completely. The manufacturer also recommends adjusting the

transmission bands at this time, since this procedure requires removing the fluid pan (all 1997 and earlier transmissions, and all 46RE, 47RE and 48RE transmissions only; see Section 36).

2    Before beginning work, purchase the specified transmission fluid (see *Recommended lubricants and fluids* at the front of this Chapter) and a new filter(s).

3    Other tools necessary for this job include a floor jack, jackstands to support the vehicle in a raised position, a drain pan capable of holding at least four quarts, newspapers and clean rags.

4    Raise the vehicle and support it securely on jackstands.

5    Place the drain pan underneath the transmission pan. Remove the rear and side pan mounting bolts, but only loosen the rear pan bolts approximately four turns.

6    Carefully pry the transmission pan loose with a screwdriver, allowing the fluid to drain (see illustration).

7    Remove the remaining bolts, pan and

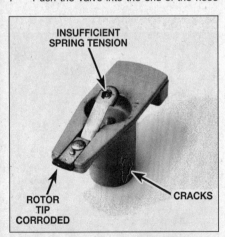

**33.12 The ignition rotor should be checked for wear and corrosion as indicated here (if in doubt about its condition, buy a new one)**

**34.1 On 3.7L V6 and 4.7L V8 engines, rotate the PCV valve 90-degrees counterclockwise and pull straight out to remove it**

**35.6 With the front bolts in place, but loose, pull the rear of the pan down to drain the fluid**

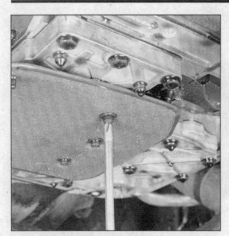

**35.9 Remove the filter screws - a special Torx-head wrench is necessary**

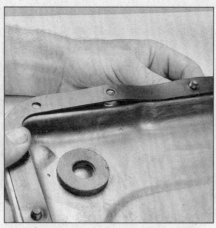

**35.11a Place a new gasket in position on the pan and install the bolts to hold it in place**

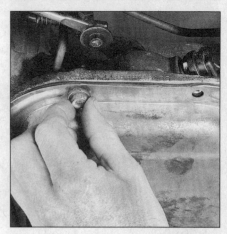

**35.11b Hold the pan in place and install all of the bolts snugly before tightening them fully**

gasket. Carefully clean the gasket surface of the transmission pan to remove all traces of the old gasket and sealant.

8    Drain the fluid from the transmission pan, clean the pan with solvent and dry it with compressed air, if available.

**Note:** *Some models are equipped with magnets in the transmission pan to catch metal debris. Clean the magnet thoroughly. A small amount of metal material is normal at the magnet. If there is considerable debris, consult a dealer or transmission specialist.*

### 1997 and earlier models

9    Remove the filter from the valve body inside the transmission (see illustration). Use a gasket scraper to remove any traces of old gasket material that remain on the valve body.

**Note:** *Be very careful not to gouge the delicate aluminum gasket surface on the valve body.*

10    Install a new gasket and filter. On many replacement filters, the gasket is attached to

the filter to simplify installation

11    Make sure the gasket surface on the transmission pan is clean, then install a new gasket on the pan (see illustration). Put the pan in place against the transmission and, working around the pan, tighten each bolt a little at a time to the torque listed in this Chapter's Specifications (see illustration).

### 1998 and later models

12    Remove the filter and seal from the valve body inside the transmission (see illustration).

13    Use a gasket scraper to remove any traces of old gasket material that remain on the valve body.

**Note:** *Be very careful not to gouge the delicate aluminum gasket surface on the valve body.*

14    If you're working on a 454RFE or a 545RFE transmission, remove the cooler return filter (see illustration). Compare the old filter with the new one to make sure they're the same type. Install the new cooler filter and tighten it to 125 inch-lbs. Install a new gasket

and filter.

15    On many replacement filters, the gasket is attached to the filter to simplify installation. On most models, the seal can be installed on the filter first, then the seal/filter can be pushed in place and secured. On models with 454RE and 545RFE transmissions, install the filter seal into the valve body first, then install the filter (see illustration).

16    Make sure the gasket surface on the transmission pan is clean, then install a new gasket on the pan. Put the pan in place against the transmission and, working around the pan, tighten each bolt a little at a time to the torque listed in this Chapter's Specifications.

**Note:** *On models with 454RFE or 545RFE transmissions, RTV sealant is used instead of a gasket. Clean the pan and transmission surfaces thoroughly with lacquer thinner and apply a continuous bead of ATF-resistant RTV sealant to the pan, then bolt it in place and tighten to Specifications within five minutes.*

**35.12 Use a seal removal tool to remove the transmission filter seal from the valve body**

**35.14 Use an oil filter wrench to remove the transmission cooler return filter**

**35.15 On 454RFE and 545RFE transmissions, install the filter seal into the valve body first**

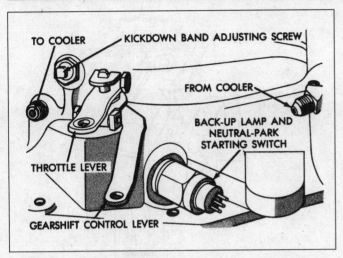

**36.4 Location of the front (kickdown) band adjusting screw**

**36.6 Loosen the rear band locknut so the adjusting screw can be turned**

## All models

17   Lower the vehicle and add the specified type and amount (minus one quart) of automatic transmission fluid through the filler tube (see Section 4).

18   With the transmission in Park and the parking brake set, run the engine at a fast idle, but don't race it.

19   Move the gear selector through each range and back to Park. Check the fluid level. It will probably be low. Add enough fluid to bring the level between the two holes on the dipstick.

20   Check under the vehicle for leaks during the first few trips. Check the fluid level again when the transmission is hot (see Section 4).

---

## 36   Automatic transmission band adjustment (all 1997 and earlier transmissions, and all 46RE, 47RE and 48RE transmissions) (every 100,000 miles)

---

**Note:** *Some models may have a shorter band adjustment interval, every 24 months/24,000 miles or 37,500 miles. Check your owners manual to verify the interval adjustment time and mileage under the maintenance section.*

1   The transmission bands should be adjusted at the specified interval when the transmission fluid and filter are being replaced (see Section 35).

### Front (kickdown) band

2   The front band adjusting screw is located on the left side (outside) of the transmission case, by the throttle valve lever.

3   Raise the front of the vehicle and support it securely on jackstands.

4   Loosen the adjusting screw locknut approximately five turns, then loosen the adjusting screw a few turns. Make sure the

adjusting screw turns freely, with no binding; lubricate it with penetrating oil if necessary (see illustration).

5   Tighten the adjusting screw to 72 in-lbs of torque, then back it off the number of turns listed in this Chapter's Specifications. Hold the adjusting screw from turning, then tighten the locknut to the torque listed in this Chapter's Specifications.

### Rear (low-reverse) band

6   To gain access to the rear band, the fluid pan must be removed (see Section 35) (see illustration).

7   Loosen the adjusting screw locknut and back it off five to six turns (see illustration). Make sure the screw turns freely in the lever.

8   Tighten the adjusting screw to 72 in-lbs of torque, then back it off the number of turns listed in this Chapter's Specifications. Hold the screw from turning, then tighten the locknut to the torque listed in this Chapter's Specifications.

9   Install the transmission fluid pan and refill the transmission (see Section 35).

---

## 37   Cooling system servicing (draining, flushing and refilling) (every 60 months)

---

**Warning:** *Wait until the engine is completely cool before beginning this procedure.*

**Warning:** *Do not allow antifreeze to come in contact with your skin or painted surfaces of the vehicle. Rinse off spills immediately with plenty of water. Antifreeze is highly toxic if ingested. Never leave antifreeze lying around in an open container or in puddles on the floor; children and pets are attracted by its sweet smell and may drink it. Check with local authorities about disposing of used antifreeze. Many communities have collection centers which will see that antifreeze is disposed of safely.*

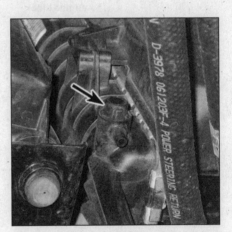

**37.4 The radiator drain fitting is located at the lower corner of the radiator**

1   Periodically, the cooling system should be drained, flushed and refilled to replenish the antifreeze mixture and prevent formation of rust and corrosion, which can impair the performance of the cooling system and cause engine damage. When the cooling system is serviced, all hoses and the radiator cap or expansion tank cap should be checked and replaced if necessary.

### Draining

2   Apply the parking brake and block the wheels. If the vehicle has just been driven, wait several hours to allow the engine to cool down before beginning this procedure.

3   Once the engine is completely cool, remove the radiator cap or expansion tank cap.

4   Move a large container under the radiator drain to catch the coolant. Attach a length of hose to the drain fitting to direct the coolant into the container, then open the drain fitting (a pair of pliers may be required to turn it) (see illustration).

**37.5 The block drain plugs are generally located about one to two inches above the oil pan - there is one on each side of the engine block**

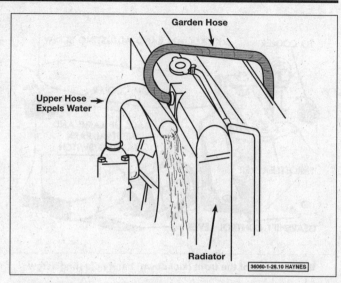

**37.10 With the thermostat removed, disconnect the upper radiator hose and flush the radiator and engine block with a garden hose**

5    After the coolant stops flowing out of the radiator, move the container under the engine block drain plugs and allow the coolant in the block to drain (see illustration).
6    While the coolant is draining, check the condition of the radiator hoses, heater hoses and clamps (refer to Section 15 if necessary). Replace any damaged clamps or hoses.
7    Reinstall the block drain plugs and tighten them securely.

### Flushing

8    Once the system has completely drained, remove the thermostat housing from the engine (see Chapter 3), then reinstall the housing without the thermostat. This will allow the system to be thoroughly flushed.
9    Disconnect the upper hose from the radiator.
10    Place a garden hose in the upper radiator inlet and flush the system until the water

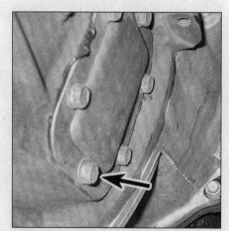

**38.3 On heavy duty models without a drain plug, remove the lower bolt from the PTO cover to drain the lubricant**

runs clear at the upper radiator hose (see illustration).
11    Severe cases of radiator contamination or clogging will require removing the radiator (see Chapter 3) and reverse flushing it. This involves inserting the hose in the bottom radiator outlet to allow the clean water to run against the normal flow, draining out through the top. A radiator repair shop should be consulted if further cleaning or repair is necessary.
12    When the coolant is regularly drained and the system refilled with the correct coolant mixture, there should be no need to employ chemical cleaners or descalers.

### Refilling

13    Close and tighten the radiator drain.
14    Place the heater temperature control in the maximum heat position.
15    Slowly add new coolant (a 50/50 mixture of water and antifreeze) to the radiator or expansion tank until the level is between the MIN and MAX marks.
16    Leave the radiator cap or expansion tank cap off and run the engine in a well-ventilated area until the thermostat opens (coolant will begin flowing through the radiator and the upper radiator hose will become hot).
17    Turn the engine off and let it cool. Add more coolant mixture to bring the level between the MIN and MAX marks on the expansion tank.
18    Squeeze the upper radiator hose to expel air, then add more coolant mixture if necessary. Replace the expansion tank cap.
19    Start the engine, allow it to reach normal operating temperature and check for leaks. Also, set the heater and blower controls to the maximum setting and check to see that the heater output from the air ducts is warm. This is a good indication that all air has been purged from the cooling system.

### 38    Manual transmission, transfer case and differential lubricant change (every 72,000 miles)

### Manual transmission

1    This procedure should be performed after the vehicle has been driven so the lubricant will be warm and therefore will flow out of the transmission more easily. Raise the vehicle and support it securely on jackstands.
2    Move a drain pan, rags, newspapers and wrenches under the transmission. Remove the fill plug from the side of the transmission case (see illustration 24.1).
3    Remove the transmission drain plug at the bottom of the case and allow the lubricant to drain into the pan. Some transmissions don't have a drain plug; remove the lower PTO cover bolt to drain the lubricant (see illustration).
4    After the lubricant has drained completely, reinstall the plug and tighten it securely.
5    Using a hand pump, syringe or funnel, fill the transmission with the specified lubricant until it begins to leak out through the hole. Reinstall the fill plug and tighten it securely.
6    Lower the vehicle.
7    Drive the vehicle for a short distance, then check the drain and fill plugs for leakage.

### Transfer case (4WD models)

8    Drive the vehicle for at least 15 minutes to warm the lubricant in the case.
9    Raise the vehicle and support it securely on jackstands.
10    Remove the drain plug from the lower part of the case and allow the old lubricant to drain completely (see illustration 24.5).
11    After the lubricant has drained com-

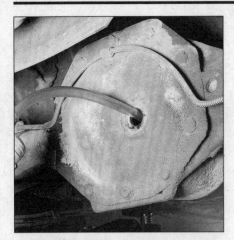

**38.18 This is the easiest way to remove the lubricant: Work the end of the hose to the bottom of the differential housing and draw out the old lubricant with a hand pump**

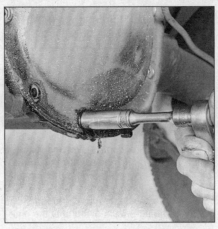

**38.19a Remove the bolts from the lower edge of the cover . . .**

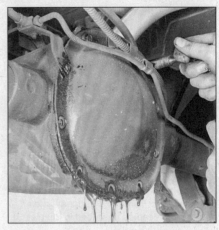

**38.19b . . . then loosen the top bolts and allow the lubricant to drain out**

pletely, reinstall the plug and tighten it securely.

12 Remove the filler plug from the case.

13 Fill the case with the specified lubricant until it is level with the lower edge of the filler hole.

14 Install the filler plug and tighten it securely.

15 Drive the vehicle for a short distance and recheck the lubricant level. In some instances a small amount of additional lubricant will have to be added.

## *Differential*

16 This procedure should be performed after the vehicle has been driven so the lubricant will be warm and therefore will flow out of the differential more easily.

17 Raise the vehicle and support it securely on jackstands. If the differential has a bolt-on cover at the rear, it is usually easiest to remove the cover to drain the lubricant (which will also allow you to inspect the differential). If there's no bolt-on cover, look for a drain plug at the bottom of the differential housing. If there's not a drain plug and no cover, you'll have to remove the lubricant through the filler plug hole with a suction pump. If you'll be draining the lubricant by removing the cover or a drain plug, move a drain pan, rags, newspapers and wrenches under the vehicle.

18 Remove the filler plug from the differential (see Section 24). If a suction pump is being used, insert the flexible hose. Work the hose down to the bottom of the differential housing and pump the lubricant out (see illustration). If you'll be draining the lubricant through a drain plug, remove the plug and allow the lubricant to drain into the pan, then reinstall the drain plug.

19 If the differential is being drained by removing the cover plate, remove the bolts on the lower half of the plate. Loosen the bolts on

**38.19c After the lubricant has drained, remove the remaining cover bolts and the cover**

the upper half and use them to keep the cover loosely attached. Allow the oil to drain into the pan, then completely remove the cover (see illustrations).

20 Using a lint-free rag, clean the inside of the cover and the accessible areas of the differential housing. As this is done, check for chipped gears and metal particles in the lubricant, indicating that the differential should be more thoroughly inspected and/or repaired.

21 Thoroughly clean the gasket mating surfaces of the differential housing and the cover plate. Use a gasket scraper or putty knife to remove all traces of the old gasket (see illustration).

22 Apply a thin layer of RTV sealant to the cover flange, then press a new gasket into position on the cover. Make sure the bolt holes align properly.

23 Place the cover on the differential housing and install the bolts. Tighten the bolts

**38.21 Carefully scrape the old gasket material off to ensure a leak-free seal**

securely.

24 Use a hand pump, syringe or funnel to fill the differential housing with the specified lubricant until it's level with the bottom of the plug hole.

25 Install the filler plug and make sure it is secure.

## 39 Power steering fluid replacement (every 90,000 miles or 72 months)

1 Apply the parking brake, raise the front of the vehicle and support the front end securely with jackstands.

2 Position a drain pan under the power steering pump, then disconnect the return line(s) from the pump (see Chapter 10). Plug the return line port(s) to prevent excessive fluid loss and the entry of contaminants.

3    Position the return line(s) so the fluid can drain into the pan.

4    Start the engine and allow it to run at idle. Turn the wheels from side-to-side, without hitting the stops, while an assistant fills the reservoir with new fluid.

5    Run about a quart of new fluid through the system, then stop the engine and install the line(s).

6    Fill the reservoir as described in Section 4, then bleed the system (see Chapter 10).

7    Repeat Steps 2 through 6, making sure all contaminated fluid is removed from the system.

8    Fill the power steering reservoir with the recommended fluid and bleed the system following the procedure described in Chapter 10.

## 40   Emissions Maintenance (MAINT REQD) Reminder light

### General information

**Note:** *The Maintenance Reminder light is used on early model Heavy Duty 5.9L V8 and 8.0L V10 gasoline powered models only.*

1    The Emissions Maintenance Reminder (EMR) light is designed as a reminder that the vehicle emissions control systems requires maintenance. It is not a warning, only a reminder to service the emissions system. The PCM will illuminate the MAINT REQD light after a predetermined mileage has elapsed. The light will stay on until the emis-

sions service is performed and the light reset. The components that require servicing are the EGR system, PCV system, EVAP system, and the oxygen sensor. Refer to the Maintenance Schedule and the appropriate sections of this Chapter for details on checking and replacing the components, if necessary.

2    Resetting the EMR light requires a special tool, usually available only at professional auto service facilities. After performing the emissions service, take the vehicle to a dealership service department or other properly equipped repair facility to have the light reset. Resetting the light without performing the required emissions service may be a violation of federal law.

# Chapter 2 Part A
# 3.7L V6 and 4.7L V8 engines

## Contents

## Specifications

### General
Displacement
  3.7L V6 .......................................... 226 cubic inches
  4.7L V8 .......................................... 287 cubic inches
Bore and stroke
  3.7L V6 .......................................... 3.66 x 3.40 inches
  4.7L V8 .......................................... 3.66 x 3.40 inches
Cylinder numbers (front-to-rear)
  3.7L V6
    Left (driver's) side .......................... 1-3-5
    Right side .................................... 2-4-6
    Firing order ................................. 1-6-5-4-3-2
  4.7L V8
    Left (driver's) side .......................... 1-3-5-7
    Right side .................................... 2-4-6-8
    Firing order ................................. 1-8-4-3-6-5-7-2
Cylinder compression pressure
  Minimum ......................................... 170 psi
  Maximum variation between cylinders ............. 40 psi

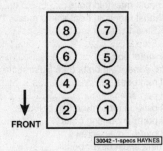

**Cylinder identification diagram - 4.7L V8 engine**

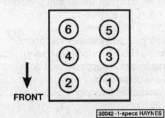

**Cylinder identification diagram - 3.7L V6 engine**

### Camshaft
Endplay .............................................. 0.003 to 0.0079 inch
Camshaft bearing oil clearance
  Standard ........................................ 0.001 to 0.0026 inch
  Service limit ................................... 0.0026 inch
Camshaft journal diameter ........................... 1.0227 to 1.0235 inch
Camshaft bore diameter .............................. 1.0245 to 1.0252 inch

## Timing chain
Idler gear endplay.................................................................... 0.004 to 0.010 inch

## Oil pump
Cover warpage limit (maximum)............................................... 0.001 inch
Inner and outer rotor thickness................................................ 0.472 inch
Outer rotor diameter (minimum) .............................................. 3.382 inches
Outer rotor-to-housing clearance (maximum).......................... 0.009 inch
Inner rotor-to-outer rotor lobe clearance (maximum)............... 0.006 inch
Oil pump housing-to-rotor side clearance (maximum)............... 0.0038 inch

## Torque specifications          Ft-lbs (unless otherwise indicated)
**Note:** *One foot-pound (ft-lb) of torque is equivalent to 12 inch-pounds (in-lbs) of torque. Torque values below approximately 15 ft-lbs are expressed in inch-pounds, because most foot-pound torque wrenches are not accurate at these smaller values.*

Camshaft sprocket bolts (non-oiled)........................................ 90
Camshaft bearing cap bolts..................................................... 100 in-lbs
Crankshaft pulley/vibration damper bolt.................................. 130
Cylinder head bolts
   3.7L V6 (see illustration 11.19a)
      Step 1
         Bolts 1 through 8 .................................................. 20
      Step 2
         Bolts 1 through 8 .................................................. 20 recheck
         Bolts 9 through 12 ................................................ 120 in-lbs
      Step 3
         Bolts 1 through 8 .................................................. Tighten an additional 90-degrees
      Step 4
         Bolts 1 through 8 .................................................. Tighten an additional 90-degrees
         Bolts 9 through 12 ................................................ 19
   4.7L V8 (see illustration 11.19b)
      Step 1
         Bolts 1 through 10 ................................................ 15
      Step 2
         Bolts 1 through 10 ................................................ 35
         Bolts 11 through 14 .............................................. 18
      Step 3
         Bolts 1 through 10 ................................................ Tighten an additional 90-degrees
         Bolts 11 through 14 .............................................. 22
Driveplate bolts
   3.7L V6.............................................................................. 70
   4.7L V8.............................................................................. 45
Exhaust manifold bolts ............................................................ 18
Exhaust manifold heat shield nuts
   Step 1 .............................................................................. 72 in-lbs
   Step 2 .............................................................................. Loosen 45-degrees
Flywheel bolts.......................................................................... 70
Intake manifold bolts (see illustrations 9.20a or 9.20b) .......... 105 in-lbs
Oil pan bolts............................................................................. 132 in-lbs
Oil pan drain plug .................................................................... 25
Oil pick-up tube mounting bolt/nut........................................... 20
Oil pump mounting bolts.......................................................... 250 in-lbs
Oil pump cover screws ............................................................ 105 in-lbs
Timing chain cover bolts.......................................................... 43
Timing chain guide bolts.......................................................... 21
Timing chain guide access plugs............................................. 15
Timing chain idler sprocket bolt .............................................. 25
Timing chain tensioner arm pivot bolt
   3.7L V6 engine................................................................. 21
   4.7L V8 engine................................................................. 150 in-lbs
Timing chain tensioner (secondary) ........................................ 21
Timing chain tensioner (primary) ............................................ 21
Transmission support brace bolts............................................ 40
Valve cover bolts ..................................................................... 105 in-lbs
Water outlet housing................................................................ 105 in-lbs

## 1 General Information

1    This Part of Chapter 2 is devoted to in-vehicle repair procedures for the 3.7L V6 and 4.7L V8 single overhead camshaft (SOHC) engines. These engines utilize a cast iron engine block with cylinders arranged in a "V" shape at a 90-degree angle between the two banks. The overhead camshaft aluminum cylinder heads are equipped with replaceable valve guides and seats. Stamped steel rocker arms with an integral roller bearing actuate the valves.

2    Information concerning engine removal and installation and engine overhaul can be found in Part E of this Chapter.

3    The following repair procedures are based on the assumption that the engine is installed in the vehicle. If the engine has been removed from the vehicle and mounted on a stand, many of the steps outlined in this Part of Chapter 2 will not apply.

## 2 Engine identification

1    Engine identification on the 3.7L V6 and 4.7L V8 engines is accomplished by matching the engine code stamped onto the engine block or by using the VIN number of the vehicle (8th position). Refer to the introductory pages in this manual for additional information.

## 3 Repair operations possible with the engine in the vehicle

1    Many major repair operations can be accomplished without removing the engine from the vehicle.

2    Clean the engine compartment and the exterior of the engine with some type of degreaser before any work is done. It will make the job easier and help keep dirt out of the internal areas of the engine.

3    Depending on the components involved, it may be helpful to remove the hood to improve access to the engine as repairs are performed (refer to Chapter 11, if necessary). Cover the fenders to prevent damage to the paint. Special pads are available, but an old bedspread or blanket will also work.

4    If vacuum, exhaust, oil or coolant leaks develop, indicating a need for gasket or seal replacement, the repairs can generally be made with the engine in the vehicle. The intake and exhaust manifold gaskets, oil pan gasket, crankshaft oil seals and cylinder head gaskets are all accessible with the engine in place.

5    Exterior engine components, such as the intake and exhaust manifolds, the oil pan, the oil pump, the water pump (see Chapter 4A), the starter motor, the alternator and the fuel system components (see Chapter 3) can be removed for repair with the engine in place.

6    Since the cylinder heads can be removed without pulling the engine, valve component servicing can also be accomplished with the engine in the vehicle. Replacement of the camshafts, timing chains and sprockets are also possible with the engine in the vehicle.

7    In extreme cases caused by a lack of necessary equipment, repair or replacement of piston rings, pistons, connecting rods and rod bearings is possible with the engine in the vehicle. However, this practice is not recommended because of the cleaning and preparation work that must be done to the components involved.

## 4 Top Dead Center (TDC) for number one piston - locating

1    Top Dead Center (TDC) is the highest point in the cylinder that each piston reaches as it travels up the cylinder bore. Each piston reaches TDC on the compression stroke and again on the exhaust stroke, but TDC generally refers to piston position on the compression stroke.

2    Positioning the piston(s) at TDC is an essential part of many procedures such as valve timing, camshaft and timing chain/sprocket removal.

3    Before beginning this procedure, be sure to place the transmission in Neutral or Park and apply the parking brake or block the rear wheels. Also, disable the ignition system by disconnecting the primary electrical connectors at the ignition coil packs and remove the spark plugs (see Chapter 1).

4    In order to bring any piston to TDC, the crankshaft must be turned using one of the methods outlined below. When looking at the front of the engine, normal crankshaft rotation is clockwise.

*a) The preferred method is to turn the crankshaft with a socket and ratchet attached to the bolt threaded into the front of the crankshaft. Turn the bolt in a clockwise direction only. Never turn the bolt counterclockwise.*

*b) A remote starter switch, which may save some time, can also be used. Follow the instructions included with the switch. Once the piston is close to TDC, use a socket and ratchet as described in the previous paragraph.*

*c) If an assistant is available to turn the ignition switch to the Start position in short bursts, you can get the piston close to TDC without a remote starter switch. Make sure your assistant is out of the vehicle, away from the ignition switch, then use a socket and ratchet as described in Paragraph (a) to complete the procedure.*

5    Install a compression pressure gauge in the number one spark plug hole (refer to Chapter 2E). It should be a gauge with a screw-in fitting and a hose at least six inches long (see illustration).

6    Rotate the crankshaft using one of the methods described above while observing for pressure on the compression gauge. The moment the gauge shows pressure indicates that the number one cylinder has begun the compression stroke.

7    Once the compression stroke has begun, TDC for the compression stroke is reached by bringing the piston to the top of the cylinder.

8    Continue turning the crankshaft until the notch in the crankshaft damper is aligned with the TDC mark on the timing chain cover (see illustration). At this point, the number one cylinder is at TDC on the compression stroke. If the marks are aligned but there was no compression, the piston was on the exhaust stroke. Continue rotating the crankshaft 360-degrees (1-turn) and realign the marks.

**Note:** *If a compression gauge is not available, you can simply place a blunt object over the spark plug hole and listen for compression as the engine is rotated. Once compression at the No.1 spark plug hole is noted, the remainder of the Step is the same.*

9    After the number one piston has been positioned at TDC on the compression stroke, TDC for any of the remaining cylinders can be located by turning the crankshaft in increments of 120-degrees for 3.7L V6 engines or

**4.5 A compression gauge can be used in the number one spark plug hole to assist in finding TDC**

**4.8 Align the groove in the damper with the TDC mark on the timing chain cover**

**5.6 Remove the left side breather tube**

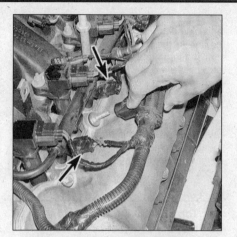

**5.8 Detach the wiring harness from the valve cover studs, then disconnect the fuel injector electrical connectors and position the harness aside**

90-degrees for 4.7L V8 engines and following the firing order (refer to the Specifications). For example on 3.7L V6 engines, rotating the engine 120-degrees past TDC #1 will put the engine at TDC compression for cylinder #6.

10   An even faster way to find TDC for any cylinder other than No. 1 is to make marks on the crankshaft damper at 120-degree intervals from the TDC mark on the crankshaft damper (V6 engine) or 90-degree intervals from the TDC mark on the crankshaft damper (V8 engine). Install the compression gauge into the cylinder for which you want to find TDC, rotate the engine until compression begins to register on the gauge, then continue turning the crankshaft until the next mark on the damper aligns with the mark on the timing chain cover.

## 5    Valve covers - removal and installation

### *Removal*

1   .Disconnect the cable from the negative terminal of the battery (see Chapter 5, Section 1).

**5.10 Remove the valve cover bolts (left side shown)**

### Right (passenger's) side cover

2   Remove the air filter housing, the air intake duct and the throttle body resonator (see Chapter 4A).
3   Drain the cooling system (see Chapter 1).
4   Remove the heater hoses (see Chapter 3).
5   Remove the drivebelt (see Chapter 1) and the air conditioning compressor (see Chapter 3). Position the A/C compressor to the side without disconnecting the refrigerant lines from the compressor.

### Left (driver's) side cover

6   Remove the PCV breather tube (see illustration).
7   Remove the air intake resonator (see Chapter 4A).

### Either cover

8   Unclip the fuel injector wiring harness from the studs on the valve cover (see illustration).
9   Disconnect the electrical connectors from the fuel injectors and ignition coil connectors on the side from which the valve cover is to be removed (see Chapter 4A). If both valve cov-

ers are to be removed, disconnect all of the connectors from the fuel injectors.
10   Remove the valve cover bolts (see illustration). Make a note of the locations of the bolts with studs before removal to ensure correct positioning during installation.
11   Detach the valve cover.
**Note:** *If the cover sticks to the cylinder head, use a block of wood and a hammer to dislodge it. If the cover still won't come loose, pry on it carefully, but don't distort the sealing flange.*

### *Installation*

12   The mating surfaces of each cylinder head and valve cover must be perfectly clean when the covers are installed.
**Caution:** *Do not use harsh cleaners when cleaning the valve covers or damage to the covers may occur.*
**Note:** *The valve cover gasket can be reused if it isn't hardened, cracked or otherwise damaged.*
13   Clean the mounting bolt or stud threads with a wire brush if necessary to remove any corrosion and restore damaged threads. Use a tap to clean the threaded holes in the heads.
14   Place the valve cover and gasket in position, then install the bolts in the correct locations from which they were removed. Tighten the bolts in several steps to the torque listed in this Chapter's Specifications.
15   Complete the installation by reversing the removal procedure. Refill the cooling system, if drained, by following the procedure in Chapter 1. Start the engine and check carefully for oil leaks.

## 6    Rocker arms and hydraulic lash adjusters - removal, inspection and installation

**Note:** *A special valve spring compressor available from most aftermarket specialty tool manufacturers will be required for this procedure. The only other alternative to accomplishing this task without the use of this special tool is to remove the timing chains and the camshafts, which requires major disassembly of the engine and surrounding components.*
**Note:** *This engine is a non-freewheeling (interference) engine and the pistons must be down in the cylinder bore before the valve and spring assembly can be compressed to allow rocker arm removal.*
1   Before beginning this procedure, be sure to place the transmission in Park and apply the parking brake or block the rear wheels. Also, disable the ignition system by disconnecting the primary electrical connectors at the ignition coils and remove the spark plugs (see Chapter 1).
2   Remove the valve cover(s) (see Section 5).
3   Before the rocker arms and lash adjusters are removed, arrange to label and store them, so they can be kept separate and reinstalled on the same valve they were removed from.

6.5 Using a special type valve spring compressor, depress the valve spring just enough to remove the rocker arm

6.7 Pull the lash adjuster up and out of its bore to remove it from the cylinder head

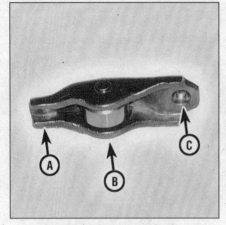

6.8 Inspect the rocker arms at the following locations

A  Valve stem seat
B  Roller
C  Lash adjuster pocket

4    Rotate the engine with a socket and ratchet in a clockwise direction by the crankshaft pulley/vibration damper bolt until the piston(s) are positioned correctly to remove the rocker arms from the corresponding cylinders as follows. Start the sequence from TDC number 1 on the compression stroke (see Section 4).

### For the 3.7L V6 engine

a)  With the No.1 piston at TDC on the compression stroke, remove the rocker arms from cylinders No. 2 and 6.
b)  Rotate the crankshaft another 180-degrees (1/2-turn) from TDC on the compression stroke to bring the No. 1 piston to BDC on the firing stroke. Remove the rocker arms from cylinder No. 1 with the No. 1 piston at Bottom Dead Center (BDC) on the firing stroke.
c)  Rotate the crankshaft another 180-degrees (1/2-turn) from BDC on the firing stroke to bring the No.1 piston to TDC on the exhaust stroke. Remove the rocker arms from cylinders No. 3 and 5 with the No. 1 piston at TDC on the exhaust stroke.
d)  Rotate the crankshaft another 180-degrees (1/2-turn) from TDC on the exhaust stroke to bring the No.1 piston to BDC on the intake stroke. Remove the rocker arms from cylinder No. 4 with the No. 1 piston at BDC on the intake stroke.

### For the 4.7L V8 engine

a)  With the No.1 piston at TDC on the compression stroke, remove the rocker arms from cylinders No. 2 and 8.
b)  Rotate the crankshaft another 360-degrees (1-turn) from TDC on the compression stroke to bring the No.1 piston to TDC on the exhaust stroke. Remove the rocker arms from cylinders No. 3

and 5 with the No. 1 piston at TDC on the exhaust stroke.
c)  Position cylinder No. 3 at TDC on the compression stroke. Remove the rocker arms from cylinder No. 4 and 6.
d)  Position cylinder No. 2 at TDC on the compression stroke. Remove the rocker arms from cylinder No. 1 and 7.

### All engines

5    Hook the valve spring compressor around the base of the camshaft. Depress the valve spring just enough to release tension on the rocker arm to be removed. Once tension on the rocker arm is relieved, the rocker arm can be removed by simply pulling it out (see illustration).
6    If you're removing or replacing only a few of the rocker arms or lash adjusters, locate the cylinder number of the rocker arm or lash adjuster you wish to remove in Step 4, then rotate the crankshaft to the corresponding position. Remember to keep the rocker arm and lash adjuster for each valve together so they can be reinstalled in the same locations. Refer to Section 4 as necessary to help position the designated cylinder at TDC.
7    Once the rocker arms are removed, the lash adjusters can be pulled out of the cylinder head and stored with the corresponding rocker arm (see illustration).
8    Inspect each rocker arm for wear, cracks and other damage. Make sure the rollers turn freely and show no signs of wear, also check the pivot area for wear, cracks and galling (see illustration).
9    Inspect the lash adjuster contact surfaces for wear or damage. Make sure the lash adjusters move up and down freely in their bores on the cylinder head without excessive side-to-side play.
10   Installation is the reverse of removal with the following exceptions: Always install the lash adjuster first and make sure they're

at least partially full of oil before installation. This is indicated by little or no lash adjuster plunger travel.

### 7    Timing chain and sprockets - removal, inspection and installation

**Warning:** *Wait until the engine is completely cool before beginning this procedure.*
**Note:** *Special tools are necessary to complete this procedure. Read through the entire procedure and obtain the special tools before beginning work.*

### Removal

**Caution:** *The timing system is complex. Severe engine damage will occur if you make any mistakes. Do not attempt this procedure unless you are highly experienced with this type of repair. If you are at all unsure of your abilities, consult an expert. Double-check all your work and be sure everything is correct before you attempt to start the engine.*
1    Disconnect the cable from the negative terminal of the battery (see Chapter 5, Section 1).
2    Drain the cooling system (see Chapter 1).
3    Refer to Chapter 3 and remove the engine cooling fan, the accessory drivebelt and the fan shroud from the engine compartment.
4    Detach the heater hoses and the lower radiator hose from the timing chain cover and position them aside.
5    Unbolt the power steering pump and set it aside without disconnecting the fluid lines (see Chapter 10).
6    Remove the alternator (see Chapter 5). Also unbolt the air conditioning compressor (if equipped) and position it aside without dis-

**7.7 Drivebelt tensioner retaining bolt**

**7.11a Right cylinder bank**

**7.11b Left cylinder bank**

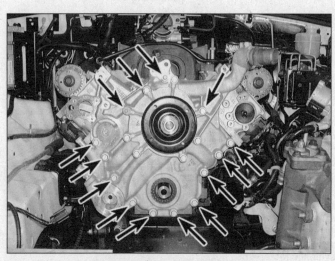

**7.13 Timing chain cover retaining bolts**

**7.14 Locking the primary timing chain tensioner in the retracted position**

**7.15 Secondary timing chain tensioner mounting bolts**

connecting the refrigerant lines.

7    Remove the accessory drivebelt tensioner from the timing chain cover (see illustration).

8    Remove the valve covers (see Section 5) and the spark plugs (see Chapter 1).

9    Remove all of the rocker arms following the procedure outlined in Section 6.

**Note:** *This step is not absolutely necessary, but it will help make alignment of the camshaft sprockets easier upon installation and also eliminate any possibility of the pistons contacting the valves during this procedure, since these are interference engines.*

10    Remove the camshaft position sensor (CMP) from the right cylinder head (see Chapter 6).

11    Position the number one piston at TDC on the exhaust stroke (one revolution from TDC on the compression stroke - see Section 4). Visually confirm the engine is at TDC on the exhaust stroke, by verifying that the timing mark on the crankshaft damper is aligned with the mark on the timing chain cover and the "V6" or "V8" marks on the camshaft sprockets are pointing straight up in the 12 o'clock position (see illustration 4.8 and the accompanying illustrations).

12    Remove the crankshaft damper/pulley (see Section 12).

13    Remove the timing chain cover and the water pump as an assembly (see illustration). Note that various types and sizes of bolts are used. They must be reinstalled in their original locations. Mark each bolt or make a sketch to help remember where they go.

14    Cover the oil pan opening with shop rags to prevent any components from falling into the engine. Collapse the primary timing chain tensioner with a pair of locking pliers and install a locking pin into the holes in the tensioner body to keep it in the retracted position (see illustration).

15    Remove the secondary timing chain tensioners (see illustration).

16    Remove the camshaft sprocket retaining bolts (see illustrations). Pull the camshaft sprockets off the camshaft hubs one at a time.

7.16a Removing the left camshaft sprocket bolt while holding the sprocket with a pin spanner wrench - note the chain guide access plug

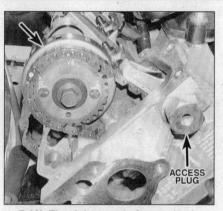

7.16b The right camshaft sprocket is identified by the camshaft position sensor ring which is fastened to the rear of the sprocket - be extremely careful not to damage or place a magnetic object of any kind near the camshaft position sensor ring or a "no start" condition may occur after installation

7.17 Remove the primary timing chain and the secondary chains as an assembly from the engine

7.18 Timing chain guide and tensioner arm pivot bolts

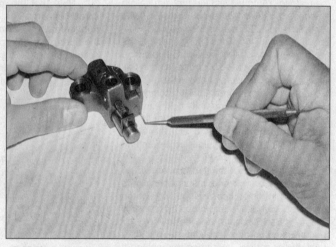

7.22 If excessive wear on the chain guides is evident, check the oil jet on the side of each secondary tensioner for clogging

Lower the sprocket(s) into the cylinder head opening until the chain can be displaced from around the sprocket, then remove the camshaft sprockets from the engine and let the secondary chains fall down between the timing chain guides.

**Caution:** *If the rocker arms were not removed as suggested in Step 9, it will be necessary to hold the camshafts from rotating with a set of locking pliers while the sprocket is being removed. Work on one camshaft and sprocket at a time starting with the left sprocket and proceeding to the right sprocket. After the sprocket is removed from the camshaft(s), let the camshaft slowly rotate to its neutral position. This is typically 15-degrees clockwise on the left camshaft sprocket and 45-degrees counterclockwise on the right camshaft. Pressure from the valve springs will make the camshafts rotate as the sprockets are removed. Sudden movement of the camshafts may allow the valves to strike the pistons.*

**Caution:** *Never install the locking pliers on a camshaft lobe as damage to the camshaft will occur. When using locking pliers, always rotate the camshaft with locking pliers by the shaft.*

**Caution:** *The right camshaft sprocket is identified by the camshaft position sensor ring which is fastened to the rear of the sprocket. Be extremely careful not to damage or place a magnetic object of any kind near the camshaft position sensor ring or a no start condition may occur after installation.*

17   Remove the idler sprocket bolt, then detach the idler sprocket, the crankshaft sprocket, the primary timing chain and the secondary timing chains as an assembly (see illustration).

18   Remove the cylinder head access plugs (see illustrations 7.16a and 7.16b). Also remove the oil fill tube (if not already removed) from the front of the right cylinder head. Detach the timing chain guides and tensioner arms (see illustration).

## Inspection

19   Inspect the camshaft and crankshaft sprockets for wear on the teeth and keyways.

20   Inspect the chains for cracks or excessive wear of the rollers.

21   Inspect the facings of the primary chain tensioner, secondary chain guides and tensioner arms for excessive wear. If any of the components show signs of excessive wear or the chain guides are grooved in excess of 0.039 inch deep, they must be replaced.

22   If any of the timing chain guides are excessively grooved or melted, the tensioner lube jet may be clogged. Be sure to remove the jet and clean it with a small metal pick, and then blow compressed air through it to remove any debris or foreign material (see illustration).

23   Inspect the idler sprocket bushing, shaft and spline joint for wear.

24   Inspect the tensioner piston and ratchet

assembly on both of the secondary chain tensioners. If it appears there has been heavy contact between the piston, and ratchet assembly, replace the tensioner arm and secondary timing chain.

**Note:** *Secondary timing chain stretch can be checked by rotating the engine clockwise until the pistons in the secondary tensioners reach their maximum travel or extension. Using a machinist's ruler or a dial caliper, measure the piston protrusion or extension from the stepped ledge on the piston to the tensioner housing on each tensioner.If the maximum extension of either tensioner piston exceeds 0.590 inch, the secondary timing chains are worn beyond their limits and should be replaced.*

## Installation

**Caution:** *Before starting the engine, carefully rotate the crankshaft by hand through at least two full revolutions (use a socket and breaker bar on the crankshaft pulley center bolt). If you feel any resistance, STOP! There is something wrong - most likely, valves are contacting the pistons. You must find the problem before proceeding. Check your work and see if any updated repair information is available.*

25   If removed, install the timing chain guides and tensioner pivot arms back onto the engine and tighten the bolts to the torque listed in this Chapter's Specifications. Apply several drops of medium strength thread-locking compound to the tensioner pivot arm bolts before installing them. Note that the silver bolts retain the guides to the cylinder head and the black colored bolts retain the guides to the engine block.

26   If the primary timing chain tensioner was removed or replaced, install it back onto the engine in the locked position and tighten the lower two bolts to the torque listed in this Chapter's Specifications (see illustration).

27   Working on one secondary timing chain tensioner at a time, compress the tensioner piston in a vise until the stepped edge is flush with the tensioner body (see illustration). Insert a small scribe or other suitable tool into the side of the tensioner body and push the spring loaded ratchet pawl away from the ratchet mechanism, then push the ratchet down into the tensioner body until it's approximately 0.080 inch away from the tensioner body. Insert the end of a paper clip into the hole on the front of the tensioner to lock the tensioner in place.

28   After the two secondary tensioners have been compressed and locked into place, install them on the engine and tighten the bolts to the torque listed in this Chapter's Specifications. Make sure the tensioner with the "R" mark is installed on the right secondary chain (passenger's side) and the tensioner with "L" mark is installed on the left secondary chain (driver's side). The secondary chain tensioners cannot be switched with one another. Also make sure the plate behind the left secondary chain tensioner is installed correctly.

29   If you purchased a new timing chain, verify that you have the correct timing chain for

**7.26 Primary timing chain tensioner/oil pump mounting bolts**

your vehicle by counting the number of links the chain has and comparing the new chain with the old chain. Also compare the position of the colored links in the new chain with the position of the colored links in the old chain.

30   Note that the idler sprocket has three sprockets and a gear incorporated into it. The front or forward facing sprocket (the largest of the three) is for the primary timing chain, the second or middle sprocket is for the left secondary chain, the third or rear sprocket is for the right secondary chain and the gear (3.7L

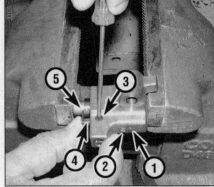

**7.27 Locking the secondary tensioner(s) in the retracted position - note the "identification" mark on the side of the tensioner, as they are not interchangeable**

1    *Insert locking pin*
2    *Identification mark*
3    *Ratchet pawl*
4    *Ratchet*
5    *Tensioner piston*

V6 engines only) is for the counterbalance shaft (the 4.7 V8 doesn't have a counterbalance shaft). The next 5 Steps will involve assembling the timing chains onto the idler sprocket on a workbench.

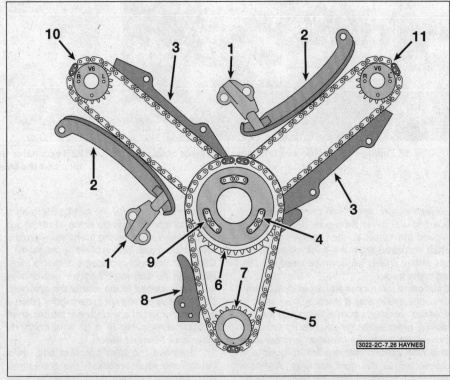

**7.31 Timing chain installation details**

1    *Secondary timing chain tensioner*
2    *Secondary tensioner arm*
3    *Chain guide*
4    *Two plated links on right camshaft chain*
5    *Primary chain*
6    *Idler sprocket*
7    *Crankshaft sprocket*
8    *Primary chain tensioner*
9    *Two plated links on left camshaft chain*
10   *Right camshaft sprocket and secondary chain*
11   *Left camshaft sprocket and secondary chain*

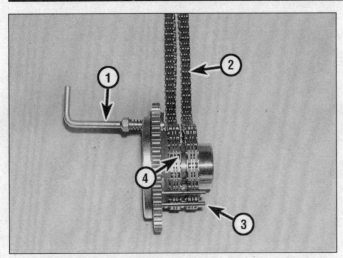

**7.33 Install the secondary chain holding tool onto the idler sprocket with the plated links on the right camshaft chain in the 4 o'clock position and the left camshaft chain in the 8 o'clock position (typical)**

1   *Secondary chain holding tool*
2   *Right camshaft timing chain*
3   *Secondary chain holding tool retaining pins*
4   *Left camshaft timing chain*

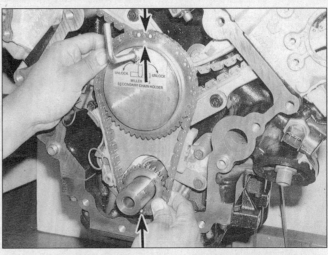

**7.39a Align the timing mark on the idler sprocket gear with the timing mark on the counterbalance shaft, then install the idler sprocket, the crankshaft sprocket, the timing chains and the chain holding tool as an assembly onto the engine with the marks aligned as shown - feed the secondary chains up through the timing chain guides and loop them over the camshaft hubs, then push the primary chain assembly the rest of the way on the engine until it's seated against the block**

31   Place the idler sprocket on a workbench with the mark on the front in the 12 o'clock position. Loop the right camshaft chain over the rear gear (farthest away from the primary chain gear) on the idler sprocket and position it so that the two plated links on the chain are visible through the lower (4 o'clock) window in the idler sprocket (see illustration).

32   Loop the left camshaft chain over the front of the idler sprocket and position it over the middle gear so that the two plated links on the chain are visible through the lower (8 o'clock) window in the idler sprocket.

**Note:** *After the left chain is in position, the two plated links on the right chain will no longer be visible through the 4 o'clock window in the idler sprocket, so be sure that the right camshaft chain is installed correctly before installing the left camshaft chain.*

33   After the secondary (camshaft) chains have been installed properly on the idler sprocket, install the special secondary chain holding tool onto the idler sprocket (see illustration). This tool serves as a third hand, to secure the camshaft chains to the idler sprocket during the installation of the idler sprocket onto the engine.

34   Install the primary timing chain onto the primary chain gear of the idler sprocket and align the double plated links with the mark on the front of the sprocket. The mark on the idler sprocket should still be in the 12 o'clock position.

35   Insert the teeth of the crankshaft sprocket into the primary timing chain with the mark on the crankshaft sprocket pointing down in the 6 o'clock position and aligned with the single plated link on the chain.

36   Lubricate the idler shaft and bushing with clean engine oil.

37   Install the idler sprocket, the crankshaft sprocket and the timing chains with the chain holding tool as an assembly onto the engine. Slide the crankshaft sprocket over the keyway on the crankshaft and position the idler sprocket partially over the idler shaft (just enough to hold the primary chain in place). Then feed the secondary chains up through the chain guides and the cylinder head.

**Note:** *It may be easier to bend a hook in the end of a coat hanger to help pull the secondary chains up through the timing chain guides and the cylinder head opening.*

38   Loop the secondary chains over the camshaft hubs and secure them with rubber bands to remove the slack from the chains.

39   Push the idler sprocket, primary timing chain and the crankshaft sprocket assembly back on to the engine until they're fully seated against the block (see illustration). If you're working on a 3.7L V6 engine, you'll have to align the timing mark on the idler sprocket gear with the timing mark on the counterbalance shaft gear while doing this.

**Note:** *On 3.7L V6 engines, make sure the single mark on the counterbalance shaft gear locks into position between the two marks on the idler sprocket gear.*

40   Thoroughly clean the idler sprocket bolt. Make sure all oil is removed from the bolt threads before installation, then lubricate the idler sprocket washer with small amount of clean engine oil making sure not to get oil on the bolt threads. Remove the secondary timing chain holding tool from the idler sprocket, then install the idler sprocket retaining bolt and tighten it to the torque listed in this Chapter's Specifications.

41   Align the "L" mark on left camshaft sprocket with the plated link on the left camshaft chain and position the camshaft sprocket over the camshaft hub (see illustration 7.31). The camshaft may have to be rotated slightly to align the dowel pin on the camshaft with the slot on the sprocket.

42   Align the "R" mark on right camshaft sprocket with the plated link on the right camshaft chain and position the camshaft sprocket over the camshaft hub. The camshaft may have to be rotated slightly to align the dowel pin on the camshaft with the slot on the sprocket.

**Note:** *If the rocker arms were not removed as suggested in Step 9, it will be necessary to rotate and hold the camshafts with a set of locking pliers while the sprocket is being installed. This is typically 15-degrees counterclockwise on the left camshaft sprocket and 45-degrees clockwise on the right camshaft (the exact opposite of removal). Work on one camshaft and sprocket at a time starting with the left sprocket and proceeding to the right sprocket and never rotate the camshaft by a camshaft lobe or damage to the camshaft will occur.*

43   Thoroughly clean the camshaft sprocket bolts. Make sure all oil is removed from the bolt threads before installation, as over-tightening of bolts may occur if oil is not removed, then lubricate the bolt washers with small amount of clean engine oil making sure not to get oil on the threads.

44   Install the camshaft sprocket bolts finger-tight.

45   Verify that all the plated timing chain links are aligned with their corresponding marks (see illustration 7.31).

**7.48 Tightening the left camshaft sprocket bolt**

**7.50 Timing chain cover tightening sequence**

46   Remove the locking pins from the primary timing chain tensioner and the secondary timing chain tensioners.
**Caution:** *Do not manually extend the tensioners; doing so will only over-extend the tensioners and lead to premature timing chain wear.*
47   Rotate the engine two complete revolutions and re-verify the position of the timing marks again. The idler sprocket mark should be located in the 12 o'clock position and the crankshaft sprocket mark should be located in the 6 o'clock position with the "V6" or "V8" marks on the camshaft sprockets located in the 12 o'clock position.
48   Using a spanner wrench to hold the sprockets from turning, tighten the camshaft sprocket bolts to the torque listed in this Chapter's Specifications (see illustration).
49   Remove all traces of old sealant or gasket material from the timing chain cover and the engine block.
50   Place the timing chain cover and gasket in position on the engine and install the bolts in their original locations and tighten the bolts to the torque listed in this Chapter's Specifications. Follow the correct tightening sequence (see illustration).

51   The remainder of the installation is the reverse of removal. Be sure to use pipe sealant on the cylinder head plugs to prevent oil leaks.
52   Change the engine oil and filter and refill the cooling system (see Chapter 1).

---

**8   Camshafts - removal, inspection and installation**

---

**Note:** *Special tools are necessary to complete this procedure. Read through the entire procedure and obtain the special tools before beginning work.*
**Note:** *The camshafts should always be thoroughly inspected before installation and camshaft endplay should always be checked prior to camshaft removal (see Step 17).*

## Removal

1   Disconnect the cable from the negative terminal of the battery (see Chapter 5, Section 1).
2   Remove the valve covers (see Section 5).

**8.6 The timing chain tensioner wedge is pushed down between the chain strands to secure the secondary chain and the tensioner in place while the camshaft is removed - this wedge is fabricated from a block of wood and a piece of wire**

3   Rotate the engine with a socket and ratchet (in a clockwise direction only) by the crankshaft pulley/vibration damper bolt until the "V6" or "V8" marks on the camshaft sprockets are located in the 12 o'clock position (see illustration 7.11a and 7.11b).
4   Using a permanent marker, apply alignment marks to the secondary timing chain links on either side of the "V6" or "V8" marks on both camshaft sprockets to help aid the installation process (4 marks total).
5   Using a spanner wrench to hold the camshaft sprockets from turning, loosen the camshaft sprocket bolts several turns, then retighten the bolts by hand until they're snug up against the sprocket. If the camshaft sprockets have rotated during the bolt-loosening process, rotate the engine clockwise until the "V6" or "V8" marks on the cam sprockets are realigned in the 12 o'clock position.
6   Install a timing chain tensioner wedge through the opening in the top of the cylinder head and force the wedge down between the narrowest section of the secondary chain (see illustration). If both camshafts are to be removed, two timing chain wedges will be necessary (one for the left camshaft chain and one for the right camshaft chain). The wedge is used to secure the chain and the secondary tensioner in place while the camshaft is removed.
**Caution** *1: Failure to use a timing chain wedge will allow the secondary tensioner to over-extend and require removal of the timing chain cover to reset the tensioners.*
**Caution** *2: Never force the wedge past the narrowest section of the secondary timing chain as damage to the tensioner will occur. If a timing chain wedge is not available, they may be fabricated using a block of wood that is 3/8 to 1/2-inch thick and a piece of wire to pull the wedge out of the cylinder head after installation.*
7   Remove the Camshaft Position Sensor (CMP) (see Chapter 6).
8   Remove the camshaft sprocket retaining

**8.9 Verify that the camshaft bearing caps are marked to ensure correct reinstallation - do not mix-up the caps from the left cylinder head with the caps from the right cylinder head**

**8.14 Inspect the cam bearing surfaces in each cylinder head for pits, score marks and abnormal wear - if wear or damage is noted, the cylinder head must be replaced**

bolt(s) and detach the camshaft sprocket(s) from the camshaft hub(s). Disengage the camshaft chain(s) from the sprocket(s) and remove the camshaft sprocket(s) from the engine.

9    Make note of the markings on the camshaft bearing caps. The caps are marked from 1 to 4 or 5 with arrow marks on the caps indicating the front of the engine (see illustration). If both camshafts are being removed, use a permanent marker to mark each bearing cap on the right cylinder head with an "R" and each bearing cap on the left cylinder head with an "L" to indicate from which cylinder head they came from. Loosen the camshaft bearing caps bolts a little at a time beginning with the bearing caps on the ends, then working inward.

**Caution:** *Keep the caps in order. They must go back in the same location they were removed from.*

10    Detach the bearing caps.

**Note:** *The rocker arms may slide out of position. Mark the rocker arms so that they will be installed in the same location.*

11    Remove the camshaft(s) from the cylinder head. Mark the camshaft(s) "Left" or "Right" to indicate which cylinder head it came from.

## Inspection

12    Inspect the camshaft sprockets for wear on the teeth.

13    Inspect the chains for cracks or excessive wear of the rollers. If any of the components show signs of excessive wear they must be replaced.

14    Visually check the camshaft bearing surfaces on the cylinder head(s) for pitting, score marks, galling and abnormal wear. If the bearing surfaces are damaged, the cylinder head may have to be replaced (see illustration).

15    Measure the outside diameter of each camshaft bearing journal and record your measurements (see illustration). Compare them to the journal outside diameter specified

in this Chapter, then measure the inside diameter of each corresponding camshaft bearing and record the measurements. Subtract each cam journal outside diameter from its respective cam bearing bore inside diameter to determine the oil clearance for each bearing. Compare the results to the specified journal-to-bearing clearance. If any of the measurements fall outside the standard specified wear limits in this Chapter, either the camshaft or the cylinder head, or both, must be replaced.

16    Check camshaft runout by placing the camshaft back into the cylinder head and set up a dial indicator on the center journal. Zero the dial indicator. Turn the camshaft slowly and note the dial indicator readings. Runout should not exceed 0.0010 inch. If the measured runout exceeds the specified runout, replace the camshaft.

17    Check the camshaft endplay by placing a dial indicator with the stem in line with the camshaft and touching the snout. Push the camshaft all the way to the rear and zero the

dial indicator. Next, pry the camshaft to the front as far as possible and check the reading on the dial indicator. The distance it moves is the endplay. If it's greater than the Specifications listed in this Chapter, check the bearing caps for wear. If the bearing caps are worn, the cylinder head must be replaced.

18    Compare the camshaft lobe height by measuring each lobe with a micrometer (see illustration). Measure each of the intake lobes and write the measurements and relative positions down on a piece of paper. Then measure of each of the exhaust lobes and record the measurements and relative positions also. This will let you compare all of the intake lobes to one another and all of the exhaust lobes to one another. If the difference between the lobes exceeds 0.005 inch the camshaft should be replaced. Do not compare intake lobe heights to exhaust lobe heights, as lobe lift may be different. Only compare intake lobes to intake lobes and exhaust lobes to exhaust lobes for this comparison.

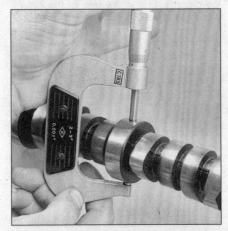

**8.15 Measure the outside diameter of each camshaft journal and the inside diameter of each bearing to determine the oil clearance measurement**

**8.18 Measuring cam lobe height with a micrometer, make sure you move the micrometer to get the highest reading (top of cam lobe)**

9.20a Intake manifold bolt tightening sequence - 3.7L V6

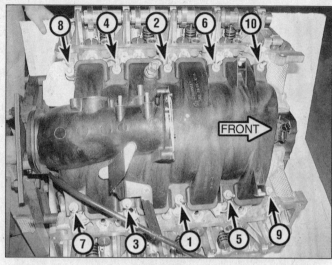

9.20b Intake manifold bolt tightening sequence - 4.7L V8

## Installation

19   Apply moly-based engine assembly lubricant to the camshaft lobes and journals and install the camshaft(s) into the cylinder head with the dowel pins in the 10 o'clock position. If the old camshafts are being used, make sure they're installed in the exact location from which they came.

20   Install the bearing caps and bolts and tighten them hand tight.

21   Tighten the bearing cap bolts a little at a time, to the torque listed in this Chapter's Specifications, starting with the middle bolts and working outward.

22   Engage the camshaft sprocket teeth with the camshaft drive chain links so that the "V6" or "V8" mark on the sprocket(s) is between the two marks made in Step 5 during removal, then position the sprocket over the dowel on the camshaft hub. At this point the chain marks and the "V6" or "V8" marks on the sprocket should be pointing up in the 12 o'clock position.

23   Thoroughly clean the camshaft sprocket bolts. Make sure all oil is removed from the bolt threads before installation, as over-tightening of bolts may occur if oil is not removed, then lubricate the bolt washers with small amount of clean engine oil making sure not to get oil on the threads.

24   Install the camshaft sprocket bolts and tighten them to the torque listed in this Chapter's Specifications (see illustration 7.48).

25   Remove the timing chain wedge(s).

26   Install the camshaft position sensor (CPS) (see Chapter 6)

27   Install the valve covers (see Section 5).

28   Connect the cable to the negative terminal of the battery.

---

## 9   Intake manifold - removal and installation

---

**Warning:** *The engine must be completely cool before beginning this procedure.*

## Removal

1   Relieve the fuel pressure (see Chapter 4A).

2   Disconnect the cable from the negative terminal of the battery (see Chapter 5, Section 1).

3   Refer to Chapter 4A and remove the air intake duct from the throttle body.

4   Label and disconnect the vacuum hoses leading to the intake manifold for the PCV valve, power brake booster, cruise control servo and evaporative emission control system.

5   Disconnect all of the electrical connectors leading to the intake manifold for the various sensors, the ignition coils and the Idle Air Control motor (IAC).

6   Disconnect the electrical connectors for the alternator and the air conditioning compressor.

7   Unbolt the ground straps attached to the intake manifold and the throttle body.

8   Remove the engine oil dipstick nut from the stud on the intake manifold, then follow the dipstick tube to the rear of the engine block and remove the bolt securing the tube at the back of the block. Pull the dipstick tube up and out of the engine block to remove it.

9   Detach the throttle cable and the cruise control cable from the throttle body and the throttle cable bracket (see Chapter 4A).

10   Remove the ignition coils (see Chapter 5).

11   Remove the fuel rails, then remove the throttle body and mounting bracket (see Chapter 4A).

12   Refer to Chapter 1 and drain the cooling system, then remove the heater hoses from the front cover and heater core tubes.

13   Refer to Chapter 6 and remove the coolant temperature sensor. This step is necessary to allow clearance for the intake manifold as it is removed.

14   Remove the intake manifold mounting fasteners in the reverse order of the tightening sequence (see illustrations 9.20a or 9.20b).

15   The manifold will probably be stuck to the cylinder heads and force may be required to break the gasket seal.

**Caution:** *Don't pry between the manifold and the heads or damage to the gasket sealing surfaces may occur, leading to vacuum leaks.*

16   Label and detach any remaining hoses which would interfere with the removal of the intake manifold.

17   Lift the manifold up level with the vehicle and remove it from the engine.

## Installation

18   Clean and inspect the intake manifold-to-cylinder head sealing surfaces. Inspect the gaskets on the manifold for tears or cracks, replacing them if necessary. The gaskets can be reused if not damaged.

19   Position the manifold on the engine making sure the gaskets and manifold are aligned correctly over the cylinder heads, then install the intake manifold bolts hand-tight.

20   Following the recommended tightening sequence, tighten the bolts to the torque listed in this Chapter's Specifications (see illustrations).

21   The remainder of the installation is the reverse of the removal procedure.

22   Fill the cooling system, run the engine and check for fuel, vacuum and coolant leaks.

---

## 10   Exhaust manifold - removal and installation

---

**Warning:** *The engine must be completely cool before beginning this procedure.*

## Removal

1   Disconnect the cable from the negative terminal of the battery (see Chapter 5).

2   Block the rear wheels, set the parking brake, raise the front of the vehicle and support it securely on jackstands.

3   Unbolt the exhaust pipe from the exhaust manifold.

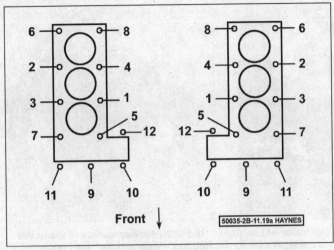

11.19a Cylinder head bolt tightening sequence - 3.7L V6

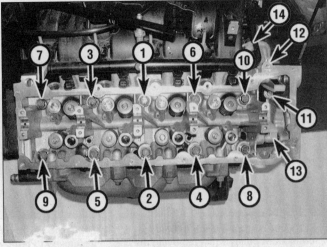

11.19b Cylinder head bolt tightening sequence - 4.7L V8

## Right side exhaust manifold, 4.7L V8 models

4    Remove the drivebelt (see Chapter 1).
5    Drain the engine coolant (see Chapter 1).
6    Remove the air inlet duct and air filter housing (see Chapter 4A).
7    Remove the air conditioning compressor (see Chapter 3).
8    Remove the accumulator bracket.
9    Remove the heater hoses at the engine (see Chapter 3).
10    Remove the starter (see Chapter 5).

## Either manifold, all models

11    Remove the exhaust manifold heat shields.
12    Remove the exhaust manifold mounting bolts and remove the manifold from the vehicle. Lower the exhaust manifold and remove it from under the vehicle.

## Installation

13    Clean the mating surfaces to remove all traces of old gasket material, then inspect the manifold for distortion and cracks. Warpage can be checked with a precision straightedge held against the mating flange. If a feeler gauge thicker than 0.030-inch can be inserted between the straightedge and flange surface, take the manifold to an automotive machine shop for resurfacing.
14    Place the exhaust manifold in position with a new gasket and install the mounting bolts finger-tight.
15    Starting in the middle and working out toward the ends, tighten the mounting bolts in several increments, to the torque listed in this Chapter's Specifications. Tighten the heat shield bolts securely.
16    Install the remaining components in the reverse order of removal. If you're working on a right-side exhaust manifold on a 4.7L engine, refill the cooling system (see Chapter 1).
17    Start the engine and check for exhaust leaks between the manifold and cylinder head and between the manifold and exhaust pipe.

## 11    Cylinder head - removal and installation

**Warning:** *The engine must be completely cool before beginning this procedure.*
Note: The following procedure describes how to remove the cylinder heads with the camshaft(s) and the exhaust manifold(s) still attached to the cylinder head.

### Removal

1    Remove the intake manifold (see Section 9).
2    Refer to Section 7 and remove the timing chains, sprockets and the timing chain guides.
3    Raise the front of the vehicle and support it securely on jackstands.
4    Unbolt the exhaust pipes from the exhaust manifolds.
5    Label and remove any remaining items attached to the cylinder head, such as coolant fittings, ground straps, cables, hoses, wires or brackets.
6    Using a breaker bar and the appropriate sized socket, loosen the cylinder head bolts in 1/4-turn increments until they can be removed by hand. Loosen the bolts in the reverse order of the tightening sequence (see illustrations 11.19a or 11.19b) to avoid warping or cracking the head.
7    Lift the cylinder head off the engine block with the camshaft in place and the exhaust manifold attached. If it's stuck, very carefully pry up at the front end of the cylinder head, beyond the gasket surface, at a casting protrusion.
8    Remove all external components from the head to allow for thorough cleaning and inspection.

### Installation

9    The mating surfaces of the cylinder head and block must be perfectly clean when the head is installed.
10    Use a gasket scraper to remove all

11.19c Using an angle measurement gauge during the final stages of tightening

traces of carbon and old gasket material from the cylinder head and engine block being careful not to gouge the aluminum, then clean the mating surfaces with lacquer thinner or acetone. If there's oil on the mating surfaces when the head is installed, the gasket may not seal correctly and leaks could develop. When working on the block, stuff the cylinders with clean shop rags to keep out debris. Use a vacuum cleaner to remove material that falls into the cylinders.
11    Check the block and head mating surfaces for nicks, deep scratches and other damage. If damage is slight, it can be removed with a file; if it's excessive, machining may be the only alternative.
12    Use a tap of the correct size to chase the threads in the head bolt holes, then clean the holes with compressed air - make sure that nothing remains in the holes.
**Warning:** *Wear eye protection when using compressed air!*
13    With a straight-edge, check each cylinder head bolt for stretching. If all threads do not contact the straight-edge, replace the bolt.

**12.4 Use a strap wrench to hold the crankshaft pulley while removing the center bolt (a chain-type wrench may be used if you wrap a section of old drivebelt or a rag around the crankshaft pulley first)**

**12.5 The use of a three jaw puller will be necessary to remove the crankshaft pulley - always place the puller jaws around the pulley hub, not the outer ring**

**12.6 If the sealing surface of the pulley hub has a wear groove from contact with the seal, repair sleeves are available at most auto parts stores**

14    Check the cylinder head for warpage. Check the head gasket, intake and exhaust manifold surfaces. Consult with an automotive machine shop.

15    Install any components that were removed from the head such as the lash adjusters, the exhaust manifold and the camshaft back onto the cylinder head.

16    Position the new cylinder head gasket over the dowel pins on the block noting which direction on the gasket faces up.

17    Carefully set the head over the dowels on the block without disturbing the gasket.

18    Before installing the M10 head bolts, apply a small amount of clean engine oil to the threads and hardened washers (if equipped). The chamfered side of the washers must face the bolt heads. Before installing the M8 head bolts, apply a small amount of thread sealant to the bolt threads.

19    Install the bolts in their original locations and tighten them finger-tight. Then tighten them, following the proper sequence, to the torque and angle of rotation listed in this Chapter's Specifications (see illustrations).

20    Install the timing chain guides, the tim-

ing chains and the timing chain sprockets as described in Section 7. The remaining installation steps are the reverse of removal.

21    Refill the cooling system and change the engine oil and filter (see Chapter 1).

22    Start the engine and check for oil and coolant leaks.

## 12   Crankshaft pulley/vibration damper - removal and installation

1    Disconnect the cable from the negative terminal of the battery (see Chapter 5, Section 1).

2    Refer to Chapter 3 and remove the cooling fans and shroud assembly.

3    Remove the drivebelts (see Chapter 1) and position the belt tensioner away from the crankshaft pulley.

4    Use a strap wrench around the crankshaft pulley to hold it while using a breaker bar and socket to remove the crankshaft pulley center bolt (see illustration).

5    Pull the damper off the crankshaft with a

puller (see illustration).

**Caution:** *The jaws of the puller must only contact the hub ofthe pulley - not the outer ring. Also, the puller screw must not contact the threads in the nose of the crankshaft; it must either bear on the end of the crankshaft nose or a spacer must be inserted into the nose of the crankshaft to protect the threads.*

6    Check the surface on the pulley hub that the oil seal rides on. If the surface has been grooved from long-time contact with the seal, a press-on sleeve may be available to renew the sealing surface (see illustration). This sleeve is pressed into place with a hammer and a block of wood and is commonly available at auto parts stores for various applications.

7    Lubricate the pulley hub with clean engine oil. Align the slot in the pulley with the key on the crankshaft and push the crankshaft pulley on the crankshaft as far as it will go. Use a vibration damper installation tool to press the pulley the rest of the way onto the crankshaft.

8    Install the crankshaft pulley retaining bolt and tighten it to the torque listed in this Chapter's Specifications.

9    The remainder of installation is the reverse of the removal.

## 13   Crankshaft front oil seal - replacement

1    Remove the crankshaft pulley from the engine (see Section 12).

2    Carefully pry the seal out of the cover with a seal removal tool or a large screwdriver (see illustration).

**Caution:** *Be careful not to scratch, gouge or distort the area that the seal fits into or an oil leak will develop.*

3    Clean the bore to remove any old seal material and corrosion. Position the new seal in the bore with the seal lip (usually the side

**13.2 Pry the seal out very carefully with a seal removal tool or screwdriver, being careful not to nick or gouge the seal bore or the crankshaft**

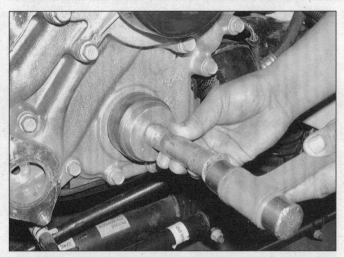

13.4 Use a seal driver or large-diameter socket to drive the new seal into the cover

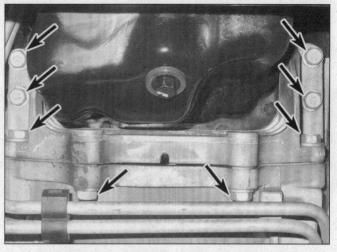

14.4 Remove the oil pan-to-transmission support brace

with the spring) facing IN (toward the engine). A small amount of oil applied to the outer edge of the new seal will make installation easier.

4    Drive the seal into the bore with a seal driver or a large socket and hammer until it's completely seated (see illustration). Select a socket that's the same outside diameter as the seal and make sure the new seal is pressed into place until it bottoms against the cover flange.

5    Lubricate the seal lips with engine oil and reinstall the crankshaft pulley.

6    The remainder of installation is the reverse of the removal. Run the engine and check for oil leaks.

## 14   Oil pan - removal and installation

### Removal

1    Disconnect the cable from the negative terminal of the battery (see Chapter 5, Section 1).

2    Apply the parking brake and block the rear wheels. Raise the front of the vehicle and place it securely on jackstands.

3    Drain the engine oil (see Chapter 1).

4    If equipped, remove the skidplate, then remove the transmission-to-oil pan support brace at the rear of the pan (see illustration).

5    Remove the transmission oil cooler line bracket.

6    Remove the front crossmember.

7    Attach an engine hoist or an engine support fixture to the lifting eyes on the engine, raise the engine just enough to take the weight of the engine off the engine mounts, then remove the engine mount through-bolts (see Section 18).

8    Raise the engine until the engine fan is almost in contact with the fan shroud.

**Caution:** *Don't allow the fan to contact the fan shroud.*

9    Remove the bolts and nuts, noting the

stud locations, then carefully separate the oil pan from the block. Don't pry between the block and the pan or damage to the sealing surfaces and gasket could occur and oil leaks may develop. Instead, tap on the side of the oil pan with a rubber mallet if necessary to break the gasket seal (see illustration).

10    Remove the two nuts and one bolt that secures the oil pump pick-up tube and windage tray. Drop the pick-up tube into the oil pan, then remove the pick-up tube, windage tray and oil pan as a unit.

### Installation

11    Clean the oil pan with solvent and remove any gasket material from the block and the pan mating surfaces. Clean the mating surfaces with lacquer thinner or acetone and make sure the bolt holes in the block are clear. Check the oil pan flange for distortion, particularly around the bolt holes.

12    Inspect the oil pan gasket for cuts and tears, replacing it if necessary. If the gasket is in good condition, it can be reused.

**Note:** *The oil pan gasket and the windage tray are a one piece design, therefore must be replaced together.*

13    Place the pick-up tube and oil pan gasket/windage tray in the oil pan and position the oil pan on the engine.

**Note:** *Always use a new O-ring on the pick-up tube and tighten the pick-up tube-to-oil pump bolt first.*

14    After the fasteners are installed, tighten all the bolts in several steps, in a criss-cross pattern starting from the center and working out to the ends, to the torque listed in this Chapter's Specifications.

15    Place the transmission-to-oil pan support brace in position and install the vertically mounted bolts. Torque the vertically mounted bolts to 10 in-lbs, then install the horizontally mounted bolts. Torque the horizontally mounted bolts to 40 ft-lbs, then retorque the vertically mounted bolts to 40 ft-lbs (see illustration 14.4).

16    The remaining steps are the reverse of the removal procedure.

14.9 If the oil pan is stuck to the gasket, gently tap on the side of the oil pan to break the gasket seal

15.3 Oil pump housing/primary timing chain tensioner retaining bolts

15.5 Remove the screws and lift the cover off

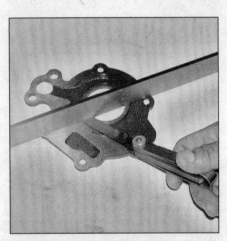

15.7a Place a straightedge across the oil pump cover and check it for warpage with a feeler gauge

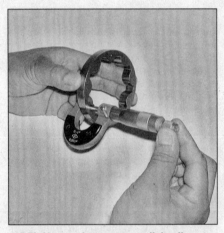

15.7b Use a micrometer or dial caliper to check the thickness and the diameter of the outer rotor

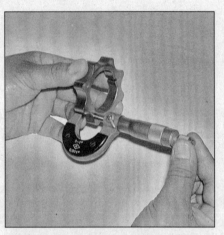

15.7c Use a micrometer or dial caliper to check the thickness of the inner rotor

15.7d Check the outer rotor-to-housing clearance

17    Refill the engine with oil (see Chapter 1), replace the oil filter, then run the engine until normal operating temperature is reached and check for leaks.

### 15   Oil pump - removal, inspection and installation

#### Removal

1    Refer to Section 7 and remove the timing chains and sprockets.
2    Remove the oil pan, windage tray and pick-up tube (see Section 14).
3    Remove the primary timing chain tensioner/oil pump bolts (see illustration), then remove the tensioner.
4    Remove the remaining oil pump bolts, then gently pry the oil pump housing outward enough to clear the flats on the crankshaft and remove it from the engine.

#### Inspection

5    Remove the screws holding the front cover on the oil pump housing (see illustration).
6    Clean all components with solvent, then inspect them for wear and damage.
**Caution:** *The oil pressure relief valve and spring are an integral part of the oil pump housing. Removal of the relief valve and spring from the oil pump housing will damage the oil pump and require replacement of the entire oil pump assembly.*
7    Check the clearance of the following oil pump components with a feeler gauge and a micrometer or dial caliper (see illustrations) and compare the measurement to the clearance specifications listed in this Chapter's Specifications.

   a)  *Cover flatness*
   b)  *Outer rotor diameter and thickness*
   c)  *Inner rotor thickness*
   d)  *Outer rotor-to-body clearance*
   e)  *Inner rotor-to-outer rotor tip clearance*
   f)  *Cover-to-inner rotor side clearance*
   g)  *Cover-to-outer rotor side clearance*

8    If any clearance is excessive, replace the entire oil pump assembly.
**Note:** *Fill the oil pump rotor cavities with clean engine oil to prime it. Assemble the oil and tighten all fasteners to the torque listed in this Chapter's Specifications.*

### Installation

10   To install the pump, turn the flats in the rotor so they align with the flats on the crankshaft and push the oil pump back into position against the block.
11   Position the primary timing chain tensioner over the oil pump and install the pump-to-block bolts. Tighten the oil pump/primary timing chain tensioner bolts to the torque listed in this Chapter's Specifications.
12   The remainder of installation is the reverse of removal.

### 16   Flywheel/driveplate - removal and installation

1    Raise the vehicle and support it securely on jackstands, then refer to Chapter 7A or Chapter 7B and remove the transmission.
2    Now would be a good time to check and replace the transmission front pump seal on automatic transmissions.
3    Use paint or a center-punch to make alignment marks on the flywheel/driveplate and crankshaft to ensure correct alignment during reinstallation.
4    Remove the bolts that secure the flywheel/driveplate to the crankshaft. If the crankshaft turns, wedge a screwdriver into the ring gear teeth to keep the crankshaft from turning.
5    Pull straight back on the flywheel/driveplate to detach it from the crankshaft.
6    Installation is the reverse of removal. Be sure to align the matching paint marks. Use thread locking compound on the bolt threads and tighten them in several steps, in a crisscross pattern, to the torque listed in this Chapter's Specifications.

### 17   Rear main oil seal - replacement

1    These models use a one-piece rear main seal that is sandwiched between the engine block and the lower main bearing cap assembly, or "bed plate" as it's often referred to. Replacing this seal requires removal of the transmission (see Chapter 7A or Chapter 7B) and flywheel/driveplate (see Section 16).
2    The seal can be removed by prying it out of the engine block with a screwdriver, being careful not to nick the crankshaft surface (see illustration). Wrap the screwdriver tip with tape to avoid damage.
3    Thoroughly clean the seal bore in the block with a shop towel. Remove all traces of oil and dirt.
4    Lubricate the seal lip with clean engine

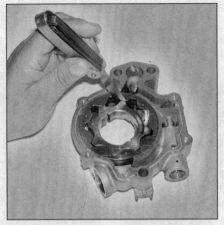

**15.7e Check the clearance between the tips of the inner and outer rotors**

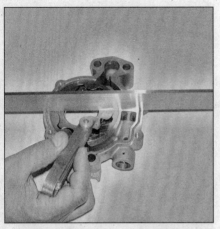

**15.7f Using a straightedge and feeler gauge, check the side clearance between the surface of the oil pump and the inner and outer rotors**

oil and install the seal over the end of the crankshaft. Make sure the lip of the seal points toward the engine.
5    Preferably, a seal installation tool (available at most auto parts stores) should be used to press the new seal back into place. Drive the new seal squarely into the seal bore and flush with the rear of the engine block.
6    The remainder of installation is the reverse of the removal procedure.

### 18   Engine mounts - check and replacement

1    There are three powertrain mounts on the vehicles covered by this manual; left and right engine mounts attached to the engine block and to the frame and a rear mount attached to the transmission and the frame. The rear transmission mount is covered in Chapter 7A. Engine mounts seldom require attention, but broken or deteriorated mounts should be replaced immediately or the added strain placed on the driveline components may cause damage or wear.

### Check

2    During the check, the engine must be raised slightly to remove the weight from the mounts.
3    Raise the vehicle and support it securely on jackstands, then position a jack under the engine oil pan. Place a large wood block between the jack head and the oil pan, then carefully raise the engine just enough to take the weight off the mounts.
**Warning:** *DO NOT place any part of your body under the engine when it's supported only by a jack!*
4    Check for relative movement between the inner and outer portions of the mount (use a large screwdriver or prybar to attempt to move the mounts). If movement is noted, lower the engine and tighten the mount fasteners.

**17.2 Pry the seal out very carefully with a seal removal tool or screwdriver - if the crankshaft is damaged, the new seal will leak!**

5    Check the mounts to see if the rubber is cracked, hardened or separated from the metal casing which would indicate a need for replacement.
6    Rubber preservative should be applied to the mounts to slow deterioration.

### Replacement

7    Disconnect the cable from the negative terminal of the battery (see Chapter 5, Section 1).
8    Remove the engine cooling fan and shroud (see Chapter 3).
**Caution:** *Raising the engine with the cooling fan in place may damage the viscous clutch.*
9    Raise the front of the vehicle and support it securely on jackstands.
10   Support the engine with a lifting device from above.. Raise the engine just enough to take the weight off the engine mounts. If you're removing the driver's side engine

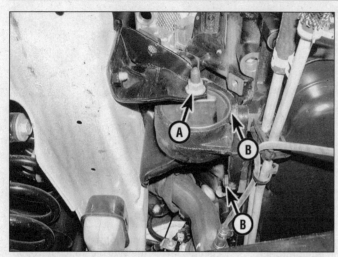

**18.12 The engine mounts are secured by the through-bolt (A) and the mount-to-engine block bolts (B) - the two upper mount-to-block bolts are not visible in this photo**

**18.19 Location of the engine mount through-bolt on a 4WD model**

mount, removal of the oil filter will be necessary.

**Caution:** *Do not connect the lifting device to the intake manifold*

### 2WD models

11    Remove the engine mount-to-frame support bracket through-bolt.

12    Remove the mount-to-engine block bolts, then remove the mount and the heat shield, if equipped (see illustration).

13    Place the heat shield and the new mount in position, install the mount-to-engine block bolts and tighten all the bolts securely.

### 4WD models

14    Use a floor jack and jackstands to support the front axle. The front axle will be partially lowered to make additional clearance for the engine mount removal.

15    Remove the engine skidplate.

16    Remove the front crossmember (see Chapter 10).

17    Remove the bolts that support the engine mount to the front axle.

18    Remove the bolts that attach the front axle to the engine.

19    Remove the engine mount-to-frame support bracket through-bolt (see illustration).

20    Remove the engine mount to engine

support bracket bolt and nuts.

21    Install the engine mount onto the engine support bracket and tighten the bolts securely.

### All models

22    After the engine mounts have been installed onto the engine, lower the engine while guiding the engine mount and through-bolt into the frame support bracket. Install the through-bolt nut and tighten it securely.

23    The remainder of the installation is the reverse of removal. Remove the engine hoist and the jackstands and lower the vehicle.

# Chapter 2 Part B
# 5.7L Hemi engines

## Contents

## Specifications

### General
| | |
|---|---|
| Firing order | 1-8-4-3-6-5-7-2 |
| Bore and stroke | 3.91 x 3.58 inches |
| Displacement | 5.7L (345 cubic inches) |
| Cylinder numbers (front-to-rear) | |
| Left (driver's) side | 1-3-5-7 |
| Right side | 2-4-6-8 |
| Compression | See Chapter 2E |

### Camshaft
| | |
|---|---|
| Journal diameters | |
| No. 1 | 2.290 inches |
| No. 2 | 2.270 inches |
| No. 3 | 2.260 inches |
| No. 4 | 2.240 inches |
| No. 5 | 1.720 inches |
| Journal oil clearance | |
| No. 1, 3 and 5 | 0.0015 to 0.0030 inch |
| No. 2 and 4 | 0.0019 to 0.0035 inch |
| Endplay | 0.0031 to 0.0114 inch |

### Oil pump
| | |
|---|---|
| Minimum pressure at curb idle | 4 psi |
| Operating pressure | 25 to 110 psi at 3,000 rpm |

30042-1-specs HAYNES

Cylinder locations on the
5.7L Hemi V8 engine

## Torque specifications

**Ft-lbs** (unless otherwise indicated)

**Note:** *One foot-pound (ft-lb) of torque is equivalent to 12 inch-pounds (in-lbs) of torque. Torque values below approximately 15 ft-lbs are expressed in inch-pounds, because most foot-pound torque wrenches are not accurate at these smaller values.*

| | |
|---|---|
| Camshaft sprocket bolt | 90 |
| Camshaft thrust plate bolts | 21 |
| Cylinder head bolts (see illustration 10.16) | |
|   Step 1 | |
|     Large bolts | 25 |
|     Small bolts | 15 |
|   Step 2 | |
|     Large bolts | 40 |
|     Small bolts | 25 |
|   Step 3 | |
|     Large bolts | Tighten an additional 90 degrees |
|     Small bolts | 25 |
| Drivebelt tensioner mounting bolt | 30 |
| Drivebelt pulley mounting bolt | 45 |
| Driveplate bolts | 70 |
| Exhaust manifold bolts/nuts | 17 |
| Exhaust manifold heat shield nuts | 132 in-lbs |
| Exhaust pipe flange nuts | 24 |
| Flywheel bolts | 55 |
| Intake manifold bolts | 105 in-lbs |
| Oil pan bolts/studs | 105 in-lbs |
| Oil pump pick-up tube bolts | 21 |
| Oil pump mounting bolts | 21 |
| Rear main seal retainer bolts | 132 in-lbs |
| Rocker arm bolts | 16 |
| Rocker arm lifter rail bolts | 106 in-lbs |
| Timing chain cover bolts | 21 |
| Transmission brace mounting bolts (see illustration 12.16) | |
|   Step 1 | 15 |
|   Step 2 | 30 |
|   Step 3 | 40 |
| Valve cover nuts/studs | 70 in-lbs |
| Vibration damper-to-crankshaft bolt | 129 |
| Water pump-to-timing chain cover bolts | 21 |

*Refer to Part E for additional specifications

## 1  General Information

1   This part of Chapter 2 is devoted to in-vehicle repair procedures for Hemi engines. Information concerning engine removal and installation and engine overhaul can be found in Part E of this Chapter.

2   Since the repair procedures included in this Part are based on the assumption that the engine is still installed in the vehicle, if they are being used during a complete engine overhaul (with the engine already out of the vehicle and on a stand) many of the steps included here will not apply.

3   These Hemi engines use a cast iron engine block with aluminum cylinder heads and intake manifold. The cylinder banks are positioned at a 90-degree angle with the camshaft mounted high in the engine block. The valvetrain includes roller lifters, with pushrods positioned between the camshaft and rocker arms in a nearly horizontal plane. The camshaft can only be removed after the cylinder heads and valvetrain components (rocker arms, pushrods and lifters) have been removed.

## 2  Repair operations possible with the engine in the vehicle

1   Many major repair operations can be accomplished without removing the engine from the vehicle.

2   Clean the engine compartment and the exterior of the engine with some type of pressure washer before any work is done. A clean engine will make the job easier and will help keep dirt out of the internal areas of the engine.

3   Depending on the components involved, it may be a good idea to remove the hood to improve access to the engine as repairs are performed (refer to Chapter 11 if necessary).

4   If oil or coolant leaks develop, indicating a need for gasket or seal replacement, the repairs can generally be made with the engine in the vehicle. The oil pan gasket, the cylinder head gaskets, intake and exhaust manifold gaskets, timing chain cover gaskets and the crankshaft front oil seal are all accessible with the engine in place.

5   Exterior engine components, such as the water pump, the starter motor, the alternator and the fuel injection components, as well as the intake and exhaust manifolds, can be removed for repair with the engine in place.

6   Since the cylinder heads can be removed without removing the engine, valve component servicing can also be accomplished with the engine in the vehicle.

7   Replacement of, repairs to or inspection of the timing chain and sprockets and the oil pump are all possible with the engine in place.

8   In extreme cases caused by a lack of necessary equipment, repair or replacement of piston rings, pistons, connecting rods and rod bearings is possible with the engine in the vehicle. However, this practice is not recommended because of the cleaning and preparation work that must be done to the components involved.

## 3  Top Dead Center (TDC) for number one piston - locating

1   Top Dead Center (TDC) is the highest point in the cylinder that each piston reaches as it travels up-and-down when the crankshaft turns. Each piston reaches TDC on the compression stroke and again on the exhaust stroke, but TDC generally refers to piston position on the compression stroke.

2   In order to bring any piston to TDC, the crankshaft must be turned using a breaker bar and socket on the vibration damper bolt. When looking at the front of the engine, normal crankshaft rotation is clockwise.

3   Disconnect the cable from the negative terminal of the battery (see Chapter 5, Section 1).

4   Remove one of the number 1 spark plugs, preferably the closest to the front of the engine, then thread a compression gauge into the spark plug hole. Turn the crankshaft with a large socket and breaker bar attached to the large bolt that is threaded into the vibration damper (see illustration). When compression registers on the gauge, the number one piston is beginning its compression stroke. Stop turning the crankshaft and remove the gauge.

5   Install a long dowel into the number one spark plug hole until it rests on top of the piston crown. Continue rotating the crankshaft slowly until the dowel levels off (piston reaches top of travel). This will be approximate TDC for number 1 piston.

6   These engines are not equipped with external components (vibration damper, flywheel, timing hole, etc.) that are marked to identify the position of number 1 TDC. Therefore the only method to double-check the exact location of TDC number 1 on Hemi engines is to remove the timing chain cover to access timing chain sprockets (see Section 9), or with the use of a degree wheel on the crankshaft vibration damper and a positive stop threaded into the spark plug hole.

## 4  Valve covers - removal and installation

### Removal

1   Disconnect the cable from the negative terminal of the battery (see Chapter 5, Section 1).

2   If you're removing the right-side valve cover, remove the air filter housing (see Chapter 4A).

3   Remove the harness clips from the valve cover studs (see illustrations).

4   Remove the ignition coils and ignition wires (see Chapter 5).

3.4 Use a breaker bar and deep socket to rotate the crankshaft

4.3a Location of the harness clips on the right side valve cover

4.3b Location of the harness clips on the left side valve cover - some hidden from view

5   Remove the ground straps from the valve cover (see illustration). Be sure to mark the location of each of the ground terminals for correct installation.

6   Remove the valve cover mounting bolts (see illustrations).

7   Remove the valve cover.

**Note:** *If the cover is stuck to the head, bump the cover with a block of wood and a hammer to release it. If it still will not come loose, try to slip a flexible putty knife between the head and cover to break the seal. Don't pry at the cover-to-head joint, as damage to the sealing surface and cover flange will result and oil leaks will develop.*

## Installation

8   The mating surfaces of each cylinder head and valve cover must be perfectly clean when the covers are installed. Wipe the mating surfaces with a cloth saturated with lacquer thinner or acetone. If there is sealant or oil on the mating surfaces when the cover is installed, oil leaks may develop.

9   If the valve cover gasket isn't damaged or hardened, it can be re-used. If it is in need of replacement, install a new one into the valve cover perimeter and new rubber seals into the grooves in the valve cover that seal the spark plug tubes (see illustration).

10   Carefully position the cover on the head and install the bolts, making sure the bolts with the studs are in the proper locations.

11   Tighten the bolts in three steps to the torque listed in this Chapter's Specifications. Start with the middle bolts and move to the outer bolts using a criss-cross pattern.

**Caution:** *DON'T over-tighten the valve cover bolts.*

12   The remaining installation steps are the reverse of removal.

13   Start the engine and check carefully for oil leaks as the engine warms up.

## 5   Rocker arms and pushrods - removal, inspection and installation

## *Removal*

1   Remove the valve covers from the cylinder heads (see Section 4).

2   Loosen the rocker arm shaft bolts one at a time, starting with the center bolt and working toward the outer bolts. When the bolts have been completely loosened, lift the rocker shaft assembly off the cylinder head (see illustration).

3   Keep track of the rocker arm positions, since they must be returned to the same locations. Store each set of rocker components in such a way as to ensure that they're reinstalled in their original locations. Remove the pushrods and store them in order as well, to make sure they don't get mixed up during

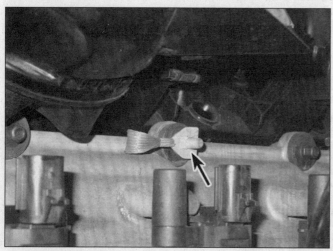

**4.5 Remove the ground straps from the valve cover studs**

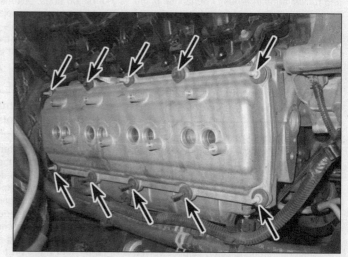

**4.6a Location of the valve cover mounting bolts on the right side valve cover**

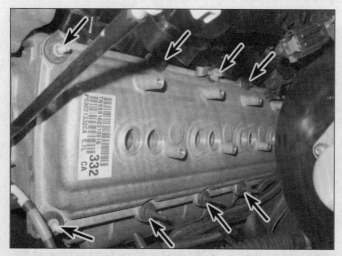

**4.6b Location of the valve cover mounting bolts on the left side valve cover**

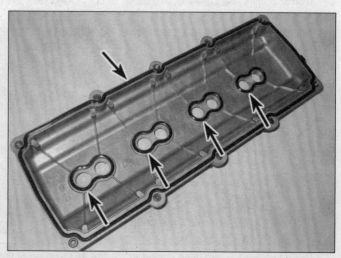

**4.9 If they're damaged or hardened, replace the rubber gasket and spark plug tube seals with new ones (if they're OK, they can be re-used)**

installation (see illustration).

**Caution:** *The exhaust pushrods are slightly longer than the intake pushrods - they aren't interchangeable.*

## Inspection

**Caution:** *If the cylinder heads have been removed and the surface milled for flatness, be sure to install correct length pushrods to compensate for the reduced distances of the rocker arms-to-camshaft dimensions. Consult with the machine shop for the correct length pushrods.*

4     Check each rocker arm for wear, cracks and other damage (see illustration), especially where the pushrods and valve stems contact the rocker arm.

5     Check the rocker arm shafts and bores of the rocker arms for wear. Look for galling, stress cracks and unusual wear patterns. If the rocker arms are worn or damaged, replace them with new ones and install new shafts as well.

**Caution:** *Do not remove the rocker arm retainers unless absolutely necessary. Each retainer has tangs at the bottom that can easily break off and get into the engine. If a retainer does break off, be sure to retrieve it from the rocker arm shaft prior to reassembly. Replace any retainers with broken tangs.*

**Note:** *Keep in mind that there is no valve adjustment on these engines, so excessive wear or damage in the valve train can easily result in excessive valve clearance, which in turn will cause valve noise when the engine is running.*

6     Make sure the hole at the pushrod end of each rocker arm is open.

7     Inspect the pushrods for cracks and excessive wear at the ends. Roll each pushrod across a piece of plate glass to see if it's bent (if it wobbles, it's bent).

## Installation

8     Lubricate the lower end of each pushrod with clean engine oil or engine assembly lube and install them in their original locations. Make sure each pushrod seats completely in the lifter socket.

9     Apply engine assembly lube to the ends of the valve stems and the upper ends of the pushrods to prevent damage to the mating surfaces on initial start-up.

10     Lubricate the rocker shafts with clean engine oil or engine assembly lube, then assemble the rocker shafts, with all of the components in their original positions. Install the rocker shafts onto the cylinder heads.

11     The rocker arm shafts must be tightened starting with the center bolt, then the center right bolt, the center left bolt, the outer right bolt and finally the outer left bolt. Follow this sequence in several steps until the torque listed in this Chapter's Specifications is reached. As the bolts are tightened, make sure the pushrods seat properly in the rocker arms.

**Caution:** *Do not continue tightening the rocker arms if the rocker arm bolts become tight before the shaft is seated or the pushrods are binding. Remove the rocker arm shafts and inspect all the components carefully before proceeding.*

12     Refer to Section 4 and install the valve covers. Start the engine, listen for unusual valve train noses and check for oil leaks at the valve cover gaskets.

## 6     Intake manifold - removal and installation

## Removal

1     Refer to Chapter 4A and relieve the fuel system pressure. Disconnect the cable from the negative terminal of the battery (see Chapter 5).

2     Remove the resonator and the intake air duct (see Chapter 4A).

**5.2 Remove the rocker arm shaft bolts - mark each rocker arm assembly and note that the upper rocker arms are the intake and the lower rocker arms are the exhaust**

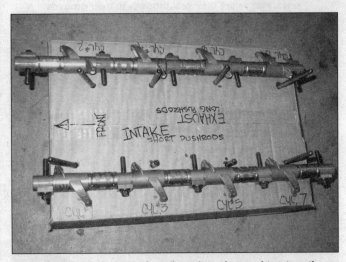

**5.3 A perforated sheet of cardboard can be used to store the rocker arms and pushrods to ensure that they're reinstalled in their original locations - note the arrow indicating the front of the engine**

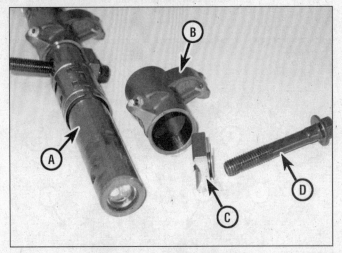

**5.4 Rocker arm component details**

| A | Rocker arm shaft | C | Retainer |
|---|---|---|---|
| B | Rocker arm | D | Rocker shaft bolt |

3   Remove the ignition wires and the ignition coils (see Chapter 5).

4   Disconnect the brake booster vacuum hose and the PCV hose.

5   Disconnect the electrical connectors at each injector, remove the fuel rails and injectors, and disconnect the throttle body linkage.

6   Remove the alternator (see Chapter 5).

7   Remove the air conditioning compressor, without disconnecting the refrigerant lines, and set it aside (see Chapter 3).

8   Refer to Chapter 6 and disconnect the electrical connectors from the IAT, MAP, TPS and ECT sensors.

9   Starting with the outer bolts and working to the inner bolts, loosen the intake manifold mounting bolts in 1/4-turn increments until they can be removed by hand (see illustration).

10   Remove the intake manifold. As the manifold is lifted from the engine, be sure to check for and disconnect anything still attached to the manifold.

## Installation

**Note:** *The mating surfaces of the cylinder heads and intake manifold must be perfectly clean when the manifold is installed.*

11   Check the O-rings on the intake manifold for damage or hardening. If they're OK, they can be re-used. If necessary, install new O-rings (see illustration).

12   Carefully set the manifold in place.

**Caution:** *Do not disturb the rubber seals and DO NOT move the manifold fore-and-aft after it contacts the cylinder heads or the seals could be pushed out of place and the engine may develop vacuum and/or oil leaks.*

13   Install the intake manifold bolts and tighten the bolts following the recommended sequence (see illustration), to the torque listed in this Chapter's Specifications. Do not overtighten the bolts.

14   The remaining installation steps are the reverse of removal. Start the engine and check carefully for vacuum leaks at the intake manifold joints.

## 7   Exhaust manifolds - removal and installation

## Removal

**Warning:** *Allow the engine to cool completely before performing this procedure.*

1   Disconnect the cable from the negative terminal of the battery (see Chapter 5).

2   Raise the vehicle and support it securely on jackstands. Disconnect the exhaust pipe-to-manifold connections. It's a good idea to apply penetrating oil on the studs/bolts and let it soak in for about 10 minutes before attempting to remove them.

3   Lower the vehicle and remove the heat shield nuts and the heat shield (see illustration).

4   Remove the bolts retaining the exhaust manifold to the cylinder head (see illustrations).

5   Remove the exhaust manifold(s).

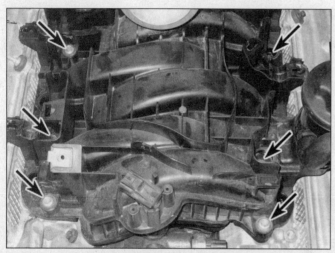

**6.9 Location of the intake manifold mounting bolts - four rear mounting bolts hidden from view**

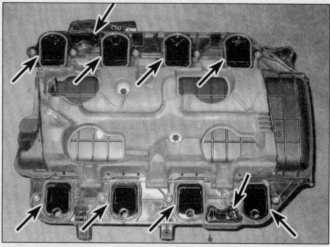

**6.11 If necessary, replace the intake manifold O-rings with new ones. Make sure they seat properly in their grooves**

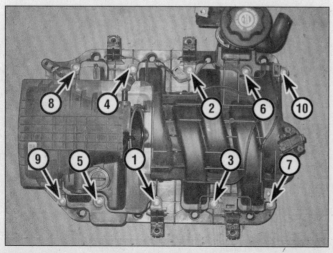

**6.13 Tightening sequence for the intake manifold mounting bolts**

**7.3 Location of the exhaust manifold heat shield nuts on the right-side exhaust manifold**

## Installation

6    Installation is the reverse of the removal procedure. Clean the manifold and head gasket surfaces and check for cracks and flatness. Replace the exhaust manifold gaskets.

7    Install the exhaust manifold(s) and fasteners. Tighten the bolts/nuts to the torque listed in this Chapter's Specifications. Work from the center to the ends and approach the final torque in three steps. Install the heat shields.

8    Apply anti-seize compound to the exhaust manifold-to-exhaust pipe bolts and tighten them securely.

---

## 8    Vibration damper and front oil seal - removal and installation

---

**Warning:** *Wait until the engine is completely cool before beginning this procedure.*

1    Disconnect the cable from the negative terminal of the battery (see Chapter 5, Section 1).

2    Remove the engine drivebelt (see Chapter 1).

3    Drain the coolant (see Chapter 1), remove the upper radiator hose and remove the engine cooling fan (see Chapter 3).

4    Remove the large vibration damper-to-crankshaft bolt. To keep the crankshaft from turning, install a chain wrench around the circumference of the pulley. Be sure to use a piece of rubber (old drivebelt, old timing belt, etc.) under the chain to protect the vibration damper from nicks or gouges (see illustration).

5    Using the proper puller (commonly available from auto parts stores), detach the vibration damper (see illustration).

**Caution:** *Do not use a puller with jaws that grip the outer edge of the pulley. The puller must be the type that utilizes bolts or arms to*

apply force to the pulley hub only. Also, the puller screw must not contact the threads in the nose of the crankshaft; it must use an adapter that allows the puller screw to apply force to the end of the crankshaft nose or a spacer must be inserted into the nose of the crankshaft to protect the threads.

6    If the seal is being removed while the cover is still attached to the engine block, carefully pry the seal out of the cover with a seal removal tool or a large screwdriver (see illustration).

**Caution:** *Be careful not to scratch, gouge or distort the area that the seal fits into or an oil leak will develop.*

7    Clean the bore to remove any old seal material and corrosion. Position the new seal in the bore with the seal lip (usually the side with the spring) facing IN (toward the engine). A small amount of oil applied to the outer edge of the new seal will make installation easier.

8    Drive the seal into the bore with a seal

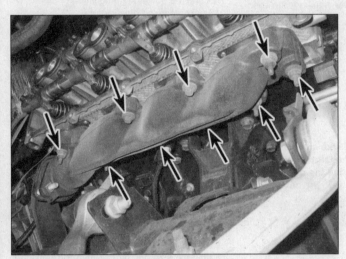

**7.4a Location of the exhaust manifold mounting bolts on the right-side exhaust manifold**

**7.4b Location of the exhaust manifold mounting bolts on the left-side exhaust manifold (not all are visible in this photo)**

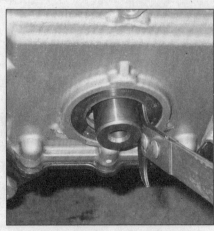

**8.4 Use a chain wrench to lock the vibration damper - be sure to position a piece of an old timing belt or drivebelt underneath the chain wrench to prevent damaging the damper**

**8.5 Use a three-jaw puller to remove the vibration damper from the crankshaft**

**8.6 Use a seal puller to remove the front seal from the timing chain cover**

driver or a large socket and hammer until it's completely seated (see illustration). Select a socket that's the same outside diameter as the seal and make sure the new seal is pressed into place until it bottoms against the cover flange.

9    Check the surface of the damper that the oil seal rides on. If the surface has been grooved from long-time contact with the seal, replace the vibration damper.

10   Lubricate the seal lips with engine oil and reinstall the vibration damper, aligning the Woodruff key on the nose of the crankshaft with the keyway in the damper hub. Use a special installation tool (available at most auto parts stores) to press the vibration damper onto the crankshaft.

11   Install the vibration damper bolt and tighten it to the torque listed in this Chapter's Specifications.

12   The remainder of installation is the reverse of the removal process.

13   Refill the cooling system (see Chapter 1).

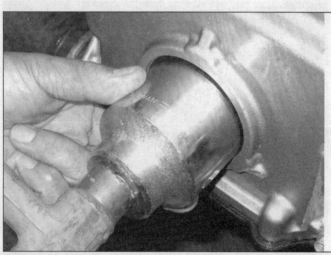

**8.8 Use a seal driver or a large socket to drive the new seal into the cover**

## 9    Timing chain cover, chain and sprockets - removal, inspection and installation

**Warning:** *Wait until the engine is completely cool before beginning this procedure.*

### Removal

**Caution:** *The timing system is complex. Severe engine damage will occur if you make any mistakes. Do not attempt this procedure unless you are highly experienced with this type of repair. If you are at all unsure of your abilities, consult an expert. Double-check all your work and be sure everything is correct before you attempt to start the engine.*

1    Disconnect the cable from the negative terminal of the battery (see Chapter 5).

2    Drain the cooling system (see Chapter 1).

3    Drain the engine oil (see Chapter 1).

4    Remove the air filter housing, the reso-

nator box and the air intake duct (see Chapter 4A).

5    Remove the drivebelt (see Chapter 1).

6    Remove the engine cooling fan and the upper and lower radiator hoses (see Chapter 3).

7    Remove the air conditioning compressor (see Chapter 3). It is not necessary to evacuate the refrigerant from the air conditioning system for this procedure. Use rope or wire to tie the compressor away from the front of the engine with the air conditioning lines attached.

8    Remove the alternator (see Chapter 5).

9    Remove the coolant reservoir (see Chapter 3).

10   Remove the drivebelt tensioner (see illustration) and the idler pulleys.

11   Remove the vibration damper (see Section 8).

12   Remove the power steering pump (see Chapter 10) and set it aside without disconnecting the power steering lines.

13   Remove the dipstick tube.

14   Remove the oil pan and the pickup tube (see Section 12).

15   Disconnect the heater hoses from the front cover.

16   Remove the water pump (see Chapter 3).

17   Remove the timing chain cover bolts (see illustration) and the front cover.

18   Remove the oil pump (see Section 13).

19   Reinstall the bolt into the end of the crankshaft and turn the crankshaft until the crankshaft sprocket timing mark is at the 6:00 o'clock position (with the crankshaft key at 2:00 o'clock) and the camshaft timing mark at the 12:00 o'clock position (see illustrations).

20   Retract the tensioner until the hole in the tensioner aligns with the hole in the camshaft tensioner thrust plate (see illustration). Install a suitable size drill bit to retain the tensioner in the retracted position.

**9.10 Details of the idler pulleys and drivebelt tensioner on the timing chain cover**

A    *Idler pulley mounting bolt*
B    *Drivebelt tensioner mounting bolt*

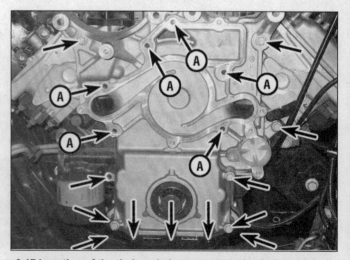

**9.17 Location of the timing chain cover mounting bolts - the bolt holes marked with an (A) secure the water pump as well as the timing chain cover**

9.19a Use a breaker bar and socket to rotate the crankshaft (clockwise) to TDC number 1 position

9.19b The single colored timing chain link should align with the camshaft sprocket timing mark . . .

**Note:** *The timing chain tensioner is an integral component of the camshaft thrust plate. If necessary, the tensioner/thrust plate assembly must be replaced as a complete unit.*

21   Remove the camshaft sprocket bolt and remove the timing chain with the camshaft and crankshaft sprockets (see illustrations).

22   Remove the camshaft tensioner thrust plate mounting bolts (see illustration 11.9) and separate the tensioner from the engine block.

### Inspection

23   Inspect the camshaft sprocket for damage or wear. The camshaft sprocket is a steel sprocket, but the teeth can become grooved or worn enough to cause a poor meshing of the sprocket and the chain.

**Caution:** *Whenever a new timing chain is required, the entire set (chain, tensioner, camshaft and crankshaft sprockets) must be replaced as an assembly.*

9.19c . . . and the two colored timing chain links (A) should straddle the crankshaft sprocket timing dot (B) - note that the keyway (C) should be at the 2:00 o'clock position

9.20 Use a large pair of pliers to retract the tensioner until the hole in the tensioner aligns with the hole in the bracket (thrust plate), then install a drill bit through the hole to keep it in the retracted position

9.21a Use a breaker bar and socket to prevent the crankshaft from rotating while loosening the camshaft sprocket bolt

9.21b Remove the camshaft sprocket, crankshaft sprocket and timing chain as a complete assembly

**9.27a The camshaft sprocket timing mark(s) must align with the single colored timing chain link . . .**

**9.27b . . . and the two colored timing chain links must straddle the crankshaft sprocket mark**

**9.34 Be sure to install a new rubber gasket into the timing chain cover groove**

24   Inspect the crankshaft sprocket for damage or wear. The crankshaft sprocket is a steel sprocket, but these teeth can also become grooved or worn enough to cause a poor meshing of the sprocket and the chain.

## Installation

**Caution:** *Before starting the engine, carefully rotate the crankshaft by hand through at least two full revolutions (use a socket and breaker bar on the crankshaft pulley center bolt). If you feel any resistance, STOP! There is something wrong - most likely, valves are contacting the pistons. You must find the problem before proceeding. Check your work and see if any updated repair information is available.*

25   Stuff a shop rag into the opening at the front of the oil pan to keep debris out of the engine, then clean off all traces of old gasket material and sealant from the engine block. Wipe the sealing surfaces with a cloth saturated with lacquer thinner or acetone.

26   If the tensioner is not compressed (retracted position), compress the tensioner until the hole aligns with the bracket hole, then insert a suitable size drill bit through both holes to keep the tensioner locked in this position (see illustration 9.20). Install the camshaft thrust plate and tighten the bolts to the torque listed in this Chapter's Specifications.

27   Assemble the timing chain and sprockets before installing them onto the engine. Loop the new chain over the camshaft sprocket with the single colored link (timing chain mark) aligned with the sprocket alignment mark (see illustration). Mesh the chain with the crankshaft sprocket, with the crankshaft sprocket alignment mark between the two colored chain links (see illustration).

28   Align the sprocket with the Woodruff key in the end of the crankshaft and assemble the chain, camshaft sprocket and crankshaft sprocket onto the crankshaft and camshaft. Tap it gently into place until it is completely seated. When the timing chain components are installed, the timing marks MUST align as shown in illustrations 9.19b and 9.19c).

**Caution:** *If resistance is encountered, do not hammer the sprocket onto the crankshaft. It may eventually move onto the shaft, but it may be cracked in the process and fail later, causing extensive engine damage.*

29   Apply a thread locking compound to the camshaft sprocket bolt threads and tighten the bolt to the torque listed in this Chapter's Specifications.

30   Lubricate the chain with clean engine oil.

31   Remove the drill bit from the tensioner and bracket. Make sure the tensioner has released and is pressing against the timing chain. Verify that the timing marks are still aligned properly.

32   Install the oil pump (see Section 13).

33   Install the oil pump pick-up tube to the bottom of the oil pump. Tighten the bolt to the torque listed in this Chapter's Specifications.

34   The timing chain cover rubber gasket can be re-used if it isn't damaged or hardened, but considering the amount of work that you've done to get to this point, it's a good idea to replace it. Double-check the surface of the timing chain cover and engine block. Make sure all old gasket material is removed and the surface is clean. Install a new rubber gasket into the groove in the timing chain cover (see illustration).

35   Check for cracks and deformation of the oil pan gasket. If the gasket has deteriorated or is damaged, replace it (see Section 12).

36   Apply a small amount of RTV sealant to the corner where the timing chain cover, engine block and oil pan meet.

37   Install the timing chain cover on the block (see illustration 9.17) and tighten the bolts, a little at a time, until you reach the torque listed in this Chapter's Specifications. Be sure to install the water pump onto the timing chain cover and tighten the timing chain cover bolts and the water pump bolts at the same time to the torque listed in this Chapter's Specifications.

38   Install the oil pan-to-timing chain cover bolts, and tighten them to the torque listed in this Chapter's Specifications.

39   Lubricate the oil seal contact surface of the vibration damper hub with clean engine oil, then install the damper on the end of the crankshaft (see Section 8). Tighten the bolt to the torque listed in this Chapter's Specifications.

40   The remaining installation steps are the reverse of removal.

41   Add coolant and engine oil. Run the engine and check for oil and coolant leaks.

## 10   Cylinder heads - removal and installation

**Warning:** *Wait until the engine is completely cool before beginning this procedure.*

## Removal

1   Relieve the fuel system pressure (see Chapter 4A), then disconnect the cable from the negative terminal of the battery (see Chapter 5).

2   Drain the cooling system (see Chapter 1).

3   Remove the intake manifold (see Section 6).

4   Remove the exhaust manifolds from the cylinder heads (see Section 7).

5   Remove the valve covers (see Section 4).

6   Remove the rocker arms and pushrods (see Section 5).

**Note:** *Again, as mentioned in Section 5, keep all the parts in order so they are reinstalled in the same locations.*

7   Loosen the head bolts in 1/4-turn increments in a pattern opposite of the tightening sequence (see illustration 10.16) until they can be removed by hand.

**Note:** *There will be different-length head bolts for different locations, so store the bolts in order as they are removed. This will ensure that the bolts are reinstalled in their original holes.*

8   Lift the heads off the engine. If resistance is felt, do not pry between the head and block

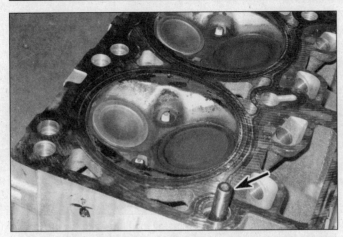

10.9 Make sure the cylinder head surface is perfectly clean, free from old gasket material, carbon deposits and dirt - note that the dowel is part of the cylinder head stand

10.12 A die should be used to remove sealant and corrosion from the bolt threads prior to installation

as damage to the mating surfaces will result. To dislodge the head, place a block of wood against the end of it and strike the wood block with a hammer, or lift on a casting protrusion. Store the heads on blocks of wood to prevent damage to the gasket sealing surfaces.

## Installation

9　The mating surfaces of the cylinder heads and block must be perfectly clean when the heads are installed (see illustration). Gasket removal solvents are available at auto parts stores and may prove helpful.

10　Use a gasket scraper to remove all traces of carbon and old gasket material, then wipe the mating surfaces with a cloth saturated with lacquer thinner or acetone. If there is oil on the mating surfaces when the heads are installed, the gaskets may not seal correctly and leaks may develop. When working on the block, cover the lifter valley with shop rags to keep debris out of the engine. Use a vacuum cleaner to remove any debris that falls into the cylinders.

11　Check the block and head mating surfaces for nicks, deep scratches and other

damage. If damage is slight, it can be removed with emery cloth. If it is excessive, machining may be the only alternative.

12　Use a tap of the correct size to chase the threads in the head bolt holes in the block. Mount each bolt in a vise and run a die down the threads to remove corrosion and restore the threads (see illustration). Dirt, corrosion, sealant and damaged threads will affect torque readings.

13　Position the new gaskets over the dowels in the block. Be sure the letter designations for the left (L) and right (R) cylinder heads and the top gasket surface (TOP) are correct (see illustration).

14　Carefully position the heads on the block without disturbing the gaskets.

15　Before installing the head bolts, coat the threads with a small amount of engine oil.

16　Install the bolts in their original locations and tighten them finger-tight. Following the recommended sequence (see illustration), tighten the bolts in several steps to the torque listed in this Chapter's Specifications.

17　The remaining installation steps are the

reverse of removal.

18　Add coolant and change the engine oil and filter (see Chapter 1). Start the engine and check for proper operation and coolant or oil leaks.

## 11　Camshaft and lifters - removal, inspection and installation

**Warning:** *Wait until the engine is completely cool before beginning this procedure.*

## Removal

1　Relieve the fuel system pressure (see Chapter 4A), then disconnect the cable from the negative terminal of the battery (see Chapter 5).

2　Drain the cooling system (see Chapter 1).

3　Remove the timing chain cover, the timing chain and the sprockets (see Section 9).

4　Remove the cylinder heads (see Section 10).

5　Remove the radiator (see Chapter 3).

10.13 Be sure the letter designations for the left (L) and right (R) cylinder heads and the top gasket surface (TOP) are correct

10.16 Cylinder head bolt tightening sequence

**11.6 Each lifter rail is secured by one bolt**

**11.7a Remove the lifters from the lifter bores and install them into the lifter rail - each lifter must be installed into the same lifter bore and in the same direction (roller rotation)**

**11.7b Install the lifters into the lifter rail and make sure the lifters are marked in their original position (UP) with number designations for the cylinders and letter designations for the valve each one operates (intake or exhaust)**

6    Remove the lifter rail mounting bolts (see illustration).

7    Remove the lifters from the lifter bores in the engine block (see illustration). Carefully place them in the correct location in the lifter rail. Each lifter must be installed into the same lifter bore and in the same direction (roller rotation) (see illustrations). Be sure to mark each lifter and lifter rail with a felt pen to designate the cylinder number and the type of lifter (intake or exhaust). There are several ways to extract the lifters from the bores. A special tool designed to grip and remove lifters is manufactured by many tool companies and is widely available, but it may not be required in every case. On newer engines without a lot of varnish buildup, the lifters can often be removed with a small magnet or even with your fingers. A machinist's scribe with a bent end can be used to pull the lifters out by positioning the point under the retainer ring inside the top of each lifter.

**Caution:** *Do not use pliers to remove the lifters unless you intend to replace them with new ones (along with the camshaft). The pliers will damage the precision machined and hardened lifters, rendering them useless. Do not attempt to withdraw the camshaft with the*

*lifters in place.*

8    Before removing the camshaft, check the endplay. Mount a dial indicator so that it contacts the nose of the camshaft. Pry the camshaft forward and back using a long screwdriver with the tip taped to prevent damage to the camshaft. Record the movement of the dial indicator and compare it to this Chapter's Specifications. If the endplay is excessive, the camshaft must be replaced.

9    Unbolt and remove the camshaft thrust plate (see illustration).

10    Thread a long bolt into the camshaft sprocket bolt hole to use as a handle when removing the camshaft from the block. Carefully pull the camshaft out. Support the cam near the block so the lobes do not nick or gouge the bearings as it is withdrawn.

## Inspection

11    After the camshaft has been removed from the engine, cleaned with solvent and dried, inspect the bearing journals for uneven wear, pitting and evidence of seizure. If the journals are damaged, the bearing inserts in

the block are probably damaged as well. Both the camshaft and bearings will have to be replaced.

12    Measure the bearing journals with a micrometer to determine if they are excessively worn or out-of-round (see illustration).

**Note:** *Camshaft bearing replacement requires special tools and expertise that place it beyond the scope of the average home mechanic. The tools for bearing removal and installation are available at stores that carry automotive tools, possibly even found at a tool rental business. It is advisable though, if bearings are bad and the procedure is beyond your ability, remove the engine block and take it to an automotive machine shop to ensure that the job is done correctly.*

13    Measure the lobe height of each cam lobe on the intake camshaft and record your measurements (see illustration). Compare the measurements for excessive variations. If the lobe heights vary more than 0.005 inch (0.125 mm), replace the camshaft. Compare

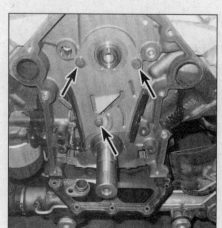

**11.9 Location of the camshaft thrust plate mounting bolts**

**11.12 Check the diameter of each camshaft bearing journal to pinpoint excessive wear and out-of-round conditions**

**11.13 Measure the camshaft lobe height (greatest dimension) with a micrometer**

**11.14 Check the cam lobes for pitting, excessive wear and scoring. If scoring is excessive, as shown here, replace the camshaft**

**11.18 The roller on the roller lifters must turn freely - check for wear and excessive play as well**

**11.19 Be sure to apply camshaft installation lube to the cam lobes and bearing journals before installing the camshaft**

the lobe height measurements on the exhaust camshaft and follow the same procedure. Do not compare intake camshaft lobe heights with exhaust camshaft lobe heights, as they are different. Only compare intake lobes with intake lobes and exhaust lobes with other exhaust lobes.

14    Check the camshaft lobes for heat discoloration, score marks, chipped areas, pitting and uneven wear (see illustration). If the lobes are in good condition and if the lobe lift variation measurements recorded earlier are within the limits, the camshaft can be reused.

15    Clean the lifters with solvent and dry them thoroughly without mixing them up.

16    Check each lifter wall, pushrod seat and foot for scuffing, score marks and uneven wear. If the lifter walls are damaged or worn (which is not very likely), inspect the lifter bores in the engine block as well. If the pushrod seats are worn, check the pushrod ends.

17    If new lifters are being installed, a new camshaft must also be installed. If a new camshaft is installed, then use new lifters as well. Never install used lifters unless the original camshaft is used and the lifters can be installed in their original locations.

18    Check the rollers carefully for wear and damage and make sure they turn freely without excessive play (see illustration).

## Installation

19    Lubricate the camshaft bearing journals and cam lobes with camshaft installation lube (see illustration).

20    Slide the camshaft slowly and gently into the engine. Support the cam near the block and be careful not to scrape or nick the bearings. Only install the camshaft far enough to install the camshaft thrust plate. Pushing it in too far could dislodge the camshaft plug at the rear of the engine, causing an oil leak. Tighten the camshaft thrust plate mounting bolts to the torque listed in this Chapter's Specifications.

21    Install the timing chain and sprockets (see Section 9). Align the timing marks on the crankshaft and camshaft sprockets.

22    Lubricate the lifters with clean engine oil and install them in the block. If the original lifters are being reinstalled, be sure to return them to their original locations, and with the numbers facing UP (exactly as they were removed). Install the lifter rail and mounting bolts. Tighten the lifter rail mounting bolts to the torque listed in this Chapter's Specifications.

**Note:** *Each lifter rail should be numbered and coincide with the correct cylinder numbers.*

23    The remaining installation steps are the reverse of removal.

24    Change the oil and install a new oil filter (see Chapter 1). Fill the cooling system with the proper type of coolant (see Chapter 1).

25    Start the engine and check for oil pressure and leaks.

**Caution:** *Do not run the engine above a fast idle until all the hydraulic lifters have filled with oil and become quiet again.*

26    If a new camshaft and lifters have been installed, the engine should be brought to operating temperature and run at a fast idle for 15 to 20 minutes to "break in" the new components. Change the oil and filter again after 500 miles of operation.

## 12   Oil pan - removal and installation

**Warning:** *Wait until the engine is completely cool before beginning this procedure.*

## Removal

1    Disconnect the cable from the negative terminal of the battery (see Chapter 5, Section 1).

2    Drain the cooling system (see Chapter 1).

3    Raise the vehicle and support it securely on jackstands (see Chapter 1).

4    Drain the engine oil and replace the oil filter (see Chapter 1). Remove the engine oil dipstick.

5    Remove the crossmember beneath the oil pan (see illustration).

6    Remove the brace between the oil pan and transmission (see illustration 12.16).

7    Support the engine from above with an engine hoist or an engine support fixture (see Chapter 2E), take a little weight off the engine

**12.5 Remove the front crossmember mounting bolts and separate the crossmember from the chassis**

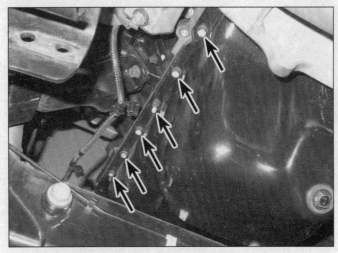

**12.8 Remove the oil pan mounting bolts from the perimeter of the oil pan - left side shown**

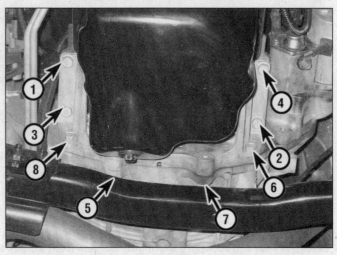

**12.16 Transmission brace bolt tightening sequence**

with the hoist or fixture, and remove the through-bolts from the engine mounts (see Section 16). Now raise the engine further.

**Caution:** *Raise the engine slightly while observing the engine cooling fan and fan shroud. Do not allow the engine cooling fan to contact the shroud or the fan and/or shroud may be damaged.*

8    Remove all of the oil pan bolts (see illustration), then lower the pan from the engine. The pan will probably stick to the engine, so strike the pan with a rubber mallet until it breaks the gasket seal. Carefully slide the oil pan out, to the rear.

**Caution:** *Before using force on the oil pan, be sure all the bolts have been removed.*

### Installation

9    Wash out the oil pan with solvent.
10    Thoroughly clean the mounting surfaces of the oil pan and engine block of old gasket material and sealer. If the oil pan is distorted at the bolt-hole areas, straighten the flange by supporting it from below on a 1x4 wood block and tapping the bolt holes with the rounded end of a ball-peen hammer. Wipe the gasket

surfaces clean with a rag soaked in lacquer thinner or acetone.
11    Apply some RTV sealant to the corners where the timing chain cover meets the block and at the rear where the rear main oil seal retainer meets the block. Then attach the one-piece oil pan gasket to the engine block with contact-cement-type gasket adhesive.
12    Make sure the alignment studs are installed in the correct locations in the engine block.
13    Lift the pan into position, slipping it over the alignment studs and being careful not to disturb the gasket, install several bolts finger-tight.
14    Check that the gasket isn't sticking out anywhere around the block's perimeter. When all the bolts are in place, install the oil pan nuts onto the studs.
15    Starting at the center and alternating from side-to-side toward the ends, tighten the fasteners to the torque listed in this Chapter's Specifications.
16    Install the transmission brace. The transmission brace must be tightened correctly or it may be damaged and cause engine noise.

Tighten the bolts in three steps and follow the correct torque sequence (see illustration).
17    The remainder of the installation procedure is the reverse of removal.
18    Add the proper type and quantity of oil, and a new oil filter (see Chapter 1), start the engine and check for leaks before placing the vehicle back in service.

### 13   Oil pump - removal and installation

**Warning:** *Wait until the engine is completely cool before beginning this procedure.*

### Removal

1    Disconnect the cable from the negative terminal of the battery (see Chapter 5, Section 1).
2    Drain the cooling system (see Chapter 1).
3    Remove the timing chain cover (see Section 9).
4    Remove the oil pan (see Section 12).
5    Remove the bolt from the pick-up tube assembly and lower it away from the oil pump (see illustration).
6    Remove the oil pump mounting bolts and detach the pump from the engine block.

### Installation

7    Position the pump on the engine. Make sure the pump rotor is aligned with the crankshaft drive. Install the oil pump mounting bolts and tighten them to the torque listed in this Chapter's Specifications.
8    Install a new O-ring onto the oil pump pick-up tube, connect the tube to the pump and tighten the bolt to the torque listed in this Chapter's Specifications.
9    The remainder of installation is the reverse of removal.
10    Fill the crankcase with the proper type and quantity of engine oil, and install a new

**13.5 Location of the oil pump pick-up tube retainer bolt (A) and the oil pump mounting bolts (B)**

16.9a Location of the through-bolt on the right side engine mount

16.9b Location of the through-bolt on the left side engine mount

oil filter (see Chapter 1). Fill the cooling system with the proper type of coolant (see Chapter 1).

11   Run the engine and check for oil pressure and leaks.

### 14   Flywheel/driveplate - removal and installation

1   This procedure is essentially the same as for the 3.7L V6 and the 4.7L V8 engines. Refer to part A and follow the procedure outlined there, but refer to the Specifications listed in this Chapter.

### 15   Rear main oil seal - replacement

1   This procedure is essentially the same as for the 3.7L V6 and the 4.7L V8 engines. Refer to part A and follow the procedure outlined there but refer to the Specifications listed in this Chapter.

### 16   Engine mounts - check and replacement

1   Engine mounts seldom require attention, but broken or deteriorated mounts should be replaced immediately or the added strain placed on the driveline components may cause damage or wear.

### Check

2   During the check, the engine must be raised slightly to remove the weight from the mounts.

3   Raise the vehicle and support it securely on jackstands, then position a jack under the engine oil pan. Place a large wood block between the jack head and the oil pan, then carefully raise the engine just enough to take the weight off the mounts.

**Warning:** *DO NOT place any part of your body under the engine when it's supported only by a jack!*

4   Check the mount insulators to see if the rubber is cracked, hardened or separated from the metal in the center of the mount.

5   Check for relative movement between the mount and the engine or frame (use a large screwdriver or prybar to attempt to move the mounts).

6   If movement is noted, lower the engine and tighten the mount fasteners.

### Replacement

7   Disconnect the cable from the negative terminal of the battery (see Chapter 5, Section 1). Raise the vehicle and support it securely on jackstands (if not already done). Support the engine as described in Step 3.

#### 2WD models

8   Remove the through-bolts, raise the engine with the jack and detach the mount from the frame bracket and engine.

9   Install the new mount(s), making sure it is correctly positioned in the bracket (see illustrations). Install the fasteners and tighten them securely.

#### 4WD models

10   Remove the skidplate from below the engine compartment.

11   Remove the engine crossmember.

12   Remove the engine oil filter (see Chapter 1).

13   Install an engine hoist (see Chapter 2E) and raise the engine slightly to take the weight off the engine mounts.

14   Use a floor jack to support the front axle.

15   Remove the engine mount through-bolts.

16   Remove the bolts that attach the engine mounts to the front axle assembly.

17   Lower the front axle slightly.

18   Remove the bolts that attach the engine mounts to the engine block.

19   Remove the engine mount(s) from the vehicle.

20   Install the new mount(s), making sure they are correctly positioned in the bracket. Install the fasteners and tighten them securely.

# Notes

# Chapter 2 Part C
# 3.9L V6, 5.2L V8, 5.9L V8 and V10 engines

## Contents

## Specifications

### General
Displacement
| | |
|---|---|
| 3.9L V6 | 239 cubic inches |
| 5.2L V8 | 318 cubic inches |
| 5.9L V8 | 360 cubic inches |
| V10 | 488 cubic inches (8.0 liters) |

Bore and stroke
| | |
|---|---|
| 3.9L V6 | 3.91 x 3.31 inches |
| 5.2L V8 | 3.91 x 3.31 inches |
| 5.9L V8 | 4.00 x 3.58 inches |
| 8.0L V10 | 4.00 x 3.88 inches |

Cylinder numbers (front-to-rear)
3.9L V6
| | |
|---|---|
| Left (driver's) side | 1-3-5 |
| Right side | 2-4-6 |
| Firing order | 1-6-5-4-3-2 |

5.2L V8 and 5.9L V8
| | |
|---|---|
| Left (driver's) side | 1-3-5-7 |
| Right side | 2-4-6-8 |
| Firing order | 1-8-4-3-6-5-7-2 |

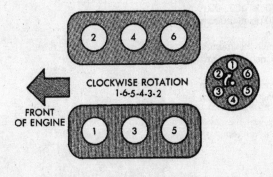

**Cylinder location and distributor rotation - V6 engines**

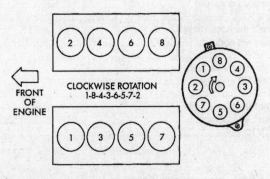

**Cylinder location and distributor rotation - V8 engines**

Cylinder numbers (front-to-rear) (continued)
V10
    Left (driver's) side ................................................... 1-3-5-7-9
    Right side.............................................................. 2-4-6-8-10
    Firing order.......................................................... 1-10-9-4-3-6-5-8-7-2
Distributor rotation on V6 and V8 engines (viewed from above) ........... Clockwise
Cylinder compression pressure
    Minimum................................................................. 100 psi
    Maximum variation between cylinders ................... 40 psi

## Camshaft

Journal diameters
  V6
    No. 1 ..................................................................... 1.998 to 1.999 inches
    No. 2 ..................................................................... 1.982 to 1.983 inches
    No. 3 ..................................................................... 1.951 to 1.952 inches
    No. 4 ..................................................................... 1.5605 to 1.5615 inches
  5.2L V8
    No. 1 ..................................................................... 1.998 to 1.999 inches
    No. 2 ..................................................................... 1.982 to 1.983 inches
    No. 3 ..................................................................... 1.967 to 1.968 inches
    No. 4 ..................................................................... 1.951 to 1.952 inches
    No. 5 ..................................................................... 1.5605 to 1.5615 inches
  5.9L V8
    No. 1 ..................................................................... 1.997 to 1.999 inches
    No. 2 ..................................................................... 1.981 to 1.983 inches
    No. 3 ..................................................................... 1.966 to 1.968 inches
    No. 4 ..................................................................... 1.950 to 1.952 inches
    No. 5 ..................................................................... 1.5595 to 1.5615 inches
  8.0L V10
    No. 1 ..................................................................... 2.091 to 2.092 inches
    No. 2 ..................................................................... 2.0745 to 2.0755 inches
    No. 3 ..................................................................... 2.059 to 2.060 inches
    No. 4 ..................................................................... 2.043 to 2.044 inches
    No. 5 ..................................................................... 2.027 to 2.028 inches
    No. 6 ..................................................................... 1.917 to 1.918 inches
Endplay
  V6 and V8 ................................................................. 0.002 to 0.010 inch
  V10 ......................................................................... 0.005 to 0.015 inch
Valve lift
  V6 and 5.2L V8, intake and exhaust ............................. 0.432 inch
  5.9L V8
    Intake ................................................................... 0.410 inch
    Exhaust ................................................................. 0.417 inch
  8.0L V10
    Intake ................................................................... 0.390 inch
    Exhaust ................................................................. 0.407 inch

## Oil pump

Minimum pressure at curb idle
  V6 and 5.2L V8 ......................................................... 8 psi
  5.9L V8 .................................................................... 6 psi
  8.0L V10 .................................................................. 12 psi
Operating pressure
  V6 and V8 engines..................................................... 30 to 80 psi at 3,000 rpm
  8.0L V10 .................................................................. 50 to 60 psi at 3,000 rpm
Outer rotor thickness limit
  V6 and V8 engines..................................................... 0.825 inch minimum
  8.0L V10 .................................................................. 0.5876 inch minimum
Outer rotor diameter limit
  V6 and V8 engines..................................................... 2.469 inches minimum
  V10 ......................................................................... 3.246 inches minimum
Inner rotor thickness limit
  V6 and V8 engines..................................................... 0.825 inch minimum
  8.0L V10 .................................................................. 0.5876 to 0.5886 inch minimum

FRONT

30042 -1-specs HAYNES

**Cylinder location and coil pack arrangement - V10 engines**

## Oil pump (continued)

Clearance over rotors

    V6 and V8 engines..........................................................................    0.004 inch maximum

    8.0L V10 ........................................................................................    0.0075 inch maximum

Outer rotor clearance limit

    V6 and V8 engines..........................................................................    0.014 inch maximum

    V10 ...............................................................................................    0.006 inch maximum

Rotor tip clearance limit

    V6 and V8 engines..........................................................................    0.008 inch maximum

    8.0L V10 ........................................................................................    0.0230 inch maximum

## Torque specifications          Ft-lbs (unless otherwise indicated)

**Note:** *One foot-pound (ft-lb) of torque is equivalent to 12 inch-pounds (in-lbs) of torque. Torque values below approximately 15 ft-lbs are expressed in inch-pounds, because most foot-pound torque wrenches are not accurate at these smaller values.*

## Camshaft sprocket bolt

    V6 and V8 engines..........................................................................    50

    8.0L V10 ........................................................................................    55

Camshaft thrust plate bolts

    V6 and V8 engines..........................................................................    210 in-lbs

    8.0L V10 ........................................................................................    192 in-lbs

Crankshaft pulley bolts ...........................................................................    210 in-lbs

Crankshaft rear main oil seal retainer bolts ...........................................    16

Crankshaft main bearing cap(s) – V6 and V8 engines

    Step 1 ...........................................................................................    20

    Step 2 ...........................................................................................    85

Cylinder head bolts (in sequence)

    V6 and V8 engines (see illustration 9.15a)

        Step 1 ...........................................................................................    50

        Step 2 ...........................................................................................    105

    8.0L V10 engines (see illustration 9.15b)

        Step 1 ...........................................................................................    43

        Step 2 ...........................................................................................    105

Exhaust manifold bolts/nuts

    V6 and V8 ......................................................................................    25

    8.0L V10 models ............................................................................    16

Exhaust pipe flange nuts .......................................................................    20 to 25

Flywheel/driveplate bolts .......................................................................    55

Intake manifold bolts

    V6 and V8

        Intake manifold (see illustrations 7.25a and 7.25b)

            Step 1 ...................................................................................    Tighten bolts 1 and 2 (V6) or 1 through 4 (V8), in increments of 12 in-lbs, to 72 in-lbs

            Step 2 ...................................................................................    Tighten bolts 3 through 12 (V6) or 5 through 12 (V8), in sequence, to 72 in-lbs

            Step 3 ...................................................................................    Check to make sure all bolts are tightened to 72 in-lbs

            Step 4 ...................................................................................    Tighten all bolts to 144 in-lbs

            Step 5 ...................................................................................    Check to make sure all bolts are tightened to 144 in-lbs

        Plenum pan

            Step 1 ...................................................................................    48 in-lbs

            Step 2 ...................................................................................    84 in-lbs

            Step 3 ...................................................................................    Recheck 84 in-lbs

    8.0L V10

        Upper intake manifold......................................................................    16

        Lower intake manifold (see illustration 7.25b)

            Step 1 ...................................................................................    40

            Step 2 ...................................................................................    Recheck 40

Oil pan bolts/studs

    V6 and V8 ......................................................................................    215 in-lbs

    8.0L V10

        Small bolts (1/4 inch)......................................................................    96 in-lbs

        Large bolts (5/16 inch).....................................................................    144 in-lbs

Oil pump cover bolts

    V6 and V8 ......................................................................................    95 in-lbs

    8.0L V10 ........................................................................................    125 in-lbs

## Torque specifications (continued)                    Ft-lbs (unless otherwise indicated)

**Note:** *One foot-pound (ft-lb) of torque is equivalent to 12 inch-pounds (in-lbs) of torque. Torque values below approximately 15 ft-lbs are expressed in inch-pounds, because most foot-pound torque wrenches are not accurate at these smaller values.*

### Camshaft sprocket bolt (continued)

| | |
|---|---|
| Oil pump mounting bolts | 30 |
| Oil drain plug | 25 |
| Rear main oil seal retainer bolts (8.0L V10) | 16 |
| Rocker arm bolts | |
|    3.9L V6 and 5.2L V8 models | 200 in-lbs |
|    5.9L V8 models | 21 |
|    8.0L V10 models | |
|       2002 | 21 |
|       2003 | 40 |
| Timing chain cover bolts | |
|    V6 and V8 | 30 |
|    8.0L V10 | 35 |
| Valve cover nuts/studs | |
|    V6 and V8 | 95 in-lbs |
|    8.0L V10 models | 144 in-lbs |
| Vibration damper-to-crankshaft bolt | |
|    3.9L V6 and 5.2L V8 models | 135 |
|    5.9L V8 | 180 |
|    8.0L V10 | 230 |
| Water pump-to-cover bolts | 30 |

*Refer to Part E for additional specifications.*

## 1 General Information

1 This part of Chapter 2 is devoted to in-vehicle repair procedures for 3.9L V6, 5.2L V8, 5.9L V8 and 8.0L V10 engines. Information concerning engine removal and installation and engine overhaul can be found in Part E of this Chapter.

2 Since the repair procedures included in this Part are based on the assumption that the engine is still installed in the vehicle, if they are being used during a complete engine overhaul (with the engine already out of the vehicle and on a stand) many of the steps included here will not apply.

3 Though the engines covered vary greatly in displacement, they all share the same basic design. The 5.2L and 5.9L V8's have been in the corporate line for decades, and the V6 is basically the same design without two of the cylinders, while the V10 shares most characteristics, but with two more cylinders added to the V8 design.

## 2 Repair operations possible with the engine in the vehicle

1 Many major repair operations can be accomplished without removing the engine from the vehicle.

2 Clean the engine compartment and the exterior of the engine with some type of pressure washer before any work is done. A clean engine will make the job easier and will help keep dirt out of the internal areas of the engine.

3 Depending on the components involved, it may be a good idea to remove the hood to improve access to the engine as repairs are performed (refer to Chapter 11 if necessary).

4 If oil or coolant leaks develop, indicating a need for gasket or seal replacement, the repairs can generally be made with the engine in the vehicle. The oil pan gasket, the cylinder head gaskets, intake and exhaust manifold gaskets, timing chain cover gaskets and the crankshaft oil seals are all accessible with the engine in place.

5 Exterior engine components, such as the water pump, the starter motor, the alternator, the distributor and the fuel injection components, as well as the intake and exhaust manifolds, can be removed for repair with the engine in place.

6 Since the cylinder heads can be removed without removing the engine, valve component servicing can also be accomplished with the engine in the vehicle.

7 Inspection or replacement of the timing chain and sprockets and the oil pump is possible with the engine in place.

8 In extreme cases caused by a lack of necessary equipment, repair or replacement of piston rings, pistons, connecting rods and rod bearings is possible with the engine in the vehicle. However, this practice is not recommended because of the cleaning and preparation work that must be done to the components involved.

## 3 Top Dead Center (TDC) for number one piston - locating

1 Top Dead Center (TDC) is the highest point in the cylinder that each piston reaches as it travels up-and-down when the crankshaft turns. Each piston reaches TDC on the compression stroke and again on the exhaust stroke, but TDC generally refers to piston position on the compression stroke. The timing marks at the front of the engine are referenced to the number one piston at TDC on the compression stroke.

2 Positioning the pistons at TDC is an essential part of many procedures such as camshaft removal, timing chain replacement and distributor removal.

**Warning:** *Before beginning this procedure, be sure to place the transmission in Neutral (manual) or Park (automatic), apply the parking brake and block the wheels. On 3.9L V6 and 5.2L V8 engines disable the ignition system by disconnecting the coil wire from the distributor cap and grounding it on the engine block. Remove the spark plugs and disable the ignition system by disconnecting the primary (low voltage) wires from the distributor (5.9L V8) or disconnecting the primary (low voltage) electrical connectors from the ignition coils (8.0L V10) (see Chapter 5).*

### V6 and V8 models

3 Scribe or paint a small mark on the distributor body directly below the number one spark plug wire terminal in the distributor cap (see illustration).

4 Remove the distributor cap as described in Chapter 1 and position it aside with the spark plug wires attached.

5 Turn the crankshaft with a socket and breaker bar attached to the large bolt that is threaded into the crankshaft vibration damper until the line on the vibration damper is aligned with the zero or "TDC" mark on the timing indicator (see illustration).

6 The rotor should now be pointing directly at the mark on the distributor body (see illustration).

7 If the rotor is 180-degrees off, the piston is at TDC on the exhaust stroke; turn the crankshaft one complete turn (360-degrees) clockwise to position it at TDC on the compression stroke. The rotor should now be pointing at the mark. When the rotor is pointing at the number one spark plug wire terminal in the distributor cap (which is indicated by the mark on the distributor body) and the timing marks are aligned, the number one piston is at TDC on the compression stroke.

3.3 Mark the body of the distributor below the number one spark plug terminal

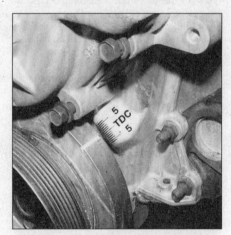

3.5 Align the full-width groove on the damper with the "0" or "TDC" mark on the timing cover

3.6 When the rotor is pointing at the number one spark plug wire terminal in the distributor cap (which is indicated by the mark on the distributor body) and the timing marks are aligned, the number one piston is at TDC on the compression stroke

**4.6 Remove the valve cover mounting bolts - some fasteners have studs, so mark their locations before removal**

**4.7 After striking the valve cover with a rubber mallet to break it loose, pull it straight up**

**5.2 Remove the mounting bolts, pivots and rocker arms**

### 8.0L V10 models

8    Install a compression pressure gauge in the number one spark plug hole. It should be a gauge with a screw-in fitting and a hose at least six inches long.

9    Rotate the crankshaft with a socket and breaker bar attached to the large bolt that is threaded into the crankshaft vibration damper while observing for pressure on the compression gauge. The moment the gauge shows pressure indicates that the number one cylinder has begun the compression stroke.

10    Once the compression stroke has begun, TDC for the compression stroke is reached by bringing the piston to the top of the cylinder.

11    Continue turning the crankshaft until the notch in the crankshaft damper is aligned with the TDC mark on the timing chain cover. At this point, the number one cylinder is at TDC on the compression stroke. If the marks are aligned but there was no compression, the piston was on the exhaust stroke. Continue rotating the crankshaft 360-degrees (1-turn).

**Note:** *If a compression gauge is not available, you can simply place a blunt object over the spark plug hole and listen for compression as the engine is rotated. Once compression at the No.1 spark plug hole is noted, the remainder of the Step is the same.*

### All models

12    After the number one piston has been positioned at TDC on the compression stroke, TDC for any of the remaining cylinders can be located by rotating the crankshaft, in the normal direction of rotation and following the firing order. If you're working on a V6 engine, make marks every 120-degrees, on 5.2L and 5.9L V8 engines, make marks on the vibration damper at 90-degree intervals from the TDC mark. If you're working on a V10, make marks on the vibration damper at 72-degree intervals from the TDC mark (a degree wheel would be helpful in this case). TDC for the next cylinder in the firing order can be found by turning the crankshaft and aligning the next mark on the damper with the TDC indicator on the timing chain cover.

## 4    Valve covers - removal and installation

### Removal

1    Disconnect the cable from the negative terminal of the battery (see Chapter 5).

2    On 8.0L V10 engines, remove the upper intake manifold to access the right-side valve cover (see Section 7).

3    Remove the spark plug wires from the spark plugs, labeling them if necessary for correct installation (see Chapter 1).

4    Remove the breather tube or PCV valve and hose from the valve cover. Remove or position aside any remaining hoses such as the power brake booster vacuum hose, the heater hoses and the evaporative emission hoses that would interfere with the removal of the valve cover(s) (see Chapter 6).

5    Remove the plastic spark plug wire holders from the valve cover studs and position the holders/wires out of the way.

**Caution:** *Pull straight up on the plastic holders - they can easily break if pulled at an angle.*

6    Remove the valve cover mounting bolts. (see illustration).

**Note:** *Some of the fasteners have studs - mark the valve covers at each stud so they can be installed in the proper location*

7    Remove the valve cover (see illustration).

**Caution:** *If the cover is stuck to the head, bump the cover with a block of wood and a hammer to release it. If it still will not come loose, try to slip a flexible putty knife between the head and cover to break the seal. Don't pry at the cover-to-head joint, as damage to the sealing surface and cover flange will result and oil leaks will develop.*

### Installation

8    The mating surfaces of each cylinder head and valve cover must be perfectly clean when the covers are installed. Use a gasket scraper to remove all traces of sealant or old

gasket, then wipe the mating surfaces with a cloth saturated with brake system cleaner. If there is sealant or oil on the mating surfaces when the cover is installed, oil leaks may develop.

**Note:** *The steel-backed silicone gaskets can be reused if they haven't been damaged and are in good condition.*

9    Make sure all threaded holes are clean. Run a tap into them to remove corrosion and restore damaged threads.

10    Mate the gaskets to the heads before installing the covers.

11    Carefully position the cover on the head and install the bolts/studs.

12    Tighten the bolts/studs in three steps to the torque listed in this Chapter's Specifications.

**Caution:** *DON'T over-tighten the valve cover bolts.*

13    The remaining installation steps are the reverse of removal.

14    Start the engine and check carefully for oil leaks as the engine warms up.

## 5    Rocker arms and pushrods - removal, inspection and installation

### Removal

1    Label and remove each spark plug wire from the spark plugs (see Chapter 1, if necessary). Refer to Section 4 and remove the valve covers from the cylinder heads.

2    Loosen the rocker arm pivot bolts one at a time and detach the rocker arms, bolts, pivots and retainer/guide plate (see illustration). Keep track of the rocker arm positions, since they must be returned to the same locations. Store each set of rocker components separately in a marked plastic bag to ensure that they're reinstalled in their original locations.

3    Remove the pushrods and store them separately to make sure they don't get mixed up during installation (see illustration).

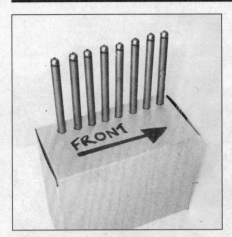

5.3 A perforated cardboard box can be used to store the pushrods to ensure they are reinstalled in their original locations - note the arrow indicating the front of the engine

5.9 Lubricate the pushrod ends and the valve stems with engine assembly lube before installing the rocker arms

5.10 Align the "V6" or "V8" neutral mark before installing and tightening rocker arms - V8 models shown

## Inspection

4    Check each rocker arm for wear, cracks and other damage, especially where the push-rods and valve stems contact the rocker arm.

5    Check the pivot seat in each rocker arm and the pivot faces. Look for galling, stress cracks and unusual wear patterns. If the rocker arms are worn or damaged, replace them with new ones and install new pivots or shafts as well.

**Note:** *Keep in mind that there is no valve adjustment on these engines, so excessive wear or damage in the valve train can easily result in excessive valve clearance, which in turn will cause valve noise when the engine is running.*

6    Make sure the hole at the pushrod end of each rocker arm is open.

7    Inspect the pushrods for cracks and excessive wear at the ends, also check that the oil hole running through each pushrod is not clogged. Roll each pushrod across a piece of plate glass to see if it's bent (if it wobbles, it's bent).

## Installation

8    Lubricate the lower end of each pushrod with clean engine oil or engine assembly lube and install them in their original locations. Make sure each pushrod seats completely in the lifter socket.

9    Apply engine assembly lube to the ends of the valve stems, the upper ends of the pushrods and to the pivot faces to prevent damage to the mating surfaces on initial start-up (see illustration).

10    The rocker arms must be tightened at a "neutral" position in the engine's rotation, to prevent valve-to-piston clearance problems, especially when the lifters have been unloaded. On V6 engines, rotate the crankshaft damper until the "V6" mark on the damper lines up with the TDC or Zero mark on the timing cover. On V8 engines, rotate the

crankshaft damper until the "V8" mark on the damper lines up with the TDC or Zero mark on the timing cover (see illustration). This represents a neutral point in the engine's directional rotation and the point at which the rocker arms can be tightened.

**Caution:** *Do not rotate the engine at all after matching these marks. Once the rockers are all bolted down, allow at least five minutes for the hydraulic lifters to "bleed down" before turning or starting the engine.*

11    Install the rocker arms, pivots, retainers and bolts. Tighten the rocker arm bolts to the torque listed in this Chapter's Specifications. As the bolts are tightened, make sure the pushrods seat properly in the rocker arms.

12    Refer to Section 4 and install the valve covers. Start the engine, listen for unusual valve train noses and check for oil leaks at the valve cover gaskets.

---

## 6    Valve springs, retainers and seals - replacement

**Note:** *Broken valve springs and defective valve stem seals can be replaced without removing the cylinder head. Two special tools and a compressed air source are normally required to perform this operation, so read through this Section carefully and rent or buy the tools before beginning the job.*

1    Remove the spark plugs (see Chapter 1).

2    Remove the valve covers (see Section 4).

3    Rotate the crankshaft until the number one piston is at Top Dead Center on the compression stroke (see Section 3).

4    Remove the rocker arms for the number 1 piston.

5    Thread an adapter into the spark plug hole and connect an air hose from a com-

pressed air source to it (see illustration). Most auto parts stores can supply the air hose adapter.

**Note:** *Many cylinder compression gauges utilize a screw-in fitting that may work with your air hose quick-disconnect fitting. If a cylinder compression gauge fitting is used, it will be necessary to remove the Schrader valve from the end of the fitting before using it in this procedure.*

6    Apply compressed air to the cylinder. The valves should be held in place by the air pressure.

**Warning:** *If the cylinder isn't exactly at TDC, air pressure may force the piston down, causing the engine to quickly rotate. DO NOT leave a wrench on the vibration damper bolt or you may be injured by the tool.*

7    Stuff shop rags into the cylinder head holes around the valves to prevent parts and tools from falling into the engine.

6.5 This is what the air hose adapter that fits into the spark plug hole looks like - they're commonly available from auto parts stores

**6.8 Once the spring is compressed, the keepers can be removed with a small magnet or needle-nose pliers (a magnet is preferred to prevent dropping the keepers)**

**6.15 Be sure to install the seals on the correct valve stems**

*1    Exhaust valve seal*

*2    Intake valve seal*

8    Using a socket and a hammer gently tap on the top of the each valve spring retainer several times (this will break the bond between the valve keeper and the spring retainer and allow the keeper to separate from the valve spring retainer as the valve spring is compressed), then use a valve-spring compressor to compress the spring. Remove the keepers with small needle-nose pliers or a magnet (see illustration).
**Note:** *Several different types of tools are available for compressing the valve springs with the head in place. One type, shown here, grips the lower spring coils and presses on the retainer as the knob is turned, while the lever-type utilizes the rocker arm bolt for leverage. Both types work very well, although the lever type is usually less expensive.*
9    Remove the valve spring and retainer.
**Note:** *If air pressure fails to retain the valve in the closed position during this operation, the valve face or seat may be damaged. If so,*

**6.19 Apply small dab of grease to each keeper as shown here before installation - it'll hold them in place on the valve stem as the spring is released**

*the cylinder head will have to be removed for repair.*
10    Remove the old valve stem seals, noting differences between the intake and exhaust seals.
11    Wrap a rubber band or tape around the top of the valve stem so the valve won't fall into the combustion chamber, then release the air pressure.
12    Inspect the valve stem for damage. Rotate the valve in the guide and check the end for eccentric movement, which would indicate that the valve is bent.
13    Move the valve up-and-down in the guide and make sure it does not bind. If the valve stem binds, either the valve is bent or the guide is damaged. In either case, the head will have to be removed for repair.
14    Reapply air pressure to the cylinder to retain the valve in the closed position, then remove the tape or rubber band from the valve stem.
15    If you're working on an exhaust valve, install the new exhaust valve seal on the valve stem and push it down to the top of the valve guide (see illustration).
16    If you're working on an intake valve, install a new intake valve stem seal over the valve stem and press it down over the valve guide. Don't force the intake valve seal against the top of the guide.
**Caution:** *Do not install an exhaust valve seal on an intake valve, as high oil consumption will result.*
17    Install the spring and retainer in position over the valve.
18    Compress the valve spring assembly only enough to install the keepers in the valve stem.
19    Position the keepers in the valve stem groove. Apply a small dab of grease to the inside of each keeper to hold it in place if necessary (see illustration). Remove the pressure from the spring tool and make sure the keepers are seated.

20    Disconnect the air hose and remove the adapter from the spark plug hole.
21    Repeat the above procedure on the remaining cylinders, following the firing order sequence (see this Chapter's Specifications). Bring each piston to Top Dead Center on the compression stroke before applying air pressure (see Section 3).
22    Reinstall the rocker arm assemblies (see Section 5), and the valve covers (see Section 4).
23    Allow the engine to sit for five minutes before starting to allow the lifters to "bleed down." Start the engine, then check for oil leaks and unusual sounds coming from the valve cover area. Allow the engine to idle for at least five minutes before revving the engine.

---

**7    Intake manifold - removal and installation**

**Warning:** *The engine must be completely cool before beginning this procedure.*

## *Removal*

1    Disconnect the cable from the negative terminal of the battery (see Chapter 5).
2    Drain the cooling system (see Chapter 1).
3    Remove the air filter housing and relieve the fuel system pressure (see Chapter 4A).
4    Rotate the accessory belt tensioner over enough to slip the serpentine belt off the idler pulley and remove the belt (see Chapter 1).
5    Remove the alternator (see Chapter 5). Remove the alternator brace.
6    On air-conditioned models, remove the air conditioning compressor and brace and set it aside (see Chapter 3).
**Warning:** *Do not disconnect the refrigerant lines.*
7    Remove the idler pulley and the alterna-

7.7a Remove the idler pulley . . .

7.7b . . . and the A/C compressor/ alternator bracket

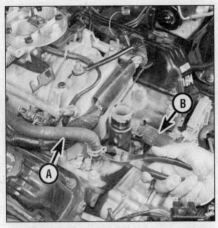

7.10 Disconnect the heater hose from the manifold (A), and the water-pump bypass hose (B)

tor/air conditioning compressor bracket from the front of the engine (see illustrations).

8   Disconnect the accelerator linkage (see Chapter 4A) and, if equipped, the cruise control linkage. On models equipped with an automatic transmission, disconnect the kickdown cable at the throttle body.

9   Disconnect any vacuum hoses attached to the intake manifold or throttle body such as the power brake booster, the PCV, EVAP control and the cruise control vacuum supply hose.

10   Remove the upper radiator hose from the engine, then disconnect the heater hose and water pump bypass hose from the intake manifold (see illustration).

11   Label and then disconnect the electrical connectors to the fuel injectors, the MAP sensor, the TPS, the IAC valve and the coolant temperature sensors (see illustration).

12   Disconnect any remaining electrical connectors connected to the intake manifold or throttle body and pull the whole engine wiring harness up and over the intake manifold to

the rear of the engine.

13   Remove the fuel rails and injectors (see Chapter 4A).

14   Label and remove each spark plug wire from the spark plugs (see Chapter 1 if necessary). If you're working on V6 or V8 engines, remove the distributor cap and spark plug wires. If you're working on a V10 engine, remove the ignition coils and spark plug wires.

15   If you're working on a V10 engine, remove the throttle body (see Chapter 4A), then loosen the upper intake manifold mounting bolts in 1/4-turn increments until they can be removed by hand. Remove the upper intake manifold, making sure there is nothing still attached to it (see illustration).

16   Remove the intake manifold-to-cylinder head bolts, working in the reverse of the tightening sequence (see illustrations 7.25a and 7.25b). The manifold will probably be stuck to the cylinder heads and force may be required to break the gasket seal. A prybar can be positioned to pry up a casting projec-

tion at the front of the manifold to break the bond made by the gasket (see illustration). As the manifold is lifted from the engine, be sure to check and disconnect anything still attached to the manifold.

**Caution:** *Do not pry between the block and manifold or the heads and manifold or damage to the gasket sealing surfaces may result and vacuum leaks could develop.*

### Installation

**Note:** *The mating surfaces of the cylinder heads, block and manifold must be perfectly clean when the manifold is installed. Gasket removal solvents in aerosol cans are available at most auto parts stores and may be helpful when removing old gasket material that is stuck to the heads and manifold. Be sure to follow the directions printed on the container.*

17   Remove carbon deposits from the exhaust crossover passages (if equipped).

18   Use a gasket scraper to remove all traces of sealant and old gasket material, then wipe the mating surfaces with a cloth saturated

7.11 Disconnect the electrical connectors from the throttle body, fuel injectors and the intake manifold - label each connector clearly to aid in the reassembly process

7.15 Pry the intake manifold upward by a casting protrusion only, not between the gasket surfaces

7.16 The intake manifold is somewhat heavy and bulky so get a good grip before lifting it up - watch for wires or hoses hanging up as you remove the manifold

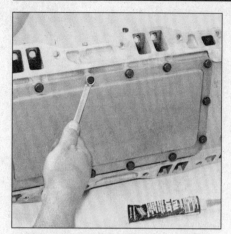

**7.20 On V6 and V8 engines, remove the plenum pan from under the intake manifold, clean the gasket surfaces and replace the gasket with a new one**

**7.22 The gaskets must be installed on the proper side; some may be marked left or right or "manifold side" - line up the ports and make sure the side gasket's cutouts clear the tabs on the head gasket front and rear**

**7.23 Apply a bead of RTV sealant to the four corners where the end gaskets meet the side gaskets - the bead should be slightly higher than the end rail gaskets**

with lacquer thinner or acetone. If there is old sealant or oil on the mating surfaces when the manifold is installed, oil or vacuum leaks may develop. Cover the lifter valley with shop rags to keep debris out of the engine. Use a vacuum cleaner to remove any gasket material that falls into the intake ports in the heads.

19   Use a tap of the correct size to chase the threads in the bolt holes, then use compressed air (if available) to remove the debris from the holes.

**Warning:** *Wear safety glasses or a face shield to protect your eyes when using compressed air.*

20   On V6 and V8 engines, the intake manifold has a stamped sheetmetal pan on the bottom, called the plenum pan (see illustration). If you have the intake manifold off for any reason, it's a good idea to replace the gasket under this pan. Use a thin film of RTV sealant on the gasket and tighten the bolts in a criss-cross pattern to the torque listed in this

Chapter's Specifications, starting in the center of the manifold and working out toward the ends, in three steps.

21   Apply a thin bead of RTV sealant to the cylinder heads around the water passages.

22   Position the side gaskets on the cylinder heads. Note that the gaskets are marked LT for left or RT for right (see illustration) or the words "Manifold Side" may appear. If so, this will ensure proper installation. Make sure they are installed on the correct side and all intake port openings, coolant passages and bolt holes are aligned correctly.

23   Apply a thin, uniform coating of quick-dry gasket cement to the intake manifold end seals and the cylinder block contact surfaces. Install the front and rear end seals on the block over the dowels (if equipped) and the end tangs. Refer to the instructions with the gasket set for further information. Apply RTV sealant at the four corners where the gaskets

meet (see illustration).

24   Carefully set the manifold in place.

**Caution:** *Do not disturb the gaskets and DO NOT move the manifold fore-and-aft after it contacts the front and rear seals or the gaskets will be pushed out of place.*

25   Install the bolts and tighten them following the recommended sequence (see illustrations) to the torque listed in this Chapter's Specifications. Do not overtighten the bolts or gasket leaks may develop.

26   If you're working on a V10 engine, install the upper intake manifold and tighten the bolts to the torque listed in this Chapter's Specifications, starting with the center bolts and working outward in a criss-cross pattern.

27   The remaining installation steps are the reverse of removal. Change the engine oil and add coolant (see Chapter 1). Start the engine and check carefully for oil, vacuum and coolant leaks at the intake manifold joints.

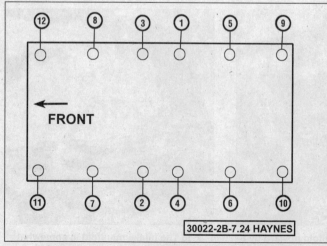

**7.25a Intake manifold bolt-tightening sequence – V6 and V8 engines**

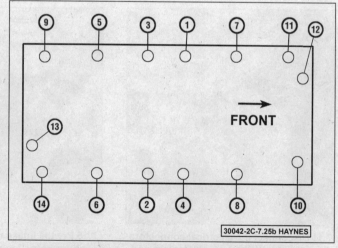

**7.25b Lower intake manifold bolt-tightening sequence – 8.0L V10 engine**

**8.2 Remove the exhaust pipe-to-manifold bolts**

**8.3 Remove the exhaust manifold heat shields**

## 8   Exhaust manifolds - removal and installation

**Warning:** *Allow the engine to cool completely before performing this procedure.*

### Removal

1   Disconnect the cable from the negative terminal of the battery (see Chapter 5).
2   Raise the vehicle and support it securely on jackstands. Disconnect the exhaust pipe-to-manifold connections (see illustration). It's a good idea to apply penetrating oil on the studs/bolts and let it soak 10 minutes before attempting to remove them.
3   Lower the vehicle and remove the heat shield from the exhaust manifold(s) (see illustration).
**Note:** *If you're working on the passenger's side exhaust manifold, it will be necessary to remove the air filter housing (see Chapter 4A) to allow access to the manifold bolts.*
4   Using a wrench remove the heat shield support extensions and washers from the exhaust manifold studs (if equipped).
5   Remove the bolts and nuts retaining the exhaust manifold to the cylinder head.
**Note:** *If any of the studs come out of the head while removing the manifolds, use new studs on reassembly. The coarse-threaded ends of the studs should be coated with a non-hardening sealant such as Permatex No. 2 to prevent the possibility of water leaks from the cylinder head. Keep track of where each of the bolts, nuts and washers go (they must be installed in the same positions).*
6   Remove the manifold(s).

### Installation

7   Clean the manifold gasket surface and check for cracks and flatness. Also clean the exhaust port gasket surface on the cylinder head.
**Note:** *V6 and V8 engines do not come equipped with exhaust manifold gaskets from*
the manufacturer although many aftermarket gasket manufacturers do provide exhaust manifold gaskets. If an exhaust leak at the manifold is noticeable, it would be wise to have the manifold resurfaced at an automotive machine shop and to use an exhaust manifold gasket when installing the manifold.
8   Install the manifold(s) and fasteners. Tighten the bolts/nuts to the torque listed in this Chapter's Specifications. Work from the center to the ends and approach the final torque in three steps. Install the heat shield extensions and washers (if equipped), then install the heat shields.
9   Apply anti-seize compound to the exhaust manifold-to-exhaust pipe bolts and tighten them securely.

## 9   Cylinder heads - removal and installation

### Removal

1   Disconnect the cable from the negative terminal of the battery (see Chapter 5) and drain the cooling system (see Chapter 1).

2   Remove the valve covers (see Section 4).
3   Remove the intake manifold (see Section 7).
4   Detach both exhaust manifolds from the cylinder heads (see Section 8). Remove the ignition coil (see Chapter 5) and the drivebelt tensioner from the right cylinder head.
5   Remove the rocker arms and pushrods (see Section 5).
**Caution:** *Again, as mentioned in Section 5, keep all the parts in order so they are reinstalled in the same location.*
6   Loosen the head bolts in 1/4-turn increments in the reverse order of the tightening sequence (see illustration 9.15a and 9.15b) until they can be removed by hand. There will be different-length head bolts for different locations, so store the bolts in a cardboard holder or some type of container as they are removed (see illustration).This will ensure that the bolts are reinstalled in their original holes.
7   Lift the heads off the engine. If resistance is felt, do not pry between the head and block as damage to the mating surfaces will result. To dislodge the head, place a block of wood against the end of it and strike the wood block

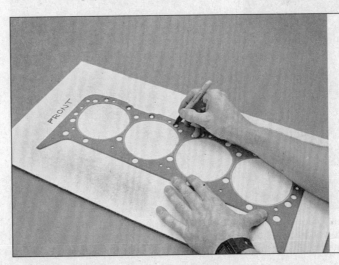

**9.6 To avoid mixing up the head bolts, use a new gasket to transfer the bolt pattern to a piece of cardboard, then punch holes to accept the bolts**

9.7a Pry on a casting protrusion to break the head loose

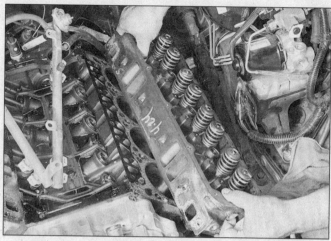

9.7b Once loose, get a good hold on the cylinder head and remove it from the engine block

with a hammer, or lift on a casting protrusion (see illustrations). Store the heads on blocks of wood to prevent damage to the gasket sealing surfaces.

8    Cylinder head disassembly, inspection and reassembly procedures should be entrusted to an automotive machine shop.

### Installation

9    The mating surfaces of the cylinder heads and block must be perfectly clean when the heads are installed. Gasket removal solvents are available at auto parts stores and may prove helpful.

10   Use a gasket scraper to remove all traces of carbon and old gasket material (see illustration), then wipe the mating surfaces with a cloth saturated with lacquer thinner or acetone. If there is oil on the mating surfaces when the heads are installed, the gaskets may not seal correctly and leaks may develop. When working on the block, cover the lifter valley with shop rags to keep debris out of the engine. Use a vacuum cleaner to remove any debris that falls into the cylinders.

11   Check the block and head mating sur-

faces for nicks, deep scratches and other damage. If damage is slight, it can be removed with emery cloth. If it is excessive, machining may be the only alternative.

12   Use a tap of the correct size to chase the threads in the head bolt holes in the block. Mount each bolt in a vise and run a die down the threads to remove corrosion and restore the threads (see illustration). Dirt, corrosion, sealant and damaged threads will affect torque readings.

13   Position the new gaskets over the dowels in the block (see illustration).

14   Carefully position the heads on the block without disturbing the gaskets.

15   Install the bolts in their original locations and tighten them finger-tight. Following the recommended sequence (see illustrations), tighten the bolts in several steps to the torque listed in this Chapter's Specifications.

16   The remaining installation steps are the reverse of removal.

17   Add coolant and change the oil and filter (see Chapter 1). Start the engine and check for proper operation and coolant or oil leaks.

### 10   Crankshaft front oil seal - replacement

1    Disconnect the cable from the negative terminal of the battery (see Chapter 5).

2    Remove the drivebelt (see Chapter 1) and the engine cooling fan (see Chapter 3).

3    Remove the bolts and separate the crankshaft pulley from the vibration damper (see illustration).

4    Remove the large vibration damper-to-crankshaft bolt. To keep the crankshaft from turning, remove the starter (see Chapter 5) and have an assistant wedge a large screwdriver against the ring gear teeth.

5    Using a puller that attaches to the hub of the damper, such as a bolt-on puller or a three-jaw puller (commonly available from auto parts stores), detach the vibration damper from the crankshaft (see illustration).

Caution: *Do not use a puller with jaws that grip the outer edge of the damper. The puller must be the type that applies force to the damper hub only. Also, the puller screw must not contact the threads in the nose of the*

9.10 Keep the intake valley covered with shop rags while removing all traces of old gasket material

9.12 A die should be used to remove sealant and corrosion from the bolt threads prior to installation

9.13 Install the new head gasket over the dowels at each end of the cylinder block

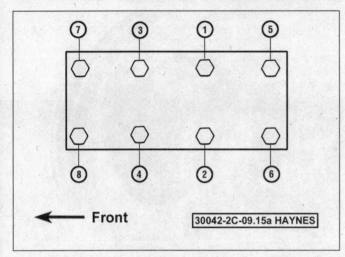

9.15a Cylinder head tightening sequence – V6 engines

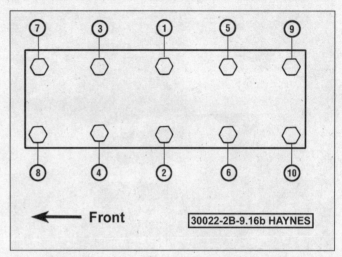

9.15b Cylinder head tightening sequence – V8 engines

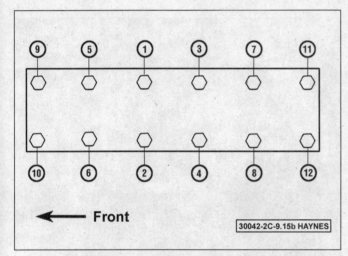

9.15c Cylinder head tightening sequence – 8.0L V10 engine

10.3 Remove the crankshaft pulley bolts and separate the pulley from the vibration damper

crankshaft; it must either bear on the end of the crankshaft nose or a spacer must be inserted into the nose of the crankshaft to protect the threads.

6    If the seal is being replaced with the timing chain cover removed, support the cover on top of two blocks of wood and drive the seal out from the backside with a hammer and punch.

**Caution:** *Be careful not to scratch, gouge or distort the area that the seal fits into or a leak will develop.*

7    If the seal is being removed while the cover is still attached to the engine block, carefully pry the seal out of the cover with a seal removal tool or a large screwdriver (see illustration).

**Caution:** *Be careful not to scratch, gouge or distort the area that the seal fits into or an oil leak will develop.*

8    Clean the bore to remove any old seal material and corrosion. Position the new seal in the bore with the seal lip (usually

10.5 Use the proper type of puller to remove the vibration damper (not one that grips the outer edge of the damper)

10.7 If you're replacing the seal with the timing chain cover installed, pry it out with a seal removal tool

**10.9 Use a seal driver or large-diameter pipe to drive the new seal into the cover**

**10.10 If the sealing surface of the damper hub has a wear groove from contact with the seal, repair sleeves are available at most auto parts stores**

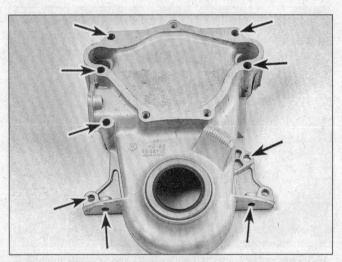

**11.9a Timing chain cover lower bolt hole locations on the V6 and V8 engines - upper through-bolts secure the water pump and the timing chain cover to the block and are detached when the water pump is removed**

**11.9b Remove the timing chain cover from the engine - being careful not to damage the oil pan gasket – V8 engine shown**

the side with the spring) facing IN (toward the engine). A small amount of oil applied to the outer edge of the new seal will make installation easier.

9    Drive the seal into the bore with a seal driver or a large socket and hammer until it's completely seated (see illustration). If you're using a socket, select one that's the same outside diameter as the seal and make sure the new seal is pressed into place until it bottoms against the cover flange.

10    Check the surface of the damper that the oil seal rides on. If the surface has been grooved from long-time contact with the seal, a press-on sleeve may be available to renew the sealing surface (see illustration). This sleeve is pressed into place with a hammer and a block of wood and is commonly available from auto parts stores.

11    Lubricate the seal lips with engine oil and

reinstall the vibration damper. Use a vibration damper installation tool to press the damper onto the crankshaft (this is a typical "draw-bolt" type puller, available at most auto parts stores).

12    Install the vibration damper-to-crankshaft bolt and tighten it to the torque listed in this Chapter's Specifications. Install the crankshaft pulley and tighten the bolts to the torque listed in this Chapter's Specifications.

13    The remainder of installation is the reverse of the removal.

---

## 11    Timing chain - removal, inspection and installation

**Warning:** *The engine must be completely cool before performing this procedure.*

### Removal and inspection

1    Remove the fan assembly (see Chapter 3) and the crankshaft pulley and damper (see Section 10).

2    Refer to Chapter 1 and drain the cooling system.

3    Remove the alternator (see Chapter 5) and the air injection pump (see Chapter 6).

4    On air-conditioned models, remove the air conditioning compressor and set it aside (see Chapter 3).

**Warning:** *Do not disconnect the refrigerant lines.*

5    Remove the idler pulley and the alternator/air conditioning compressor bracket from the front of the engine (see illustrations 7.7a and 7.7b).

6    Remove the water pump (see Chapter 1).

7    Remove and set aside the power steering pump with the lines still connected (see

**11.14 Loosen the camshaft sprocket bolt (A), then rotate the engine clockwise by the crankshaft bolt until the timing marks (B) align**

**11.15a The sprocket on the camshaft can be removed with a two or three-jaw puller . . .**

**11.15b . . . or with two screwdrivers**

Chapter 10).

**Note:** *On some models it may only be necessary to remove the bolt securing the power steering oil cooler to help facilitate removal of the timing chain cover.*

8    Loosen the oil pan bolts, then remove the front two oil pan bolts that thread into the timing chain cover - they're most easily accessed from below. Even though this procedure can be done without the removal of the oil pan, it is difficult on some models and oil pan removal may actually simplify the job (see Section 13).

9    Remove the remaining timing chain cover mounting bolts and separate the timing chain cover from the block and oil pan (see illustrations). The cover may be stuck; if so, use a putty knife to break the gasket seal. The cover is easily damaged, so DO NOT attempt to pry it off.

**Caution:** *Remove the cover as carefully as possible, so as not to tear the one-piece oil pan gasket. If the gasket becomes torn, the oil pan will have to be removed and a new gasket installed*

10    Inspect the timing chain for stretching. Attach a socket and torque wrench to the camshaft sprocket bolt and apply force in the normal direction of crankshaft rotation (30 ft-lbs if the cylinder heads are still in position complete with rocker arms, or 15 ft-lbs if the cylinder heads have been removed). Don't allow the crankshaft to rotate. If necessary, wedge a screwdriver into the flywheel ring gear teeth (with the starter removed) so that it can't move.

11    Place a ruler on top of the chain above the camshaft gear. Line up a mark on the ruler with the edge of a chain link. Apply the same amount of force as in Step 10 in the opposite direction of rotation and note the amount of movement of the chain. If it exceeds 1/8-inch, a new timing chain set will be required.

**Note:** *Always replace the timing chain, camshaft and crankshaft sprockets as set.*

12    Inspect the camshaft sprocket for damage or wear. The camshaft sprocket on some

models is steel, but most original-equipment cam sprockets will be an aluminum sprocket with a nylon coating on the teeth. This nylon coating may be cracked or breaking off in small pieces. These pieces tend to end up in the oil pan and may eventually plug the oil pump pickup screen. If the pieces have come off the camshaft sprocket, the oil pan should be removed to properly clean or replace the oil pump pickup screen.

13    Inspect the crankshaft sprocket for damage or wear. The crankshaft sprocket is a steel sprocket, but the teeth can be grooved or worn enough to cause a poor meshing of the sprocket and the chain.

14    After inspection has been completed, loosen the camshaft sprocket bolt, then rotate the engine in the normal direction of rotation (clockwise) until the timing marks are aligned (see illustration). Remove the bolt from the camshaft sprocket.

15    The sprockets on the camshaft and crankshaft can be removed with a two or three-jaw puller or by using two screwdrivers (see illustrations), but be careful not to damage the threads in the end of the crankshaft.

**Note:** *If the crankshaft front oil seal has been leaking, refer to Section 10 and install a new one.*

## Installation

**Note:** *Timing chains must be replaced as a set with the camshaft and crankshaft sprockets. Never put a new chain on old sprockets.*

16    Use a gasket scraper to remove all traces of old gasket material and sealant from the cover and engine block. Stuff a shop rag into the opening at the front of the oil pan to keep debris out of the engine. Wipe the cover and block sealing surfaces with a cloth saturated with lacquer thinner or acetone.

**Note:** *Some models are equipped with a timing chain tensioner. This tensioner must be compressed prior to installing the timing chain.*

17    On models with a timing chain tensioner, align the crankshaft sprocket keyway with the crankshaft Woodruff key and install the

**11.19 Slip the chain and camshaft sprocket in place over the crankshaft sprocket with the camshaft sprocket timing mark at the bottom**

sprocket. Carefully place a large flat-blade screwdriver between the crankshaft sprocket and the tensioner shoe. Compress the tensioner shoe until the shoe hole aligns with the bracket hole, then insert a suitable size pin through both holes to keep the shoe locked in this position. Remove the screwdriver and the crankshaft sprocket.

18    lign the crankshaft sprocket with the Woodruff key and press the sprocket onto the crankshaft with the vibration damper bolt, a large socket and some washers or tap it gently into place until it is completely seated.

**Caution:** *If resistance is encountered, do not hammer the sprocket onto the crankshaft. It may eventually move onto the shaft, but it may be cracked in the process and fail later, causing extensive engine damage.*

19    Loop the new chain over the camshaft sprocket, then turn the sprocket until the timing mark is at the bottom (see illustration). Mesh the chain with the crankshaft sprocket and position the camshaft sprocket on the end of the camshaft. If necessary, turn the

**12.3 Pull up on the distributor drive gear to remove it, rotating it clockwise until it can be removed through the distributor hole in the block - upon installation be sure the slot is aligned so that a line drawn through the slot crosses the front intake bolt hole in the left (driver's side) cylinder head, when the No. 1 piston is at TDC**

**12.4 Before removing the lifters note the paint marks that indicate which side of the roller lifters face the valley - apply marks if none are visible**

**12.7 Arrange a method of storing the lifters in order before removing them - a divided cardboard box is handy for storage of the lifters**

camshaft so the key fits into the sprocket keyway with the timing mark in the 6 o'clock position (see illustration 11.14). When the chain is installed, the timing marks MUST align as shown.

20  Apply a thread locking compound to the camshaft sprocket bolt threads and tighten the bolt to the torque listed in this Chapter's Specifications.

21  Lubricate the chain with clean engine oil.

22  Verify that the timing marks are still aligned properly (see illustration 11.14) and readjust if necessary.

23  Check for cracks and deformation of the oil pan gasket before installing the timing cover. If the gasket has deteriorated or is damaged, it must be replaced before reinstalling the timing chain cover.

24  Apply a thin layer of RTV sealant to both sides of the new cover gasket and the corners of the pan and block, then position the new

cover gasket on the engine. The sealant will hold it in place.

25  Install the timing chain cover on the block and tighten the bolts, a little at a time, until you reach the torque listed in this Chapter's Specifications.

26  Install the two oil pan bolts, bringing the oil pan up against the timing chain cover, and tighten the rest of the pan bolts, if they were previously loosened.

27  Lubricate the oil seal contact surface of the vibration damper hub with clean engine oil, then install the damper (see Section 10).

28  The remaining installation steps are the reverse of removal.

29  Change the engine oil and filter and refill the cooling system (see Chapter 1). Run the engine and check for oil and coolant leaks.

---

## 12  Camshaft and lifters - removal and installation

**Warning:** *The engine must be completely cool before performing this procedure.*

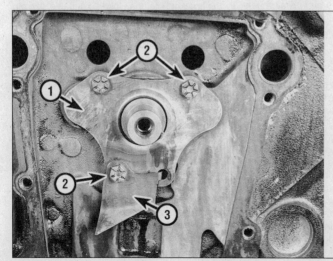

**12.8 Remove the camshaft thrust plate and oil tab**

1  *Thrust plate*
2  *Thrust plate bolts*
3  *Oil tab*

### Removal

1  Remove the intake manifold (see Section 7), valve covers (see Section 4), rocker arms, pushrods (see Section 5) and the timing chain (see Section 11).

2  Remove the radiator and air conditioning condenser (see Chapter 3).

3  On V6 and V8 engines, remove the distributor (see Chapter 5) and the distributor drive gear (see illustration).

4  Before removing the lifters and yokes note the marks showing which side of the lifter faces the lifter "valley." If they aren't marked, apply some paint dabs before removing the yokes (see illustration).

**Caution:** *The lifters must be installed the same way to aim the oil feed holes properly.*

5  Remove the lifter yoke retainer.

6  There are several ways to extract the lifters from the bores. A special tool designed to grip and remove lifters is manufactured by many tool companies and is widely available, but it may not be required in every case. On newer engines without a lot of varnish buildup, the lifters can often be removed with a small magnet or even with your fingers. A machinist's scribe with a bent end can be used to pull the lifters out by positioning the point under the retainer ring inside the top of each lifter.

**Caution:** *Do not use pliers to remove the lifters unless you intend to replace them with new ones. The pliers will damage the precision machined and hardened lifters, rendering them useless.*

7  Remove the lifter guides (aligning yokes) and lifters. Store the lifters in a clearly labeled box to ensure that they are reinstalled in their original locations (see illustration).

8  Unbolt and remove the camshaft thrust plate and oil tab (see illustration). Note how the oil tab is installed so you can return it to its original location on reassembly.

9  Thread a long bolt into the camshaft sprocket bolt hole to use as a handle when removing the camshaft from the block.

**12.10 Thread a long bolt into the camshaft sprocket bolt hole to use as a handle - as the camshaft is being removed, support it near the block so the lobes do not nick the bearings**

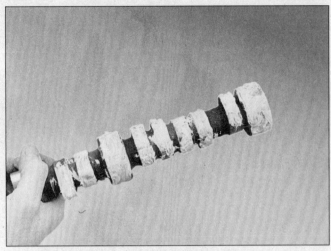

**12.11 Be sure to apply camshaft installation lube to the cam lobes and bearing journals before installing the camshaft**

10   Carefully pull the camshaft out. Support the cam near the block so the lobes do not nick or gouge the bearings as it is withdrawn (see illustration).

## Installation

**Caution:** *When replacing any of the valve-train components on V6 engines, make sure the replacement parts are for the exact year of your engine. Match the design of the replacement part to your old part when making any replacement, or serious oiling problems could develop.*

11   Lubricate the camshaft bearing journals and cam lobes with camshaft installation lube (see illustration).

12   Slide the camshaft slowly and gently into the engine. Support the cam near the block and be careful not to scrape or nick the bearings. Only install the camshaft far enough to allow the installation of the camshaft thrust plate. Pushing it in too far could dislodge the camshaft plug at the rear of the engine, causing an oil leak.

13   Install the camshaft thrust plate and oil tab (see illustration 12.8).

14   Align the timing marks on the crankshaft and camshaft sprockets, install the timing chain and sprockets (see Section 11), then check the camshaft endplay.

15   With the timing chain marks aligned, rotate the engine 360-degrees to bring the No.1 piston to TDC on the compression stroke. On the 5.9L V8 engine, install the distributor drive gear (see illustration 12.3).

**Note:** *Removing the spark plugs will allow the engine to rotate easier.*

16   Lubricate the lifters with clean engine oil and install them in the block. If the original lifters are being reinstalled, be sure to return them to their original locations, and with the paint marks facing the valley and the oil-feed holes on the side of the lifter body facing UP, away from the crankshaft. Install the lifter yokes and the lifter yoke retainer.

**Note:** *The lifter yokes must be installed with their arrows pointing toward the camshaft.*

17   Refer to the appropriate Sections and install the timing chain cover, vibration damper, pushrods and rocker arms.

18   The remaining installation steps are the reverse of removal.

19   Change the oil and install a new oil filter (see Chapter 1).

20   Start the engine, check for oil pressure and leaks.

**Caution:** *Do not run the engine above a fast idle until all the hydraulic lifters have filled with oil and become quiet again.*

21   If a new camshaft and lifters have been installed, the engine should be brought to operating temperature and run at a fast idle for 15 to 20 minutes to "break in" the new components. Change the oil and filter again after 500 miles of operation.

---

## 13   Oil pan - removal and installation

### Removal

1   Disconnect the cable from the negative terminal of the battery (see Chapter 5). Raise the vehicle and support it securely on jackstands (see Chapter 1).

2   Drain the engine oil (see Chapter 1). Remove the engine oil dipstick.

3   Remove the flywheel inspection cover.

4   Disconnect and lower the exhaust Y pipe from the engine (see illustration 8.2).

5   Support the engine from above with an engine hoist. Take the weight off the engine mounts with the hoist, being careful not to let the distributor cap come in contact with the firewall. On V6 and V8 engines, remove the distributor cap if necessary. On 4WD vehicles, remove the front axle assembly (see Chapter 8).

6   Remove the engine mounts and, on 4WD models, the engine mount support brackets (see Section 17).

**Note:** *On 8.0L V10 models, remove the transmission support strut from the left side of the transmission/engine.*

7   Remove all the oil pan bolts (see illustration), then lower the pan from the engine. The pan will probably stick to the engine, so strike the pan with a rubber mallet until it breaks the gasket seal. Carefully slide the oil pan out, to the rear.

**Caution:** *Before using force on the oil pan, be sure all the bolts have been removed.*

## Installation

8   Wash out the oil pan with solvent.

9   Thoroughly clean the mounting surfaces of the oil pan and engine block of old gasket material and sealer. If the oil pan is distorted at the bolt-hole areas, straighten the flange by supporting it from below on a 1x4 wood block and tapping the bolt holes with the rounded

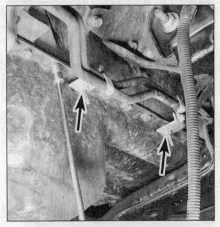

**13.7 Remove the bolts around the perimeter of the oil pan - if the vehicle is equipped with an automatic transmission remove and note the location of the transmission cooler line retainers**

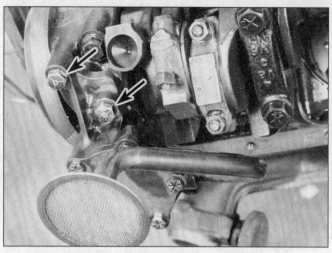

**14.2 Remove the bolts and detach the oil pump**

**14.10 Inspect the end of the oil pump driveshaft for excessive wear, position the pump body over the rear main cap, then slowly rotate the oil pump until it aligns with the driveshaft, install the mounting bolts and tighten them to the correct specification**

end of a ball-peen hammer. Wipe the gasket surfaces clean with a rag soaked in brake system cleaner.

10   Apply some RTV sealant to the corners where the front cover meets the block and at the rear where the rear main cap meets the block. Then attach the one-piece oil pan gasket to the engine block with contact cement-type gasket adhesive.

11   Prepare four pan alignment dowels from 5/16-inch bolts, 1-1/2 inches long. Cut off the bolt heads and slot the ends with a hacksaw.

12   Install the four alignment dowels into the frontmost and rearmost pairs of pan bolt holes in the block.

13   Lift the pan into position, slipping it over the alignment dowels and being careful not to disturb the gasket, install several bolts finger-tight.

14   Check that the gasket isn't sticking out anywhere around the block's perimeter. When all the bolts are in place, replace the align-

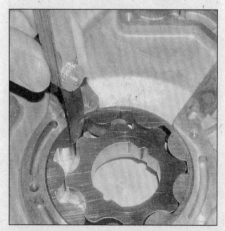

**14.18a Use a feeler gauge to check the inner-to-outer rotor tip clearance . . .**

ment dowels with four pan bolts.

15   Starting at the ends and alternating from side-to-side toward the center, tighten the bolts to the torque listed in this Chapter's Specifications.

16   The remainder of installation is the reverse of removal.

17   Add the proper type and quantity of oil (see Chapter 1), start the engine and check for leaks before placing the vehicle back in service.

---

## 14   Oil pump - removal, inspection and installation

### V6 and V8 models
#### Removal

1   Remove the oil pan (see Section 13).

2   While supporting the oil pump, remove the oil pump mounting bolts (see illustration).

3   Lower the pump and pickup screen assembly from the vehicle.

#### Inspection

4   Remove the oil pump cover and withdraw the rotors from the pump body. Clean the components with solvent, dry them thoroughly and inspect for any obvious damage.

5   Place a straightedge across the inner surface of the oil pump cover and try to insert a 0.0015-inch feeler gauge under it. If the gauge fits, the oil pump assembly should be replaced.

6   Measure the thickness of the inner and outer rotors with a micrometer. If either is less than the minimum thickness listed in this Chapter's Specifications, the pump assembly should be replaced.

7   Install the rotors into the pump body and measure the clearance between the outer rotor and the body, between the inner

and outer rotors, and the clearance over the rotors. Compare these measurements to this Chapter's Specifications. If any components are scored, scratched or worn beyond the Specifications, replace the oil pump assembly. If the parts are OK, reinstall the cover and tighten the bolts to the torque listed in this Chapter's Specifications.

#### Installation

8   If removed, thread the oil pickup tube and screen into the oil pump and tighten it.

**Caution:** *Be absolutely certain that the pickup tube is securely tightened so that no air can be sucked into the oiling system at this connection.*

9   Prime the pump by pouring clean motor oil into the pickup tube, while turning the pump by hand.

10   Position the pump on the engine with a new gasket, if required. Make sure the pump driveshaft is aligned with the oil pump (see illustration).

11   Install the mounting bolts and tighten them to the torque listed in this Chapter's Specifications.

12   Install the oil pan and add oil.

13   Run the engine and check for oil pressure and leaks.

### 8.0L V10 models

14   Remove the timing chain cover (see Section 11).

15   Remove the oil pump cover mounting bolts.

16   Remove the oil pump inner and outer rotors and inspect the oil pump for wear.

#### Inspection

17   Clean all components with solvent, then inspect them for wear and damage.

18   Check the clearance of the following oil pump components with a feeler gauge and a micrometer or dial caliper (see illustrations)

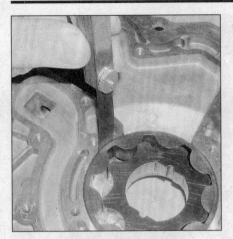

**14.18b . . . and the outer rotor-to-housing clearance**

**14.18c Use a straightedge and a feeler gauge to check the rotor-to-cover clearance**

**15.4 Remove the bolts and detach the rear main bearing cap from the engine**

and compare the measurement to the clearance specifications listed in this Chapter's Specifications.

  a) *Cover flatness*
  b) *Outer rotor diameter and thickness*
  c) *Inner rotor thickness*
  d) *Outer rotor-to-body clearance*
  e) *Inner rotor-to-outer rotor tip clearance*
  f) *Cover-to-inner rotor side clearance*
  g) *Cover-to-outer rotor side clearance*

19   If any clearance is excessive, replace the entire oil pump assembly.

20   Pack the oil pump rotor cavities with petroleum jelly to prime it. Assemble the oil pump and tighten all fasteners to the torque listed in this Chapter's Specifications.

### Installation

21   Install the oil pump cover and tighten the screws to the torque listed in this Chapter's Specifications.

22   To install the pump, turn the flats in the inner rotor so they align with the flats on the crankshaft, then install the timing chain cover back into position against the block (see Section 11).

23   Tighten the timing chain cover mounting bolts to the torque listed in this Chapter's Specifications.

24   The remainder of installation is the reverse of removal.

25   Run the engine and check for oil leaks.

---

## 15   Rear main oil seal - replacement

### V6 and V8 models

**Note:** *If you're installing a new seal during a complete engine overhaul, ignore the steps in this procedure that concern removal of external parts. Also, since the crankshaft is already removed, it's not necessary to use any special tools to remove the upper seal half (remove and install the upper seal half the same way as the lower seal half).*

1   The rear main seal can be replaced with the engine in the vehicle. The rear main seal is a two-piece design, made from Viton rubber.

2   Remove the oil pan (see Section 13).

3   Remove the oil pump (see Section 14).

4   Remove the bolts and detach the rear main bearing cap from the engine (see illustration).

5   Remove the lower half of the oil seal from the bearing cap and the upper half from the block.

**Note:** *It may be easier to remove the upper rear seal when the two main bearing caps ahead of the rear cap are loosened slightly. ALL the main bearing caps must be retightened to Specifications after the new seal and rear cap are installed.*

6   Clean the bearing cap and engine block surfaces carefully to degrease them and remove any sealant.

7   Lightly oil the lips of the new crankshaft seals.

**Caution:** *Always wipe the crankshaft surface clean, then oil it lightly before installing a new seal.*

8   Rotate a new seal half into the cylinder block with the paint stripe (yellow on some models, white on others) toward the rear of the engine.

**Caution:** *Hold your thumb firmly against the outside diameter of the seal as you're rotating it into place. This will prevent the seal outside diameter from being shaved from contact with the sharp edge of the engine block. If the seal gets damaged, oil leaks may occur.*

9   Place the other seal half in the bearing cap with the paint stripe toward the rear.

10   Apply a drop of Loctite 515 or equivalent on either side of the cap (on the surface that mates with the block), and a small amount of RTV sealant in the slots on either side of the cap. Install the cap quickly after applying the Loctite and sealant. Tighten the rear main bearing cap (and ALL the other bearing caps if you loosened any of the others) to the torque Specifications listed in this Chapter.

11   Install the oil pump and oil pan.

12   The remainder of installation is the reverse of removal. Fill the pan with oil, run the engine and check for leaks.

### 8.0L V10 models

13   Rear seal removal and installation for the 8.0L V10 engine is the same as for the 3.7L V6 and 4.7L V8 engines. Refer to Chapter 2A, for the seal replacement procedure.

14   The rear seal can be removed with the rear seal retainer plate in place, or by removing the retainer plate and replacing the seal off the engine. If the seal is replaced with the retainer plate still on the engine, use a special seal removal tool.

15   If the rear seal retainer plate is to be removed, follow the procedure in Chapter 2A but use the torque Specifications listed in this Chapter's Specifications.

---

## 16   Flywheel/driveplate - removal and installation

1   Flywheel/driveplate removal and installation for the 5.9L V8 and 8.0L V10 is principally the same for the 3.7L V6 and 4.7L V8 engines (see illustration). Refer to Chapter 2A, but use the torque Specifications in this Chapter's Specifications. Always apply Loctite 242 on

**16.1 Before removing the flywheel or driveplate, mark its relationship to the crankshaft**

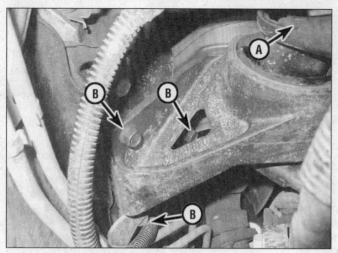

**17.11a Driver's side engine mount details**

A    *Through-bolt*    B    *Mount-to-engine block bolts*

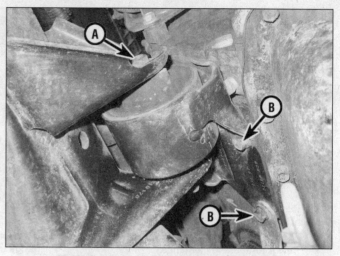

**17.11b Passenger's side engine mount details**

A    *Through-bolt*
B    *Mount-to-engine block bolts (not all are visible in this photo)*

the threads.

**Note:** *The pilot bearing (on manual transmission models) is pressed into the end of the crankshaft. If the pilot bearing is worn or has been damaged in transmission removal, refer to Chapter 8 for replacement.*

## 17    Engine mounts - check and replacement

1    Engine mounts seldom require attention, but broken or deteriorated mounts should be replaced immediately or the added strain placed on the driveline components may cause damage or wear.

### Check

2    During the check, the engine must be raised slightly to remove the weight from the mounts.

3    Raise the vehicle and support it securely on jackstands, then position a jack under the engine oil pan. Place a large wood block between the jack head and the oil pan, then carefully raise the engine just enough to take the weight off the mounts.

**Warning:** *DO NOT place any part of your body under the engine when it's supported only by a jack!*

4    Check for relative movement between the mount plates and the engine or frame (use a large screwdriver or prybar to attempt to move the mounts). If movement is noted,

lower the engine and tighten the mount fasteners.

5    Check the mounts to see if the rubber is cracked, hardened or separated from the bushing in the center of the mount, which would indicate a need for replacement.

6    Rubber preservative should be applied to the mounts to slow deterioration.

### Replacement

7    Disconnect the cable from the negative terminal of the battery (see Chapter 5, Section 1).

8    Raise the front of the vehicle and support it securely on jackstands. Drain the engine oil and remove the oil filter (see Chapter 1).

9    Support the engine with a lifting device from above. Raise the engine just enough to take the weight off the engine mounts.

**Caution:** *Do not connect the lifting device to the intake manifold.*

**Caution:** *Remove the engine cooling fan (see Chapter 3). Raising the engine with the cooling fan in place may damage the viscous clutch.*

#### 2WD models

10    Remove the engine mount-to-frame support bracket through-bolt.

11    Remove the mount-to-engine block bolts, then remove the mount and the heat shield (if equipped) (see illustrations).

12    Place the heat shield and the new mount in position, install the mount-to-engine block bolts and tighten the bolts securely.

**Note:** *Be sure to install the rubber restrictors*

onto the engine support bracket cushion, if equipped.

#### 4WD models

13    Remove the front axle assembly (see Chapter 5). If removing the driver's side engine mount, remove the starter (see Chapter 8).

14    Remove the engine mount to frame support bracket through-bolt.

15    Remove the engine mount to engine support bracket bolt and nuts.

16    Raising the engine more, if necessary, remove the engine mount(s).

17    To remove the engine support brackets simply remove the bolts from the engine block and transmission housing.

18    If removed, place the engine support bracket(s) in position and install the engine support bracket to engine block and transmission housing. Tighten the bolts securely.

19    Install the engine mount onto the engine support bracket and tighten the bolts securely.

#### All models

20    After the engine mounts have been installed onto the engine, lower the engine while guiding the engine mount and through-bolt into the frame support bracket. Install the through-bolt nut and tighten it securely.

21    The remainder of the installation is the reverse of removal. Remove the engine hoist and the jackstands and lower the vehicle.

# Chapter 2 Part D
# Diesel engines

## Contents

## Specifications

### General

| | |
|---|---|
| Displacement | 5.9L (360 cu.in.) or 6.7L (409 cu. in.) |
| Cylinder numbers (front to rear) | 1-2-3-4-5-6 |
| Firing order | 1-5-3-6-2-4 |
| Bore and stroke | |
| 5.9L | 4.02 x 4.72 inches |
| 6.7L | 4.21 x 4.88 inches |

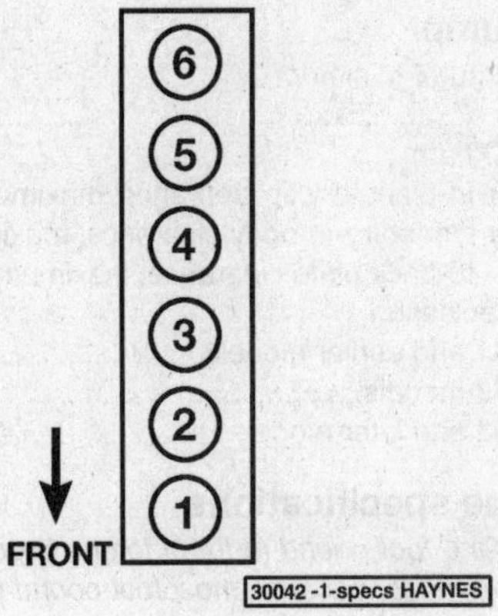

### Cylinder head and block

| | |
|---|---|
| Cylinder head warpage limit | |
| End-to-end | 0.012 inch |
| Side-to-side | 0.003 inch |
| Cylinder block deck warpage limit | |
| End-to-end | 0.003 inch |
| Side-to-side | 0.002 inch |
| Cylinder head bolt length (maximum) | 5.200 inches |

### Camshaft

| | |
|---|---|
| Journal diameter | |
| 1994 through 1998 | 2.1245 inches |
| 1999 through 2001 | |
| Journal No. 1 | 2.1270 inches |
| Journal Nos. 2 through 7 | 2.1245 inches |
| 2002 and later | |
| Journal No. 1 and 7 | |
| Minimum | 2.1270 inches |
| Maximum | 2.1280 inches |
| Journals 2 through 6 | |
| Minimum | 2.1245 inches |
| Maximum | 2.1265 inches |

6
5
4
3
2
1

FRONT

30042-1-specs HAYNES

**Cylinder locations**

## Camshaft (continued)

Lobe height, minimum

1994 through 1998

| | |
|---|---|
| Intake | 1.852 inches |
| Exhaust | 1.841 inches |
| Fuel pump lobe | 1.398 inches |

1999 and later

| | |
|---|---|
| Intake | 1.857 inches |
| Exhaust | 1.797 inches |

Endplay

| | |
|---|---|
| 2006 and earlier | 0.006 to 0.010 inch |
| 2007 and later | 0.004 to 0.020 inch |

Gear backlash

| | |
|---|---|
| 2006 and earlier | 0.003 to 0.013 inch |
| 2007 and later | 0.003 to 0.016 inch |

## Camshaft thrust plate

| | |
|---|---|
| Thrust plate minimum thickness | 0.368 inch |
| Thrust plate maximum thickness | 0.377 inch |

## Rocker arms and shafts (1999 and later models)

| | |
|---|---|
| Rocker arm bore diameter (maximum) | 0.867 inch |
| Rocker arm shaft diameter (minimum) | 0.865 inch |

## Valve clearance

1998 and earlier models

| | |
|---|---|
| Intake | 0.010 inch |
| Exhaust | 0.020 inch |

1999 through 2006 models

Intake

| | |
|---|---|
| Allowable | 0.006 to 0.015 inch |
| Desired | 0.010 inch |

Exhaust

| | |
|---|---|
| Allowed | 0.015 to 0.030 inch |
| Desired | 0.022 inch |

2007 and later models

Intake

| | |
|---|---|
| Allowable | 0.006 to 0.015 inch |
| Desired | 0.010 inch |

Exhaust

| | |
|---|---|
| Allowed | 0.021 to 0.034 inch |
| Desired | 0.026 inch |

## Oil pump

Oil pressure, minimum

| | |
|---|---|
| Idle | 10 psi |
| 2,500 rpm | 30 psi |
| Gerotor-to-planetary tip clearance, maximum | 0.007 inch |
| Gerotor planetary-to-body clearance, maximum | 0.015 inch |
| Gerotor-to-back plate clearance, maximum | 0.005 inch |

Gear backlash

| | |
|---|---|
| 2001 and earlier models | 0.003 to 0.013 inch |
| 2002 models | 0.030 to 0.034 inch |
| 2003 and later models | 0.006 to 0.010 inch |

## Torque specifications                    Ft-lbs (unless otherwise indicated)

**Note:** *One foot-pound (ft-lb) of torque is equivalent to 12 inch-pounds (in-lbs) of torque. Torque values below approximately 15 ft-lbs are expressed in inch-pounds, because most foot-pound torque wrenches are not accurate at these smaller values.*

| | |
|---|---|
| Alternator mounting bolts | 30 |
| Camshaft thrust plate bolts | 18 |

Crankshaft damper bolts

| | |
|---|---|
| 1994 through 1996 models | 135 |
| 1997 through 2002 models | 92 |

2003 and later models

| | |
|---|---|
| Step 1 | 30 |
| Step 2 | Tighten an additional 60-degrees |

## Torque specification (continued)

**Ft-lbs (unless otherwise indicated)**

**Note:** *One foot-pound (ft-lb) of torque is equivalent to 12 inch-pounds (in-lbs) of torque. Torque values below approximately 15 ft-lbs are expressed in inch-pounds, because most foot-pound torque wrenches are not accurate at these smaller values.*

Cylinder head bolts (in sequence - see illustration 11.21)

1998 and earlier models
| | |
|---|---|
| Step 1, all bolts | 66 |
| Step 2, long bolts | 89 |
| Step 3, all bolts | Tighten an additional 90-degrees |

1999 through 2002 models
| | |
|---|---|
| Step 1 | 59 |
| Step 2 | 77 |
| Step 3 | 77 (re-check) |
| Step 4 | Tighten an additional 90-degrees |

2003 and later models
| | |
|---|---|
| Step 1 | 52 |
| Step 2 | Loosen 360-degrees |
| Step 3 | 77 |
| Step 4 | 77 (re-check) |
| Step 5 | Tighten an additional 90-degrees |

| | |
|---|---|
| Drivebelt tensioner bolt | 32 |
| Exhaust manifold bolts | 32 |
| Fan support hub assembly bolts | |
|     2002 models | 16 |
|     2003 and later models | 24 |
| Flywheel/driveplate bolts | 101 |
| Flywheel housing adapter | 57 |
| Gear housing bolts | 18 |
| Gear housing cover bolts | 18 |
| Intake manifold bolts | 18 |
| Oil pressure relief valve plug | 60 |
| Oil pan drain plug | See Chapter 1 |
| Oil pan bolts | |
|     2002 and earlier models | 18 |
|     2003 and later models | 21 |
| Oil pump mounting bolts | |
|     Step 1 | 44 in-lbs |
|     Step 2 | 18 |
| Rear main oil seal retainer bolts | 80 in-lbs |
| Rocker arm bolts | |
|     1994 through 1998 | |
|         12 mm | Use cylinder head bolt torque specification (and sequence shown in illustration 5.11) |
|         8 mm | 18 |
|     1999 on | 27 |
| Valve cover bolts | 18 |
| Valve adjusting lock nut | 18 |

## 1   General Information

1    This part of Chapter 2 is devoted to in-vehicle repair procedures for the 5.9L and 6.7L Cummins inline six-cylinder diesel engines. Information concerning engine removal and installation and engine overhaul can be found in Part E of this Chapter.

2    Since the repair procedures included in this Part are based on the assumption that the engine is still installed in the vehicle, if they are being used during a complete engine overhaul (with the engine already out of the vehicle and on a stand) many of the steps included here will not apply.

3    The 5.9L and 6.7L diesel engines are of an extremely rugged, proven design, incorporating a turbocharger and intercooler for efficient power production and low-end torque.

## 2   Repair operations possible with the engine in the vehicle

1    Many major repair operations can be accomplished without removing the engine from the vehicle.

2    Clean the engine compartment and the exterior of the engine with some type of pressure washer before any work is done. A clean engine will make the job easier and will help keep dirt out of the internal areas of the engine.

3    Depending on the components involved, it may be a good idea to remove the hood to improve access to the engine as repairs are performed (refer to Chapter 11 if necessary).

4    If oil or coolant leaks develop, indicating a need for gasket or seal replacement, the repairs can generally be made with the engine in the vehicle. The cylinder head gasket, intake and exhaust manifold gaskets, gear cover gaskets and the crankshaft oil seals are all accessible with the engine in place. The oil pan gasket, however, does require discon-

necting the engine mounts and raising the engine.

5    Exterior engine components, such as the water pump, the starter motor, the alternator, turbocharger and the fuel injection components, as well as the intake manifold cover and exhaust manifold, can be removed for repair with the engine in place.

6    Since the cylinder head can be removed without pulling the engine, valve component servicing can also be accomplished with the engine in the vehicle.

7    Replacement of, repairs to or inspection of the gear case components and the oil pump are all possible with the engine in place.

## 3   Top Dead Center (TDC) - locating

### 1998 and earlier models

1    On 1994 through 1998 models, a timing pin is located on the back of the gear housing, below the injection pump and above the power steering pump (see illustration). It is normally pulled out, but when timing the engine, it is pushed in until it contacts a hole in the camshaft gear, locking the camshaft gear in the TDC position. There is no timing pin on 1999 and later models. The Camshaft Position (CMP) sensor is installed at this location.

2    To remove the timing pin, use a small screwdriver to remove the snap-ring, and pull out the timing pin (see illustration). When installing the timing pin, use a new O-ring.

3    To find TDC, remove the fuel injector nozzles (see Chapter 4B) to allow the engine to rotate smoothly. Remove the timing pin as described in Step 2. Use a breaker bar and a large socket on the crankshaft damper bolt to turn the engine over, while watching the timing pin hole (use a small bright flashlight and a small mirror) until the hole in the back of the camshaft gear is visible through the hole.

**Note:** *A special "barring" tool, available from specialty tool manufacturers, fits into a hole in the bellhousing and engages the flywheel ring-gear teeth(see illustrations 3.6a and 3.6b). Remove the rubber plug from the bellhousing, insert the tool, and the engine can be turned slowly and precisely with the tool, a ratchet and an extension.*

4    When the gear hole appears directly in line with the timing pin hole, push the timing pin back in to lock the camshaft in the TDC position.

**Caution:** *Do not attempt to rotate the engine while the timing pin is pushed in.*

### 1999 through 2002 models

5    Remove the fuel injection pump gear cover from the engine front cover.

6    Rotate the engine and align the pump gear mark with the TDC mark at the top of the gear housing cover (see illustration). A special "barring" tool, available from specialty tool manufacturers, fits into a hole in the bellhousing and engages the flywheel ring-gear teeth (see illustrations). Remove the rubber plug from the bellhousing, insert the tool, and the engine can be turned slowly and precisely with the tool, a ratchet and an extension.

7    When the pump gear mark is aligned with the TDC mark on the gear housing, the engine is at TDC compression for cylinder number 1.

### 2003 and later models

8    Remove the valve cover (see Section 4).

9    Using the special "barring" tool described in Step 6, rotate the engine until the TDC mark on the crankshaft vibration damper is in the 12 o'clock position.

10    Check the rocker arms for the number one cylinder. If they're both loose, the engine is at TDC compression for cylinder number 1.

**Note:** *This is an approximate TDC setting, but it is close enough for checking valve lash.*

11    If both rocker arms for cylinder number 1 are not loose, turn the crankshaft 360-degrees

**3.1 The timing pin is located on the left rear side of the gear housing, below the injection pump (1994 through 1998 models)**

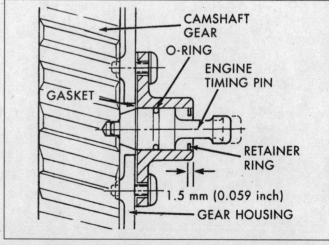

CAMSHAFT GEAR

O-RING

ENGINE TIMING PIN

GASKET

RETAINER RING

1.5 mm (0.059 inch)

GEAR HOUSING

**3.2 Timing pin details (1994 through 1998 models)**

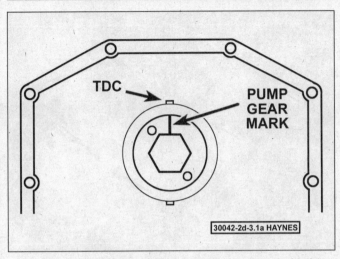

3.6a The fuel injection pump mark should be aligned with the TDC casting on the gear housing for TDC number 1 – remove the timing pump cover to access the marks (1999 through 2002 models)

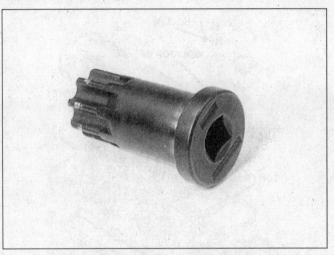

3.6b A special "barring" tool is available from specialty tool manufacturers

(one turn), bringing the mark on the vibration damper to the 12 o'clock position.

3.6c Remove the cover or rubber plug and insert the special barring tool into the bellhousing - used in conjunction with a ratchet and extension, the engine can be rotated by hand

## 4  Valve cover - removal and installation

### 1998 and earlier models

1    Remove the two bolts and remove the plastic decorative panel over the valve covers (see illustration).

2    There is an individual valve cover for every cylinder of the engine, six in all. Remove the bolt and pull off the valve cover for one or all of the cylinders, as necessary (see illustration).

**Caution:** *Do not pry between the valve cover and the cylinder head. If the cover sticks, tap it with a rubber mallet or a hammer and block of wood.*

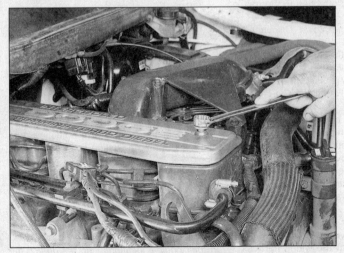

4.1 Remove the plastic cover over the individual valve covers (1994 through 1998 models)

4.2 Each of the individual valve covers is retained by one bolt (1994 through 1998 models)

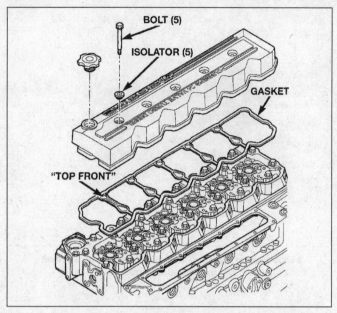

**4.4 Valve cover installation details (1999 and later models)**

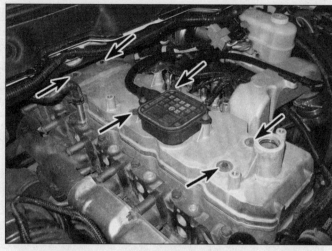

**4.10 Valve cover bolt locations - 2003 and later models**

3    The original gaskets are steel-backed silicone and are reusable, unless damaged. Place the gasket on the valve cover, install the valve cover on the cylinder head and tighten the bolt to the torque listed in this Chapter's Specifications.

### 1999 through 2001 models

4    Loosen all five valve cover bolts (see illustration). Remove the front three bolts and leave the two rear bolts in the cover. Remove the valve cover.
5    Using clean solvent, wipe off and dry the gasket mating surfaces of the cylinder head and the valve cover. Wipe off the gasket and inspect its condition. The gasket and isolators (the rubber grommets for the valve cover bolts) can be reused if they're not cracked. If an isolator or the valve cover gasket is

**5.4 Remove the bolts and the rocker arm/ pedestal assembly - arrow indicates the locating dowel ring on the bottom of the pedestal (1994 through 1998 models)**

cracked, replace it to avoid leaks.
6    Installation is the reverse of removal. Make sure that the words "TOP FRONT" are facing up and toward the front of the cylinder head. Install the three valve cover bolts you removed. Starting with the center bolt and working toward the outer bolts, tighten the valve cover bolts to the torque listed in this Chapter's Specifications.

### 2002 and later models

**Note:** *On 2007 and later models, the injector wiring harness is integrated into the valve cover gasket. Use care to avoid damaging the wiring.*
7    Disconnect the cables from the negative terminals of the batteries (see Chapter 5, Section 1).
8    Remove the oil filler cap. On 2007 and later models, disconnect the two injector wiring harness connectors attached to the gasket assembly.
9    Remove the breather cover. Disconnect the breather hose and drain tube from the breather housing. On 2007 and later models, disassemble and remove the Closed Crankcase Ventilation (CCV) assembly and the Crankcase Depression Regulator (CDR) (see Chapter 6).
10    Unscrew the valve cover bolts (see illustration). If you're working on a 2002 model, remove the front bolts and leave the two rear bolts in the cover. Remove the valve cover.
**Note:** *The valve cover on some later models is equipped with a grounding spring that fits into a hole in the underside of the cover. Be careful not to lose it.*
11    On 2007 and later models, remove the nuts that secure the valve cover gasket/wiring harness and disconnect the wiring harness from the injectors. Remove the gasket/wiring harness.

12    Clean the gasket mating surfaces of the cylinder head and the valve cover. Wipe off the gasket and inspect its condition. The gasket and isolators (the rubber grommets for the valve cover bolts) can be reused if they're not hardened, cracked or otherwise damaged. If an isolator or the valve cover gasket is cracked, replace it to avoid leaks.
13    Installation is the reverse of removal. Make sure the gasket is installed properly (some are marked TOP FRONT). Tighten the bolts a little at a time, starting with the center bolts, to the torque listed in this Chapter's Specifications.

### 5    Rocker arms and pushrods - removal, inspection and installation

1    Disconnect the cables from the negative terminals of the batteries (see Chapter 5, Section 1).
2    Remove the valve cover (see Section 4).

### Removal

#### 1998 and earlier models

**Note:** *The following procedure should be performed on a cold engine.*
3    Loosen the rocker arm adjusting nuts and back out the adjusting screws until they stop.
4    Remove the rocker arm pedestal bolts (which are also cylinder head bolts) and remove the rocker arm/pedestal assemblies (see illustration).
**Caution:** *Keep the rocker arm/pedestal assemblies in order so they can be installed in their original locations - do not detach the rocker arms from the pedestals unless they are being replaced.*

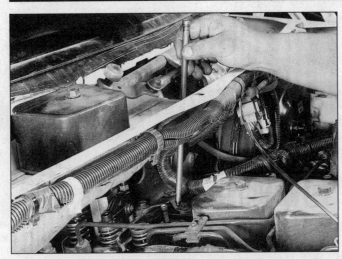

5.5 The pushrods for the two rearmost cylinders must be removed through holes in the cowl above the rear of the engine (1994 through 1998 models)

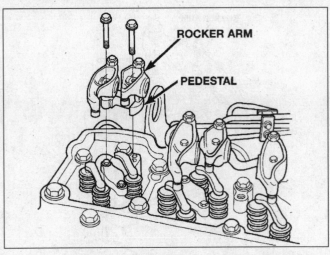

5.6 Rocker arm /pedestal details (1999 and later models)

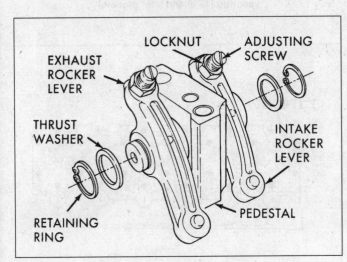

5.9 Rocker arm, shaft and pedestal installation details (1994 through 1998 models)

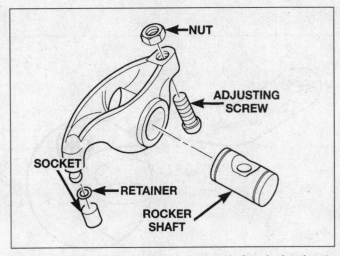

5.13 Exploded view of a rocker arm, rocker shaft and related parts (1999 and later models)

5    Remove the pushrods. Keep the push-rods in order so they can be installed in their original locations. Remove the rubber access plugs and withdraw the pushrods and long pedestal bolts for the two rearmost cylinders through holes in the cowl panel directly above the rear section of the engine (see illustration).

### 1999 and later models
6    Mark the rocker arm/pedestal assemblies to ensure that they will be reinstalled in their original locations. Remove the rocker arm/pedestal bolts and remove the rocker arm/pedestal assemblies (see illustration).
7    Mark the crossheads (the pieces that bridge each pair of intake and exhaust valves) to ensure that they will be reinstalled in their original locations. Remove the crossheads.
**Caution:** *The sockets may drop from the rocker arms when lifting them from the cylinder head. Be sure to secure the rocker arm*

*sockets before lifting them from the cylinder head.*
8    Mark the pushrods to ensure that they will be reinstalled in their original locations. Remove the pushrods.
**Note:** *Lift out the intake and exhaust pushrods for the No. 5 and No. 6 cylinders through access holes in the cowl.*

## Inspection
### 1998 and earlier models
9    Check each rocker arm for wear, cracks and other damage, especially where the pushrods and valve stems contact the rocker arm faces. Also check the rocker arm shafts for wear. If the rocker arms are disassembled from the pedestal shafts, mark the rocker arms first so they can be installed in their original locations. The rocker arms can be removed by removing the snap-ring and thrust washer at each end of the shaft (see illustration).
10    Make sure the oil feed holes in each

rocker arm shaft are not plugged so that each rocker arm gets proper lubrication.
11    Check each rocker arm pivot area and wear area on the shaft for excessive wear, scoring, cracks and galling. If the rocker arms or shafts are worn or damaged, replace them with new ones.
12    Inspect the pushrods for cracks and excessive wear at the ends. Roll each pushrod across a piece of plate glass to see if it is bent (if it wobbles, it is bent). Replace the pushrods if any of these conditions are present.

### 1999 and later models
13    Disassemble the rocker arms, pedestals and shafts (see illustration) and wash them, along with the crossheads, in clean solvent. Keep each rocker arm pair, the rocker shafts, the pedestal and related parts together. If necessary, use a wire brush to remove deposits. Rinse the parts in hot water and blow them dry with compressed air.

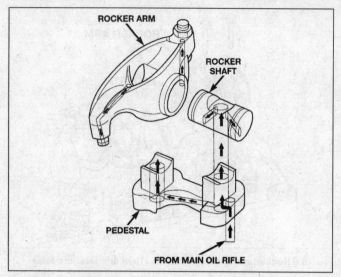

**5.14 Blow out the oil passages inside each rocker arm, rocker shaft and pedestal (1999 and later models)**

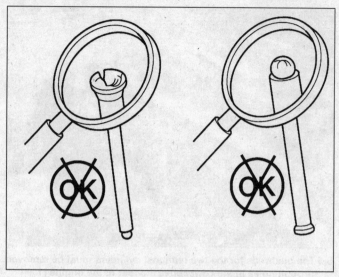

**5.17 Inspect each pushrod socket and ball for signs of cracks or scoring (1999 and later models)**

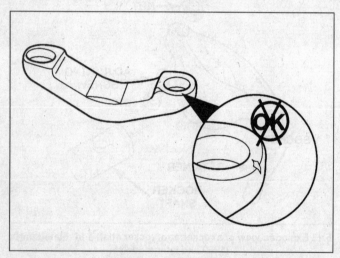

**5.18 Inspect each crosshead for cracks and excessive wear, especially in the rim around each crosshead/calve tip contact area (1999 and later models)**

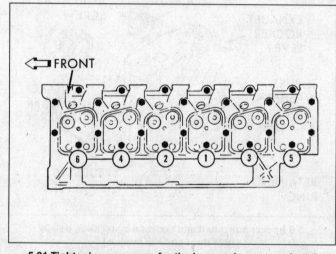

**5.21 Tightening sequence for the long rocker arm pedestal retaining bolts (which are also cylinder head bolts) (1994 through 1998 models)**

14   Inspect the oil passages in the rocker arms, rocker shafts and pedestals (see illustration). Blow out all lubrication passages with compressed air to remove any debris.

15   Inspect the bearing surface of each rocker shaft for scoring, cracks and galling, and for any other excessive wear. Inspect the socket and the ball insert for excessive wear. If the retainer is weak, replace it.

16   Measure the inside diameter of each rocker arm bore and the outside diameter of each rocker shaft. Compare your measurements to the maximum allowable diameter for rocker arm bores and to the minimum allowable diameter for rocker shafts. If a rocker arm or rocker shaft is worn excessively, replace it.

17   Inspect each pushrod ball and socket for cracks and any signs of scoring (see illustration). Roll each pushrod on a clean flat surface with the socket end hanging off the end

of the bench. If a pushrod is bent, or excessively worn, replace it.

18   Inspect each crosshead for cracks and excessive wear, especially around the rim of the crosshead/valve tip contact area (see illustration). If a crosshead is damaged or excessively worn, replace it.

## Installation

### 1998 and earlier models

19   Reinstall the pushrods in their original locations.

20   If the rocker arms were removed from their shafts, lube the shafts with engine assembly lube and reinstall the rocker arms, thrust washers and snap-rings.

21   Place the rocker arm/pedestal assemblies onto the cylinder head, making sure that the dowel rings on the bottom of the pedestals locate properly into the cylinder head holes

(see illustration 5.3). Tighten the long bolts to the torque listed in this Chapter's Specifications for the cylinder head bolts, in the proper sequence (see illustration). Tighten the smaller rocker arm bolts to the torque listed in this Chapter's Specifications.

**Note:** *If a pedestal will not sit flush against the cylinder head before tightening the bolt, rotate the crankshaft to relieve pressure from the pushrod, then tighten the bolt to the torque listed in this Chapter's Specifications.*

22   Refer to Section 3 to position the engine at TDC for number 1 piston. Be sure to pull the timing pin back out after locating TDC.

23   Refer to Chapter 1 and adjust the valve clearance.

24   Install the valve covers.

25   The remainder of installation is the reverse of removal. Don't forget to plug the holes in the cowl.

## 1999 and later models

26  Install the pushrods, with the ball ends facing down, in their original locations. Make sure that the pushrods are fully seated in the tappets.

27  Lubricate the valve tips with clean engine oil and install the crossheads in their original locations.

28  Lubricate the rocker shafts and the rocker shaft bores in the rocker arms with clean engine oil. Reassemble the rocker arm/ rocker shaft/pedestal assemblies.

29  Lubricate the crossheads and the push-rod sockets with clean engine oil and install the rocker arm/pedestal assemblies in their original locations. Install the rocker arm/ped-estal bolts and tighten them to the torque listed in this Chapter's Specifications.

30  Before installing the valve cover, check and, if necessary, adjust the valve clearance (see below).

31  After the valve clearance has been checked and, if necessary, adjusted, install the valve cover (see Section 4).

### Valve clearance check and adjustment

32  Position the engine at Top Dead Center (TDC) for cylinder number 1 (see Section 3).

33  With the engine in this position, measure the valve clearance at the following rocker arms:

INTAKE - 1, 2 and 4
EXHAUST - 1, 3 and 5

34  Measure the valve clearance by inserting a feeler gauge between the rocker arm socket and the crosshead. Compare your measurements to the valve clearance ranges listed in this Chapter's Specifications.

35  If the valve clearance is incorrect for any of the above intake or exhaust valves, loosen the locknut and then turn the adjusting screw until the clearance is correct. Set the clearances to the torque listed in this Chapter's Specifications. When the clearance is correct, tighten the locknut securely (see this Chapter's Specifications for the proper torque read-

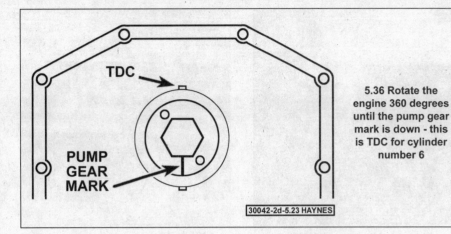

5.36 Rotate the engine 360 degrees until the pump gear mark is down - this is TDC for cylinder number 6

ing) and then re-check the clearance to make sure that it didn't change as a result of tightening the nut.

36  Using the barring tool, rotate the engine one complete revolution (360-degrees). The mark on the pump gear will be at the six o'clock position in relation to the TDC mark on the gear housing cover (see illustration). With the engine in this position, measure the valve clearance at the following rocker arms:

INTAKE - 3, 5 and 6
EXHAUST - 2, 4 and 6

37  Following the procedure described in Steps 34 and 35, measure and, if necessary, adjust the valve clearances for the remaining intake and exhaust valves.

38  Install the valve cover (see Section 4).

## 6  Intake manifold cover - removal and installation

**Note:** *The intake manifold on the diesel engine is integral with the cylinder head and is not removable. The only service procedures are replacement of the air intake heating ele-*

*ment and the intake manifold cover gasket.*

### 1998 and earlier models

1  Refer to Chapter 4B and remove the high-pressure fuel lines that cross over the intake manifold. Remove the fuel line retaining brackets (see illustration).

2  Loosen the clamp and disconnect the duct from the intercooler to the intake manifold (see Chapter 4B).

3  Mark the two air intake heater wires with tape so they can be installed in their original locations and remove the nuts and wires from the studs. Unbolt the oil dipstick bracket from the air intake.

4  Refer to Chapter 6, and disconnect the wire to the charge air temperature sensor and disconnect the air temperature switch.

5  Remove the four bolts retaining the air intake housing and gasket from the manifold cover. Avoid dropping gasket pieces or foreign matter into the manifold.

6  Two of the cover fasteners are a stud and bolt retaining the fuel filter to the intake cover (see illustration). Pull the heating element from the manifold, then unbolt the intake

6.1 Remove the two fuel line brackets (arrows) (1998 and earlier models)

6.6a At the rear of the intake manifold cover, disconnect the charge air temperature sensor (1), pull the wiring harness clip (2) from the fuel filter bolt (3), and remove the fuel filter bolt and stud (1998 and earlier models)

6.6b Remove the remaining bolts retaining the intake manifold cover and remove the cover (1998 and earlier models)

**6.10 Loosen this clamp attaching the intercooler duct to the air intake housing**

**7.2 On models so equipped, remove the bolt retaining the heater pipe(s) to the exhaust manifold. Be careful not to lose the spacers**

**7.4 Remove the exhaust manifold bolts**

manifold cover and gasket (see illustration).

7   Stuff the intake manifold with rags to keep debris from falling into the manifold and scrape the sealing surface clean. Clean the bottom of the intake manifold cover as well.

8   Install the new gasket and the intake manifold cover, using liquid Teflon sealant on all the bolt threads. Tighten the bolts to the torque listed in this Chapter's Specifications.

9   Install the heating element and a new gasket for the air inlet housing. The remainder of installation is the reverse of removal. Install the high-pressure fuel lines and bleed the fuel system (see Chapter 4B).

### 1999 and later models

10   Loosen the hose clamp attaching the intercooler duct to the air intake housing (see illustration).

11   Remove the mounting bolt from the dipstick tube bracket and move the dipstick tube aside.

12   Remove the cable mounting studs and disconnect the electrical cables from the air grid heater.

13   Remove the four air intake housing bolts and remove the housing from the air intake heating element.

14   Remove the air intake heater from the manifold cover (see Chapter 4B).

15   Remove the high-pressure fuel lines that cross over the intake manifold cover.

16   On 2003 and later models, remove the Accelerator Pedal Position Sensor (APPS) bracket from the front of the cylinder head.

17   Disconnect the Manifold Air Temperature/Pressure sensor from the cylinder head (see Chapter 6).

18   Remove the intake manifold cover-to-cylinder head bolts.

19   Remove the intake manifold cover and gasket.

20   Stuff the air intake with shop rags and then carefully remove any old gasket material. Also clean off any gasket material from the intake manifold cover.

21   Installation is the reverse of removal. Be sure to use a new gasket. Tighten the intake manifold cover bolts to the torque listed in this Chapter's Specifications.

### 7   Exhaust manifold - removal and installation

1   Remove the turbocharger (see Chapter 4B).

2   Remove the bolts and brackets retaining the heater line(s) to the exhaust manifold (see illustration).

3   On models so equipped, remove the heat shield from the exhaust manifold. On 2007 and later 6.7L engines, remove the EGR Cooler (see Chapter 6).

4   Remove the exhaust manifold bolts, exhaust manifold, gaskets and the spacers (see illustration).

5   Clean the mounting surfaces of the manifold and the cylinder head, and clean the threads of the exhaust manifold mounting bolts.

6   Install the manifold using new gaskets and anti-seize compound on the bolt threads. Tighten the manifold bolts a little at a time, starting with the center bolts and working outward, to the torque listed in this Chapter's Specifications.

7   The remainder of installation is the reverse of removal.

### 8   Crankshaft front oil seal - replacement

1   Disconnect the cables from the negative terminals of the batteries (see Chapter 5).

2   Remove the drivebelt (see Chapter 1).

3   Remove the bolts retaining the damper to the crankshaft (see illustration).

4   Mark the relationship of the damper to the crankshaft and to the crankshaft position sensor (see illustration). Remove the crankshaft damper.

5   Using a drill with an 1/8-inch bit, drill two holes opposite each other in the front seal.

6   Using a slide-hammer with a #10 sheet-metal screw, thread the screw into each of the

**8.3 Remove the four bolts retaining the vibration damper to the crankshaft**

**8.4 Mark the damper's relationship to both the crankshaft and the sensor (above)**

**8.6 Use a sheetmetal screw and a small slide-hammer to pull the front seal out of the housing**

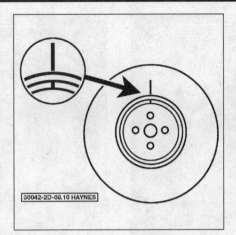

**8.10 The crankshaft damper index marks should not be more than 1/16 inch out of alignment**

**9.7a Loosen the clamp bolt (right arrow) on the oil filler tube, then remove the bolt retaining the clamp to the engine (left arrow) (1998 and earlier models)**

holes and pull out on the seal (see illustration). Alternate pulling on each hole until the seal is free from the housing.

7    Clean the sealing surface of the crankshaft snout thoroughly. There should be no oil on the sealing surface or the new seal may leak.

8    Apply sealant, such as Loctite 277 or equivalent, to the outer diameter of the new seal.

9    Using the plastic alignment/installation tool included with the new seal, drive the seal into the housing until it is seated to the same depth as the original seal.

10    Inspect the crankshaft damper before installing it onto the crankshaft. Inspect the index lines on the damper hub and the inertia member for alignment (see illustration). If they are more than 1/16-inch out of alignment, replace the crankshaft damper.

11    Reinstall the crankshaft damper, making sure the hole in the damper is positioned over the dowel pin.

12    Use the barring tool (see illustration 3.6b) to hold the flywheel stationary and tighten the crankshaft damper bolts to the torque listed in this Chapter's Specifications.

13    Install the drivebelt (refer to Chapter 1).

## 9    Gear housing cover - removal and installation

**Warning:** *Wait until the engine is completely cool before beginning this procedure.*

### *Removal*

1    Disconnect the cables from the negative terminals of the batteries (see Chapter 5, Sec-tion 1).

2    Remove the drivebelt, belt tensioner (see Chapter 1), the engine cooling fan and fan shroud (see Chapter 3).

3    Raise the vehicle and support it securely on jackstands.

4    Drain the coolant (see Chapter 1).

5    Remove the upper radiator hose (see Chapter 3).

6    Remove the windshield washer reservoir, if necessary.

7    On 1994 through 1998 models, remove the oil filler tube and elbow from the gear housing cover (see illustrations). On 2000 and later models, remove the crankcase breather and vent hose.

8    On 2003 and later models, remove the crankshaft sensor (see Chapter 6).

9    Remove the crankshaft damper (see Section 8). On 2003 and later models, remove

**9.7b Twist the upper portion of the oil filler tube and unscrew it from the lower elbow (arrow) (1998 and earlier models)**

**9.7c The oil filler elbow can now be twisted counterclockwise out of the front cover - note that the elbow covers the nut on the fuel injection pump (1998 and earlier models)**

**9.10a Use large pliers to grip the fan drive pulley while removing the bolts**

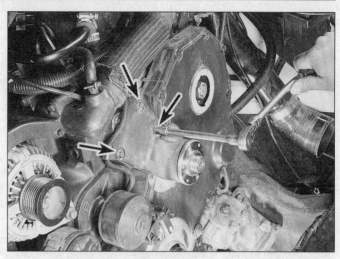

**9.10b Remove the three bolts and remove the fan support/hub assembly**

the crankshaft gear timing ring.

10   Unbolt the fan support/hub assembly from the engine block (see illustrations).

11   Remove the power steering pump (see Chapter 10).

12   On 1994 through 1998 models, remove the engine speed sensor retaining nuts and the sensor (see Chapter 6), and then remove the sensor mounting studs (see illustration). (On these models, the sensor mounting studs also serve as two of the gear housing cover bolts.) On all models, remove all bolts retaining the cover to the gear housing. Carefully pry off the cover.

**Note:** *Be careful not to damage the gasket sealing areas of the cover or the gear housing or oil leaks may result.*

## Installation

13   Visually inspect the camshaft, crankshaft

and oil pump drive gears for excessive wear, chips or cracks (see illustration).

14   Pry the original front seal from the cover. Clean the mounting surfaces of the cover and gear housing. Clean the front seal area of the crankshaft completely, or the new front seal may leak. Lubricate the gears with clean engine oil.

15   Install the cover, with a new gasket, onto the gear housing. Install the bolts, but leave them slightly loose. Install a special alignment tool onto the crankshaft to center the gear housing cover around the crankshaft. Tighten the cover bolts to the torque listed in this Chapter's Specifications.

16   Install the crankshaft front seal (see Section 8).

17   The remainder of the installation is the reverse of the removal procedure.

## 10   Camshaft and tappets - removal, inspection and installation

**Note:** *Camshaft and tappet replacement in the diesel engine is a very involved process. The diesel engine tappets have a head larger than the tappet body and must be inserted into their bores from the bottom of the bore. This results in a specialized procedure which requires several special tools. There are two methods for retaining the tappets for camshaft removal; read through the entire Section and obtain the special tools before beginning the procedure.*

1   If the vehicle is equipped with air conditioning, and you're planning to remove the camshaft with the engine installed in the vehicle, have the air conditioning system discharged by an automotive air condition-

**9.12 On 1998 and earlier models, remove the crankshaft position sensor retaining nuts, remove the sensor and then remove the two sensor mounting studs (arrows); on all models, remove the gear housing cover bolts**

**9.13 Inspect all of the gears in the case with the cover off**

| 1 | Oil pump gear | 5 | Vacuum pump/power |
|---|---|---|---|
| 2 | Idler gear | | steering pump gear |
| 3 | Crankshaft gear | 6 | Fuel injection pump gear |
| 4 | Camshaft gear | | |

**10.9a Remove the crankcase vent tube, the two screws and pull the plastic cover off**

**10.9b Remove these six bolts and pull off the side cover and its gasket**

ing shop before proceeding (you will have to remove the grille, radiator and condenser to remove the camshaft).

2    Remove the crankshaft damper (see Section 8) and the gear housing cover (see Section 9).

3    If you're planning to retain the tappets using Method Two, refer to Chapter 4B and remove the fuel transfer pump, the fuel filter/ water separator and the fuel injection pump.

4    Refer to Section 3 and position the engine at TDC for cylinder number 1.

5    Remove the valve covers (see Section 4), rocker arms and pushrods (see Section 5).

## Tappet retention

**Note:** *The tappets must be retained up in their bores, away from the camshaft lobes, in order to remove the camshaft.*

### Method one

6    A set of 12 wooden dowels, four inches longer than the pushrods and the correct diameter to just fit snugly into the top of the tappets, will be necessary for the procedure.

If you make your own and size them to fit, make sure that they are well-sanded with fine sandpaper and cleaned of sanding residue before use, so that no wood chips or sawdust contaminates the engine.

7    Insert the dowels down through the pushrod holes until they lodge firmly in the tappets. For each cylinder, pull up the two dowels (intake and exhaust) and secure them to each other with large rubber bands. There must be enough tension on the rubber bands to keep the tappets raised as far as they can go up in their bores.

8    When all of the tappets are secured at the top of their bores, the camshaft can be removed.

### Method two

9    A somewhat easier method of tappet retention can be accomplished if the engine is out of the vehicle for overhaul, or in-vehicle, if the fuel filter/water separator and fuel injection pump are removed (see Chapter 4B) allowing removal of the engine side cover (see illustrations).

10    Slip a small hose clamp over each tappet. Pull up the tappet to the top of its travel with a magnetic tool and tighten the hose clamp to keep the tappet at the top of its bore. Repeat this procedure for all of the tappets, tightening the clamps only enough to retain them at the top (see illustration).

## Camshaft removal

11    With the engine positioned at TDC, remove the two bolts retaining the camshaft thrust plate (see illustration).

**Caution:** *Be careful not to let the thrust plate fall into the crankcase.*

12    Pull the camshaft out as straight as possible. Be very careful not to nick any of the camshaft bearings in the block with the lobes or journals. Work slowly - it's a long and heavy camshaft.

**Note:** *Refer to Chapter 11 for removal of the radiator and air conditioning condenser, Chapter 4B for the intercooler removal and Chapter 3 for removal of the grille to allow room for camshaft extraction.*

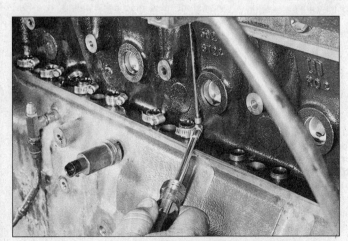

**10.10 With the side cover off, use a magnetic tool to lift each tappet up, then tighten a small hose clamp around the tappet to keep it there**

**10.11 Remove the two bolts retaining the camshaft thrust plate**

10.14 Insert the trough-like tool into the camshaft bore with the open side up - then pull the dowels, or as shown, release the hose clamp from one tappet at a time until it falls into the trough and can be withdrawn from the engine

10.17 Measure the camshaft lobe at its greatest dimension to determine the lobe height

## Tappet removal

13   A special tool is necessary to extract the tappets from the block. The tool is a long 1/2-section of pipe slightly smaller than the camshaft bore. The top of the pipe is removed, lengthwise, and one end capped. This "trough" may be available through your local dealer, or you can fabricate your own from copper tubing.

14   Insert the trough-like tool the full length of the camshaft bore, with the open side up (see illustration). Remove the rubber bands from two of the dowels, pull the dowel out of one tappet, and re-tie the other dowel with rubber bands to the valve spring or other nearby component. As the dowel is pulled out, that tappet will fall into the trough. Look through the trough with a flashlight to ensure that the tappet is laying on its side in the trough. If not, jiggle the trough to make it fall over and then extract the trough and retrieve the tappet.

15   Repeat this procedure for each tappet, keeping the tappets in order so they can be reinstalled in their original locations, until all of the tappets have been removed for inspection.

## Inspection

16   After the camshaft has been removed from the engine, cleaned with solvent and dried, inspect the bearing journals for uneven wear, pitting and evidence of seizure. If the journals are damaged, the bearing inserts in the block are probably damaged as well. Both the camshaft and bearings will have to be replaced.

**Note:** *Camshaft bearing replacement requires special tools and expertise that place it beyond the scope of the average home mechanic. Although the tool for bearing removal/ installation is available at stores that carry automotive tools and possibly even found at a tool rental business, if the bearings are bad and bearing replacement is beyond your ability, remove the engine and take the block to an automotive machine shop to ensure that the job is done correctly.*

17   Measure the bearing journals with a micrometer to determine if they are excessively worn or out-of-round. Measure the camshaft lobe height (see illustration). Compare your measurements with this Chapter's Specifications to determine if the camshaft is worn.

18   Check the camshaft lobes for heat discoloration, score marks, chipped areas, pitting and uneven wear. If the lobes are in good condition and if the journal diameters and lobe height measurements are as specified, the camshaft can be reused.

19   Check each tappet wall, pushrod seat and foot for scuffing, score marks and uneven wear. Each tappet foot (the surface that rides on the cam lobe) should be perfectly flat, although it may be slightly concave in normal wear (see illustration). If there are signs of uneven wear or scoring, the tappets and camshaft must be replaced. If the tappet walls are damaged or worn (which is not very likely), inspect the tappet bores in the engine block as well, using a small inspection mirror with a long handle. If the pushrod seats are worn, check the pushrod ends.

20   If new tappets are being installed, a new camshaft must also be installed. If a new camshaft is installed, then use new tappets as well. Never install used tappets unless the original camshaft is used and the tappets can be installed in their original locations.

21   Measure the thickness of the camshaft thrust plate with a micrometer. Refer to the Specifications listed in this Chapter. If the camshaft thrust plate is too thin or thick, replace it with a new one.

## Camshaft and tappet installation

22   A special tappet installation tool is needed to "fish" the new tappets up into their bores before the camshaft is installed. The installation tool is basically a long wire attached to a short plug that fits inside the tappet. This special tool is available through your dealer, or you can make your own.

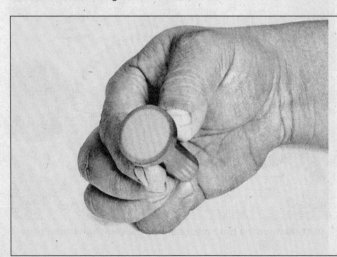

10.19 Examine the foot of the tappet for uneven wear or pitting - it should be perfectly flat

**10.23 You can make your own tappet installation tools: Our trough was made from a length of copper tubing, and the retrieval tool is a short section of hose that just fits into the tappet and is attached to a long piece of wire (you can get by without the hooked retrieval tool - simply pull the trough out to retrieve each tappet)**

**10.27 Lube the camshaft thoroughly with camshaft installation lube**

**10.28 Align the timing marks on the crankshaft and camshaft gears**

23    Insert the tappet trough tool fully into the camshaft bore and drop the tappet retrieval tool down through the pushrod hole from above until it hits the trough. Using the hooked retrieval tool (included with the tappet installation tool kit), pull the tappet installation tool out of the trough, then push the plug into the tappet, lubricate the sides and foot of the tappet with engine assembly lube and pull the wire back out the tappet hole until the tappet is seated in its bore. If you don't have the factory installation tools, make your own (see illustration). You can get by without the hooked retrieval tool; instead, carefully pull the trough out of the engine until the tappet installation tool is exposed.

24    Push the trough back into the engine fully, if removed, then from above, pull up on the wire until the tappet is at the top of its bore.

25    Now rotate the trough around until its closed side is UP, which will keep the tappet from falling out of its bore. The "fishing" tool can now be pulled out of the tappet and the dowel inserted and secured, retaining that tappet in place. If the side cover is off, secure the tappet with a hose clamp, as in Step 10.

26    Repeat Steps 22 to 24 for the remaining tappets until all are held high in their proper bores with the dowels and rubber bands, or hose clamps.

27    Lubricate the camshaft lobes and journals thoroughly with camshaft installation lubricant (see illustration) and insert the camshaft into the block, again being careful to insert it straight without nicking the bearings with the lobes or journals.

28    As the camshaft is close to being fully inserted, align the timing marks on the camshaft gear with the timing mark on the crankshaft gear (see illustration). When the camshaft is fully inserted and the gears properly

meshed, install the camshaft thrust plate bolts and tighten them to the torque listed in this Chapter's Specifications.

**Caution:** *Do not push the camshaft any further into the block than is necessary, or the camshaft plug at the back of the block could be loosened, creating an oil leak.*

29    All of the tappet retaining dowels or clamps may now be removed, and the pushrods, rocker arms and other components installed. Adjust the valve clearance as described in Section 5.

30    The remainder of the installation is the reverse of the removal procedure. If the side cover had been removed, install it with a new gasket. Change the engine oil and oil filter (see Chapter 1).

31    Have the air conditioning system evacuated, recharged and leak tested by the shop that discharged it.

## 11    Cylinder head - removal, inspection and installation

**Warning:** *Make sure the engine is completely cool before beginning this procedure.*

### Removal

1    Disconnect the cables from the negative terminals of the batteries (see Chapter 5).

2    Remove the drivebelt (see Chapter 6). Disconnect the water-in-fuel and fuel heater electrical connectors. Detach all engine harnesses and ground cables from the cylinder head. Remove the alternator (see Chapter 5) and unbolt the alternator bracket from the cylinder head. Disconnect the electrical connectors from the engine coolant temperature sensor, the Intake Air Temperature (IAT) sensor and the Manifold Air Pressure (MAP) sensor (see Chapter 1).

3    Drain the engine coolant (see Chapter 3). Detach the heater hoses from the exhaust manifold and from the cylinder head. Disconnect the upper radiator hose from the thermostat housing (see Chapter 1). Remove the heater hoses

and the radiator hose.

4    Remove the turbocharger and remove all fuel lines (see Chapter 4B). Don't forget to detach the fuel return lines at the rear of the cylinder head, if equipped. Remove the intake manifold cover (see Section 6) and the exhaust manifold (see Section 7). Remove the fuel filter/water separator (see Chapter 4B).

5    Remove the throttle linkage cover, remove the Accelerator Pedal Position Sensor (APPS)-to-cylinder head bracket bolts, set the APPS assembly aside and disconnect the APPS electrical connector (see Chapter 6). Disconnect the injector harness connectors (2003 and later models).

6    Remove the valve cover(s) (see Section 4) and the rocker arm assemblies and pushrods (see Section 5).

7    Using a new head gasket, make a template of the bolt hole locations on a piece of cardboard (see illustration). Loosen the head bolts, working in the order opposite that of the tightening sequence (see illustration 11.21). As each head bolt is removed, insert it into its location on the cardboard template.

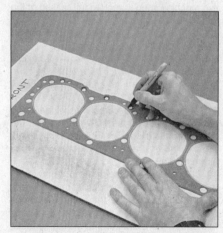

**11.7 Use a new head gasket to trace the bolt pattern on a piece of cardboard - punch holes for the head bolts and use the cardboard to keep track of the locations of the bolts**

**11.12 Use a gasket scraper and gasket removing solvent to clean the cylinder head and block sealing surfaces**

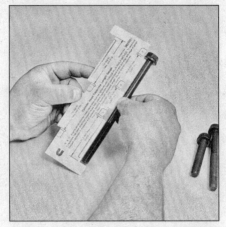

**11.15 A head bolt stretch gauge (included with the gasket set) is used to determine if the cylinder heads bolts can be reused**

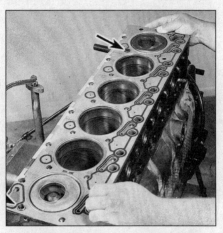

**11.18 Position the new head gasket over the dowels in the block - note any markings on the gasket that indicate Top or Front**

8    Make a thorough inspection of the head for any wiring harnesses and/or ground cables that might still be attached to the head. Make sure that all components have been removed or detached from the head. When you're sure that nothing more is attached to the head, carefully pry on a casting protrusion between the head and the block to break the head gasket seal. The cylinder head is quite heavy, so have an assistant help you lift it off the engine. If any assistant is not available, attach an engine lifting hoist to the lifting brackets at the front and rear of the cylinder head and lift out the head.
**Warning:** *Do NOT attempt to remove the head by yourself!*

## Inspection

9    The cylinder head is a vital part of the engine's efficiency. If you have gone to the trouble to remove it, to replace the head gasket, for example, and the engine has accumulated many, many miles, consider having the valves and seats refaced at an automotive machine shop to restore full sealing of the valves.
10    Remove the fuel injectors and rocker housing from the cylinder head.
**Note:** *Fuel injector removal requires special tools (see Chapter 4B). These tools are commonly available through aftermarket tool suppliers.*
11    The mating surfaces of the cylinder head and block must be perfectly clean when the heads are installed. Gasket removal solvents are available at auto parts stores and may prove helpful.
12    Use a gasket scraper to remove all traces of carbon and old gasket material (see illustration), then wipe the mating surfaces with a cloth saturated with lacquer thinner or acetone. If there is oil on the mating surfaces when the head is installed, the gasket may not seal correctly and leaks may develop. When working on the block, fill the cylinders with shop rags to keep debris out of the engine. Use a vacuum cleaner to remove any debris

that falls into the cylinders.
**Note:** *Clean any carbon from the injector nozzle seats with a brass or nylon brush.*
13    Check the block and head mating surfaces for nicks, deep scratches and other damage. If imperfections are slight, they can be removed with emery cloth. If excessive, machining may be the only alternative. Use a straightedge and feeler gauge to check the cylinder head for warpage. If it is not within Specifications, the head must be machined to restore flatness. Consult with an automotive machine shop.
**Note:** *There is a raised pad at the rear of the cylinder head. There may be stampings there to indicate whether the head has been machined before. More than 0.010-inch removal may require valve regrinding as well. Consult with an automotive machine shop.*
14    The block deck surface should also be checked for warping by using a precision straightedge and feeler gauges. Compare your findings with the limits listed in this Chapter's Specifications.
15    Use a tap of the correct size to chase the threads in the head bolt holes in the block. Mount each bolt in a vise and run a die down the threads to remove corrosion and restore the threads. Dirt, corrosion, sealant and damaged threads will affect torque readings. Measure the length of each cylinder head bolt, from under the bolt head to the end of the threads, comparing your measurements to the maximum bolt length listed in this Chapter's Specifications. Most engine gaskets sets will include a bolt stretch gauge for the head bolts (see illustration). If the head bolts are longer than the allowable length indicated on the gauge, they are stretched and must be replaced with new bolts.
16    If removed, have the rocker housing and fuel injectors reinstalled by the shop that removed them.

## Installation

17    2003 and later models only: Using a surface micrometer or a vernier or dial caliper,

measure the protrusion of each piston from the block deck. Calculate the average piston protrusion; this will be necessary when you go to purchase a new head gasket, as two different thicknesses of gasket are available. One gasket is for an average piston protrusion of less than 0.011-inch, the other for an average piston protrusion of greater than 0.011-inch.
18    Position the new gasket over the dowels in the block (see illustration).
19    Carefully position the cylinder head on the block without disturbing the gasket.
20    Apply engine oil to the threads and underneath the bolt heads.
21    Install the bolts in their original locations and tighten them finger-tight. Following the recommended sequence (see illustration), tighten the bolts in several steps to the torque listed in this Chapter's Specifications.
22    The remainder of the installation is the reverse of the removal procedure. Refer to Chapter 1 and change the oil and filter and refill the cooling system.
23    Refer to Chapter 4B and bleed or prime the fuel system before attempting to start the engine.

## 12  Oil pump - removal, inspection and installation

1    Disconnect the cables from the negative terminals of the batteries (see Chapter 5).
2    Drain the engine oil (see Chapter 1).
3    Remove the gear housing cover (see Section 9).
4    Measure the backlash between the gears using a dial indicator. Install the dial indicator tip against one of the teeth on the idler gear and twist the idler gear back and forth (see illustration). This will give the backlash measurement between the crankshaft gear and the idler gear. Compare it to this Chapter's Specifications.
5    Place the dial indicator tip on the oil pump drive gear and check the backlash between it and the idler gear while securely holding the

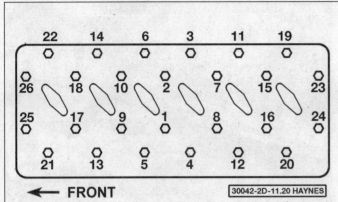

11.21 Cylinder head bolt tightening sequence

12.4 With the dial indicator tip positioned against the idler gear, rotate the idler gear and compare its backlash to the Specifications

idler gear from moving (see illustration). If the backlash is greater than that listed in this Chapter's Specifications for either gear, the gears must be replaced.

6    Remove the four mounting bolts and remove the oil pump assembly from the gear case (see illustration).

7    Remove the back plate of the oil pump assembly (see illustration). Clean the top of the gerotor planetary of oil and mark it with the word TOP with a felt pen or paint.

8    Remove the components, clean them with solvent and dry them thoroughly. Assemble the components back in the oil pump housing.

**Note:** *The chamfer on the outside diameter of the gerotor planetary must face down, into the housing. Using a feeler gauge measure the* planetary-to-body clearance, the tip clearance and the gerotor-to-back plate clearance (see illustrations). If any clearance is beyond that listed in this Chapter's Specifications, replace the oil pump assembly.

9    If the original pump is being reused, fill

12.5 Check the backlash at the drive gear while holding the idler gear

12.6 Remove the four mounting bolts to remove the oil pump from the gear case

12.7 Remove the two screws on the back plate, then mark the top of the gerotor planetary with a felt marker

12.8a Measure the gerotor-to-planetary tip clearance with a feeler gauge

12.8b Measure the gerotor planetary-to-body clearance

12.8c Using the feeler gauge and a straightedge, measure the gerotor-to-back plate clearance

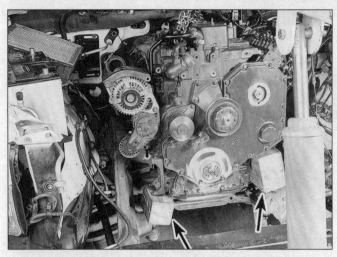

**13.3 Support the engine with an engine hoist, two large wood blocks, and place a floor jack under the transmission**

**13.5 With the engine safely supported, remove the oil pan bolts**

the pump cavity with engine oil and reinstall the back cover, then install the pump assembly in the gear case and tighten the mounting bolts to the torque listed in this Chapter's Specifications.

10   The remainder of the installation is the reverse of the disassembly procedure. Refill the crankcase with oil, start the engine, check for leaks and proper oil pressure.

## 13   Oil pan - removal and installation

### *Removal*

1   Disconnect the cables from the negative terminals of the batteries (see Chapter 5, Section 1).

2   Drain the engine oil (see Chapter 1).

3   Attach an engine hoist to the engine lift brackets, raise the engine slightly and remove the through-bolts from the engine mounts (see Section 17). Continue to raise the engine until the engine mounts clear the brackets, then remove the engine mounts. Place two large wood blocks on the frame rails and lower the

weight of the engine onto the wood blocks (see illustration). Support the transmission with a floor jack.

**Caution:** *Check the clearance of the engine components as you raise the engine. If necessary, remove the cooling fan and fan shroud.*

4   If equipped with an automatic transmission, disconnect the transmission oil cooler line clips at the oil pan.

5   Remove the oil pan bolts and use a putty knife between the block and the pan to break the gasket seal (see illustration).

**Caution:** *Do not gouge the sealing surfaces with a screwdriver or pry tool.*

6   Lower the pan to access and remove the two bolts retaining the oil suction tube near the front of the block (see illustration). Lower the suction tube into the oil pan and remove the oil pan and suction tube together.

### *Installation*

7   Clean the interior of the oil pan with rags and solvent and clean the oil suction tube, blowing it out with compressed air if available. Also clean the pan mounting surface of the block of any sealant, gasket material or oil.

8   On the engine, apply a small bead of RTV sealant to the block and front cover joints, and the block and the rear seal retainer joints.

9   Attach a new gasket to the oil suction tube mounting flange and place the suction tube into the pan, with the mounting flange at the front.

10   Raise the oil pan up next to the block and attach the oil suction tube to the block. Install the oil pan. Tighten the bolts, starting in the center and working toward the ends, to the torque listed in this Chapter's Specifications.

11   Install the oil pan drain plug with a new sealing washer and tighten it to the torque listed in this Chapter's Specifications.

12   Refill the engine with new oil (see Chapter 1). The remainder of installation is the reverse of removal. Start the engine and check for oil leaks.

## 14   Oil pressure relief valve - replacement

1   Disconnect the cables from the negative terminals of the batteries (see Chapter 5).

2   Remove the threaded plug, spring and plunger from the oil filter/cooler assembly.

3   Clean the oil pressure relief valve bore thoroughly with solvent and compressed air.

4   Install the plunger, spring and plug and torque the oil pressure relief valve plug to the torque values listed in this Chapter's Specifications.

## 15   Flywheel/driveplate - removal and installation

1   Flywheel/driveplate removal and installation for the diesel engine is principally the same as for the gasoline engines. Refer to Chapter 2A for procedures, but use the torque

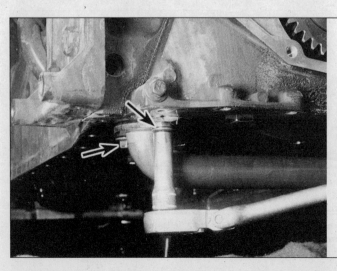

**13.6 Lower the oil pan and remove the suction tube bolts at the front of the engine**

**16.3a Remove the bolts to remove the engine-to-transmission adapter . . .**

**16.3b . . . for access to the rear main seal retainer, held to the block with six bolts**

Specifications in this Chapter's Specifications. Always use new bolts when the flywheel/driveplate is reinstalled, and apply Loctite 242 on the threads.

## 16   Rear main oil seal - replacement

1    Rear seal removal and installation for the diesel engine is the same as for the gasoline engines (refer to Chapter 2A).
2    The rear seal can be removed with the rear seal retainer plate in place, or by removing the retainer plate and replacing the seal off the engine. If the seal is replaced with the retainer plate still on the engine, an alternate method may be used to remove it; drill holes in the seal and use a slide-hammer as described in Section 8.
3    If the rear seal retainer plate is to be removed, the engine-to-transmission adapter must be removed first (see illustrations).
4    There are two types of rear seals. On seals with a rubber outer diameter, use soapy water around the outside during installation into the retainer plate. The seals without a rubber edge should be installed with Loctite 277 around the outer diameter.

**Caution:** *DO NOT use oil on the seal lip or crankshaft during installation - the crankshaft sealing surface and the oil seal must be clean and dry or oil leaks may result.*

## 17   Engine mounts – inspection and replacement

1    Refer to Chapter 2A for this procedure. Tighten all the engine mount and through-bolts securely.

# Notes

# Chapter 2 Part E
# General engine overhaul procedures

## Contents

## Specifications

### General

Displacement
| | |
|---|---|
| 3.7L V6 | 226 cubic inches |
| 3.9L V6 | 239 cubic inches |
| 4.7L V8 | 287 cubic inches |
| 5.2L V8 | 318 cubic inches |
| 5.7L V8 (Hemi) | 345 cubic inches |
| 5.9L V8 | 360 cubic inches |
| 8.0L V10 | 488 cubic inches |
| 5.9L diesel | 360 cubic inches |
| 6.7L diesel | 409 cubic inches |

Bore and stroke
| | |
|---|---|
| 3.7L V6 | 3.66 x 3.40 inches |
| 3.9L V6 | 3.91 x 3.31 inches |
| 4.7L V8 | 3.66 x 3.40 inches |
| 5.7L V8 (Hemi) | 3.91 x 3.58 inches |
| 5.2L V8 | 3.91 x 3.31 inches |
| 5.9L V8 | 4.00 x 3.58 inches |
| 8.0L V10 | 4.00 x 3.88 inches |
| 5.9L diesel | 4.02 x 4.72 inches |
| 6.7L diesel | 4.21 x 4.88 inches |

Cylinder compression pressure

3.7L V6 and 4.7L V8
| | |
|---|---|
| Minimum | 170 psi |
| Maximum variation between cylinders | 40 psi |

5.7L V8 (Hemi) ... Not available, but pressure should not vary more than 40 psi between cylinders

3.9L V6, 5.2L V8, 5.9L V8 and 8.0L V10
| | |
|---|---|
| Minimum | 100 psi |
| Maximum variation between cylinders | 40 psi |

Diesel*
| | |
|---|---|
| Minimum | 350 psi |
| Maximum variation between cylinders | 70 psi |

### Oil pump pressure

3.7L V6, 4.7L V8 and 5.7L V8 (Hemi)
| | |
|---|---|
| Minimum pressure at curb idle | 4 psi |
| Operating pressure | 25 to 110 psi at 3,000 rpm |

3.9L V6, 5.2L V8 and 5.9L V8
| | |
|---|---|
| Minimum pressure at curb idle | 6 psi |
| Operating pressure | 30 to 80 psi at 3,000 rpm |

Diesel
| | |
|---|---|
| Minimum pressure at curb idle | 10 psi |
| Operating pressure | 30 psi at 2,500 rpm |

8.0L V10
| | |
|---|---|
| Minimum pressure at curb idle | 12 psi |
| Operating pressure | 50 to 60 psi at 3,000 rpm |

**Warning:***Checking compression on the diesel engine requires several special tools in addition to a special compression gauge, therefore the procedure is not included in this manual.*

## Torque specifications

**Ft-lbs** (unless otherwise indicated)

**Note:** *One foot-pound (ft-lb) of torque is equivalent to 12 inch-pounds (in-lbs) of torque. Torque values below approximately 15 ft-lbs are expressed in inch-pounds, because most foot-pound torque wrenches are not accurate at these smaller values.*

Connecting rod cap bolts
  3.7L V6 and 4.7L V8 engines
    Step 1 ................................................................. 20
    Step 2 ................................................................. Tighten an additional 90-degrees
  5.7L V8 (Hemi) engines
    Step 1 ................................................................. 15
    Step 2 ................................................................. Tighten an additional 90-degrees
  3.9L V6, 5.2L V8, 5.9L V8 and 8.0L V10 engines ............. 45
  5.9L diesel engines
    2002 and earlier models
      Step 1
        2001 and earlier models.............................. 26
        2002 models................................................ 28
      Step 2 ......................................................... 51
      Step 3 ......................................................... 73
    2003 and later models
      Step 1 ......................................................... 22
      Step 2 ......................................................... 44
      Step 3 ......................................................... Tighten an additional 60-degrees
  6.7L diesel engines
    Step 1 ................................................................. 22
    Step 2 ................................................................. 44
    Step 3 ................................................................. Tighten an additional 60-degrees
Main bearing cap bolts/bedplate assembly
  3.7L V6 bedplate fasteners (see illustration 10.20a)
    Step 1, bolts 4, 7 and 6.................................... Hand-tight until bedplate contacts block mating surface
    Step 2, bolts 1 through 10................................. 40
    Step 3, bolts 11 through 18............................... 60 in-lbs
    Step 4, bolts 11 through 18............................... Tighten an additional 90-degrees
    Step 5, bolts 19 through 23............................... 20
  4.7L V8 bedplate fasteners (see illustration 10.20b)
    Step 1, bolts 1 through 12................................. 40
    Step 2, bolts 13 through 22............................... 25 in-lbs
    Step 3, bolts 13 through 22............................... Tighten an additional 90-degrees
    Step 4, bolts 23 through 28............................... 20
  5.7L V8 (Hemi) engine* (see illustration 10.20c)
    Step 1, bolts 1 through 10................................. 20
    Step 2, bolts 1 through 10................................. Tighten an additional 90-degrees
    Step 3, crossbolts 11 through 20 ...................... 21
    Step 4, crossbolts 11 through 20 ...................... 21 (re-check)
  3.6L V6, 5.2L V8, 5.9L V8 and 8.0L V10 engines
    Step 1 ................................................................. 20
    Step 2 ................................................................. 85
  5.9L diesel engine
    2001 and earlier models
      Step 1 ......................................................... 44
      Step 2 ......................................................... 88
      Step 3 ......................................................... 129
    2002 and later models
      Step 1 ......................................................... 37
      Step 2 ......................................................... 59
      Step 3 ......................................................... Tighten an additional 90-degrees
  6.7L diesel engines
    Used bolts
      Step 1 ......................................................... 44
      Step 2 ......................................................... 59
      Step 3 ......................................................... Tighten an additional 90-degrees
    New bolts
      Step 1 ......................................................... 89
      Step 2 ......................................................... Loosen one full turn
      Step 3 ......................................................... 44
      Step 4 ......................................................... 63
      Step 5 ......................................................... Tighten an additional 120-degrees

*\*Install a new washer/seal onto each crossbolt before tightening. First, install main bearing bolts and main bearing crossbolts all finger-tight. Next torque the main bearing bolts completely (Steps 1 and 2) before torquing the crossbolts.*

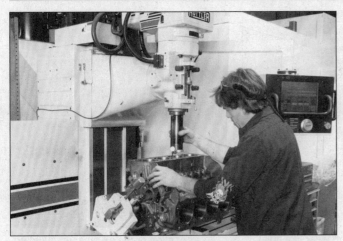

**1.10a An engine block being bored. An engine rebuilder will use special machinery to recondition the cylinder bores**

**1.10b If the cylinders are bored, the machine shop will normally hone the engine on a machine like this**

## 1 General information - engine overhaul

1 Included in this portion of Chapter 2 are general information and diagnostic testing procedures for determining the overall mechanical condition of your engine.

2 The information ranges from advice concerning preparation for an overhaul and the purchase of replacement parts and/or components to detailed, step-by-step procedures covering removal and installation.

3 The following Sections have been written to help you determine whether your engine needs to be overhauled and how to remove and install it once you've determined it needs to be rebuilt. For information concerning in-vehicle engine repair, see Chapter 2A, Chapter 2B, Chapter 2C or Chapter 2D.

4 The Specifications included in this Part are general in nature and include only those necessary for testing the oil pressure and checking the engine compression. Refer to Chapter 2A, Chapter 2B, Chapter 2C or Chapter 2D for additional engine Specifications.

5 It's not always easy to determine when, or if, an engine should be completely overhauled, because a number of factors must be considered.

6 High mileage is not necessarily an indication that an overhaul is needed, while low mileage doesn't preclude the need for an overhaul. Frequency of servicing is probably the most important consideration. An engine that's had regular and frequent oil and filter changes, as well as other required maintenance, will most likely give many thousands of miles of reliable service. Conversely, a neglected engine may require an overhaul very early in its service life.

7 Excessive oil consumption is an indication that piston rings, valve seals and/or valve guides are in need of attention. Make sure that oil leaks aren't responsible before deciding that the rings and/or guides are bad. Perform a cylinder compression check to determine

the extent of the work required (see Section 4). Also, on gasoline engines, check the vacuum readings under various conditions (see Section 3).

8 Check the oil pressure with a gauge installed in place of the oil pressure sending unit (see Section 2) and compare it to this Chapter's Specifications. If it's extremely low, the bearings and/or oil pump are probably worn out.

9 Loss of power, rough running, knocking or metallic engine noises, excessive valve train noise and high fuel consumption rates may also point to the need for an overhaul, especially if they're all present at the same time. If a complete tune-up doesn't remedy the situation, major mechanical work is the only solution.

10 An engine overhaul involves restoring the internal parts to the specifications of a new engine. During an overhaul, the piston rings are replaced and the cylinder walls are reconditioned (rebored and/or honed) (see illustrations 1.10a and 1.10b). If a rebore is done by an automotive machine shop, new oversize pistons will also be installed. The main bearings, connecting rod bearings and camshaft

bearings are generally replaced with new ones and, if necessary, the crankshaft may be reground to restore the journals (see illustration 1.10c). Generally, the valves are serviced as well, since they're usually in less-than-perfect condition at this point. While the engine is being overhauled, other components, such as the distributor, starter and alternator, can be rebuilt as well. The end result should be similar to a new engine that will give many trouble free miles.

**Note:** *Critical cooling system components such as the hoses, drivebelts, thermostat and water pump should be replaced with new parts when an engine is overhauled. The radiator should be checked carefully to ensure that it isn't clogged or leaking (see Chapter 3). If you purchase a rebuilt engine or short block, some rebuilders will not warranty their engines unless the radiator has been professionally flushed. Also, we don't recommend overhauling the oil pump - always install a new one when an engine is rebuilt.*

11 Overhauling the internal components on today's engines is a difficult and time-consuming task which requires a significant amount of specialty tools and is best left to a

**1.10c A crankshaft having a main bearing journal ground**

**1.11a A machinist checks for a bent connecting rod, using specialized equipment**

**1.11b A bore gauge being used to check a cylinder bore**

**1.11c Uneven piston wear like this indicates a bent connecting rod**

**2.2a Location of the oil pressure sending unit on 3.7L V6 and 4.7L V8 engines**

professional engine rebuilder (see illustrations 1.11a, 1.11b and 1.11c). A competent engine rebuilder will handle the inspection of your old parts and offer advice concerning the reconditioning or replacement of the original engine. Never purchase parts or have machine work done on other components until the block has been thoroughly inspected by a professional machine shop. As a general rule, time is the primary cost of an overhaul, especially since the vehicle may be tied up for a minimum of two weeks or more. Be aware that some engine builders only have the capability to rebuild the engine you bring them while other rebuilders have a large inventory of rebuilt exchange engines in stock. Also be aware that many machine shops could take as much as two weeks time to completely rebuild your engine depending on shop workload. Sometimes it makes more sense to simply exchange your engine for another engine that's already rebuilt to save time.

## 2   Oil pressure check

1    Low engine oil pressure can be a sign of an engine in need of rebuilding. A "low oil pressure" indicator (often called an "idiot light") is not a test of the oiling system. Such indicators only come on when the oil pressure is dangerously low. Even a factory oil pressure gauge in the instrument panel is only a relative indication, although much better for driver information than a warning light. A better test is with a mechanical (not electrical) oil pressure gauge.

2    Locate the oil pressure indicator sending unit on the engine block. The oil pressure sending unit is located in various locations depending upon engine type:

a)  *On 3.7L V6 and 4.7L V8 engines, the oil pressure sending unit is located near the timing chain cover next to the oil filter (see illustration).*

b)  *On Hemi engines, the oil pressure sending unit is located on the oil filter housing above the oil filter (see illustration).*

c)  *On 3.9L V6, 5.2L V8 and 5.9L V8 engines, the oil pressure sending unit is located next to the distributor (see illustration).*

d)  *On 8.0L V10 engines, the oil pressure sending unit is below the starter at the top of the oil filter housing (see illustration).*

e)  *On diesel engines, the oil pressure sending unit is located on the left side of the engine block, under the fuel transfer pump (see illustration).*

3    Unscrew and remove the oil pressure sending unit and then screw in the hose for your oil pressure gauge (see illustration). If necessary, install an adapter fitting. Use Teflon tape or thread sealant on the threads of the adapter and/or the fitting on the end of your gauge's hose.

**2.2b Location of the oil pressure sending unit on Hemi engines**

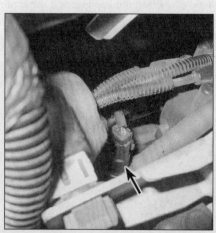

**2.2c Location of the oil pressure sending unit on 3.9L V6, 5.2L V8 and 5.9L V8 engines**

**2.2d Location of the oil pressure sending unit on 8.0L V10 engines**

**2.2e Location of the oil pressure sending unit on the diesel engine**

4   Connect an accurate tachometer to the engine, according to the tachometer manufacturer's instructions.

5   Check the oil pressure with the engine running (normal operating temperature) at the specified engine speed, and compare it to this Chapter's Specifications. If it's extremely low, the bearings and/or oil pump are probably worn out.

## 3   Cylinder compression check

### Gasoline engines

1   A compression check will tell you what mechanical condition the upper end of your engine (pistons, rings, valves, head gaskets) is in. Specifically, it can tell you if the compression is down due to leakage caused by worn piston rings, defective valves and seats or a blown head gasket.

**Note:** *The engine must be at normal operating temperature and the battery must be fully charged for this check.*

2   Begin by cleaning the area around the spark plugs before you remove them (compressed air should be used, if available). The idea is to prevent dirt from getting into the cylinders as the compression check is being done.

3   Disable the ignition system by unplugging the primary (low voltage) electrical connector from the distributor (3.9LV6, 2.5L V8 and 5.9L V8 engines) or from the ignition coil assemblies (all other engines) (see Chapter 4A) and by removing the fuel pump relay (see Chapter 5).

4   If you're working on a 5.7L V8 (Hemi) engine, remove one spark plug from each cylinder; on all other engines, remove all of the spark plugs from the engine (see Chapter 1).

5   Block the throttle wide open.

6   Install a compression gauge in the spark plug hole (see illustration).

7   Crank the engine over at least seven compression strokes and watch the gauge. The compression should build up quickly in a healthy engine. Low compression on the first stroke, followed by gradually increasing pressure on successive strokes, indicates worn piston rings. A low compression reading on the first stroke, which doesn't build up during successive strokes, indicates leaking valves or a blown head gasket (a cracked head could also be the cause). Deposits on the undersides of the valve heads can also cause low compression. Record the highest gauge reading obtained.

8   Repeat the procedure for the remaining cylinders and compare the results to this Chapter's Specifications.

9   Add some engine oil (about three squirts from a plunger-type oil can) to each cylinder, through the spark plug hole, and repeat the test.

10   If the compression increases after the oil is added, the piston rings are definitely worn. If the compression doesn't increase significantly, the leakage is occurring at the valves or head gasket. Leakage past the valves may

be caused by burned valve seats and/or faces or warped, cracked or bent valves.

11   If two adjacent cylinders have equally low compression, there's a strong possibility that the head gasket between them is blown. The appearance of coolant in the combustion chambers or the crankcase would verify this condition.

12   If one cylinder is slightly lower than the others, and the engine has a slightly rough idle, a worn lobe on the camshaft could be the cause.

13   If the compression is unusually high, the combustion chambers are probably coated with carbon deposits. If that's the case, the cylinder head(s) should be removed and decarbonized.

14   If compression is way down or varies greatly between cylinders, it would be a good idea to have a leak-down test performed by an automotive repair shop. This test will pinpoint exactly where the leakage is occurring and how severe it is.

### Diesel engine

15   To test the compression on the diesel engine, the fuel injectors must be removed and a special compression gauge installed to measure the much higher compression readings. Have the compression checked by a dealer service department or other qualified automotive repair facility.

## 4   Vacuum gauge diagnostic checks

**Note:** *This procedure applies only to gasoline engines.*

1   A vacuum gauge provides inexpensive but valuable information about what is going on in the engine. You can check for worn rings or cylinder walls, leaking head or intake manifold gaskets, incorrect carburetor adjustments, restricted exhaust, stuck or burned valves, weak valve springs, improper ignition or valve timing and ignition problems.

**2.3 Install an oil pressure gauge into the block after removing the oil pressure sending unit - Hemi engine shown**

**3.6 Use a compression gauge with a threaded fitting for the spark plug hole, not the type that requires hand pressure to maintain the seal**

**4.4 A simple vacuum gauge can be handy in diagnosing engine condition and performance**

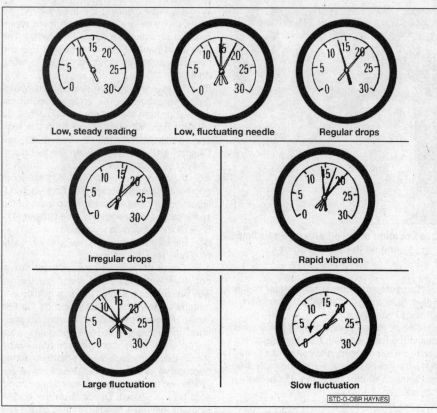

Low, steady reading     Low, fluctuating needle     Regular drops

Irregular drops     Rapid vibration

Large fluctuation     Slow fluctuation

STD-O-OBR HAYNES

**4.6 Typical vacuum gauge readings**

2    Unfortunately, vacuum gauge readings are easy to misinterpret, so they should be used in conjunction with other tests to confirm the diagnosis.

3    Both the absolute readings and the rate of needle movement are important for accurate interpretation. Most gauges measure vacuum in inches of mercury (in-Hg). The following references to vacuum assume the diagnosis is being performed at sea level. As elevation increases (or atmospheric pressure decreases), the reading will decrease. For every 1,000 foot increase in elevation above approximately 2,000 feet, the gauge readings will decrease about one inch of mercury.

4    Connect the vacuum gauge directly to the intake manifold vacuum, not to ported (throttle body) vacuum (see illustration). Some models are equipped with a vacuum fitting built into the brake booster vacuum hose grommet at the brake booster. Other models are equipped with a vacuum hose fitting on the intake manifold. Use a T-fitting to access the vacuum signal. Be sure no hoses are left disconnected during the test or false readings will result.

5    Before you begin the test, allow the engine to warm up completely. Block the wheels and set the parking brake. With the transmission in Park, start the engine and allow it to run at normal idle speed. **Warning:** *Keep your hands and the vacuum gauge clear of the fans.*

6    Read the vacuum gauge; an average, healthy engine should normally produce about 17 to 22 in-Hg with a fairly steady needle (see illustration). Refer to the following vacuum gauge readings and what they indicate about the engine's condition:

7    A low, steady reading usually indicates a leaking gasket between the intake manifold and cylinder head(s) or throttle body, a leaky vacuum hose, late ignition timing or incorrect camshaft timing. Check ignition timing with a timing light and eliminate all other possible causes, utilizing the tests provided in this

Chapter before you remove the timing chain cover to check the timing marks.

8    If the reading is three to eight inches below normal and it fluctuates at that low reading, suspect an intake manifold gasket leak at an intake port or a faulty fuel injector.

9    If the needle has regular drops of about two-to-four inches at a steady rate, the valves are probably leaking. Perform a compression check or leak-down test to confirm this.

10    An irregular drop or down-flick of the needle can be caused by a sticking valve or an ignition misfire. Perform a compression check or leak-down test and read the spark plugs.

11    A rapid vibration of about four in-Hg vibration at idle combined with exhaust smoke indicates worn valve guides. Perform a leak-down test to confirm this. If the rapid vibration occurs with an increase in engine speed, check for a leaking intake manifold gasket or head gasket, weak valve springs, burned valves or ignition misfire.

12    A slight fluctuation, say one inch up and down, may mean ignition problems. Check all the usual tune-up items and, if necessary, run the engine on an ignition analyzer.

13    If there is a large fluctuation, perform a compression or leak-down test to look for a weak or dead cylinder or a blown head gasket.

14    If the needle moves slowly through a wide range, check for a clogged PCV system, incorrect idle fuel mixture, throttle body or intake manifold gasket leaks.

15    Check for a slow return after revving the engine by quickly snapping the throttle open until the engine reaches about 2,500 rpm and let it shut. Normally the reading should drop to near zero, rise above normal idle reading (about 5 in-Hg over) and then return to the previous idle reading. If the vacuum returns slowly and doesn't peak when the throttle is snapped shut, the rings may be worn. If there is a long delay, look for a restricted exhaust system (often the muffler or catalytic converter). An easy way to check this is to temporarily disconnect the exhaust ahead of the suspected part and redo the test.

## 5   Engine rebuilding alternatives

1    The do-it-yourselfer is faced with a number of options when purchasing a rebuilt engine. The major considerations are cost, warranty, parts availability and the time required for the rebuilder to complete the project. The decision to replace the engine block, piston/connecting rod assemblies and crankshaft depends on the final inspection results of your engine. Only then can you make a cost effective decision whether to have your engine overhauled or simply purchase an exchange engine for your vehicle.

2    Some of the rebuilding alternatives include:

3    **Individual parts** - If the inspection procedures reveal that the engine block and most

**6.3a After tightly wrapping water-vulnerable components, use a spray cleaner on everything, with particular concentration on the greasiest areas, usually around the valve cover and lower edges of the block. If one section dries out, apply more cleaner**

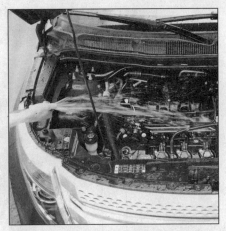

**6.3b Depending on how dirty the engine is, let the cleaner soak in according to the directions and then hose off the grime and cleaner. Get the rinse water down into every area you can get at; then dry important components with a hair dryer or paper towels**

**6.6 Get an engine stand sturdy enough to firmly support the engine while you're working on it. Stay away from three-wheeled models; they have a tendency to tip over more easily, so get a four-wheeled unit**

engine components are in reusable condition, purchasing individual parts and having a rebuilder rebuild your engine may be the most economical alternative. The block, crankshaft and piston/connecting rod assemblies should all be inspected carefully by a machine shop first.

4    **Short block** - A short block consists of an engine block with a crankshaft and piston/connecting rod assemblies already installed. All new bearings are incorporated and all clearances will be correct. The existing camshafts, valve train components, cylinder head and external parts can be bolted to the short block with little or no machine shop work necessary.

5    **Long block** - A long block consists of a short block plus an oil pump, oil pan, cylinder head, valve cover, camshaft and valve train components, timing sprockets and chain or gears and timing cover. All components are installed with new bearings, seals and gaskets incorporated throughout. The installation of manifolds and external parts is all that's necessary.

6    **Low mileage used engines** – Some companies now offer low mileage used engines which is a very cost effective way to get your vehicle up and running again. These engines often come from vehicles which have been totaled in accidents or come from other countries which have a higher vehicle turn over rate. A low mileage used engine also usually has a similar warranty like the newly remanufactured engines.

7    Give careful thought to which alternative is best for you and discuss the situation with local automotive machine shops, auto parts dealers and experienced rebuilders before ordering or purchasing replacement parts.

## 6    Engine removal - methods and precautions

1    If you've decided that an engine must be removed for overhaul or major repair work, several preliminary steps should be taken. Read all removal and installation procedures carefully prior to committing to this job.

2    Locating a suitable place to work is extremely important. Adequate work space, along with storage space for the vehicle, will be needed. If a shop or garage isn't available, at the very least a flat, level, clean work surface made of concrete or asphalt is required.

3    Cleaning the engine compartment and engine before beginning the removal procedure will help keep tools clean and organized (see illustrations).

4    An engine hoist will also be necessary. Make sure the hoist is rated in excess of the weight of the engine. Safety is of primary importance, considering the potential hazards involved in removing the engine from the vehicle. If you're removing a diesel or a V10 engine, you'll need a heavy duty engine hoist and a heavy duty engine stand.

5    If you're a novice at engine removal, get at least one helper. One person cannot easily do all the things you need to do to remove a big heavy engine and transmission assembly from the engine compartment. Also helpful is to seek advice and assistance from someone who's experienced in engine removal.

6    Plan the operation ahead of time. Arrange for or obtain all of the tools and equipment you'll need prior to beginning the job (see illustration). Some of the equipment necessary to perform engine removal and installation safely and with relative ease are

(in addition to an engine hoist) a heavy duty floor jack (preferably fitted with a transmission jack head adapter), complete sets of wrenches and sockets as described in the front of this manual, wooden blocks, plenty of rags and cleaning solvent for mopping up spilled oil, coolant and gasoline.

7    Plan for the vehicle to be out of use for quite a while. A machine shop can do the work that is beyond the scope of the home mechanic. Machine shops often have a busy schedule, so before removing the engine, consult the shop for an estimate of how long it will take to rebuild or repair the components that may need work.

## 7    Engine - removal and installation

**Warning:** *Gasoline and diesel fuel is extremely flammable, so take extra precautions when you work on any part of the fuel system. Don't smoke or allow open flames or bare light bulbs near the work area, and don't work in a garage where a gas-type appliance (such as a water heater or clothes dryer) is present. Since gasoline is carcinogenic, wear fuel-resistant gloves when there's a possibility of being exposed to fuel, and, if you spill any fuel on your skin, rinse it off immediately with soap and water. Mop up any spills immediately and do not store fuel-soaked rags where they could ignite. The fuel system is under constant pressure, so, if any fuel lines are to be disconnected, the fuel pressure in the system must be relieved first (see Chapter 4A or Chapter 4B for more information). When you perform any kind of work on the fuel system, wear safety glasses and have a Class B type fire extinguisher on hand.*

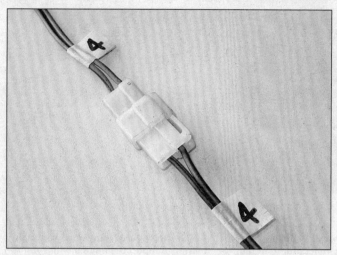

**7.14 Label both ends of each wire or vacuum connection before disconnecting them**

**7.29 Lift the engine carefully up and forward with the engine hoist, making sure everything is disconnected**

**Warning:** *The air conditioning system is under high pressure. Do not loosen any hose fittings or remove any components until after the system has been discharged. Air conditioning refrigerant must be properly discharged into an EPA-approved recovery/recycling unit at a dealer service department or an automotive air conditioning repair facility. Always wear eye protection when disconnecting air conditioning system fittings.*
**Warning:** *The engine must be completely cool before beginning this procedure.*

## *Removal*

1    Have the air conditioning system discharged by an automotive air conditioning technician.
2    If you're working on a gasoline-powered model, relieve the fuel system pressure (see Chapter 4A).
3    Disconnect the cable(s) from the negative battery terminal(s) (see Chapter 5).
4    Remove the hood (see Chapter 11).
5    Remove the air filter housing, air intake duct and, on models so equipped, the resonator (see Chapter 4A or Chapter 4B).
6    Drain the cooling system and remove the drivebelts (see Chapter 1).
7    Remove the radiator, shroud and engine cooling fan (see Chapter 3). Also remove the upper crossmember and the radiator support.
8    Detach the radiator and heater hoses from the engine.
9    If equipped, remove the air conditioning condenser and automatic transmission oil cooler (see Chapter 3).
10    On diesel engines, remove the intercooler (see Chapter 4B).
11    Disconnect the accelerator cable or accelerator pedal position switch (APPS) (see Chapter 4A or Chapter 4B) and throttle valve cable (automatic transmission only - see Chapter 7B).
12    Remove the power steering pump, without disconnecting the hoses, and tie it out of

the way (see Chapter 10).
13    Remove the alternator (see Chapter 5).
14    Label and disconnect all wires from the engine (see illustration). Masking tape and/or a touch-up paint applicator work well for marking items.
**Note:** *Take instant photos or sketch the locations of components and brackets to help with reassembly.*
15    Disconnect the fuel line to the engine (see Chapter 4A or Chapter 4B) and plug the lines.
16    Label and remove all vacuum lines between the engine and the firewall (or other components in the engine compartment).
17    If you're working on a model with a manual transmission and a diesel or V10 engine, remove the shift lever (see Chapter 7A).
18    Raise the vehicle and support it securely on jackstands.
**Note:** *On some models this step may not be necessary, because some models already have sufficient ground clearance to allow disconnection of the exhaust system, the engine mounts, etc., from underneath the vehicle. Raising these vehicles any higher might even make engine removal more difficult because it might position the vehicle too high to lift the engine out of the engine compartment with a hoist.*
19    On automatic transmission vehicles, detach the transmission cooler lines from the engine.
20    On 4WD models, remove the axle isolator bracket from the axle, engine and transmission.
21    Drain the engine oil (see Chapter 1).
22    Disconnect the exhaust pipes from the exhaust manifolds or, if you're working on a diesel, from the turbocharger outlet pipe.
23    Remove the starter (see Chapter 5).
24    Support the engine from above with a hoist. Attach the hoist chain to the engine lifting brackets. If no brackets are present, you'll have to fasten the chains to some substantial

part of the engine - one that is strong enough to take the weight, but in a location that will provide good balance. If you're attaching the chain to a stud on the engine, or are using a bolt passing through the chain and into a threaded hole, place a washer between the nut or bolt head and the chain, and tighten the nut or bolt securely.
**Caution:** *Do not lift the engine by the intake manifold.*
25    If you're working on a model with a diesel or a V10 engine, remove the transmission (see Chapter 7A).
26    On automatic transmission models (except those equipped with a diesel or V10 engine), remove the torque converter-to-driveplate bolts (see Chapter 7B).
27    Use the hoist to take the weight off the engine mounts, then remove the engine mount through bolts (see Chapter 2A, Chapter 2B, Chapter 2C or Chapter 2D).
28    On all models except the diesel or the V10, support the transmission with a floor jack. Place a block of wood on the jack head to protect the transmission.
29    Check to make sure everything is disconnected, then lift the engine out of the vehicle (see illustration). The engine will probably need to be tilted and/or maneuvered as it's lifted out, so have an assistant handy.
**Warning:** *Do not place any part of your body under the engine when it is supported only by a hoist or other lifting device.*
30    Remove the flywheel/driveplate and mount the engine on an engine stand or set the engine on the floor and support it so it doesn't tip over. Then disconnect the engine hoist.

## *Installation*

31    Check the engine mounts. If they're worn or damaged, replace them.
32    On manual transmission models, inspect the clutch components (see Chapter 8). On automatic transmission-equipped models,

**9.1 Before you try to remove the pistons, use a ridge reamer to remove the raised material (ridge) from the top of the cylinders**

**9.3 Checking the connecting rod endplay (side clearance)**

**9.4 If the connecting rods or caps are not marked, use permanent ink or paint to mark the caps to the rods by cylinder number (for example, this would be number 4 cylinder connecting rod)**

inspect the front seal and bushing.

33   Apply a dab of grease to the pilot bearing on manual transmission models.

34   Attach the hoist to the engine, remove the engine from the engine stand and install the flywheel or driveplate (see Chapter 2A, Chapter 2B, Chapter 2C or Chapter 2D).

35   Carefully guide the engine into place, lowering it slowly and moving it back into the engine compartment until the engine mounts can be secured.

36   If you're working on a diesel or a V10, reinstall the transmission (see Chapter 7A or Chapter 7B).

37   Tighten the transmission-to-engine bolts to the torque listed in the Chapter 7A, Specifications or Chapter 7B, Specifications).

38   On automatic transmission models, install the torque converter-to-driveplate bolts (see Chapter 7B).

39   Tighten all the bolts on the engine mounts and remove the hoist and jack.

40   Reinstall the remaining components in the reverse order of removal.

41   Add coolant, oil, power steering and transmission fluid as needed (see Chapter 1).

42   If you're working on a diesel engine, prime the fuel system (see Chapter 4B).

43   Run the engine and check for proper operation and leaks. Shut off the engine and recheck the fluid levels.

## 8   Engine overhaul - disassembly sequence

1   It's much easier to remove the external components if it's mounted on a portable engine stand. A stand can often be rented quite cheaply from an equipment rental yard. Before the engine is mounted on a stand, the flywheel/driveplate should be removed from the engine.

2   If a stand isn't available, it's possible to remove the external engine components with

it blocked up on the floor. Be extra careful not to tip or drop the engine when working without a stand.

3   If you're going to obtain a rebuilt engine, all external components must come off first, to be transferred to the replacement engine. These components include:

 *Flywheel/driveplate*
 *Ignition system components*
 *Emissions-related components*
 *Engine mounts and mount brackets*
 *Engine rear cover (spacer plate between flywheel/driveplate and engine block)*
 *Intake/exhaust manifolds*
 *Fuel injection components*
 *Oil filter*
 *Spark plug wires and spark plugs*
 *Thermostat and housing assembly*
 *Water pump*

**Note:** *When removing the external components from the engine, pay close attention to details that may be helpful or important during installation. Note the installed position of gaskets, seals, spacers, pins, brackets, washers, bolts and other small items.*

4   If you're going to obtain a short block (assembled engine block, crankshaft, pistons and connecting rods), then remove the timing chain, cylinder head, oil pan, oil pump pick-up tube, oil pump and water pump from your engine so that you can turn in your old short block to the rebuilder as a core. See Section 5 *Engine rebuilding alternatives* for additional information regarding the different possibilities to be considered.

## 9   Pistons and connecting rods - removal and installation

### *Removal*

**Note:** *Prior to removing the piston/connecting rod assemblies, remove the cylinder head and oil pan (see Chapter 2A, Chapter 2B, Chapter*

2C or Chapter 2D).

1   Use your fingernail to feel if a ridge has formed at the upper limit of ring travel (about 1/4-inch down from the top of each cylinder). If carbon deposits or cylinder wear have produced ridges, they must be completely removed with a special tool (see illustration). Follow the manufacturer's instructions provided with the tool. Failure to remove the ridges before attempting to remove the piston/connecting rod assemblies may result in piston breakage.

2   After the cylinder ridges have been removed, turn the engine so the crankshaft is facing up.

3   Before the main bearing cap assembly and connecting rods are removed, check the connecting rod endplay with feeler gauges. Slide them between the first connecting rod and the crankshaft throw until the play is removed (see illustration). Repeat this procedure for each connecting rod. The endplay is equal to the thickness of the feeler gauge(s). Check with an automotive machine shop for the endplay service limit (a typical end play limit should measure between 0.005 to 0.015 inch [0.127 to 0.381 mm]). If the play exceeds the service limit, new connecting rods will be required. If new rods (or a new crankshaft) are installed, the endplay may fall under the minimum allowable. If it does, the rods will have to be machined to restore it. If necessary, consult an automotive machine shop for advice.

4   Check the connecting rods and caps for identification marks. If they aren't plainly marked, use paint or a marker (see illustration) to clearly identify each rod and cap (1, 2, 3, etc., depending on the cylinder they're associated with). Do not interchange the rod caps. Install the exact same rod cap onto the same connecting rod.

**Caution:** *Do not use a punch and hammer to mark the connecting rods or they may be damaged.*

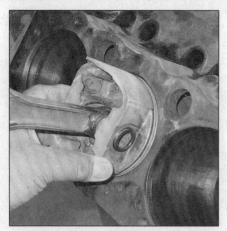

**9.13 Install the piston ring into the cylinder then push it down into position using a piston so the ring will be square in the cylinder**

**9.14 With the ring square in the cylinder, measure the ring end gap with a feeler gauge**

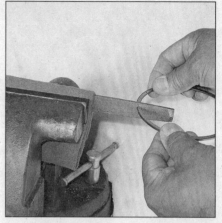

**9.15 If the ring end gap is too small, clamp a file in a vise as shown and file the piston ring ends - be sure to remove all raised material**

5    Loosen each of the connecting rod cap bolts or nuts 1/2-turn at a time until they can be removed by hand.

**Note:** *On the 3.7L V6 and the 4.7L and Hemi V8 engines, new connecting rod cap bolts must be used when reassembling the engine, but save the old bolts for use when checking the connecting rod bearing oil clearance.*

6    Remove the number one connecting rod cap and bearing insert. Don't drop the bearing insert out of the cap.

7    Remove the bearing insert and push the connecting rod/piston assembly out through the top of the engine. Use a wooden or plastic hammer handle to push on the upper bearing surface in the connecting rod. If resistance is felt, double-check to make sure that all of the ridge was removed from the cylinder.

8    Repeat the procedure for the remaining cylinders.

9    After removal, reassemble the connecting rod caps and bearing inserts in their respective connecting rods and install the cap bolts finger-tight. Leaving the old bearing inserts in place until reassembly will help pre-

vent the connecting rod bearing surfaces from being accidentally nicked or gouged.

10    The pistons and connecting rods are now ready for inspection and overhaul at an automotive machine shop.

### Piston ring installation

11    Before installing the new piston rings, the ring end gaps must be checked. It's assumed that the piston ring side clearance has been checked and verified correct.

12    Lay out the piston/connecting rod assemblies and the new ring sets so the ring sets will be matched with the same piston and cylinder during the end gap measurement and engine assembly.

13    Insert the top (number one) ring into the first cylinder and square it up with the cylinder walls by pushing it in with the top of the piston (see illustration). The ring should be near the bottom of the cylinder, at the lower limit of ring travel.

14    To measure the end gap, slip feeler gauges between the ends of the ring until a gauge equal to the gap width is found

(see illustration). The feeler gauge should slide between the ring ends with a slight amount of drag. A typical ring gap should fall between 0.010 and 0.020 inch [0.25 to 0.50 mm] for compression rings (0.033 to 0.045 inch [0.85 to 1.15 mm] for the second compression ring on the diesel engine) and up to 0.030 inch [0.76 mm] for the oil ring steel rails. If the gap is larger or smaller than specified, double-check to make sure you have the correct rings before proceeding.

15    If the gap is too small, it must be enlarged or the ring ends may come in contact with each other during engine operation, which can cause serious damage to the engine. If necessary, increase the end gaps by filing the ring ends very carefully with a fine file. Mount the file in a vise equipped with soft jaws, slip the ring over the file with the ends contacting the file face and slowly move the ring to remove material from the ends. When performing this operation, file only by pushing the ring from the outside end of the file toward the vise (see illustration).

16    Excess end gap isn't critical unless it's greater than 0.040 inch (1.01 mm) (the exception to this is the second compression ring on the 5.9L diesel). Again, double-check to make sure you have the correct ring type.

17    Repeat the procedure for each ring that will be installed in the first cylinder and for each ring in the remaining cylinders. Remember to keep rings, pistons and cylinders matched up.

18    Once the ring end gaps have been checked/corrected, the rings can be installed on the pistons.

19    The oil control ring (lowest one on the piston) is usually installed first. It's composed of three separate components. Slip the spacer/expander into the groove (see illustration). If an anti-rotation tang is used, make sure it's inserted into the drilled hole in the ring groove. Next, install the upper side rail in the same manner (see illustration). Don't use a piston ring installation tool on the oil ring side rails, as they may

**9.19a Installing the spacer/expander in the oil ring groove**

**9.19b DO NOT use a piston ring installation tool when installing the oil control side rails**

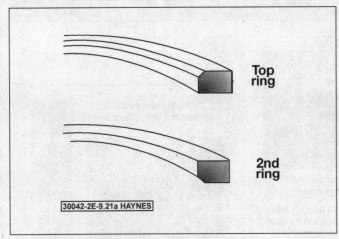

9.21a Top and middle piston ring profiles - 3.9L V6, 5.2L V8, 5.9L
V8 and 8.0L V10 engines (on all other gasoline engine models,
just be sure the second compression ring is installed with
the dot on the ring facing up)

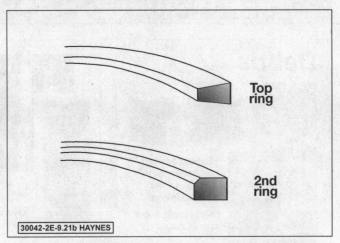

9.21b Top and middle piston ring profiles - 5.9L diesel engine

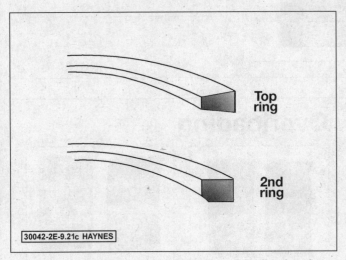

9.21c Top and middle piston ring profiles - 6.7L diesel engine

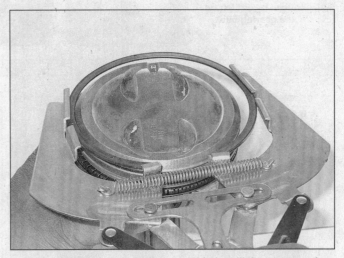

9.22 Use a piston ring installation tool to install the compression
rings - on some engines the number two compression ring has a
directional mark that must face toward the top of the piston

be damaged. Instead, place one end of the side rail into the groove between the spacer/expander and the ring land, hold it firmly in place and slide a finger around the piston while pushing the rail into the groove. Finally, install the lower side rail.

20   After the three oil ring components have been installed, check to make sure that both the upper and lower side rails can be rotated smoothly inside the ring grooves.

21   The number two (middle) ring is installed next. It's usually stamped with a mark which must face up, toward the top of the piston. Do not mix up the top and middle rings, as they have different cross-sections (see illustrations).

**Note:** *Always follow the instructions printed on the ring package or box - different manufacturers may require different approaches.*

22   Use a piston ring installation tool and make sure the identification mark is facing the top of the piston, then slip the ring into the middle groove on the piston (see illustration). Don't expand the ring any more than necessary to slide it over the piston.

23   Install the number one (top) ring in the same manner. Be careful not to confuse the number one and number two rings.

24   Repeat the procedure for the remaining pistons and rings.

## Installation

25   Before installing the piston/connecting rod assemblies, the cylinder walls must be perfectly clean, the top edge of each cylinder bore must be chamfered, and the crankshaft must be in place.

26   Remove the cap from the end of the number one connecting rod (refer to the marks made during removal). Remove the original bearing inserts and wipe the bearing surfaces of the connecting rod and cap with a clean, lint-free cloth. They must be kept spotlessly clean.

### Connecting rod bearing oil clearance check

27   Clean the back side of the new upper bearing insert, then lay it in place in the connecting rod.

28   Make sure the tab on the bearing fits into the recess in the rod. Don't hammer the bearing insert into place and be very careful not to nick or gouge the bearing face. Don't lubricate the bearing at this time.

29   Clean the back side of the other bearing insert and install it in the rod cap. Again, make sure the tab on the bearing fits into the recess in the cap, and don't apply any lubricant. It's critically important that the mating surfaces of the bearing and connecting rod are perfectly clean and oil free when they're assembled.

# ENGINE BEARING ANALYSIS

## Debris

**Babbitt bearing embedded with debris from machinings**

Microscopic detail of debris

Microscopic detail of gouges

**Overplated copper alloy bearing gouged by cast iron debris**

Aluminum bearing embedded with glass beads

Microscopic detail of glass beads

Damaged lining caused by dirt left on the bearing back

## Misassembly

Result of a lower half assembled as an upper - blocking the oil flow

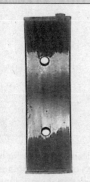

Excessive oil clearance is indicated by a short contact arc

Polished and oil-stained backs are a result of a poor fit in the housing bore

Result of a wrong, reversed, or shifted cap

## Overloading

Damage from excessive idling which resulted in an oil film unable to support the load imposed

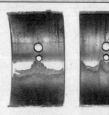

Damaged upper connecting rod bearings caused by engine lugging; the lower main bearings (not shown) were similarly affected

The damage shown in these upper and lower connecting rod bearings was caused by engine operation at a higher-than-rated speed under load

# Misalignment

A warped crankshaft caused this pattern of severe wear in the center, diminishing toward the ends

A poorly finished crankshaft caused the equally spaced scoring shown

A tapered housing bore caused the damage along one edge of this pair

A bent connecting rod led to the damage in the "V" pattern

# Lubrication

Result of dry start: The bearings on the left, farthest from the oil pump, show more damage

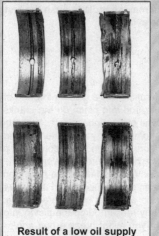

Result of a low oil supply or oil starvation

Severe wear as a result of inadequate oil clearance

# Corrosion

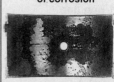

Microscopic detail of corrosion

Corrosion is an acid attack on the bearing lining generally caused by inadequate maintenance, extremely hot or cold operation, or inferior oils or fuels

Microscopic detail of cavitation

Example of cavitation - a surface erosion caused by pressure changes in the oil film

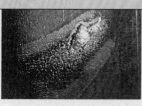

Damage from excessive thrust or insufficient axial clearance

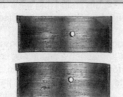

Bearing affected by oil dilution caused by excessive blow-by or a rich mixture

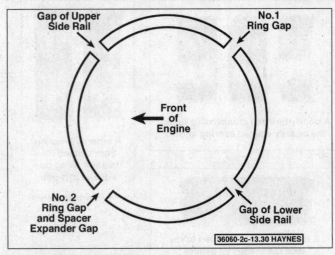

9.30a Position the piston ring end gaps as shown for the 3.7L V6, 4.7L V8, Hemi and 5.9L V8 engines

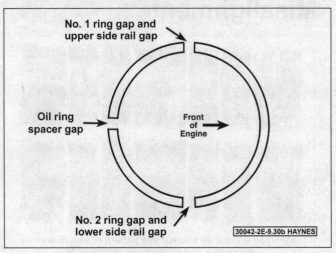

9.30b Ring end gap positions for the 8.0L V10 engine

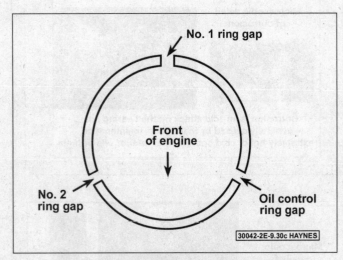

9.30c Ring end gap positions for the diesel engine

9.35 Use a plastic or wooden hammer handle to push the piston into the cylinder

30    Position the piston ring gaps at the intervals around the piston as shown (see illustrations).

31    Lubricate the piston and rings with clean engine oil and attach a piston ring compressor to the piston. Leave the skirt protruding about 1/4-inch to guide the piston into the cylinder. The rings must be compressed until they're flush with the piston.

32    Rotate the crankshaft until the number one connecting rod journal is at BDC (bottom dead center) and apply a liberal coat of engine oil to the cylinder walls. Refer to the TDC locating procedure in Chapter 2A, Chapter 2B, Chapter 2C or Chapter 2D for additional information.

33    With the "front" mark on the piston facing the front (timing chain end) of the engine, gently insert the piston/connecting rod assembly into the number one cylinder bore and rest the bottom edge of the ring compressor on the engine block.

**Note:** *Some engines have a letter "F" marking on the side of the piston near the wrist pin, others have an arrow, an "F" or a dimple or groove on the top of the piston. All of these are marks that indicate the front of the piston.*

34    Tap the top edge of the ring compressor to make sure it's contacting the block around its entire circumference.

35    Gently tap on the top of the piston with the end of a wooden or plastic hammer handle

(see illustration) while guiding the end of the connecting rod into place on the crankshaft journal. The piston rings may try to pop out of the ring compressor just before entering the cylinder bore, so keep some downward pressure on the ring compressor. Work slowly, and if any resistance is felt as the piston enters the cylinder, stop immediately. Find out what's hanging up and fix it before proceeding. Do not, for any reason, force the piston into the cylinder - you might break a ring and/or the piston.

36    Once the piston/connecting rod assembly is installed, the connecting rod bearing oil clearance must be checked before the rod cap is permanently installed.

**9.37 Place Plastigage on each connecting rod bearing journal parallel to the crankshaft centerline**

**9.41 Use the scale on the Plastigage package to determine the bearing oil clearance - be sure to measure the widest part of the Plastigage and use the correct scale; it comes with both standard and metric scales**

**10.1 Checking crankshaft endplay with a dial indicator**

37   Cut a piece of the appropriate size Plastigage slightly shorter than the width of the connecting rod bearing and lay it in place on the number one connecting rod journal, parallel with the journal axis (see illustration).

38   Clean the connecting rod cap bearing face and install the rod cap. Make sure the mating mark on the cap is on the same side as the mark on the connecting rod (see illustration 9.4).

39   Install the old rod bolts at this time, and tighten them to the torque listed in this Chapter's Specifications.

**Note:** *Use a thin-wall socket to avoid erroneous torque readings that can result if the socket is wedged between the rod cap and the bolt or nut. If the socket tends to wedge itself between the fastener and the cap, lift up on it slightly until it no longer contacts the cap. DO NOT rotate the crankshaft at any time during this operation.*

40   Remove the fasteners and detach the rod cap, being very careful not to disturb the Plastigage. Discard the cap bolts at this time as they cannot be reused.

**Note:** *You MUST use new connecting rod bolts.*

41   Compare the width of the crushed Plastigage to the scale printed on the Plastigage envelope to obtain the oil clearance (see illustration). The connecting rod bearing oil clearance is usually about 0.001 to 0.002 inch. Consult an automotive machine shop for the clearance specified for the rod bearings on your engine.

42   If the clearance is not as specified, the bearing inserts may be the wrong size (which means different ones will be required). Before deciding that different inserts are needed, make sure that no dirt or oil was between the bearing inserts and the connecting rod or cap when the clearance was measured. Also, recheck the journal diameter. If the Plasti-

gage was wider at one end than the other, the journal may be tapered. If the clearance still exceeds the limit specified, the bearing will have to be replaced with an undersize bearing.

**Caution:** *When installing a new crankshaft always use a standard size bearing.*

### Final installation

43   Carefully scrape all traces of the Plastigage material off the rod journal and/or bearing face. Be very careful not to scratch the bearing - use your fingernail or the edge of a plastic card.

44   Make sure the bearing faces are perfectly clean, then apply a uniform layer of clean moly-base grease or engine assembly lube to both of them. You'll have to push the piston into the cylinder to expose the face of the bearing insert in the connecting rod.

**Caution:** *If you're working on a 3.7L V6, a 4.7L V8 or a Hemi engine, install new connecting rod cap bolts. Do NOT reuse old bolts - they have stretched and cannot be reused.*

45   Slide the connecting rod back into place on the journal, install the rod cap, install the nuts or bolts and tighten them to the torque listed in this Chapter's Specifications. Again, work up to the torque in three steps.

46   Repeat the entire procedure for the remaining pistons/connecting rods.

47   The important points to remember are:

 a) *Keep the back sides of the bearing inserts and the insides of the connecting rods and caps perfectly clean when assembling them.*

 b) *Make sure you have the correct piston/rod assembly for each cylinder.*

 c) *The mark on the piston must face the front (timing chain end) of the engine.*

 d) *Lubricate the cylinder walls liberally with clean oil.*

 e) *Lubricate the bearing faces when installing the rod caps after the oil clearance has been checked.*

48   After all the piston/connecting rod assemblies have been correctly installed, rotate the crankshaft a number of times by hand to check for any obvious binding.

49   As a final step, check the connecting rod endplay again. If it was correct before disassembly and the original crankshaft and rods were reinstalled, it should still be correct. If new rods or a new crankshaft were installed, the endplay may be inadequate. If so, the rods will have to be removed and taken to an automotive machine shop for resizing.

## 10   Crankshaft - removal and installation

### Removal

**Note:** *The crankshaft can be removed only after the engine has been removed from the vehicle. It's assumed that the flywheel or driveplate, crankshaft pulley, timing chain, oil pan, oil pump, oil filter and piston/connecting rod assemblies have already been removed. The rear main oil seal retainer must be unbolted and separated from the block before proceeding with crankshaft removal.*

1   Before the crankshaft is removed, measure the endplay. Mount a dial indicator with the indicator in line with the crankshaft and touching the end of the crankshaft (see illustration).

2   Pry the crankshaft all the way to the rear and zero the dial indicator. Next, pry the crankshaft to the front as far as possible and check the reading on the dial indicator. The distance traveled is the endplay. A typical crankshaft endplay will fall between 0.003

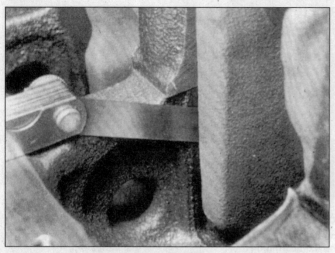

**10.3 Checking crankshaft endplay with feeler gauges at the thrust bearing journal**

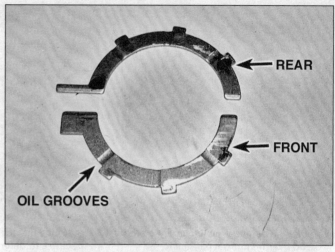

**10.11a Thrust washer identification on the 3.7L V6 engine - 4.7L V8 similar**

to 0.010 inch (0.076 to 0.254 mm). If it is greater than that, check the crankshaft thrust washer/bearing assembly surfaces for wear after it's removed. If no wear is evident, new main bearings should correct the endplay. Refer to Step 11 for the location of the thrust washer/bearing assembly on each engine.

3   If a dial indicator isn't available, feeler gauges can be used. Gently pry the crankshaft all the way to the front of the engine. Slip feeler gauges between the crankshaft and the front face of the thrust bearing or washer to determine the clearance (see illustration).

4   Loosen the main bearing cap/bedplate bolts 1/4-turn at a time each, until they can be removed by hand.

**Note:** *The main bearing caps on the Hemi engine are each secured by four bolts, two of which are accessed from the sides of the engine block.*

**10.11b Insert the thrust washer into the machined surface between the crankshaft and the upper bearing saddle, then rotate it down into the block until it's flush with the parting line on the main bearing saddle - make sure the oil grooves on the thrust washer face the crankshaft**

5   Gently tap the main bearing caps/bedplate assembly with a soft-faced hammer around the perimeter of the assembly. Pull the main bearing cap/bedplate assembly straight up and off the cylinder block. Try not to drop the bearing inserts if they come out with the assembly.

**Note:** *The bedplate on 3.7L V6 and 4.7L V8 engines has built in pry points; don't pry anywhere else or damage to the bedplate will occur.*

6   Carefully lift the crankshaft out of the engine. It may be a good idea to have an assistant available, since the crankshaft is quite heavy and awkward to handle. With the bearing inserts in place inside the engine block and main bearing caps, reinstall the main bearing cap assembly onto the engine block and tighten the bolts finger-tight. Make sure you install the main bearing cap assembly with the arrow facing the front end (timing chain) of the engine.

### Installation

7   Crankshaft installation is the first step in engine reassembly. It's assumed at this point that the engine block and crankshaft have been cleaned, inspected and repaired or reconditioned.

8   Position the engine block with the bottom facing up.

9   Remove the mounting bolts and lift off the main bearing cap assembly.

10   If they're still in place, remove the original bearing inserts from the block and from the main bearing cap assembly. Wipe the bearing surfaces of the block and main bearing cap assembly with a clean, lint-free cloth. They must be kept spotlessly clean. This is critical for determining the correct bearing oil clearance.

### Main bearing oil clearance check

11   Without mixing them up, clean the back sides of the new upper main bearing inserts

(with grooves and oil holes) and lay one in each main bearing saddle in the block. Each upper bearing has an oil groove and oil hole in it.

**Caution:** *The oil holes in the block must line up with the oil holes in the upper bearing inserts. Locate the thrust washers.*

    a) *On 3.7L V6 engines, the thrust washers are located on the number 2 main journal (see illustrations).*

    b) *On 3.9L V6, V8 and V10 engines, the thrust washers are located on the number 3 main journal.*

    c) *On diesel engines, the thrust washer/main bearing is located the number 6 main journal.*

12   The thrust washers must be installed in the correct journal. Clean the back sides of the lower main bearing inserts and lay them in the corresponding location in the main bearing cap. Make sure the tab on the bearing insert fits into the recess in the block or main bearing cap. The upper bearings with the oil holes are installed into the engine block while the lower bearings without the oil holes are installed in the caps or bedplate.

**Caution:** *Do not hammer the bearing insert into place and don't nick or gouge the bearing faces. DO NOT apply any lubrication at this time.*

13   Clean the faces of the bearing inserts in the block and the crankshaft main bearing journals with a clean, lint-free cloth.

14   Check or clean the oil holes in the crankshaft, as any dirt here can go only one way - straight through the new bearings.

15   Once you're certain the crankshaft is clean, carefully lay it in position in the cylinder block.

**Note:** *On 3.7L V6 and 4.7L V8 engines, install the thrust washers with the groove in the thrust washer facing the crankshaft with the smooth sides facing the main bearing saddle.*

16   Before the crankshaft can be permanently installed, the main bearing oil clearance must be checked.

10.18 Place the Plastigage onto the crankshaft bearing journal as shown

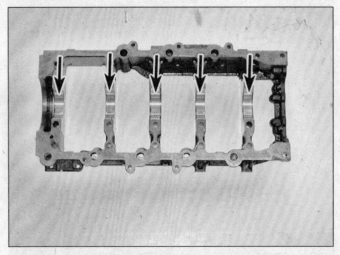

10.19a On the 3.7L V6 engines, the bearings are installed into the corresponding saddles in the bedplate . . .

10.19b . . . then the bedplate is set over the crankshaft onto the dowels on the engine block

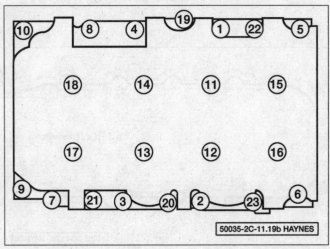

10.20a Main bearing caps/bedplate bolts tightening sequence on the 3.7L V6 engine

17    Cut several strips of the appropriate size of Plastigage. They must be slightly shorter than the width of the main bearing journal.

18    Place one piece on each crankshaft main bearing journal, parallel with the journal axis as shown (see illustration).

19    Clean the faces of the bearing inserts in the main bearing caps or bedplate assembly (see illustrations). Hold the bearing inserts in place and install the assembly onto the crankshaft and cylinder block. DO NOT disturb the Plastigage. Make sure you install the main bearing cap assembly with the arrow facing the front (timing chain end) of the engine.

20    Apply clean engine oil to all bolt threads prior to installation, then install all bolts finger-tight. Tighten main bearing caps/bedplate assembly bolts in the sequence shown (see illustrations) progressing in steps, to the torque listed in this Chapter's Specifications. DO NOT rotate the crankshaft at any time during this operation.

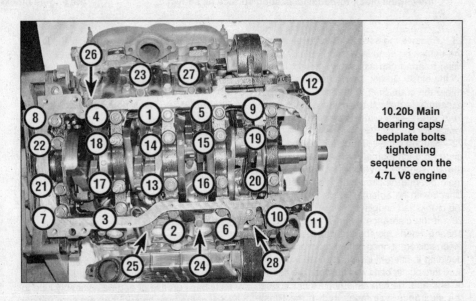

10.20b Main bearing caps/ bedplate bolts tightening sequence on the 4.7L V8 engine

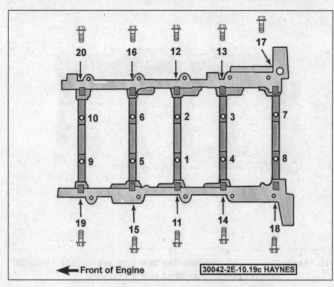

**10.20c Main bearing caps and crossbolts tightening sequence on the Hemi engine**

**10.22 Use the scale on the Plastigage package to determine the bearing oil clearance - be sure to measure the widest part of the Plastigage and use the correct scale; it comes with both standard and metric scales**

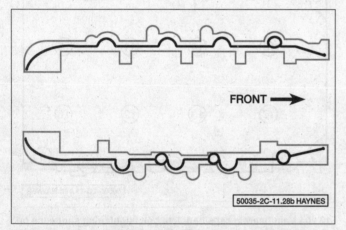

**10.29a On 3.7L V6 engines, apply a 2.5 mm bead of RTV sealant to the engine block-to-bedplate sealing surface as shown**

**10.29b On 4.7L V8 engines, apply a 2.5 mm bead of RTV sealant to the engine block-to-bedplate sealing surface as shown**

21    Remove the bolts in the reverse order of the tightening sequence and carefully lift the main bearing cap assembly straight up and off the block. Do not disturb the Plastigage or rotate the crankshaft. If the main bearing cap assembly is difficult to remove, tap it gently from side-to-side with a soft-faced hammer to loosen it.

22    Compare the width of the crushed Plastigage on each journal to the scale printed on the Plastigage envelope to determine the main bearing oil clearance (see illustration). Check with an automotive machine shop for the crankshaft endplay service limits.

23    If the clearance is not as specified, the bearing inserts may be the wrong size (which means different ones will be required). Before deciding if different inserts are needed, make sure that no dirt or oil was between the bearing inserts and the cap assembly or block when the clearance was measured. If the Plasti-

gage was wider at one end than the other, the crankshaft journal may be tapered. If the clearance still exceeds the limit specified, the bearing insert(s) will have to be replaced with an undersize bearing insert(s).

**Caution:** *When installing a new crankshaft always install a standard bearing insert set.*

24    Carefully scrape all traces of the Plastigage material off the main bearing journals and/or the bearing insert faces. Be sure to remove all residue from the oil holes. Use your fingernail or the edge of a plastic card - don't nick or scratch the bearing faces.

### Final installation

25    Carefully lift the crankshaft out of the cylinder block.

26    Clean the bearing insert faces in the cylinder block, then apply a thin, uniform layer of moly-base grease or engine assembly lube to each of the bearing surfaces. Be sure to coat

the thrust faces as well as the journal face of the thrust washers.

**Note:** *Install the thrust washers on 3.7L V6, 4.7L V8 and Hemi engines after the crankshaft has been installed.*

27    Make sure the crankshaft journals are clean, then lay the crankshaft back in place in the cylinder block.

28    Clean the bearing insert faces and then apply the same lubricant to them. Clean the engine block thoroughly. The surfaces must be free of oil residue. On 3.7L V6, 4.7L V8 and Hemi engines, install the thrust washers.

29    On 3.7L V6 and 4.7L V8 models, apply a 2.5 mm bead of Mopar Engine RTV sealant or equivalent to the bedplate sealing area on the block (see illustrations). Install each main bearing cap (or the bedplate) onto the crankshaft and cylinder block. On engines with individual main bearing caps, make sure the arrow faces the front (timing chain) of the engine.

**10.30a Install the new neoprene upper seal half into the engine block . . .**

**10.30b . . . with the seal lip facing the front of the engine**

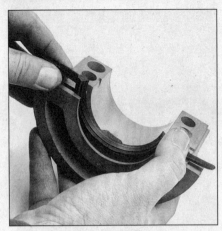

**10.30c Install the new neoprene lower seal half into the rear main cap**

30   On 3.9L V6, 5.2L V8 and 5.9L V8 engines, install the upper half of the rear main oil seal into the block (see illustration) with the paint facing the rear of the engine and the seal lip facing the front of the engine (see illustration). Install the other half of the new rear main oil seal into the rear main cap (see illustration). Apply a drop of Loctite 515 or equivalent on either side of the rear cap, then install the cap and apply RTV sealant to the slots between the cap and engine block (after the bolts have been installed) (see illustration).

31   Prior to installation, apply clean engine oil to all bolt threads, wiping off any excess, then install all bolts finger-tight.

32   Tighten the main bearing cap bolts or bedplate assembly bolts to the torque listed in this Chapter's Specifications (in the proper sequence on 3.7L V6, 4.7L V8 and Hemi engines) (see illustrations 10.19a, 10.19b and 10.19c). On 3.9L V6, 5.2L V8, 5.9L V8, 8.0L V10 and diesel engines, start with the center cap bolts and work toward the ends.

33   Recheck crankshaft endplay with a feeler gauge or a dial indicator. The endplay should be correct if the crankshaft thrust faces aren't worn or damaged and if new bearings have been installed.

34   Rotate the crankshaft a number of times by hand to check for any obvious binding. It should rotate with a running torque of 50 in-lbs or less. If the running torque is too high, identify and correct the problem at this time.

35   On all engines except the 3.9L V6, 5.2L V8 and 5.9L V8, install the new rear main oil seal (see Chapter 2A, Chapter 2B, Chapter 2C or Chapter 2D).

## 11   Engine overhaul - reassembly sequence

1   Before beginning engine reassembly, make sure you have all the necessary new parts, gaskets and seals as well as the following items on hand:

*Common hand tools*
*A 1/2-inch drive torque wrench*
*New engine oil*
*Gasket sealant*
*Thread locking compound*

2   If you obtained a short block it will be necessary to install the cylinder head, the oil pump and pick-up tube, the oil pan, the water pump, the timing chain and timing cover, and the valve cover (see Chapter 2A, Chapter 2B, Chapter 2C or Chapter 2D). In order to save time and avoid problems, the external components must be installed in the following general order:

*Thermostat and housing cover*
*Water pump*
*Intake and exhaust manifolds*
*Fuel injection components*
*Emission control components*
*Spark plugs*
*Ignition coils*
*Oil filter*
*Engine mounts and mount brackets*
*Flywheel/driveplate*

## 12   Initial start-up and break-in after overhaul

**Warning:** *Have a fire extinguisher handy when starting the engine for the first time.*

1   Once the engine has been installed in the vehicle, double-check the engine oil and coolant levels.

2   With the spark plugs out of the engine and the ignition system and fuel pump disabled, crank the engine until oil pressure registers on the gauge or the light goes out.

3   Install the spark plugs, hook up the plug wires and restore the ignition system and fuel pump functions. If you're working on a diesel, prime the fuel system (see Chapter 4B).

4   Start the engine. It may take a few moments for the fuel system to build up pressure, but the engine should start without a great deal of effort.

5   After the engine starts, it should be allowed to warm up to normal operating temperature. While the engine is warming up, make a thorough check for fuel, oil and coolant leaks.

6   Shut the engine off and recheck the engine oil and coolant levels.

7   Drive the vehicle to an area with minimum traffic, accelerate from 30 to 50 mph, then allow the vehicle to slow to 30 mph with the throttle closed. Repeat the procedure 10 or 12 times. This will load the piston rings and cause them to seat properly against the cylinder walls. Check again for oil and coolant leaks.

8   Drive the vehicle gently for the first 500 miles (no sustained high speeds) and keep a constant check on the oil level. It is not unusual for an engine to use oil during the break-in period.

9   At approximately 500 to 600 miles, change the oil and filter.

10   For the next few hundred miles, drive the vehicle normally. Do not pamper it or abuse it.

11   After 2000 miles, change the oil and filter again and consider the engine broken in.

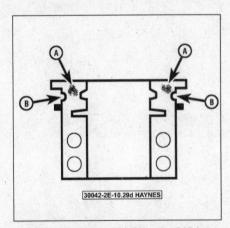

30042-2E-10.29d HAYNES

**10.30d Apply a drop of Loctite 515 (or equivalent) on either side of the rear main cap (A). Apply RTV sealant into the slot in each side of the cap (B) after the cap has been installed**

**Notes**

# Chapter 3
# Cooling, heating and air conditioning systems

## Contents

## Specifications

### General

| | |
|---|---|
| Coolant capacity | See Chapter 1 |
| Drivebelt tension | See Chapter 1 |
| Radiator cap pressure rating | 14 to 18 psi (94 to 124 kPa) |
| Thermostat opening temperature | |
|   Diesel engines | |
|     2001 and earlier models | 188-degrees F (86.7-degrees C) |
|     2002 models | 181-degrees F (83-degrees C) |
|     2003 and later models | 186-degrees F (85-degrees C) |
|   Gasoline engines | |
|     2001 and earlier models | 192 to 199-degrees F (88.9 to 93-degrees C) |
|     2002 and later models | 195-degrees F (90-degrees C) |

### Torque specifications                    Ft-lbs (unless otherwise indicated)

**Note:** *One foot-pound (ft-lb) of torque is equivalent to 12 inch-pounds (in-lbs) of torque. Torque values below approximately 15 ft-lbs are expressed in inch-pounds, since most foot-pound torque wrenches are not accurate at these smaller values.*

| | |
|---|---|
| Thermostat housing bolts | |
|   3.7L V6, 4.7L V8 and Hemi engines | 112 in-lbs |
|   3.9L V6, 5.2L V8 and 5.9L V8 engine | 17 |
|   Diesel engine | |
|     2002 and earlier | 18 |
|     2003 and later | 89 in-lbs |
|   8.0L V10 engine | 18 |
| Water pump bolts | |
|   3.7L V6, 4.7L V8 engines | 43 |
|   Hemi and diesel engines | 18 |
|     3.9L V6, 5.2L V8, 5.9L V8 and 8.0L V10 engines | 30 |
| Water pump pulley attaching bolts | |
|   3.9L V6, 5.2L V8 and 5.9L V8 engines | 20 |
|   V10 | 16 |
| Fan drive hub pulley bolts (diesel) | 18 |
| Fan clutch-to-fan blade bolts | 17 |
| Fan assembly-to-drive hub nut | 42 |

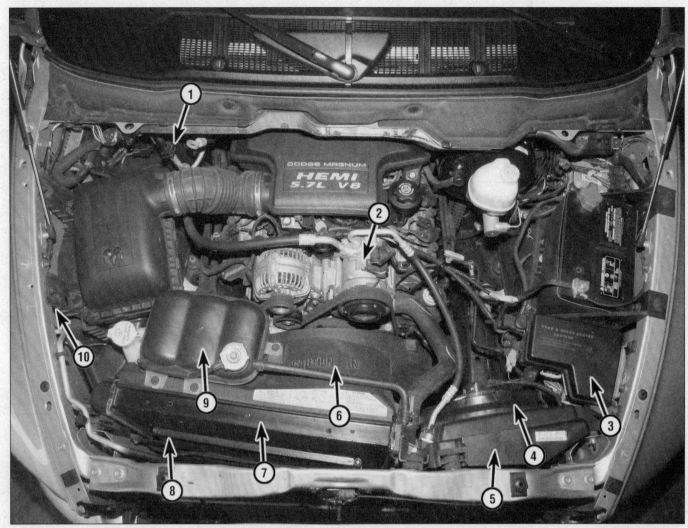

**1.1a Cooling and air conditioning component locations on the Hemi engine**

1   Accumulator
2   Air conditioning compressor
3   Fuse/relay box
4   Condenser cooling fan
5   Condenser

6   Engine cooling fan (under fan shroud)
7   Radiator
8   Automatic transmission fluid cooler
(see Chapter 7B)

9   Expansion tank
10  Orifice tube (behind air filter housing)

## 1   General Information

### Engine cooling system

1   All vehicles covered by this manual employ a pressurized engine cooling system with thermostatically controlled coolant circulation (see illustrations). An impeller-type water pump mounted on the front of the block pumps coolant through the engine. The coolant flows around each cylinder and toward the rear of the engine. Cast-in coolant passages direct coolant around the intake and exhaust ports, near the spark plug areas and in close proximity to the exhaust valve guides.

Because of the design of the accessories, pulleys and drivebelts, some engines are equipped with reverse rotating water pumps, cooling fans and viscous fan clutches. Always check with a parts department and install only components marked REVERSE on these components.

2   A wax-pellet type thermostat is located in a housing near the front of the engine. During warm up, the closed thermostat prevents coolant from circulating through the radiator. As the engine nears normal operating temperature, the thermostat opens and allows hot coolant to travel through the radiator, where it's cooled before returning to the engine.

3   Some models are equipped with a cool-

ant reservoir. These systems incorporate the pressure cap on top of the radiator. Other models are equipped with an expansion tank on top of the cooling fan shroud. These models incorporate the pressure cap on the expansion tank. Both type pressure caps (radiator and expansion tank) raise the boiling point of the coolant. If the system pressure exceeds the cap pressure-relief value, the excess pressure in the system forces the spring-loaded valve inside the cap off its seat. This allows either excess pressure or overheated coolant to escape through an overflow tube into a separate coolant reservoir or on models with an expansion tank, to the atmosphere.

**1.1b Cooling and air conditioning component locations on the 4.7L V8 engine**

| | | | | | |
|---|---|---|---|---|---|
| 1 | Fuse/relay box | 4 | Engine cooling fan | 7 | Expansion tank |
| 2 | Condenser fan | 5 | Radiator | 8 | Accumulator |
| 3 | Condenser | 6 | Air conditioning compressor | | |

4   The radiator cooling fan is mounted on the front of the water pump on gasoline engines or the fan pulley on diesel engines. Gasoline-engined models and 2002 diesel models are equipped with a viscous fan clutch while 2003 and later diesel models are equipped with an electronic viscous clutch that is controlled by the Powertrain Control Module (PCM).

## Heating system

5   The heating system consists of a blower fan and heater core located in the heater/air conditioning unit under the dash, the hoses connecting the heater core to the engine cooling system and the heater/air conditioning control head on the instrument panel. Hot engine coolant is circulated through the heater core. When the heater mode is activated, a flap door opens to expose the heater box to the passenger compartment. A fan switch on the control head activates the blower motor, which forces air through the core, heating the air.

## Air conditioning system

6   The air conditioning system consists of a condenser mounted in front of the radiator (diesel and 8.0L V10 models) or adjacent to the radiator (all other models), an evaporator mounted adjacent to the heater core under the dash, a compressor mounted on the engine, an accumulator mounted near the firewall and the plumbing that connects all of these components.

7   A blower fan forces the warmer air of the passenger compartment through the evaporator core (sort of a radiator-in-reverse), transferring the heat from the air to the refrigerant. The liquid refrigerant boils off into low-pressure vapor, taking the heat with it when it leaves the evaporator.

**2.2 The cooling system pressure tester is connected in place of the pressure cap, then pumped up to pressurize the system**

**2.5a The combustion leak detector consists of a bulb, syringe and test fluid**

**2.5b Place the tester over the cooling system filler neck and use the bulb to draw a sample into the tester**

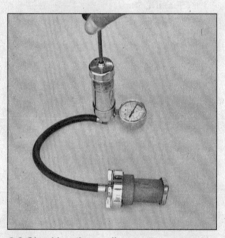

**2.8 Checking the cooling system pressure cap with a cooling system pressure tester**

## 2   Troubleshooting

### Coolant leaks

1    A coolant leak can develop anywhere in the cooling system, but the most common causes are:

a) *A loose or weak hose clamp*
b) *A defective hose*
c) *A faulty pressure cap*
d) *A damaged radiator*
e) *A bad heater core*
f) *A faulty water pump*
g) *A leaking gasket at any joint that carries coolant*

2    Coolant leaks aren't always easy to find. Sometimes they can only be detected when the cooling system is under pressure. Here's where a cooling system pressure tester comes in handy. After the engine has cooled completely, the tester is attached in place of the pressure cap, then pumped up to the pressure value equal to that of the pressure cap rating (see illustration). Now, leaks that only exist when the engine is fully warmed up will become apparent. The tester can be left connected to locate a nagging slow leak.

### Coolant level drops, but no external leaks

3    If you find it necessary to keep adding coolant, but there are no external leaks, the probable causes include:

a) *A blown head gasket*
b) *A leaking intake manifold gasket (only on engines that have coolant passages in the manifold)*
c) *A cracked cylinder head or cylinder block*

4    Any of the above problems will also usually result in contamination of the engine oil, which will cause it to take on a milkshake-like appearance. A bad head gasket or cracked head or block can also result in engine oil contaminating the cooling system.

5    Combustion leak detectors (also known as block testers) are available at most auto parts stores. These work by detecting exhaust gases in the cooling system, which indicates a compression leak from a cylinder into the coolant. The tester consists of a large bulb-type syringe and bottle of test fluid (see illustration). A measured amount of the fluid is added to the syringe. The syringe is placed over the cooling system filler neck and, with the engine running, the bulb is squeezed and a sample of the gases present in the cooling system are drawn up through the test fluid (see illustration). If any combustion gases are present in the sample taken, the test fluid will change color.

6    If the test indicates combustion gas is present in the cooling system, you can be sure that the engine has a blown head gasket or a crack in the cylinder head or block, and will require disassembly to repair.

### Pressure cap

**Warning:** *Wait until the engine is completely cool before beginning this check.*

7    The cooling system is sealed by a spring-loaded cap, which raises the boiling point of the coolant. If the cap's seal or spring are worn out, the coolant can boil and escape past the cap. With the engine completely cool, remove the cap and check the seal; if it's cracked, hardened or deteriorated in any way, replace it with a new one.

8    Even if the seal is good, the spring might not be; this can be checked with a cooling system pressure tester (see illustration). If the cap can't hold a pressure within approximately 1-1/2 lbs of its rated pressure (which is marked on the cap), replace it with a new one.

9    The cap is also equipped with a vacuum relief spring. When the engine cools off, a vacuum is created in the cooling system. The vacuum relief spring allows air back into the system, which will equalize the pressure and prevent damage to the radiator (the radiator tanks could collapse if the vacuum is great enough). If, after turning the engine off and allowing it to cool down you notice any of the cooling system hoses collapsing, replace the pressure cap with a new one.

## Thermostat

10    Before assuming the thermostat (see illustration) is responsible for a cooling system problem, check the coolant level (see Chapter 1), drivebelt tension (see Chapter 1) and temperature gauge (or light) operation.

11    If the engine takes a long time to warm up (as indicated by the temperature gauge or heater operation), the thermostat is probably stuck open. Replace the thermostat with a new one.

12    If the engine runs hot or overheats, a thorough test of the thermostat should be performed.

13    Definitive testing of the thermostat can only be made when it is removed from the vehicle. If the thermostat is stuck in the open position at room temperature, it is faulty and must be replaced.

**Caution:** *Do not drive the vehicle without a thermostat. The computer may stay in open loop and emissions and fuel economy will suffer.*

14    To test a thermostat, suspend the (closed) thermostat on a length of string or wire in a pot of cold water.

15    Heat the water on a stove while observing the thermostat. The thermostat should fully open before the water boils.

16    If the thermostat doesn't open and close as specified, or sticks in any position, replace it.

## Cooling fan

### Electric cooling fan

17    If the engine is overheating and the cooling fan is not coming on when the engine temperature rises to an excessive level, unplug the fan motor electrical connector(s) and connect the motor directly to the battery with fused jumper wires. If the fan motor doesn't come on, replace the motor.

18    If the radiator fan motor is okay, but it isn't coming on when the engine gets hot, the fan relay might be defective. A relay is used to control a circuit by turning it on and off in response to a control decision by the Powertrain Control Module (PCM). These control circuits are fairly complex, and checking them should be left to a qualified automotive technician. Sometimes, the control system can be fixed by simply identifying and replacing a bad relay.

19    Locate the fan relays in the engine compartment fuse/relay box.

20    Test the relay (see Chapter 12).

21    If the relay is okay, check all wiring and

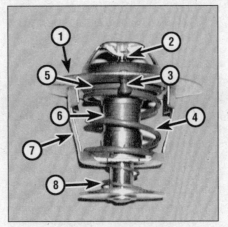

**2.10 Typical thermostat:**

| | | | |
|---|---|---|---|
| 1 | *Flange* | 5 | *Valve seat* |
| 2 | *Piston* | 6 | *Valve* |
| 3 | *Jiggle valve* | 7 | *Frame* |
| 4 | *Main coil spring* | 8 | *Secondary coil spring* |

connections to the fan motor. Refer to the wiring diagrams at the end of Chapter 12. If no obvious problems are found, the problem could be the Engine Coolant Temperature (ECT) sensor or the Powertrain Control Module (PCM). Have the cooling fan system and circuit diagnosed by a dealer service department or repair shop with the proper diagnostic equipment.

**Note:** *These models are equipped with a cooling fan motor resistor. Have the resistor checked if the fan motor does not respond to the speed variations signaled by the PCM.*

### Belt-driven cooling fan

22    Disconnect the cable from the negative terminal of the battery (see Chapter 5) and rock the fan back and forth by hand to check for excessive bearing play.

23    With the engine cold (and not running), turn the fan blades by hand. The fan should turn freely.

24    Visually inspect for substantial fluid leakage from the clutch assembly. If problems are noted, replace the clutch assembly.

25    With the engine completely warmed up, turn off the ignition switch and disconnect the negative battery cable from the battery. Turn the fan by hand. Some drag should be evident. If the fan turns easily, replace the fan clutch.

## Water pump

26    A failure in the water pump can cause serious engine damage due to overheating.

### Drivebelt-driven water pump

27    There are two ways to check the operation of the water pump while it's installed on the engine. If the pump is found to be defective, it should be replaced with a new or rebuilt unit.

28    Water pumps are equipped with weep (or vent) holes (see illustration). If a failure occurs in the pump seal, coolant will leak from

**2.28 The water pump weep hole is generally located on the underside of the pump and can be seen through the pulley holes**

the hole.

29    If the water pump shaft bearings fail, there may be a howling sound at the pump while it's running. Shaft wear can be felt with the drivebelt removed if the water pump pulley is rocked up and down (with the engine off). Don't mistake drivebelt slippage, which causes a squealing sound, for water pump bearing failure.

### Timing chain or timing belt-driven water pump

30    Water pumps driven by the timing chain or timing belt are located underneath the timing chain or timing belt cover.

31    Checking the water pump is limited because of where it is located. However, some basic checks can be made before deciding to remove the water pump. If the pump is found to be defective, it should be replaced with a new or rebuilt unit.

32    One sign that the water pump may be failing is that the heater (climate control) may not work well. Warm the engine to normal operating temperature, confirm that the coolant level is correct, then run the heater and check for hot air coming from the ducts.

33    Check for noises coming from the water pump area. If the water pump impeller shaft or bearings are failing, there may be a howling sound at the pump while the engine is running.

**Note:** *Be careful not to mistake drivebelt noise (squealing) for water pump bearing or shaft failure.*

34    It you suspect water pump failure due to noise, wear can be confirmed by feeling for play at the pump shaft. This can be done by rocking the drive sprocket on the pump shaft up and down. To do this you will need to remove the tension on the timing chain or belt as well as access the water pump.

### All water pumps

35    In rare cases or on high-mileage vehicles, another sign of water pump failure may be the presence of coolant in the engine oil.

This condition will adversely affect the engine in varying degrees.

**Note:** *Finding coolant in the engine oil could indicate other serious issues besides a failed water pump, such as a blown head gasket or a cracked cylinder head or block.*

36    Even a pump that exhibits no outward signs of a problem, such as noise or leakage, can still be due for replacement. Removal for close examination is the only sure way to tell. Sometimes the fins on the back of the impeller can corrode to the point that cooling efficiency is diminished significantly.

## Heater system

37    Little can go wrong with a heater. If the fan motor will run at all speeds, the electrical part of the system is okay. The three basic heater problems fall into the following general categories:

a) *Not enough heat*
b) *Heat all the time*
c) *No heat*

38    If there's not enough heat, the control valve or door is stuck in a partially open position, the coolant coming from the engine isn't hot enough, or the heater core is restricted. If the coolant isn't hot enough, the thermostat in the engine cooling system is stuck open, allowing coolant to pass through the engine so rapidly that it doesn't heat up quickly enough. If the vehicle is equipped with a temperature gauge instead of a warning light, watch to see if the engine temperature rises to the normal operating range after driving for a reasonable distance.

39    If there's heat all the time, the control valve or the door is stuck wide open.

40    If there's no heat, coolant is probably not reaching the heater core, or the heater core is plugged. The likely cause is a collapsed or plugged hose, core, or a frozen heater control valve. If the heater is the type that flows coolant all the time, the cause is a stuck door or a broken or kinked control cable.

## Air conditioning system

41    If the cool air output is inadequate:

a) *Inspect the condenser coils and fins to make sure they're clear.*
b) *Check the compressor clutch for slippage.*
c) *Check the blower motor for proper operation.*
d) *Inspect the blower discharge passage for obstructions.*
e) *Check the system air intake filter for clogging.*

42    If the system provides intermittent cooling air:

a) *Check the circuit breaker, blower switch and blower motor for a malfunction.*
b) *Make sure the compressor clutch isn't slipping.*
c) *Inspect the plenum door to make sure it's operating properly.*
d) *Inspect the evaporator to make sure it isn't clogged.*

e) *If the unit is icing up, it may be caused by excessive moisture in the system, incorrect super heat switch adjustment or low thermostat adjustment.*

43    If the system provides no cooling air: Inspect the compressor drivebelt. Make sure it's not loose or broken.

a) *Make sure the compressor clutch engages. If it doesn't, check for a blown fuse.*
b) *Inspect the wire harness for broken or disconnected wires.*
c) *If the compressor clutch doesn't engage, bridge the terminals of the A/C pressure switch(es) with a jumper wire; if the clutch now engages, and the system is properly charged, the pressure switch is bad.*
d) *Make sure the blower motor is not disconnected or burned out.*
e) *Make sure the compressor isn't partially or completely seized.*
f) *Inspect the refrigerant lines for leaks.*
g) *Check the components for leaks.*
h) *Inspect the receiver-drier/accumulator or expansion valve/tube for clogged screens.*

44    If the system is noisy:

a) *Look for loose panels in the passenger compartment.*
b) *Inspect the compressor drivebelt. It may be loose or worn.*
c) *Check the compressor mounting bolts. They should be tight.*
d) *Listen carefully to the compressor. It may be worn out.*
e) *Listen to the idler pulley and bearing and the clutch. Either may be defective.*
f) *The winding in the compressor clutch coil or solenoid may be defective.*
g) *The compressor oil level may be low.*
h) *The blower motor fan bushing or the motor itself may be worn out.*
i) *If there is an excessive charge in the system, you'll hear a rumbling noise in the high pressure line, a thumping noise in the compressor, or see bubbles or cloudiness in the sight glass.*
j) *If there's a low charge in the system, you might hear hissing in the evaporator case at the expansion valve, or see bubbles or cloudiness in the sight glass.*

---

## 3    Air conditioning and heating system - check and maintenance

---

## Air conditioning system

**Warning:** *The air conditioning system is under high pressure. Do not loosen any hose fittings or remove any components until after the system has been discharged. Air conditioning refrigerant should be properly discharged into an EPA-approved recovery/recycling unit at a dealer service department or an automotive air conditioning repair facility. Always wear eye protection when disconnecting air conditioning*

system fittings.

**Caution:** *All models covered by this manual use environmentally friendly R-134a. This refrigerant (and its appropriate refrigerant oils) are not compatible with R-12 refrigerant system components and must never be mixed or the components will be damaged.*

**Caution:** *When replacing entire components, additional refrigerant oil should be added equal to the amount that is removed with the component being replaced. Read the can before adding any oil to the system, to make sure it is compatible with the R-134a system.*

1    The following maintenance checks should be performed on a regular basis to ensure that the air conditioning continues to operate at peak efficiency.

a) *Inspect the condition of the compressor drivebelt. If it is worn or deteriorated, replace it (see Chapter 1).*
b) *Check the drivebelt tension (see Chapter 1).*
c) *Inspect the system hoses. Look for cracks, bubbles, hardening and deterioration. Inspect the hoses and all fittings for oil bubbles or seepage. If there is any evidence of wear, damage or leakage, replace the hose(s).*
d) *Inspect the condenser fins for leaves, bugs and any other foreign material that may have embedded itself in the fins. Use a fin comb or compressed air to remove debris from the condenser.*
e) *Make sure the system has the correct refrigerant charge.*

2    It's a good idea to operate the system for about ten minutes at least once a month. This is particularly important during the winter months because long term non-use can cause hardening, and subsequent failure, of the seals. Note that using the Defrost function operates the compressor.

3    If the air conditioning system is not working properly, proceed to Step 6 and perform the general checks outlined below.

4    Because of the complexity of the air conditioning system and the special equipment necessary to service it, in-depth troubleshooting and repairs beyond checking the refrigerant charge and the compressor clutch operation are not included in this manual. However, simple checks and component replacement procedures are provided in this Chapter. For more complete information on the air conditioning system, refer to the *Haynes Automotive Heating and Air Conditioning Manual.*

5    The most common cause of poor cooling is simply a low system refrigerant charge. If a noticeable drop in system cooling ability occurs, one of the following quick checks will help you determine if the refrigerant level is low.

### Checking the refrigerant charge

6    Warm the engine up to normal operating temperature.

7    Place the air conditioning temperature selector at the coldest setting and put the blower at the highest setting.

**3.9 Insert a thermometer in the center vent, turn on the air conditioning system and wait for it to cool down; depending on the humidity, the output air should be 35 to 40 degrees cooler than the ambient air temperature**

**3.11 R-134a automotive air conditioning charging kit**

**3.13 Location of the low-side charging port (2003 Hemi model shown)**

8    After the system reaches operating temperature, feel the larger pipe exiting the evaporator at the firewall. The outlet pipe should be cold (the tubing that leads back to the compressor). If the evaporator outlet pipe is warm, the system probably needs a charge.

9    Insert a thermometer in the center air distribution duct (see illustration) while operating the air conditioning system at its maximum setting - the temperature of the output air should be 35 to 40 degrees F below the ambient air temperature (down to approximately 40 degrees F). If the ambient (outside) air temperature is very high, say 110 degrees F, the duct air temperature may be as high as 60 degrees F, but generally the air conditioning is 35 to 40 degrees F cooler than the ambient air.

10    Further inspection or testing of the system requires special tools and techniques and is beyond the scope of the home mechanic.

### Adding refrigerant

**Caution:** *Make sure any refrigerant, refrigerant oil or replacement component you purchase is designated as compatible with R-134a systems.*

11    Purchase an R-134a automotive charging kit at an auto parts store (see illustration). A charging kit includes a can of refrigerant, a tap valve and a short section of hose that can be attached between the tap valve and the system low side service valve.

**Caution:** *Never add more than one can of refrigerant to the system. If more refrigerant than that is required, the system should be evacuated and leak tested.*

12    Back off the valve handle on the charging kit and screw the kit onto the refrigerant can, making sure first that the O-ring or rubber seal inside the threaded portion of the kit is in place.

**Warning:** *Wear protective eyewear when dealing with pressurized refrigerant cans.*

13    Remove the dust cap from the low-side charging port and attach the hose's quick-connect fitting to the port (see illustration).

**Warning:** *DO NOT hook the charging kit hose to the system high side! The fittings on the charging kit are designed to fit only on the low side of the system.*

14    Warm up the engine and turn On the air conditioning. Keep the charging kit hose away from the fan and other moving parts.

**Note:** *The charging process requires the compressor to be running. If the clutch cycles off, you can put the air conditioning switch on High and leave the car doors open to keep the clutch on and compressor working. The compressor can be kept on during the charging by removing the connector from the pressure switch and bridging it with a paper clip or jumper wire during the procedure.*

15    Turn the valve handle on the kit until the stem pierces the can, then back the handle out to release the refrigerant. You should be able to hear the rush of gas. Keep the can upright at all times, but shake it occasionally. Allow stabilization time between each addition.

**Note:** *The charging process will go faster if you wrap the can with a hot-water-soaked rag to keep the can from freezing up.*

16    If you have an accurate thermometer, you can place it in the center air conditioning duct inside the vehicle and keep track of the output air temperature. A charged system that is working properly should cool down to approximately 40 degrees F. If the ambient (outside) air temperature is very high, say 110 degrees F, the duct air temperature may be as high as 60 degrees F, but generally the air conditioning is 35 to 40 degrees F cooler than the ambient air.

17    When the can is empty, turn the valve handle to the closed position and release the connection from the low-side port. Reinstall the dust cap.

18    Remove the charging kit from the can and store the kit for future use with the piercing valve in the UP position to prevent inadvertently piercing the can on the next use.

### Heating systems

19    If the carpet under the heater core is damp, or if antifreeze vapor or steam is coming through the vents, the heater core is leaking. Remove it (see Section 12) and install a new unit (most radiator shops will not repair a leaking heater core).

20    If the air coming out of the heater vents isn't hot, the problem could stem from any of the following causes:

a)  *The thermostat is stuck open, preventing the engine coolant from warming up enough to carry heat to the heater core. Replace the thermostat (see Section 4).*

b)  *There is a blockage in the system, preventing the flow of coolant through the heater core. Feel both heater hoses at the firewall. They should be hot. If one of them is cold, there is an obstruction in one of the hoses or in the heater core, or the heater control valve is shut. Detach the hoses and back flush the heater core with a water hose. If the heater core is clear but circulation is impeded, remove the two hoses and flush them out with a water hose.*

c)  *If flushing fails to remove the blockage from the heater core, the core must be replaced (see Section 12).*

### Eliminating air conditioning odors

21    Unpleasant odors that often develop in air conditioning systems are caused by the growth of a fungus, usually on the surface of the evaporator core. The warm, humid environment there is a perfect breeding ground for mildew to develop.

3.24 Insert the nozzle of the disinfectant can into the return-air intake behind the glove box

4.4 Thermostat housing location on the 3.7L V6 engine (4.7L V8 similar) - view here is from below at the front of the engine

4.6a Thermostat housing location on the Hemi engine - the air conditioning compressor is removed for clarity

4.6b On 1994 through 1998 diesel engines, the alternator bracket (large arrow) must be removed, then remove the bolts (three small arrows) and lift the thermostat cover off

22   The evaporator core on most vehicles is difficult to access, and factory dealerships have a lengthy, expensive process for eliminating the fungus by opening up the evaporator case and using a powerful disinfectant and rinse on the core until the fungus is gone. You can service your own system at home, but it takes something much stronger than basic household germ-killers or deodorizers.

23   Aerosol disinfectants for automotive air conditioning systems are available in most auto parts stores, but remember when shopping for them that the most effective treatments are also the most expensive. The basic procedure for using these sprays is to start by running the system in the RECIRC mode for ten minutes with the blower on its highest speed. Use the highest heat mode to dry out the system and keep the compressor from engaging by disconnecting the wiring connector at the compressor.

24   The disinfectant can usually comes

with a long spray hose. Insert the nozzle into an intake port inside the cabin, and spray according to the manufacturer's recommendations (see illustration). Try to cover the whole surface of the evaporator core by aiming the spray up, down and sideways. Follow the manufacturer's recommendations for the length of spray and waiting time between applications.

## Automatic heating and air conditioning systems

25   Some vehicles are equipped with an optional automatic climate control system. This system has its own computer that receives inputs from various sensors in the heating and air conditioning system. This computer, like the PCM, has self-diagnostic capabilities to help pinpoint problems or faults within the system. Vehicles equipped with automatic heating and air conditioning systems are very complex and considered beyond the scope of the home mechanic. Vehicles equipped with automatic heating and air conditioning systems should be taken to a dealer service department or other qualified facility for repair.

---

### 4   Thermostat - replacement

**Warning:** *Do not remove the radiator cap or expansion tank cap, drain the coolant or replace the thermostat until the engine has cooled completely.*

1   Disconnect the cable(s) from the negative battery terminal(s) (see Chapter 5, Section 1).

2   Drain the cooling system (see Chapter 1). If the coolant is relatively new or in good condition (see Section 1), save it and reuse it.

### 3.7L V6 and 4.7L V8 engines

3   Raise the vehicle and support it securely on jackstands.

4   Follow the lower radiator hose to the engine to locate the thermostat housing (see illustration).

### Hemi, diesel and 8.0L V10 engines

5   On 1999 and earlier diesel models, unbolt the alternator (see Chapter 5) and alternator mounting bracket, then set it aside for access to the thermostat.

6   Follow the upper radiator hose to the engine to locate the thermostat housing (see illustrations).

### 3.9L V6, 5.2L V8 and 5.9L V8 engines

7   Remove the alternator bracket and the alternator (see Chapter 5).

**Note:** *On 4WD models, unplug the 4WD indicator lamp harness located behind the alternator.*

8   Follow the upper radiator to the engine to locate the thermostat housing.

### All models

9   Squeeze the tabs on the hose clamp to loosen it from the hose(s), then reposition the clamp several inches back up the hose. Detach the hose(s) from the thermostat housing.

**Note:** *Special hose clamp pliers are available at most auto parts stores. If the hose is stuck, grasp it near the end with a pair of adjustable pliers and twist it to break the seal, then pull it off. If the hose is old or deteriorated, cut it off and install a new one.*

10   If the outer surface of the thermostat housing that mates with the hose is deteriorated (corroded, pitted, etc.) it may be damaged further by hose removal. If it is, the thermostat housing will have to be replaced.

11   Remove the thermostat housing from the engine. If the housing is stuck, tap it with a soft-faced hammer to jar it loose. Be pre-

4.12 Location of the jiggle valve on the Hemi engine's thermostat

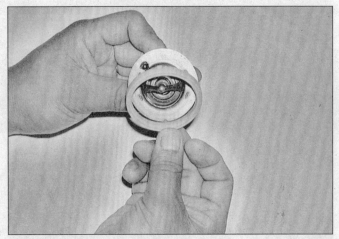

4.17a On 3.7L V6 engines, align the notch on the thermostat with the rubber tab on the gasket's inner groove . . .

pared for some coolant to spill as the gasket seal is broken.

**Note:** *On 8.0L V10 engines, a smaller hose and the sensor harness connector must be disconnected from the thermostat cover.*

12   Note how the thermostat is installed (which end is facing up, or out, and the position of the air bleed "jiggle valve," if equipped) and remove it from the engine (see illustration).

13   On 3.9L V6, 5.2L V8 and 5.9L V8 engines, stuff a rag into the engine opening, then remove all traces of old gasket material and sealant from the housing and cover with a gasket scraper. Remove the rag from the opening and clean the gasket mating surfaces with chemical gasket remover or lacquer thinner or acetone.

14   On all other models, simply remove the rubber gasket from around the thermostat.

15   On 3.9L V6, 5.2L V8 and 5.9L V8 engines, install the new thermostat in the machined groove on the intake manifold. Make sure the correct end faces into the engine. Apply a thin, uniform layer of RTV sealant to both sides of the new gasket and position it over the thermostat on the intake manifold.

16   On 8.0L V10 engines, install a new rubber seal constructed with a metal shoulder (sleeve) into the intake manifold. Apply a small amount of RTV sealant around the edge before installing it. Use a special tool to drive the seal into the manifold.

17   On all other models, install a new rubber gasket around the thermostat. Make sure to align the rubber tab on the inside of the O-ring groove with the notch on the thermostat (see illustration). Then align the rubber tab on the outside of the gasket with the notch on the thermostat housing and insert the thermostat and gasket into the thermostat housing (see illustration).

**Note:** *Some models are not equipped with alignment notches on the thermostat. Simply install the rubber gasket around the thermostat.*

18   Install the thermostat housing and bolts

onto the engine. Tighten the bolts to the torque listed in 2E this Chapter's Specifications.

**Note:** *On Hemi, diesel, 3.9L V6, 5.2L V8 and 5.9L V8 engines, install the thermostat housing with the word FRONT towards the front of the engine. This positions the slightly angled thermostat housing into the correct alignment.*

19   Reattach the hose(s) to the fitting(s) and tighten the hose clamp(s) securely.

20   Refill the cooling system (see Chapter 1).

21   Start the engine and allow it to reach normal operating temperature, then check for leaks and proper thermostat operation.

## 5   Engine and condenser cooling fan(s) - component replacement

### *Engine cooling fan*

**Warning:** *To avoid possible injury or damage, DO NOT operate the engine with a damaged fan. Do not attempt to repair fan blades - replace a damaged fan with a new one.*

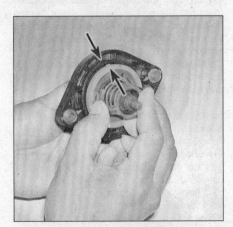

4.17b . . . then align the tab (lower arrow) on the outer edge of the gasket with the notch in the thermostat housing (upper arrow) and insert the thermostat into the housing

1   Disconnect the cable(s) from the negative battery terminal(s) (see Chapter 5).

### Gasoline engines and 2002 and earlier diesel engines

2   Remove the expansion tank (see Section 6). If you're working on a V10, detach the upper radiator hose from the radiator.

3   A special pin spanner wrench (obtainable at most auto parts stores) may be required to hold the water pump pulley while a large open-end wrench is used to loosen the fan clutch nut (see illustration). Sometimes it is possible to hold the water pump pulley by applying considerable hand pressure to the serpentine belt while the large nut is loosened, but it may require the tool if the fan drive nut is excessively tight. Carefully lower the fan and clutch assembly into the fan shroud. Be very careful not to damage the radiator fins while doing so.

**Note:** *On all models except 2002 diesels, turn the nut counterclockwise to loosen it. On 2002 diesel models the nut has left hand threads - turn the nut clockwise to loosen it.*

5.3 Use a pin spanner wrench to prevent the water pump pulley from turning, then loosen the fan clutch nut with an open end wrench

**5.4 Location of the engine cooling fan shroud mounting bolts (A) and the radiator mounting bolts (B) on a Hemi engine - other models similar**

**5.5 Remove the four bolts retaining the cooling fan to the fan clutch - Hemi engine shown, others similar**

**5.18 Location of the condenser mounting bolts**

**5.20 Slide the clip off the stud in the direction of the arrow and separate the cooling fan from the electric motor**

4   Remove the fan shroud mounting bolts and, on models so equipped, pull the shroud up to detach the clips at the bottom of the shroud (see illustration). Remove the fan shroud and the cooling fan components as one assembly.

**Note:** *On some models the shroud is retained by two bolts.On others it's retained by four bolts.*

5   Working on the bench, remove the cooling fan mounting bolts from the viscous fan clutch (see illustration).

6   Installation is the reverse of removal. Tighten the fan clutch-to-cooling fan bolts to the torque Specifications listed in this Chapter. Tighten the fan clutch securely.

### 2003 and later diesel engines

7   Remove the fan shroud bolts.

8   Install a large screwdriver between the fan pulley bolts while a large open-end wrench is used to loosen the fan drive nut on the cooling fan. Turn the large nut counterclockwise (right-hand threads). Carefully lower the fan and clutch assembly into the fan shroud. Be very careful not to damage the radiator fins while doing so.

**Caution:** *Do not remove any of the cooling fan pulley bolts. The pulley is under spring tension and could release.*

9   Disconnect the electronic fan clutch connector located at the lower fan shroud bracket.

10   Detach the electronic fan clutch harness from the fan shroud bracket.

11   Lift the assembly from the engine compartment.

12   Remove the bolts and separate the fan from the fan clutch.

13   Installation is the reverse of removal. Tighten the fan clutch-to-cooling fan bolts to the torque Specifications listed in this Chapter. Tighten the fan clutch securely.

### Condenser cooling fan

**Warning:** *The air conditioning system is under high pressure. Do not loosen any hose fittings or remove any components until after the system has been discharged. Air conditioning refrigerant must be properly discharged into an EPA-approved recovery/recycling unit at a dealer service department or an automotive air conditioning repair facility. Always wear eye protection when disconnecting air conditioning system fittings.*

**Note:** *2003 and later diesel engines and 8.0L V10 engines are equipped with a condenser that is mounted in front of the radiator. These models are not equipped with an electric cooling fan.*

14   Have the air conditioning system discharged (see Warning above).

15   Disconnect the cable(s) from the negative battery terminal(s) (see Chapter 5).

16   Disconnect the air conditioning lines at the condenser. Install a piece of tape or special plugs into the openings to prevent dirt or contamination from entering.

17   Disconnect the harness connector from the cooling fan.

18   Remove the two upper bolts that attach the condenser to the upper crossmember (see illustration).

19   Lift the condenser and cooling fan assembly from the engine compartment.

20   Remove the clip and separate the cooling fan from the electric motor (see illustration).

21   Remove the mounting bolts and separate the cooling fan motor from the frame (see illustration).

22   Installation is the reverse of removal.

23   When installing the fan and fan shroud assembly, make sure that the dowels on the bottom of the condenser are seated in their rubber grommets.

24   Have the air conditioning system evacuated, charged and leak tested by the shop that discharged it.

5.21 Remove the fan motor mounting bolts

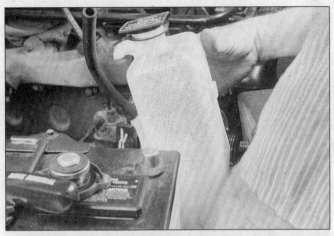

6.3a Pull straight up on the coolant reservoir to separate it from the fan shroud

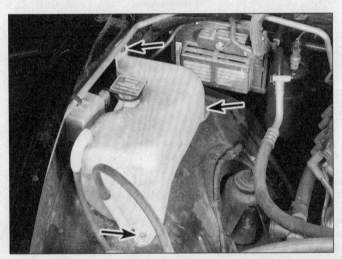

6.3b The coolant reservoir on early V10 models is attached to the inner fender panel with screws

6.5 Disconnect the supply hose (A) and return hose (B), then remove the expansion tank mounting bolts (C)

## 6   Coolant reservoir/expansion tank - removal and installation

**Warning:** *Wait until the engine is completely cool before beginning this procedure.*
**Note:** *Some models are equipped with a coolant reservoir mounted on the side of the cooling fan shroud or at the right rear corner of the engine compartment. These systems incorporate the radiator cap on top of the radiator and the coolant reservoir stores excess coolant that is transferred through the overflow hose. Other models are equipped with an expansion tank on top of the cooling fan shroud. These models incorporate the pressure cap on the expansion tank.*

1   Drain the cooling system (see Chapter 1).

### Coolant reservoir systems

2   Disconnect the hose from the coolant reservoir.
3   Remove the coolant reservoir:

a) *If you're working on a diesel, remove the right-side battery (see Chapter 5).*
b) *Some models use T-slots to lock the reservoir into brackets. Lift the coolant reservoir from the T-slots and separate it from the cooling fan shroud (see illustration).*
c) *Some models use bolts and pins to retain the reservoir to the shroud and radiator or inner fender (see illustration). Remove the mounting bolts and separate it from the cooling fan shroud. Be sure to align the pins into the slots on installation.*

### Expansion tank systems

4   Disconnect the hoses from the expansion tank.
5   Remove the expansion tank mounting bolts (see illustration). Remove the tank.

### All models

6   Installation is the reverse of removal.
7   Refill the cooling system (see Chapter 1).

## 7   Radiator - removal and installation

**Warning:** *If vehicle is equipped with airbags, refer to Chapter 12 to disarm the airbag system prior to performing any work described below.*
**Warning:** *Wait until the engine is completely cool before beginning this procedure.*

### Removal

1   Disconnect the cable(s) from the negative battery terminal(s) (see Chapter 5, Section 1).
2   Drain the cooling system (see Chapter 1). If the coolant is relatively new or in good condition, save it and reuse it.
3   On models with the expansion tank or coolant reservoir mounted to the radiator, remove the expansion tank or reservoir (see Section 6).
4   Unclip the power steering hoses from the cooling fan shroud.

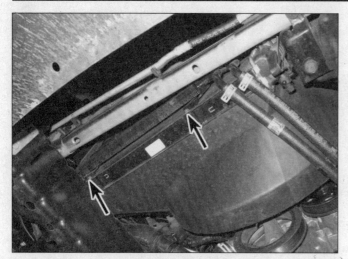

**7.9 Remove the mounting nut and bolt and detach the power steering cooler from the radiator**

**7.10 Location of the upper radiator hose spring tension clamp on the Hemi engine**

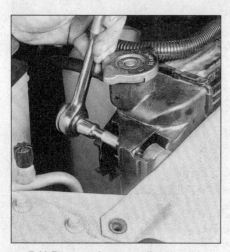

**7.11 Remove the two radiator upper mounting bolts - 2008 and earlier models shown, other models similar**

5    Remove the condenser cooling fan, on models so equipped (see Section 5). On other models, unbolt the fan shroud, move it away from the radiator and allow it to rest on the fan.

6    Remove the windshield washer fluid reservoir.

7    On diesel models, remove the air filter housing (see Chapter 4A).

8    Remove the transmission fluid cooler bolt and slide the cooler away from the radiator (see Chapter 7B).

9    Remove the mounting fasteners and separate the power steering cooler from the radiator (see illustration).

10    Loosen the hose clamps, then detach the radiator hoses from the fittings on the radiator (see illustration). If they're stuck, grasp each hose near the end with a pair of adjustable pliers and twist it to break the seal, then pull it off - be careful not to distort the radiator fittings. If

the hoses are old or deteriorated, cut them off and install new ones.

11    Remove the radiator mounting bolts from the upper crossmember (see illustration).

12    Lift the radiator from the engine compartment (see illustration). Don't spill coolant on the vehicle or scratch the paint. Also be careful not to damage the cooling fins of the transmission cooler or power steering cooler.

13    Whenever the radiator is removed from the vehicle, make note of the location of all rubber mounting cushions and their location (see illustration). If they're cracked, hardened or otherwise deteriorated, replace them.

## Installation

14    With the radiator removed, it can be inspected for leaks and damage. If it needs repair, have a radiator shop or dealer service department perform the work as special techniques are required.

**7.12 After prying the bottom of the radiator loose from the rubber insulators, pull the radiator straight up and out**

**7.13 Inspect the radiator mounts for damage**

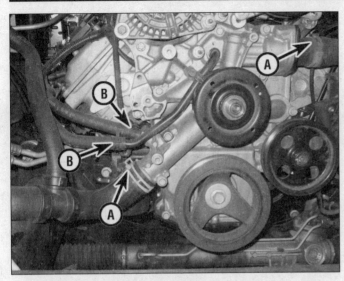

8.7 Location of the radiator (A) and heater hoses (B) on the Hemi engine

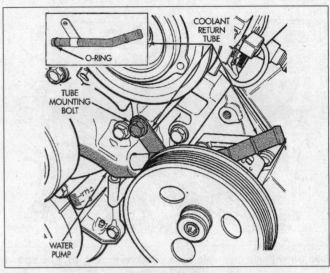

8.8 On 3.9L V6, 5.2L V8 or 5.9L V8 models, the coolant return tube must be unbolted and twisted out of the pump

15   Bugs and dirt can be removed from the front of the radiator with a garden hose, followed by compressed air and a soft brush. Don't bend the cooling fins as this is done. When blowing out the core, direct the hose or air line only from the engine side out.

16   Inspect the radiator mounts for deterioration and make sure there's nothing in them when the radiator is installed.

17   Installation is the reverse of the removal procedure.

18   After installation, fill the cooling system with the proper mixture of antifreeze and water (see Chapter 1).

19   Start the engine and check for leaks. Allow the engine to reach normal operating temperature, indicated by the inlet radiator hose becoming hot. Recheck the coolant level and add more if required.

## 8   Water pump - replacement

**Warning:** *Wait until the engine is completely cool before beginning this procedure.*

### Removal

1   Disconnect the cable(s) from the negative battery terminal(s) (see Chapter 5, Section 1).

2   Drain the cooling system (see Chapter 1). If the coolant is relatively new or in good condition, save it and reuse it.

3   On all models except those equipped with a diesel engine, remove the engine cooling fan and shroud (see Section 5).

4   Remove the drivebelt (see Chapter 1).

### Hemi engines

5   Unbolt the air conditioning compressor and alternator and reposition them so they're out of the way. Don't disconnect the refrigerant lines from the compressor.

6   Remove the idler pulley and the drivebelt tensioner.

### All engines

7   Detach the radiator hose(s) and the heater hose(s) from the water pump (see illustration). If a hose sticks, grasp it near the end with a pair of adjustable pliers and twist it to break the seal, then pull it off. If the hose is deteriorated, cut it off and install a new one.

8   If you're working on a 3.9L V6, 5.2L V8 or 5.9L V8, remove the bolt and pull the coolant tube out of the water pump using a twisting motion (see illustration).

9   Remove the bolts and detach the water pump from the engine. Note the locations of the various lengths and different types of bolts as they're removed to ensure correct installation (see illustrations).

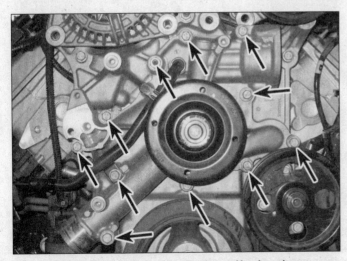

8.9a Water pump bolt locations on a Hemi engine

8.9b Water pump removal on a diesel engine

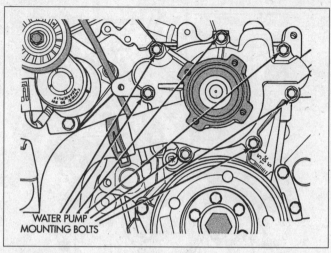

**8.9c Water pump mounting bolts locations on 3.9L V6, 5.2L V8 and 5.9L V8 engines**

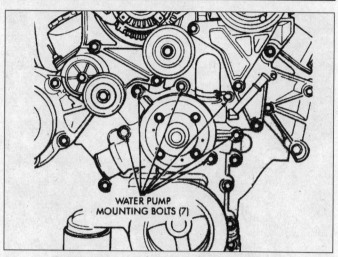

**8.9d Water pump bolt locations V10 engines**

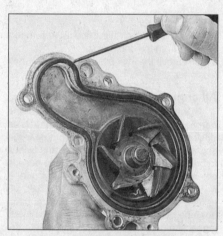

**8.13a On 3.7L V6/4.7L V8 models, first remove the rubber O-ring from the water pump flange**

10   If you're working on 3.9L V6, 5.2L V8 and 5.9L V8 engines, loosen the clamp and disconnect the bypass hose as the water pump is being removed.

**Note:** *The bypass hose on 3.9L V6, 5.2L V8 and 5.9L V8 engines is difficult to access. After the water pump has been removed, it is recommended that the bypass hose be replaced with a new one.*

### Installation

11   Clean the bolt threads and the threaded holes in the engine to remove corrosion and sealant.

12   Compare the new pump to the old one to make sure they're identical. If the old pump is being reused, check the impeller blades on the backside for corrosion. If any fins are missing or badly corroded, replace the pump with a new one.

13   Remove all traces of old gasket material from the engine (and water pump, if the same one is to be installed) (see illustrations).

14   Clean the engine and water pump mating surfaces with lacquer thinner or acetone.

15   On water pumps equipped with an O-ring seal, apply a thin coat of RTV sealant to the new water pump O-ring and position it in the groove on the back of the water pump (see illustrations).

**Caution:** *Make sure the O-ring is correctly seated in the water pump groove to avoid a coolant leak.*

16   On water pumps equipped with a gasket, apply a thin film of RTV sealant to the gasket mating surface of the new pump, and position the gasket on the pump. Apply a thin film of RTV sealant to the engine-side of the gasket and slip a couple of bolts through the pump mounting holes to hold the gasket in place.

17   Carefully attach the pump and O-ring/

**8.13b Remove all traces of sealant or gasket material - use care to avoid gouging the soft aluminum**

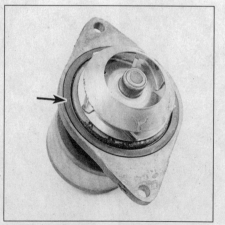

**8.15a Install a new rubber O-ring in the groove on the back of the pump (diesel water pump shown)**

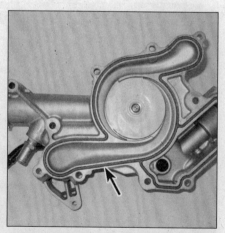

**8.15b Here's the rubber O-ring on a Hemi water pump - make sure it rests properly in its groove**

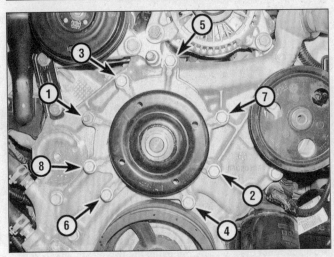
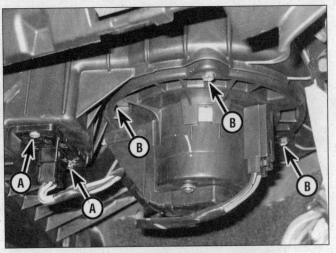

**8.18 Tighten the water pump bolts in a criss-cross pattern (3.7L V6/4.7L V8 engine shown)**

**10.3 Blower motor and resistor details**
A    Blower motor resistor mounting screws
B    Blower motor mounting bolts

gasket to the engine and thread the bolts into the holes finger-tight. On diesel engines, make sure the weep hole is pointing down.
18    Install the remaining bolts and tighten them in a criss-cross pattern to the torque listed in this Chapter's Specifications in 1/4-turn increments (see illustration). Turn the water pump by hand to make sure it rotates freely.
19    If you're working on 3.9L V6, 5.2L V8 or 5.9L V8, install a new O-ring on the coolant tube. Lubricate the O-ring with clean coolant, then insert the tube into the pump using a twisting motion. Install the bolt and tighten it securely.
20    Reinstall all parts removed for access to the pump.
**Caution:** *Make sure the serpentine drivebelt is installed as originally routed or overheating could result.*
21    Refill the cooling system (see Chapter 1). Run the engine and check for leaks.

**9    Coolant temperature sending unit**

1    All models covered in this manual utilize a variety of electronic sensors and an onboard computer to monitor various engine parameters, engine temperature being one of them. The Powertrain Control Module (PCM) controls the temperature gauge on the instrument cluster. An individual sending unit for the temperature gauge is not necessary with the use of this technology.

**10    Blower motor resistor and blower motor - replacement**

**Warning:** *The models covered by this manual are equipped with a Supplemental Restraint*

System (SRS), more commonly known as airbags. Always disarm the airbag system before working in the vicinity of any airbag system component to avoid the possibility of accidental deployment of the airbag, which could cause personal injury (see Chapter 12). Do not use a memory saving device to preserve the PCM's memory when working on or near airbag system components.
1    Disconnect the cable(s) from the negative battery terminal(s) (see Chapter 5).

**Blower motor resistor**

2    Working in the passenger's compartment under the glove box, remove the lower dash panel (see Chapter 11).
3    Disconnect the electrical connector from the blower motor resistor (see illustration).
4    Remove the blower motor resistor mounting screws and remove it from the blower housing.

5    Installation is the reverse of removal.
6    Reconnect the battery.

**Blower motor**

7    Working in the passenger's compartment under the glove box, remove the lower dash panel (see Chapter 11).
8    Disconnect the electrical connector from the blower motor, then remove the mounting screws and lower the blower motor out of the housing (see illustration 10.3).
9    On 2001 and earlier models, the blower motor and fan are both replaceable individually. To remove the fan from the blower motor, squeeze the spring clip together and slip the fan off the shaft (see illustration).
10    On 2002 and later models, if either the fan or motor is damaged, the entire unit must be replaced as an assembly.
11    Installation is the reverse of removal.

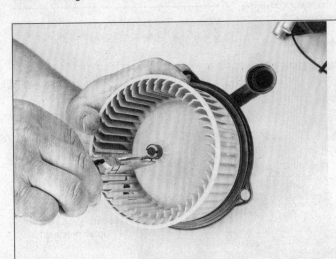

**10.9 Remove the fan by squeezing the spring clip together and slipping the fan off the shaft (2001 and earlier models)**

**11.3 Remove the four screws retaining the heater/air conditioning control assembly to the instrument panel - 2001 and earlier models**

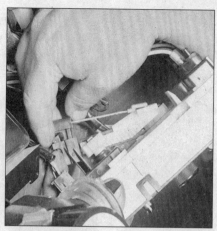

**11.4a Pull the control assembly away from the instrument panel, disconnect the blend cable by depressing the red "flag" tab, then disconnect the cable housing from the control assembly - 2001 and earlier models**

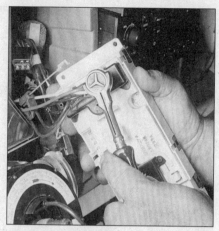

**11.4b Disconnect the vacuum connector by removing the two plastic nuts - 2001 and earlier models**

## 11 Heater/air conditioning control assembly - removal and installation

**Warning:** *The models covered by this manual are equipped with a Supplemental Restraint System (SRS), more commonly known as airbags. Always disarm the airbag system before working in the vicinity of any airbag system component to avoid the possibility of accidental deployment of the airbag, which could cause personal injury (see Chapter 12). Do not use a memory saving device to preserve the PCM's memory when working on or near airbag system components.*

1    Disconnect the cable(s) from the negative battery terminal(s) (see Chapter 5).
2    Refer to Chapter 11 and remove the center trim bezel.
3    On 2001 and earlier models, remove the four control assembly retaining screws (see illustration).
4    On 2001 and earlier models, remove

the heater/air conditioning control assembly from the instrument panel and disconnect the blend-air control cable, electrical connector and vacuum lines from the control assembly (see illustrations).
**Caution:** *Be careful when removing the vacuum lines to avoid cracking the plastic connectors and causing a vacuum leak (possibly internal within the control assembly).*
5    On 2002 and later models, pull the bezel forward and disconnect the electrical connectors (see illustration).
6    Remove the four mounting screws and detach the air conditioning and heater control assembly.
7    Installation is the reverse of the removal procedure.

## 12 Heater core - replacement

**Warning:** *The models covered by this manual are equipped with a Supplemental Restraint*

*System (SRS), more commonly known as airbags. Always disarm the airbag system before working in the vicinity of any airbag system component to avoid the possibility of accidental deployment of the airbag, which could cause personal injury (see Chapter 12). Do not use a memory saving device to preserve the PCM's memory when working on or near airbag system components.*
**Warning:** *The air conditioning system is under high pressure. Do not loosen any hose fittings or remove any components until after the system has been discharged. Air conditioning refrigerant must be properly discharged into an EPA-approved recovery/recycling unit at a dealer service department or an automotive air conditioning repair facility. Always wear eye protection when disconnecting air conditioning system fittings.*
**Warning:** *Wait until the engine is completely cool before beginning this procedure.*
**Note:** *Heater core removal is a difficult task for the home mechanic. It can be done with slow, careful attention to detail, but many fasteners and wiring connectors are difficult to get at behind the instrument panel. The entire instrument panel must be removed to allow the heater/air conditioning unit to be removed from the vehicle.*

### 2001 and earlier 1500 models/ 2002 and earlier 2500 and 3500 models

#### Removal

1    If equipped with air conditioning, have the system discharged at a dealer service department or automotive air conditioning facility.
2    Disconnect the cable(s) from the negative battery terminal(s) (see Chapter 5). Drain the cooling system (see Chapter 1).
3    Disconnect the heater hoses at the heater core inlet and outlet on the engine side

**11.5 Depress the tabs and detach the electrical connectors from the back of the heater/air conditioning control assembly - 2002 and later models**

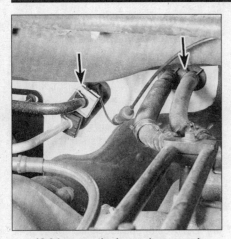

12.3 Loosen the hose clamps and disconnect the heater hoses from the heater core tubes at the firewall (right arrow), then disconnect the two refrigerant lines (left arrow)

12.6 Remove the nuts from the studs on the engine compartment side of the firewall - one more (not seen here) is at the center of the firewall above the engine

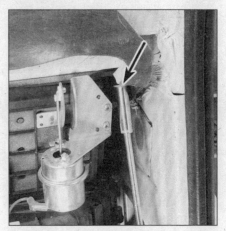

12.8a Remove the right-side kick panel and remove the bolt holding the heater/air conditioning unit to the cowl . . .

of the firewall (see illustration). Cap the open fittings.

4    Using spring-lock coupling tools, disconnect the refrigerant lines at the firewall. Cap the open lines to prevent entry of contaminants.

5    On V10 models, refer to Section 6 and remove the coolant reservoir. Refer to Chapter 6 and remove the PCM without disconnecting its wires. On diesel models, remove the air cleaner housing for access to the PCM (see Chapter 4B).

6    Remove the four nuts from the heater/air conditioning unit studs on the engine compartment side of the firewall (see illustration). Refer to Section 14 for removal of the accumulator. After it is removed, remove the nut from the mounting stud that held the accumulator to the firewall. One stud/nut is at the

center of the firewall, to the right of the heater hose connections.

7    Refer to Chapter 11 for removal of the instrument panel, and Section 11 of this Chapter for removal and disconnection of the heater/air conditioning controls.

8    Remove the bolts retaining the heater/air conditioning unit to the cowl (see illustrations).

9    Move the heater housing to the rear until it clears the studs and remove the unit from the vehicle (see illustration). Make sure the heater core inlet and outlet pipes are securely plugged to prevent coolant from spilling into the passenger compartment.

**Note:** *The heater blend door cable must be disconnected, either at the controls (see Section 11) or at the heater/air conditioning housing assembly.*

10    The heater core itself is retained by three screws in the housing, one that clamps the tubes near the firewall, and two on a clamp near the core (see illustration). Remove the three screws and clamps, then pull the heater core straight out of the housing.

11    Remove and save any sealing material around the core or tubes.

## Installation

12    Installation is the reverse of removal. Be sure to reinstall any sealing materials around the heater core, doors, or ducting.

13    Refill the cooling system (see Chapter 1).

14    Start the engine and check for proper operation. If equipped with air conditioning, have the air conditioning system evacuated and recharged by the shop that discharged it.

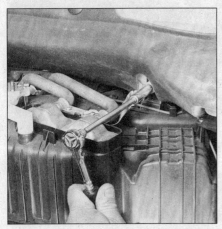

12.8b . . . then remove the nut from this stud - remove the ground strap from the stud, then the final nut (on the same stud) holding the unit to the firewall

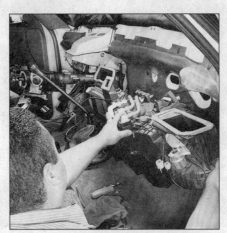

12.9 With everything disconnected, the entire heater/air conditioner unit can be removed from the vehicle

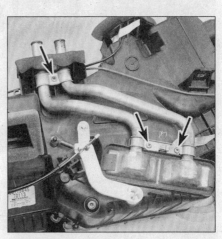

12.10 Remove these three screws and the clamps and slide the heater core straight out of the housing

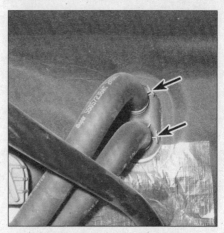

**12.18 Slide the clamps away and detach the hoses from the heater core at the engine compartment firewall**

**12.22 Remove the two heater/air conditioning unit nuts from the studs in the engine compartment**

**12.24 Location of the heater/air conditioning unit mounting fasteners - later models shown, earlier models similar**

## *2002 and later 1500 models/ 2003 and later 2500 and 3500 models*

### Removal

15   On models with air conditioning, have the system discharged (see Warning above).

16   Disconnect the cable(s) from the negative battery terminal(s) (see Chapter 5).

17   Drain the cooling system (see Chapter 1).

18   Disconnect the heater hoses at the heater core on the right side of the engine compartment at the firewall (see illustration). Tape or plug all openings.

19   On models with air conditioning, detach the accumulator and mounting bracket (see Section 14) and disconnect both air conditioning lines from the evaporator.

20   Remove the instrument panel (see Chapter 11).

21   Remove the Powertrain Control Module (PCM) from the engine compartment (see Chapter 6).

22   Remove the two heater/air conditioning unit nuts from the studs in the engine compartment (see illustration).

23   From inside the vehicle, disconnect the electrical connector from the blower motor resistor (see Section 10). Disconnect the electrical connector and vacuum hoses from the heater/air conditioning unit.

24   Remove the heater/air conditioning unit mounting nuts and bolt located in the passenger compartment (see illustration).

25   Remove the heater/air conditioning unit from the interior of the vehicle.

26   Detach the linkage rod, if equipped, remove the two heater core retaining screws, then lift the heater core out of the heater/air conditioning unit (see illustrations).

**12.26a Location of the heater core retaining screws**

**12.26b Pinch the release tabs and lift the heater core from the housing**

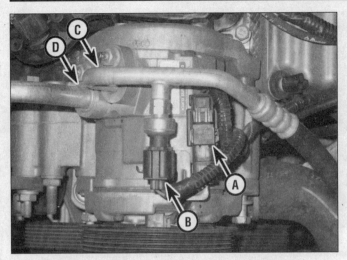

13.3a Air conditioning compressor details on the Hemi

A  Compressor clutch harness connector
B  High pressure switch
C  High pressure line (discharge) fitting
D  Low pressure line (suction) fitting

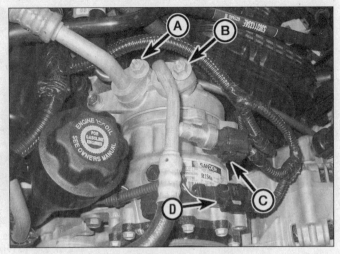

13.3b Air conditioning compressor details on the 3.7L V6

A  Low pressure line (suction) fitting
B  High pressure line (discharge) fitting
C  High pressure switch
D  Compressor clutch harness connector

## Installation

27  Before installing the heater core, make sure all foam seals are in place on the heater core and evaporator coil tubes.
28  Slide the heater core into the housing and install the screws.
29  Reinstall the remaining components in the reverse order of removal.
**Note:** When installing the heater/air conditioning unit, avoid pinching any wiring harnesses between the body and the housing.
30  Refill the cooling system (see Chapter 1).
31  Start the engine and check for proper operation.
32  On models with air conditioning, have the system evacuated, recharged and leak-tested by the shop that discharged it.

## 13  Air conditioning compressor - removal and installation

**Warning:** The air conditioning system is under high pressure. Do not loosen any hose fittings or remove any components until after the system has been discharged. Air conditioning refrigerant must be properly discharged into an EPA-approved recovery/recycling unit at a dealer service department or an automotive air conditioning repair facility. Always wear eye protection when disconnecting air conditioning system fittings.
**Note:** The accumulator (see Section 14) should be replaced whenever the compressor is replaced.

1  Have the air conditioning system discharged (see Warning above).
2  Disconnect the cable(s) from the negative battery terminal(s) (see Chapter 5).
3  Disconnect the compressor clutch electrical connector (see illustrations).
4  Remove the drivebelt (see Chapter 1).
5  Disconnect the refrigerant lines from the compressor. Plug the open fittings to prevent entry of dirt and moisture.
6  Unbolt the compressor from the mounting brackets and lift it out of the vehicle (see illustrations).
**Note:** On Hemi engines, remove the alternator bracket mounting bolts and the compressor bracket.
7  If a new compressor is being installed,

13.6a Right side compressor mounting bolts - 3.7L V6 engine

13.6b Left side compressor mounting bolt - 3.7L V6 engine

13.6c On diesel models, the compressor is mounted low on the right side of the engine - three of the four bolts (arrows) are shown, one is further back and accessible from underneath

**14.4a Remove the clip that protects the fitting . . .**

**14.4b . . . then use a special A/C spring lock tool to release the coupler**

**15.3a Remove the protective cover from the refrigerant line…**

follow the directions with the compressor regarding the draining of excess oil prior to installation.

**Note:** *Any replacement compressor used must be designated as compatible with refrigerant R-134a.*

8    The clutch may have to be transferred from the original to the new compressor.

9    Installation is the reverse of removal. Replace all O-rings with new ones specifically made for air conditioning system use and compatible with refrigerant R-134a. Lubricate them with refrigerant oil. Any refrigerant oil added must also be compatible with refrigerant R-134a.

10    Have the system evacuated, recharged and leak-tested by the shop that discharged it.

---

## 14   Air conditioning accumulator - removal and installation

**Warning:** *The air conditioning system is under high pressure. Do not loosen any hose fittings or remove any components until after the system has been discharged. Air conditioning refrigerant must be properly discharged into an EPA-approved recovery/recycling unit at a dealer service department or an automotive*

air conditioning repair facility. Always wear eye protection when disconnecting air conditioning system fittings.

1    Have the air conditioning system discharged (see Warning above).

2    Disconnect the cable(s) from the negative battery terminal(s) (see Chapter 5).

3    On gasoline-engine models, remove the air filter housing and the air intake duct (see Chapter 4A).

4    Disconnect the refrigerant line from the accumulator outlet tube (see illustrations).

5    Disconnect the accumulator line to the evaporator at the firewall.

6    Plug the open fittings to prevent entry of dirt and moisture.

7    Remove the accumulator and bracket from the firewall. If a new accumulator is being installed, remove the Schrader valve (under the pressure switch) from the old accumulator, if equipped. Add 2 oz (60 ml) of new refrigerant oil (a type designated as compatible with refrigerant R-134a) to the new accumulator.

8    Installation is the reverse of removal.

**Note:** *New R-134a compatible O-rings should be used in each fitting during reassembly.*

9    Take the vehicle back to the shop that discharged it. Have the air conditioning system evacuated, charged and leak tested.

---

## 15   Air conditioning condenser - removal and installation

**Warning:** *The air conditioning system is under high pressure. Do not loosen any hose fittings or remove any components until after the system has been discharged. Air conditioning refrigerant must be properly discharged into an EPA-approved recovery/recycling unit at a dealer service department or an automotive air conditioning repair facility. Always wear eye protection when disconnecting air conditioning system fittings.*

**Note:** *The accumulator (Section 13) should be replaced whenever the condenser is replaced.*

1    Have the air conditioning system discharged (see Warning above).

2    Disconnect the cable(s) from the negative battery terminal(s) (see Chapter 5).

### All models except diesel and 8.0L V10 models

3    Unbolt and disconnect the refrigerant lines from the condenser (see illustrations). Plug the lines and fittings to prevent the entry of moisture and contaminants.

**Note:** *On some models, the refrigerant lines are equipped with spring-lock connectors instead of nuts.*

4    Disconnect the condenser cooling fan motor connector (see Section 5).

5    On 2001 and earlier models, remove the condenser mounting bolts (see illustration).

6    On 2002 and later models, remove the two upper condenser mounting bolts from the upper crossmember (see Section 5).

7    Remove the condenser cooling fan and condenser assembly from the vehicle.

### Diesel and 8.0L V10 models

8    Unbolt and disconnect the refrigerant lines from the condenser. Plug the lines and fittings to prevent the entry of moisture and contaminants.

9    On diesel models, remove the brackets that secure the condenser to the intercooler

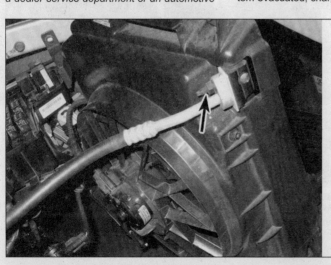

**15.3b … then remove the nut and disconnect the refrigerant line from the condenser**

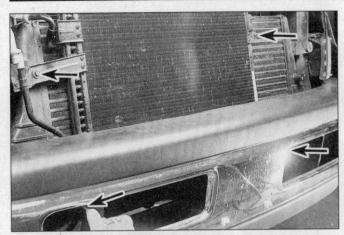

**15.5 The air conditioning condenser is located in front of the radiator - arrows indicate mounting bolts, two of which are accessible through holes in the front bumper**

**15.12 On V10 models, and as optional equipment on other models, the left condenser mount is slightly different, to make room for the auxiliary transmission oil cooler (arrow)**

on the passenger's side of the vehicle and the nuts/studs from the driver's side of the condenser/intercooler.

10   On 8.0L V10 models, remove the front bumper (see Chapter 11).

11   On 8.0L V10 models, remove the front hood latch assembly (see Chapter 11).

12   Remove the mounting bolts from the condenser brackets (see illustration).

13   Lift the condenser straight up and out of the condenser brackets. Plug the open fittings to prevent entry of dirt and moisture.

### All models

14   If the original condenser will be reinstalled, store it with the line fittings on top to prevent oil from draining out.

15   If a new condenser is being installed, pour 1 oz (30 ml) of refrigerant oil into it prior to installation (an oil designated as compatible with refrigerant R-134a).

**Note:** *New R-134a compatible O-rings should be used in each fitting during reassembly.*

16   Install new O-rings onto the refrigerant lines (see illustration).

17   Reinstall the components in the reverse order of removal.

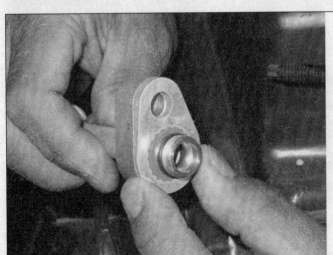

**15.16 Install new O-rings onto the refrigerant lines**

18   Have the system evacuated, recharged and leak-tested by the shop that discharged it.

### 16   Air conditioning high-pressure switch - replacement

**Warning:** *The air conditioning system is under high pressure. Do not loosen any hose fittings or remove any components until after the system has been discharged. Air conditioning refrigerant must be properly discharged into an EPA-approved recovery/recycling unit at a dealer service department or an automotive air conditioning repair facility. Always wear eye protection when disconnecting air conditioning system fittings.*

**Note:** *The air conditioning high pressure switch is mounted on the high pressure line at the compressor.*

1   Have the air conditioning system discharged (see Warning above).

2   Disconnect the cable(s) from the negative battery terminal(s) (see Chapter 5).

3   Unplug the electrical connector from the air conditioning pressure switch (see Section 13)

4   Unscrew the pressure cycling switch.

Use a back-up wrench to prevent damaging the refrigerant line.

5   Lubricate the switch O-ring with clean refrigerant oil of the correct type.

6   Screw the new switch onto the refrigerant line until hand tight, and then tighten it securely.

7   Reconnect the electrical connector.

8   Have the air conditioning system evacuated, recharged and leak tested by the shop that discharged it.

### 17   Air conditioning orifice tube - removal and installation

**Warning:** *The air conditioning system is under high pressure. Do not loosen any hose fittings or remove any components until after the system has been discharged. Air conditioning refrigerant must be properly discharged into an EPA-approved recovery/recycling unit at a dealer service department or an automotive air conditioning repair facility. Always wear eye protection when disconnecting air conditioning system fittings.*

**Note:** *After operating a fully-charged air conditioner for five minutes, the liquid line should be hot near the condenser and it should be cold near the evaporator (be careful - it can get very hot!). If there isn't a significant temperature difference, the orifice tube may be plugged. If the system is checked with the appropriate gauges, and the high-pressure reads extremely high and the low-pressure reads almost a vacuum, the orifice tube is plugged. In either case, the liquid line, which contains the orifice tube, must be replaced.*

1   The fixed orifice tube is an inline metering restrictor that is located in the liquid line, between the condenser and the evaporator. Have the air conditioning system discharged (see Warning above).

2   Disconnect the cable(s) from the negative battery terminal(s) (see Chapter 5, Section 1).

### 2001 and earlier models

3   Access the condenser line in front of the radiator by opening the hood.

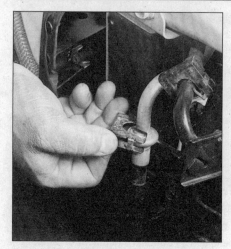

**17.4a To disconnect any of the air conditioning lines, first pull off the factory clip . . .**

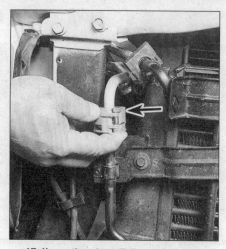

**17.4b . . . then install the spring-lock coupling tool, push the two connected lines together . . .**

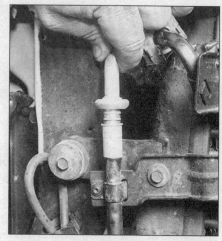

**17.4c . . . then remove the tool and pull the lines apart**

4    Using a spring-lock coupling tool, disconnect the refrigerant line fittings. Use needle-nose pliers to withdraw the fixed-orifice tube from the condenser outlet line. Cap the open fittings to prevent the entry of dirt and moisture (see illustrations).

## 2002 and later models

5    Remove the inner fender splash shield (see Chapter 11).
6    Remove the air filter housing (see Chapter 4A) and support tray (see illustrations).
7    Using a special refrigerant line spring lock tool, disconnect the liquid line at each end (see illustration). Cap or plug the refrigerant openings to prevent any dirt or moisture from entering the system.
8    Reinstall the new line/orifice tube.
**Note:** *New R-134a compatible O-rings should be used in each fitting during reassembly.*
9    Have the system evacuated, recharged and leak-tested by the shop that discharged it.

**17.4d The fixed-orifice tube is located in the condenser outlet line**

**17.6a After removing the air filter housing, remove these bolts from the support tray . . .**

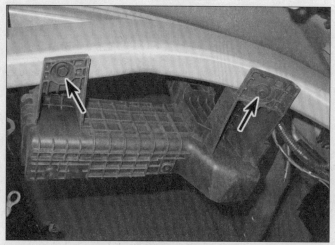

**17.6b . . . and these bolts from the underside of the support tray, then remove the tray**

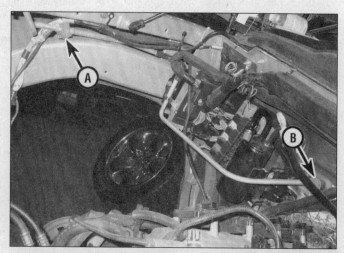

**17.7 Detach the liquid line at its connection below the lip of the right fender (A) and at the evaporator inlet tube (B)**

# Chapter 4 Part A
# Fuel and exhaust systems - gasoline engines

## Contents

## Specifications

### General

Fuel pressure (engine running at idle speed)
| | |
|---|---|
| 1994 and 1995 | 35 to 45 psi |
| 1996 through 2003 | 44.2 to 54.2 psi |
| 2004 on | 54 to 64 psi |

Fuel injector resistance (at 68° F [20° C])
| | |
|---|---|
| 2001 and earlier | 12.4 ohms |
| 2002 | 10.8 to 13.2 ohms |
| 2003 on | Not specified, but the injectors can still be checked with an ohmmeter to verify that the solenoid coils are not open or shorted |

### Torque specifications — Ft-lbs (unless otherwise indicated)

**Note:** *One foot-pound (ft-lb) of torque is equivalent to 12 inch-pounds (in-lbs) of torque. Torque values below approximately 15 ft-lbs are expressed in inch-pounds, since most foot-pound torque wrenches are not accurate at these smaller values.*

Throttle body mounting bolts
| | |
|---|---|
| 3.7L V6 | 100 in-lbs |
| 4.7L V8 | 105 in-lbs |
| 5.7L V8 (Hemi) | 105 in-lbs |
| 3.9L V6 and 5.2L V8 | 19 |
| 5.9L V8 | 16.5 |
| 8.0L V10 | 16 |

Fuel rail mounting nuts/bolts
| | |
|---|---|
| 3.7L V6, 4.7L V8 and 5.7L V8 (Hemi) | 100 in-lbs |
| 3.9L V6 and 5.2L V8 | 108 in-lbs |
| 5.9L V8 | 16.5 |
| 8.0L V10 | 136 in-lbs |

## 1   General Information, precautions and troubleshooting

### *General information*
#### Fuel system warnings

**Warning:** *Gasoline is extremely flammable, so take extra precautions when you work on any part of the fuel system. Don't smoke or allow open flames or bare light bulbs near the work area, and don't work in a garage where a gas-type appliance (such as a water heater or a clothes dryer) is present. Since gasoline is carcinogenic, wear fuel-resistant gloves when there's a possibility of being exposed to fuel, and, if you spill any fuel on your skin, rinse it off immediately with soap and water. Mop up any spills immediately and do not store fuel-soaked rags where they could ignite. The fuel system is under constant pressure, so, if any fuel lines are to be disconnected, the fuel pressure in the system must be relieved first. When you perform any kind of work on the fuel system, wear safety glasses and have a Class B type fire extinguisher on hand.*

a) *Don't smoke or allow open flames or bare light bulbs near the work area*
b) *Don't work in a garage with a gas-type appliance (water heater, clothes dryer)*
c) *Use fuel-resistant gloves. If any fuel spills on your skin, wash it off immediately with soap and water*
d) *Clean up spills immediately*
e) *Do not store fuel-soaked rags where they could ignite*
f) *Prior to disconnecting any fuel line, you must relieve the fuel pressure (see Section 2)*
g) *Wear safety glasses*
h) *Have a proper fire extinguisher on hand*

#### Fuel system

1   The fuel system consists of the fuel tank, electric fuel pump/fuel level sending unit (located in the fuel tank), fuel rail, fuel injectors and, on turbocharged models, a high-pressure fuel pump mounted to the end of the cylinder head. The fuel injection system is a multi-port system; multi-port fuel injection uses timed impulses to inject the fuel directly into the intake port of each cylinder. The Powertrain Control Module (PCM) controls the injectors. The PCM monitors various engine parameters and delivers the exact amount of fuel required into the intake ports.
2   Fuel is circulated from the fuel pump to the fuel rail through fuel lines running along the underside of the vehicle. Various sections of the fuel line are either rigid metal or nylon, or flexible fuel hose. The various sections of the fuel hose are connected either by quick-connect fittings or threaded metal fittings.

#### Electronic throttle control system

3   The Accord uses an electronically actuated throttle body; there is no direct cable link between the accelerator pedal and the throttle body. Instead, an electric actuator within the throttle body operates the throttle based on a signal it receives from the Powertrain Control Module (PCM). The Accelerator Pedal Position sensor provides input to the PCM of the actual position of the accelerator pedal.

#### Exhaust system

4   The exhaust system consists of the exhaust manifold, catalytic converter(s), muffler(s), tailpipe and all connecting pipes, flanges and clamps. The catalytic converters are an emission control device added to the exhaust system to reduce pollutants. On some models, the exhaust manifold is incorporated into the cylinder head, and the primary catalytic converter bolts directly to it.

### *Troubleshooting*
#### Fuel pump

5   The fuel pump is located inside the fuel tank. Sit inside the vehicle with the windows closed, turn the ignition key to On (not Start) and listen for the sound of the fuel pump as it's briefly activated. You will only hear the sound for a second or two, but that sound tells you that the pump is working. Alternatively, have an assistant listen at the fuel filler cap.
6   If the pump does not come on, check the fuel pump fuse in the engine compartment (underhood fuse/relay box) and the fuel pump relay (see illustration). If the fuse and relays are okay, check the wiring back to the fuel pump. If the fuse, relay and wiring are okay, the fuel pump is probably defective. If the pump runs continuously with the ignition key in the On position, the Powertrain Control Module (PCM) is probably defective. Have the PCM checked by a professional mechanic.

#### Fuel injection system

**Note:** *The following procedure is based on the assumption that the fuel pump is working and the fuel pressure is adequate (see Section 3).*
7   Check all electrical connectors that are related to the system. Check the ground wire connections for tightness.
8   Verify that the battery is fully charged (see Chapter 5).
9   Inspect the air filter element (see Chapter 1).
10   Check all fuses related to the fuel system (see Chapter 12).
11   Check the air induction system between the throttle body and the intake manifold for air leaks. Also inspect the condition of all vacuum hoses connected to the intake manifold and to the throttle body.
12   Remove the air intake duct from the throttle body and look for dirt, carbon, varnish, or other residue in the throttle body, particularly around the throttle plate. If it's dirty, clean it with carb cleaner, a toothbrush and a clean shop towel.
13   With the engine running, place an automotive stethoscope against each injector, one at a time, and listen for a clicking sound that indicates operation (on models where the injectors are accessible).
**Warning:** *Stay clear of the drivebelt and any rotating or hot components.*
14   If you can hear the injectors operating, but the engine is misfiring, the electrical circuits are functioning correctly, but the injectors might be dirty or clogged. Try a commercial injector cleaning product (available at auto parts stores). If cleaning the injectors doesn't help, replace the injectors.
15   If an injector is not operating (it makes no sound), disconnect the injector electrical connector and measure the resistance across the injector terminals with an ohmmeter. Compare this measurement to the other injectors. If the resistance of the non-operational injector is quite different from the other injectors, replace it.
16   If the injector is not operating, but the resistance reading is within the range of resistance of the other injectors, the PCM or the circuit between the PCM and the injector might be faulty.

## 2   Fuel pressure relief procedure

**Warning:** *See the Warning in Section 1.*

### *Models with a test port on the fuel rail*

1   Detach the cable from the negative battery terminal (see Chapter 5). Unscrew the fuel filler cap to relieve pressure built up in the fuel tank.

**1.6 Check the fuel pump fuse (A) and the fuel pump relay (B) located in the under-hood fuse/relay box (2003 1500 model with a 5.7L Hemi shown; be sure to check the underside of the fuse/relay box lid for the locations of the fuse and relay on your vehicle)**

 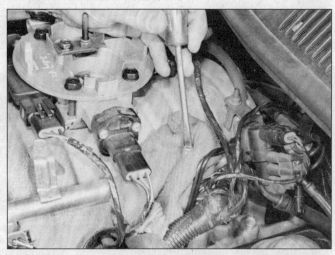

**2.3a Connect a fuel pressure gauge to the fuel rail at the test port and use the valve to bleed off the excess fuel into an approved fuel container**

**2.3b Use a small screwdriver or punch to depress the Schrader valve within the fuel pump test port. Be sure to catch any residual fuel using a rag (cover the screwdriver tip and valve with a rag to prevent fuel spray)**

2    Remove the cap from the fuel pressure test port located on the fuel rail.

3    Use one of the two following methods:

a) *Attach a fuel pressure gauge equipped with a bleeder hose (commonly available at auto parts stores) to the test port Schrader valve on the fuel rail (see illustration). Place the gauge bleeder hose in an approved fuel container. Open the valve on the gauge to relieve pressure.*

b) *Place several shop towels around the test port and the fuel rail. Remove the cap and, using the tip of a screwdriver, depress the Schrader valve and let the fuel drain into the shop towels (see illustration). Be careful to catch any fuel that might spray up by using another shop towel.*

4    Unless this procedure is followed before servicing fuel lines or connections, fuel spray (and possible injury) may occur.

5    Install the cap onto the fuel pressure test port.

### Models without a test port on the fuel rail

6    Remove the fuel filler cap (this will relieve any pressure that has built up in the tank).

7    Remove the fuel pump relay from the fuse and relay box in the engine compartment. You can locate any relay by looking at the relay guide printed on the underside of the fuse box cover (see illustration).

8    Turn the ignition key to Start and crank over the engine for several seconds. It will either start momentarily and immediately stall, or it won't start at all.

9    Turn the ignition key to the Off position.

10   Install the fuel pump relay.

11   Disconnect the cable from the negative battery terminal before beginning work on the fuel system (see Chapter 5, Section 1).

12   After all work on the fuel system has been completed, the CHECK ENGINE light or

Malfunction Indicator Light (MIL) might come on during operation because the engine was cranked with the fuel pump relay unplugged. The light will likely go out after a period of normal operation. If it does not go out, refer to Chapter 6.

---

### 3   Fuel pump/fuel pressure - check

**Warning:** *See the Warning in Section 1.*

### *Preliminary check*

1    The fuel pump is located inside the fuel tank, which muffles its sound when the engine is running. But you can actually hear the fuel pump. Turn the ignition key to On (not Start) and listen carefully for the whirring sound made by the fuel pump as it's briefly turned on by the PCM to pressurize the fuel system prior to starting the engine. You will only hear the sound for a second or two, but that indicates that the pump is working. If you can't hear the pump from inside the vehicle, remove the fuel filler cap and have an assistant turn the igni-

tion switch to On while you listen for the sound of the pump. If the pump does not come on when the ignition key is turned to On, check the fuel pump fuse and relay (both of which are located in the engine compartment fuse and relay box). If the fuse and relay are okay, check the wiring back to the fuel pump (see Section 6 if you need help locating the fuel pump electrical connector). If the fuse, relay and wiring are okay, the fuel pump is probably defective. If the pump runs continuously with the ignition key in its On position, the Powertrain Control Module (PCM) is probably defective. Have the PCM checked by a dealer service department or other qualified repair shop.

### *Pressure check*

**Note:** *In order to perform the fuel pressure test, you will need a fuel pressure gauge capable of measuring high fuel pressure. You'll also need the right fittings or adapters to attach it to the fuel rail.*

2    Relieve the fuel system pressure (see Section 2).

**2.7 To depressurize the fuel system, remove the fuel pump relay (B), which is located inside the fuse and relay box in the engine compartment. If the pump ever fails to operate, check the fuel pump fuse (A), then check the fuel pump relay. (The location of all the fuses and relays is displayed on the underside of the fuse box cover)**

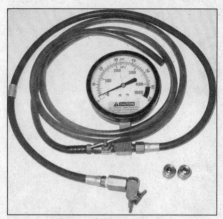

**3.3 To check the fuel pressure, you'll need to obtain a fuel pressure gauge capable of reading the fuel pressure within the specified operating system pressure, a hose to connect the gauge to the fuel pressure test port and an adapter suitable for connecting the hose to the test port**

**3.4a Fuel pressure test port location for 3.7L V6 and 4.7L V8 engines (V8 engine shown, V6 similar)**

**3.4b Fuel pressure test port location for Hemi engines**

3    For this check, you'll need to obtain a fuel pressure gauge with a hose and an adapter suitable for connecting it to the Schrader valve type test port on the injector fuel rail (see illustration).

4    The test port is located on the fuel rail (see illustrations). Look at the photos accompanying this step. If you can see - or if you can see but can't access - the fuel pressure test port, remove the air intake duct and, if necessary, the air resonator box (see Section 10). (On 8.0L V10 engines, the test port is located at the right front corner of the fuel rail.)

5    Unscrew the threaded cap from the test port and connect the fuel pressure gauge hose to the test port (see illustration).

6    Start the engine and check the pressure on the gauge, comparing your reading with the pressure listed in this Chapter's Specifications.

7    If the fuel pressure is not within specifications, check the following:

a) *If the pressure is lower than specified, check for a restriction in the fuel system (this includes the inlet strainer and the fuel filter at the fuel pump module).*

b) *If the fuel pressure is higher than specified, replace the fuel pressure regulator (see Section 7).*

---

4    **Fuel lines and fittings - general information and disconnection**

**Warning:** *Gasoline is extremely flammable. See Fuel system warnings in Section 1.*

1    Relieve the fuel pressure before servicing fuel lines or fittings (see Section 2), then disconnect the cable from the negative battery terminal (see Chapter 5) before proceeding.

2    The fuel supply line connects the fuel pump in the fuel tank to the fuel rail on the engine. The Evaporative Emission (EVAP)

system lines connect the fuel tank to the EVAP canister and connect the canister to the intake manifold.

3    Whenever you're working under the vehicle, be sure to inspect all fuel and evaporative emission lines for leaks, kinks, dents and other damage. Always replace a damaged fuel or EVAP line immediately.

4    If you find signs of dirt in the lines during disassembly, disconnect all lines and blow them out with compressed air. Inspect the fuel strainer on the fuel pump pick-up unit for damage and deterioration.

### Steel tubing

5    It is critical that the fuel lines be replaced with lines of equivalent type and specification.

6    Some steel fuel lines have threaded fittings. When loosening these fittings, hold the stationary fitting with a wrench while turning the tube nut.

### Plastic tubing

7    When replacing fuel system plastic tubing, use only original equipment replacement plastic tubing.

**Caution:** *When removing or installing plastic*

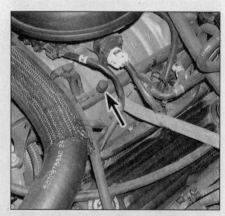

**3.4c Fuel pressure test port location for 3.9L V6, 5.2L V8 and 5.9L V8 engines**

*fuel line tubing, be careful not to bend or twist it too much, which can damage it. Also, plastic fuel tubing is NOT heat resistant, so keep it away from excessive heat.*

### Flexible hoses

8    When replacing fuel system flexible hoses, use only original equipment replacements.

9    Don't route fuel hoses (or metal lines) within four inches of the exhaust system or within ten inches of the catalytic converter. Make sure that no rubber hoses are installed directly against the vehicle, particularly in places where there is any vibration. If allowed to touch some vibrating part of the vehicle, a hose can easily become chafed and it might start leaking. A good rule of thumb is to maintain a minimum of 1/4-inch clearance around a hose (or metal line) to prevent contact with the vehicle underbody.

### Direct-injection high-pressure fuel lines

10    The high pressure fuel lines between the high-pressure fuel pump and injectors must be replaced if removed.

**3.5 Unscrew the cap from the test port and, using an adapter that fits the Schrader valve type test port, connect the fuel pressure gauge hose to the test port**

# Disconnecting Fuel Line Fittings

Two-tab type fitting; depress both tabs with your fingers, then pull the fuel line and the fitting apart

On this type of fitting, depress the two buttons on opposite sides of the fitting, then pull it off the fuel line

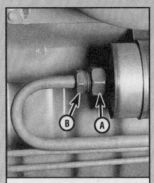

Threaded fuel line fitting; hold the stationary portion of the line or component (A) while loosening the tube nut (B) with a flare-nut wrench

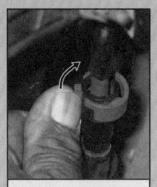

Plastic collar-type fitting; rotate the outer part of the fitting

Metal collar quick-connect fitting; pull the end of the retainer off the fuel line and disengage the other end from the female side of the fitting . . .

. . . insert a fuel line separator tool into the female side of the fitting, push it into the fitting and pull the fuel line off the pipe

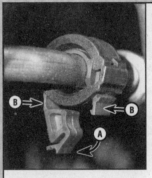

Some fittings are secured by lock tabs. Release the lock tab (A) and rotate it to the fully-opened position, squeeze the two smaller lock tabs (B) . . .

. . . then push the retainer out and pull the fuel line off the pipe

Spring-lock coupling; remove the safety cover, install a coupling release tool and close the tool around the coupling . . .

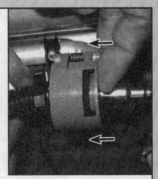

. . . push the tool into the fitting, then pull the two lines apart

Hairpin clip type fitting: push the legs of the retainer clip together, then push the clip down all the way until it stops and pull the fuel line off the pipe

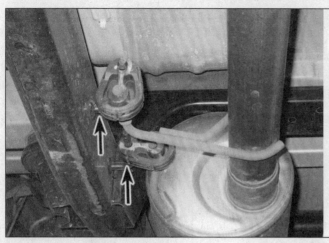

**5.1 Typical exhaust system hangers. Inspect regularly and replace at the first sign of damage or deterioration**

## 5   Exhaust system servicing - general information

**Warning:** *Allow exhaust system components to cool before inspection or repair. Also, when working under the vehicle, make sure it is securely supported on jackstands.*

1   The exhaust system consists of the exhaust manifolds, catalytic converter, muffler, tailpipe and all connecting pipes, flanges and clamps. The exhaust system is isolated from the vehicle body and from chassis components by a series of rubber hangers (see illustration). Periodically inspect these hangers for cracks or other signs of deterioration, replacing them as necessary.

2   Conduct regular inspections of the exhaust system to keep it safe and quiet. Look for any damaged or bent parts, open seams, holes, loose connections, excessive corrosion or other defects which could allow exhaust fumes to enter the vehicle. Do not repair deteriorated exhaust system components; replace them with new parts.

3   If the exhaust system components are extremely corroded, or rusted together, a cutting torch is the most convenient tool for removal. Consult a properly-equipped repair shop. If a cutting torch is not available, you can use a hacksaw, or if you have compressed air, there are special pneumatic cutting chisels that can also be used. Wear safety goggles to protect your eyes from metal chips and wear work gloves to protect your hands.

4   Here are some simple guidelines to follow when repairing the exhaust system:

a) *Work from the back to the front when removing exhaust system components.*

b) *Apply penetrating oil to the exhaust system component fasteners to make them easier to remove.*

c) *Use new gaskets, hangers and clamps.*

d) *Apply anti-seize compound to the threads of all exhaust system fasteners during reassembly.*

e) *Be sure to allow sufficient clearance between newly installed parts and all points on the underbody to avoid overheating the floor pan and possibly damaging the interior carpet and insulation. Pay particularly close attention to the catalytic converter and heat shield.*

## 6   Fuel tank - removal and installation

**Warning:** *See the Warning in Section 1.*

1   Relieve the fuel system pressure (see Section 2).

2   Disconnect the cable(s) from the negative battery terminal(s) (see Chapter 5, Section 1).

3   If the vehicle is a four-door model with a six-foot bed (short bed), loosen the left rear wheel lug nuts.

4   Raise the vehicle and place it securely on jackstands.

5   If the vehicle is a four-door model with a six-foot bed (short bed), remove the left rear wheel.

6   Loosen the hose clamps for the fuel filler neck hose and the fuel tank vent hose (see illustration) and disconnect both hoses from their metal pipes.

**Warning:** *Never start the siphoning action by mouth!*

**Note:** *If the fuel tank still has a lot of fuel in it, now is the time to siphon the remaining fuel from the tank through the rubber fuel filler neck hose. Using a siphoning kit (available at most auto part stores), siphon the fuel from the tank, through the filler neck hose, into an approved gasoline container.*

7   Support the fuel tank with a transmission jack or with a floor jack. If you're going to use a floor jack, be sure to put a piece of wood between the jack head and the fuel tank to protect the tank.

8   Remove the fuel tank retaining strap nuts (see illustration) and remove both retaining straps. The hinged straps are secured with fasteners on the right side of the tank. To disengage the left end of each strap from its hinge, lift up the left end of the strap, then move it to the left.

9   Carefully lower the fuel tank just far enough to disconnect the electrical connector and fuel supply line from the fuel pump/fuel

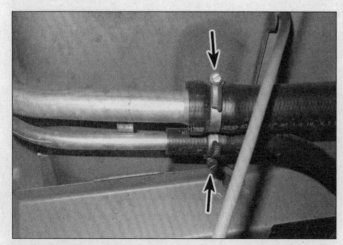

**6.6 To disconnect the fuel filler neck hose and the fuel tank vent hose from their metal pipes, loosen these two hose clamps**

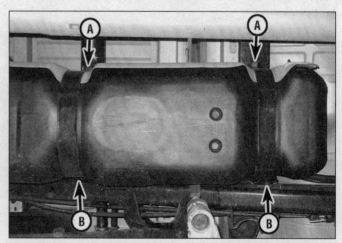

**6.8 To detach the fuel tank from the underside of the vehicle, remove these two fuel tank strap nuts (A), then allow the fuel tank straps to swing down (they're hinged on the left side) and disengage the left end of each strap from its hinge (B) by lifting up the end of the strap (jack removed for clarity)**

**6.9a Lower the fuel tank just enough to access the fuel pump/fuel level sending unit module, then disconnect the electrical connector and the fuel supply line fitting from the module**

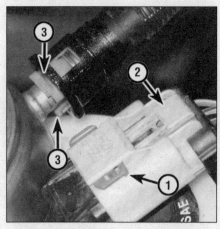

**6.9b To unplug the connector from the fuel pump module, push the lock (1) toward the fuel line fitting, depress the release button (2) and unplug the connector. To detach the fuel line, depress the tabs (3) and pull off the fitting (see Section 4 for more information about this type of fitting)**

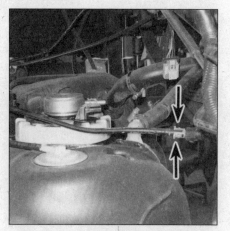

**6.10 After lowering the fuel tank to the floor, disconnect the EVAP line fitting. (The EVAP line fitting has already been disconnected in this photo. If you don't know how to disconnect this type of fitting, see Section 4)**

level sending unit module (see illustrations). Remove the fuel tank.

10   Lower the fuel tank to the floor, then disconnect the EVAP line fitting (see illustration).

11   Installation is basically the reverse of removal. Please note the following guidelines:

a) *If the fuel tank is being replaced, remove the necessary components from the old fuel tank and install them on the new tank. If you need help with any of the EVAP hoses, refer to Chapter 6.*

b) *Tighten the fuel tank strap nuts securely.*

---

## 7   Fuel filter/fuel pressure regulator - removal and installation

**Warning:** *See the Warning in Section 1.*
**Note:** *Replacing the fuel filter is not part of the*
*regular maintenance schedule for the vehicles covered in this manual. The main fuel filter, which is an integral part of the fuel pressure regulator, and the inlet fuel filter, at the lower end of the fuel pump, are extended-life parts that should be replaced only if diagnostic tests indicate excessive contamination inside the fuel tank. If this condition occurs, have the fuel tank professionally cleaned, then replace the filter.*

1   The fuel filter/fuel pressure regulator is located on top of the fuel pump/fuel level sending unit module, which is located in the upper part of the fuel tank.

2   Relieve the fuel system pressure (see Section 2).

3   Remove the fuel tank (see Section 6).

4   To prevent dirt from entering the fuel system, clean the area surrounding the fuel filter/fuel pressure regulator.

5   To remove the fuel filter/fuel pressure regulator assembly, grasp it firmly and pull it straight up (see illustration). If the filter/regulator is difficult to extract from its mounting grommet, twist it back and forth to "unstick" it from the grommet and try again.

6   Inspect the condition of the mounting grommet. A defective mounting grommet will cause the EVAP leak detection system to set a Diagnostic Trouble Code, so if the grommet is cracked, torn, deteriorated or otherwise damaged, replace it.

7   To prevent leaks (and Diagnostic Trouble Codes) make sure that the fuel filter/fuel pressure regulator is fully seated against its mounting grommet (see illustration). Also make sure that the fuel pipe on the fuel filter/fuel pressure regulator is pointing toward the driver's side of the truck (see illustration). Installation is otherwise the reverse of removal.

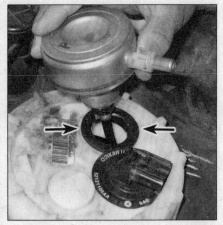

**7.5 To detach the filter/pressure regulator from the fuel pump module, grasp it firmly and pull it straight up. After removing the filter/regulator, inspect the condition of the mounting grommet**

**7.7a When installing the fuel filter/fuel pressure regulator, make sure it's fully seated against the mounting grommet . . .**

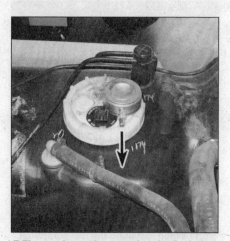

**7.7b . . . also make sure that the fuel pipe on the fuel filter/fuel pressure regulator is pointing toward the left (driver's side) of the vehicle**

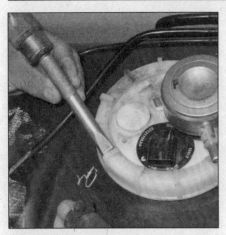

**8.8a Use a large pair of pliers or a hammer and drift to loosen the lockring that secures the fuel pump/fuel level sending unit module**

**8.8b Carefully remove the fuel pump/fuel level sending unit module from the fuel tank. Be sure to inspect the large rubber gasket that seals the mounting hole for the pump/sending unit**

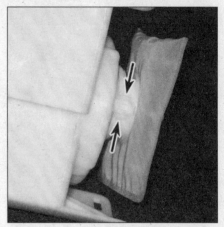

**8.10 To detach the fuel pump inlet filter from the pump, release the two locking tabs on either side (other locking tab not visible in this photo) and pull off the filter. To install the filter, push it onto the pump until it snaps into place**

## 8   Fuel pump and fuel level sending unit module - removal and installation

**Warning:** *See the Warning in Section 1.*
1    The fuel pump/fuel level sending unit module includes the fuel filter/fuel pressure regulator, the electric fuel pump assembly (including the fuel pump inlet filter) and the fuel level sending unit. This section covers the removal and installation of the complete module, which is removed as a complete assembly. But you can replace the components separately. The replacement procedure for the fuel filter/fuel pressure regulator is in Section 7. The replacement procedures for the fuel pump and for the fuel level sending unit are in Section 9.

**8.11 When installing the fuel pump/fuel level sending unit module, make sure the alignment arrow on top of the module is aligned with the center mark of the three hash marks on top of the fuel tank**

2    Relieve the fuel system pressure (see Section 2).
3    Disconnect the cable(s) from the negative battery terminal(s) (see Chapter 5).
4    Raise the vehicle and place it securely on jackstands.
5    Remove the fuel tank (see Section 6).
6    To prevent dirt from entering the fuel tank, clean the area surrounding the fuel pump/fuel level sending unit.
7    Disconnect the fuel line from the fuel filter/fuel pressure regulator and disconnect the fuel pump/fuel level sending unit electrical connector (see illustration 6.9b).
8    Using a pair of large pliers to turn the lockring, or using a hammer and a drift (see illustration), tap on the lockring to turn it counterclockwise. When the lockring is loose, unscrew it. Carefully remove the fuel pump/

**9.2 Disconnect the electrical connector for the fuel level sending unit**

fuel level sending unit module from the tank (see illustration).
9    Inspect the large rubber gasket. If it's cracked, torn, deteriorated or otherwise damaged, replace it.
10    The fuel pump inlet filter is attached to the bottom of the fuel pump module. Any time you remove the fuel pump for any reason, always inspect the inlet filter. If it's dirty, remove it (see illustration) and scrub it thoroughly with clean solvent and an old toothbrush (don't use a wire brush to clean the inlet filter - you'll damage it if you do). If you're unable to clean the inlet filter, replace it.
11    When installing the fuel pump/fuel level sending unit module, rotate the module until the embossed alignment arrow on the module is aligned with the center mark of the three hash marks on the top of the fuel tank (see illustration). Also make sure that the fuel pipe on the fuel filter/fuel pressure regulator is pointing toward the driver's side of the truck (see illustration 7.7b).
12    The remainder of installation is the reverse of removal.

## 9   Fuel pump/fuel level sending unit - replacement

**Warning:** *See the Warning in Section 1.*
1    Remove the fuel pump/fuel level sending unit module (see Section 8).
2    Locate the electrical connector for the fuel pump and fuel level sending unit in the upper part of the fuel pump module (see illustration) and disconnect it.
3    On 2001 and earlier models, to detach the fuel level sending unit from the fuel pump module, remove the screws that retain the fuel level sending unit to the assembly (see illustration) and on 2002 and later models, pry the plastic locking tab loose from its detent in

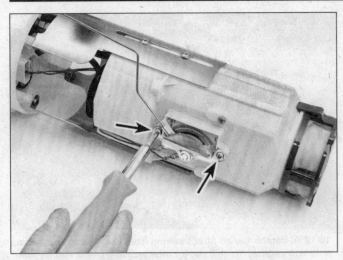

**9.3a Remove the fuel level sending unit mounting screws (2001 and earlier models)**

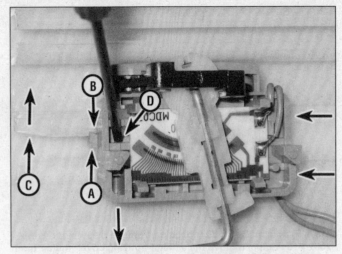

**9.3b Fuel level sending unit removal and installation details (2002 and later models):**

A   Locking tab (locks into detent in mounting rail)
B   Detent in mounting rail
C   Mounting rail
D   Insert small screwdriver here and carefully pry the mounting rail detent away from the locking tab, then slide the fuel level sending unit off the rail

the mounting rail (see illustration), then slide the sending unit down the rail (toward the inlet fuel filter) to remove it.

4   On 2001 and earlier models, mark the location, then disconnect the electrical connectors to the fuel level sending unit terminals.

5   On 2002 and later models, the electrical connector is shared with the fuel pump, so the wires from the old sending unit must be disengaged from the connector and the wires to the new sending unit must be installed in their place. To separate the fuel level sending unit wire terminals from the electrical connector:

a) Remove the locking collar from the connector receptacle (see illustration).
b) Using a small pick, depress the locking finger on the terminal and push the terminal in (see illustration).
c) Pull the wire and terminal out of the connector from the backside.

6   Except for the fuel pump inlet filter (see Step 10 in Section 8), no further disassembly of the fuel pump module is recommended. You may now replace either the fuel pump module or the fuel level sending unit.

7   Installation is the reverse of removal.

---

**10   Air filter housing, air intake duct and resonator box - removal and installation**

## Air intake duct

1   Loosen the hose clamps and remove the air intake duct (see illustration).

2   Inspect the condition of the air intake duct. Look for cracks, tears, deterioration and other damage. If the air intake duct is

damaged in any way, replace it. A leaking air intake duct will allow the introduction of "false air" (unmetered air) into the air intake manifold, which will cause the air/fuel mixture to become excessively lean. A lean air/fuel mixture can cause rough running at idle, and even misfires if the leak is big enough.

3   Installation is the reverse of removal.

## Air filter housing

### All engines except 2002 and earlier 3.9L V6, 5.2L V8, 5.9L V8 engine and V10 engine

4   If you're going to remove the air filter housing from the engine compartment, remove the air intake duct (see Step 1). If you're simply raising up the air filter housing

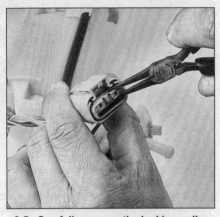

**9.5a Carefully remove the locking collar from the electrical connector**

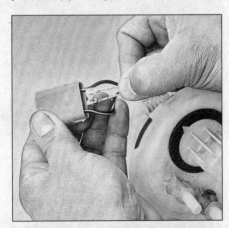

**9.5b Using a small pick, depress the terminal locking finger and push the terminal into the connector, then pull the two fuel level sending unit wires and terminals out of the connector**

**10.1 To remove the air intake duct, loosen the hose clamps at each end and disconnect the duct from the air filter housing and the air resonator box**

10.5 To detach the air filter housing from the throttle body on a 2002 V10 engine, remove the air filter housing cover and air filter element (see Chapter 1), then remove these four nuts

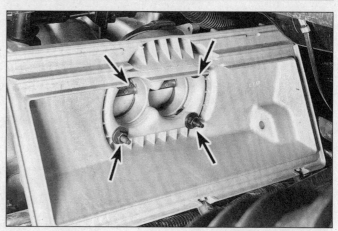

10.12 To detach the air filter housing from the throttle body on a 2002 V10 engine, remove the air filter housing cover and air filter element (see Chapter 1), then remove these four nuts

10.15 To detach the air resonator box from a Hemi engine, disconnect the electrical connector (1) from the Intake Air Temperature (IAT) sensor, remove the resonator mounting bolts (2), pull the box forward to disengage it from the throttle body, then lift it up slightly to disconnect the PCV fresh air inlet hose (3) from the underside

10.16a To detach the air resonator box from a 3.7L V6 or from a 4.7L V8 engine, remove this mounting bolt from the left side of the box . . .

to access some component(s) underneath the housing, it's not necessary to remove the air intake duct.

5    To remove the air filter housing on all engines except 2002 and earlier 3.9L V6, 5.2L V8, 5.9L V8 engine and V10 engines, grasp it firmly and lift it straight up (see illustration). The air filter housing is secured to the vehicle by four grommets that fit onto four locator pins. Two of the grommets and one of the locator pins are visible in the accompanying photograph. The other two grommets are located in the underside of the air filter housing.

6    Inspect the condition of the four mounting grommets. If they're cracked, torn, deteriorated or otherwise damaged, replace them.

7    Installation is the reverse of removal.

### 2002 and earlier 3.9L V6, 5.2L V8, 5.9L V8 engines

8    On these models, the air filter hous-ing is a black plastic rectangular box located on top of the throttle body (the mouth of the throttle body faces straight up on these models). Remove the air filter housing cover clips, remove the cover and remove the air filter element.

9    To detach the air filter housing from the throttle body, remove the nut that secures the lower half of the housing to the mounting stud on the throttle body.

10    Installation is the reverse of removal.

### 2002 and earlier V10 engines

11    On these models, the air filter housing is a plastic rectangular box located on the left side of the intake manifold (the mouth of the throttle body faces toward the left on these models). Remove the air filter housing cover clips, remove the cover and remove the air filter element.

12    Remove the four nuts that attach the air filter housing to the filter housing mounting studs on the throttle body (see illustration).

13    Installation is the reverse of removal.

### Air resonator box

14    Remove the air intake duct or disconnect it from the air resonator box (see illustration 10.1).

15    On Hemi engines, disconnect the electrical connector from the Intake Air Temperature (IAT) sensor (see illustration).

16    Remove the air resonator box mounting bolts (3.7L V6 and 4.7L V8 engines, see illustrations; Hemi engine, see illustration 10.15).

17    Grasp the air resonator box firmly and pull it forward to disengage it from the throttle body. Lift up the air resonator box slightly and disconnect the PCV fresh air inlet hose from the underside of the left front corner of the resonator. Remove the air resonator box.

18    Installation is the reverse of removal.

10.16b . . . remove this mounting bolt from the right side of the box . . .

10.16c . . . grasp the box firmly and pull it forward slightly to disengage it from the throttle body, then reach around behind the left rear corner of the box and disconnect the PCV fresh air inlet hose from the box (4.7L V8 engine shown, 3.7L V6 similar)

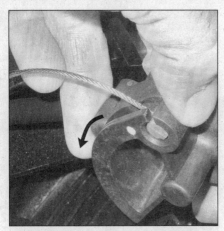

11.2 To disconnect the accelerator cable from the throttle lever, rotate the throttle lever to the wide-open position, then slide the cable end plug out of its socket in the throttle lever

## 11   Accelerator cable - replacement

**Note:** *All engines use a conventional accelerator cable except for the Hemi. On Hemi engines, the "accelerator cable" connects the accelerator pedal to the Accelerator Pedal Position Sensor (APPS), which is located under the battery tray. But the cable is NOT connected to the throttle lever on the throttle body. The throttle plate is electronically controlled by the Powertrain Control Module (PCM). The APPS is sold as a complete assembly, including the sensor, the plastic housing and the cable. To replace the APPS, refer to Chapter 6. However-*

*er, if you just want to replace the APPS cable, it's available separately, and is removed and installed just like any other accelerator cable (except that you disconnect it from the APPS instead of the throttle body).*

1    Remove the air intake duct and, if equipped, the air resonator box (see Section 10).

2    Rotate the throttle lever to the wide-open position and detach the cable end (see illustration). If you're replacing the cable on a Hemi model, disconnect the cable from the APPS (see Accelerator Pedal Position Sensor - replacement in Chapter 6).

3    Using a small screwdriver, press the tab

to release the accelerator cable retainer from the cable bracket (see illustration) and slide the cable out of the bracket.

4    Trace the accelerator cable to the firewall and note its routing. Then detach the cable from any clamps, clips and/or brackets.

5    Working underneath the dash, disconnect the accelerator cable from the accelerator pedal (see illustration).

6    Remove the retaining clip (see illustration) that secures the cable housing to its hole in the firewall.

7    Pull the cable through the firewall and into the engine compartment.

8    Installation is the reverse of removal.

11.3 To disengage the accelerator cable from the cable bracket, use a small flat-blade screwdriver to press the tab to release the cable from the bracket

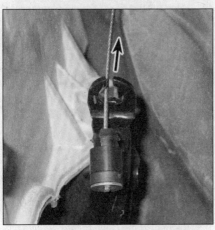

11.5 To disengage the cable from the accelerator pedal, push the upper end of the pedal forward and thread the cable through the slot in the top of the pedal

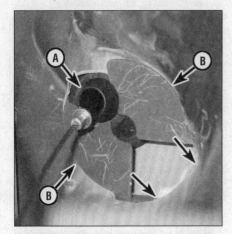

11.6 The accelerator cable housing (A) is secured to its hole in the firewall by this retaining clip (B). To access the clip, which looks like a pair of butterfly wings, carefully peel back the rubber floor liner until you can see the entire clip. To remove the clip, disengage it from the cable housing by prying it loose with a screwdriver or pulling it off with a pair of needle-nose pliers

12.3 To remove the throttle body from a 3.7L V6 or a 4.7L V8 engine, disconnect the electrical connectors from the Throttle Position (TP) sensor (1) and the Idle Air Control (IAC) motor (2), label all vacuum lines connected to the throttle body and disconnect them, then remove the throttle body mounting bolts (3) (4.7L V8 engine shown, 3.7L V6 similar)

12.12 To remove the throttle body from a Hemi engine, simply disconnect the electrical connector and remove the four mounting bolts

## 12   Throttle body - removal and installation

### 3.7L V6 and 4.7L V8 engines

1     Disconnect the cable from the negative terminal of the battery (see Chapter 5, Section 1).
2     Remove the air intake duct and the air box resonator (see Section 10).
3     Disconnect the electrical connectors from the Throttle Position (TP) sensor and from the Idle Air Control motor (see illustration).
4     Clearly label all vacuum hoses connected to the throttle body, then disconnect them. Be sure to inspect the vacuum hoses for cracks, tears and deterioration. If any of them are damaged, replace them.
5     Disconnect the accelerator cable from the throttle body (see Section 7B) and, if equipped, the transmission control cable (see Chapter 11) and the cruise control cable. (Disconnect the cruise control cable using the same procedure you used to disconnect the accelerator cable.)
6     Remove the three mounting bolts and remove the throttle body.
7     Remove the throttle body O-ring and inspect it for cracks, tears and deterioration. If it's damaged, replace it.
8     Wipe off the gasket mating surfaces of the throttle body and the intake manifold.
**Caution:** *Do NOT use spray carburetor cleaners or silicone lubricants on any part of the throttle body.*
9     Installation is the reverse of removal. Be sure to tighten the throttle body mounting bolts to the torque listed in this Chapter's Specifications.

### Hemi engine

10    Disconnect the cable from the negative terminal of the battery (see Chapter 5, Section 1).
11    Remove the air intake duct and the air box resonator (see Section 10).
12    Disconnect the electrical connector from the throttle body (see illustration).
13    Remove the four throttle body mounting bolts and remove the throttle body.
14    Remove and inspect the throttle body O-ring for cracks, tears and deterioration. If it's damaged, replace it.
15    Wipe off the gasket mating surfaces of the throttle body and the intake manifold.
**Caution:** *Do NOT use spray carburetor cleaners or silicone lubricants on any part of the throttle body.*
16    Installation is the reverse of removal (if you're installing a new throttle body, be sure to see the next Step). Tighten the throttle body mounting bolts to the torque listed in this Chapter's Specifications.

#### Installing a NEW throttle body on a Hemi engine

17    If you've just replaced the old throttle body with a new unit, disconnect the cable from the negative battery terminal for about 90 seconds.
18    Reconnect the cable to the negative battery terminal.
19    Turn the ignition switch to On, but don't start the engine.
20    Leave the ignition switch in the On position for at least 10 seconds. The Powertrain Control Module (PCM) uses this time to learn the new throttle body's electrical parameters.

### 3.9L V6, 5.2L V8 and 5.9L V8 engine

21    Disconnect the cable from the negative terminal of the battery (see Chapter 5, Section 1).
22    Remove the air intake duct (see Section 10).
23    Disconnect the electrical connectors from the Idle Air Control (IAC) motor, the Throttle Position (TP) sensor and the Manifold Absolute Pressure (MAP) sensor (see illustration).
24    Clearly label all vacuum hoses connected to the throttle body, then disconnect them.
25    Disconnect the accelerator cable from the throttle body (see Section 7B) and, if equipped, the transmission control cable (see Chapter 11) and the cruise control cable. (Disconnect the cruise control cable using the same procedure you used to disconnect the accelerator cable.)
26    Remove the throttle body mounting bolts.
27    Remove the throttle body.
28    Remove the old throttle body gasket. If any gasket material is stuck to the gasket surfaces of the throttle body or the intake manifold, carefully remove it. Do NOT scratch these surfaces, which might cause an air leak.
29    Even if the gasket surfaces are free of old gasket material, clean them thoroughly.
30    Using a new throttle body gasket, place the throttle body in position, install the mounting bolts and tighten them to the torque listed in this Chapter's Specifications. Installation is otherwise the reverse of removal.

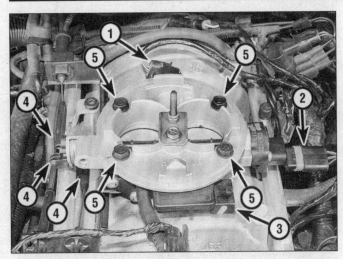

12.23 To remove the throttle body from 3.9L V6, 5.2L V8 and 5.9L
V8 engines, disconnect or remove the following:

1  *Idle Air Control (IAC) motor electrical connector*
2  *Throttle Position (TP) sensor electrical connector*
3  *Manifold Absolute Pressure (MAP) sensor electrical connector
   (already unplugged in this photo)*
4  *Accelerator, cruise control and Throttle Valve (TV) cables*
5  *Throttle body mounting bolts*

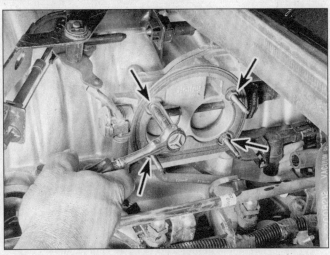

12.35 To detach the throttle body from the intake manifold on a
V10 engine, remove these four bolts. The TP sensor (A) is located
on the rear of the throttle body

## 8.0L V10 engine

31  Disconnect the cable from the negative terminal of the battery (see Chapter 5, Section 1).
32  On 2002 and earlier models, remove the air filter housing (see Section 10). On 2003 and later models, remove the air intake duct/resonator.
33  Disconnect the electrical connectors from the Throttle Position (TP) sensor and from the Idle Air Control (IAC) motor.
34  Disconnect the accelerator cable from the throttle body (see Section 7B) and, if equipped, the transmission control cable (see Chapter 11) and the cruise control cable. (Disconnect the cruise control cable using the same procedure you used to disconnect the accelerator cable.)

35  Remove the four throttle body mounting bolts (see illustration).
36  Remove the throttle body.
37  Remove the old throttle body gasket. If any gasket material is stuck to the gasket surfaces of the throttle body or the intake manifold, carefully remove it. Do NOT scratch these surfaces, which might cause an air leak.
38  Even if the gasket surfaces are free of old gasket material, clean them thoroughly.
39  Using a new throttle body gasket, place the throttle body in position, install the mounting bolts and tighten them to the torque listed in this Chapter's Specifications.
40  Installation is otherwise the reverse of removal.

## 13  Fuel rail and injectors - removal and installation

**Warning:** *See the Warning in Section 1.*
**Warning:** *The engine must be completely cool before beginning this procedure.*

### 3.7L V6 and 4.7L V8 engines

1  Remove the fuel tank filler neck cap to relieve any pressure inside the fuel tank. Then relieve the fuel system pressure (see Section 2).
2  Disconnect the cable from the negative terminal of the battery (see Chapter 5).
3  Remove the air intake duct and the air box resonator (see Section 10).
4  Disconnect the fuel supply line from the fuel rail.
5  Clearly label any vacuum hoses that will interfere with fuel rail removal, then disconnect them from the throttle body and from the intake manifold.
6  Disconnect the electrical connectors from all throttle body information sensors (see Section 12) and set the wiring harnesses for those sensors aside. Also disconnect the electrical connectors for any other wiring harnesses that will interfere with fuel rail removal and set the wiring harnesses aside.
7  Disconnect the fuel injector electrical connectors (see illustrations) and set the injector wiring harness aside.
**Note:** *Each connector should be numbered with the corresponding cylinder number. If the number tag is obscured or missing, renumber the connectors.*
8  Remove all of the ignition coils from the engine (see Chapter 5).

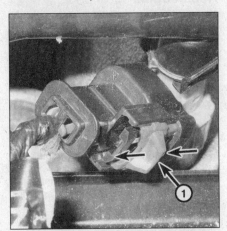

13.7a To disconnect the electrical
connector from the injector on a 3.7L
V6 or 4.7L V8, move the red slider (1) up
(away from the injector) . . .

13.7b . . . then depress the tab (2) and pull
the connector off of the injector

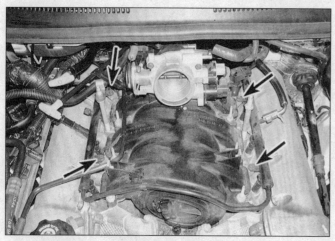

**13.9 Fuel rail mounting bolts (4.7L V8 engine, shown, 3.7L V6 similar)**

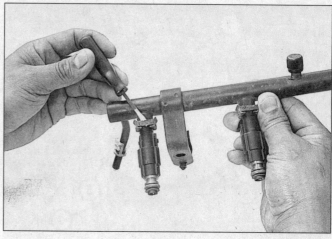

**13.10a Using a screwdriver or pliers, remove the injector retaining clip . . .**

9    Clean any debris from around the injectors. Remove the fuel rail mounting nuts/bolts (see illustration). Gently rock the fuel rail and injectors to loosen the injectors and remove the fuel rail and fuel injectors as an assembly. **Caution:** *Do not attempt to separate the left and right fuel rails. Both sides are serviced together as an assembly.*

10    Remove the injectors from the fuel rail, then remove and discard the O-rings (see illustrations).
**Note:** *Whether you're replacing an injector or a leaking O-ring, it's a good idea to remove all the injectors from the fuel rail and replace all the O-rings.*

11    Coat the new O-rings with clean engine oil and install them on the injector(s), then insert each injector into its corresponding bore in the fuel rail. Install the injector retaining clip.

12    Clean the injector bores on the intake manifold.

13    Guide the injectors/fuel rail assembly into the injector bores on the intake manifold. Make sure the injectors are fully seated, then tighten the fuel rail mounting nuts/bolts to the torque listed in this Chapter's Specifications.

14    The remainder of installation is the reverse of removal.

15    After the injector/fuel rail assembly installation is complete, turn the ignition switch to On, but don't operate the starter. This activates the fuel pump for about two seconds, which builds up fuel pressure in the fuel lines and the fuel rail. Repeat this step two or three times, then check the fuel lines, fuel rail and injectors for fuel leakage.

### Hemi engine

16    Remove the fuel tank filler neck cap to relieve any pressure inside the fuel tank. Then relieve the fuel system pressure (see Section 2).

17    Disconnect the cable from the negative terminal of the battery (see Chapter 5).

18    Remove the air intake duct and the air box resonator (see Section 10).

19    Clearly label each end of each spark plug wire, then disconnect the plug wires from the ignition coils and from the spark plugs. When all the wires are disconnected, release the four tabs that attach the spark plug wire tray to the intake manifold and remove the spark plug wire tray and plug wires as an assembly (see illustrations).

20    Disconnect the electrical connectors from all eight ignition coils (see Chapter 5).

21    Disconnect the fuel supply line from the fuel rail.

22    Look at the wiring harness for the ignition coils and for the fuel injectors. Note how each

**13.10b . . . and withdraw the injector from the fuel rail**

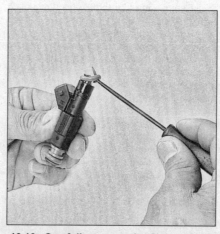

**13.10c Carefully remove the O-rings from the injectors**

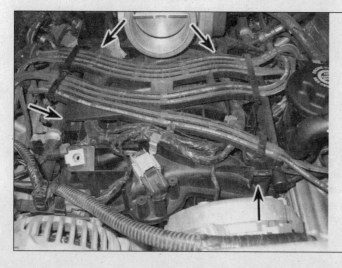

**13.19a To remove the spark plug wire tray from the intake manifold on a Hemi engine, disengage these four retaining clips . . .**

13.19b . . . then lift the spark plug wire tray and plug wires off the manifold as a single assembly

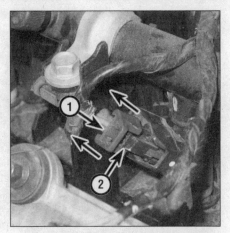

13.22 To disconnect an electrical connector from an injector on a Hemi engine, move the red slider (1) away from the injector, then depress the release tab (2) and pull off the connector

13.23a To disconnect the main electrical connector for the fuel injector/ignition coil/throttle body wiring harness, depress this release tab

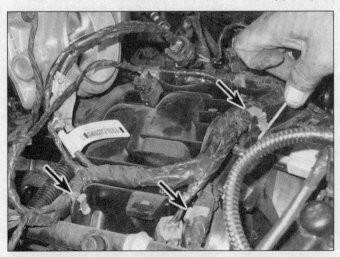

13.23b To detach the fuel injector/ignition coil/throttle body wiring harness from the intake manifold, remove these retaining clips

13.24 To detach the fuel rail from the intake manifold, remove these four bolts and hold-down clamps

branch of the main harness branches into two leads - one for the coil and one for the injector - for each cylinder. And to make sure that you don't accidentally plug the wrong connector into the wrong injector, each injector lead is identified by a numeric designation - 1, 2, 3, 4, etc. - imprinted on the electrical tape protecting the lead. If the harness does not have these numbers on the eight injector leads, be sure to label them now, before disconnecting the electrical connectors from the fuel injectors. Then disconnect the electrical connectors from all eight fuel injectors (see illustration).

23   Disconnect the electrical connector from the throttle body (see illustration 12.12), and from any information sensors to which the harness connected. Then disconnect the main electrical connector (see illustration) for the fuel injector/ignition coil/throttle body wiring harness, detach the harness clips from the intake manifold (see illustration) and set the wiring harness aside.

24   Remove the four fuel rail mounting bolts and hold-down clamps (see illustration).
25   Starting with the left side of the fuel rail, carefully pull on the injectors while wiggling them from side to side at the same time until all four injectors start to clear their mounting holes. Then go the right side and repeat this step. Go back and forth between the two sides of the engine, gradually working the injectors out of their mounting holes, until all eight injectors are free. When all of the injectors are free, remove the fuel rail and injectors as a single assembly (see illustration).
26   To remove an injector from the fuel rail, remove the injector retainer clip (see illustration 13.10a) and pull the injector out of the fuel rail.
27   Remove the O-rings from the injector (see illustration 13.10c), discard them and install new O-rings. Be sure to lubricate the new O-rings with clean engine oil before installing the injector into the fuel rail.

13.25 Carefully lift the fuel rail and injectors off the engine as a single assembly

28    Installation is the reverse of removal. Be sure to tighten the fuel rail mounting bolts to the torque listed in this Chapter's Specifications.

### 3.9L V6, 5.2L V8 and 5.9L V8 engines

29    Remove the fuel tank filler neck cap to relieve any pressure inside the fuel tank. Then relieve the fuel system pressure (see Section 2).
30    Disconnect the cable from the negative terminal of the battery (see Chapter 5).
31    Remove the air intake duct (see Section 10).
32    Remove the throttle body (see Section 12).
33    If the vehicle is equipped with air conditioning, remove the A-shaped air conditioning compressor support bracket from the intake manifold (the bracket is attached to the manifold by three bolts).
34    Disconnect the electrical connectors from all eight fuel injectors. These connectors are identical to the connectors used on Hemi engines and are disconnected the same way (see illustration 13.22).
35    Disconnect the fuel supply line from the fuel rail.
36    Remove the fuel rail mounting bolts (see illustration).
37    Starting with the left side of the fuel rail, carefully pull on the injectors while wiggling them from side to side at the same time until all four injectors start to clear their mounting holes. Then go to the right side and repeat this step. Go back and forth between the two sides of the engine, gradually working the injectors out of their mounting holes, until all eight injectors are free. When all of the injectors are free, remove the fuel rail and injectors as a single assembly.
38    To remove the injectors from the fuel rail and replace the injector O-rings, refer to Step 10.
**Note:** *Whether you're replacing an injector or a leaking O-ring, it's a good idea to remove all the injectors from the fuel rail and replace all the O-rings.*

13.36 To detach the fuel rail from the intake manifold on 5.9L V8 engines, remove these two bolts from the right side of the fuel rail and the other two bolts (not shown) from the left side

39    Installation is the reverse of removal. Be sure to tighten the fuel rail mounting bolts to the torque listed in this Chapter's Specifications.

### 8.0L V10 engine

40    Remove the fuel tank filler neck cap to relieve any pressure inside the fuel tank. Then relieve the fuel system pressure (see Section 2).
41    Disconnect the cable from the negative terminal of the battery (see Chapter 5).
42    On 2002 models, remove the air intake duct and the air filter housing (see Section 10). On 2003 models, remove the air intake duct and the resonator.
43    Remove the throttle body (see Section 12).
44    Remove the ignition coil pack (see Chapter 5) and remove the coil pack mounting bracket.
45    Remove the upper half of the intake manifold (see Chapter 2C).
46    Disconnect the electrical connectors from all eight fuel injectors. These connectors are identical to the connectors used on Hemi engines and are disconnected the same way (see illustration 13.22).

47    Disconnect the fuel supply line from the fuel rail.
48    Remove the six fuel rail mounting bolts.
49    Starting with the left side of the fuel rail, carefully pull on the injectors while wiggling them from side to side at the same time until all four injectors start to clear their mounting holes. Then go to the right side and repeat this step. Go back and forth between the two sides of the engine, gradually working the injectors out of their mounting holes, until all eight injectors are free. When all of the injectors are free, remove the fuel rail and injectors as a single assembly.
50    To remove the injectors from the fuel rail and replace the injector O-rings, refer to Step 10.
**Note:** *Whether you're replacing an injector or a leaking O-ring, it's a good idea to remove all the injectors from the fuel rail and replace all the O-rings.*
51    Installation is the reverse of removal. Be sure to tighten the fuel rail mounting bolts to the torque listed in this Chapter's Specifications.

# Chapter 4 Part B
# Fuel and exhaust systems - diesel engines

## Contents

## Specifications

| Fuel injector washer thickness | |
| --- | --- |
| 1994 through 1998 models | See dealer parts department |
| 1999 and later models | 0.060 inch |
| Transfer pump output fuel pressure | |
| 1994 through 1996 | 25 psi minimum |
| 1997 and 1998 | |
| Idle | 17 to 22 psi |
| 2500 rpm | 25 to 30 psi |
| 1999 on | |
| Engine cranking | 5 to 7 psi |
| Engine running, at idle | 10 psi |
| Fuel return line vacuum | Approximately 4 in-Hg |

## Torque specifications

**Ft-lbs (unless otherwise indicated)**

*Note:* *One foot-pound (ft-lb) of torque is equivalent to 12 inch-pounds (in-lbs) of torque. Torque values below approximately 15 ft-lbs are expressed in inch-pounds, since most foot-pound torque wrenches are not accurate at these smaller values.*

| | |
|---|---|
| Banjo bolt (test port fitting on 2002 and earlier models) | 18 |
| Fuel valve holder (2001 and earlier models) | |
|     Initial torque | 29 |
|     Final torque | 85 |
| Fuel control actuator mounting bolts | |
|     First stage | 27 in-lbs |
|     Second stage | 62 in-lbs |
| Fuel injection pump mounting nuts/bolts | |
|     2001 and earlier models | 18 |
|     2002 models | |
|         Pump mounting nuts | 32 |
|         Rear lower pump mounting bracket-to-pump bolts | 18 |
|     2003 and later models | 71 in-lbs |
| Fuel injection pump shaft nut (drive gear-to-pump shaft nut) | |
|     2001 and earlier models | |
|         Initial torque | 7 to 12 |
|         Final torque | 144 |
|     2002 models | |
|         Initial torque | 15 to 22 |
|         Final torque | 125 |
|     2003 and later models | 77 |
| Fuel injection pump oil fill plug (2001 and earlier models) | 21 |
| Fuel injector hold-down nut (1998 and earlier models) | 44 |
| Fuel injector hold-down clamp bolt (1999 through 2002 models) | 89 in-lbs |
| Fuel injector mounting bolts (2003 and later models) | 89 in-lbs |
| Fuel injector wire nuts (2003 and later models) | 11 in-lbs |
| Fuel injector connector tube nuts (2003 and later models) | 37 |
| Fuel line banjo bolts | |
|     2002 and earlier models | 18 |
|     2003 and later models | 17 |
| High-pressure fuel line fittings | |
|     1998 and earlier models | 18 |
|     1999 through 2002 | |
|         At pump | 18 |
|         At cylinder head | 28 |
|     2003 and later models | |
|         Between Injector connector tubes and fuel rail | 22 |
|         Between pump and fuel rail | 27 |
| Intake air heater manifold mounting bolts | 18 |

## Torque specifications

**Ft-lbs** (unless otherwise indicated)     **Nm**

*Note:* *One foot-pound (ft-lb) of torque is equivalent to 12 inch-pounds (in-lbs) of torque. Torque values below approximately 15 ft-lbs are expressed in inch-pounds, because most foot-pound torque wrenches are not accurate at these smaller values.*

| | |
|---|---|
| Timing pin access cover (1998 and earlier models) | 18 |
| Transfer pump | |
|     2002 models | |
|         Pump mounting bracket nuts | 108 in-lbs |
|         Banjo bolts | 18 |
|     2003 and later models | |
|         Pump mounting bolts | 61 in-lbs |
| Turbocharger | |
|     Turbocharger-to-exhaust manifold stud mounting nuts | |
|         2002 models | 24 |
|         2003 and later models | 32 |
|     Turbocharger oil return line bolts | 18 |
|     Turbocharger oil supply line fitting | |
|         2002 models | 133 in-lbs |
|         2003 and later models | 18 |
|     Exhaust pipe flange-to-turbo outlet elbow flange bolts (2002 models) | 25 |

## 1   General Information

### General information

1   The fuel system is what most sets diesel engines apart from their gasoline powered cousins. Simply stated, fuel is injected directly into the combustion chambers, and the extremely high pressures produced in the cylinders is what ignites the charge. Unlike gasoline engines, diesels have no throttle plate to limit the entry of air into the intake manifold. The only control is the amount of fuel injected; an unrestricted supply of air is always available through the intake. (And because there is no throttle plate, there is no intake manifold vacuum either.)

2   There are two major sub-systems in the fuel injection system: the low pressure (also known as the supply or transfer) portion and the high-pressure injection (delivery) portion.

3   The low pressure system moves fuel from the fuel tank to the injection pump. Fuel is drawn from the fuel tank by a transfer pump and then pumped through a fuel filter/water separator and then into the high-pressure injection pump. A bypass system allows excess fuel to return to the tank.

4   On 2002 and earlier models, the fuel injection pump meters fuel to the cylinders in metered high-pressure squirts. These fuel pulses are directed to the fuel injectors of each cylinder in the firing order of the engine. When more power and speed is desired, the fuel injection system simply sprays more fuel into the cylinders. When a preset maximum engine speed is reached, a governor limits the delivery of fuel, thereby limiting speed. The injection pump also controls combustion timing just as a distributor controls spark timing in a gasoline engine. As engine speed increases, injection timing is advanced.

5   On 2003 and later models, the fuel injection pump supplies high-pressure fuel to a fuel rail, which is attached by high-pressure fuel lines to the fuel injectors. The injectors are electrically actuated, in firing order sequence, by the ECM.

6   Fuel system problems are by far the most frequent cause of breakdowns and loss of power in diesel-powered vehicles. Whenever a diesel engine quits running or loses power for no apparent reason, check the fuel system first. Begin with the most obvious items, such as the fuel filter and damaged fuel lines. If the vehicle has multiple fuel tanks, suspect a faulty tank switchover valve.

7   The fuel system on diesel engines is extremely sensitive to contamination. Because of the very small clearances in the injection pump and the minute orifices in the injection nozzles, fuel contamination can be a serious problem. The injection pump and the injectors can be damaged or ruined by contamination. Water-contaminated diesel fuel is a major problem. If it remains in the fuel system too long, water will cause serious and expensive damage. The fuel lines and the fuel filter can also become plugged with rust particles, or clogged with ice in cold weather.

### Diesel fuel contamination

**Warning:** *The pressure in the high-pressure fuel lines can reach extremely high pressure (as much as 23,200 psi), so use extreme caution when working near any part of the fuel injection system with the engine running.*

8   Before you replace an injection pump or some other expensive component, find out what caused the failure. If water contamination is present, buying a new or rebuilt pump or other component won't do much good. The following procedure will help you determine if water contamination is present:

a) *Remove the engine fuel filter and inspect the contents for the presence of water or gasoline (see Chapter 1).*

b) *If the vehicle has been stalling, performance has been poor or the engine has been knocking loudly, suspect fuel contamination. Gasoline or water must be removed by flushing (see below).*

c) *If you find a lot of water in the fuel filter, remove the injection pump fuel return line and check for water there. If the pump has water in it, flush the system.*

d) *Small quantities of surface rust won't create a problem. If contamination is excessive, the vehicle will probably stall.*

e) *Sometimes contamination in the system becomes severe enough to cause damage to the internal parts of the pump. If the damage reaches this stage, have the damaged parts replaced and the pump rebuilt by an authorized fuel injection shop, or buy a rebuilt pump.*

### Storage

9   Good quality diesel fuel contains inhibitors to stop the formation of rust in the fuel lines and the injectors, so as long as there are no leaks in the fuel system, it's generally safe from water contamination. Diesel fuel is usually contaminated by water as a result of careless storage. There's not much you can do about the storage practices of service stations where you buy diesel fuel, but if you keep a small supply of diesel fuel on hand at home, as many diesel owners do, follow these simple rules:

a) *Diesel fuel "ages" and goes stale. Don't store containers of diesel fuel for long periods of time. Use it up regularly and replace it with fresh fuel.*

b) *Keep fuel storage containers out of direct sunlight. Variations in heat and humidity promote condensation inside fuel containers.*

c) *Don't store diesel fuel in galvanized containers. It may cause the galvanizing to flake off, contaminating the fuel and clogging filters when the fuel is used.*

d) *Label containers properly, as containing diesel fuel.*

### Fighting fungi and bacteria with biocides

10   If there's water in the fuel, fungi and/or bacteria can form in warm or humid weather. Fungi and bacteria plug fuel lines, fuel filters and injection nozzles; they can also cause corrosion in the fuel system.

11   If you've had problems with water in the fuel system and you live in a warm or humid climate, have a diesel specialist correct the problem. Then, use a diesel fuel biocide to sterilize the fuel system in accordance with the manufacturer's instructions. Biocides are available from your dealer, service stations and auto parts stores. Consult your dealer or a diesel specialist for advice on using biocides in your area and for recommendations on which ones to use.

### Cleaning the low-pressure fuel system

**Warning:** *Diesel fuel is flammable, so take extra precautions when you work on any part of the fuel system. Don't smoke or allow open flames or bare light bulbs near the work area, and don't work in a garage where a gas-type appliance (such as a water heater or a clothes dryer) is present. Since diesel fuel is carcinogenic, wear latex gloves when there's a possibility of being exposed to fuel, and, if you spill any fuel on your skin, rinse it off immediately with soap and water. Mop up any spills immediately and do not store diesel fuel-soaked rags where they could ignite. When you perform any kind of work on the fuel system, wear safety glasses and have a Class B type fire extinguisher on hand.*

#### "Water-In-Fuel" (WIF) warning system

12   The WIF system detects the presence of water in the fuel filter when it reaches excessive amounts. Water is detected by a probe located in the fuel filter that completes a circuit through a wire to a light in the instrument cluster that reads "WATER IN FUEL" on 2002 models, and shows a gas station pump surrounded by water drops on 2003 and later models.

13   The WIF system includes a bulb-check feature: When the ignition is turned to On, the bulb glows momentarily, then fades away.

14   If the light comes on immediately after you've filled the tank or let the vehicle sit for an extended period of time, drain the water from the system immediately. Do not start the engine. There might be enough water in the system to shut the engine down before you've driven even a short distance. If, however, the light comes on during a cornering or braking maneuver, there's less water in the system; the engine probably won't shut down immediately, but you still should drain the water soon.

15   Water is heavier than diesel fuel, so it sinks to the bottom of the fuel tank. An extended return pipe on the fuel tank sending unit, which reaches down into the bottom of the tank, enables you to siphon most of the

water from the tank without having to remove the tank. But siphoning won't remove all of the water; you'll still need to remove the tank and thoroughly clean it.

**Warning:** *Do not start a siphon by mouth - use a siphoning kit (available at most auto parts stores).*

### Removing water from the fuel system

16   Disconnect the ground cables from the negative terminals of the batteries (see Chapter 5, Section 1).

17   Drain the fuel tank into an approved container and dispose of it properly.

18   Remove the fuel tank and the gauge sending unit (see Chapter 4A).

19   Thoroughly clean the fuel tank. If it's rusted inside, send it to a repair shop or replace it. Clean or replace the fuel pick-up filter.

20   Reinstall the fuel tank but don't connect the fuel lines to the fuel tank yet.

21   Disconnect the main fuel line from the low-pressure fuel pump. Remove the fuel filter (see Chapter 1). Using low air pressure, blow out the line toward the rear of the vehicle.

**Warning:** *Wear eye protection when using compressed air.*

22   Temporarily disconnect the fuel return fuel line at the injection pump and again, using low air pressure, blow out the line toward the rear of the vehicle.

23   Reconnect the main fuel and return lines at the tank. Fill the tank to a fourth of its capacity with clean diesel fuel. Install the cap on the fuel filler neck.

24   Discard the fuel filter.

25   Connect the fuel line to the fuel pump.

26   Reconnect the battery cables.

27   Purge the fuel pump and pump-to-filter line by cranking the engine until clean fuel is pumped out. Catch the fuel in a closed metal container.

28   Install a new fuel filter.

29   Install a hose from the fuel return line (from the injection pump) to a closed metal container with a capacity of at least two gallons.

30   Crank the engine until clean fuel appears at the return line. Don't crank the engine for more than 30 seconds at a time. If it's necessary to crank it again, allow a three-minute interval before resuming.

31   Loosen each high-pressure line fitting at the injector nozzles. Loosen the fittings only enough to allow fuel to seep out.

32   Crank the engine until clean fuel appears at each nozzle, then tighten the fitting securely. Don't crank the engine for more than 30 seconds at a time. If it's necessary to crank it again, allow a three-minute interval before resuming.

### Gasoline in the fuel system

**Warning:** *Gasoline and diesel fuel is flammable, so take extra precautions when you work on any part of the fuel system. Don't smoke or allow open flames or bare light bulbs near the work area, and don't work in a garage where a gas-type appliance (such as a water heater*

or a clothes dryer) is present. Since diesel fuel is carcinogenic, wear latex gloves when there's a possibility of being exposed to fuel, and, if you spill any fuel on your skin, rinse it off immediately with soap and water. Mop up any spills immediately and do not store diesel fuel-soaked rags where they could ignite. When you perform any kind of work on the fuel system, wear safety glasses and have a Class B type fire extinguisher on hand.

33   If gasoline has been accidentally pumped into the fuel tank, it should be drained immediately. Gasoline in the fuel in small amounts - up to 30 percent - isn't usually noticeable. At higher ratios, the engine may make a knocking noise, which will get louder as the ratio of gasoline increases. Here's how to rid the fuel system of gasoline:

a)   *Drain the fuel tank into an approved container and fill the tank with clean, fresh diesel fuel (see Chapter 4A).*

b)   *Remove the fuel line between the fuel filter and the injection pump.*

c)   *Connect a short pipe and hose to the fuel filter outlet and run it to a closed metal container.*

d)   *Crank the engine to purge gasoline out of the fuel pump and fuel filter. Don't crank the engine more than 30 seconds. Allow two or three minutes between cranking intervals for the starter to cool.*

e)   *Remove the short pipe and hose and install the fuel line between the fuel filter and the injection pump.*

f)   *Try to start the engine. If it doesn't start, purge the injection pump and lines: Loosen the fuel line fittings a little, just enough for fuel to leak out. Depress the accelerator pedal to the floor and, holding it there, crank the engine until all gasoline is removed, i.e., diesel fuel leaks out of the fittings. Tighten the fittings. Limit cranking to 30 seconds with two or three minute intervals between cranking.*

**Warning:** *Avoid sources of ignition and have a fire extinguisher handy.*

g)   *Start the engine and run it at idle for 15 minutes.*

---

## 2   Fuel system priming

**Warning:** *Diesel fuel is flammable, so take extra precautions when you work on any part of the fuel system. Don't smoke or allow open flames or bare light bulbs near the work area, and don't work in a garage where a gas-type appliance (such as a water heater or a clothes dryer) is present. Since diesel fuel is carcinogenic, wear latex gloves when there's a possibility of being exposed to fuel, and, if you spill any fuel on your skin, rinse it off immediately with soap and water. Mop up any spills immediately and do not store diesel fuel-soaked rags where they could ignite. When you perform any kind of work on the fuel system, wear safety glasses and have a Class B type fire extinguisher on hand.*

**Warning:** *The pressure in the high-pressure*

fuel lines can reach extremely high pressure (as much as 23,200 psi), so use extreme caution when working near any part of the fuel injection system with the engine running.

**Note:** *Anytime that fuel system components or fuel lines are opened up or removed, you need to bleed the air from the system or "prime" the fuel system. On 2002 and earlier models, air must be bled from the system manually. For 2001 and earlier models (see Chapter 1, Section 22).*

### 2002 models

1   Loosen but don't remove the banjo bolt (for the low-pressure fuel supply line) from the test port fitting on the fuel injection pump. (Put a shop rag around the fitting.)

2   Turn the ignition key to the Crank position and quickly release the key to the On position before the engine starts. This will operate the fuel transfer pump for about 25 seconds.

3   If there is no fuel present at the fuel supply line after 25 seconds, turn the ignition key to Off and repeat the previous step until fuel is coming out at the fuel supply line banjo bolt.

4   Tighten the banjo bolt to the torque listed in this Chapter's Specifications. Primary air bleeding is now complete.

5   Try to start the engine. If it starts it will probably run erratically and noisily for a few minutes. This is normal. If the engine won't start, proceed to the next step.

6   If the fuel tank is empty, or if you replaced the injection pump or the high-pressure lines, or if the truck has not been operated for an extended period of time, proceed to the next step.

7   Perform the previous air bleeding procedure steps. Make sure that there is fuel in the fuel supply line (i.e., that it's coming out at the banjo bolt).

8   Crank the engine over for about 30 seconds at a time to allow the air trapped in the injection pump to vent out the drain manifold.

9   Thoroughly clean the area around the injector fittings where they're connected to the connector tubes.

10   Bleed out the air by loosening the high-pressure fuel line fittings at cylinders 3, 4 and 5.

11   Once the engine starts (remember: it might be erratic and noisy for a few minutes), continue bleeding until it runs smoothly. (This might take a few minutes.)

### 2003 and later models

12   The fuel system is primed by the transfer (lift) pump. When the key is turned to On (without cranking over the engine), the pump runs for about two seconds, then it shuts off. It will also operate for as much as 25 seconds after the starter has been quickly engaged, then disengaged without allowing the engine to start. (The pump shuts off immediately if the key is turned to On and the engine stops running.)

13   Turn the ignition key to the Crank position, then quickly release the key to the On position before the engine starts. This step will energize the transfer pump for about 25 seconds.

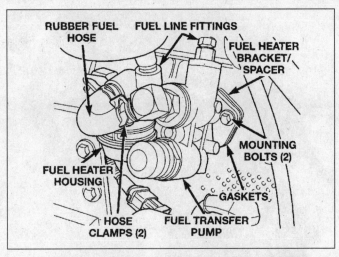

**3.9 Fuel transfer pump assembly installation details (1998 and earlier models)**

**3.10 Remove the transfer pump mounting bolts (arrows) (1998 and earlier models)**

14   If the engine doesn't start after 25 seconds, turn the key to Off and repeat the previous step until the engine does start.

15   The fuel system is now primed.

16   Try to start the engine again. If it starts but runs erratically and noisily, that's normal. It will clean out in a few minutes. If the engine won't start, proceed to the next step.

17   Perform the previous fuel priming procedure steps. Make sure that there is fuel in the tank.

18   Crank the engine for 30 seconds at a time to allow the fuel system to prime.

## 3   Fuel transfer pump - check and replacement

**Warning:** *Diesel fuel is flammable, so take extra precautions when you work on any part of the fuel system. Don't smoke or allow open flames or bare light bulbs near the work area, and don't work in a garage where a gas-type appliance (such as a water heater or a clothes dryer) is present. Since diesel fuel is carcinogenic, wear latex gloves when there's a possibility of being exposed to fuel, and, if you spill any fuel on your skin, rinse it off immediately with soap and water. Mop up any spills immediately and do not store diesel fuel-soaked rags where they could ignite. When you perform any kind of work on the fuel system, wear safety glasses and have a Class B type fire extinguisher on hand.*

1   The transfer pump draws fuel from the fuel tank, pumps it through the fuel filter/water separator and delivers it to the fuel injection pump. A transfer pump that is operating incorrectly can cause low engine power, excessive white smoke and/or a hard-to-start engine. There are some simple tests you can perform to determine whether the transfer pump is operating satisfactorily. But first, do the following preliminary inspection:

### Check

**Note:** *The following check procedures applies to 2004 and earlier models, with the transfer pump externally mounted. The transfer pump on 2005 and later models is mounted inside the fuel tank and is a part of the fuel pump module (see Chapter 4A).*

2   Check the fuel line fittings and connections. Make sure that they're tight. If a fitting is loose, it can allow air and/or fuel leaks to occur.

3   Inspect the fuel lines for bends and kinks. Replace any damaged fuel lines immediately.

4   Start the engine and let it warm up. With the engine idling, conduct the following preliminary inspection before proceeding to the actual transfer pump tests:

a)  *Look for leaks at the pressure (outlet) side of the pump.*

b)  *Look for leaks on the suction (inlet) side of the pump. A leak on the suction side will let air into the pump and reduce the volume of fuel on the pressure (outlet) side of the pump.*

c)  *Inspect the fittings on the transfer pump for leaks. Tighten or replace the fittings as necessary.*

d)  *Look for leaks around the diaphragm, the flange and the breather holes in the pump housing. If any of them are leaking, replace the pump.*

5   If the preceding inspection fails to turn up any obvious problem, have the transfer pump and the low-pressure side of the system diagnosed by a dealer service department or other qualified repair shop. Further testing is beyond the scope of the home mechanic. However, you can save money by replacing the transfer pump yourself.

### Replacement

6   Disconnect the negative battery cables from both batteries (see Chapter 5).

7   Remove the starter from the engine (see

Chapter 5).

8   Place a drain pan below the transfer pump.

### 1998 and earlier models

**Note:** *The transfer pump is located on the left side of the engine, behind and below the fuel filter/water separator, and above the starter.*

9   Clean the area around the fuel line fittings on the fuel heater housing and on the transfer pump. Disconnect the fuel line fittings from the transfer pump and from the fuel heater housing (see illustration).

10   Remove the bolts that retain the transfer pump to the side of the engine block (see illustration).

11   Lift the transfer pump and fuel heater from the block and remove the drive rod from the assembly (see illustration).

12   Installation is the reverse of removal. Be sure to use new gaskets and lubricate the ends of the drive rod with engine assembly lube.

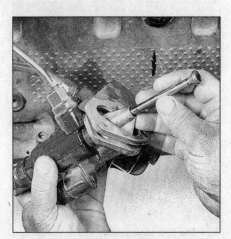

**3.11 Remove the drive rod from the transfer pump (1998 and earlier models)**

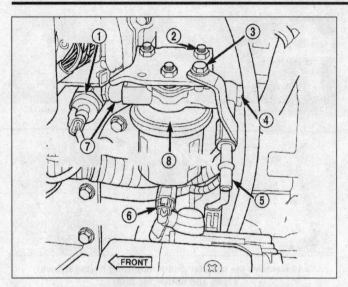

**3.13 Fuel transfer pump assembly installation details (1999 through 2002 models)**

| | | | |
|---|---|---|---|
| 1 | Oil pressure sensor | 5 | Fuel supply line |
| 2 | Pump bracket nuts (3) | 6 | Electrical connector |
| 3 | Support bracket bolt | 7 | Front banjo bolt |
| 4 | Rear banjo bolt | 8 | Fuel transfer pump |

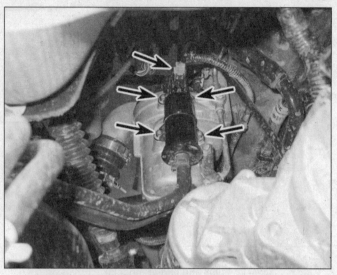

**3.20 To remove the transfer pump from the fuel filter/water separator on 2003 and later models, disconnect the electrical connector and remove the pump mounting bolts**

### 1999 through 2002 models

**Note:** *The fuel transfer pump is located on the left-rear side of the engine block, above the starter motor.*

13   Disconnect the fuel line quick-connecting fitting from the fuel supply line at the rear of the pump (see illustration).

14   Remove the pump support bracket bolt, then detach the support bracket from the pump bracket.

15   Remove the banjo bolts from the front and rear of the pump. Discard the sealing washers.

16   Unplug the pump wiring harness connector.

17   Remove the three pump mounting

**3.21 The fuel tank supply line is connected to the fuel transfer pump extension line inside the left frame rail**

bracket nuts and remove the pump.

18   Installation is the reverse of removal. Be sure to use new gaskets and lubricate the ends of the drive rod with engine assembly lube. Be sure to use new sealing washers when installing the banjo bolts and then tighten the banjo bolts to the torque listed in this Chapter's Specifications.

### 2003 and 2004 models

**Note:** *The fuel transfer pump is located on the rear side of the fuel filter/water separator, which is located on the left side of the engine block.*

19   Drain the fuel from the fuel filter/water separator (see Chapter 1).

20   Disconnect the electrical connector from the fuel transfer pump (see illustration).

21   Disconnect the fuel tank supply line from the fuel transfer pump extension line at the disconnection point on the inside of the left frame rail (see illustration).

**Note:** *For a general overview of the fuel lines and fittings used on diesel models, refer to the next Section. For specific step-by-step instructions showing how to disconnect the various types of quick-connect fittings used on these models, refer to Chapter 4A, Section 4.*

22   Remove the four transfer pump mounting bolts and remove the pump.

23   Remove the old transfer pump O-ring and discard it.

24   Installation is the reverse of removal. Be sure to use a new O-ring, and tighten the transfer pump mounting bolts to the torque listed in this Chapter's Specifications.

### 2005 and later models

25   The transfer pump is located in the fuel tank and is a part of the fuel pump module (see Chapter 4A).

### 4   Fuel lines and fittings - general information

**Warning:** *Diesel fuel is flammable, so take extra precautions when you work on any part of the fuel system. Don't smoke or allow open flames or bare light bulbs near the work area, and don't work in a garage where a gas-type appliance (such as a water heater or a clothes dryer) is present. Since diesel fuel is carcinogenic, wear latex gloves when there's a possibility of being exposed to fuel, and, if you spill any fuel on your skin, rinse it off immediately with soap and water. Mop up any spills immediately and do not store diesel fuel-soaked rags where they could ignite. When you perform any kind of work on the fuel system, wear safety glasses and have a Class B type fire extinguisher on hand.*

**Warning:** *The pressure in the high-pressure fuel lines can reach extremely high pressure (as much as 23,200 psi), so use extreme caution when inspecting for high-pressure fuel leaks. Do not move your hand near a suspect leak - instead, use a piece of cardboard. High-pressure fuel leaks can cause severe injury.*

**Caution:** *Do not attempt to weld high-pressure fuel lines or repair lines that are bent, kinked or otherwise damaged. Replace them with factory replacement fuel lines.*

# Disconnecting Fuel Line Fittings

Two-tab type fitting; depress both tabs with your fingers, then pull the fuel line and the fitting apart

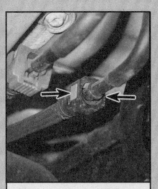

On this type of fitting, depress the two buttons on opposite sides of the fitting, then pull it off the fuel line

Threaded fuel line fitting; hold the stationary portion of the line or component (A) while loosening the tube nut (B) with a flare-nut wrench

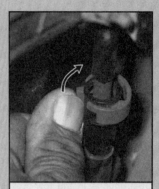

Plastic collar-type fitting; rotate the outer part of the fitting

Metal collar quick-connect fitting; pull the end of the retainer off the fuel line and disengage the other end from the female side of the fitting . . .

. . . insert a fuel line separator tool into the female side of the fitting, push it into the fitting and pull the fuel line off the pipe

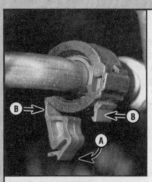

Some fittings are secured by lock tabs. Release the lock tab (A) and rotate it to the fully-opened position, squeeze the two smaller lock tabs (B) . . .

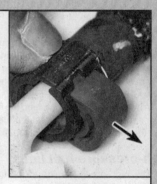

. . . then push the retainer out and pull the fuel line off the pipe

Spring-lock coupling; remove the safety cover, install a coupling release tool and close the tool around the coupling . . .

. . . push the tool into the fitting, then pull the two lines apart

Hairpin clip type fitting: push the legs of the retainer clip together, then push the clip down all the way until it stops and pull the fuel line off the pipe

## Low-pressure fuel lines

1    The low-pressure side of the fuel system includes the following lines:

a) *Fuel supply line from the fuel tank to the fuel transfer pump*

b) *Fuel return line back to the fuel tank*

c) *Fuel drain manifold line at the rear of the cylinder head*

d) *Fuel supply line from the fuel filter to the fuel injection pump*

2    Leaks in the low-pressure fuel lines can cause fuel starvation, which will result in low power. You should be able to smell a leak on the low-pressure side of the fuel system. If you find a leak at a fuel line connection, tighten the fitting and see if the leak stops. If it doesn't, the fitting might be stripped, and must therefore be replaced.

3    Obstructions in the low-pressure fuel lines can cause starting problems and, because they're restricting the fuel supply to the fuel injection pump, they can prevent the engine from accelerating. The usual symptoms are low power and/or a white fog-like exhaust. Inspect the low-pressure fuel lines for bends, kinks and other damage. If you find a damaged line, don't try to repair it. Replace it.

4    The low-pressure lines use various types of quick-connect fittings at connection points. For step-by-step instructions showing how to disconnect and reconnect these fittings, see Chapter 4A, Section 4.

5    When you're done tightening the fitting(s) and/or replacing any low-pressure fuel lines, prime the fuel system (see Section 2).

## High-pressure fuel lines

6    The high-pressure side of the fuel system includes the following lines:

a) *Six fuel lines from the fuel injection pump to the fuel injectors (2002 and earlier models)*

b) *Fuel line from the fuel injection pump to the fuel rail (2003 and later models)*

c) *Six fuel lines from the fuel rail to the fuel injector connector tubes (2003 and later models)*

7    Leaks in the high-pressure fuel lines are usually pretty obvious, and can be extremely dangerous. Not only as a fire hazard, but a stream of high-pressure fuel can cut right through your skin. Start the engine, put on a pair of safety goggles and protective clothing and move a piece of clean cardboard over and around the high-pressure fuel lines and their connections. If a high-pressure line connection is leaking, it will spray the cardboard. Tighten the fitting, then prime the fuel system (see Section 2). If a line itself is leaking, the line must be replaced - don't attempt to repair a damaged line.

8    Unless you're replacing the injection pump or some other component on the high-pressure side of the fuel system, we don't recommend disassembling the high-pressure side of the fuel system.

## 5    Fuel Control Actuator (FCA) - replacement

**Warning:** *Diesel fuel is flammable, so take extra precautions when you work on any part of the fuel system. Don't smoke or allow open flames or bare light bulbs near the work area, and don't work in a garage where a gas-type appliance (such as a water heater or a clothes dryer) is present. Since diesel fuel is carcinogenic, wear fuel-resistant gloves when there's a possibility of being exposed to fuel, and, if you spill any fuel on your skin, rinse it off immediately with soap and water. Mop up any spills immediately and do not store diesel fuel-soaked rags where they could ignite. When you perform any kind of work on the fuel system, wear safety glasses and have a Class B type fire extinguisher on hand.*

**Note:** *The FCA, which is used on 2003 and later models, is located on the rear of the fuel-injection pump.*

1    Disconnect the cables from the negative terminals of both batteries (see Chapter 5).

2    Thoroughly clean off the area around the FCA with brake system cleaner, then disconnect the electrical connector from the FCA (see illustration).

3    Remove the FCA mounting bolts and remove the FCA. Discard the bolts; the manufacturer states that new ones must be used upon installation.

4    Remove and discard the old FCA O-rings. Always install new O-rings before installing the FCA.

5    Inspect the FCA for corrosion and damage. Shake the FCA. It should rattle. If it doesn't, replace it.

6    Apply a little clean light grease to the new O-rings and install the FCA on the fuel injection pump. Make sure that the FCA is flush with its mounting surface on the injection pump, then tighten the FCA mounting bolts, in two stages, to the torque listed in this Chapter's Specifications.

**Caution:** *Do not wait between the tightening stages - the new bolts might lose their ability to retain the torque.*

## 6    Fuel injection pump - removal and installation

**Warning:** *Diesel fuel is flammable, so take extra precautions when you work on any part of the fuel system. Don't smoke or allow open flames or bare light bulbs near the work area, and don't work in a garage where a gas-type appliance (such as a water heater or a clothes dryer) is present. Since diesel fuel is carcinogenic, wear fuel-resistant gloves when there's a possibility of being exposed to fuel, and, if you spill any fuel on your skin, rinse it off immediately with soap and water. Mop up any spills immediately and do not store diesel fuel-soaked rags where they could ignite. When you perform any kind of work on the fuel system, wear safety glasses and have a Class B type fire extinguisher on hand.*

### *1998 and earlier models*

**Removal**

1    Disconnect the negative battery cable from both batteries (see Chapter 5).

2    If equipped with an automatic transmission, disconnect the electrical connector from the TPS sensor located on the side of the fuel injection pump (see Chapter 6).

3    Disconnect the electrical connector at the fuel shutdown solenoid (see Section 9).

4    Disconnect the main engine wiring harness at the top of the fuel injection pump and move it to the side.

5    Remove the intake manifold-to-intercooler air duct (see illustration).

6    Remove the engine oil dipstick tube from the engine (see Chapter 2D).

7    Disconnect the intake air heater wires and remove the intake air heater assembly from the intake manifold (see Section 10).

**5.2 To detach the FCA from the back of the fuel injection pump, disconnect the electrical connector and remove the two FCA mounting bolts (2003 and later models)**

**6.5 Remove the intercooler-to-intake manifold air duct (1998 and earlier models)**

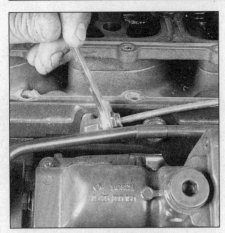

**6.10a Disconnect the injection pump oil feed line (1998 and earlier models)**

**6.10b Disconnect the fuel line from the back of the fuel injection pump (1998 and earlier models)**

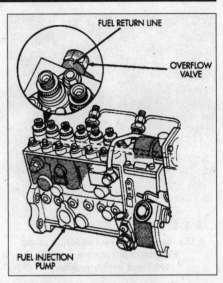

**6.11 Location of the injection pump overflow valve (1998 and earlier models)**

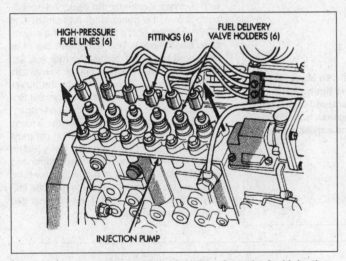

**6.12 Remove the high-pressure fuel lines from the fuel injection pump (1998 and earlier models)**

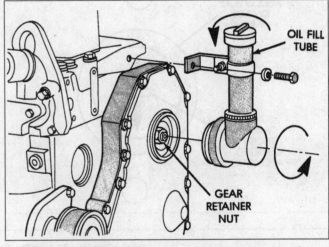

**6.13 Remove the oil fill tube mounting bolt and rotate the assembly counterclockwise to remove it from the front cover (1998 and earlier models)**

8   Remove the accelerator cable, bracket and linkage assembly from the side of the fuel injection pump.

9   Disconnect the turbocharger wastegate oil line and pressure line from the air flow control valve at the rear of the fuel injection pump.

10   Disconnect the lines from the pump (see illustrations) and the fuel filter/water separator (see Section 4). Place a shop rag or towel beneath the fuel lines to catch any residual fuel.

11   Remove the fuel overflow valve and the fuel return line from the fuel injection pump (see illustration).

12   Disconnect the six high-pressure fuel lines from the fuel delivery valve holders (see illustration) at the top of the injection pump. Place shop rags beneath to catch any residual fuel. Cap the fuel lines, the high-pressure fittings on the fuel injection pump and the fuel injectors to prevent the entry of dirt or contamination.

13   Remove the oil fill tube bracket mounting bolt (see illustration) and twist the assembly counterclockwise to remove it from the gear housing cover.

14   Locate the camshaft gear timing pin and set the engine on TDC for cylinder number 1 by following the procedure in Chapter 2D, Section 3. Apply a paint mark on the front pulley indicating the position of the engine at TDC (see illustration).

**Caution:** *The engine and the fuel injection pump must be set on number 1 TDC before removing or installing the fuel injection pump to maintain proper fuel injection pump timing.After locating TDC for number one cylinder, remove the timing pin to prevent accidental shearing of the pin.*

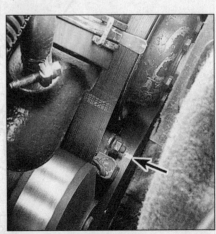

**6.14 Paint an alignment mark on the front pulley directly in front of the cover and bolt assembly (1998 and earlier models)**

**6.15a Remove the fuel injection pump alignment pin access cover (1998 and earlier models)**

**6.15b Be prepared to catch the oil as the cover is removed (1998 and earlier models)**

**6.15c Reverse the alignment pin and install it with the notched end facing into the fuel injection pump (1998 and earlier models)**

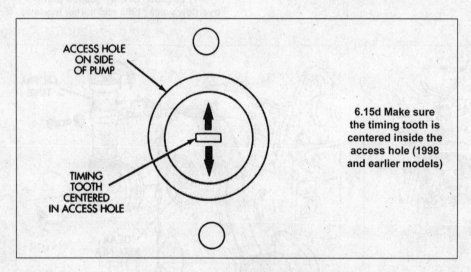

**6.15d Make sure the timing tooth is centered inside the access hole (1998 and earlier models)**

15   The fuel injection pump is equipped with another alignment pin designed specifically to lock the pump shaft on number one TDC while the pump remains off the engine (see illustrations). This alignment pin must be locked into place before the fuel injection pump is removed from the engine to maintain the pump timing. Before removing the pump, remove the access cover and reverse the timing pin, installing it with the slotted end engaging the timing tooth and reinstall the access cover (see illustrations). The timing pin must be reversed (unlocked) once the fuel injection pump is installed back onto the engine and ready to start. If a new or rebuilt pump will be installed, the pump should come from the factory with the slotted end of the pin engaged with the timing tooth.

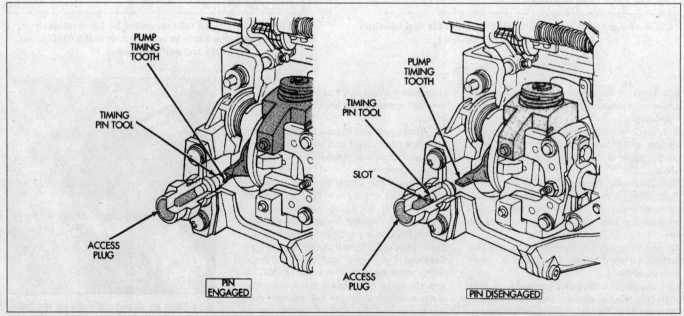

**6.15e Fuel injection pump timing pin installation details - with the timing pin engaged the fuel injection pump is locked at number one TDC (1998 and earlier models)**

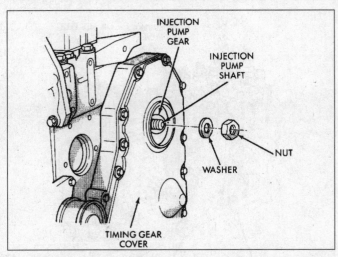

6.16 Remove the injection pump gear nut and washer (1998 and earlier models)

6.17 Pull the gear loose from the fuel injection pump - cover removed for clarity (1998 and earlier models)

16   Remove the nut and washer retaining the gear to the fuel injection pump shaft (see illustration).

**Note:** *Position a shop rag or towel into the housing cover opening to prevent the nut or washer from falling into the gear housing. If the gear nut or washer is accidentally dropped into the housing, the cover must be completely removed to retrieve them.*

17   Using a gear puller and two metric bolts (M8 X 1.24 mm), pull the fuel injection pump gear forward until it loosens from the injection pump shaft (see illustration).

**Caution:** *Pull the gear out until it's just loose from the fuel injection pump shaft. Do not continue pulling or damage to the cover may occur.*

18   Remove the two fuel injection pump bracket mounting bolts (see illustration).

19   Remove the four fuel injection pump-to-gear housing mounting nuts (see illustration).

20   Remove the pump from the gear housing. Be careful not to damage the injection pump shaft when removing the fuel injection pump.

**Warning:** *The pump is very heavy - you may require the help of an assistant.*

21   Clean the injection pump O-ring mounting surfaces on both the gear housing and the fuel injection pump.

## Installation

**Caution:** *The engine must be positioned on TDC for number one cylinder before the fuel injection pump is installed to maintain proper fuel injection pump timing. Engage the cam-*

*shaft gear timing pin before proceeding with installation (see Chapter 2D).*

22   In the event the original pump or new pump is not locked in place at TDC with the fuel injection pump timing pin, it will be necessary to rotate the pump shaft until the timing tooth is visible in the plug opening (see illustration 6.15e). Install the slotted end of the timing pin tool over the timing tooth and lock it into place. Do not force the slots in the tool over the timing tooth.

**Note:** *New or rebuilt pumps should have the pin locked in place. Be sure to verify this before proceeding with the installation.*

23   Check the condition of the rubber O-ring at the fuel injection pump mounting area. If the seal is worn or damaged, replace it with a new part.

6.18 Remove the two fuel injection pump bracket mounting bolts (arrows) (1998 and earlier models)

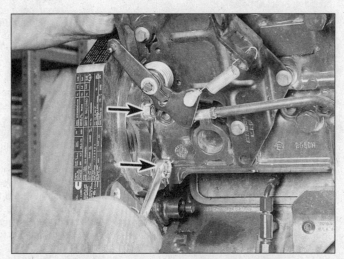

6.19 Remove the four fuel injection pump mounting nuts (arrows) - two of the nuts are not visible in this photo (1998 and earlier models)

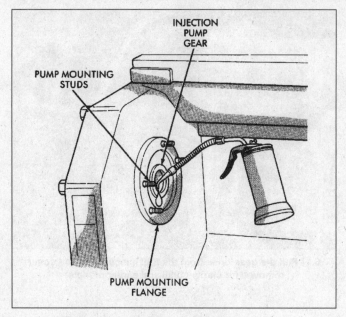

**6.24 Apply a light film of oil to the gear cover (1998 and earlier models)**

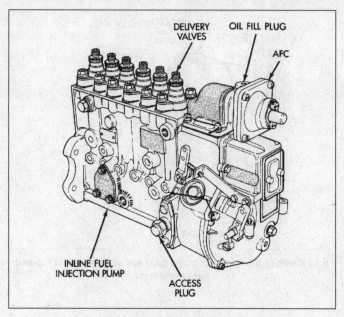

**6.41 Location of the oil fill plug on top of the injection pump (1998 and earlier models)**

24   Apply clean engine oil to the injection pump mounting flange opening in the gear cover housing to allow easier fuel injection pump installation (see illustration).

**Note:** *Make sure that there is no oil residue on the fuel injection pump shaft or camshaft gear. This is crucial when obtaining the correct camshaft-to-injection pump torque specifications.*

25   Install the fuel injection pump onto the mounting flange while inserting the pump shaft through the gear.

26   Install the four pump mounting nuts finger-tight. Do not attempt to "pull-in" the pump by tightening the mounting nuts. This will damage the gear and shaft assembly. Make sure the pump is seated onto the gear housing before the nuts are tightened.

27   Install the two vertical fuel injection pump mounting bracket bolts.

28   Tighten the four pump mounting nuts to the torque listed in this Chapter's Specifications, then tighten the bracket bolts securely.

29   Install the injection pump drive shaft washer and nut and tighten the nut in two stages. First, tighten it to the initial torque listed in this Chapter's Specifications. This will keep it from moving while you remove the timing pins.

30   Disengage the camshaft gear timing pin from the camshaft gear.

31   Unscrew the access plug on the side of the pump and remove the injection pump tooth alignment pin.

32   Tighten the injection pump drive shaft nut to its final torque, which is listed in this Chapter's Specifications. Use the barring tool (see Chapter 2D, Section 3) to hold the engine while tightening the pump shaft nut to its final torque.

33   Retighten the fuel injection pump mounting nuts to the torque listed in this Chapter's Specifications.

34   Verify that the fuel injection pump is timed correctly as follows:

*Step 1)   Rotate the engine clockwise (as viewed from the front of the engine compartment) with the barring tool. Continue rotating the engine until the camshaft gear timing pin engages the hole in the camshaft gear. The engine is now at TDC (see Chapter 2D).*

*Step 2)   Remove the access cover and check the position of the fuel injection pump timing tooth. Install the alignment pin to check the position. If the timing pin will not engage the timing tooth, remove the pump gear nut and loosen the pump gear from the pump shaft with the puller. With the gear loose, rotate the injection pump shaft until the timing tooth is centered in the access hole. Remove the timing pins, tighten the fuel injection pump gear and remove the barring tool.*

35   This step is simply to get the pump timing close to the correct setting. The fuel injection pump still must be timed properly in order to insure proper operation of the fuel system. Follow the adjustment procedure beginning with Step 56.

36   Remove the timing pin from the fuel injection pump. Reverse the position of the pin and install it into the pump. The slotted end should be facing OUT. Install the access cover, with the sealing washer, and tighten it to the torque listed in this Chapter's Specifications.

37   Install the engine oil supply line and fuel return line/overflow valve to the fuel injection pump.

38   Install the six high-pressure fuel lines to

the top of the fuel injection pump. Tighten the line fittings to the torque listed in this Chapter's Specifications.

39   Install the low-pressure fuel supply line to the fuel injection pump.

40   Install the wastegate line to the turbocharger and AFC sensing line to the fuel injection pump.

41   Pre-lubricate the fuel injection pump before operation. All new and rebuilt units must be lubricated to ensure safe operation initially. Failure to lubricate the pump may result in premature governor wear. Remove the 10 mm hex fill plug on the top of the fuel injection pump governor (see illustration). Add 25 ounces of clean engine oil through this opening. Install the oil fill plug and tighten it to the torque listed in this Chapter's Specifications.

42   Connect the throttle linkage to the fuel injection pump.

43   Connect the electrical connector to the fuel shutdown solenoid.

44   Connect the main engine wiring harness to the top of the fuel injection pump.

45   Install the engine oil dipstick tube mounting clamp at the opening to the intake manifold.

46   Install the oil fill tube and tube adapter.

47   Install the oil fill tube bracket and mounting bolt.

48   Plug in the TPS electrical connector.

49   Install the air cleaner housing-to-turbocharger tube at the air cleaner housing.

50   Install the intake manifold air heater assembly (see Section 10). Be sure to use a new gasket.

51   Install the intake manifold intercooler tube.

52   Check and adjust throttle linkage.

53   Bleed the air from the fuel injection pump and system (refer to Chapter 1).

**6.57 Remove the number one cylinder high-pressure line from the pump (1998 and earlier models)**

**6.58 Use a special socket to loosen the delivery valve holder (1998 and earlier models)**

**6.59 Remove the delivery valve holder, spring, fill piece and shims (1998 and earlier models)**

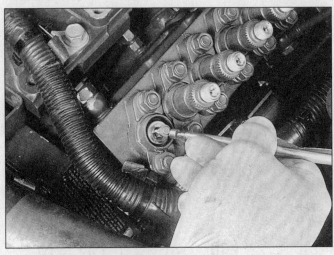

**6.60 Use a magnet to lift out the two-piece delivery valve assembly (1998 and earlier models)**

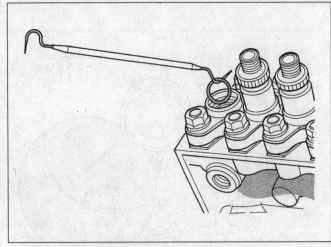

**6.61 If equipped, remove the copper delivery valve washer (1998 and earlier models)**

54   Adjust the low idle speed if necessary (refer to Section 11).

55   Be sure to check the engine oil level (see Chapter 1).

## Timing adjustment

**Note:** *It is necessary to check the fuel injection pump timing when the original pump is removed or a rebuilt pump is installed in place of the original. The following procedure is difficult, requires special tools, and must be set exactly to the manufacturer's specifications. It is recommended that the pump timing be performed by a dealer service department or other qualified diesel technician.*

56   Locate the camshaft gear timing pin and position the engine on TDC for cylinder number 1 by following the procedure in Chapter 2D, Section 3. Apply a paint mark on the front

pulley to indicate the position of TDC (see illustration 6.14). It is a good idea to remove the star-shaped clip on the locating tool to allow free movement through the housing into the camshaft gear. This will give the hand an easy touch when the hole approaches the tip of the locating pin, allowing the pin to drop easily into place.

**Caution:** *After locating TDC for number one cylinder, remove the timing pin to prevent accidental shearing of the pin.*

57   Remove the number 1 cylinder high-pressure line from the fuel injection pump (see illustration).

58   Loosen (but don't remove) the delivery valve holder using a special socket, available at most auto parts stores (see illustration). There is an external O-ring on the holder to help prevent debris from dropping down into

the fuel injection pump.

59   Remove the delivery valve holder by carefully tipping the holder outward with one hand while using the other hand to hold the spring, fill piece and shims from falling out of the holder (see illustration). Carefully place these parts as an assembly onto a clean work area.

60   If equipped, use a magnet and remove the two-piece delivery valve assembly from the pump (see illustration).

61   Using a pick, remove the copper delivery valve washer from the top of the pumping element (see illustration). Be careful not to scratch the top of the plunger (barrel assembly) during this process. Discard the used delivery valve washer. A new washer will be used for reassembly.

62   Install the dial indicator adapter in place

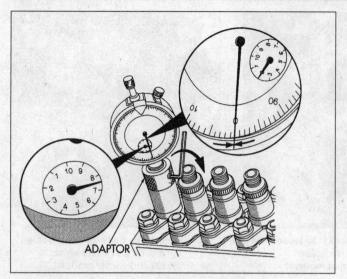

**6.63a Set the dial indicator between 7 and 9 mm and tighten the set screw (1998 and earlier models)**

**6.64 Observe the paint mark as the engine is rotated counterclockwise (as viewed from the front) then zero the dial indicator on the bottom of its stroke (1998 and earlier models)**

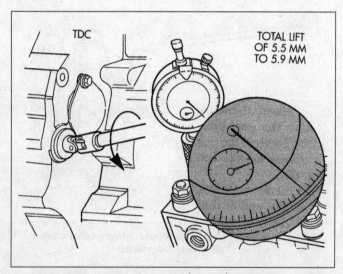

**6.65a Count the complete rotations of the dial (first digit) then the decimal reading (second and third digit) as the plunger reaches the top of its travel (1998 and earlier models)**

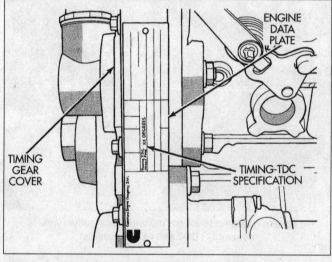

**6.65b Location of the engine data plate (1998 and earlier models)**

of the number 1 delivery valve holder and tighten the set screw lightly.

63   Install the dial indicator and tip into the adapter. Loosen the set screw, position the dial indicator to read between 7.0 and 9.0 mm and tighten the set screw (see illustration).

**Note:** *The dial indicator is capable of measuring from 0 to 20.00 mm lift. The small inner dial is marked in increments of 1 mm. The large outer dial is marked in increments of 0.01 mm. One revolution of the outer dial is equal to 1 mm. The inner dial indicates 0 to 10 mm but will rotate twice as the indicator goes through the full range.*

64   Using the engine barring tool, rotate the engine opposite of normal engine rotation (counterclockwise as viewed from the front) until you see the dial indicator reading stop dropping (see illustration). This is the inner base circle (bottom travel) of the fuel injection pump cam. Zero the dial indicator and note the reading on the small inner dial. This action will drop the plunger to the lowest point of travel within the fuel injection pump.

**Note:** *Do not be confused by the direction of rotation. Follow the directions carefully, rotating the front pulley in the correct direction by turning the barring tool opposite to the direc-* *tion specified.*

65   Rotate the engine slowly clockwise, until the paint marks you made on the pulley align (TDC). Note the fuel injection pump lift setting on the dial indicator (see illustration). This will give the total travel of the plunger from top to bottom. Locate the engine data plate on the left side of the timing gear cover (see illustration). Record the "Timing - TDC" specification listed in degrees. Compare these specifications to the chart for your specific model. Use the CPL number stamped onto the engine plate to cross-reference the pump plunger lift specification.

## 49 STATE MODELS

### CPL 1549, 1550, 1815, 1816, 1959

| Static timing (degrees BTDC) | Plunger lift (mm) at TDC |
|---|---|
| 11.5 | 5.5 |
| 12.0 | 5.6 |
| 12.5 | 5.7 |
| 13.0 | 5.8 |
| 13.5 | 5.9 |

## 49 STATE, AUTOMATIC TRANSMISSION

### CPL 2022

| Static timing(degrees BTDC) | Plunger lift (mm) at TDC |
|---|---|
| 12.0 | 4.1 |
| 12.5 | 4.2 |
| 13.0 | 4.3 |
| 13.5 | 4.4 |
| 14.0 | 4.5 |

## 49 STATE, MANUAL TRANSMISSION

### CPL 2023

| Static timing (degrees BTDC) | Plunger lift (mm) at TDC |
|---|---|
| 11.5 | 4.7 |
| 12.0 | 4.8 |
| 12.5 | 4.9 |
| 13.0 | 5.0 |
| 13.5 | 5.1 |

## CALIFORNIA, AUTOMATIC TRANSMISSION, FROM JANUARY 1995

### CPL 1968

| Static timing (degrees BTDC) | Plunger lift (mm) at TDC |
|---|---|
| 12.5 | 4.20 |
| 13.0 | 4.28 |
| 13.5 | 4.36 |
| 14.0 | 4.44 |
| 14.5 | 4.52 |

## CALIFORNIA with EGR system

### CPL 1863

| Static timing (degrees BTDC) | Plunger lift (mm) at TDC |
|---|---|
| 11.5 | 4.0 |
| 12.0 | 4.1 |
| 12.5 | 4.2 |
| 13.0 | 4.3 |
| 13.5 | 4.4 |

66   If the specifications do not match, it will be necessary to adjust the pump timing. The fuel injection pump must be released from the gear and adjusted until the exact lift measurement is attained as follows:

67   Remove the oil filler tube and adapter elbow from the front of the gear housing (see illustration 6.13).

68   Loosen the fuel injection pump gear nut (see illustration) and using a magnet, remove the nut and washers. Use the barring tool and a breaker bar to prevent the engine from rotating when loosening the nut.

**Caution:** *Be very careful not to drop the nut and washer into the gear housing.*

69   It is recommended that a special washer and bearing kit be used to prevent losing the timing setting. It is possible to time the pump without them but it will require a steady hand

to prevent the pump from rotating when the gear is loosened. The barring tool, extension and breaker bar must be held firmly when loosening or tightening the gear nut. If the home mechanic chooses to use this procedure, using a magnet, install the special bearing and thrust washer kit onto the shaft. Position the parts in this order:

a) *Thrust washer*
b) *Bearing*
c) *Thrust washer*

70   Do not tighten the nut at this time

71   Slowly rotate the engine clockwise until reaching the required lift setting on the dial indicator.

**Note:** *The injection pump shaft should rotate with the engine since the injection pump gear is still locked to the fuel injection pump shaft.*

72   With the fuel injection pump at the cor-

**6.68 Remove the nut from the fuel injection pump gear (1998 and earlier models)**

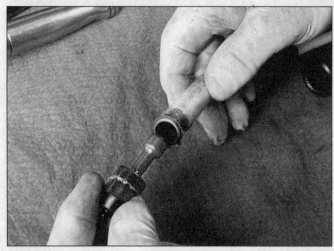

**6.86 Use a small pipe to install the retaining clip over the locating pin after it is installed in the housing (1998 and earlier models)**

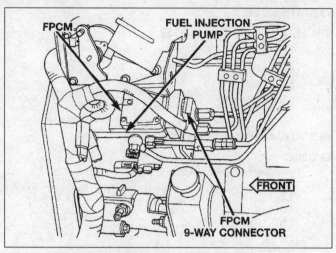

**6.89 Unplug the electrical connector from the Fuel Pump Control Module (FPCM) on the rear of the injection pump (1999 through 2002 models)**

rect plunger lift setting, use a gear puller to pull the injection pump gear off the taper of the fuel injection pump input shaft (see illustration 6.17). With the gear loose, double-check to make sure that the lift setting has not changed. Leave the gear puller installed.

73   Rotate the engine 20 to 30-degrees counterclockwise, then clockwise back to TDC (paint mark). This will remove any backlash from the gears. The setting on the dial indicator should not move at this time because the pump shaft has been disconnected from the gear.

74   Loosen but do not remove the gear puller bolts. Using the gear puller, rotate the pump gear (by hand) counterclockwise while pushing the gear onto the shaft. This will remove backlash between the injection pump and the camshaft gears.

75   Install the pump gear nut and washer.

76   Hand-tighten the pump gear nut and remove the gear puller.

77   Tighten the pump gear nut to its initial torque, listed in this Chapter's Specifications, to seat the gear to the pump shaft taper.

78   If the special washers and bearing tools were used, remove them from the pump shaft using a magnet on the end of the shaft to prevent the parts from dropping down into the gear housing.

79   Prevent the engine from turning using the barring tool and torque the fuel injection pump gear nut to the torque listed in this Chapter's Specifications.

80   Repeat Steps 63 and 64 to verify the final timing adjustment. If the Specifications are not correct, repeat the timing adjustment procedure.

81   Remove the dial indicator and adapter from the fuel injection pump.

82   If equipped, install a new copper delivery

valve washer to the fuel injection pump (see illustration 6.60). Install the delivery valve assembly on top of the sealing washer.

**Caution:** *Follow the installation procedure exactly. Incorrect installation and tightening of the delivery valve will result in damage and fuel leaks.*

83   Lubricate the threads and clamping surface of the delivery valve holder using a few drops of the SAE 90 hypoid gear oil. Install the delivery valve holder assembly taking care not to displace the delivery valve spring, fill piece or any shims.

84   Pre-tighten the delivery valve holder to its initial torque, which is listed in this Chapter's Specifications. Using a single motion, tighten the holder to its final torque, listed in this Chapter's Specifications.

85   Install the other engine components removed during the adjustment procedure. Leave the number 1 injector line loose to facilitate bleeding the air out of the system. Refer to Section 4 for the correct high-pressure bleeding procedure.

86   The remainder of installation is the reverse of removal. An easy way to install the star-shaped clip back onto the TDC locating pin is to use a small diameter pipe (see illustration). Install the pin into the housing, place the clip on the end of the pin and slide it over the handle into the housing. The clip will snap once it's in place. This clip retains the pin inside the housing, preventing it from falling out when the engine is running.

### 1999 through 2002 models

#### Removal

87   Disconnect the negative cables from both batteries (see Chapter 5).

88   Thoroughly wipe off the fuel supply lines, the fuel injection pump and the high-pressure

fuel lines.

89   Unplug the electrical connector from the Fuel Pump Control Module (FPCM) on the rear of the injection pump (see illustration).

90   On 1999 models, remove the overflow valve (see illustration); on 2000 through 2002 models, detach the fuel return line from the injection pump (see illustration). Catch any spilled fuel with a rag.

91   Remove the fuel supply line banjo bolt (1999 models, see illustration 6.90a; 2000 through 2002 models, see illustration 6.90b) and detach the fuel supply line from the injection pump. Detach the other end of the same line from the fuel filter.

92   Remove the intake air duct (see Section 12).

93   Remove the engine oil dipstick tube (see Chapter 2D).

94   Remove all wiring harness clips and disconnect the electrical cables from the air intake heater (see illustration).

95   Remove the air intake housing (see Section 12).

96   Remove the Accelerator Pedal Position Sensor (APPS) (see Chapter 6, Section 3).

97   Remove the rear engine lifting bracket and remove the high-pressure lines (see Section 4).

98   On 1999 models, unscrew the plastic access cap from the front gear cover (see illustration). Remove the nut and washer that attach the injection pump gear to the pump shaft. On 2000 through 2002 models, remove the crankcase breather assembly (see illustration) from the front gear cover.

99   Remove the rubber access plug for the barring tool and then insert the barring tool into the flywheel housing (see Chapter 2D, Section 3). Rotate the engine until the keyway is at the 12 o'clock position (see illustration).

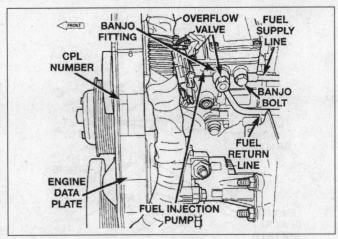

6.90a The overflow valve is located on the side of the injection pump, next to the banjo bolt for the fuel supply line (1999 models)

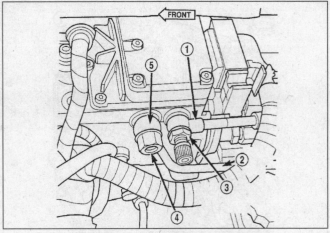

6.90b Overflow valve assembly installation details (2000 through 2002 models)

1   Fuel supply line
2   Fuel return line
3   Banjo bolt (test port fitting)
4   Overflow valve
5   Banjo fitting

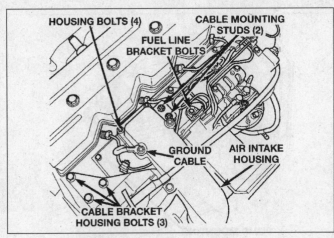

6.94 Disconnect the heating element electrical cables, remove the four air intake housing bolts and remove the housing (1999 and later models)

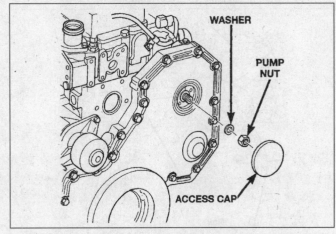

6.98a On 1999 models, unscrew the plastic access cap from the front gear cover and then remove the nut and washer that attach the injection pump gear to the pump shaft (1999 through 2002 models)

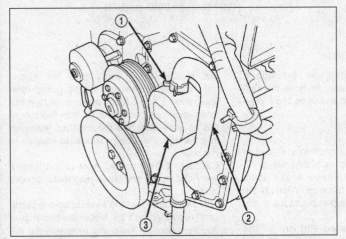

6.98b On 2000 and later models, loosen the hose clamp (1), detach the crankcase breather hose (2) and remove the crankcase breather (3); then remove the nut and washer that attach the injection pump to the pump shaft (see previous illustration) (1999 through 2002 models)

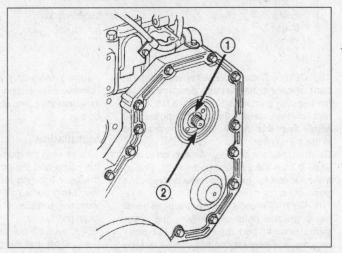

6.99 Rotate the engine with the barring tool until the keyway is at the 12 o'clock position (1999 through 2002 models)

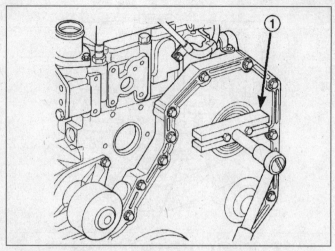

**6.100 Using a T-bar type puller, insert two M8 X 1.24 mm (metric) screws through the puller, screw them into the threaded holes provided in the pump gear and then separate the injection pump gear from the injection pump shaft (1999 and later models)**

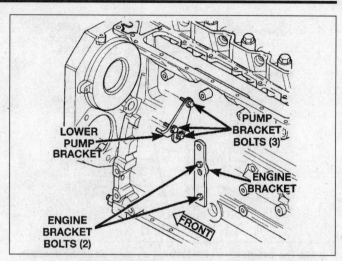

**6.101a On 1999 models, remove the three lower pump bracket bolts and remove the lower pump bracket, then loosen, but don't remove, the two engine bracket bolts (1999 through 2002 models)**

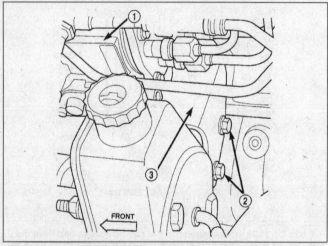

**6.101b On 2000 and later models, remove the two lower pump bracket bolts (1999 through 2002 models)**

| 1 | Fuel injection pump | 3 | Rear/lower bracket |
| 2 | Bolts (2) | | |

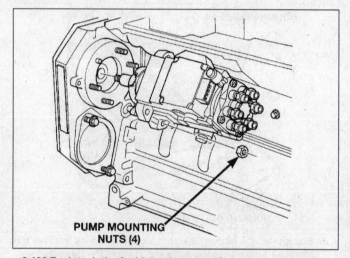

**6.102 To detach the fuel injection pump from the gear housing, remove the four injection pump-to-gear housing mounting nuts (1999 through 2002 models)**

100  Using a T-bar type puller (see illustration), separate the injection pump gear from the injection pump shaft. Insert two M8 X 1.24 mm (metric) screws through the puller and screw them into the threaded holes provided in the pump gear.
**Caution:** *Pull the gear only far enough to separate it from the injection pump shaft. Pulling the gear too far might damage or break the gear cover.*
101  On 1999 models, remove the three lower pump bracket bolts and remove the lower pump bracket and then loosen, but don't remove, the two engine bracket bolts (see illustration). On 2000 through 2002 models, remove the two lower pump bracket bolts (see illustration).
102  Remove the four injection pump-to-gear

housing mounting nuts (see illustration). Remove the injection pump. Remove the keyway from the pump shaft and store it in a plastic bag.

## Installation

103  Inspect the pump mounting surfaces of the pump and the pump mounting flange on the gear housing for damage. Also inspect the O-ring surfaces for damage. Wipe off the mounting surfaces of the pump and the pump mounting flange.
104  Clean off the tapered surfaces of the pump shaft and the pump gear (see illustration) with brake system cleaner.
105  Coat the new injection pump O-ring with clean engine oil and then install the O-ring (see illustration).

106  Install the keyway with the arrow pointed toward the rear of the pump (see illustration 6.105). Also, make sure that the three-digit number stamped into the top of the keyway matches the number stamped into the injection pump data plate (see illustration).
**Caution:** *If the incorrect keyway is installed, the PCM might display a diagnostic trouble code.*
107  Make sure that the keyway on the pump shaft is aligned with the slot in the pump gear and then position the pump assembly on the gear housing mounting flange. The dowel on the mounting flange (see illustration 6.104) must be aligned with the hole in the front of the pump.
108  When the pump is flat against the mount-

Chapter 4 Part B

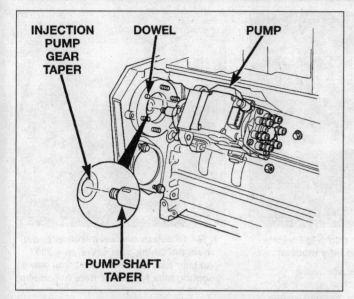

**6.104 Clean off the tapered surfaces of the pump shaft and the pump gear with an evaporative type cleaning agent such as brake cleaner; and, when installing the pump, make sure that the hole in the pump face is aligned with the dowel on the mounting flange (1999 through 2002 models)**

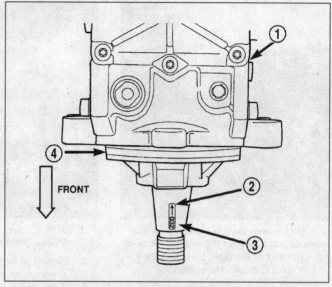

**6.105 Coat the new injection pump O-ring with clean engine oil and then install the O-ring (4); when installing the keyway, make sure that the arrow (2) faces toward the rear of the pump (1); also make sure that the number (3) on the keyway matches the three-digit number on the pump data plate (see next illustration) (1999 and later models)**

ing flange, install the four pump mounting nuts and hand-tighten them. Do NOT torque the pump mounting nuts at this time.

**Caution:** *Do NOT try to "pull" the pump to the gear cover using the pump mounting nuts. Doing so might damage the pump and/or the cover. The pump MUST be positioned flat against the mounting flange before tightening the mounting nuts.*

109  To prevent damage to any components, tighten the pump-related fasteners in the following sequence:

a)  *Install the injection pump shaft washer and nut on the pump shaft and tighten the shaft nut finger-tight.*

b)  *Place the lower pump bracket in position and install the three bracket bolts (1999 models) or two rear/lower pump mounting bolts (2000 through 2002 models) finger-tight.*

c)  *Tighten the injection pump shaft nut to its preliminary torque, which is listed in this Chapter's Specifications.*

d)  *Tighten the four pump mounting nuts to the torque listed in this Chapter's Specifications.*

e)  *Tighten the three lower pump bracket-to-pump bolts (1999 models) or two rear/lower pump bracket-to-pump bolts (2000 through 2002 models) to the torque listed in this Chapter's Specifications.*

f)  *On 1999 models, tighten the two engine bracket-to-engine bolts to the torque listed in this Chapter's Specifications.*

g)  *Using the barring tool to prevent the engine from rotating, tighten the injection pump shaft nut to its final torque, which is listed in Chapter 2D, Section 3.*

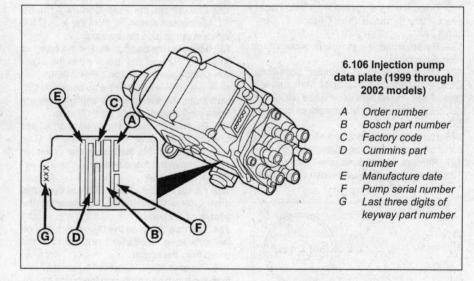

**6.106 Injection pump data plate (1999 through 2002 models)**

A   *Order number*
B   *Bosch part number*
C   *Factory code*
D   *Cummins part number*
E   *Manufacture date*
F   *Pump serial number*
G   *Last three digits of keyway part number*

110  Install the plastic access cap (1999 models) or the crankcase breather and hose (2000 through 2002 models).

111  Using new sealing washers, reconnect the fuel return line and overflow valve to the injection pump. Tighten the overflow valve to the torque listed in this Chapter's Specifications.

112  Using new sealing washers, reconnect the fuel supply line between the fuel filter housing and the injection pump. Tighten the banjo bolts to the torque listed in this Chapter's Specifications.

113  Install the engine rear lifting bracket and the high-pressure fuel lines (see this Chapter's Specifications).

114  Install the Accelerator Pedal Position

Sensor (APPS) (see Chapter 6, Section 3).

115  Install the air intake housing (see Section 10).

116  Reconnect the electrical cables to the air intake heater and install all wiring harness clips (see Section 10).

117  Install the engine oil dipstick tube.

118  Install the intake air duct (see Section 12).

119  Plug in the electrical connector for the Fuel Pump Control Module (FPCM) on the rear of the injection pump.

120  Reconnect the negative cables to both batteries.

121  Bleed air from the fuel system (see Chapter 1, Section 22).

122  Check for fuel and engine oil leaks.

**6.124 Loosen the hose clamps on the connecting tubes for the intercooler duct at each end of the duct, then remove the duct (2003 and later models)**

**6.130 Fuel injection pump-to-fuel line fittings (2003 and later models)**

*A  Banjo bolt for fuel filter/water separator-to-injection pump line*
*B  Banjo bolt for fuel pressure limiting valve (on fuel rail) to injection pump line*
*C  Tube nut type fitting for high-pressure line to fuel rail*

**6.134 To detach the fuel injection pump from the timing gear cover on a 2003 and later model, remove the three pump mounting nuts (other two nuts not shown)**

## 2003 and later models

### Removal

123  Disconnect the cables from both negative battery terminals (see Chapter 5, Section 1).

124  Remove the left-side intercooler duct (see illustration).

125  Remove the ECM mounting bolts (see Chapter 6), detach the ECM from the left side of the engine and set it aside (DO NOT disconnect the electrical connectors from the ECM).

126  Remove the cooling fan shroud and the cooling fan assembly (see Chapter 3).

127  Remove the drivebelt (see Chapter 1).

128  Thoroughly clean off the rear of the injec-

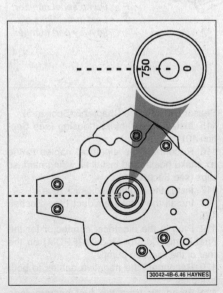

**6.139 Set the fuel injection pump phasing with the digit "5" in the 9 o'clock position**

tion pump and the connections for its three fuel lines. Also clean off the connections at the opposite ends of the three fuel lines.

129  Disconnect the Fuel Control Actuator (FCA) electrical connector from the rear of the injection pump (see illustration 5.2).

130  Unscrew the banjo bolts and the tube nut fitting that connect the fuel lines to the injection pump (see illustration). Remove the old sealing washers from the banjo bolts and discard them. Always use new sealing washers when reconnecting these banjo fittings.

131  Remove the fuel pump drive gear access cover plate with a 1/2-inch drive ratchet. (The plate is screwed into the timing gear cover.)

132  Remove the fuel pump drive gear mounting nut and washer.

133  Attach a suitable gear puller to the pump drive gear with two bolts and separate the gear from the pump.

134  Remove the three injection pump mounting nuts (see illustration) and remove the pump from the engine.

135  Remove the old injection pump O-ring from the machined groove in the pump mounting surface. Discard the O-ring.

### Installation

136  Using an evaporative cleaner (such as brake cleaner), thoroughly clean off the pump mounting surfaces of the pump and the timing gear cover. Also clean off the machined tapers on both the injection pump shaft and on the injection pump gear. These surfaces must be absolutely dry and free of all dirt and oil to ensure correct gear-to-shaft torque.

137  Apply a little clean engine oil to the new injection pump O-ring, then install a new O-ring into the machined groove in the pump mounting surface.

138  On 5.9L engines, place the injection pump in position on the backside of the timing

gear cover and insert the pump shaft through the hole in the cover and through the drive gear.

139  On 6.7L engines, check the fuel injection pump phasing before installing the pump onto the engine. Locate the numbers on the fuel injection pump shaft. There should be 0 and a 750 stamped onto the shaft. Set the number "5" digit at the 9 o'clock position (see illustration). Place the pump in position on the backside of the timing gear cover with the digit "5" set in the 9 o'clock position. Make sure the engine is at TDC (see Chapter 2D).

**Note:** *The engine can be positioned in TDC number 1 or TDC number 6 for this procedure.*

140  Once the pump is flush with the mounting surface on the timing gear cover, install the three pump mounting nuts and tighten them finger-tight. To prevent damage to any components, tighten the injection pump mounting nuts and the drive gear-to-pump shaft nut in the following sequence:

a) *Install the washer and nut on the injection pump shaft and hand-tighten the nut until it's finger-tight, then carefully tighten it a bit more.*

b) *Tighten the three injection pump mounting nuts to the torque listed in this Chapter's Specifications.*

c) *Tighten the injection pump shaft-to-gear nut to the torque listed in this Chapter's Specifications.*

141  Using new sealing washers, reconnect the fuel line banjo bolts and tighten them to the torque listed in this Chapter's Specifications. Reconnect the tube nut fitting for the high-pressure fuel line and tighten it to the torque listed in this Chapter's Specifications.

142  The remainder of installation is the reverse of removal.

**7.4a Remove the fuel drain manifold fitting from each injector and from the top fitting on the fuel filter/water separator (1994 through 1998 models)**

**7.4b Lift the fuel drain manifold from the engine (1994 through 1998 models)**

**7.7 Hold the injector with one wrench while loosening the nut with another (1998 and earlier models)**

143  When you're done, reconnect the cables to the negative battery terminals.
144  Prime the fuel system (see Section 2).
145  Start the engine and check for fuel leaks.

## 7   Fuel injectors - replacement

**Warning:** *Diesel fuel is flammable, so take extra precautions when you work on any part of the fuel system. Don't smoke or allow open flames or bare light bulbs near the work area, and don't work in a garage where a gas-type appliance (such as a water heater or a clothes dryer) is present. Since diesel fuel is carcinogenic, wear latex gloves when there's a possibility of being exposed to fuel, and, if you spill any fuel on your skin, rinse it off immediately with soap and water. Mop up any spills immediately and do not store diesel fuel-soaked rags where they could ignite. When you perform any kind of work on the fuel system, wear safety glasses and have a Class B type fire extinguisher on hand.*

### Check
1   A leaking fuel injector could cause various symptoms, depending on the severity of the leak. Fuel knock, poor acceleration and performance, low fuel economy and rough engine idle can be caused by pintle-valve leaks. Defective needle valve operation might cause the engine to misfire. Any checks on diesel fuel injectors should be performed by a dealer service department or other qualified diesel repair facility. Injector tests require special high-pressure testing equipment and adapters for accurate results.
**Note:** *A leak in the high-pressure fuel line(s) can cause many of the same problems and symptoms. Check for fuel line leaks before proceeding (see Section 4).*

**7.8 Use a special slide hammer to remove the fuel injectors (1998 and earlier models)**

### 1998 and earlier models

#### Removal
2   Disconnect the negative battery cable from each battery (see Chapter 5).
3   Remove the high-pressure fuel lines from the fuel injection pump (see Section 4).
**Warning:** *Allow the engine to rest for approximately three minutes before disconnecting the high-pressure fuel lines. The extremely high fuel pressure in the lines may cause skin damage and leak excess amounts of fuel over the engine area. Fuel pressure will dissipate after a three-minute period. The pressure in the high-pressure fuel lines can reach up to 17,400 psi; therefore, use extreme caution when inspecting for fuel leaks. Do not move your hand near a suspect leak - instead, use a piece of cardboard. High-pressure fuel leaks can injure your skin upon contact.*

**7.9 Clean the injector bore and threads with a small wire brush (1998 and earlier models)**

4   Remove the fuel drain manifold (see illustrations).
5   Clean the area around the injector. Make sure there is no grease, oil or rust around the injector hold-down nut.
**Note:** *It is a good idea to spray penetrating lubricant around the hold-down nuts at the top of the injector to loosen the rust from the threads.*
6   Strike the injector using a brass drift to break the rust loose, if necessary.
7   Remove the injector (see illustration).
8   If the injector is difficult to remove, use a special injector puller, available at most auto parts stores (see illustration).

#### Installation
9   Clean the cylinder head bore for each injector with a wire brush that is capable of reaching the injector threads (see illustration).

**7.10a Measure the diameter of the injector tip to determine correct washer size...**

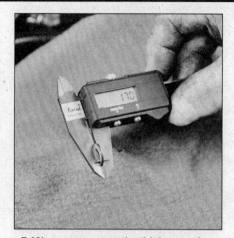

**7.10b ... or measure the thickness of an original copper washer (1998 and earlier models)**

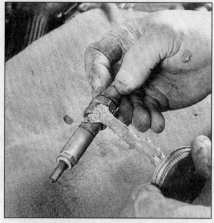

**7.11 Apply a small amount of anti-seize compound to the threads of the injector (1998 and earlier models)**

10   Install a new copper washer onto the tip of the injector.

**Note:** *Washer thickness varies, depending upon the diameter of the injector tip (see illustration), CPL number and part number stamped onto the injector body. Measure the thickness of an original washer (see illustration) and replace it with one of the same thickness. If an old washer is not available, consult a dealer parts department for the necessary information.*

11   Apply a coating of anti-seize to the threads of the injector hold-down nut and between the top of the nut and injector body (see illustration).

12   Install the injector into the cylinder head. Align the tab on the injector body with the notch in the cylinder bore (see illustration).

**Note:** *Install the O-ring onto the injector if equipped.*

13   Tighten the injector hold-down nut to the torque listed in this Chapter's Specifications.

14   Connect the fuel drain manifold to the injectors.

15   Connect the high-pressure fuel lines and bleed the system (see Section 4).

16   Connect the negative battery cable to each battery.

## 1999 and later models
### Removal

17   Disconnect the negative battery cable from each battery (see Chapter 5).

18   1999 through 2002 models: If the injector(s) for cylinders 1 or 2 are being removed, remove the intake air heater (see Section 10). If the injector for cylinder 5 is being removed, remove the engine lifting bracket.

19   2003 and later models: Remove the breather assembly.

20   Remove the valve cover (see Chapter 2D).

21   Clean the area around the high pressure fuel line fittings at each end, then remove the high-pressure fuel line from the injector and the high-pressure fuel pump

(1999 through 2002 models) or fuel rail (2003 and later models).

**Warning:** *Allow the engine to rest for approximately three minutes before disconnecting the high-pressure fuel lines. The extremely high fuel pressure in the lines may cause skin damage and leak excess amounts of fuel over the engine area. Fuel pressure will dissipate after a three-minute period. The pressure in the high-pressure fuel lines can reach up to 17,400 psi; therefore, use extreme caution when inspecting for fuel leaks. Do not move your hand near a suspect leak - instead, use a piece of cardboard. High-pressure fuel leaks can injure your skin upon contact.*

**Caution:** *On 2003 and later models, hold the injector connector tube retaining nut stationary with one wrench while loosening the high-pressure fuel line nut with another wrench. This will prevent damage to the fuel line. Once the fuel line is removed, unscrew the the connector tube retaining nut.*

22   Pull the fuel injector connector tube from the cylinder head. Sometimes this can be done by grasping the tube and pulling it straight out, but if it is stuck, a special tool that threads onto the connector tube must be used (these tools are commonly available from special tool vendors and diesel specialist shops). Remove the O-ring from the connector tube.

23   1999 through 2002 models: Remove the front bolt from the injector hold-down clamp and slide the clamp from the shoulder on the rear bolt (do not loosen the rear bolt).

24   2003 and later models: Remove the exhaust rocker arm assembly (see Chapter 2E). Remove the nuts securing the wires to the top of the injector and detach the wires.

25   1999 through 2002 models: Using special injector removal tool no. 8318 (or equivalent) (see illustration), thread the tool onto the injector and tighten the nut on the bolt; this will draw the injector from its bore in the cylinder head. Remove the injector shim from the bore if it did not come out with the injector. Also remove the O-ring from the injector.

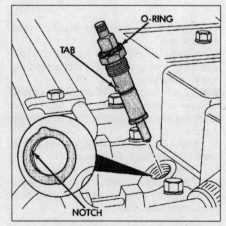

**7.12 Align the tab on the injector with the notch in the injector bore (1998 and earlier models)**

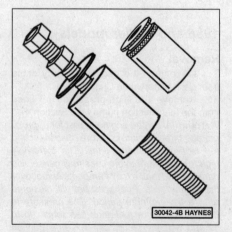

**7.25 Injector removal tool - 1999 through 2002 models**

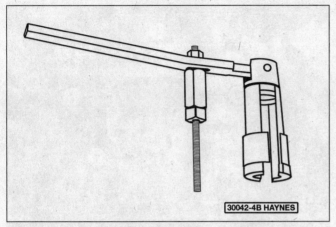

**7.26 Injector removal tool - 2003 and later models**

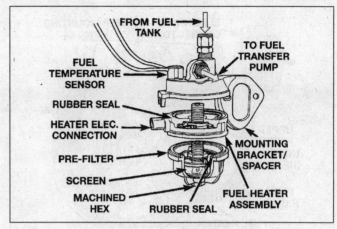

**8.4 An exploded view of fuel heater and pre-filter assembly (1994 through 1998 models)**

26   2003 and later models:

a) *Remove the injector mounting bolts. Special injector removal tool no. 9010 (or equivalent) is used to remove the injector (see illustration).*

b) *Remove one of the rocker housing mounting bolts and thread the stud of the tool into the hole.*

c) *Place the handle of the tool onto the stud and install the nut, leaving it a bit loose.*

d) *Place the clamshell halves of the tool over the injector, then slide the sleeve down to lock the tool to the injector.*

e) *Push the tool's handle down to pull the injector from its bore in the cylinder head.*

f) *Remove the injector shim from the bore if it did not come out with the injector.*

g) *Also remove the O-ring from the injector.*

## Installation

**Note:** *If you are installing a new injector (or injectors) on a 6.7L model, record the injector calibration correction code (printed on the intake side of each injector) for each injector replaced, along with its cylinder number. This information must be programmed into the PCM after the job is completed.*

27   Clean the cylinder head bore for each injector with a wire brush, then blow out the hole with compressed air.

**Warning:** *Wear eye protection.*

28   Install a new copper washer of the proper thickness (see this Chapter's Specifications) onto the tip of the injector. Also install a new injector O-ring. Lubricate the shim and O-ring with clean engine oil.

29   Install the injector into its bore, with the fuel inlet hole in the side of the injector aligned with the hole for the injector connector tube. Push the injector into place until it seats.

**Caution:** *Use hand pressure only, and do not allow the injector tip to contact the sides of the bore.*

### 1999 through 2002 models

30   Install the hold-down clamp and bolt, tightening the bolt to the torque listed in this Chapter's Specifications.

31   Lubricate a new O-ring with clean engine oil and install it onto the connector tube. Push the connector tube into its bore in the cylinder head until it is seated.

**Caution:** *Use hand pressure only.*

32   Install the high-pressure fuel line, tightening the tube nuts to the torque listed in this Chapter's Specifications.

### 2003 and later models

33   Install the two mounting bolts and tighten them to 44 inch-lbs to center and seat the injector, then back them off but leave them threaded in place.

34   Lubricate a new O-ring with clean engine oil and install it onto the connector tube. Also lubricate the connector tube bore and threads in the cylinder head. Push the connector tube into its bore in the cylinder head, with the locating pins on the side of the tube aligned with the groove in the bore, until it is seated.

**Caution:** *Use hand pressure only.*

35   Install the injector tube retaining nut and tighten it to 132 inch-lbs, then tighten the injector mounting bolts, a little at a time, to the torque listed in this Chapter's Specifications.

36   Tighten the connector tube retaining nut to the torque listed in this Chapter's Specifications.

37   Connect the wires to the injector terminals and install the nuts, then tighten the nuts to the torque listed in this Chapter's Specifications.

### All models

38   Install the rocker arms (see Chapter 2D).

39   Adjust the valve clearance (see Chapter 1).

40   Install the high-pressure fuel line, tightening the fitting nuts to the torque listed in this Chapter's Specifications.

**Caution:** *On 2003 and later models, hold the injector connector tube retaining nut with one wrench while tightening the high-pressure fuel line fitting nut. If this is not done, the line could twist and break.*

41   Install the valve cover (see Chapter 2D).

42   The remainder of installation is the reverse of removal.

43   If you're working on a 6.7L model, the injector calibration correction code (printed on the intake side of the injector) must be entered

into the PCM using a scan tool capable of performing this operation.

## 8   Fuel heater and fuel heater relay - replacement

**Warning:** *Diesel fuel is flammable, so take extra precautions when you work on any part of the fuel system. Don't smoke or allow open flames or bare light bulbs near the work area, and don't work in a garage where a gas-type appliance (such as a water heater or a clothes dryer) is present. Since diesel fuel is carcinogenic, wear latex gloves when there's a possibility of being exposed to fuel, and, if you spill any fuel on your skin, rinse it off immediately with soap and water. Mop up any spills immediately and do not store diesel fuel-soaked rags where they could ignite. When you perform any kind of work on the fuel system, wear safety glasses and have a Class B type fire extinguisher on hand.*

### *Fuel heater*

1   The fuel heater prevents diesel fuel from waxing during cold weather operation. A defective fuel heater can cause wax build-up in the fuel filter/water separator. This clogging effect can make the engine difficult to start and prevent the engine from revving up. This condition can also cause a fog-like blue or white exhaust. If the heater doesn't operate in a cold climate, the engine might not operate at all because of fuel waxing. The fuel heater is located on the fuel filter/water separator housing on all models.

### 1998 and earlier models

2   Remove the starter motor (see Chapter 5).

3   Unplug the electrical connector from the fuel heater housing.

4   Place a drain pan below the fuel heater. A machined hex is located on the bottom of the pre-filter housing (see illustration). Working from underneath the vehicle, unscrew and remove the pre-filter.

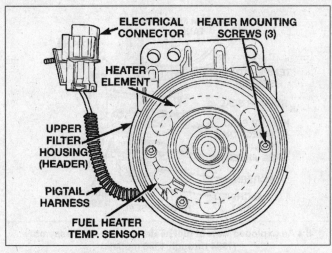

**8.9 To detach the heater assembly from the header on 1999 models, remove the three heater mounting screws**

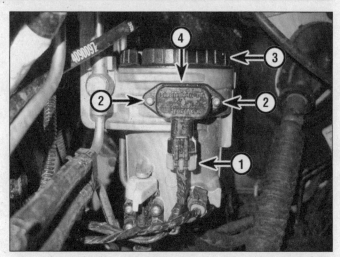

**8.19 Disconnect the fuel heater electrical connector (1), remove the heater retaining screws (2), unscrew the filter housing cap (3), remove the filter element from the housing and remove the fuel heater (4)**

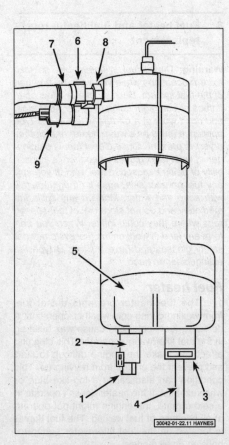

**8.26 Fuel filter assembly details on the 6.7L diesel engine**

1    *WIF harness connector*
2    *WIF sensor*
3    *Drain valve*
4    *Drain tube*
5    *Fuel filter canister*
6    *Fuel line connector*
7    *Fuel line*
8    *Filter screen*
9    *Fuel heater element connector*

5    Remove the fuel heater assembly from the housing.
6    Installation is the reverse of removal.

## 1999 models

7    Remove the fuel filter (see Chapter 1).
8    Unplug the heater electrical connector from the main engine wiring harness (near the upper/rear of the filter). The connector must be removed in order to snake the harness through the top of the filter. Mark the color of each wire on the connector, and then remove the clip retaining the wires to the connector. Remove the wires from the connector.
9    The heater mounting plate, heating element, temperature sensor and wiring harness are housed in the underside of the filter canister header (mounting flange). They must be serviced as a single assembly. To detach the heater assembly from the header, remove the three heater mounting screws (see illustration).
10    To remove the heater from the filter canister header, press down on the heater sealing grommet in the top of the header.
11    Remove the heater assembly from the header and pull the harness through its hole in the header.
12    Installation is the reverse of removal. Be sure to clean the inside of the canister header before installing the heater.

## 2000 through 2002 models

13    Remove the fuel filter (see Chapter 1).
14    Disconnect the fuel heater electrical connector.
15    Remove the two temperature sensor housing retaining screws and remove the sensor from the fuel filter housing.
16    The heater side of the round electrical connector goes through the fuel filter housing and is plugged directly into the heater element. Pry the connector from the fuel filter housing and disconnect it from the heater element.

17    Unlock the heater element fingers and pry the heater element out of the filter housing.
18    Installation is the reverse of removal. Be sure to clean the inside of the fuel filter housing before installing the heater.

## 2003 and later models

### 5.9L diesel engines

19    Disconnect the fuel heater electrical connector (see illustration).
20    Remove the fuel heater retaining screws.
21    Remove the fuel filter cover and filter element (see Chapter 1). Remove and discard the old filter cover O-ring.
22    Remove the fuel heater from the fuel filter housing.
23    Be sure to clean the inside of the fuel filter housing and the underside of the filter housing cap.
24    Installation is the reverse of removal. Be sure to install a new O-ring on the filter housing cap.

### 6.7L diesel engines

25    Drain the water fuel contaminants from the fuel filter assembly (see Chapter 1).
26    Disconnect the fuel heater element connector (see illustration).
27    Remove the two fuel heater element mounting screws.
28    Remove the fuel heater element from the fuel filter assembly.
29    Replace the O-ring with a new one.
30    Installation is the reverse of removal.

## *Fuel heater relay*

**Note:** *On 2006 and later models, there is no serviceable fuel heater relay. It is an integral part of the underhood fuse/relay box - which the manufacturer calls the Totally Integrated Power Module (TIPM). Have the fuel heater relay circuit diagnosed using a scan tool at a* *dealer service department or other qualified automotive repair facility.*

31   The fuel heater relay (see illustration) is located in the engine compartment fuse and relay box. The actual location of the relay inside the fuse box might be different from the one you see here (a 2004 model). Refer to the fuse and relay guide on the underside of the fuse and relay box cover.

mediately and do not store diesel fuel-soaked rags where they could ignite. When you perform any kind of work on the fuel system, wear safety glasses and have a Class B type fire extinguisher on hand.

**Note:** *There is no fuel shutdown solenoid on 1999 and later models. They use an Automatic Shutdown (ASD) relay that is controlled by the Electronic Control Module (ECM). For more information on the ASD relay, refer to Chapter 6.*

**8.31 The fuel heater relay is located in the engine compartment fuse and relay box. The actual location of the fuel heater relay on your vehicle's fuse box might be slightly different from what you see here. Refer to the fuse and relay guide on the fuse box cover**

---

## 9   Fuel shutdown solenoid (1998 and earlier models) - check and replacement

**Warning:** *Diesel fuel is flammable, so take extra precautions when you work on any part of the fuel system. Don't smoke or allow open flames or bare light bulbs near the work area, and don't work in a garage where a gas-type appliance (such as a water heater or a clothes dryer) is present. Since diesel fuel is carcinogenic, wear latex gloves when there's a possibility of being exposed to fuel, and, if you spill any fuel on your skin, rinse it off immediately with soap and water. Mop up any spills im-*

### Check

1   The fuel shutdown solenoid is used to electrically shut off the flow of diesel fuel to the high pressure fuel injection pump. It is mounted on the side of the fuel injection pump and is connected to the pump with a lever (see illustration). The fuel shutdown solenoid and relay are not controlled by the PCM. The solenoid controls the stopping and starting of the engine regardless of the position of the accelerator pedal. With the ignition key in the Off position, the solenoid plunger is spring loaded in the down position. When the ignition is turned to Start (engine cranking), current

---

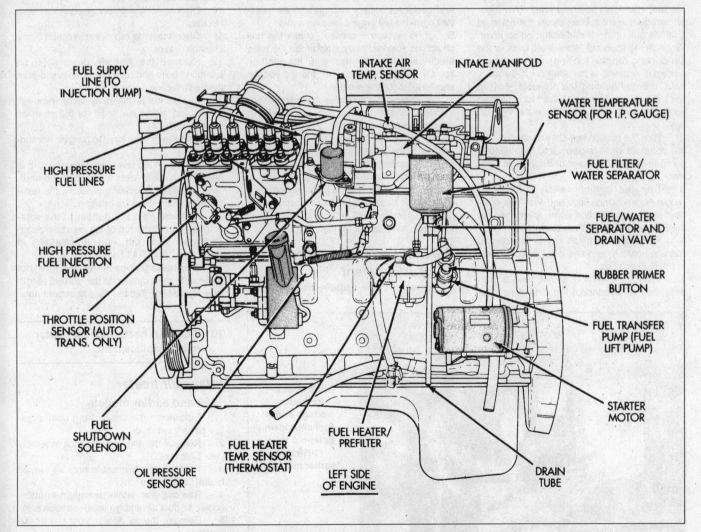

**9.1 1998 and earlier model fuel system component locations**

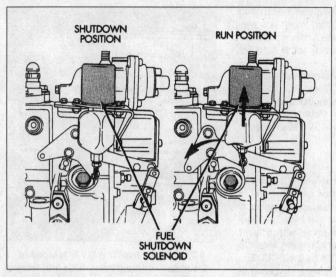

**9.3 Fuel solenoid shutdown positions (1998 and earlier models)**

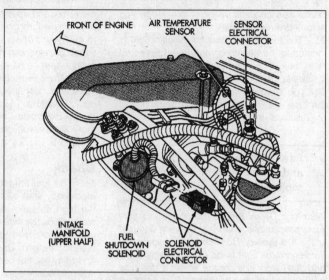

**9.5 Disconnect the fuel shutdown solenoid electrical connector (1998 and earlier models)**

is supplied to the shutdown solenoid through the fuel shutdown solenoid relay. This high-amperage current supply allows the solenoid shaft to pull-up on the injection pump lever. When the ignition key is released back in the On position (engine running), low-amperage current is supplied to the other coil in the solenoid, thereby holding the solenoid shaft in the UP position. Voltage to the fuel shutdown solenoid relay is supplied from the ignition key.

2   Turn the ignition key Off and confirm that the solenoid shaft is down and the injection pump lever is in the down or Shut Down position.

3   Turn the ignition switch to the Start (engine cranking) position and see if the solenoid shaft and injection pump lever move to the Run position (see illustration).

4   Release the ignition key to On (engine running position) and see if the pump lever is in the Run position.

5   If the pump lever does not move or partially moves, disconnect the three-wire electrical connector to the fuel shutdown solenoid and check for battery voltage with an assistant cranking the engine (see illustration).

6   If no voltage is present, check the fuel shutdown solenoid relay. Backprobe the relay electrical connector and with the ignition key On (engine not running), battery voltage should exist (see illustration).

7   If voltage is present to the relay, check the relay itself for correct operation. Refer to the relay checks in Chapter 12).

8   If voltage is present, check for battery voltage at the three-wire electrical connector when the ignition key is in the On (engine running position). Refer to the wiring diagrams at the end of Chapter 12 for a circuit schematic.
**Note:** *In the event that the fuel shutdown solenoid is defective, it will be necessary to adjust the shaft (see Steps 9 through 17).*

### Solenoid replacement and shaft adjustment

9   Disconnect the negative battery cables from both batteries.

10   Disconnect the solenoid electrical connector.

11   Disconnect the clip at the injection pump shutdown lever.

12   Remove the fuel shutdown solenoid mounting bolts and remove the solenoid from the fuel injection pump.

13   Installation is the reverse of removal. Check and adjust the length of the shaft on the solenoid.

14   Turn the ignition key On (engine not running).

15   Pull up on the lever using your hand and hold the solenoid lever in place. If the shutdown solenoid is working properly, the lever should remain in the Up position.

16   Measure from the bottom of the solenoid bracket to the top of the injection pump shutdown lever pin. (see illustration). It should be 2.64 (2-41/64) inches.

17   If necessary, loosen the shaft locknut and rotate the adjuster to the correct length (see illustration). Tighten the adjustment nut.

---

### 10   Intake air heater and air heater relay - replacement

### *Intake air heater*
#### 1998 and earlier models

1   Disconnect the cables from both negative battery terminals.

2   Remove the engine oil dipstick assembly (see Chapter 2D).

3   Remove the two cable nuts at the air heater (see illustration).

4   Remove the intake manifold-to-intercooler air duct assembly (see illustration 6.5).

5   Remove the air heater from the intake manifold.

6   Installation is the reverse of removal.

**9.6 Check for battery voltage at the fuel shutdown solenoid relay (1998 and earlier models)**

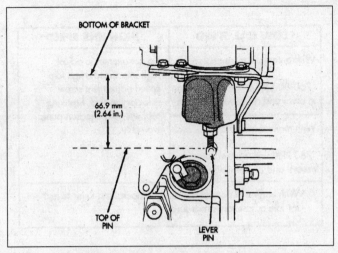

**9.16 Measure the distance from the top of the lever pin to the bottom of the bracket (1998 and earlier models)**

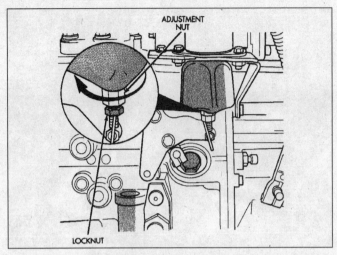

**9.17 Loosen the locknut and turn the adjustment nut (1998 and earlier models)**

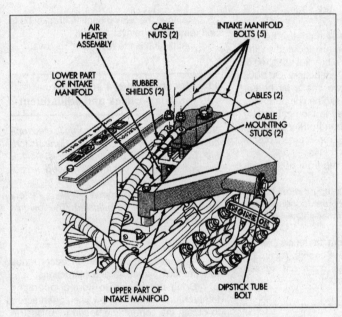

**10.3 Remove the cable nuts from the heater cable ends (1998 and earlier models)**

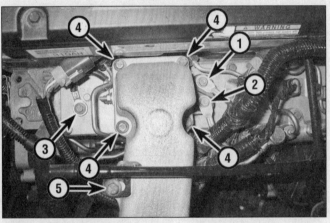

**10.11 To access the intake air heater elements on 2003 and later models, disconnect or remove the following:**

1   *Heater grid positive cable nut*
2   *Heater grid positive cable nut*
3   *Heater grid ground cable - it's not necessary to remove this bolt unless you're replacing the ground cable; instead disconnect the other end of the ground cable from its terminal stud (see next illustration)*
4   *Intake air heater manifold bolts*
5   *Dipstick tube mounting bracket bolt*

Be sure to use new gaskets on the lower and upper side of the air intake heater.

### 1999 and later models

**Note:** *The two intake air heater elements are housed inside a metal block that's bolted to the top of the intake manifold cover by the four intake air heater manifold bolts. The metal block and intake air heater elements are not serviceable separately. They must be replaced as a single assembly.*

7   The two intake air heater grids are housed inside a metal box, which is located on top of the intake manifold cover. The intake air heater elements heat incoming air to make the engine easier to start during cold start-ups and to improve driveability in cool and cold ambient temperatures. The Engine Control Module (ECM) controls the current to the heater elements through two heater relays located in the engine compartment.

8   Disconnect the cables from both negative battery terminals (see Chapter 5, Section 1).

9   Remove the intake manifold air intake duct (see illustration 6.124).

10   Lift up the two rubber covers (if equipped) to gain access to the two heater cable nuts.

11   Remove the two heater cable nuts (see illustration) and disconnect the two heater cables from their terminals.

12   Remove the ground strap nut (see illustration) and disconnect the ground strap from its heater element stud terminal.

**10.12 To disconnect the heater element ground strap from its stud terminal remove this nut**

**10.20 The two heater relays are located next to the right battery on 2003 and later models**

| LOW IDLE SPEED | HIGH IDLE SPEED |
|---|---|
| With automatic transmission...<br><br>*750-800 RPM with transmission in drive and air conditioning on.<br><br>With manual transmission...<br><br>*780 RPM with transmission in neutral and air conditioning on. | Do not attempt to adjust high idle speed. High idle speed adjustment screw is factory sealed. Breaking seal will void injection pump warranty. |
| * With engine at normal operating temperature. Refer to text for idle adjustment procedures. | |

**11.2a Idle speed specifications (1998 and earlier models)**

13   Detach the wiring harness clips.

14   Detach the engine oil dipstick tube bracket from the air inlet connection and from the fuel filter housing.

15   Remove the four intake air heater manifold bolts and detach the dipstick tube from the manifold (see illustration 10.11), then remove the manifold.

16   Remove the intake air heater block and heater element assembly from the intake manifold.

17   Remove the two old heater housing gaskets.

18   Clean the old gasket material from the air intake housing and intake manifold and from both ends of the heater block.

19   Installation is the reverse of removal. Be sure to use new upper and lower heater block gaskets and tighten the air intake housing bolts to the torque listed in this Chapter's Specifications.

### Heater relays

20   On 2002 and earlier models, the two intake air heater relays are located in the engine compartment, on a bracket attached to the left fender below the left battery. On 2003 and later models, the two intake air heater relays are located in the engine compartment, on a bracket that is bolted to the right battery tray (see illustration). Though their locations are different, the following replacement procedure applies to all heater relays.

21   Disconnect the cables from both negative battery terminals.

22   Clearly label the four trigger wires to both relays, then disconnect all four trigger wires.

23   Remove the four rubber shields from all four cable terminals.

24   Remove the nuts from the four cable terminals and disconnect the cables. Again, be sure to label all four wires to prevent crossed wires during reassembly.

25   Remove the relay mounting bracket bolts and remove the relays.

26   Installation is the reverse of removal.

### 11   Idle speed (1994 and 1998 models) - check and adjustment

**Note:** *Because the injection pump is electronically controlled by the Electronic Control Module (ECM) on 1999 and later models, neither the high idle speed nor low idle speed are adjustable on these later models.*

**Note:** *The high idle speed screw is factory sealed and cannot be adjusted. The low idle speed screw is adjustable.*

### Idle speed

1   Connect a tachometer in accordance with the tool manufacturer's instructions.

2   Bring the engine to normal operating temperature. Adjust the low idle speed screw to obtain the correct idle speed (see illustrations).

3   Tighten the locknut after the correct idle is obtained.

### 12   Air filter housing - removal and installation

### 2002 and earlier models

1   Loosen the big hose clamp that secures the air intake duct to the upper half of the air filter housing (see illustration).

2   Unlatch the four clips from the air filter housing cover, then remove the cover and the filter element.

3   Remove the three air filter housing mounting bolts (see illustration), then remove the air filter housing.

4   Installation is the reverse of removal.

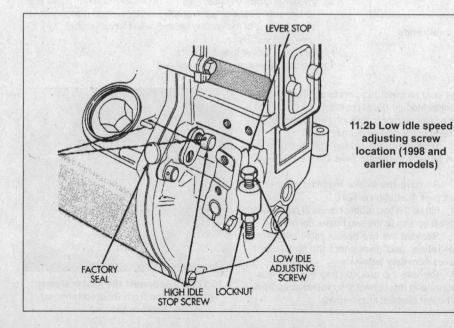

**11.2b Low idle speed adjusting screw location (1998 and earlier models)**

LEVER STOP

FACTORY SEAL

HIGH IDLE STOP SCREW

LOCKNUT

LOW IDLE ADJUSTING SCREW

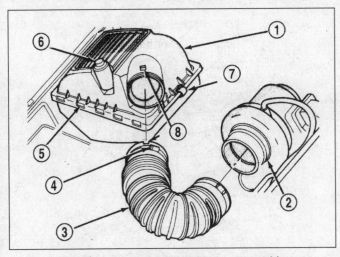

**12.1 Typical early model air cleaner assembly**

| | | | |
|---|---|---|---|
| 1 | Air filter housing cover | 5 | Hinge tabs |
| 2 | Turbocharger | 6 | Filter Minder® |
| 3 | Air intake tube | 7 | Clips (4) |
| 4 | Hose clamp | 8 | Duct alignment notches |

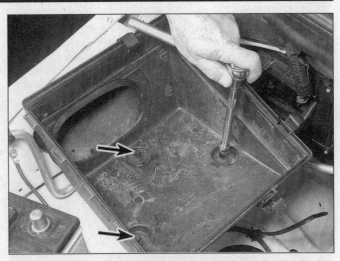

**12.3 To detach the lower half of the air filter housing on 2002 and earlier models, remove these three bolts**

### 2003 and later models

5    Disconnect the electrical connector from the inlet air temperature sensor (see illustration).

6    Loosen the big hose clamp that secures the air intake duct to the upper half of the air filter housing.

7    Remove the air filter housing retaining bolt, then remove the air filter housing. Besides the mounting bolt up top, there are a couple of locator pins on the underside of the air filter housing that are secured by grommets. Pull the air filter housing straight up to disengage these locator pins from their grommets.

8    While the air filter housing is removed, inspect the rubber locator pin grommets for cracks, tears and deterioration. If they're damaged, replace them.

9    Installation is the reverse of removal.

### 13  Accelerator cable - removal and installation

### 1998 and earlier models

1    Use a screwdriver to pry the cable end off of the throttle lever (see illustration).

2    Separate the accelerator cable casing from its bracket by lubricating both sides of the grommet and working the grommet through the bracket with a screwdriver (see illustration).

3    Working underneath the dash, detach the cable from the accelerator pedal.

4    Pinch the tabs on the cable housing retainer and push the cable through the firewall and into the engine compartment.

5    Installation is the reverse of removal.

### 1999 through 2002 models

6    Working underneath the dash, disconnect the accelerator cable from the accelerator pedal (see illustration 11.5 in Chapter 4A).

7    Remove the retaining clip (see illustration 11.6 in Chapter 4A) that secures the cable housing to its hole in the firewall.

**12.5 Air filter housing details - 2003 and later models**

1    Inlet air temperature sensor connector
2    Hose clamp
3    Mounting bolt

**13.1 Pry the cable end off the throttle lever ballstud**

**13.2 Press on the sides of the grommet with a screwdriver to work it through the bracket (1998 and earlier models)**

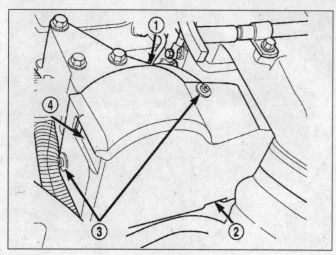

**13.8 Accelerator cable/throttle lever/throttle linkage cover installation details**

1   Cover
2   Push up on lower tab
3   Phillips screws (and retention clips, not visible)
4   Push upper tab here

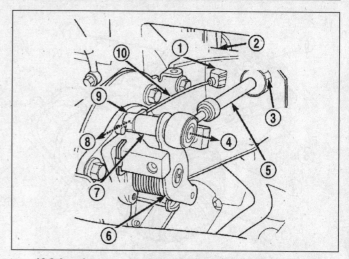

**13.9 Accelerator cable at throttle lever installation details**

1   Squeeze the two cable housing pinch tabs together
2   Accelerator cable mounting bracket
3   Squeeze the two cable housing pinch tabs together
4   To detach the accelerator cable socket from the throttle lever ball, pry it off with screwdrivers
5   Accelerator cable
6   Throttle lever
7   Throttle lever pin
8   To detach the cruise control cable from the throttle lever pin, pull it this way
9   Connector
10  Cruise control cable

8    Working in the engine compartment, remove the cable cover (see illustration). The cable cover is secured by two Phillips screws (screwed into a pair of plastic retention clips) and by two push tabs. Remove the two Phillips screws and pry out the retention clips. Then push the cover to the rear at the front tab, and upward at the lower tab.

9    Using a couple of screwdrivers, pry the cable connector socket off the throttle lever ball (see illustration).

10   Squeeze the two pinch tabs on the sides of the throttle cable at the mounting bracket and disengage the cable from the bracket.

11   Trace the cable back to the firewall. Note the routing of the cable, then detach any cable clips that secure the cable to any engine compartment components.

12   Pull the cable through the firewall and into the engine compartment.

13   Installation is the reverse of removal.

### 2003 and later models

14   These models do not have a conventional accelerator cable between the accelerator pedal and the throttle lever. What they do have is a cable connecting the accelerator pedal to the Accelerator Pedal Position Sensor (APPS), which is located underneath the left battery tray. The procedure for removing and installing this cable is identical to the procedure for the APPS cable used on Hemi gasoline engines (see Chapter 4A, Section 11).

## 14   Turbocharger - description and inspection

### Description

1    A turbocharger improves engine performance, lowers the density of exhaust smoke, improves fuel economy, reduces engine noise and mitigates the effects of lower density air at higher altitude. The turbocharger uses an exhaust gas-driven turbine to pressurize the air entering the combustion chambers.

2    The amount of "boost" (intake manifold pressure) is controlled by a "wastegate" (exhaust bypass valve). The wastegate is operated by a spring-loaded actuator assembly, which controls the maximum boost level by allowing a certain amount of exhaust gas to bypass the turbine in accordance with the intake manifold pressure.

3    Turbocharged models are equipped with an "intercooler," a heat exchanger through which the compressed air intake charge is routed to lower the temperature of the intake charge. Cooler air is denser, which promotes combustion efficiency, increasing power and reducing emissions.

### Inspection

#### Turbocharger

4    Though it's a relatively simple device, the turbocharger is a precision component. Special tools are needed to disassemble and overhaul a turbocharger, so servicing should be left to a dealer service department. However, you can inspect some things yourself, such as a cracked turbo mounting flange, a blocked or restricted oil supply line, a worn out or overheated turbine/compressor shaft bearing or a defective wastegate actuator.

5    A turbocharger has its own distinctive sound, so a change in the quality or the quantity of noise can be a sign of potential problems. But before assuming that a funny sound is caused by a defective turbocharger, inspect the exhaust manifold for cracks and loose connections. For example, a high-pitched or whistling sound might indicate an intake air or exhaust gas leak. Inspect the turbocharger mounting flange at the exhaust manifold and make sure that the hose clamp that attaches the air intake duct to the turbocharger is tight.

6    If an unusual sound is coming from the turbocharger, turn off the engine and allow it to cool completely. Remove the intake duct between the air cleaner housing and the turbocharger. Turn the compressor wheel to make sure it spins freely. If it doesn't, it's possible the turbo lubricating oil has sludged or coked-up from overheating. Push in on the turbine wheel and check for binding. The turbine should rotate freely with no binding or rubbing on the housing. If it does, the turbine or compressor shaft bearing is worn out.

**Warning:** *Inspect the turbocharger with the engine off and cool to the touch.*

**Warning:** *The turbine or compressor wheels have very sharp blades; do not turn the blades with your fingers. Use a plastic pen.*

**15.2 To disconnect the air intake duct from the turbocharger, loosen this hose clamp screw. Then disconnect the other end of the air intake duct from the air filter housing and remove the duct (and, if you need even more room, remove the air filter housing too [see Section 10])**

**15.3 To disconnect the turbocharger outlet duct from the turbocharger, loosen this hose clamp screw and pull off the duct**

**15.4 To disconnect the exhaust discharge elbow (A) from the turbocharger, loosen this clamp (B) and separate the elbow from the turbocharger. If you need more room, loosen the hose clamp (C) at the lower end of the elbow and remove the elbow entirely**

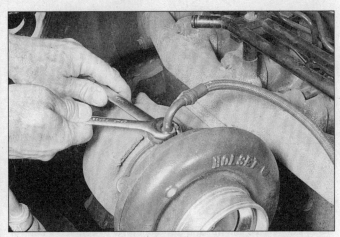

**15.5a Disconnect the oil supply line from the top of the turbocharger. Use a back-up wrench to protect the elbow in the line from kinks**

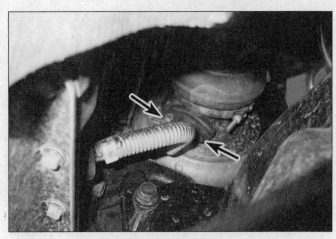

**15.5b To disconnect the oil return line from the underside of the turbocharger, remove these two bolts**

7    The turbocharger is lubricated by engine oil that has been pressurized, cooled and filtered. Oil is delivered to the turbocharger by a supply line that's tapped into the oil filter head. Oil travels to the turbocharger's bearing housing, where it lubricates the shaft and bearings. A return pipe at the bottom of the turbocharger routes the engine oil back to the crankcase. Because the turbine and compressor wheels spin at speeds up to 140,000 rpm, severe damage can result from the interruption or contamination of the oil supply to the turbocharger bearings. Look for leaks in the oil supply line (the one on top). If a fitting is leaking, tighten it and note whether the leak stops. If the supply line itself is leaking, replace it. Remove the oil return line (on the bottom) and inspect it for obstructions. A blocked return line can cause a loss of oil through the turbocharger seals. Burned oil on the turbine housing is a sign of a blocked return line.

**Caution:** *Whenever a major engine bearing such as a main, connecting rod or camshaft bearing is replaced, flush the turbocharger oil passages with clean oil.*

## 15   Turbocharger - removal and installation

### Removal

**Caution:** *The turbocharger is a precision component that has been assembled and balanced to very fine tolerances. Do not disassemble it or try to repair it. Turbochargers should only be overhauled or repaired by authorized turbocharger repair facilities. An incorrectly assembled turbocharger could result in damage to the turbocharger and/or the engine.*

1    Disconnect the negative battery cables from both batteries.

2    Loosen the big hose clamp (see illustration) that secures the air intake duct to the turbocharger and disconnect the air intake duct from the turbocharger. (Although it's not absolutely necessary to remove the air filter housing, you might wish to do so to provide extra working room.)

3    Working from the underside of the engine, loosen the clamp (see illustration) and disconnect the turbocharger outlet duct (the intercooler inlet duct) from the bottom of the compressor.

4    Disconnect the exhaust downpipe from the rear of the turbocharger. If you're planning to replace the turbocharger, also remove the exhaust discharge elbow (see illustration).

5    Disconnect the oil supply line from the top of the turbocharger (see illustration) and the oil return line from the bottom of the turbocharger (see illustration). Be ready with a rag to catch any oil from the lines as they are disconnected.

**15.6a Spray a small amount of penetrant onto the turbocharger mounting nuts, wait awhile, then remove the nuts**

**15.6b Carefully lift the turbocharger out of the engine compartment**

**15.12 Apply 15 to 20 psi to the actuator with a hand-held pressure pump (1998 and earlier models)**

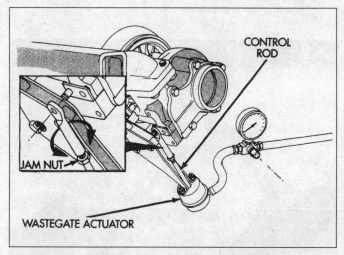

**15.15 Loosen the jam nut and turn the clevis to adjust the control rod travel (1998 and earlier models)**

6    Remove the four nuts holding the turbo-charger to the exhaust manifold and remove the turbocharger, being careful not to damage the wastegate actuator assembly (see illustrations).
**Note:** *The wastegate actuator is precisely adjusted. Be careful when laying the complete turbocharger unit on the bench, so as not to disturb wastegate actuator alignment.*

### Installation

7    Use a die to clean the studs in the turbocharger mounting portion of the exhaust manifold and coat them with anti-seize compound. Bolt the turbocharger onto the exhaust manifold, using a new gasket.
8    Reinstall the oil drain line fitting with a new gasket.
9    Prime the center bearing of the turbocharger with oil by squirting some clean engine oil into the oil supply hole on top, while turning the compressor wheel, then install the supply line.
**Warning:** *The turbine or compressor wheels have very sharp blades; do not turn the blades with your fingers. Use a plastic pen.*
10    The remainder of installation is the reverse of removal. Be sure to tighten the turbocharger-to-exhaust manifold nuts to the torque listed in this Chapter's Specifications.

### Wastegate control rod adjustment (1998 and earlier models)

**Note:** *No adjustment is necessary on 1999 and later models.*
11    Adjustment of the wastegate control rod length is critical. The wastegate is precisely adjusted at the factory. It does not need to be readjusted unless it is damaged or replaced.
**Caution:** *Do not adjust the wastegate to increase the operating pressure (boost) or damage to the turbocharger may result.*
12    Install a dial indicator to check the movement of the actuator rod at the turbocharger.

Position the dial indicator so that the plunger is touching the clevis end of the control rod (see illustration). Disconnect the pressure hose from the actuator and apply 15 to 20 psi of air pressure to the actuator. This will seat the components.
13    Release the air pressure and zero the dial indicator. Apply 19.3 psi of air pressure to the actuator with a hand pump while watching the dial indicator. The rod should move a total of 0.013 to 0.050 (1/64 to 3/64) inch.
14    If adjustment is necessary, apply air pressure again to allow the rod to remove the pressure from the wastegate lever. Remove the nut and pull the clevis off the lever.
15    Loosen the jam nut and turn the clevis either in or out as necessary (see illustration), then replace the clevis on the lever. Retest the actuator control rod travel (see Steps 11 through 13).
16    Once the adjustment is correct, tighten the jam nut on the clevis.

## 16  Intercooler - removal and installation

**Note:** *The intercooler, which is standard equipment on all diesel models, is located at the front of the vehicle, right behind the air conditioning condenser, if equipped. If the vehicle doesn't have air conditioning, the intercooler is the front heat exchanger. (The automatic transmission oil cooler, if equipped, is behind the intercooler, and the radiator is behind the transmission cooler.)*

1   If the vehicle is equipped with air conditioning, have the air conditioning system discharged.
2   On 2002 and earlier models, remove the front bumper cover (see Chapter 11).
3   Remove the air conditioning condenser, if equipped (see illustration).
4   Remove the transmission oil cooler, if equipped (see Chapter 7B).
5   Disconnect the air inlet and outlet ducts from the intercooler (see illustration 16.3).
6   Remove the intercooler mounting bolts.
7   Pivot the intercooler forward, then lift it up to remove it.
8   Inspect the intercooler for cracks and damage to the flanges, tubes and fins. Replace it or have it repaired if necessary. Also inspect the rubber mounts, replacing them if necessary.
9   Installation is the reverse of removal.
10  Have the air conditioning system recharged, if applicable, when you're done.

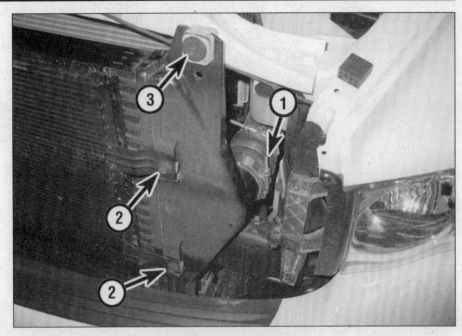

**16.3 Intercooler removal details:**

1   Loosen the hose clamps and disconnect the left and right air ducts (this is the outlet duct, which goes to the intake manifold; the other duct, on the right end of the intercooler, is identical)
2   Remove the condenser mounting bolts to detach the condenser from the intercooler
3   Remove the intercooler mounting bolts to detach the intercooler from the radiator crossmember

# Notes

# Chapter 5
# Engine electrical systems

## Contents

## Specifications

### General

Battery voltage
Engine off ............................................................... 12.66 volts minimum
Engine running ....................................................... 13.5 to 15 volts
Firing order
V6 engine ............................................................... 1-6-5-4-3-2
V8 engines ............................................................. 1-8-4-3-6-5-7-2
V10 engine ............................................................. 1-10-9-4-3-6-5-8-7-2

### Ignition system

Ignition coil resistance (at 70 to 80-degrees F)
3.7L V6 and 4.7L V8 engines
Primary resistance ........................................... 0.6 to 0.9 ohms
Secondary resistance ...................................... 6 to 9 k-ohms
5.7L V8 (Hemi) engine
Primary resistance ........................................... 0.5 to 0.8 ohms
Secondary resistance ...................................... N/A
3.9L V6, 5.2L V8 and 5.9L V8 engine
Diamond
Primary resistance ....................................... 0.97 to 1.18 ohms
Secondary resistance ................................... 11.3 to 15.3 k-ohms
Toyodenso
Primary resistance ....................................... 0.95 to 1.20 ohms
Secondary resistance ................................... 11.3 to 13.3 k-ohms
V10 engine
Primary resistance ........................................... 0.53 to 0.65 ohms
Secondary resistance ...................................... 10.9 to 14.7 k-ohms
Spark plug wire resistance
Minimum.................................................................. 250 ohms per inch/3000 ohms per foot
Maximum................................................................. 1,000 ohms per inch/12,000 ohms per foot

## 1 General Information

1    The engine electrical systems include all ignition, charging and starting components. Because of their engine-related functions, these components are discussed separately from chassis electrical devices such as the lights, the instruments, etc. (which are included in Chapter 12).

2    Always observe the following precautions when working on the electrical systems:

Be extremely careful when servicing engine electrical components. They are easily damaged if checked, connected or handled improperly.

a)  *Never leave the ignition switch on for long periods of time with the engine off.*

b)  *Don't disconnect the battery cables while the engine is running.*

c)  *Maintain correct polarity when connecting a battery cable from another vehicle during jump-starting.*

d)  *Always disconnect the negative cable first and hook it up last or the battery may be shorted by the tool being used to loosen the cable clamps.*

3    It's also a good idea to review the safety-related information regarding the engine electrical systems located in the Safety First! Section near the front of this manual before beginning any operation included in this Chapter.

## 2 Troubleshooting

### *Ignition system*

1    If a malfunction occurs in the ignition system, do not immediately assume that any particular part is causing the problem. First, check the following items:

a)  *Make sure that the cable clamps at the battery terminals are clean and tight.*

b)  *Test the condition of the battery (see Steps 15 through 18). If it doesn't pass all the tests, replace it.*

c)  *Check the ignition coil or coil pack connections.*

d)  *Check any relevant fuses in the engine compartment fuse and relay box (see Chapter 12). If they're burned, determine the cause and repair the circuit.*

### Check

**Warning:** *Because of the high voltage generated by the ignition system, use extreme care when performing a procedure involving ignition components.*

**Note:** *The ignition system components on these vehicles are difficult to diagnose. In the event of ignition system failure that you can't diagnose, have the vehicle tested at a dealer service department or other qualified auto repair facility.*

**Note:** *You'll need a spark tester for the following test. Spark testers are available at most auto supply stores.*

2    If the engine turns over but won't start, verify that there is sufficient ignition voltage to fire the spark plugs as follows.

3    Remove an ignition coil and install the tester between the boot at the lower end of the coil and the spark plug (see illustration).

4    Crank the engine and note whether or not the tester flashes.

**Caution:** *Do NOT crank the engine or allow it to run for more than five seconds; running the engine for more than five seconds may set a Diagnostic Trouble Code (DTC) for a cylinder misfire.*

5    If the tester flashes during cranking, the coil is delivering sufficient voltage to the spark plug to fire it. Repeat this test for each cylinder to verify that the other coils are OK.

6    If the tester doesn't flash, remove a coil from another cylinder and swap it for the one being tested. If the tester now flashes, you know that the original coil is bad. If the tester still doesn't flash, the PCM or wiring harness is probably defective. Have the PCM checked out by a dealer service department or other qualified repair shop (testing the PCM is beyond the scope of the do-it-yourselfer because it requires expensive special tools).

7    If the tester flashes during cranking but a misfire code (related to the cylinder being tested) has been stored, the spark plug could be fouled or defective.

### *Charging system*

8    If a malfunction occurs in the charging system, do not automatically assume the alternator is causing the problem. First check the following items:

a)  *Check the drivebelt tension and condition, as described in Chapter 1. Replace it if it's worn or deteriorated.*

b)  *Make sure the alternator mounting bolts are tight.*

c)  *Inspect the alternator wiring harness and the connectors at the alternator and voltage regulator. They must be in good condition, tight and have no corrosion.*

d)  *Check the fusible link (if equipped) or main fuse in the underhood fuse/relay box. If it is burned, determine the cause, repair the circuit and replace the link or fuse (the vehicle will not start and/or the accessories will not work if the fusible link or main fuse is blown).*

e)  *Start the engine and check the alternator for abnormal noises (a shrieking or squealing sound indicates a bad bearing).*

f)  *Check the battery. Make sure it's fully charged and in good condition (one bad cell in a battery can cause overcharging by the alternator).*

g)  *Disconnect the battery cables (negative first, then positive). Inspect the battery posts and the cable clamps for corrosion. Clean them thoroughly if necessary (see Chapter 1). Reconnect the cables (positive first, negative last).*

### Alternator - check

9    Use a voltmeter to check the battery voltage with the engine off. It should be at least 12.6 volts (see illustration 2.15).

10    Start the engine and check the battery voltage again. It should now be approximately 13.5 to 15 volts.

11    If the voltage reading is more or less than the specified charging voltage, the voltage regulator is probably defective, which will require replacement of the alternator (the voltage regulator is not replaceable separately). Remove the alternator and have it bench tested (most auto parts stores will do this for you).

12    The charging system (battery) light on the instrument cluster lights up when the ignition key is turned to On, but it should go out when the engine starts.

13    If the charging system light stays on after the engine has been started, there is a problem with the charging system. Before replacing the alternator, check the battery condition, alternator belt tension and electrical cable connections.

14    If replacing the alternator doesn't restore voltage to the specified range, have the charging system tested by a dealer service department or other qualified repair shop.

### Battery - check

**Warning:** *Hydrogen gas is produced by the battery, so keep open flames and lighted cigarettes away from it at all times. Always wear eye protection when working around a battery. Rinse off spilled electrolyte immediately with large amounts of water.*

15    Check the battery state of charge. Visually inspect the indicator eye on the top of the

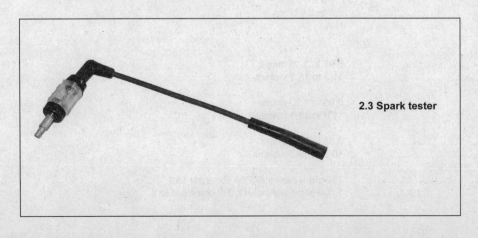

**2.3 Spark tester**

**2.15 To test the open circuit voltage of the battery, touch the black probe of the voltmeter to the negative terminal and the red probe to the positive terminal of the battery; a fully charged battery should be at least 12.6 volts**

**2.17 Connect a battery load tester to the battery and check the battery condition under load following the tool manufacturer's instructions**

battery (if equipped with one); if the indicator eye is black in color, charge the battery as described in Section 1. Next perform an open circuit voltage test using a digital voltmeter. With the engine and all accessories off, touch the negative probe of the voltmeter to the negative terminal of the battery and the positive probe to the positive terminal of the battery (see illustration). The battery voltage should be 12.6 volts or slightly above. If the battery is less than the specified voltage, charge the battery before proceeding to the next test. Do not proceed with the battery load test unless the battery charge is correct.

**Note:** *The battery's surface charge must be removed before accurate voltage measurements can be made. Turn on the high beams for ten seconds, then turn them off and let the vehicle stand for two minutes.*

16   Disconnect the negative battery cable, then the positive cable from the battery.

17   Perform a battery load test. An accurate check of the battery condition can only be performed with a load tester (see illustration). This test evaluates the ability of the battery to operate the starter and other accessories during periods of high current draw. Connect the load tester to the battery terminals. Load test the battery according to the tool manufacturer's instructions. This tool increases the load demand (current draw) on the battery.

18   Maintain the load on the battery for 15 seconds and observe that the battery voltage does not drop below 9.6 volts. If the battery condition is weak or defective, the tool will indicate this condition immediately.

**Note:** *Cold temperatures will cause the minimum voltage reading to drop slightly. Follow the chart given in the manufacturer's instructions to compensate for cold climates. Minimum load voltage for freezing temperatures (32 degrees F) should be approximately 9.1 volts.*

## Starting system

### The starter rotates, but the engine doesn't

19   Remove the starter (see Section 8). Check the overrunning clutch and bench test the starter to make sure the drive mechanism extends fully for proper engagement with the flywheel ring gear. If it doesn't, replace the starter.

20   Check the flywheel ring gear for missing teeth and other damage. With the ignition turned off, rotate the flywheel so you can check the entire ring gear.

### The starter is noisy

21   If the solenoid is making a chattering noise, first check the battery (see Steps 15 through 18). If the battery is okay, check the cables and connections.

22   If you hear a grinding, crashing metallic sound when you turn the key to Start, check for loose starter mounting bolts. If they're tight, remove the starter and inspect the teeth on the starter pinion gear and flywheel ring gear. Look for missing or damaged teeth.

23   If the starter sounds fine when you first turn the key to Start, but then stops rotating the engine and emits a zinging sound, the problem is probably a defective starter drive that's not staying engaged with the ring gear. Replace the starter.

### The starter rotates slowly

24   Check the battery (see Steps 15 through 18).

25   If the battery is okay, verify all connections (at the battery, the starter solenoid and motor) are clean, corrosion-free and tight. Make sure the cables aren't frayed or damaged.

26   Check that the starter mounting bolts are tight so it grounds properly. Also check the pinion gear and flywheel ring gear for evidence of a mechanical bind (galling, deformed

gear teeth or other damage).

### The starter does not rotate at all

27   Check the battery (see Steps 15 through 18).

28   If the battery is okay, verify all connections (at the battery, the starter solenoid and motor) are clean, corrosion-free and tight. Make sure the cables aren't frayed or damaged.

29   Check all of the fuses in the underhood fuse/relay box.

30   Check that the starter mounting bolts are tight so it grounds properly.

31   Check for voltage at the starter solenoid "S" terminal when the ignition key is turned to the start position. If voltage is present, replace the starter/solenoid assembly. If no voltage is present, the problem could be the starter relay, the Transmission Range (TR) switch (see Chapter 6) or clutch start switch (see Chapter 8), or with an electrical connector somewhere in the circuit (see the wiring diagrams at the end of Chapter 12). Also, on many modern vehicles, the Powertrain Control Module (PCM) and the Body Control Module (BCM) control the voltage signal to the starter solenoid; on such vehicles a special scan tool is required for diagnosis.

---

**3    Battery and battery tray - removal and installation**

**Warning:** *Hydrogen gas is produced by the battery, so keep open flames and lighted cigarettes away from it at all times. Always wear eye protection when working around a battery. Rinse off spilled electrolyte immediately with large amounts of water.*

**Caution:** *Always disconnect the negative cable first and hook it up last or you might accidentally short the battery with the tool that you're using to loosen the cable clamps.*

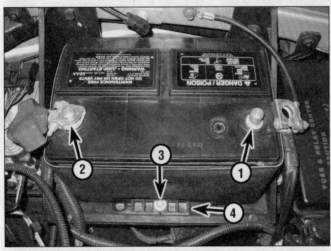

**3.1a When disconnecting the battery cables, always disconnect the cable from the negative terminal (1) first, then disconnect the cable from the positive terminal (2). After the battery cables are disconnected, remove the battery hold-down bolt (3) and the hold-down clamp (4) - later model shown**

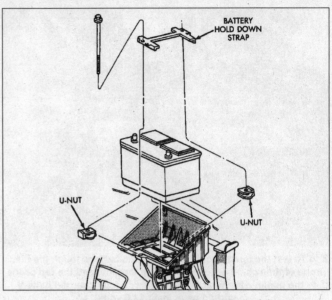

**3.1b Battery mounting details - early models**

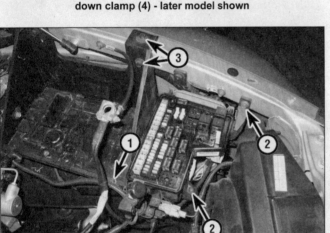

**3.9 Topside battery tray mounting details**

| 1 | Wiring harness clips | 3 | Tray mounting bolts |
| 2 | Fuse/relay box mounting fasteners | 4 | ABS controller bolt |

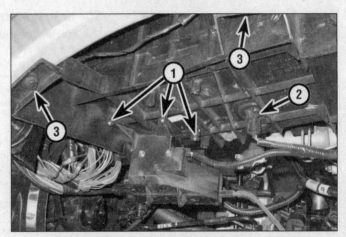

**3.15 Underside battery tray mounting details**

| 1 | APPS mounting screws (Hemi and some diesel models only) |
| 2 | Battery temperature sensor |
| 3 | Tray mounting bolts |

**Note:** *On 2001 and earlier models, if the vehicle will be stored (no starting) for more than 20 days, it will be necessary to remove the IOD fuse in the Power Distribution Center to avoid excessive battery discharging.*

### Battery

1   Disconnect the cable from the negative battery terminal (see illustrations), then disconnect the cable from the positive terminal.
2   Remove the battery hold-down bolt(s) and hold-down clamp.
3   Lift out the battery. Be careful - it's heavy.
**Note:** *Battery straps and handlers are available at most auto parts stores for a reasonable price. They make it easier to remove and carry the battery.*
4   While the battery is out, inspect the area underneath the tray for corrosion. Clean the battery tray, then use a baking soda/water

solution to neutralize any deposits to prevent further oxidation. If the metal around the tray is corroded, too, clean it as well and spray the area with a rust-inhibiting paint.
5   If corrosion has leaked down past the battery tray, remove the tray for further cleaning.
6   If you are replacing the battery, make sure you get one that's identical, with the same dimensions, amperage rating, cold cranking rating, etc.
7   Installation is the reverse of removal.

### Battery tray

#### Left side

8   Remove the battery (see Steps 1 through 3).
9   Detach the wiring harness clips from the battery tray (see illustration).
10   Remove the engine compartment fuse and relay box mounting bolts.

11   Slide the fuse and relay box toward the center of the engine compartment to disengage the two locator pins from their respective slots in the front wall of the battery box, then lift up the fuse and relay box.
12   Remove the ABS controller mounting bolt, then support the controller with some wire or with a bungee cord.
13   Loosen the lug nuts for the left front wheel. Raise the front of the vehicle and place it securely on jackstands. Remove the left front wheel. Remove the left front wheelhouse splash shield (see Chapter 11).
14   Mark the location of the cruise control servo (if equipped), then remove the servo retaining screws and detach the servo from the battery tray.
15   On models so equipped, remove the three screws that attach the Accelerator Pedal Position Sensor (APPS) assembly to the bottom of the battery tray (see illustration) and

**3.17 To detach the EVAP purge solenoid from its mounting bracket, depress this locking tang and slide the solenoid off its bracket**

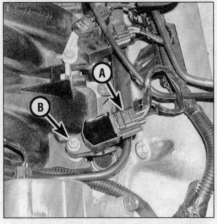

**5.2 To remove an ignition coil from a 3.7L V6 or a 4.7L V8 engine, push down on the release lock on top of the electrical connector (A) and disconnect the connector, remove the coil mounting nut (B), then detach the coil from the spark plug by pulling it straight up**

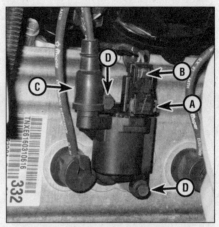

**5.7 To remove an ignition coil from a Hemi engine, push the slide lock (A) sideways to unlock the electrical connector, push down on the connector release tab (B), disconnect the connector, pull off the spark plug wire boot (C) for the companion cylinder and remove the two coil mounting bolts (D)**

detach the APPS assembly from the tray.

16   Unplug the electrical connector from the battery temperature sensor.

17   Detach the Evaporative Emissions (EVAP) system purge solenoid from its mounting bracket (see illustration). It's not necessary to disconnect the electrical connector from the purge solenoid or to detach the solenoid mounting bracket from the battery tray, which is attached to the underside of the tray by a pair of retaining screws (unless you're planning to replace the tray).

18   Disconnect the ground cable from the left front fender (see illustration 4.4a).

19   Remove the battery tray mounting bolts and remove the battery tray.

20   Installation is the reverse of removal.

### Right side

21   Removal of the right-side battery tray, on models so equipped, is similar to the removal procedure of the left side battery tray, except that the air filter housing must be removed (see Chapter 4A or Chapter 4B), and some of the steps related to left side tray removal will not apply.

---

## 4   Battery cables - replacement

1   When removing the cables, always disconnect the cable from the negative battery terminal first and hook it up last, or you might accidentally short out the battery with the tool you're using to loosen the cable clamps. Even if you're only replacing the cable for the positive terminal, be sure to disconnect the negative cable from the battery first.

2   Disconnect the old cables from the battery, then trace each of them to their opposite ends and disconnect them. Be sure to note the routing of each cable before disconnecting it to ensure correct installation.

3   If you are replacing any of the old cables, take them with you when buying new cables. It is vitally important that you replace the cables with identical parts.

4   Clean the threads of the solenoid or ground connection with a wire brush to remove rust and corrosion. Apply a light coat of battery terminal corrosion inhibitor or petroleum jelly to the threads to prevent future corrosion.

5   Attach the cable to the solenoid or ground connection and tighten the mounting nut/bolt securely.

6   Before connecting a new cable to the battery, make sure that it reaches the battery post without having to be stretched.

7   Connect the cable to the positive battery terminal first, then connect the ground cable to the negative battery terminal.

---

## 5   Ignition coil - replacement

### 3.7L V6 and 4.7L V8 engines

1   Depending on which coil you're planning to replace, remove either the air intake duct or the air intake resonator box (see Chapter 4A).

2   Disconnect the electrical connector from the coil (see Illustration). (To release the connector, push down on the release lock on top of the connector and pull off the connector.)

3   To prevent dirt and debris from falling down into the spark plug well, use compressed air to blow out the area around the base of the ignition coil.

4   Remove the ignition coil mounting nut and detach the coil from the spark plug (see Illustration 5.2).

5   Installation is the reverse of removal.

### Hemi engine

6   If you're planning to replace the ignition coils for cylinder numbers 2, 4, 6 and/or 8, remove the air intake duct and the resonator box (see *Air filter housing - removal and*

*installation* in Chapter 4A).

7   Disconnect the electrical connector and the spark plug wire boot for the companion cylinder from the ignition coil (see illustration).

8   To prevent dirt and debris from falling into the spark plug well, blow out the area surrounding the base of the ignition coil with compressed air.

9   Remove the coil mounting bolts. To remove the coil, carefully pull it up with a twisting motion.

10   Installation is the reverse of removal.

### 3.9L V6, 5.2L V8 and 5.9L V8 engines

11   Disconnect the electrical connector from the ignition coil (see illustration).

12   Remove the coil mounting bolts and remove the coil.

13   Installation is the reverse of removal.

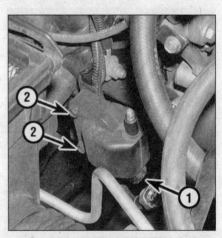

**5.11 To detach the ignition coil from a 3.9L V6, 5.2L V8 or 5.9L V8 engine, disconnect the electrical connector (1) and remove the two mounting bolts (2)**

**5.16 To detach the coil packs from a V10 engine, disconnect the electrical connectors and remove the four mounting bolts from each coil pack**

## V10 engine

14　Clearly label all spark plug wires, then disconnect them from the coil pack(s).

15　Disconnect the electrical connectors from the two coil packs.

16　Remove the coil pack mounting bolts (see illustration) and remove the coil packs.

17　Installation is the reverse of removal.

## 6　Distributor (3.9L V6, 5.2L V8 and 5.9L V8 engines) - removal and installation

### Removal

1　Disconnect the cable from the negative battery terminal (see Section 3).

2　Disconnect the electrical connector from the distributor. Also detach all clamps, clips and wiring harnesses attached to the distributor. Mark the wires to insure correct reinstallation.

**7.4 To detach the alternator from a 3.7L V6 or a 4.7L V8 engine, remove these mounting bolts (4.7L V8 engine shown, 3.7L V6 similar)**

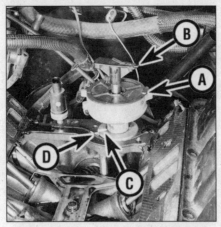

**6.5 Before removing the distributor from a 3.9L V6, 5.2L V8 and 5.9L V8 engine, bring the number one piston to TDC on its compression stroke and remove the distributor cap. Then make a mark on the edge of the distributor body (A) directly underneath and in line with the center of the rotor tip (B), and make another mark across the distributor mounting flange (C) and the engine block (D)**

3　Look for a raised letter or number on the distributor cap. This marks the location of the terminal for the number one spark plug wire going to the number one cylinder. If the cap doesn't already have a mark for the number one terminal, go to the number one spark plug (front cylinder on the left cylinder bank), trace the plug wire back to its terminal on the distributor cap and mark it.

4　Remove the distributor cap (see Chapter 1) and rotate the engine until the rotor is pointing toward the terminal for the number one spark plug wire (see the Top Dead Center locating procedure in Chapter 2C).

5　Make a mark on the edge of the distributor body directly below the rotor tip and in line with it (if the rotor on your engine has more than one tip, use the center one for reference). Also mark the orientation of the distributor base to the engine (see illustration) to ensure correct reinstallation.

6　Remove the distributor hold-down bolt and remove the distributor assembly by pulling it straight up.

**Caution:** *Do NOT turn the crankshaft while the distributor is out of the engine or the alignment marks that you made will be useless.*

7　Remove the old O-ring from the distributor.

### Installation

**Note:** *If the crankshaft was accidentally moved while the distributor was removed, you must reposition the number one piston at Top Dead Center. You can do this by removing the number one spark plug, rotating the crankshaft and feeling for compression pressure at the spark plug hole. Once you feel compression, align the ignition timing zero mark with the pointer.*

**7.2 Remove the nut from the battery (B+) output terminal stud (A) and disconnect the battery cable from the stud, then disconnect the electrical connector (B) for the field terminals (4.7L V8 engine shown, 3.7L V6 engine similar)**

8　Install a new O-ring on the distributor housing.

9　Before installing the distributor, insert it into the engine block in exactly the same relationship to the block that it was in when removed, then turn the rotor until it aligns with the mark that you made on the distributor housing in Step 5. When the distributor and the rotor are both correctly aligned, lower the distributor the rest of the way into the distributor hole, install the hold-down clamp and bolt and tighten the hold-down bolt to the torque listed in this Chapter's Specifications.

10　The remainder of installation is the reverse of removal.

## 7　Alternator - removal and installation

1　Disconnect the cable from the negative terminal of the battery (see Section 3). On diesel engines, disconnect the cables from the negative battery terminals on both batteries.

### 3.7L V6 and 4.7L V8 engines

2　Disconnect the battery cable from the B+ output terminal and disconnect the field wire electrical connector from the field terminal (see illustration).

3　Remove the drivebelt (see Chapter 1).

4　Remove the mounting bolts (see illustration) and remove the alternator.

5　If you are replacing the alternator, take the old one with you when purchasing a replacement unit. Make sure the new/rebuilt unit looks identical to the old alternator. Look at the terminals - they should be the same in number, size and location as the terminals on the old alternator. Finally, look at the identification numbers - they will be stamped into the housing or printed on a tag attached to

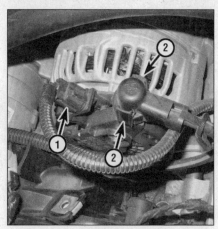

**7.11 Disconnect the field wire electrical connector (1) from the field terminal, then depress the two release tabs (2) on the plastic insulator cap, pull off the cap and remove the nut that secures the battery cable to the B+ terminal (Hemi engine)**

**7.13 To detach the alternator support bracket, remove these three nuts and the bolt (Hemi engine)**

**7.14 To detach the alternator from its mounting bracket, remove this bolt and stud/bolt (Hemi engine)**

the housing. Make sure the numbers are the same on both alternators.

6  Many new and remanufactured alternators do not have a pulley installed, so you may have to switch the pulley from the old unit to the new/rebuilt one. When buying an alternator, find out the shop's policy regarding pulleys; some shops will perform this service free of charge.

7  Installation is the reverse of removal.

8  Install the drivebelt (see Chapter 1).

9  Check the charging voltage (see Section 2) to verify that the alternator is operating correctly.

## 5.7L V8 (Hemi) engine

10  Remove the drivebelt (see Chapter 1).

11  Disconnect the field wire electrical connector from the field terminal (see illustration).

12  Unsnap the plastic insulator cap from the B+ output terminal, remove the battery cable retaining nut from the B+ output terminal and disconnect the battery cable from the B+ output terminal.

13  Remove the alternator support bracket nuts and bolts (see illustration) and remove the alternator support bracket.

14  Remove the alternator mounting bolts (see illustration) and remove the alternator.

15  Installation is the reverse of removal.

## 3.9L V6, 5.2L V8 and 5.9L V8 engines

16  Remove the drivebelt (see Chapter 1).

17  Remove the air conditioning hose support bracket and the alternator support bracket (see illustration).

18  Disconnect the field wire electrical connector from the field terminal and disconnect the alternator output cable from the B+ terminal.

19  Remove the alternator mounting bolts and nut (see illustration) and remove the alternator.

20  Installation is the reverse of removal.

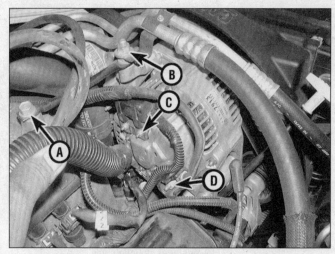

**7.17 Alternator assembly removal details (3.9L V6, 5.2L V8 and 5.9L V8 engines):**

*A*  Loosen this bolt

*B*  Remove this nut, detach the air conditioning hose bracket and swing the alternator support strut out of the way

*C*  Disconnect the field wire electrical connector from the field wire terminal

*D*  Disconnect the alternator output cable from the B+ terminal

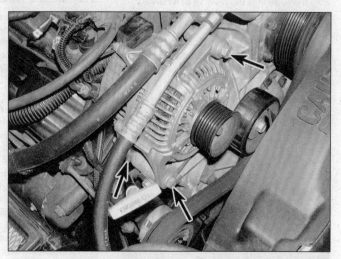

**7.19 To detach the alternator from its mounting bracket, remove the upper mounting bolt and the lower mounting bolt and nut (3.9L V6, 5.2L V8 and 5.9L V8 engines)**

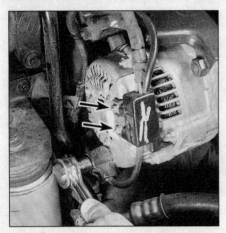

**7.22 Disconnect the alternator electrical connections**

**8.4 If the starter motor is equipped with a heat shield, remove these two bolts (A) to detach it from the starter. To remove the starter from an automatic transmission (shown), remove these two bolts (B) (starter motor on 3.7L V6 with automatic and 4WD shown, starters on other 3.7L V6 engines and 4.7L V8 engines similar)**

**8.5 Disconnect the electrical connector (A) from the spade terminal on the solenoid, then remove the nut and disconnect the battery cable (B) from the terminal stud on the solenoid (starter motor on 3.7L V6 shown, starters on 4.7L V8 similar)**

### Diesel engines

21    Remove the drivebelt (see Chapter 1).
22    Unsnap the plastic insulator cap from the B+ output terminal, remove the nut that secures the battery cable to the B+ output terminal and disconnect the cable from the B+ terminal (see illustration). Disconnect the field wire electrical connector from the field terminal.
23    Remove the upper alternator mounting bolt.
24    Remove the lower alternator mounting bolt and nut and remove the alternator from its mounting bracket.
25    Installation is the reverse of removal.

### V10 engine

26    Remove the drivebelt (see Chapter 1).
27    Unsnap the plastic insulator cap from the B+ output terminal, remove the nut that

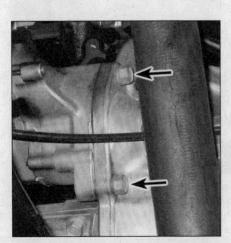

**8.10 To detach the starter motor from the transmission on a Hemi engine, remove these two bolts**

secures the battery cable to the B+ output terminal and disconnect the cable from the B+ terminal. Disconnect the field wire electrical connector from the field terminal.
28    Remove the upper alternator mounting bolt and nut.
29    Remove the lower alternator mounting bolt and remove the alternator from its mounting bracket.
30    Installation is the reverse of removal.

---

### 8    Starter motor - removal and installation

---

1    Disconnect the cable from the negative terminal of the battery (see Section 3). (On diesels, disconnect the cable from the negative terminal of each battery.)
2    Raise the vehicle and support it securely on jackstands.

### 3.7L V6 and 4.7L V8 engines

3    On 4WD models with certain transmissions, there's a support bracket between the front axle and the side of the transmission that blocks access to the lower starter mounting bolt. If your vehicle has this support bracket, remove the two support bracket bolts at the transmission, then pry the support bracket aside enough to gain access to the lower starter mounting bolt.
4    Remove the heat shield, if equipped, from the starter motor (see illustration).
5    Remove the nut that secures the battery cable to the terminal stud on the starter solenoid, disconnect the cable from the terminal stud and disconnect the electrical connector from the spade terminal on the solenoid (see illustration).
**Note:** *If you have difficulty disconnecting the battery cable or the electrical connector*

*from the solenoid, leave them connected until you detach the starter from the transmission bellhousing and move it to a position where you can access the wiring connectors more easily.*
6    On models with a manual transmission, remove the starter mounting bolt and nut. On models with an automatic transmission, remove the two starter mounting bolts (see illustration 8.4).
7    Move the starter motor toward the front of the vehicle until the nose of the starter pinion housing clears the transmission bellhousing, then tilt the nose down and, if you haven't already done so, lower the starter until you can disconnect the electrical connector and remove the nut that secures the battery cable to the terminal stud on the starter solenoid. Once everything is disconnected, remove the starter.
**Caution:** *The starter motor is fairly heavy, so be sure to support it while removing it. Do NOT allow it to hang by the wiring harness.*
8    Installation is the reverse of removal.

### 5.7L V8 (Hemi) engine

9    On some 4WD models with certain transmissions, there's a support bracket between the front axle and the side of the transmission that blocks access to the lower starter mounting bolt. If your vehicle has this support bracket, remove the two support bracket bolts at the transmission, then pry the support bracket aside enough to gain access to the lower starter mounting bolt.
10    Remove the two starter motor mounting bolts (see illustration).
11    Move the starter toward the front of the vehicle until the starter pinion housing clears the transmission bellhousing.
**Caution:** *The starter motor is fairly heavy, so be sure to support it while removing it. Do NOT allow it to hang by the wiring harness.*

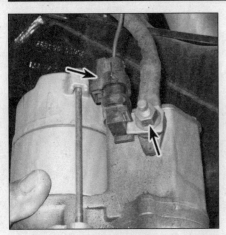

**8.12 After unbolting the starter motor and moving it forward, remove the nut that secures the battery positive cable to the stud terminal on the solenoid, disconnect the positive cable from the stud, then disconnect the electrical connector from the spade terminal on the solenoid**

**8.15 Remove this nut and disconnect the battery positive cable from the stud terminal on the starter motor solenoid, then disconnect the electrical connector (not shown) from its receptacle on the starter solenoid (5.9L V8 engine shown, other engines similar)**

**8.16 To detach the starter motor from the transmission, remove the nut and lockwasher from the lower mounting stud and remove the upper mounting bolt (5.9L V8 engine shown, other engines similar)**

12   Disconnect the battery cable and electrical connector from the terminals on the starter motor solenoid (see illustration).
13   Installation is the reverse of removal.

### 3.9L V6, 5.2L V8, 5.9L V8 and 8.0L V10 engines

14   On some 4WD models with certain transmissions, there's a support bracket between the front axle and the side of the transmission that blocks access to the lower starter mounting bolt. If your vehicle has this support bracket, remove the two support bracket bolts at the transmission, then pry the support bracket aside enough to gain access to the lower starter mounting bolt.
15   Disconnect the battery positive cable from the starter motor solenoid (see illustration) and disconnect the electrical connector from its receptacle on the starter solenoid.
**Note:** *If you have difficulty disconnecting the battery cable or the electrical connector from the solenoid, leave them connected until you*

*detach the starter from the transmission bell-housing and move it to a position where you can access the wiring connectors more easily.*
16   Remove the nut and lock washer from the starter motor lower mounting stud (see illustration), then support the starter and remove the upper mounting bolt.
17   If the vehicle is equipped with an automatic transmission, slide the transmission cooler line bracket forward on the cooler lines far enough to allow the starter motor flange to clear the starter's lower mounting stud.
18   Move the starter forward until the nose of the starter pinion housing clears the transmission bellhousing.
19   Tilt the nose of the starter down and, if you haven't already done so, lower the starter until you can disconnect the electrical connector and remove the nut that secures the battery cable to the terminal stud on the starter solenoid. Once everything is disconnected, remove the starter.

**Caution:** *The starter motor is fairly heavy, so be sure to support it while removing it. Do NOT allow it to hang by the wiring harness.*
20   Installation is the reverse of removal.

### Diesel engine

21   Remove the three starter motor mounting bolts.
22   Move the starter motor forward far enough for the nose of the starter pinion housing to clear the transmission bellhousing.
23   Tilt the nose of the starter down and lower the starter motor until you can access the electrical connections, then remove the two nuts that attach the battery cable and electrical wiring to the starter solenoid.
24   Remove the starter motor and, if equipped, the aluminum spacer that goes between the starter and the transmission.
25   If your vehicle is equipped with this spacer, be sure to note the orientation of the spacer before removing it.
26   Installation is the reverse of removal.

# Notes

# Chapter 6
# Emissions and engine control systems

## Contents

## Specifications

### Torque specifications

**Ft-lbs (unless otherwise indicated)**

**Note:** *One foot-pound (ft-lb) of torque is equivalent to 12 inch-pounds (in-lbs) of torque. Torque values below approximately 15 ft-lbs are expressed in inch-pounds, since most foot-pound torque wrenches are not accurate at these smaller values.*

| | |
|---|---|
| Air injection system (HDC 5.9L V8 or 8.0L V10 with air injection) | |
|     Air injection pump pulley bolts | 105 in-lbs |
|     One-way check valves | 25 |
| Camshaft position (CMP) sensor bolt | |
|     3.7L V6/4.7L V8/5.7L V8 engines | 106 in-lbs |
|     V10 engine | |
|         2003 and earlier models | 50 in-lbs |
|         2004 and later models | 95 in-lbs |
|     Diesel engine | 18 |
| Crankshaft position (CKP) sensor | |
|     3.9L V6, 5.2L V8, 5.9L V8 and 8.0L V10 engines | 70 in-lbs |
|     3.7L V6, 4.7L V8 and 5.7L V8 engines | 21 |
|     Diesel engine | |
|         2000 and earlier models | 18 |
|         2002 and 2003 models | Not available |
|         2003 and later models | 80 in-lbs |
| Engine Coolant Temperature (ECT) sensor | |
|     3.7L V6, 4.7L V8, Hemi and 8.0L V10 | 96 in-lbs |
|     3.9L V6 and 5.2L V8 | 120 in-lbs |
|     5.9L V8 | 75 in-lbs |
|     Diesel | 156 in-lbs |
| EGR tube mounting bolts | 204 in-lbs |
| EGR valve bolts | 200 in-lbs |
| Knock sensor mounting bolts (3.7L V6, 4.7L V8 and Hemi) | 176 in-lbs |
| Manifold Absolute Pressure (MAP) sensor (diesel) | 120 in-lbs |
| Oxygen sensors | 22 |

## 1   General information

1   To prevent pollution of the atmosphere from incompletely burned and evaporating gases, and to maintain good driveability and fuel economy, a number of emission control systems are incorporated. They include the:

### Catalytic converter

2   A catalytic converter is an emission control device in the exhaust system that reduces certain pollutants in the exhaust gas stream. There are two types of converters: oxidation converters and reduction converters.

3   Oxidation converters contain a monolithic substrate (a ceramic honeycomb) coated with the semi-precious metals platinum and palladium. An oxidation catalyst reduces unburned hydrocarbons (HC) and carbon monoxide (CO) by adding oxygen to the exhaust stream as it passes through the substrate, which, in the presence of high temperature and the catalyst materials, converts the HC and CO to water vapor ($H_2O$) and carbon dioxide ($CO_2$).

4   Reduction converters contain a monolithic substrate coated with platinum and rhodium. A reduction catalyst reduces oxides of nitrogen (NOx) by removing oxygen, which in the presence of high temperature and the catalyst material produces nitrogen (N) and carbon dioxide ($CO_2$).

5   Catalytic converters that combine both types of catalysts in one assembly are known as "three-way catalysts" or TWCs. A TWC can reduce all three pollutants.

### Evaporative Emissions Control (EVAP) system

6   The Evaporative Emissions Control (EVAP) system prevents fuel system vapors (which contain unburned hydrocarbons) from escaping into the atmosphere. On warm days, vapors trapped inside the fuel tank expand until the pressure reaches a certain threshold. Then the fuel vapors are routed from the fuel tank through the fuel vapor vent valve and the fuel vapor control valve to the EVAP canister, where they're stored temporarily until the next time the vehicle is operated. When the conditions are right (engine warmed up, vehicle up to speed, moderate or heavy load on the engine, etc.) the PCM opens the canister purge valve, which allows fuel vapors to be drawn from the canister into the intake manifold. Once in the intake manifold, the fuel vapors mix with incoming air before being drawn through the intake ports into the combustion chambers where they're burned up with the rest of the air/fuel mixture. The EVAP system is complex and virtually impossible to troubleshoot without the right tools and training.

### Secondary Air Injection (AIR) system

7   Some models are equipped with a Secondary Air Injection (AIR) system. The secondary air injection system is used to reduce tailpipe emissions on initial engine start-up. The system uses an electric motor/pump assembly, relay, vacuum valve/solenoid, air shut-off valve, check valves and tubing to inject fresh air directly into the exhaust manifolds. The fresh air (oxygen) reacts with the exhaust gas in the catalytic converter to reduce HC and CO levels. The air pump and solenoid are controlled by the PCM through the AIR relay. During initial start-up, the PCM energizes the AIR relay, the relay supplies battery voltage to the air pump and the vacuum valve/solenoid, engine vacuum is applied to the air shut-off valve which opens and allows air to flow through the tubing into the exhaust manifolds. The PCM will operate the air pump until closed loop operation is reached (approximately four minutes). During normal operation, the check valves prevent exhaust backflow into the system.

### Powertrain Control Module (PCM)

8   The Powertrain Control Module (PCM) is the brain of the engine management system. It also controls a wide variety of other vehicle systems. In order to program the new PCM, the dealer needs the vehicle as well as the new PCM. If you're planning to replace the PCM with a new one, there is no point in trying to do so at home because you won't be able to program it yourself.

### Positive Crankcase Ventilation (PCV) system

9   The Positive Crankcase Ventilation (PCV) system reduces hydrocarbon emissions by scavenging crankcase vapors, which are rich in unburned hydrocarbons. A PCV valve or orifice regulates the flow of gases into the intake manifold in proportion to the amount of intake vacuum available.

10   The PCV system generally consists of the fresh air inlet hose, the PCV valve or orifice and the crankcase ventilation hose (or PCV hose). The fresh air inlet hose connects the air intake duct to a pipe on the valve cover. The crankcase ventilation hose (or PCV hose) connects the PCV valve or orifice in the valve cover to the intake manifold.

## 2   On Board Diagnosis (OBD) system and diagnostic trouble codes

### Scan tool information

1   Because extracting the Diagnostic Trouble Codes (DTCs) from an engine management system is now the first step in troubleshooting many computer-controlled systems and components, a code reader, at the very least, will be required (see illustration). More powerful scan tools can also perform many of the diagnostics once associated with expensive factory scan tools (see illustration). If you don't plan to purchase a code reader or scan tool and don't have access to one, you can have the codes extracted by a dealer service department or an independent repair shop.
**Note:** *Some auto parts stores even provide this service.*
**Note:** *Trouble codes on models equipped with an OBD-I system can be obtained without the use of a scan tool (see Steps 4 and 5).*

### Obtaining and clearing Diagnostic Trouble Codes (DTCs)

2   Before outputting any DTCs stored in the PCM, thoroughly inspect ALL electrical connectors and hoses. Make sure that all electrical connections are tight, clean and free of corrosion. Make sure that all hoses are correctly connected, fit tightly and are in good condition (no cracks or tears). Also, make sure that the engine is tuned up. A poorly running engine is probably one of the biggest causes of emission-related malfunctions. Often, simply giving the engine a good tune-up will correct the problem.

#### 1994 and 1995 models, and 1996 and 1997 OBD-I models

3   The PCM turns on the CHECK ENGINE light (also known as the Malfunction Indicator Lamp) on the instrument cluster when it recognizes a fault in the system. The light will remain illuminated until the problem is repaired and the code is cleared, or until the

**2.1a Simple code readers are an economical way to extract trouble codes when the CHECK ENGINE light comes on**

**2.1b Hand-held scan tools like these can extract computer codes and also perform diagnostics**

# Information Sensors

**Accelerator Pedal Position (APP) sensor** - as you press the accelerator pedal, the APP sensor alters its voltage signal to the PCM in proportion to the angle of the pedal, and the PCM commands a motor inside the throttle body to open or close the throttle plate accordingly

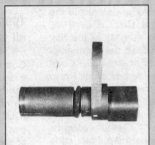

**Camshaft Position (CMP) sensor** - produces a signal that the PCM uses to identify the number 1 cylinder and to time the firing sequence of the fuel injectors

**Crankshaft Position (CKP) sensor** - produces a signal that the PCM uses to calculate engine speed and crankshaft position, which enables it to synchronize ignition timing with fuel injector timing, and to detect misfires

**Engine Coolant Temperature (ECT) sensor** - a thermistor (temperature-sensitive variable resistor) that sends a voltage signal to the PCM, which uses this data to determine the temperature of the engine coolant

**Fuel tank pressure sensor** - measures the fuel tank pressure and controls fuel tank pressure by signaling the EVAP system to purge the fuel tank vapors when the pressure becomes excessive

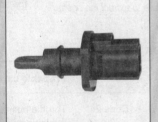

**Intake Air Temperature (IAT) sensor** - monitors the temperature of the air entering the engine and sends a signal to the PCM to determine injector pulse-width (the duration of each injector's on-time) and to adjust spark timing (to prevent spark knock)

**Knock sensor** - a piezoelectric crystal that oscillates in proportion to engine vibration which produces a voltage output that is monitored by the PCM. This retards the ignition timing when the oscillation exceeds a certain threshold

**Manifold Absolute Pressure (MAP) sensor** - monitors the pressure or vacuum inside the intake manifold. The PCM uses this data to determine engine load so that it can alter the ignition advance and fuel enrichment

**Mass Air Flow (MAF) sensor** - measures the amount of intake air drawn into the engine. It uses a hot-wire sensing element to measure the amount of air entering the engine

**Oxygen sensors** - generates a small variable voltage signal in proportion to the difference between the oxygen content in the exhaust stream and the oxygen content in the ambient air. The PCM uses this information to maintain the proper air/fuel ratio. A second oxygen sensor monitors the efficiency of the catalytic converter

**Throttle Position (TP) sensor** - a potentiometer that generates a voltage signal that varies in relation to the opening angle of the throttle plate inside the throttle body. Works with the PCM and other sensors to calculate injector pulse width (the duration of each injector's on-time)

*Photos courtesy of Wells Manufacturing, except APP and MAF sensors.*

**2.6 The 16-pin Data Link Connector (DLC), also referred to as the diagnostic connector, is located under the left part of the dash**

PCM no longer detects the malfunction for several consecutive drive cycles.

4    The trouble code(s) can be determined by counting the number of flashes of the CHECK ENGINE light. To extract the diagnostic trouble codes using this method, proceed as follows:

a) *Without starting the engine, turn the ignition key On, Off, On, Off and finally On. The CHECK ENGINE light on the dash will begin to flash.*

b) *If any trouble codes are stored in the PCM memory, the CHECK ENGINE light will flash the number of the first digit, pause and flash the number of the second digit. For example: Code 23, air temperature sensor circuit would be indicated by two flashes, pause three flashes. A long pause will appear between individual codes if more than one code is present. Carefully observe the flashes and record the exact code number(s) onto paper.*

c) *After the stored codes have been indicated (or if everything in the self diagnosis system is functioning properly), the CHECK ENGINE light will flash a Code 55. Refer to the "Check Engine Light Flash Code" column of the trouble code chart for trouble code identification.*

d) *If the ignition key is turned Off during the code extraction process and then turned back On, the self diagnostic system will automatically invalidate the procedure. Restart the procedure to extract the codes.*

**Note:** *The self diagnostic system cannot be accessed with the engine running.*

5    Diagnostic trouble codes can also be extracted from the PCM with an OBD-I scan tool.

### 1996 and 1997 OBD-II models and all 1998 and later models

6    On these models, the Diagnostic Trouble Codes (DTCs) can only be accessed with a code reader or a scan tool (see illustrations 2.1a and 2.1b). Simply plug the connector of the tool into the Data Link Connector (DLC) or diagnostic connector (see illustration), which is located under the lower edge of the dash, just to the right of the steering column. Then follow the instructions included with the scan tool to extract the DTCs.

7    Once you have outputted all of the stored DTCs, look them up on the accompanying DTC chart.

8    After troubleshooting the source of each DTC, make any necessary repairs or replace the defective component(s).

### Clearing the DTCs

9    Clear the DTCs with the scan tool in accordance with the instructions provided by the scan tool's manufacturer.

## OBD-I Diagnostic Trouble Codes - gasoline engines

| Code | Probable cause |
| --- | --- |
| Code 11 | No distributor reference signal detected during engine cranking. Check the circuit between the distributor and the PCM. |
| Code 12 | Problem with the battery connection. Direct battery input to PCM disconnected within the last 50 ignition key-on cycles. |
| Code 13** | Indicates a problem with the MAP sensor vacuum system. |
| Code 14** | MAP sensor voltage too low or too high. |
| Code 15** | A problem with the vehicle distance/speed signal. No distance/speed sensor signal detected during road load conditions. |
| Code 17 | Engine is cold too long. Engine coolant temperature remains below normal operating temperatures during operation (check the thermostat). |
| Code 21** | Problem with oxygen sensor signal circuit. Sensor voltage to computer not fluctuating. |
| Code 22** | Coolant sensor voltage too high or too low. Test coolant temperature sensor. |
| Code 23** | Indicates that the air temperature sensor input is below the minimum acceptable voltage or sensor input is above the maximum acceptable voltage. |

| Code | Probable cause |
| --- | --- |
| Code 24** | Throttle position sensor voltage high or low. Test the throttle position sensor. |
| Code 25** | Idle Air Control (IAC) valve circuits. A shorted condition is detected in one or more of the IAC valve circuits. |
| Code 27 | One of the injector control circuit output drivers does not respond properly to the control signal. Check the circuits. |
| Code 31** | Problem with the canister purge solenoid circuit. |
| Code 32** | An open or shorted condition detected in the EGR solenoid circuit. Possible air/fuel ratio imbalance not detected during diagnosis. |
| Code 33 | Air conditioner clutch relay circuit. An open or shorted condition detected in the air conditioning clutch relay circuit. |
| Code 34 | Open or shorted condition detected in the speed control vacuum or vent solenoid circuits. |
| Code 35 | Open or shorted condition detected in the radiator fan low speed relay circuit. |
| Code 41** | Problem with the charging system. Occurs when battery voltage from the ASD relay is below 11.75 volts. |
| Code 42 | Auto shutdown relay (ASD) control circuit indicates an open or shorted circuit condition. |

| Code | Probable cause |
|------|----------------|
| Code 43** | Peak primary circuit current not achieved with the maximum dwell time. |
| Code 44 | Battery temperature sensor volts malfunction. Problem with the battery temperature voltage circuit in the PCM. |
| Code 45 | Transmission overdrive solenoid circuit malfunction. An open or short circuit problem exists in the transmission overdrive solenoid circuit. |
| Code 46** | Charging system voltage too high. Computer indicates that the battery voltage is not properly regulated. |
| Code 47** | Charging system voltage too low. Battery voltage sense input below target charging voltage during engine operation and no significant change in voltage detected during active test of alternator output. |
| Code 51 | Oxygen sensor signal input indicates lean fuel/air ratio condition during engine operation. |
| Code 52** | Oxygen sensor signal input indicates rich fuel/air ratio condition during engine operation. |

| Code | Probable cause |
|------|----------------|
| Code 53 | Internal PCM failure detected. |
| Code 54 | No camshaft position sensor signal from distributor. Problem with the distributor synchronization circuit. |
| Code 55 | Completion of fault code display on CHECK ENGINE lamp. This is an end of message code. |
| Code 62 | PCM failure to update the SRI (service reminder indicator) mileage setting in the EEPROM. |
| Code 63 | Controller failure. EEPROM write denied. Check the PCM. |
| Code 71** | Auxiliary 5 volt supply output voltage signal is low. The 5 volt output signal from the regulator is not reaching the required voltage amount. |
| Code 72** | Catalytic converter efficiency failure. The catalytic converter is not converting emissions in the proper ratio. |

**Note:** **These codes light up the CHECK ENGINE light on the instrument panel during engine operation once the trouble code has been recorded.*

## OBD-I Diagnostic Trouble Codes - diesel engines

| Code | Probable cause |
|------|----------------|
| Code 11 | No crank reference signal detected during engine cranking |
| Code 12 | No codes. Problem with the battery connection. Direct battery input to the PCM disconnected within the last 50 ignition key-on cycles. |
| Code 15** | No vehicle speed sensor signal. No VSS signal detected by the PCM during driving conditions. |
| Code 23** | Intake air temperature sensor voltage high or low. Intake manifold air temperature sensor circuit signals above or below the acceptable voltage. |
| Code 24** | Throttle position sensor (TPS) voltage high or low. Test the throttle position sensor. |
| Code 33 | Air conditioner clutch relay circuit. An open or shorted condition detected in the air conditioning clutch relay circuit. |
| Code 34 | Open or shorted condition detected in the speed control vacuum or vent solenoid circuits. |
| Code 37** | Torque Converter Clutch (TCC) solenoid circuit open or shorted. |
| Code 37** | Transmission temperature sensor voltage signal above or below acceptable voltage values. |
| Code 41** | Problem with the charging system. Occurs when battery voltage from the ASD relay is below 11.75-volts. |

| Code | Probable cause |
|------|----------------|
| Code 42 | Auto shutdown relay (ASD) control circuit indicates an open or shorted circuit condition. |
| Code 44 | Battery temperature sensor volts malfunction. Problem with the battery temperature voltage circuit in the PCM. |
| Code 45 | Transmission overdrive solenoid circuit malfunction. An open or short circuit problem exists in the transmission overdrive solenoid circuit. |
| Code 46** | Charging system voltage too high. Computer indicates that the battery voltage is not properly regulated. |
| Code 47** | Charging system voltage too low. Battery voltage sense input below target charging voltage during engine operation and no significant change in voltage detected during active test of alternator output. |
| Code 53 | Internal PCM failure detected. |
| Code 55 | Completion of fault code display on CHECK ENGINE lamp. This is an end of message code. |
| Code 63 | Controller failure. EEPROM write denied. Check the PCM. |
| Code 68** | PCM not active or a fault condition of the EGR sensors and/or EGR solenoid. |

**Note:** **These codes light up the CHECK ENGINE light on the instrument panel during engine operation once the trouble code has been recorded.*

## OBD-II Diagnostic Trouble Codes -
### 1996 through 2001 gasoline-engine models, 1998 through 2002 diesel-engine models

| Code | Probable cause | Code | Probable cause |
|------|----------------|------|----------------|
| P0100 | Mass air flow or volume air flow circuit malfunction | P0124 | Throttle position or pedal position sensor/switch circuit, intermittent |
| P0101 | Mass air flow or volume air flow circuit, range or performance problem | P0125 | Coolant temperature signal incorrect |
| P0102 | Mass air flow or volume air flow circuit, low input | P0126 | Insufficient coolant temperature for stable operation |
| P0103 | Mass air flow or volume air flow circuit, high input | P0128 | Engine is cold too long |
| P0104 | Mass air flow or volume air flow circuit, intermittent | P0130 | O2 sensor circuit malfunction (cylinder bank no. 1, sensor no. 1) |
| P0105 | Manifold absolute pressure or barometric pressure circuit malfunction | P0131 | O2 sensor circuit, low voltage (cylinder bank no. 1, sensor no. 1) |
| P0106 | Manifold absolute pressure or barometric pressure circuit, range or performance problem | P0132 | O2 sensor circuit, high voltage (cylinder bank no. 1, sensor no. 1) |
| P0107 | Manifold absolute pressure or barometric pressure circuit, low input | P0133 | O2 sensor circuit, slow response (cylinder bank no. 1, sensor no. 1) |
| P0108 | Manifold absolute pressure or barometric pressure circuit, high input | P0134 | O2 sensor circuit - no activity detected (cylinder bank no. 1, sensor no. 1) |
| P0109 | Manifold absolute pressure or barometric pressure circuit, intermittent | P0135 | O2 sensor heater circuit malfunction (cylinder bank no. 1, sensor no. 1) |
| P0110 | Intake air temperature circuit malfunction | P0136 | O2 sensor circuit malfunction (cylinder bank no. 1, sensor no. 2) |
| P0111 | Intake air temperature circuit, range or performance | P0137 | O2 sensor circuit, low voltage (cylinder bank no. 1, sensor no. 2) |
| P0112 | Intake Air Temperature (IAT) sensor voltage too low (diesel models) | P0138 | O2 sensor circuit, high voltage (cylinder bank no. 1, sensor no. 2) |
| P0112 | Intake air temperature circuit, low input | P0139 | O2 sensor circuit, slow response (cylinder bank no. 1, sensor no. 2) |
| P0113 | Intake Air Temperature (IAT) sensor voltage too high (diesel models) | P0140 | O2 sensor circuit - no activity detected (cylinder bank no. 1, sensor no. 2) |
| P0114 | Intake air temperature circuit, intermittent | P0141 | O2 sensor heater circuit malfunction (cylinder bank no. 1, sensor no. 2) |
| P0117 | Engine Coolant Temperature (ECT) sensor voltage too low (diesel models) | P0142 | O2 sensor circuit malfunction (cylinder bank no. 1, sensor no. 3) |
| P0118 | Engine Coolant Temperature (ECT) sensor voltage too high (diesel models) | P0143 | O2 sensor circuit, low voltage (cylinder bank no. 1, sensor no. 3) |
| P0119 | Engine coolant temperature circuit, intermittent | P0144 | O2 sensor circuit, high voltage (cylinder bank no. 1, sensor no. 3) |
| P0120 | Throttle position or pedal position sensor/switch circuit malfunction | P0145 | O2 sensor circuit, slow response (cylinder bank no. 1, sensor no. 3) |
| P0121 | Throttle Position Sensor (TPS)/Accelerator Pedal Position Sensor (APPS) circuit voltage range problem | P0146 | O2 sensor circuit - no activity detected (cylinder bank no. 1, sensor no. 3) |
| P0122 | Throttle Position Sensor (TPS)/Accelerator Pedal Position Sensor (APPS) signal voltage too low | | |
| P0123 | Throttle Position Sensor (TPS)/Accelerator Pedal Position Sensor (APPS) signal voltage high | | |

| Code | Probable cause |
|------|----------------|
| P0147 | O2 sensor heater circuit malfunction (cylinder bank no. 1, sensor 3) |
| P0150 | O2 sensor circuit malfunction (cylinder bank no. 2, sensor no. 1 |
| P0151 | O2 sensor circuit, low voltage (cylinder bank no. 2, sensor no. 1) |
| P0152 | O2 sensor circuit, high voltage (cylinder bank no. 2, sensor no. 1) |
| P0153 | O2 sensor circuit, slow response (cylinder bank no. 2, sensor no. 1) |
| P0154 | O2 sensor circuit - no activity detected (cylinder bank no. 2, sensor no. 1) |
| P0155 | O2 sensor heater circuit malfunction (cylinder bank no. 2, sensor no. 1) |
| P0156 | O2 sensor circuit malfunction (cylinder bank no. 2, sensor no. 2) |
| P0157 | O2 sensor circuit, low voltage (cylinder bank no. 2, sensor no. 2) |
| P0158 | O2 sensor circuit, high voltage (cylinder bank no. 2, sensor no. 2) |
| P0159 | O2 sensor circuit, slow response (cylinder bank no. 2, sensor no. 2) |
| P0160 | O2 sensor circuit - no activity detected (cylinder bank no. 2, sensor no. 2) |
| P0161 | O2 sensor heater circuit malfunction (cylinder bank no. 2, sensor no. 2) |
| P0162 | O2 sensor circuit malfunction (cylinder bank no. 2, sensor no. 3) |
| P0163 | O2 sensor circuit, low voltage (cylinder bank no. 2, sensor no. 3) |
| P0164 | O2 sensor circuit, high voltage (cylinder bank no. 2, sensor no. 3) |
| P0165 | O2 sensor circuit, slow response (cylinder bank no. 2, sensor no. 3) |
| P0166 | O2 sensor circuit - no activity detected (cylinder bank no. 2, sensor no. 3) |
| P0167 | O2 sensor heater circuit malfunction (cylinder bank no. 2, sensor 3) |
| P0168 | Decreased engine performance caused by high fuel temperature inside the injection pump (diesel models) |
| P0170 | Fuel trim malfunction (cylinder bank no. 1) |
| P0171 | System too lean (cylinder bank no. 1) |

| Code | Probable cause |
|------|----------------|
| P0172 | System too rich (cylinder bank no. 1) |
| P0173 | Fuel trim malfunction (cylinder bank no. 2) |
| P0174 | System too lean (cylinder bank no. 2) |
| P0175 | System too rich (cylinder bank no. 2) |
| P0176 | Fuel composition sensor circuit malfunction |
| P0177 | Fuel composition sensor circuit, range or performance problem; water in fuel (diesel models) |
| P0178 | Fuel composition sensor circuit, low input; Water-In-Fuel (WIF) sensor voltage low (diesel models) |
| P0179 | Fuel composition sensor circuit, high input |
| P0180 | Fuel temperature sensor A circuit malfunction; fuel injection pump temperature out of range (diesel models) |
| P0181 | Fuel temperature sensor A circuit, range or performance problem; fuel injection pump failure (diesel models) |
| P0182 | Fuel temperature sensor A circuit, low input |
| P0183 | Fuel temperature sensor A circuit, high input |
| P0184 | Fuel temperature sensor A circuit, intermittent |
| P0185 | Fuel temperature sensor B circuit malfunction |
| P0186 | Fuel temperature sensor B circuit, range or performance problem |
| P0187 | Fuel temperature sensor B circuit, low input |
| P0188 | Fuel temperature sensor B circuit, high input |
| P0189 | Fuel temperature sensor B circuit, intermittent |
| P0190 | Fuel rail pressure sensor circuit malfunction |
| P0191 | Fuel rail pressure sensor circuit, range or performance problem |
| P0192 | Fuel rail pressure sensor circuit, low input |
| P0193 | Fuel rail pressure sensor circuit, high input |
| P0194 | Fuel rail pressure sensor circuit, intermittent |
| P0195 | Engine oil temperature sensor malfunction |
| P0196 | Fuel rail pressure sensor circuit, range or performance problem |
| P0197 | Fuel rail pressure sensor circuit, low input |
| P0198 | Fuel rail pressure sensor circuit, high input |
| P0199 | Fuel rail pressure sensor circuit, intermittent |
| P0200 | Injector circuit malfunction |

## OBD-II Diagnostic Trouble Codes -
### 1996 through 2001 gasoline-engine models, 1998 through 2002 diesel-engine models (continued)

| Code | Probable cause |
|------|----------------|
| P0201 | Injector circuit malfunction - cylinder no. 1 |
| P0202 | Injector circuit malfunction - cylinder no. 2 |
| P0203 | Injector circuit malfunction - cylinder no. 3 |
| P0204 | Injector circuit malfunction - cylinder no. 4 |
| P0205 | Injector circuit malfunction - cylinder no. 5 |
| P0206 | Injector circuit malfunction - cylinder no. 6 |
| P0207 | Injector circuit malfunction - cylinder no. 7 |
| P0208 | Injector circuit malfunction - cylinder no. 8 |
| P0209 | Injector circuit malfunction - cylinder no. 9 |
| P0210 | Injector circuit malfunction - cylinder no. 10 |
| P0211 | Injector circuit malfunction - cylinder no. 11 |
| P0212 | Injector circuit malfunction - cylinder no. 12 |
| P0213 | Cold start injector no. 1 malfunction |
| P0214 | Cold start injector no. 2 malfunction |
| P0215 | Engine shut-off solenoid malfunction; fuel injection pump control circuit problem (diesel models) |
| P0216 | Injection timing control circuit malfunction; fuel injection pump timing failure (diesel models) |
| P0217 | Engine overheating condition; diminished engine performance due to engine overheating (diesel models) |
| P0218 | Transmission overheating condition |
| P0219 | Engine overspeed condition |
| P0220 | Throttle position or pedal position sensor/switch B circuit malfunction |
| P0221 | Throttle position or pedal position sensor/switch B, range or performance problem |
| P0222 | Throttle position or pedal position sensor/switch B circuit, low input; both idle validation signals low (diesels) |
| P0223 | Throttle position or pedal position sensor/switch B circuit, high input; both idle validation signals high (diesels) |
| P0224 | Throttle position or pedal position sensor/switch B circuit, intermittent |
| P0225 | Throttle position or pedal position sensor/switch C circuit malfunction |

| Code | Probable cause |
|------|----------------|
| P0226 | Throttle position or pedal position sensor/switch C, range or performance problem |
| P0227 | Throttle position or pedal position sensor/switch C circuit, low input |
| P0228 | Throttle position or pedal position sensor/switch C circuit, high input |
| P0229 | Throttle position or pedal position sensor/switch C circuit, intermittent |
| P0230 | Fuel pump primary circuit malfunction; transfer pump circuit out of range (diesel models) |
| P0231 | Fuel pump secondary circuit low voltage |
| P0232 | Fuel pump secondary circuit high voltage; fuel shutoff signal voltage too high (diesel models) |
| P0233 | Fuel pump secondary circuit, intermittent |
| P0234 | Engine overboost condition; turbo boost limit exceeded (diesel models) |
| P0235 | Turbocharger boost sensor A circuit malfunction |
| P0236 | Turbocharger boost sensor A circuit, range or performance problem; Manifold Absolute Pressure (MAP) sensor voltage too high for too long (diesel models) |
| P0237 | Turbocharger boost sensor A circuit, low; Manifold Absolute Pressure (MAP) sensor voltage too low (diesels) |
| P0238 | Turbocharger boost sensor A circuit, high; Manifold Absolute Pressure (MAP) sensor voltage too high (diesels) |
| P0239 | Turbocharger boost sensor B circuit malfunction |
| P0240 | Turbocharger boost sensor B circuit, range or performance problem |
| P0241 | Turbocharger boost sensor B circuit, low |
| P0242 | Turbocharger boost sensor B circuit, high |
| P0243 | Turbocharger wastegate solenoid A malfunction |
| P0244 | Turbocharger wastegate solenoid A, range or performance problem |
| P0245 | Turbocharger wastegate solenoid A, low |
| P0246 | Turbocharger wastegate solenoid A, high |
| P0247 | Turbocharger wastegate solenoid B malfunction |

| Code | Probable cause |
|------|----------------|
| P0248 | Turbocharger wastegate solenoid B, range or performance problem |
| P0249 | Turbocharger wastegate solenoid B, low |
| P0250 | Turbocharger wastegate solenoid B, high |
| P0251 | Injection pump fuel metering control A malfunction (cam/rotor/injector); fuel injection pump mechanical failure fuel valve feedback circuit (diesel models) |
| P0252 | Injection pump fuel metering control A, range or performance problem (cam/rotor/injector); fuel valve signal missing (diesel models) |
| P0253 | Injection pump fuel metering control A, low (cam/rotor/injector); fuel injection pump fuel valve open circuit (diesels) |
| P0254 | Injection pump fuel metering control A, high (cam/rotor/injector); fuel injection pump fuel valve current too high (diesel models) |
| P0255 | Injection pump fuel metering control A, intermittent (cam/rotor/injector) |
| P0256 | Injection pump fuel metering control B malfunction (cam/rotor/injector) |
| P0257 | Injection pump fuel metering control B, range or performance problem (cam/rotor/injector) |
| P0258 | Injection pump fuel metering control B, low (cam/rotor/injector) |
| P0259 | Injection pump fuel metering control B, high (cam/rotor/injector) |
| P0260 | Injection pump fuel metering control B, intermittent (cam/rotor/injector) |
| P0261 | Cylinder no. 1 injector circuit, low |
| P0262 | Cylinder no. 1 injector circuit, high |
| P0263 | Cylinder no. 1 contribution/balance fault |
| P0264 | Cylinder no. 2 injector circuit, low |
| P0265 | Cylinder no. 2 injector circuit, high |
| P0266 | Cylinder no. 2 contribution/balance fault |
| P0267 | Cylinder no. 3 injector circuit, low |
| P0268 | Cylinder no. 3 injector circuit, high |
| P0269 | Cylinder no. 3 contribution/balance fault |
| P0270 | Cylinder no. 4 injector circuit, low |
| P0271 | Cylinder no. 4 injector circuit, high |
| P0272 | Cylinder no. 4 contribution/balance fault |

| Code | Probable cause |
|------|----------------|
| P0273 | Cylinder no. 5 injector circuit, low |
| P0274 | Cylinder no. 5 injector circuit, high |
| P0275 | Cylinder no. 5 contribution/balance fault |
| P0276 | Cylinder no. 6 injector circuit, low |
| P0277 | Cylinder no. 6 injector circuit, high |
| P0278 | Cylinder no. 6 contribution/balance fault |
| P0279 | Cylinder no. 7 injector circuit, low |
| P0280 | Cylinder no. 7 injector circuit, high |
| P0281 | Cylinder no. 7 contribution/balance fault |
| P0282 | Cylinder no. 8 injector circuit, low |
| P0283 | Cylinder no. 8 injector circuit, high |
| P0284 | Cylinder no. 8 contribution/balance fault |
| P0285 | Cylinder no. 9 injector circuit, low |
| P0286 | Cylinder no. 9 injector circuit, high |
| P0287 | Cylinder no. 9 contribution/balance fault |
| P0288 | Cylinder no. 10 injector circuit, low |
| P0289 | Cylinder no. 10 injector circuit, high |
| P0290 | Cylinder no. 10 contribution/balance fault |
| P0291 | Cylinder no. 11 injector circuit, low |
| P0292 | Cylinder no. 11 injector circuit, high |
| P0293 | Cylinder no. 11 contribution/balance fault |
| P0294 | Cylinder no. 12 injector circuit, low |
| P0295 | Cylinder no. 12 injector circuit, high |
| P0296 | Cylinder no. 12 contribution/balance fault |
| P0300 | Random/multiple cylinder misfire detected |
| P0301 | Cylinder no. 1 misfire detected |
| P0302 | Cylinder no. 2 misfire detected |
| P0303 | Cylinder no. 3 misfire detected |
| P0304 | Cylinder no. 4 misfire detected |
| P0305 | Cylinder no. 5 misfire detected |
| P0306 | Cylinder no. 6 misfire detected |
| P0307 | Cylinder no. 7 misfire detected |

## OBD-II Diagnostic Trouble Codes -
### 1996 through 2001 gasoline-engine models, 1998 through 2002 diesel-engine models (continued)

| Code | Probable cause | Code | Probable cause |
|------|----------------|------|----------------|
| P0308 | Cylinder no. 8 misfire detected | P0338 | Crankshaft Position (CKP) sensor A circuit, high input |
| P0309 | Cylinder no. 9 misfire detected | P0339 | Crankshaft Position (CKP) sensor A circuit, intermittent |
| P0310 | Cylinder no. 10 misfire detected | P0340 | Camshaft Position (CMP) sensor circuit malfunction |
| P0311 | Cylinder no. 11 misfire detected | P0341 | Camshaft Position (CMP) sensor circuit, range or performance problem |
| P0312 | Cylinder no. 12 misfire detected | | |
| P0320 | Ignition/distributor engine speed input circuit malfunction; no crank reference signal at PCM (diesel models) | P0342 | Camshaft Position (CMP) sensor circuit, low input |
| | | P0343 | Camshaft Position (CMP) sensor circuit, high input |
| P0321 | Ignition/distributor engine speed input circuit, range or performance problem | P0344 | Camshaft Position (CMP) sensor circuit, intermittent |
| | | P0350 | Ignition coil primary or secondary circuit malfunction |
| P0322 | Ignition/distributor engine speed input circuit, no signal | P0351 | Ignition coil A primary or secondary circuit malfunction |
| P0323 | Ignition/distributor engine speed input circuit, intermittent | P0352 | Ignition coil B primary or secondary circuit malfunction |
| | | P0353 | Ignition coil C primary or secondary circuit malfunction |
| P0325 | Knock sensor no. 1 circuit malfunction (cylinder bank no. 1 or single sensor) | P0354 | Ignition coil D primary or secondary circuit malfunction |
| P0326 | Knock sensor no. 1 circuit, range or performance problem (cylinder bank no. 1 or single sensor) | P0355 | Ignition coil E primary or secondary circuit malfunction |
| | | P0356 | Ignition coil F primary or secondary circuit malfunction |
| P0327 | Knock sensor no. 1 circuit, low input (cylinder bank no. 1 or single sensor) | P0357 | Ignition coil G primary or secondary circuit malfunction |
| P0328 | Knock sensor no. 1 circuit, high input (cylinder bank no. 1 or single sensor) | P0358 | Ignition coil H primary or secondary circuit malfunction |
| | | P0359 | Ignition coil I primary or secondary circuit malfunction |
| P0329 | Knock sensor no. 1 circuit, intermittent (cylinder bank no. 1 or single sensor) | P0360 | Ignition coil J primary or secondary circuit malfunction |
| P0330 | Knock sensor no. 2 circuit malfunction (cylinder bank no. 2) | P0361 | Ignition coil K primary or secondary circuit malfunction |
| | | P0362 | Ignition coil L primary or secondary circuit malfunction |
| P0331 | Knock sensor no. 2 circuit, range or performance problem (cylinder bank no. 2) | P0370 | Timing reference high resolution signal A malfunction; fuel injection pump speed/position sensor signal lost (diesel models) |
| P0332 | Knock sensor no. 2 circuit, low input (cylinder bank no. 2) | | |
| P0333 | Knock sensor no. 2 circuit, high input (cylinder bank no. 2) | P0371 | Timing reference high resolution signal A, too many pulses |
| P0334 | Knock sensor no. 2 circuit, intermittent (cylinder bank no. 2) | P0372 | Timing reference high resolution signal A, too few pulses |
| P0335 | Crankshaft Position (CKP) sensor A circuit, malfunction | P0373 | Timing reference high resolution signal A, intermittent/erratic pulses |
| | | P0374 | Timing reference high resolution signal A, no pulse |
| P0336 | Crankshaft Position (CKP) sensor A circuit, range or performance problem | P0375 | Timing reference high resolution signal B malfunction |
| P0337 | Crankshaft Position (CKP) sensor A circuit, low input | P0376 | Timing reference high resolution signal B, too many pulses |

| Code | Probable cause |
|------|----------------|
| P0377 | Timing reference high resolution signal B, too few pulses |
| P0378 | Timing reference high resolution signal B, intermittent/erratic pulses |
| P0379 | Timing reference high resolution signal B, no pulse |
| P0380 | Intake air heater relay no. 1 control circuit malfunction (diesel models) |
| P0381 | Wait-to-start lamp malfunction (diesel models) |
| P0382 | Intake air heater relay no. 2 control circuit malfunction (diesel models) |
| P0385 | Crankshaft position sensor B circuit malfunction |
| P0386 | Crankshaft position sensor B circuit, range or performance problem |
| P0387 | Crankshaft position sensor B circuit, low input |
| P0388 | Crankshaft position sensor B circuit, high input |
| P0389 | Crankshaft position sensor B circuit, intermittent |
| P0400 | Exhaust gas recirculation flow malfunction |
| P0401 | Exhaust gas recirculation, insufficient flow detected |
| P0402 | Exhaust gas recirculation, excessive flow detected |
| P0403 | Exhaust gas recirculation circuit malfunction |
| P0404 | Exhaust gas recirculation circuit, range or performance problem |
| P0405 | Exhaust gas recirculation sensor A circuit low |
| P0406 | Exhaust gas recirculation sensor A circuit high |
| P0407 | Exhaust gas recirculation sensor B circuit low |
| P0408 | Exhaust gas recirculation sensor B circuit high |
| P0410 | Secondary air injection system malfunction |
| P0411 | Secondary air injection system, incorrect flow detected |
| P0412 | Secondary air injection system switching valve A, circuit malfunction |
| P0413 | Secondary air injection system switching valve A, open circuit |
| P0414 | Secondary air injection system switching valve A, shorted circuit |
| P0415 | Secondary air injection system switching valve B, circuit malfunction |
| P0416 | Secondary air injection system switching valve B, open circuit |

| Code | Probable cause |
|------|----------------|
| P0417 | Secondary air injection system switching valve B, shorted circuit |
| P0418 | Secondary air injection system, relay A circuit malfunction |
| P0419 | Secondary air injection system, relay B circuit malfunction |
| P0420 | Catalyst system efficiency below threshold (cylinder bank no. 1) |
| P0421 | Warm-up catalyst efficiency below threshold (cylinder bank no. 1) |
| P0422 | Main catalyst efficiency below threshold (cylinder bank no. 1) |
| P0423 | Heated catalyst efficiency below threshold (cylinder bank no. 1) |
| P0424 | Heated catalyst temperature below threshold (cylinder bank no. 1) |
| P0430 | Catalyst system efficiency below threshold (cylinder bank no. 2) |
| P0431 | Warm-up catalyst efficiency below threshold (cylinder bank no. 2) |
| P0432 | Main catalyst efficiency below threshold (cylinder bank no. 2) |
| P0433 | Heated catalyst efficiency below threshold (cylinder bank no. 2) |
| P0434 | Heated catalyst temperature below threshold (cylinder bank no. 2) |
| P0440 | Evaporative emission control system malfunction |
| P0441 | Evaporative emission control system, incorrect purge flow |
| P0442 | Evaporative emission control system, small leak detected |
| P0443 | Evaporative emission control system, purge control valve circuit malfunction |
| P0444 | Evaporative emission control system, open purge control valve circuit |
| P0445 | Evaporative emission control system, short in purge control valve circuit |
| P0446 | Evaporative emission control system, vent control circuit malfunction |
| P0447 | Evaporative emission control system, open vent control circuit |
| P0448 | Evaporative emission control system, shorted vent control circuit |

## OBD-II Diagnostic Trouble Codes -
### 1996 through 2001 gasoline-engine models, 1998 through 2002 diesel-engine models (continued)

| Code | Probable cause |
|------|----------------|
| P0449 | Evaporative emission control system, vent valve/ solenoid circuit malfunction |
| P0450 | Evaporative emission control system, pressure sensor malfunction |
| P0451 | Evaporative emission control system, pressure sensor range or performance problem |
| P0452 | Evaporative emission control system, pressure sensor low input |
| P0453 | Evaporative emission control system, pressure sensor high input |
| P0454 | Evaporative emission control system, pressure sensor intermittent |
| P0460 | Fuel level sensor circuit malfunction |
| P0461 | Fuel level sensor circuit, range or performance problem |
| P0462 | Fuel level sensor circuit, low input |
| P0463 | Fuel level sensor circuit, high input |
| P0464 | Fuel level sensor circuit, intermittent |
| P0465 | Purge flow sensor circuit malfunction |
| P0466 | Purge flow sensor circuit, range or performance problem |
| P0467 | Purge flow sensor circuit, low input |
| P0468 | Purge flow sensor circuit, high input |
| P0469 | Purge flow sensor circuit, intermittent |
| P0470 | Exhaust pressure sensor malfunction |
| P0471 | Exhaust pressure sensor, range or performance problem |
| P0472 | Exhaust pressure sensor, low |
| P0473 | Exhaust pressure sensor, high |
| P0474 | Exhaust pressure sensor, intermittent |
| P0475 | Exhaust pressure control valve malfunction |
| P0476 | Exhaust pressure control valve, range or performance problem |
| P0477 | Exhaust pressure control valve, low |
| P0478 | Exhaust pressure sensor, high |
| P0479 | Exhaust pressure sensor, intermittent |
| P0480 | Cooling fan no. 1, control circuit malfunction |

| Code | Probable cause |
|------|----------------|
| P0481 | Cooling fan no. 2, control circuit malfunction |
| P0482 | Cooling fan no. 3, control circuit malfunction |
| P0483 | Cooling fan rationality check malfunction |
| P0484 | Cooling fan circuit, high current |
| P0485 | Cooling fan power/ground circuit malfunction |
| P0500 | Vehicle speed sensor malfunction |
| P0501 | Vehicle speed sensor, range or performance problem |
| P0502 | Vehicle speed sensor circuit, low input |
| P0503 | Vehicle speed sensor circuit, intermittent, erratic or high input |
| P0505 | Idle control system malfunction |
| P0506 | Idle control system, rpm lower than expected |
| P0507 | Idle control system, rpm higher than expected |
| P0510 | Closed throttle position switch malfunction |
| P0520 | Engine oil pressure sensor/switch circuit malfunction |
| P0521 | Engine oil pressure sensor/switch circuit, range or performance problem |
| P0522 | Engine oil pressure sensor/switch circuit, low voltage |
| P0523 | Engine oil pressure sensor/switch circuit, high voltage |
| P0524 | Oil pressure too low (diesel models) |
| P0530 | A/C refrigerant pressure sensor, circuit malfunction |
| P0531 | A/C refrigerant pressure sensor, range or performance problem |
| P0532 | A/C refrigerant pressure sensor, low input |
| P0533 | A/C refrigerant pressure sensor, high input |
| P0534 | A/C refrigerant charge loss |
| P0550 | Power steering pressure sensor, circuit malfunction |
| P0551 | Power steering pressure sensor circuit, range or performance problem |
| P0552 | Power steering pressure sensor circuit, low input |
| P0553 | Power steering pressure sensor circuit, high input |
| P0554 | Power steering pressure sensor circuit, intermittent input |

| Code | Probable cause |
|------|----------------|
| P0560 | System voltage malfunction |
| P0561 | System voltage unstable |
| P0562 | Charging system voltage too low |
| P0563 | Charging system voltage too high |
| P0565 | Cruise control on signal malfunction |
| P0566 | Cruise control off signal malfunction |
| P0567 | Cruise control resume signal malfunction |
| P0568 | Cruise control set signal malfunction |
| P0569 | Cruise control coast signal malfunction |
| P0570 | Cruise control accel signal malfunction |
| P0571 | Cruise control/brake switch A, circuit malfunction |
| P0572 | Cruise control/brake switch A, circuit low |
| P0573 | Cruise control/brake switch A, circuit high |
| P0600 | Serial communication link malfunction |
| P0601 | Powertrain Control Module (PCM) internal controller failure |
| P0602 | Electronic Control Module (ECM)/Powertrain Control Module (PCM) calibration/programming error |
| P0603 | Internal control module, keep alive memory (KAM) error |
| P0604 | Internal control module, random access memory (RAM) error |
| P0605 | Internal control module, read only memory (ROM) error |
| P0606 | Electronic Control Module (ECM)/Powertrain Control Module (PCM) processor failure |
| P0608 | Control module VSS, output A malfunction |
| P0609 | Control module VSS, output B malfunction |
| P0620 | Generator control circuit malfunction |
| P0621 | Generator lamp L, control circuit malfunction |
| P0622 | Generator lamp F, control circuit malfunction; generator field not switching correctly |
| P0645 | Air conditioning clutch relay circuit |
| P0650 | Malfunction indicator lamp (MIL), control circuit malfunction |
| P0654 | Engine rpm output, circuit malfunction |
| P0655 | Engine hot lamp output control, circuit malfunction |
| P0656 | Fuel level output, circuit malfunction |

| Code | Probable cause |
|------|----------------|
| P0700 | Transmission control system malfunction |
| P0701 | Transmission control system, range or performance problem |
| P0702 | Transmission control system, electrical |
| P0703 | Torque converter/brake switch B, circuit malfunction |
| P0704 | Clutch switch input circuit malfunction |
| P0705 | Transmission range sensor, circuit malfunction (PRNDL input) |
| P0706 | Transmission range sensor circuit, range or performance problem |
| P0707 | Transmission range sensor circuit, low input |
| P0708 | Transmission range sensor circuit, high input |
| P0709 | Transmission range sensor circuit, intermittent input |
| P0710 | Transmission fluid temperature sensor, circuit malfunction |
| P0711 | Transmission fluid temperature sensor circuit, range or performance problem |
| P0712 | Transmission fluid temperature sensor circuit, low input |
| P0713 | Transmission fluid temperature sensor circuit, high input |
| P0714 | Transmission fluid temperature sensor circuit, intermittent input |
| P0715 | Input/turbine speed sensor circuit malfunction |
| P0716 | Input/turbine speed sensor circuit, range or performance problem |
| P0717 | Input/turbine speed sensor circuit, no signal |
| P0718 | Input/turbine speed sensor circuit, intermittent signal |
| P0719 | Torque converter/brake switch B, circuit low |
| P0720 | Output speed sensor malfunction |
| P0721 | Output speed sensor circuit, range or performance problem |
| P0722 | Output speed sensor circuit, no signal |
| P0723 | Output speed sensor circuit, intermittent signal |
| P0724 | Torque converter/brake switch B circuit, high |
| P0725 | Engine speed input circuit malfunction |
| P0726 | Engine speed input circuit, range or performance problem |
| P0727 | Engine speed input circuit, no signal |

## OBD-II Diagnostic Trouble Codes -
### 1996 through 2001 gasoline-engine models, 1998 through 2002 diesel-engine models (continued)

| Code | Probable cause | Code | Probable cause |
|------|----------------|------|----------------|
| P0728 | Engine speed input circuit, intermittent signal | P0761 | Shift solenoid C, performance problem or stuck in off position |
| P0730 | Incorrect gear ratio | P0762 | Shift solenoid C, stuck in on position |
| P0731 | Incorrect gear ratio, first gear | P0763 | Shift solenoid C, electrical problem |
| P0732 | Incorrect gear ratio, second gear | P0764 | Shift solenoid C, intermittent operation |
| P0733 | Incorrect gear ratio, third gear | P0765 | Shift solenoid D malfunction |
| P0734 | Incorrect gear ratio, fourth gear | P0766 | Shift solenoid D, performance problem or stuck in off position |
| P0735 | Incorrect gear ratio, fifth gear | P0767 | Shift solenoid D, stuck in on position |
| P0736 | Incorrect gear ratio, reverse gear | P0768 | Shift solenoid D, electrical problem |
| P0740 | Torque converter clutch, circuit malfunction | P0769 | Shift solenoid D, intermittent operation |
| P0741 | Torque converter clutch, circuit performance or stuck in off position | P0770 | Shift solenoid E malfunction |
| P0742 | Torque converter clutch circuit, stuck in on position | P0771 | Shift solenoid E, performance problem or stuck in off position |
| P0743 | Torque converter clutch circuit, electrical problem | P0772 | Shift solenoid E, stuck in on position |
| P0744 | Torque converter clutch circuit, intermittent | P0773 | Shift solenoid E, electrical problem |
| P0745 | Pressure control solenoid malfunction | P0774 | Shift solenoid E, intermittent operation |
| P0746 | Pressure control solenoid, performance problem or stuck in off position | P0780 | Shift malfunction |
| P0747 | Pressure control solenoid, stuck in on position | P0781 | First-to-second shift malfunction |
| P0748 | Pressure control solenoid, electrical problem | P0782 | Second-to-third shift malfunction |
| P0749 | Pressure control solenoid, intermittent operation | P0783 | Third-to-fourth shift malfunction |
| P0750 | Shift solenoid A malfunction | P0784 | Fourth-to-fifth shift malfunction |
| P0751 | Shift solenoid A, performance problem or stuck in off position | P0785 | Shift/timing solenoid malfunction |
| P0752 | Shift solenoid A, stuck in on position | P0786 | Shift/timing solenoid, range or performance problem |
| P0753 | Shift solenoid A, electrical problem | P0787 | Shift/timing solenoid, low |
| P0754 | Shift solenoid A, intermittent operation | P0788 | Shift/timing solenoid, high |
| P0755 | Shift solenoid B malfunction | P0789 | Shift/timing solenoid, intermittent |
| P0756 | Shift solenoid B, performance problem or stuck in off position | P0790 | Normal/performance switch circuit malfunction |
| P0757 | Shift solenoid B, stuck in on position | P0801 | Reverse inhibit control circuit malfunction |
| P0758 | Shift solenoid B, electrical problem | P0803 | First-to-fourth upshift (skip shift) solenoid control circuit malfunction |
| P0759 | Shift solenoid B, intermittent operation | P0804 | First-to-fourth upshift (skip shift) lamp control circuit malfunction |
| P0760 | Shift solenoid C malfunction | | |

## OBD-II Diagnostic Trouble Codes (DTCs) -
## 2002 and later gasoline engines (includes transmission codes)

| Code | Probable cause | Code | Probable cause |
|------|----------------|------|----------------|
| P0016 | Crankshaft/camshaft timing misalignment | P0117 | Engine Coolant Temperature (ECT) sensor circuit, voltage too low |
| P0031 | Upstream oxygen sensor (left cylinder bank), heater circuit low voltage | P0118 | Engine Coolant Temperature (ECT) sensor circuit, voltage too high |
| P0032 | Upstream oxygen sensor (left cylinder bank), heater circuit high voltage | P0121 | Throttle Position (TP) sensor, voltage doesn't agree with MAP sensor signal |
| P0037 | Downstream oxygen sensor (left cylinder bank), heater circuit low voltage | P0121 | Throttle Position (TP) sensor No. 1, performance |
| P0038 | Downstream oxygen sensor (left cylinder bank), heater circuit high voltage | P0122 | Throttle Position (TP) sensor circuit, voltage too low |
| P0051 | Upstream oxygen sensor (right cylinder bank), heater circuit low voltage | P0123 | Throttle Position (TP) sensor circuit, voltage too high |
| P0052 | Upstream oxygen sensor (right cylinder bank), heater circuit high voltage | P0124 | Throttle Position (TP) sensor intermittent |
| P0057 | Downstream oxygen sensor (right cylinder bank), heater circuit low voltage | P0125 | Coolant temperature insufficient to go into closed-loop operation |
| P0058 | Downstream oxygen sensor (right cylinder bank), heater circuit high voltage | P0128 | Thermostat rationality |
| P0068 | MAP sensor/TP sensor correlation, vacuum leak detected | P0129 | Barometric pressure out-of-range |
| P0070 | Ambient temperature sensor stuck | P0131 | Upstream oxygen sensor (left cylinder bank), circuit voltage too low |
| P0071 | Ambient temperature sensor performance | P0132 | Upstream oxygen sensor (left cylinder bank), circuit voltage too high |
| P0071 | Battery temperature sensor performance | P0133 | Upstream oxygen sensor (left cylinder bank), slow response |
| P0072 | Ambient temperature sensor circuit, low voltage | P0135 | Upstream oxygen sensor (left cylinder bank), heater failure |
| P0073 | Ambient temperature sensor circuit, high voltage | P0136 | Downstream oxygen sensor (left cylinder bank), heater circuit malfunction |
| P0106 | Manifold Absolute Pressure (MAP) sensor performance | P0137 | Downstream oxygen sensor (left cylinder bank), circuit voltage too low |
| P0107 | Manifold Absolute Pressure (MAP) sensor circuit, voltage too low | P0138 | Downstream oxygen sensor (left cylinder bank), circuit voltage too high |
| P0108 | Manifold Absolute Pressure (MAP) sensor circuit, voltage too high | P0139 | Downstream oxygen sensor (left cylinder bank), slow response |
| P0110 | Intake Air Temperature (IAT) sensor stuck | P0141 | Downstream oxygen sensor (left cylinder bank), heater failure |
| P0111 | Intake Air Temperature (IAT) sensor performance | P0151 | Upstream oxygen sensor (right cylinder bank), heater circuit low voltage |
| P0112 | Intake Air Temperature (IAT) sensor circuit, voltage too low | P0152 | Upstream oxygen sensor (right cylinder bank), circuit voltage too high |
| P0113 | Intake Air Temperature (IAT) sensor circuit, voltage too high | P0153 | Upstream oxygen sensor (right cylinder bank), slow response |
| P0116 | Engine Coolant Temperature (ECT) sensor circuit performance | | |

## OBD-II Diagnostic Trouble Codes (DTCs) - 2002 and later gasoline engines (includes transmission codes) (continued)

| Code | Probable cause | Code | Probable cause |
|------|----------------|------|----------------|
| P0155 | Upstream oxygen sensor (right cylinder bank), heater failure | P0303 | Cylinder No. 3 misfire |
| P0157 | Downstream oxygen sensor (right cylinder bank), circuit voltage too low | P0304 | Cylinder No. 4 misfire |
| | | P0305 | Cylinder No. 5 misfire |
| P0158 | Downstream oxygen sensor (right cylinder bank), circuit voltage too high | P0306 | Cylinder No. 6 misfire |
| | | P0307 | Cylinder No. 7 misfire |
| P0159 | Downstream oxygen sensor (right cylinder bank), slow response | P0308 | Cylinder No. 8 misfire |
| | | P0309 | Cylinder No. 9 misfire |
| P0161 | Downstream oxygen sensor (right cylinder bank), heater failure | P0310 | Cylinder No. 10 misfire |
| P0171 | Fuel system lean at upstream oxygen sensor (left cylinder bank) | P03165 | No crank sensor learned |
| P0172 | Fuel system rich at upstream oxygen sensor (left cylinder bank) | P0320 | No crank reference signal from the CKP sensor at the PCM |
| P0174 | Fuel system lean at upstream oxygen sensor (right cylinder bank) | P0325 | Knock sensor No. 1 circuit |
| | | P0330 | Knock sensor No. 2 circuit |
| P0175 | Fuel system rich at upstream oxygen sensor (right cylinder bank) | P0335 | Crankshaft Position (CKP) sensor circuit |
| P0201 | Fuel injector No. 1 control circuit | P0339 | Crankshaft Position (CKP) sensor intermittent |
| P0202 | Fuel injector No. 2 control circuit | P0340 | No cam reference signal from the CMP sensor at the PCM |
| P0203 | Fuel injector No. 3 control circuit | P0344 | Camshaft Position (CMP) sensor intermittent |
| P0204 | Fuel injector No. 4 control circuit | P0351 | Ignition coil No. 1 primary circuit |
| P0205 | Fuel injector No. 5 control circuit | P0352 | Ignition coil No. 2 primary circuit |
| P0206 | Fuel injector No. 6 control circuit | P0353 | Ignition coil No. 3 primary circuit |
| P0207 | Fuel injector No. 7 control circuit | P0354 | Ignition coil No. 4 primary circuit |
| P0208 | Fuel injector No. 8 control circuit | P0355 | Ignition coil No. 5 primary circuit |
| P0209 | Fuel injector No. 9 control circuit | P0356 | Ignition coil No. 6 primary circuit |
| P0210 | Fuel injector No. 10 control circuit | P0357 | Ignition coil No. 7 primary circuit |
| P0218 | High-temperature operation activated | P0358 | Ignition coil No. 8 primary circuit |
| P0221 | Throttle Position (TP) sensor No. 2, performance | P0420 | Upstream catalytic converter (left cylinder bank) efficiency |
| P0222 | Throttle Position (TP) sensor No. 2, low voltage | P0432 | Upstream catalytic converter (right cylinder bank) efficiency |
| P0223 | Throttle Position (TP) sensor No. 2, high voltage | | |
| P0300 | Multiple cylinder misfire | P0440 | General EVAP system failure |
| P0301 | Cylinder No. 1 misfire | P0441 | EVAP system purge system performance |
| P0302 | Cylinder No. 2 misfire | P0442 | EVAP system leak monitor, medium (0.40) leak detected |

| Code | Probable cause |
|------|----------------|
| P0443 | EVAP system purge solenoid circuit |
| P0452 | Natural Vacuum Leak Detection (NVLD) pressure switch stuck closed |
| P0453 | Natural Vacuum Leak Detection (NVLD) pressure switch stuck open |
| P0455 | EVAP system leak monitor, large leak detected |
| P0456 | EVAP system leak monitor, small (0.20) leak detected |
| P0460 | Fuel level sending unit, no change over miles |
| P0461 | Fuel level sending unit, no change over time |
| P0462 | Fuel level sending unit, voltage too low |
| P0463 | Fuel level sending unit, voltage too high |
| P0480 | Low-speed fan control relay circuit |
| P0498 | Natural Vacuum Leak Detection (NVLD) canister vent valve solenoid circuit low |
| P0499 | Natural Vacuum Leak Detection (NVLD) canister vent valve solenoid circuit high |
| P0500 | No vehicle speed signal |
| P0501 | Vehicle Speed Sensor (VSS) signal performance |
| P0503 | Vehicle Speed Sensor (VSS), erratic signal |
| P0505 | Idle air control motor circuit |
| P0506 | Idle speed performance lower than expected |
| P0507 | Idle speed performance higher than expected |
| P0508 | Idle Air Control (IAC) valve signal, circuit low voltage |
| P0509 | Idle Air Control (IAC) valve signal, circuit high voltage |
| P0513 | Invalid Sentry Key Immobilizer Module (SKIM) key |
| P0516 | Battery temperature sensor, low voltage |
| P0517 | Battery temperature sensor, high voltage |
| P0522 | Oil pressure circuit, low voltage |
| P0523 | Oil pressure circuit, high voltage |
| P0532 | Air conditioning pressure switch circuit, low voltage |
| P0533 | Air conditioning pressure switch circuit, high voltage |
| P0551 | Power steering switch performance |
| P0562 | Low battery voltage |
| P0563 | High battery voltage |
| P0571 | Brake switch performance |

| Code | Probable cause |
|------|----------------|
| P0572 | Brake switch, low circuit voltage |
| P0573 | Brake switch, high circuit voltage |
| P0579 | Speed control switch No. 1 performance |
| P0580 | Speed control switch No. 1, low voltage |
| P0581 | Speed control switch No. 1, high voltage |
| P0582 | Speed control vacuum solenoid circuit |
| P0585 | Speed control switch No. 1 and No. 2 correlation |
| P0586 | Speed control vent solenoid circuit |
| P0591 | Speed control switch No. 2, performance |
| P0592 | Speed control switch No. 2, low voltage |
| P0593 | Speed control switch No. 2, high voltage |
| P0594 | Speed control servo power circuit |
| P0600 | Serial communication link |
| P0601 | PCM Internal controller failure (internal memory checksum invalid) |
| P0604 | Internal Transmission Control Module (TCM) |
| P0605 | Internal Transmission Control Module (TCM) |
| P0613 | Internal Transmission Control Module (TCM) |
| P0606 | ECM/PCM processor failure |
| P0622 | Alternator field control circuit not switching correctly |
| P0627 | Fuel pump relay circuit |
| P0630 | Vehicle Identification Number (VIN) not programmed into PCM |
| P0632 | Odometer not programmed into PCM |
| P0633 | Sentry Key Immobilizer Module (SKIM) not programmed into PCM |
| P0642 | Primary 5-volt supply low |
| P0643 | Primary 5-volt supply high |
| P0645 | Air conditioning clutch relay circuit |
| P0652 | Auxiliary 5-volt supply low |
| P0653 | Auxiliary 5-volt supply high |
| P0685 | Automatic Shut Down (ASD) relay control circuit |
| P0688 | Automatic Shut Down (ASD) sense circuit, low voltage |
| P0700 | Transmission control system (MIL request) |

## OBD-II Diagnostic Trouble Codes (DTCs) -
### 2002 and later gasoline engines (includes transmission codes) (continued)

| Code | Probable cause | Code | Probable cause |
|------|----------------|------|----------------|
| P0706 | Check shifter signal | P770 | 4C solenoid circuit |
| P0711 | Transmission temperature sensor performance, no temperature increase after start-up | P0836 | 4WD MUX switch stuck |
| P0712 | Transmission temperature sensor, low voltage | P0837 | 4WD MUX switch performance |
| | | P0838 | 4WD mode sensor circuit, low voltage |
| P0713 | Transmission temperature sensor, high voltage | P0839 | 4WD mode sensor circuit, high voltage |
| P0714 | Transmission temperature sensor, intermittent voltage | P0841 | LR pressure switch sense circuit |
| P0715 | Input Speed Sensor (ISS) error | P0845 | 2C hydraulic pressure test failure |
| P0720 | Output Speed Sensor (OSS) error, low rpm above 15 mph | P0846 | 2C hydraulic pressure switch sense circuit |
| P0725 | Engine speed sensor circuit | P0850 | Park/Neutral Position (PNP) switch performance |
| P0731 | Gear ratio error in first gear | P0868 | Line pressure low |
| P0732 | Gear ratio error in second gear | P0869 | Line pressure high |
| P0733 | Gear ratio error in third gear | P0870 | Overdrive hydraulic pressure test failure |
| P0734 | Gear ratio error in fourth gear | P0871 | Overdrive pressure switch sense circuit |
| P0735 | Gear ratio error fourth prime | P0875 | UD hydraulic pressure test failure |
| P0736 | Gear ratio error in REVERSE | P0876 | UD hydraulic switch sense circuit |
| P0740 | Torque Converter Clutch (TCC) control circuit | P0884 | Power up at speed |
| P0743 | Torque Converter Clutch (TCC) solenoid/transmission relay circuits | P0888 | Relay output always off |
| P0748 | Pressure SOL control/transmission relay circuits | P0890 | Switched battery |
| | | P0891 | Transmission relay always on |
| P0750 | LR solenoid circuit | P0932 | Line pressure sensor circuit fault |
| P0751 | Overdrive switch pressed LO for more than 5 minutes | P0934 | Line pressure sensor circuit, low voltage |
| P0753 | Transmission 3-4 shift SOL/transmission relay circuits | P0935 | Line pressure sensor circuit, high voltage |
| P0755 | 2C solenoid circuit | P0944 | Loss of prime |
| P0760 | OD solenoid circuit | P0987 | 4C hydraulic pressure test failure |
| P0765 | UD solenoid circuit | P0988 | 4C pressure switch sense circuit |

## OBD-II Diagnostic Trouble Codes (DTCs) - 2003 and later diesel engines (for transmission codes, refer to gasoline engines)

| Code | Probable cause | Code | Probable cause |
|------|----------------|------|----------------|
| P0016 | Engine speed signal mismatch | P0236 | Manifold Absolute Pressure (MAP) sensor voltage too high for too long |
| P0071 | Inlet Air Temperature (IAT) sensor rationality | P0237 | Manifold Absolute Pressure (MAP) sensor circuit, voltage too low |
| P0072 | Inlet Air Temperature (IAT) sensor circuit, voltage too low | P0238 | Manifold Absolute Pressure (MAP) sensor circuit, voltage too high |
| P0073 | Inlet Air Temperature (IAT) sensor circuit, voltage too high | P0251 | CP3 pump regulator control |
| P0088 | Fuel rail pressure signal above maximum limit | P0300 | Multiple cylinder misfire |
| P0106 | Inlet air pressure sensor rationality | P0301 | Cylinder No. 1 misfire |
| P0107 | Inlet air pressure sensor circuit, voltage too low | P0302 | Cylinder No. 2 misfire |
| P0108 | Inlet air pressure sensor circuit, voltage too high | P0303 | Cylinder No. 3 misfire |
| P0111 | Intake Air Temperature (IAT) sensor rationality | P0304 | Cylinder No. 4 misfire |
| P0112 | Intake Air Temperature (IAT) sensor, voltage too low | P0305 | Cylinder No. 5 misfire |
| P0113 | Intake Air Temperature (IAT) sensor, voltage too high | P0306 | Cylinder No. 6 misfire |
| P0116 | Engine Coolant Temperature (ECT) sensor rationality | P0335 | Crankshaft Position (CKP) sensor lost |
| P0117 | Engine Coolant Temperature (ECT) sensor, voltage too low | P0336 | Crankshaft Position (CKP) sensor signal |
| P0118 | Engine Coolant Temperature (ECT) sensor, voltage too high | P0337 | Crankshaft Position (CKP) sensor circuit, voltage too low |
| P0128 | Thermostat rationality | P0338 | Crankshaft Position (CKP) sensor circuit, voltage too high |
| P0148 | High-Pressure Common Rail (HPCR) checksum | P0340 | Camshaft Position (CMP) sensor lost |
| P0169 | Water-In-Fuel (WIF) light on too long | P0341 | Camshaft Position (CMP) sensor signal |
| P0192 | Fuel pressure sensor circuit, voltage too low | P0381 | WAIT TO START light inoperative |
| P0193 | Fuel pressure sensor circuit, voltage too high | P0461 | Fuel level sending unit, no change over time |
| P0201 | Injector No. 1 control circuit | P0462 | Low voltage detected at fuel level sensor |
| P0202 | Injector No. 2 control circuit | P0463 | High voltage detected at fuel level sensor |
| P0203 | Injector No. 3 control circuit | P0477 | Low voltage on the engine brake driver |
| P0204 | Injector No. 4 control circuit | P0478 | High voltage on the engine brake driver |
| P0205 | Injector No. 5 control circuit | P0480 | Fan clutch |
| P0206 | Injector No. 6 control circuit | P0483 | Fan speed |
| P0217 | Decreased engine performance because of engine overheating condition | P0500 | No Vehicle Speed Sensor (VSS) signal |
| P0219 | Crankshaft Position (CKP) sensor over speed signal | P0514 | Battery temperature sensor rationality |
|  |  | P0516 | Low voltage at battery temperature sensor |
| P0234 | Turbocharger boost limit exceeded | P0521 | Oil pressure switch rationality |

## OBD-II Diagnostic Trouble Codes (DTCs) -
## 2003 and later diesel engines (for transmission codes, refer to gasoline engines)

| Code | Probable cause | Code | Probable cause |
|---|---|---|---|
| P0524 | Oil pressure too low | P0622 | Alternator field circuit not switching correctly |
| P0533 | Air conditioning sending unit, voltage too high | P0628 | Low voltage detected at fuel lift pump |
| P0541 | Low voltage at the No. 1 intake air heater relay | P0629 | High voltage detected at fuel lift pump |
| P0542 | High voltage at the No. 1 intake air heater relay | P0630 | Vehicle Identification Number (VIN) not entered error |
| P0562 | Battery voltage low | P0633 | Sentry Key Immobilizer Module (SKIM) secret key not entered |
| P0563 | Battery voltage high | | |
| P0572 | Low voltage detected at brake switch | P0646 | Low voltage detected at air conditioning clutch relay |
| P0573 | High voltage detected at brake switch | P0647 | High voltage detected at air conditioning clutch relay |
| P0580 | Low voltage detected at cruise control switch | P0652 | Low voltage detected at the No. 1 sensor supply circuit |
| P0581 | High voltage detected at cruise control switch | P0653 | High voltage detected at the No. 1 sensor supply circuit |
| P0602 | Check sum error | P0698 | Accelerator Pedal Position (APP) sensor, supply voltage too low |
| P0604 | Engine Control Module (ECM) software error | P0699 | Accelerator Pedal Position (APP) sensor, supply voltage too high |
| P0606 | Engine Control Module (ECM) hardware error | | |
| P0607 | Engine Control Module (ECM) internal failure | P0700 | Transmission message |

## 3  Accelerator Pedal Position Sensor (APPS) - replacement

### Hemi engine

1    Disconnect the cable from the negative terminal of the battery (see Chapter 5). Working inside the vehicle, disconnect the APPS cable from the accelerator pedal and detach it from the firewall (see Chapter 4A Section 11).

2    Loosen the lug nuts for the left front wheel. Raise the front of the vehicle and place it securely on jackstands. Remove the left front wheel.

3    Remove the left inner fender panel (see Chapter 11).

4    To access the APPS electrical connector open the swing-down door on the APPS assembly (see illustration).

**3.4 To access the APPS electrical connector, open the swing-down door on the APPS assembly**

**3.6 To detach the APPS assembly from the underside of the left battery tray, remove these three screws**

**3.7 To detach the accelerator cable from the APPS assembly, push this locking tab to the rear with a small screwdriver, then slide the cable housing out of its slot in the APPS housing**

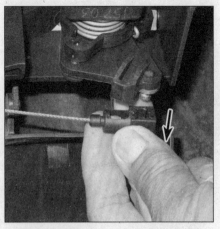

**3.8 To disconnect the accelerator cable clip from the ball socket on the APPS lever arm, simply pull it straight down with your fingers (it's not necessary to pry off the clip with a screwdriver)**

5    Disconnect the APPS electrical connector.

6    Remove the three APPS mounting screws (see illustration) and pull down the APPS assembly to access the cable.

7    Detach the cable housing from the APPS housing (see illustration).

8    Disconnect the clip on the end of the cable from the ball socket on the APPS lever arm (see illustration).

9    Installation is the reverse of removal.

10   When you're done be sure to perform the following procedure to enable the PCM to learn the electrical parameters of the APPS (if you don't do this step, the PCM will set a Diagnostic Trouble Code for the APPS):
Connect the cable to the negative battery terminal.

a)  *Turn the ignition switch to On, but do not start the engine (do not turn the ignition switch to Start).*

b)  *Leave the ignition switch turned to On for at least 10 seconds.*

c)  *If the PCM sets any diagnostic trouble codes, you'll have to erase them with a scan tool. Some generic scan tools can perform this function. Others cannot. If you don't have a scan tool, or your scan tool is unable to erase DTCs, have them erased at a dealer service department or other qualified repair shop.*

## Diesel engines

### 1999 through 2002 models and early 2003 models

11   The APPS is located at the throttle lever, under a plastic cover. The APPS assembly consists of the throttle lever, the mounting bracket and the actual sensor, all of which is replaced as a single assembly.

12   Disconnect the cables from both negative battery terminals (see Chapter 5).

13   Remove the cable cover. The cable cover is retained by two Phillips screws, two plastic retention clips and two push tabs. First, remove the two Phillips screws and carefully pry out the two plastic retention clips, then push the front tab to the rear and push the lower tab upward to remove the cover.

14   Disconnect the end of the speed control servo cable from the throttle lever pin. To disconnect the speed control servo cable from the throttle lever pin, pull forward on the connector while holding the lever to the rear.
**Caution:** *Do NOT try to pull the connector off perpendicular to the lever pin. Doing so will break the connector.*

15   Using two small screwdrivers pry the throttle cable connector socket from the throttle lever ball.

16   Disconnect the transmission control cable, if applicable, from the lever arm.

17   Squeeze the pinch tabs on the speed control cable and pull the cable to the rear to disengage it from the mounting bracket.

18   Squeeze the pinch tabs on the throttle cable and pull the cable to the rear to disengage it from the mounting bracket.

19   If the vehicle is equipped with an automatic transmission, remove the transmission control cable (see Chapter 7B).

20   Detach the wiring harness clip from the bottom of the bracket.

21   Remove the six APPS mounting bolts and partially remove the APPS assembly to access the electrical connector.

22   Disconnect the electrical connector from the bottom of the APPS sensor by pushing on the connector release tab.

23   Remove the APPS.

24   Installation is the reverse of removal.

### Late 2003 models and 2004 and later models

25   The APPS is located under the left battery tray. It's identical to the APPS used on Hemi vehicles (see steps 1 through 10).

## 4    Camshaft Position (CMP) sensor - replacement

1    Disconnect the cable(s) from the negative battery terminal(s) (see Chapter 5).

### 3.7L V6 and 4.7L V8 engines

**Note:** *The CMP sensor is located on the outer side of the front end of the right cylinder head, just ahead of the exhaust manifold.*

2    Raise the front end of the vehicle and place it securely on jackstands.

3    Disconnect the electrical connector from the CMP sensor (see illustrations).

4    Remove the sensor mounting bolt and remove the CMP sensor.

5    Inspect the CMP sensor O-ring for cracks, tears and other deterioration. If it's damaged, replace it.

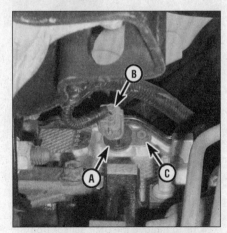

**4.3a To detach the CMP sensor (A) from a 3.7L V6 engine, disconnect the electrical connector (B) and remove the sensor mounting bolt (C) (as seen from underneath the engine)**

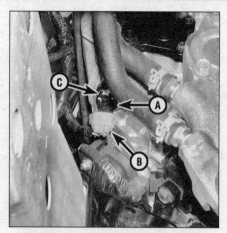

**4.3b To detach the CMP sensor (A) from a 4.7L V8 engine, disconnect the electrical connector (B) and remove the sensor mounting bolt (C) (as seen from underneath the engine)**

**4.9 To detach the CMP sensor from the timing chain cover on a Hemi engine, disconnect the electrical connector and remove the sensor mounting bolt**

**4.11 Remove the old CMP sensor O-ring and inspect it for cracks, tears and deterioration. If it's damaged, replace it**

6    When installing the CMP sensor, apply a small dab of clean engine oil to the sensor O-ring, then use a slight rocking motion to work the O-ring into the sensor mounting bore. Do not use a twisting motion or you will damage the O-ring.

7    Make sure that the CMP sensor mounting flange is fully seated flat against the mounting surface around the sensor mounting hole.

**Caution:** *If the CMP sensor is not fully seated against its mounting surface, the sensor mounting tang will be damaged when the sensor mounting bolt is tightened to the specified torque.*

8    Installation is otherwise the reverse of removal. Be sure to tighten the CMP sensor mounting bolt to the torque listed in this Chapter's Specifications.

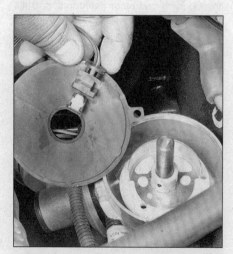

**4.18 To remove the CMP sensor from the distributor, simply disconnect the electrical connector, then carefully lift out the sensor assembly - V8 models shown, V6 models similar**

### 5.7L V8 (Hemi) engine

**Note:** *The CMP sensor is located on the upper right side of the timing chain cover.*

9    Disconnect the electrical connector from the CMP sensor (see illustration).

10    Remove the CMP sensor mounting bolt and remove the CMP sensor from the timing chain cover.

11    Remove the old CMP sensor O-ring (see illustration) and inspect it for cracks, tears and deterioration. If the old O-ring is damaged, replace it.

12    When installing the CMP sensor, apply a small dab of clean engine oil to the sensor O-ring, then use a slight rocking motion to work the O-ring into the sensor mounting bore. Do NOT use a twisting motion or you will damage the O-ring.

13    Make sure that the CMP sensor mounting flange is fully seated flat against the mounting surface around the sensor mounting hole.

**Caution:** *If the CMP sensor is not fully seated against its mounting surface, the sensor mounting tang will be damaged when the sensor mounting bolt is tightened to the specified torque.*

14    Installation is otherwise the reverse of removal. Be sure to tighten the CMP sensor mounting bolt to the torque listed in this Chapter's Specifications.

### 3.9L V6, 5.2L and 5.9L V8 engine

**Note:** *The CMP sensor is located inside of the distributor.*

15    Remove the air intake duct (see Air filter housing, air intake duct and resonator box - removal and installation in Chapter 4A).

16    Remove the distributor cap and rotor from the distributor (see Chapter 1).

17    Disconnect the CMP sensor electrical connector.

18    Remove the CMP sensor from the dis-

tributor (see illustration).

19    When installing the CMP sensor be sure align the tab on the CMP sensor with the notch in the distributor housing.

20    Installation is otherwise the reverse of removal.

### V10 engine

**Note:** *The CMP sensor is located on the left side of the timing chain cover.*

21    Disconnect the cable from the negative terminal of the battery (see Chapter 5).

22    Disconnect the electrical connector from the sensor.

23    Remove the bolt from the camshaft sensor and lift the sensor from the timing chain cover.

24    Installation is the reverse of removal. Be sure to install the paper spacer (which should come with the new sensor) onto the tip of the camshaft sensor and tighten the camshaft sensor bolt to the torque listed in this Chapter's Specifications.

**Caution:** *On 2006 and later models, the camshaft sprocket has a low area machined into its hub - the sensor must not be installed with this area of the sprocket positioned at the sensor mounting hole. Measure the distance from the mounting hole surface to the camshaft sprocket; if the depth to the sprocket approximately 1-13/16 inches, the sensor can be installed. If the depth is approximately 2-1/64 inches, the engine will have to be rotated until the depth measures 1-13/16 inches (otherwise the sensor will break when the engine is started).*

**Note:** *The paper spacer sets the gap between the sensor and the camshaft sprocket.*

### Diesel engine

**Note:** *The CMP sensor is located on the left backside of the timing gear cover.*

25    Disconnect the electrical connector from the CMP sensor (see illustration).

26    As you can see, the CMP sensor is very

4.25 To remove the CMP sensor from the backside of the timing gear cover on diesel engines, disconnect the electrical connector, remove the sensor mounting bolt and pull the sensor out of the timing cover

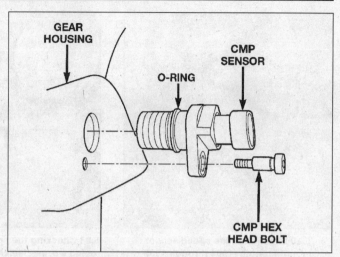

4.27 1999 and later CMP sensor assembly details

difficult to reach! You might want to unbolt the power steering pump mounting bracket (see Chapter 10) for better access.

27   Remove the CMP sensor mounting bolt and remove the CMP sensor from its mounting hole (see illustration).

28   Remove the CMP sensor O-ring and inspect it for cracks, tears and deterioration. If it's damaged, replace it.

29   Clean out the CMP sensor mounting hole.

30   Apply a small dab of clean engine oil on the CMP sensor O-ring, then install the sensor using a slight rocking (side-to-side) motion. Do not twist the sensor into position or you will damage the O-ring.

31   The remainder of installation is the reverse of removal.

## 5   Crankshaft Position (CKP) sensor - replacement

1   Disconnect the cable(s) from the negative battery terminal(s) (see Chapter 5).

### 3.7L V6, 4.7L V8 and Hemi engines

**Note:** *The CKP sensor is located on the right rear side of the engine block.*

2   Raise the front end of the vehicle and place it securely on jackstands.

3   Disconnect the electrical connector from the CKP sensor (see illustrations).

4   Remove the CKP sensor mounting bolt and remove the sensor from the engine.

5   Remove the CKP sensor O-ring and inspect it for cracks, tears and deterioration. If

it's damaged, replace it.

6   Apply a small amount of engine oil on the O-ring and, using a slight rocking motion, push the sensor into its mounting hole in the engine block until the sensor is fully seated.

7   Installation is otherwise the reverse of removal.

### 3.9L V6, 5.2L V8 and 5.9L V8 engine

**Note:** *The CKP sensor is located at the rear of the engine, adjacent to the starter ring gear on the flywheel.*

8   Disconnect the CKP sensor electrical connector from the main engine harness.

9   Remove the two sensor mounting bolts (recessed hex heads) and remove the sensor.

10   Installation is the reverse of removal.

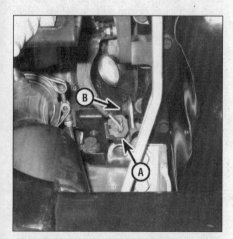

5.3a To detach the CKP sensor from the block on a 3.7L V6 engine, disconnect the electrical connector (A) and remove the sensor mounting bolt (B)

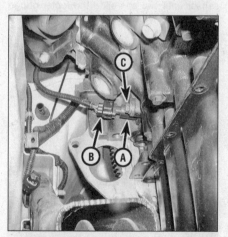

5.3b To detach the CKP sensor (A) from the block on a 4.7L V8 engine, disconnect the electrical connector (B) and remove the sensor mounting bolt (C)

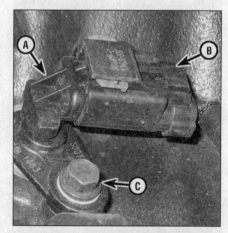

5.3c To detach the CKP sensor (A) from the (right-rear side of the) block on a Hemi engine, disconnect the electrical connector (B) and remove the sensor mounting bolt (C)

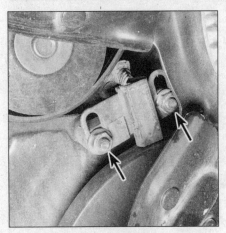

**5.20 Location of the speed sensor mounting nuts (1994 through 1998 diesel engines)**

**5.23 Checking the speed sensor clearance using a brass feeler gauge (1994 through 1998 diesel engines)**

**5.27 To detach the CKP sensor from a 1999 or later diesel engine, disconnect the electrical connector and remove the sensor mounting bolt**

## 8.0L V10 engine

**Note:** *The CKP sensor is located on the lower right side of the block, ahead of the right engine mount, right above the oil pan.*

11    Raise the front of the vehicle and place it securely on jackstands.

12    Cut the cable tie that secures the CKP sensor electrical lead to the main engine wiring harness, then disconnect the CKP sensor electrical connector from the main harness.

13    Remove the CKP sensor mounting bolt.

14    Carefully pry the CKP sensor from the block with a couple of small screwdrivers.

15    Remove the old CKP sensor O-ring and inspect it for cracks, tears and deterioration. If it's damaged, replace it.

16    Apply a small amount of engine oil on the O-ring and, using a slight rocking motion, push the sensor into its mounting hole in the engine block until the sensor is fully seated.

17    Installation is otherwise the reverse of removal.

18    When you're done, be sure to secure the CKP sensor electrical lead to the main engine wiring harness with a new cable tie.

## Diesel engine

### Crankshaft position sensor (1994 through 1996 models)/engine speed sensor (1997 and 1998 models)

19    The crankshaft position sensor/engine speed sensor is located on the front of the engine, between the water pump pulley and the crankshaft pulley. Disconnect the sensor electrical connector.

20    Remove the nuts that retain the sensor to the timing gear cover studs (see illustration).

21    Install the new sensor. Install the mounting spacers from the old sensor and tighten the nuts finger-tight.

22    Route the sensor wiring harness behind the pulleys and tighten the harness clips to the engine.

23    Adjust the sensor-to-damper clearance with a 0.050-inch brass feeler gauge positioned between the sensor and the vibration damper (see illustration). Gently position the sensor until you can slide the feeler gauge between the sensor and vibration damper

with a slight amount of drag.

24    Tighten the sensor mounting nuts to the torque listed in this Chapter's Specifications.

25    Remove the feeler gauge and connect the speed sensor electrical connector.

### 1999 and later models

**Note:** *The CKP sensor is located on the front left side of the engine, next to the crankshaft pulley.*

26    Raise the front of the vehicle and support it securely on jackstands.

27    Disconnect the electrical connector from the CKP sensor (see illustration).

28    Remove the CKP sensor mounting bolt and remove the CKP sensor.

29    Remove and inspect the old sensor O-ring. If it's cracked, torn or deteriorated, replace it.

30    Before installing the CKP sensor, clean out the sensor's mounting hole and apply a little clean engine oil to the sensor O-ring.

31    Install the CKP sensor using a slight rocking motion. Make sure that the sensor is flush with its mounting surface before installing and tightening the sensor mounting bolt to the torque listed in this Chapter's Specifications.

32    Installation is otherwise the reverse of removal.

---

## 6    Engine Coolant Temperature (ECT) sensor - replacement

---

1    Partially drain the cooling system (see Chapter 1).

2    Disconnect the cable(s) from the negative battery terminal(s) (see Chapter 5).

## 3.7L V6 and 4.7L V8 engines

**Note:** *The ECT sensor is located at the front of the intake manifold.*

3    Disconnect the electrical connector from the ECT sensor (see illustrations).

4    Using a deep socket, carefully unscrew

**6.3a To remove the ECT sensor from the intake manifold on a 3.7L V6 engine, disconnect the electrical connector (A) and unscrew the sensor (B) from the manifold**

**6.3b To remove the ECT sensor from the intake manifold on a 4.7L V8 engine, disconnect the electrical connector and unscrew the sensor from the manifold**

**6.5 Before installing the ECT sensor, be sure to wrap the threads of the sensor with Teflon tape to prevent leaks**

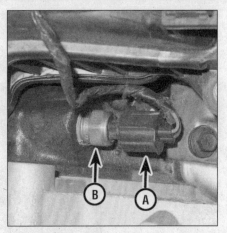

**6.10 To remove the ECT sensor from the intake manifold on a Hemi engine, disconnect the electrical connector (A) and unscrew the sensor (B) from the manifold**

**6.16 Use an end-wrench to remove the Engine Coolant Temperature sensor from the intake manifold (V8 engine shown, V6 similar)**

the ECT sensor from the intake manifold.

5    To prevent leakage and thread corrosion, wrap the threads of the ECT sensor with Teflon sealing tape (see illustration) before installing the sensor. (Seal the sensor threads whether you're installing the old sensor or a new unit.)

6    Installation is otherwise the reverse of removal. Be sure to tighten the ECT sensor to the torque listed in this Chapter's Specifications.

7    Refill the cooling system (see Chapter 1).

## Hemi engine

**Note:** *The ECT sensor is located at the front of the engine block, under the air conditioning compressor.*

8    Remove the drivebelt (see Chapter 1).

9    To access the ECT sensor, you'll need to unbolt the air conditioning compressor from the engine (see Chapter 3). It is NOT necessary to disconnect any air conditioning hoses from the compressor. Set the compressor aside and support it with a bungee cord or a

**6.25 ECT sensor location - diesel engine**

piece of wire.

10    Disconnect the electrical connector from the ECT sensor (see illustration).

11    Using a deep socket, carefully unscrew the ECT sensor from the intake manifold.

12    To prevent leakage and thread corrosion, wrap the threads of the ECT sensor with Teflon sealing tape (see illustration 6.5) before installing the sensor. (Seal the sensor threads whether you're installing the old sensor or a new unit.)

13    Installation is otherwise the reverse of removal. Be sure to tighten the ECT sensor to the torque listed in this Chapter's Specifications.

14    When you're done, be sure to refill the cooling system (see Chapter 1).

## 3.9L V6, 5.2L and 5.9L V8 engine

**Note:** *The ECT sensor is located at the front of the intake manifold.*

15    Disconnect the electrical connector from the ECT sensor.

16    Unscrew the ECT sensor from the intake

manifold (see illustration).

17    To prevent leakage and thread corrosion, wrap the threads of the ECT sensor with Teflon sealing tape before installing the sensor. (Seal the sensor threads whether you're installing the old sensor or a new unit.)

18    Installation is otherwise the reverse of removal. Be sure to tighten the ECT sensor to the torque listed in this Chapter's Specifications.

19    When you're done, be sure to refill cooling system (see Chapter 1).

## 8.0L V10 engine

**Note:** *The ECT sensor is located on the thermostat housing.*

20    Disconnect the electrical connector from the ECT sensor.

21    Unscrew the ECT sensor from the intake manifold.

22    To prevent leakage and thread corrosion, wrap the threads of the ECT sensor with Teflon® sealing tape (see illustration 6.5) before installing the sensor. (Seal the sensor threads whether you're installing the old sensor or a new unit.)

23    Installation is otherwise the reverse of removal. Be sure to tighten the ECT sensor to the torque listed in this Chapter's Specifications.

24    When you're done, be sure to refill cooling system (see Chapter 1).

## Diesel engine

**Note:** *The ECT sensor is located at the right front corner of the cylinder head, near the thermostat housing.*

25    Disconnect the electrical connector from the ECT sensor (see illustration).

26    Unscrew the ECT sensor from the cylinder head and then discard the O-ring, if equipped.

27    On models without an O-ring, to prevent leakage and thread corrosion, wrap the threads of the ECT sensor with Teflon® seal-

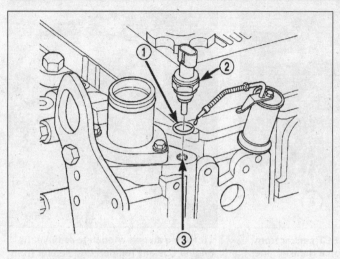

**6.28 Installation details of the ECT sensor assembly
(1999 and later diesel models)**

1    O-ring                    3    Mounting hole
2    ECT sensor

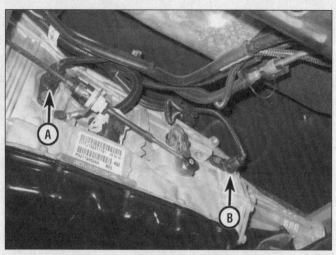

**7.3 The ISS sensor (A) and OSS sensor (B) are located on the left
side of 45RFE and 545RFE automatic transmissions**

ing tape (see illustration 6.5) before installing the sensor. (Seal the sensor threads whether you're installing the old sensor or a new unit.)

28    On models with an O-ring replace the O-ring and apply a small amount of oil to the O-ring (see illustration).

29    Installation is otherwise the reverse of removal. Be sure to tighten the ECT sensor to the torque listed in this Chapter's Specifications.

30    When you're done, be sure to refill the cooling system (see Chapter 1).

### 7    Input Shaft Speed (ISS) and Output Shaft Speed (OSS) sensors - replacement

**Note:** *ISS and OSS sensors are located on the left side of the transmission. They're used*

*only on 45RFE and 545RFE automatic transmissions.*

1    Disconnect the cable(s) from the negative battery terminal(s) (see Chapter 5).

2    Raise the vehicle and place it securely on jackstands.

3    The ISS and OSS sensors (see illustration) are identical in appearance (and are replaced exactly the same way), so make sure that you've correctly identified the sensor that you wish to replace.

4    Disconnect the electrical connector from the ISS or OSS sensor (see illustration).

5    Place a drain pan underneath the sensor that you're going to replace. Remove the sensor mounting bolt and pull out the sensor.

6    Installation is the reverse of removal.

7    When you're done, check the transmission fluid level (see Chapter 1) and add fluid as necessary.

### 8    Intake Air Temperature (IAT) sensor - replacement

1    Disconnect the cable(s) from the negative battery terminal(s) (see Chapter 5).

### 3.7L V6, 4.7L V8 and Hemi engines

**Note:** *On 3.7L V6 and 4.7L V8 engines, the IAT sensor is located on the left side of the intake manifold. On Hemi engines the IAT sensor is located at the right front corner of the air resonator box.*

2    Disconnect the electrical connector from the IAT sensor (see illustrations).

3    To remove the IAT sensor, lift up the release tab (see illustration) slightly, then turn the sensor 1/4-turn to the left and pull it out.

4    Remove the old O-ring from the IAT sen-

**7.4 To remove an ISS or OSS sensor from the transmission, disconnect the electrical connector (1), then remove the sensor mounting bolt (2)**

**8.2a On 3.7L V6 engines, the IAT sensor (A) is located on the left side of the intake manifold. The MAP sensor (B) is located at the front of the intake manifold**

**8.2b On 4.7L V8 engines the IAT sensor is also located on the left side of the intake manifold**

8.2c On Hemi engines the IAT sensor is located at the right front corner of the air resonator box

8.2d To disconnect the electrical connector from an IAT sensor, depress this tab and pull off the connector (IAT sensor on Hemi engine shown, IAT sensor connectors on 3.7L V6 and 4.7L V8 are disconnected in a similar fashion)

8.3 To remove the IAT sensor, lift up the release tab slightly and rotate the sensor counterclockwise 1/4-turn and pull it out (IAT sensor on Hemi engine shown, 3.7L V6 and 4.7L V8 sensors are removed in a similar fashion)

sor (see illustration) and inspect it for cracks, tears and deterioration. If the O-ring is damaged, replace it.

5    To install the IAT sensor, insert it into its mounting hole and rotate it clockwise 1/4-turn. Make sure that the release tab locks the sensor into place. Installation is otherwise the reverse of removal.

### 3.9L V6, 5.2L V8 and 5.9L V8 engines

**Note:** *The IAT sensor is located at the front of the intake manifold.*

6    Disconnect the electrical connector from the IAT sensor (see illustration).

7    Unscrew the IAT sensor from the intake manifold.

8    Installation is the reverse of removal.

### 8.0L V10 engine

**Note:** *The IAT sensor is located on the left side of the intake manifold, ahead of the throttle body.*

9    Disconnect the electrical connector from the IAT sensor.

10    Unscrew the IAT sensor from the intake manifold.

11    Installation is the reverse of removal.

### Diesel engine

#### 2002 and earlier models

#### Intake Air Temperature (IAT) sensor

**Note:** *The IAT sensor is located on the left rear side of the intake manifold, to the right of the MAP sensor.*

12    Disconnect the electrical connector from the IAT sensor.

13    Unscrew the IAT sensor from the intake manifold (see illustration).

14    Remove and inspect the old sensor O-ring. If it's cracked, torn or deteriorated, replace it.

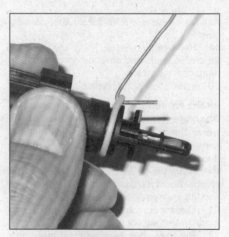

8.4 Be sure to remove the O-ring from the IAT sensor and inspect it for cracks, tears and deterioration. If the O-ring is damaged, replace it

8.6 To remove the IAT sensor from the intake manifold on V6 or V8 engine, disconnect the electrical connector and unscrew the sensor from the manifold

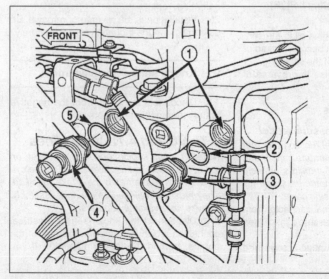

8.13 Intake Air Temperature (IAT) sensor electrical connector terminal guide (2002 and earlier diesel models)

1   *Sensor mounting holes*
2   *IAT sensor O-ring*
3   *IAT sensor*
4   *MAP sensor*
5   *MAP sensor O-ring*

**8.17 To remove the inlet air temperature sensor from the air filter housing cover on a diesel engine, disconnect the electrical connector and remove the two sensor mounting screws**

**9.9 To detach a knock sensor from the block on a Hemi engine, disconnect the electrical connector (A) and remove the knock sensor mounting bolt (B)**

15   Apply a little clean engine oil to the sensor O-ring so that it doesn't become kinked or twisted during installation of the sensor.
16   Installation is otherwise the reverse of removal.

## 2003 and later models

### Inlet air temperature/pressure sensor
**Note:** *This sensor is a dual-function unit that serves as the inlet air temperature sensor and as the pressure sensor. It monitors ambient air temperature and barometric pressure. It's located on the air filter housing cover.*
17   Disconnect the electrical connector from the inlet air temperature/pressure sensor (see illustration).
18   Remove the two mounting screws and

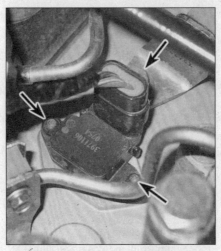

**8.21 To remove the IAT/MAP sensor from the top of the intake manifold on a diesel engine, disconnect the electrical connector and remove the two Torx mounting screws**

remove the sensor from the air filter housing cover.
19   Remove the sensor O-ring and inspect it for cracks, tears and other deterioration. If it's damaged, replace it.
20   Installation is the reverse of removal.

### Intake Air Temperature/Manifold Absolute Pressure (IAT/MAP) sensor
**Note:** *This sensor is a dual-function unit that serves as the intake air temperature sensor and as the manifold absolute pressure sensor. It monitors the air temperature and the turbocharger boost pressure inside the intake manifold. It's located on top of the intake manifold.*
21   Disconnect the electrical connector from the IAT/MAP sensor (see illustration).
22   Remove the two sensor mounting screws.
23   Remove the IAT/MAP sensor from the intake manifold.
24   Remove the sensor O-ring and inspect it for cracks, tears and other deterioration. If it's damaged, replace it.
25   Installation is the reverse of removal. Be sure to tighten the mounting screws securely.

## 9   Knock sensor - replacement

1   Disconnect the cable from the negative battery terminal (see Chapter 5).

### *3.7L V6 and 4.7L V8 engines*
**Note:** *The two knock sensors are located on top of the block, in the valley between the cylinder heads, underneath the intake manifold. They must be replaced as a single assembly. They're not available separately.*
2   Disconnect the knock sensor electrical connector, which is located at the rear of the engine, behind the intake manifold. (If you

can't find the knock sensor electrical connector, wait until you have removed the intake manifold. Then locate the two knock sensors and trace their leads back to this common connector.)
3   Remove the intake manifold (see Chapter 2A).
4   Remove the knock sensor mounting bolts and remove the knock sensor assembly.
**Note:** *The foam strips on the knock sensor mounting bolt threads are used to retain the bolts during vehicle assembly at the manufacturing plant. They have no other purpose. They are not some form of adhesive, thread sealant or locking compound. Do NOT use any type of adhesive, thread sealant or locking compound when installing these bolts again.*
5   Make sure that the holes for the knock sensor mounting bolts are thoroughly cleaned before installing the knock sensor mounting bolts.
6   Note that the left knock sensor is identified by an identification tag (Left) and that it has a larger mounting bolt. Do not switch the knock sensors, i.e., do not install the left knock sensor in the right sensor mounting position and vice versa. The PCM assumes that the knock sensors are installed in their correct locations.
**Caution:** *Switching the sensor locations will confuse the PCM and cause it to set a Diagnostic Trouble Code.*
7   Installation is otherwise the reverse of removal. Be sure to tighten the knock sensor mounting bolts to the torque listed in this Chapter's Specifications.
**Caution:** *Over- or under-tightening the knock sensor mounting bolts will affect knock sensor performance, which might affect the PCM's spark control ability.*

### *Hemi engine*
**Note:** There are two knock sensors. One is located on the left side of the block, below the exhaust manifold, and the other is located in the same place on the right side of the block.
8   Raise the front of the vehicle and place it securely on jackstands.
9   Disconnect the electrical connector from the knock sensor (see illustration).
10   Remove the knock sensor mounting bolt and remove the knock sensor from the engine.
**Note:** *The foam strips on the knock sensor mounting bolt threads are used to retain the bolts during vehicle assembly at the manufacturing plant. They have no other purpose. They are not some form of adhesive, thread sealant or locking compound. Do not use any type of adhesive, thread sealant or locking compound when installing these bolts again.*
11   Installation is the reverse of removal. Be sure to tighten the knock sensor mounting bolts to the torque listed in this Chapter's Specifications.
**Caution:** *Over- or under-tightening the knock sensor mounting bolts will affect knock sensor performance, which might affect the PCM's spark control ability.*

10.2 On 4.7L V8 engines the MAP sensor is located on the front of the intake manifold (3.7L V6 similar)

10.6 To disconnect the electrical connector from the MAP sensor on a Hemi engine, slide the release lock (1) away from the sensor (toward the harness), then depress the release tab (2) and pull off the connector

10.7 To remove the MAP sensor from the intake manifold, rotate it 1/4-turn counterclockwise and pull it out of its mounting hole. Be sure to remove and inspect the MAP sensor O-ring

## 10  Manifold Absolute Pressure (MAP) sensor - replacement

1    Disconnect the cable(s) from the negative battery terminal(s) (see Chapter 5).

### 3.7L V6 and 4.7L V8 engines

**Note:** *The MAP sensor is located on the front of the intake manifold.*

2    Disconnect the electrical connector from the MAP sensor (see illustration).
3    Remove the two MAP sensor mounting screws and remove the MAP sensor from the intake manifold.
4    Remove the MAP sensor O-ring and inspect it for cracks, tears and deterioration. If the O-ring is damaged, replace it.
5    Installation is the reverse of removal.

### Hemi engine

**Note:** *The MAP sensor is located on the front of the intake manifold.*

6    Disconnect the electrical connector from the MAP sensor (see illustration).
7    Remove the MAP sensor from the intake manifold (see illustration).
8    Remove the old MAP sensor O-ring (see illustration 10.7) and inspect it for cracks and deterioration. If it's damaged, replace it.
9    To install the MAP sensor, place it in position, insert it into the mounting hole in the intake manifold and turn it 1/4-turn clockwise.
10    Installation is otherwise the reverse of removal.

### 3.9L V6, 5.2L V8 and 5.9L V8 engine

**Note:** *The MAP sensor is located on the front of the throttle body.*

11    Disconnect the electrical connector from the MAP sensor.
12    Remove the MAP sensor mounting screws, disconnect the rubber elbow fitting from the throttle body (see illustration) and remove the MAP sensor.
13    Remove the rubber elbow from the MAP sensor and inspect it for cracks, tears and deterioration. If it's damaged, replace it.
14    Installation is the reverse of removal.

### 8.0L V10 engine

**Note:** *The MAP sensor is located on the upper right side of the intake manifold.*

15    Disconnect the electrical connector from the MAP sensor.
16    Remove the two MAP sensor mounting bolts and remove the MAP sensor from the intake manifold.
17    The MAP sensor is sealed by a permanent rubber gasket, i.e., it cannot be removed from the sensor. Inspect the rubber gasket for cracks, tears and deterioration. If it's damaged, replace the MAP sensor.
18    If the MAP sensor's rubber gasket is in good condition, lubricate it with a little clean engine oil.
19    Installation is the reverse of removal. Be sure to tighten the MAP sensor mounting bolts to the torque listed in this Chapter's Specifications.

### Diesel engine
#### 2002 and earlier models

20    Unplug the electrical connector from the CKP sensor.
21    Unscrew and remove the MAP sensor and then discard the old O-ring (see illustration 8.13).
22    Installation is the reverse of removal. Be sure to use a new O-ring and apply engine oil to the O-ring before installing the MAP sensor. Tighten the MAP sensor to the torque listed in this Chapter's Specifications.

#### 2003 and later models

**Note:** *The MAP sensor is located on top of the intake manifold.*

10.12 To detach the MAP sensor from the throttle body, remove the two mounting screws (1) and disconnect the rubber elbow (2) from the throttle body

23    The MAP sensor is one-half of the dual-function Intake Air Temperature/Manifold Absolute Pressure (IAT/MAP) sensor. The replacement procedure is in Section 8.

## 11  Oxygen sensors - general description and replacement

### General description

1    The oxygen in the exhaust reacts with the elements inside the oxygen sensor to produce a voltage output that varies from 0.1 volt (high oxygen, lean mixture) to 0.9 volt (low oxygen, rich mixture). The pre-converter oxygen sensor (mounted in the exhaust system before the catalytic converter) provides a feedback signal to the PCM that indicates the amount of leftover oxygen in the exhaust. The PCM monitors this variable voltage continuously

**11.8a The upstream oxygen sensor is located ahead of the catalytic converter. To find the electrical connector, trace the electrical lead from the sensor to the connector and disconnect it (Hemi exhaust system shown, other models similar)**

**11.8b The downstream oxygen sensor (not visible in this photo, but shown in the next photo) is located behind the catalyst. First, disconnect the electrical connector, then trace the lead up to the sensor**

**11.9 Remove an oxygen sensor with a wrench if you can (this is the downstream sensor). If there's not enough room for a wrench you might have to use an oxygen sensor socket (available at most auto parts stores)**

tinuously to determine the required fuel injector pulse width and to control the engine air/fuel ratio. A mixture ratio of 14.7 parts air to 1 part fuel is the ideal ratio for minimum exhaust emissions, as well as the best combination for fuel economy and engine performance. Based on oxygen sensor signals, the PCM tries to maintain this air/fuel ratio of 14.7:1 at all times.

2    The post-converter oxygen sensor (mounted in the exhaust system after the catalytic converter) has no effect on PCM control of the air/fuel ratio. However, the post-converter sensor is identical to the pre-converter sensor and operates in the same way. The PCM uses the post-converter signal to monitor the efficiency of the catalytic converter. A post-converter oxygen sensor will produce a slower fluctuating voltage signal that reflects the lower oxygen content in the post-catalyst exhaust.

3    Oxygen sensor configuration varies depending on the model and on where it is sold, i.e., "Federal" (49-State) model or "California" model. On vehicles equipped with the Federal (49-State) emissions package and on some California models, there is one upstream and one downstream oxygen sensor. On these vehicles, the upstream oxygen sensor is located in the exhaust pipe ahead of the catalyst and the downstream sensor is located on the pipe behind the catalyst. On some vehicles equipped with the California emissions package (those with two catalysts, one for each cylinder bank) there are two upstream sensors (one in each exhaust pipe between the exhaust manifold and the catalyst) and two downstream sensors (one behind each catalyst).

4    An oxygen sensor produces no voltage when it is below its normal operating temperature of about 600-degrees F. During this warm-up period, the PCM operates in an open-loop fuel control mode. It does not use the oxygen sensor signal as a feedback

indication of residual oxygen in the exhaust. Instead, the PCM controls fuel metering based on the inputs of other sensors and its own programs.

5    An oxygen sensor depends on four conditions in order to operate correctly:
**Electrical** - The low voltage generated by the sensor requires good, clean connections. Always check the connectors whenever an oxygen sensor problem is suspected or indicated.
**Outside air supply** - The sensor needs air circulation to the internal portion of the sensor. Whenever the sensor is installed, make sure that the air passages are not restricted.
**Correct operating temperature** - The PCM will not react to the sensor signal until the sensor reaches approximately 600-degrees F. This factor must be considered when evaluating the performance of the sensor.
**Unleaded fuel** - Unleaded fuel is essential for correct sensor operation.

6    The PCM can detect several different oxygen sensor problems and set Diagnostic Trouble Codes (DTCs) to indicate the specific fault (see Section 2). When an oxygen sensor DTC occurs, the PCM disregards the oxygen sensor signal voltage and reverts to open-loop fuel control as described previously.

### Replacement

**Warning:** *Be careful not to burn yourself during the following procedure.*
**Note:** *Since the exhaust pipe contracts when cool, the oxygen sensor may be hard to loosen. To make sensor removal easier, start the engine and let it run for a minute or two, then turn it off.*

7    Raise the vehicle and place it securely on jackstands.

8    Locate the upstream or downstream oxygen sensor (see illustrations), trace the sensor's electrical lead to the sensor electrical connector and disconnect it.

9    Remove the upstream or downstream oxygen sensor. On some models you can

remove the sensor with a wrench (see illustration). On others, you will have to use an oxygen sensor socket (available at most auto parts stores).

10    Clean the threads inside the sensor mounting hole in the exhaust pipe with an appropriate tap.

11    If you're installing the old sensor, clean off the threads, then apply a coat of anti-seize compound to the threads before installing the sensor. If you're installing a new sensor, do NOT apply anti-seize compound; new sensors are already coated with anti-seize.

12    Installation is otherwise the reverse of removal. Be sure to tighten the oxygen sensor to the torque listed in this Chapter's Specifications.

---

### 12    Throttle Position (TP) sensor - replacement

---

1    Disconnect the cable(s) from the negative battery terminal(s) (see Chapter 5).

### 3.7L V6 and 4.7L V8 engines

**Note:** *This procedure applies to 2006 and earlier models only. On later models the TP sensor is an integral part of the throttle body.*

2    Remove the air intake duct and the air resonator box (see Chapter 4A).

3    Disconnect the electrical connector from the TP sensor (see illustration), remove the TP sensor mounting screws and remove the TP sensor from the throttle body.

4    When installing the TP sensor on the throttle body, align the sensor so that the locating tangs on the backside of the TP sensor fit over each side of the flat end of the throttle shaft (see illustration). If the sensor fits flush against the throttle body and you're able to rotate the TP sensor a few degrees in order to align the sensor mounting holes with the mounting holes in the throttle body, then you've installed the sensor correctly. If

**12.3 Locations of the TP sensor (A) and IAC motor (B) on 3.7L V6 and 4.7L V8 engines. To disconnect the TP sensor electrical connector, slide the red lock tab (1) away from the sensor, then depress the tab (2) and pull off the connector. To disconnect the electrical connector from the IAC motor, depress the tab (3) and pull off the connector**

the sensor doesn't fit flush against the throttle body and/or you're unable to rotate it a few degrees to align the mounting holes, then pull it off and verify that the locating tangs are correctly positioned above and below the flat end of the throttle shaft and try again.

5   Installation is otherwise the reverse of removal.

### 3.9L V6, 5.2L V8 and 5.9L V8 engine

6   Remove the air intake duct (see Chapter 4A).
7   Disconnect the electrical connector from the TP sensor (see illustration).
8   Remove the TP sensor mounting screws (see illustration).
9   When installing the TP sensor on the throttle body, align the sensor so that the locating tangs on the backside of the TP sensor fit over each side of the flat end of the throttle shaft (see illustration 12.4). If the sensor fits flush against the throttle body and you're able to rotate the TP sensor a few degrees in order to align the sensor mounting holes with the mounting holes in the throttle body, then you've installed the sensor correctly. If the sensor doesn't fit flush against the throttle body and/or you're unable to rotate it a few degrees to align the mounting holes, then pull it off and verify that the locating tangs are correctly located above and below the flat end of the throttle shaft and try again.
10   Installation is otherwise the reverse of removal.

### 8.0L V10 engine

11   Remove the air filter housing (2002 models) or the air intake duct (2003 models) (see Chapter 4A).
12   Locate the TP sensor on the rear (firewall) side of the throttle body (see illustration 12.35 in Chapter 4A).

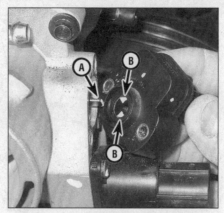

**12.4 When installing the TP sensor, make sure that the flat end of the throttle shaft (A) fits between the two locating tangs (B) on the backside of the TP sensor (3.7L V6 shown, 4.7L V8 similar)**

13   Disconnect the electrical connector from the TP sensor, remove the TP sensor mounting screws and remove the sensor from the throttle body.
14   When installing the TP sensor on the throttle body, align the sensor so that the locating tangs on the backside of the TP sensor fit over each side of the flat end of the throttle shaft (see illustration 12.4). If the sensor fits flush against the throttle body and you're able to rotate the TP sensor a few degrees in order to align the sensor mounting holes with the mounting holes in the throttle body, then you've installed the sensor correctly. If the sensor doesn't fit flush against the throttle body and/or you're unable to rotate it a few degrees to align the mounting holes, then pull it off and verify that the locating tangs are correctly located above and below the flat end of the throttle shaft and try again.
15   Installation is otherwise the reverse of removal.

**12.8 To detach the TP sensor from the throttle body on V6 and V8 engines, remove these two mounting screws**

**12.7 On V6 and V8 engines, the TP sensor is located on the left side of the throttle body**

### 13   Transmission Range (TR) sensor - replacement

**Note:** *All automatic transmissions used by the vehicles covered in this manual are equipped with TR sensors. But not all of them can be replaced at home. The TR sensor used by 45RFE and 545RFE automatics is an integral part of the solenoid module, which is located inside the transmission, on top of the valve body. We don't recommend tackling TR sensor replacement on one of these transmissions because of their complexity. However, if you own a vehicle with a 46RE or a 48RE transmission, you can replace the TR sensor yourself.*

1   Disconnect the cable(s) from the negative battery terminal(s) (see Chapter 5).
2   Raise the vehicle and place it securely on jackstands.
3   Place a drain pan under the TR sensor to catch any spilled transmission fluid.
4   Disconnect the electrical connector from the TR sensor (see illustration).

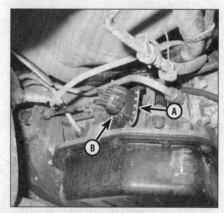

**13.4 To remove the TR sensor (A) from a 46RE or 48RE automatic transmission, disconnect the electrical connector (B), then remove the two TR sensor mounting bolts and pull the sensor straight out of the transmission case**

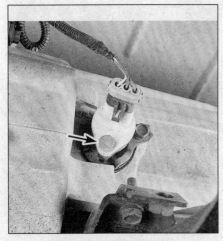

**14.1 Remove the VSS mounting bolt (arrow) (NV 4500 transmission shown)**

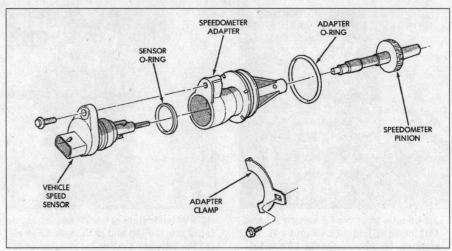

**14.3 Typical Vehicle Speed Sensor, adapter and speedometer pinion installation details**

5    Place the shift lever in the Low position.
6    Remove the two TR sensor mounting bolts and remove the TR sensor by pulling it straight out of its mounting bracket. Once you've removed the TR sensor, do not move the shift lever.
7    Before installing the TR sensor, make sure that the shift lever is still in the Low position.
8    Insert the TR sensor into its mounting hole with the electrical terminal facing toward the front of the vehicle, then install the TR sensor mounting bolts and tighten them securely.
9    Reconnect the TR sensor electrical connector.
10    Check the fluid level in the automatic transmission, adding fluid as necessary (see Chapter 1).
11    Lower the vehicle, reconnect the battery and verify that the engine can be started only in Park and Neutral.

**14    Vehicle Speed Sensor (VSS) - replacement**

## 2001 and earlier models

1    To replace the VSS, disconnect the electrical connector from the VSS. Remove the retaining bolt and withdraw the VSS from the speedometer adapter (see illustration).
2    Thoroughly clean the adapter flange and mounting area in the transmission and note the relationship of the adapter-to-transmission for proper alignment.
3    Remove the adapter clamp bolt and clamp and withdraw the adapter and speedometer pinion from the transmission (see illustration).
4    Remove the speedometer pinion from the adapter and check the gear teeth for damage. Count the number of teeth on the speedometer pinion and note the corresponding index number on the speedometer adapter (see illustration).
5    Install VSS into speedometer adapter and tighten the mounting screw. Install the speedometer pinion into the adapter.
6    Install new O-rings on the adapter and lubricate the O-rings and the speedometer pinion with automatic transmission fluid.
7    Install the assembly into the transmission or transfer case.
8    Turn the VSS assembly until the correct index numbers on the speedometer adapter are positioned at 6 o'clock. For example: If the speedometer pinion has 35 teeth, position the 32-38 index number straight down (6 o'clock).
9    Install the speedometer adapter clamp and retaining screw. Tighten the screw securely.
10    Installation is the reverse of removal.

## 2002 and later models

**Note:** *The VSS is located on the overdrive gear case of 46RE and 48RE automatic transmissions. (On 45RFE and 545RFE transmissions, the VSS function is handled by the Output Shaft Speed [OSS] sensor.)*
11    Disconnect the cable(s) from the negative battery terminal(s) (see Chapter 5).
12    Raise the vehicle and place it securely on jackstands.
13    Place a drain pan under the VSS to catch any spilled transmission fluid.
14    Disconnect the electrical connector from the VSS.
15    Unscrew the VSS from the transmission.
16    Apply Teflon tape or some other suitable thread sealant to the threads of the VSS to prevent leaks.
17    Installation is the reverse of removal.
18    Check the fluid level in the automatic transmission, adding fluid as necessary (see Chapter 1).

**15    Powertrain Control Module (PCM)/Engine Control Module (ECM) - removal and installation**

**Caution:** *Avoid static electricity damage to the Powertrain Control Module (PCM) (gasoline engines) or the Engine Control Module (ECM) (diesel engines) by grounding yourself to the body of the vehicle before touching the PCM or ECM and using a special anti-static pad on which to store the PCM or ECM once it's removed.*
**Note:** *Anytime the PCM or ECM is replaced with a new unit, it must be reprogrammed with a scan tool by a dealership service department or other qualified repair shop.*
**Note:** *Anytime the battery is disconnected, stored operating parameters may be lost from the PCM or ECM, causing the engine to run rough for a period of time while the PCM or ECM relearns the information.*

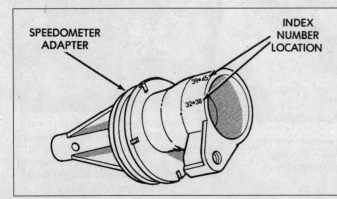

**14.4 The number of teeth on the speedometer pinion should fall within one of the groups of numbers on the speedometer adapter**

15.4 Remove the PCM electrical connector retaining bolt
(1998 and earlier models)

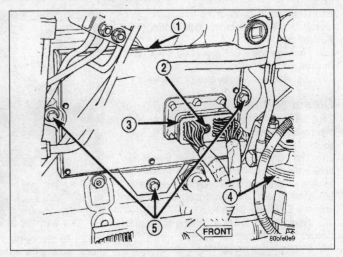

15.8 The Electronic Control Module (ECM) is bolted to the left side
of the engine block (1999 through 2001 models)

1   ECM
2   ECM electrical connector retaining bolt (hex-head)
3   ECM electrical connector
4   Fuel transfer pump
5   ECM mounting bolts (3)

## Gasoline engines

### 1998 and earlier models

**Note:** *Avoid static electricity damage to the PCM by grounding yourself to the body of the vehicle before touching the PCM and using a special anti-static pad to store the PCM on once it is removed.*

1   Disconnect the cable from the negative battery terminal.
2   Remove the air cleaner assembly (see Chapter 4A).
3   Remove the bolts that retain the PCM to the engine compartment and lift the assembly from the vehicle.
4   Remove the harness retaining bolt for the PCM electrical connector (see illustration).
5   Installation is the reverse of removal.

### 1999 through 2001 models

6   Be sure to extract any diagnostic trouble codes from the ECM or PCM before removing it (see Section 2).
7   Disconnect both negative battery cables.

### Engine Control Module (ECM)

8   The ECM (see illustration) is bolted to the left side of the engine block.
9   Remove the electrical connector retaining bolt (female 4 mm hex head) and carefully unplug the connector.
**Note:** *To remove the retaining bolt, you'll need a ball-hex bit or a ball-hex screwdriver, such as a Snap-On 4 mm SDABM4, or a suitable equivalent. (A 5/32-inch ball-hex bit or screwdriver will also work.)*
10  Remove the three ECM mounting bolts and remove the ECM.
11  Installation is the reverse of removal.
12  After the ECM has been installed, turn

the ignition key to the On position, but do not start the engine. With the key in the On position, slowly press the accelerator pedal all the way to the floor, and then slowly release it. This step ensures that the Accelerator Pedal Position Sensor (APPS) calibration has been "learned" by the ECM. If the APPS calibration is not learned by the ECM, diagnostic trouble codes might be set.

### Powertrain Control Module (PCM)

13  The PCM (see illustration) is located on the firewall, at the right rear corner of the engine compartment.
14  Remove the plastic cover from the PCM electrical connectors. The cover snaps off.
15  Carefully unplug the three electrical connectors from the PCM.
16  Remove the three PCM mounting bolts

and remove the PCM.
17  Installation is the reverse of removal.
18  After a new PCM has been installed, it must be reprogrammed by a DRB scan tool (the factory scan tool) with the Vehicle Identification Number (VIN) and with the original mileage. An aftermarket scan tool won't work for this procedure. Drive the vehicle to a dealer service department and have the new PCM reprogrammed. Failure to do so will result in diagnostic trouble codes being set.

### 2002 and later models

19  The PCM is located in the right rear corner of the engine compartment, on the firewall.
20  Disconnect the cable from the negative terminal of the battery (see Chapter 5, Section 1).

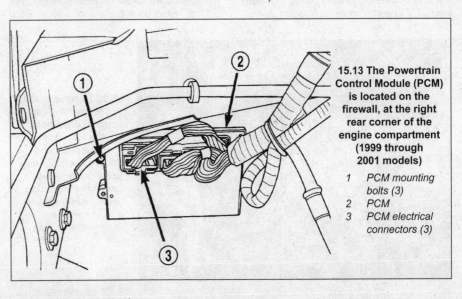

15.13 The Powertrain Control Module (PCM) is located on the firewall, at the right rear corner of the engine compartment (1999 through 2001 models)

1   PCM mounting bolts (3)
2   PCM
3   PCM electrical connectors (3)

21　Carefully disconnect the three (JTEC) or four (NGC) PCM electrical connectors (see illustration).
22　Remove the PCM mounting bolts (see illustration).
23　Installation is the reverse of removal.

### Diesel engines

24　Disconnect the cable(s) from the negative battery terminal(s) (see Chapter 5, Section 1).
25　The ECM is located on the left side of the engine block. For access, raise the front of the vehicle and support it securely on jackstands.
26　Disconnect the electrical connectors from the ECM (see illustration).
27　Remove the ECM mounting bolts and remove the ECM from the engine.
28　Installation is the reverse of removal.

---

**16　Air injection system - general description, check and component replacement**

---

### General description

**Note:** *Only 2003 and earlier Heavy Duty Cycle (HDC) models with a 5.9L V8 or an 8.0L V10 engine are equipped with an air injection system.*

1　The air injection exhaust emission control system reduces carbon monoxide and hydrocarbon content in the exhaust gases by injecting fresh air into the hot exhaust gases leaving the exhaust ports. When fresh air is mixed with the hot exhaust gases, oxidation is increased, reducing the concentration of hydrocarbons and carbon monoxide and converting them into harmless carbon dioxide and water. The system does not interfere with the NOx emission controls of the engine.
2　The air injection system is used on Heavy Duty Cycle (HDC) 5.9L V8 and 8.0L V10 engines. The air injection system consists of the belt-driven AIR pump, two air pressure relief valves, two one-way check valves, and the rubber hoses and metal tubes that connect all of these components together.

**15.21 To disconnect each of the electrical connectors from the Powertrain Control Module (PCM), slide the red lock (1) away from the PCM, then depress the release tab (2) and pull off the connector**

3　On V8 models, air is drawn into the pump through a rubber tube connected to a fitting on the air filter housing. On V10 models, air is drawn into the pump through a rubber tube connected to a fitting on the air injection pump filter housing.
4　Air is compressed by the air injector pump. Then it's expelled from the pump and routed into a rubber tube where it reaches the air pressure relief valve. Pressure relief holes in the relief valve prevent excess downstream pressure. If excess pressure occurs at the relief valve, it's vented into the atmosphere. Air is routed from the relief valve to a "Y" connector through two one-way check valves before being injected into the catalytic converters. The two-way valves protect the hoses, air pump and injection tubes from hot exhaust gases backing up into the system. Air is allowed to flow through these valves in ONE direction only.
5　The air pump is mounted on the front of the engine and driven by a belt connected to the front pulley. Under normal operating conditions, noise from the pump rises in pitch

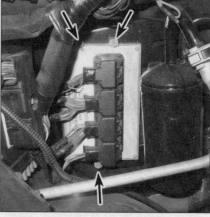

**15.22 To detach the PCM from the firewall, remove these three bolts**

as engine speed increases. Do not attempt to lubricate the air injection pump with oil or any spray penetrant. Lubricating the pump will damage it.

### Check

#### Air injection pump

6　Check the drivebelt tension (see Chapter 1).
7　Disconnect the air supply hose from the pressure relief valve.
8　If you can feel airflow at the pump outlet with the engine running at idle, and if the airflow increases as the engine speed increases, then the pump is operating satisfactorily.
9　If you feel little or no airflow, replace the pump with a rebuilt or new unit.

#### One-way check valves

10　Disconnect the rubber air tube from the intake side of the check valves.
11　Start the engine and verify that no exhaust fumes escape through the valve. If there are signs of leakage, replace the check valves with new parts.

### Component replacement

#### One-way check valves

12　Loosen the hose clamp and disconnect the hose from the inlet side of the check valve.
13　Unscrew the valve from the catalyst tube. Use a back-up wrench on the catalyst tube to protect the tube from kinking.
14　Installation is the reverse of removal. Be sure to tighten the one-way check valve to the torque listed in this Chapter's Specifications.

#### Air injection pump filter

**Note:** *The air injection pump filter is used only on 8.0L V10 engines. The air pump filter is located inside a housing on the right side of the engine compartment. A rubber hose connects the filter housing to the air injection pump.*

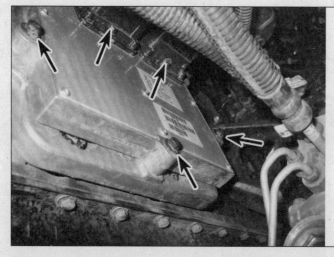

**15.26 To remove the ECM from a diesel engine, disconnect the electrical connectors and remove the mounting bolts (some models use three mounting bolts, while others have five mounting bolts)**

15   Disconnect the rubber tubes from the filter housing.

16   Remove the filter housing mounting nut and remove the housing.

17   Remove the lid from the filter housing (it snaps off).

18   Remove the filter element from the housing.

19   Clean out the inside of the filter housing before installing the new filter element.

20   Installation is otherwise the reverse of removal.

## Air injection pump

21   Disconnect the hoses or tubes from the air injection pump.

22   Loosen, but do not remove, the three bolts from the air injection pump pulley.

23   Relieve tension on the automatic belt tensioner and remove the drivebelt (see Chapter 1).

24   Remove the three bolts from the air injection pump pulley and remove the pulley from the pump.

25   Remove the two air injection pump mounting bolts and remove the pump from its mounting bracket.

26   Installation is the reverse of removal. Be sure to tighten the pulley bolts to the torque listed in this Chapter's Specifications.

## 17   Idle Air Control (IAC) motor - replacement

1   Disconnect the cable(s) from the negative battery terminal(s) (see Chapter 5).

### 3.7L V6 and 4.7L V8 engines

**Note:** *This procedure applies to 2006 and earlier models only. On later models the idle speed is controlled by the Electronic Throttle Control (ETC) system.*

2   Remove the air intake duct and the air resonator box (see Chapter 4A).

3   Disconnect the electrical connector from the IAC motor (see illustration 12.3).

4   Remove the two IAC motor mounting screws and remove the IAC motor from the throttle body.

5   Installation is the reverse of removal.

### 3.9L V6, 5.2L V8 and 5.9L V8 engine

6   Remove the air intake duct (see Chapter 4A).

7   Disconnect the electrical connector from the IAC motor (see illustration).

8   Remove the IAC mounting screws and remove the IAC motor.

9   Installation is the reverse of removal.

### 8.0L V10 engine

10   Remove the air filter housing (2002 models) or the air intake duct (2003 models) (see Chapter 4A).

11   Locate the IAC motor on the rear (firewall) side of the throttle body, right above the TP sensor (see illustration 12.35 in Chapter 4A).

**17.7 To detach the IAC motor from the throttle body, disconnect the electrical connector (1) and remove the two IAC motor mounting screws (2)**

12   Disconnect the electrical connector from the IAC motor.

13   Remove the IAC motor mounting screws and remove the IAC motor from the throttle body.

14   Installation is the reverse of removal.

## 18   Catalytic converter - general description, check and replacement

**Note:** *Because of a Federally-mandated extended warranty which covers emission-related components such as the catalytic converter, check with a dealer service department before replacing the converter at your own expense.*

### General description

1   A catalytic converter (or catalyst) is an emission control device in the exhaust system that reduces certain pollutants in the exhaust gas stream. There are two types of converters. An oxidation catalyst reduces hydrocarbons (HC) and carbon monoxide (CO). A reduction catalyst reduces oxides of nitrogen (NOx). A catalyst that can reduce all three pollutants is known as a "Three-Way Catalyst" (TWC). All models covered by this manual are equipped with TWCs.

### Check

2   The test equipment for a catalytic converter (a "loaded-mode" dynamometer and a 5-gas analyzer) is expensive. If you suspect that the converter on your vehicle is malfunctioning, take it to a dealer or authorized emission inspection facility for diagnosis and repair.

3   Whenever you raise the vehicle to service underbody components, inspect the converter for leaks, corrosion, dents and other damage. Carefully inspect the welds and/or flange bolts and nuts that attach the front and rear ends of the converter to the exhaust system. If you note any damage, replace the converter.

4   Although catalytic converters don't break too often, they can become clogged or even plugged up. The easiest way to check for a restricted converter is to use a vacuum gauge to diagnose the effect of a blocked exhaust on intake vacuum.

a)   *Connect a vacuum gauge to an intake manifold vacuum source (see Chapter 2A).*

b)   *Warm the engine to operating temperature, place the transaxle in Park (automatic models) or Neutral (manual models) and apply the parking brake.*

c)   *Note the vacuum reading at idle and jot it down.*

d)   *Quickly open the throttle to near its wide-open position and then quickly get off the throttle and allow it to close. Note the vacuum reading and jot it down.*

e)   *Do this test three more times, recording your measurement after each test.*

f)   *If your fourth reading is more than one in-Hg lower than the reading that you noted at idle, the exhaust system might be restricted (the catalytic converter could be plugged, or an exhaust pipe or muffler could be restricted).*

### Replacement

**Warning:** *Make sure that the exhaust system is completely cooled down before proceeding. If the vehicle has just been driven, the catalytic converter can be hot enough to cause serious burns.*

**Note:** *The photos accompanying this procedure are of a 2003 Hemi model with a single catalyst, two short pipes welded to either end of the catalyst, a two-hole mounting flange at the front end of the forward pipe and a straight pipe behind the catalyst that uses a clamp to secure it to the pipe going to the muffler. Most models use this same setup. If your vehicle doesn't use a slip joint behind the catalyst, but is welded to the rear exhaust pipe instead, you will have to either cut it off yourself with a hacksaw or have it cut off at an automotive repair shop.*

5   Raise the vehicle and place it securely on jackstands.

6   Spray a liberal amount of penetrant onto the threads of the exhaust pipe-to-exhaust manifold bolts and the clamp bolt behind the

**18.6a To disconnect the exhaust pipe ahead of the catalyst from the exhaust manifold, remove these two bolts. If they're difficult to loosen, spray some penetrant onto the threads, wait awhile and try again. Discard these bolts and use new ones when reconnecting the pipe to the manifold**

**18.6b To disconnect the exhaust pipe behind the catalyst from the exhaust pipe going to the muffler, back off this nut to loosen the clamp. If it's hard to loosen, spray some penetrant onto the threads and wait awhile. If the clamp is in bad shape, replace it with a new one**

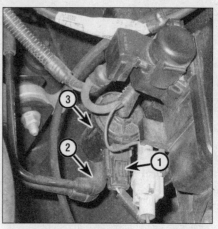

**19.2 To remove the EVAP canister purge solenoid, disconnect the electrical connector (1), disconnect the vacuum hoses (2) and disengage the solenoid (3) from its mounting bracket**

catalytic converter (see illustrations) and wait awhile for the penetrant to loosen things up.

7    While you're waiting for the penetrant to do its work, disconnect the electrical connectors for the upstream and downstream oxygen sensor and remove both oxygen sensors (see Section 11).

8    Unscrew the upper exhaust pipe-to-exhaust manifold flange bolts. If they're still difficult to loosen, spray the threads with some more penetrant, wait awhile and try again.

9    To loosen the clamp that secures the slip joint between the exhaust pipe behind the catalytic converter and the pipe ahead of the muffler, back off the nut. If it's still difficult to loosen, spray the threads with some more penetrant, wait awhile and try again.

10    Remove the catalytic converter assembly. Remove and discard the old flange gasket.

11    Installation is the reverse of removal. Be sure to use a new flange gasket at the exhaust manifold mounting flange. Use new bolts at the front flange. Although the slip joint clamp doesn't get as overheated as the exhaust manifold flange bolts, it's still a good idea to use a new clamp. Coat the threads of the clamp and the exhaust manifold bolts with anti-seize compound to facilitate future removal. Tighten the fasteners securely.

## 19   Evaporative emissions control (EVAP) system - component replacement

### EVAP canister purge solenoid

1    Disconnect the cable(s) from the negative battery terminal(s) (see Chapter 5).

2    Disconnect the electrical connector from the EVAP canister purge solenoid (see illustration).

3    Clearly label the vacuum hoses, then disconnect them from the EVAP canister purge solenoid.

4    Disengage the EVAP canister purge solenoid from its mounting bracket.

5    Installation is the reverse of removal.

### *Leak Detection Pump (LDP)*

**Note:** *The LDP is located on the front of the EVAP canister mounting bracket, which is located ahead of the fuel tank. The LDP looks similar to the NVLD (see illustration 19.13)but the two components are not interchangeable. Even though you're going to detach the LDP and its air filter from one another and remove them separately, they're actually available only as a single assembly, i.e., if you have to replace either component, you have to replace the entire assembly.*

6    Raise the vehicle and place it securely on jackstands.

7    Disconnect the electrical connector from the LDP.

8    Disconnect the hose that connects the LDP filter to the LDP, then remove the LDP filter mounting bolt and remove the filter.

9    Clearly label all vacuum and vapor hoses that are connected to the LDP, then disconnect them from the LDP.

10    Remove the LDP mounting bolt and remove the LDP.

11    Installation is the reverse of removal.

### *Natural Vacuum Leak Detection (NVLD) assembly*

**Note:** *The NVLD is located on the front of the EVAP canister mounting bracket, which is located ahead of the fuel tank. Even though you're going to detach the NVLD and its air filter from one another and remove them separately, they're actually available only as a single assembly, i.e., if you have to replace either component, you have to replace the en-*

*tire assembly.*

12    Raise the vehicle and place it securely on jackstands.

13    Locate the NVLD on the front side of the EVAP canister mounting brackets (see illustration).

14    Clearly label the vapor hoses connected to the NVLD, then disconnect them from the NVLD.

15    To detach the NVLD from its mounting bracket, push the release tab (see illustration) toward the NVLD, then push the NVLD straight up.

16    Disconnect the electrical connector from the NVLD (see illustration) and remove the NVLD.

17    Installation is the reverse of removal.

### *EVAP canisters*

18    Raise the vehicle and place it securely on jackstands.

19    Disconnect the vapor hoses from the EVAP canisters (see illustration).

20    Remove the lower support bracket bolts (see illustration) and remove the lower support bracket.

21    Remove the EVAP canister mounting nuts from the top of the upper support bracket and remove the EVAP canisters.

22    Installation is the reverse of removal.

## 20   Positive Crankcase Ventilation (PCV) system - general description and check

### *General information*

**Note:** *For specific information on how to replace the PCV valves on the engines covered by this manual, see Chapter 1.*

1    The Positive Crankcase Ventilation (PCV) system reduces hydrocarbon emis-

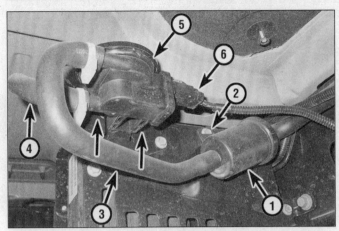

**19.13 The Natural Vacuum Leak Detection (NVLD) assembly, which is used on vehicles with New Generation Controller (NGC), is located on the front side of the EVAP canister mounting brackets. To disengage the NVLD from its mounting bracket, depress the release tab (see illustration 19.24) and push the NVLD straight up**

1   Air filter
2   Air filter mounting bolt
3   Air filter-to-LDP hose
4   LDP-to-EVAP canister hose
5   LDP
6   Electrical connector
    (see illustration 19.25)

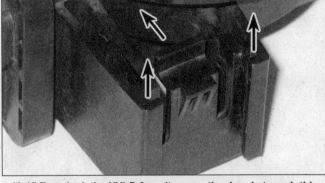

**19.15 To unlock the NVLD from its mounting bracket, push this release tab toward the NVLD (toward the front of the vehicle) and slide the NVLD straight up until the two NVLD mounting rails are free of the bracket**

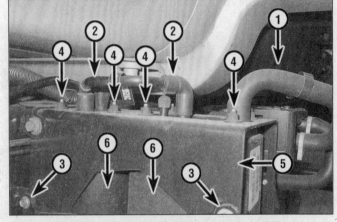

**19.19 To remove the EVAP canisters from their mounting brackets:**

1   Disconnect the vapor hose that connects the NVLD to the EVAP canisters
2   Disconnect the connecting hose that connects the two EVAP canisters
3   Remove the two rear bolts that attach the lower support bracket to the upper support bracket
4   Remove the four nuts that attach the two EVAP canisters to the upper support bracket
5   Upper support bracket
6   EVAP canisters

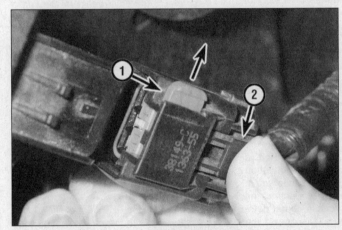

**19.16 To disconnect the electrical connector from the NVLD, push the sliding lock (1) to its released position (away from the connector), then depress the release tab (2) and pull off the connector**

sions by scavenging crankcase vapors, which are rich in unburned hydrocarbons. A PCV valve regulates the flow of gases into the intake manifold in proportion to the amount of intake vacuum available. At idle, when intake vacuum is very high, the PCV valve restricts the flow of vapors so that the engine doesn't run poorly. As the throttle plate opens and intake vacuum begins to diminish, the PCV valve opens more to allow vapors to flow more freely.

2    On 3.7L V6 and 4.7L V8 engines, the PCV system consists of a fresh air inlet hose that connects a pipe at the left rear corner of the air resonator box to a pair of breather pipes at the inner rear corner of each valve

**19.20 To detach the lower support bracket from the upper support bracket, remove these two bolts and remove the two bolts on the rear side (see illustration 19.28)**

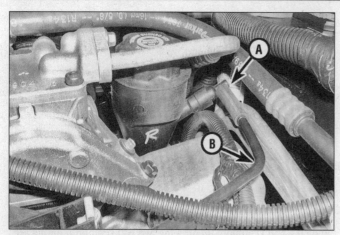

**20.2 On 3.7L V6 and 4.7L V8 engines, the PCV valve (A) is located on the side of the engine oil filler tube. The crankcase ventilation hose (B) connects the PCV valve to the intake manifold (4.7L V8 shown, 3.7L V6 similar)**

**20.3 On Hemi engines, the PCV system consists of a fresh air inlet hose (A) that connects the air resonator box (removed in this photo) to the oil filler tube and the PCV valve (B), which is located on the intake manifold, to the right of the throttle body**

cover; the PCV valve, (see illustration) which is located on the oil filler tube; and the crankcase ventilation hose that connects the PCV valve to the intake manifold.

3    On Hemi engines, the PCV system consists of a fresh air inlet hose that connects a pipe on the underside of the left front corner of the air resonator box to another pipe on the oil filler tube (see illustration), the PCV valve, which is located on the intake manifold, to the right of the throttle body, and the internal passages connecting the PCV to the intake manifold (there is no external crankcase ventilation hose on these models).

4    On 3.9L V6, 5.2L V8 and 5.9L V8 engines, the PCV system consists of a fresh air inlet hose that connects a pipe on the left valve cover to the air filter housing or the air intake duct; a PCV valve (see illustration), which is located on the right valve cover; and the crankcase ventilation hose that connects the PCV hose to the intake manifold.

5    The 8.0L V10 engine is equipped with a Crankcase Ventilation (CCV) system. This

system operates the same as the conventional PCV system but it does not use the vacuum control valve. Instead, a molded vacuum tube connects manifold vacuum to the top of the right cylinder head valve cover. The vacuum tube contains a fixed orifice of a calibrated size. It meters the amount of crankcase vapors drawn out of the engine. A fresh air supply hose from the air cleaner is connected to the front of the cylinder head at the valve cover. When the engine is running, fresh air enters the engine and mixes with the crankcase vapors. Manifold vacuum draws the vapor/air mixture through the fixed orifice and into the intake manifold and consumes them during combustion.

### Check

6    An engine that is operated without a properly functioning crankcase ventilation system can be damaged. So anytime you're servicing the engine, be sure to inspect the PCV system hose(s) for cracks, tears, deterioration and other damage. Disconnect the hose(s) and inspect it/them for damage and obstructions. If a hose is clogged, clean it out. If you're unable to clean it satisfactorily, replace it.

7    A plugged PCV hose might cause any or all of the following conditions: A rough idle, stalling or a slow idle speed, oil leaks or sludge in the engine. So if the engine is running roughly, stalling and idling at a lower than normal speed, or is losing oil, or has oil in the throttle body or air intake manifold plenum, or has a build-up of sludge, a PCV system hose might be clogged. Repair or replace the hose(s) as necessary.

8    A leaking PCV hose might cause any or all of the following conditions: a rough idle, stalling or a high idle speed. So if the engine is running roughly, stalling and idling at a higher than normal speed, a PCV system hose might be leaking. Repair or replace the hose(s) as necessary.

9    Here's an easy functional check of the

PCV system on a vehicle with a fresh air inlet hose and a crankcase ventilation hose with a PCV valve in it:

a) *Disconnect the crankcase ventilation hose (the crankcase ventilation hose, or simply "the PCV hose," is the hose that connects the PCV valve to the intake manifold).*

b) *Start the engine and let it warm up to its normal idle.*

c) *Verify that there is vacuum at the PCV hose. If there is no vacuum, look for a plugged hose or a clogged port or pipe on the intake manifold. Also look for a hose that collapses when it's blocked (i.e., when vacuum is applied). Replace clogged or deteriorated hoses.*

d) *Remove the engine oil dipstick and install a vacuum gauge on the upper end of the dipstick tube.*

e) *Pinch off or plug the PCV system's fresh air inlet hose.*

f) *Run the engine at 1500 rpm for 30 seconds, then read the vacuum gauge while the engine is running at 1500 rpm.*

g) *If there's vacuum present, the crankcase ventilation system is operating correctly.*

h) *If there's no vacuum present, the engine might be drawing in outside air. The PCV system won't function correctly unless the engine is a sealed system. Inspect the valve cover(s), oil pan gasket or other sealing areas for leaks.*

i) *If the vacuum gauge indicates positive pressure, look for a plugged hose or engine blow-by.*

10    If the PCV system is functioning correctly, but there's evidence of engine oil in the throttle body or air filter housing, it could be caused by excessive crankcase pressure. Have the crankcase pressure tested by a dealer service department.

11    In the PCV system, excessive blow-by (caused by worn rings, pistons and/or cylinders, or by constant heavy loads) is discharged into the intake manifold and con-

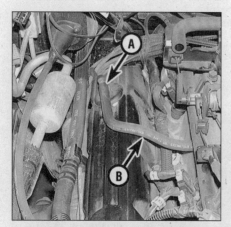

**20.4 On 3.9L V6, 5.2L V8 and 5.9L V8 engines, the PCV valve (A) is located on the right valve cover. The crankcase ventilation hose (B) connects the PCV valve to the intake manifold**

**21.6 To detach the crankcase breather cover from the valve cover, remove these four bolts. When you're installing the breather cover, don't forget to reattach the wiring harness clip at the left rear cover bolt**

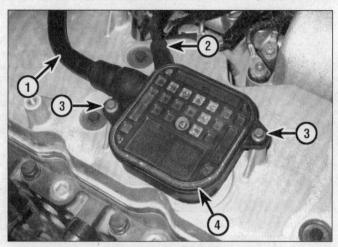

**21.7 To detach the crankcase breather, disconnect or remove the following items:**

| | | | |
|---|---|---|---|
| 1 | Breather tube | 4 | Crankcase breather |
| 2 | Lube oil drain tube | | assembly |
| 3 | Breather mounting bolts | | |

sumed. If you discover heavy sludge deposits or a dilution of the engine oil, even though the PCV system is functioning correctly, look for other causes (see Troubleshooting and Chapter 2E) and correct them as soon as possible.

## 21  Crankcase breather system (diesel engines) - general description and component replacement

### 2002 and early 2003 models

**Note:** *The crankcase breather assembly is located at the front of the engine, on the timing gear cover. Dodge recommends emptying the contents of the vapor canister when changing the engine oil and filter. It's also a good idea to empty the canister anytime you remove it for any reason.*

1  Loosen the cap on top of the vapor canister.
2  Remove the canister mounting nut and remove the vapor canister.
3  Loosen the hose clamp and slide it up the hose, then disconnect the hose from the crankcase breather.
4  Remove the crankcase breather from the timing gear cover.
5  Installation is the reverse of removal.

### *(Late) 2003 through 2006 models*

**Note:** *The crankcase breather is located on top of the valve cover, underneath the breather cover.*

6  Remove the crankcase breather cover bolts (see illustration) and remove the breather cover.
7  Disconnect the breather tube and the lube oil drain tube from the breather (see illustration).
8  Remove the breather mounting bolts and

remove the breather assembly from the valve cover.
9  Remove the old breather assembly O-ring from the valve cover and discard it. Install a new O-ring and apply a little engine oil to it to facilitate breather installation.
10  Installation is the reverse of removal.

### *2007 and later models*

### Closed Crankcase Ventilation (CCV) system - description

11  2007 and later models use a Closed Crankcase Ventilation (CCV) system, which vents crankcase gases into the intake manifold for combustion.
12  The CCV system incorporates a filter, which is located in the valve cover. Should this filter become clogged, a CCV valve, located under the filter, will prevent oil from being siphoned into the engine. It is recommended that the CCV filter be replaced at 60,000-mile intervals.

### CCV filter replacement

13  The CCV filter is located inside the breather cover at the top of the valve cover. Remove any covers or hoses that are in the way.
14  If equipped, remove the EGR heat shield.
15  Disconnect any hoses attached to the breather cover.
16  Remove the breather cover mounting bolts, then remove the breather cover from the valve cover.
17  Lift the CCV filter straight up out of its cavity in the breather cover.
18  Clean the CCV filter sealing surfaces on the valve cover.
19  Seat the new CCV filter in the breather cover, pressing down until it is fully seated.
20  The remainder of installation is the reverse of removal.

### Crankcase Depression Regulator (CDR) - description

21  The Crankcase Depression Regulator (CDR) is used to maintain a constant positive pressure in the crankcase. Crankcase gases are directed through the CDR valve, into the fresh air side of the turbocharger. The CDR valve is non-serviceable and is located on the underside of the breather cover.

## 22  Exhaust Gas Recirculation (EGR) system - description and component replacement

### *Description*

1  Oxides of nitrogen, nitrogen oxide, or simply NOx, is a compound that is formed in the combustion chambers when the oxygen and nitrogen in the incoming air mix together. NOx is a natural byproduct of high combustion chamber temperatures (2500 degrees F and higher). When NOx is emitted from the tailpipe, it mixes with reactive organic compounds (ROCs), hydrocarbons (HC) and sunlight to form ozone and photochemical smog. The EGR system reduces NOx by recirculating exhaust gases from the exhaust manifold, through the EGR valve and intake manifold, then back to the combustion chambers, where it mixes with the incoming air/fuel mixture before being consumed. These recirculated exhaust gases "dilute" the incoming air/fuel mixture, which cools the combustion chambers, thereby reducing NOx emissions.
2  The EGR system consists of the Powertrain Control Module (PCM), the EGR valve and various information sensors (ECT, TP, MAP, IAT, RPM and VSS sensors) that the PCM uses to determine when to open the EGR valve. When the PCM closes the power/control circuit for the EGR valve, a solenoid inside the EGR valve is energized. This cre-

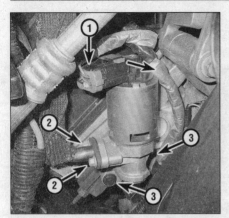

**22.5 To remove the EGR valve on a typical V6 or V8 engine, disconnect the electrical connector (1), remove the EGR pipe flange (2), then remove the EGR valve bolts (3)**

ates an electromagnetic field, which causes an armature to pull up, lifting the pintle off its seat. The exhaust gas then flows from the exhaust manifold port to the intake manifold.

3   Once activated by the PCM, the EGR valve uses a position feedback circuit to control the position of the pintle valve. The feedback circuit, which functions like a potentiometer, puts out a variable output voltage signal with an operating range between approximately 0.5 and 5.4 volts. This variable output enables the PCM to control the position of the pintle with a high degree of precision. A pintle position sensor monitors the position of the pintle, and the PCM adjusts the current to match the actual pintle position to the optimal pintle position.

4   If there is too much EGR flow at idle, cruise or during cold running conditions, the engine will stop after a cold start, stop at idle after deceleration, surge during cruising speeds or idle roughly. If there is too little EGR flow, combustion chamber temperature can become too high during acceleration or under a heavy load, which can cause spark knock (detonation) and/or engine overheating.

**Note:** *If the EGR valve control solenoid becomes disconnected or damaged, the electrical signal will be lost and the EGR valve will be open at all times during warm-up and driving conditions. The associated symptoms will be rough idle and poor performance.*

## Component replacement
### V6 and V8 engines

#### EGR valve
**Note:** *The EGR valve is located at the rear of the left cylinder head on V6 and 4.7L V8 models. It is located at the front of the right cylinder head on Hemi V8 engines.*

5   Disconnect the electrical connector from the EGR valve (see illustration).
6   Remove the EGR pipe mounting flange bolts.
7   Remove the EGR valve mounting bolts and remove the EGR valve. Remove and dis-

card the old gasket.
8   Clean the EGR valve mounting surfaces on the cylinder head and on the valve itself.
9   Installation is the reverse of removal. Be sure to use new gaskets between the EGR valve and the cylinder head and between the EGR pipe mounting flange and the EGR valve and tighten the EGR valve and EGR pipe mounting bolts to the torque listed in this Chapter's Specifications.

#### EGR pipe
**Note:** *The EGR pipe connects the EGR valve to the intake manifold.*
10   Remove the engine cover.
11   Remove the EGR pipe mounting flange bolts. Remove and discard the old EGR pipe mounting flange gasket.
12   Disconnect the EGR pipe from the intake manifold.
13   Remove the old gasket from the EGR pipe flange and replace it with a new one. Remove the old seal(s) from the EGR pipe. To ensure a positive seal, you should always replace the seal(s) whenever you disconnect the EGR pipe.
14   Clean the EGR pipe mounting surfaces on the EGR valve and on the EGR pipe mounting flange.
15   Installation is the reverse of removal. Be sure to tighten the EGR pipe mounting flange bolts securely.

### Diesel engines
**Note:** *On 2001 and earlier models, the 1997 and 1998 diesel engine with the California Emission Package is the only diesel engine equipped with an EGR system. A vacuum pump supplies vacuum for the EGR valve and the EGR valve vacuum regulator solenoid. This pump also supplies vacuum for the power brake booster, the speed control servo and the heating/air conditioning system.*

#### EGR valve
16   The EGR valve is located at the front of the engine, on top of the intake manifold.
17   Disconnect both negative battery terminals.
18   Remove the bolts (there are usually four of them) and remove the EGR crossover tube cover.
19   Remove the EGR valve heat shield.
20   Loosen, but do not remove, the clamp at the end of the EGR crossover tube.
21   Disconnect the electrical connector at the end of the EGR valve assembly.
22   Remove the two EGR valve assembly mounting bolts and two nuts.
23   Disconnect the EGR valve assembly from the intake connector by prying up.
24   Remove the crossover tube doughnut gasket and clean the EGR valve. Also clean the end of the EGR tube, being sure to remove all old gasket material.
25   Installation is the reverse of removal.

#### EGR cooler
26   Diesel models incorporate an EGR cooler that uses engine coolant to cool the hot diesel exhaust gases to a temperature where

they will better do their job of reducing combustion temperature when they are routed into the engine. The EGR cooler/bypass valve assembly is mounted on the top of the exhaust manifold, on the passenger's side of the engine.
27   Remove the engine trim cover.
28   Drain the level of engine coolant below the EGR cooler.
29   Disconnect the electrical connector from the EGR bypass controller, remove the mounting bolts and set EGR bypass control aside.
30   Loosen, but do not remove, the EGR valve mounting bolts
31   Disconnect the EGR temperature sensor electrical connector, center retaining clamp, crossover tube-to-EGR valve and crossover tube-to-EGR cooler clamps, then remove the crossover tube.
32   Remove front and rear coolant, breather, EGR transfer connection tube and hoses from the EGR Cooler Housing and set aside.
33   Remove the EGR cooler support bracket, flange and mounting bolts and nuts.
34   Remove the EGR cooler and discard the gaskets.

## 23   Multi-Displacement System (MDS) (5.7L Hemi engine) - description and component replacement

### Description
1   The Multi Displacement System (MDS) improves the fuel economy of the Hemi V8 engine by deactivating four of the cylinders when certain conditions are met. Under acceleration or heavy loads, the engine runs on all eight cylinders, allowing full power. But when the conditions are right - cruising at light loads or driving in city traffic, for example - the Powertrain Control Module (PCM) deactivates cylinders 1, 4, 6 and 7 (cylinders 2, 3, 5 and 8 run all the time).
2   The MDS components include an oil temperature sensor, four control valve/solenoids, special roller lifters that can be deactivated, the wiring harness that connects these components and a specially-designed camshaft.

### Component replacement
#### Control valve/solenoid
**Note:** *The four solenoids are located in the valley between the cylinder heads. This procedure applies to any of the four units.*
3   Remove the intake manifold (see Chapter 2B).
4   Disconnect the electrical connector from the solenoid.
5   Remove the solenoid hold-down bolt and remove the solenoid.
6   Installation is the reverse of removal.

#### Lifters and camshaft
7   Refer to Chapter 2B.

# Chapter 7 Part A
# Manual transmission

## Contents

## Specifications

### General

Transmission lubricant type .................................................................... See Chapter 1

### Torque specifications

**Ft-lbs (unless otherwise indicated)**

**Note:** *One foot-pound (ft-lb) of torque is equivalent to 12 inch-pounds (in-lbs) of torque. Torque values below approximately 15 ft-lbs are expressed in inch-pounds, because most foot-pound torque wrenches are not accurate at these smaller values.*

| | |
|---|---|
| Back-up light switch | 20 to 25 |
| Crossmember-to-frame rail bolts | 50 |
| Shift tower-to-transmission bolts | |
| NV3500 | 70 in-lbs |
| NV4500 and NV5600 | 96 in-lbs |
| G56 | 204 in-lbs |
| T56 | 156 in-lbs |
| Structural dust cover bolts | |
| NV3500 | |
| 2002 and 2003 | 54 |
| 2004 on | 40 |
| G56 | 40 |
| Transmission-to-engine mounting bolts | |
| NV3500 and G56 | |
| 2001 and earlier models | |
| Transmission-to-engine bolts | 30 |
| Engine-to-transmission nuts | 110 in-lbs |
| 2002 and later models | |
| Transmission-to-engine bolts (no washers) | 30 |
| Engine-to-transmission bolts (washers) | 50 |
| NV4500 | 40 to 45 |
| NV4500 (transmission-to-clutch housing bolts) | 80 |
| T56 (transmission-to-clutch housing bolts) | 26 |

## 1   General Information

1    Vehicles equipped with a manual transmission use an NV3500, an NV4500, an NV5600, a G56 or a T56. The NV3500 and NV4500 are five-speed transmissions. The NV5600, G56 and T56 are six-speed transmissions.

2    Depending on the cost of having a transmission overhauled, it might be a better idea to replace it with a used or rebuilt unit. Your local auto parts store, dealer or transmission shop should be able to supply information concerning cost, availability and exchange policy. Regardless of how you decide to remedy a transmission problem, you can still save a lot of money by removing and installing the unit yourself.

## 2   Extension housing oil seal - replacement

**Note:** *This procedure also applies to the transfer case extension housing seal on 4WD models.*

1    Oil leaks at the extension housing oil seal are usually caused by a worn seal lip. Replacing this seal is relatively easy, since you can do so without removing the transmission from the vehicle. The extension housing oil seal is located at the rear tip of the transmission extension housing, where the driveshaft is attached. (If the vehicle is a 4WD model, there is no extension housing. Instead, the transfer case is bolted to the rear of the transmission housing. But the following procedure applies to replacing the rear seal on 4WD models too.)

2    If you suspect that the extension housing seal is leaking (because you've seen puddles right below the extension housing seal and/or because the transmission seems to be losing lubricant all the time), raise the vehicle and support it securely on jackstands. If the seal is leaking, gear lube will be oozing or dripping

from the rear of the transmission, coating the forward end of the driveshaft and leaking onto the ground.

3    Remove the driveshaft (see Chapter 8).

4    Some seals have a metal casing with a lip. With this type of seal you can use a chisel and hammer to carefully pry the oil seal out of the rear of the transmission (see illustration). Do not damage the splines on the transmission output shaft.

5    If the seal doesn't have a metal lip, obtain a special oil seal removal tool (available at most auto parts stores) to do the job.

6    Using a seal driver or a very large socket as a drift, install the new oil seal (see illustration). Drive it into the bore squarely and make sure that it's completely seated.

7    Lubricate the splines of the transmission output shaft and the outside of the driveshaft yoke with lightweight grease, then install the driveshaft (see Chapter 1). Be careful not to damage the lip of the new seal.

## 3   Shift lever - removal and installation

**Note:** *On NV3500 models, the shift lever assembly can be disassembled for cleaning, but the only part that can be replaced separately is the boot. The tower, shift lever and and other components are NOT available separately; if the shift lever, tower or any other part is defective or worn out, you must replace the entire shift lever assembly.*

1    If equipped, remove the center console (see Chapter 11). With the parking brake on and the wheels blocked, place the shift lever in Neutral.

2    Remove the retaining screws for the shift lever boot (see illustrations) and slide the shift lever boot up the shift lever.

3    Remove the four shift tower mounting bolts and remove the shift lever and tower from the transmission as a single assembly.

**2.4 Use a hammer and chisel to dislodge the rear seal from the extension housing on 2WD models (shown) or, on 4WD models, from the transfer case**

**2.6 Use a large socket (shown) or a seal driver to drive the new seal into the extension housing (shown) or transfer case. The outside diameter of the socket must be slightly smaller than the outside diameter of the seal, just enough to clear the edges of the seal bore**

**3.2a On early NV4500 models, to detach the extension lever boot from the floor, remove these retainer screws, then slide the boot up the lever so that it's out of the way**

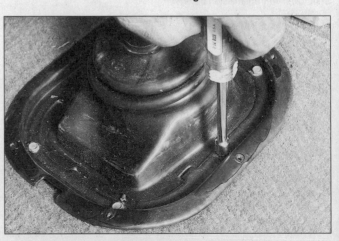

**3.2b To detach the boot retainer plate from the floor, remove these screws**

4   Disassemble the shift lever assembly, clean the parts in solvent, blow everything dry with compressed air, then coat all friction surfaces with clean multi-purpose grease and reassemble.

5   Installation is the reverse of removal. Be sure to tighten the shift tower mounting bolts to the torque listed in this Chapter's Specifications.

## 4   Back-up light switch - check and replacement

### Check

1   The back-up light switch is located on the side of the transmission case (see illustration).

2   Turn the ignition key to the On position, move the shift lever to the Reverse position and verify that the back-up lights come on.

3   If the back-up lights don't go on, check the back-up light fuse, which is located in the engine compartment fuse and relay box (see Chapter 12).

4   If the fuse is blown, troubleshoot the back-up light circuit for a short circuit.

5   If the fuse is okay, put the shift lever in Reverse, then raise the vehicle and support it securely on jackstands.

6   Working under the vehicle, disconnect the electrical connector from the back-up light switch. Using an ohmmeter, check for continuity across the terminals of the switch (not the connector). There should be continuity.

7   If there is no continuity between the switch terminals with the shift lever in Reverse, replace the switch.

8   If there is continuity at the switch, check for voltage at the electrical connector. One of the two terminals should have battery voltage present with the ignition key in the On position.

9   If there is no voltage at the switch electrical connector, troubleshoot the circuit between the engine compartment fuse and relay box and the back-up light switch connector for an open circuit condition.

10   If there is voltage at the switch electrical connector, trace the back-up light circuit between the electrical connector and the back-up light bulbs for an open circuit condition.

**Note:** *Although not very likely, the back-up light bulbs could both be burned out, but don't rule out this possibility.*

### Replacement

11   Raise the vehicle and support it securely on jackstands, if not already done.

12   Disconnect the electrical connector from the back-up light switch.

13   Using a wrench, unscrew the back-up light switch from the transmission case.

14   Apply RTV sealant or Teflon tape to the threads of the new switch to prevent leakage. Install the switch in the transmission case and tighten it to the torque listed in this

**4.1 Location of the back-up light switch - T56 transmission shown**

Chapter's Specifications.

15   The remainder of installation is the reverse of removal.

## 5   Transmission mount - check and replacement

### Check

1   Raise the vehicle and support it securely on jackstands.

2   Insert a large screwdriver or prybar into the space between the transmission extension housing and the crossmember and try to pry the transmission up slightly (see illustration).

3   The transmission should not move much at all and the rubber in the center of the mount should fully insulate the center of the mount from the mount bracket around it.

### Replacement

4   To replace the mount, remove the bolts attaching the mount to the crossmember and the bolts attaching the mount to the transmission.

5   Raise the transmission slightly with a jack and remove the mount.

6   Installation is the reverse of the removal procedure. Be sure to tighten all nuts and bolts securely.

## 6   Transmission - removal and installation

### Removal

1   Disconnect the cable(s) from the negative battery terminal(s) (see Chapter 5).

2   Put the transmission shift lever into the Neutral position.

3   Remove the retaining screws for the shift lever boot and slide the boot up the shift lever. Remove the shift tower and lever assembly (see Section 3).

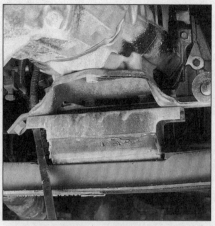

**5.2 To check the transmission mount, insert a large screwdriver or prybar between the crossmember and the extension housing and try to lever the transmission up and down and back and forth - it should move very little; if the mount yields easily, it's probably cracked or torn**

4   Raise the vehicle and support it securely on jackstands.

5   Remove the skid plate, if equipped.

6   Disconnect the electrical connector from the back-up light switch and detach the wiring harness from any clips on the transmission. If the engine has a Crankshaft Position (CKP) sensor located at the flywheel, disconnect the electrical connector from the Crankshaft Position (CKP) sensor and remove the sensor (see Chapter 6).

7   Drain the transmission lubricant (see Chapter 1).

8   Remove the driveshaft (see Chapter 8).

9   Detach the exhaust pipe(s) between the exhaust manifolds and the catalytic converter(s) and remove them. Remove any other exhaust system components that are routed under the transmission and/or transfer case.

10   On 4WD models, remove the transfer case shift linkage, then remove the transfer case (see Chapter 7C).

11   Detach the clutch release cylinder from the clutch housing (see Chapter 8), then move the cylinder aside for clearance. If you're careful, you should be able to set the release cylinder aside without actually disconnecting the clutch hydraulic line from the release cylinder.

12   Remove the starter motor (see Chapter 5).

13   Remove the structural dust cover, if equipped.

14   Remove the dust shield.

15   Remove the suspension crossmember.

16   Support the engine from above with an engine hoist, or place a jack (with a block of wood as an insulator) under the engine oil pan. The engine must remain supported at all times while the transmission is out of the vehicle.

17   Support the transmission with a trans-

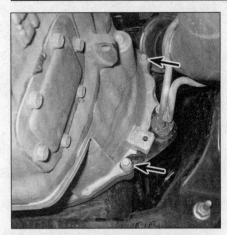

**6.21a Right-side transmission mounting bolts (not all bolts are visible in this photo)**

**6.21b Left-side transmission mounting bolts (not all bolts are visible in this photo; the two center bolts are the starter mounting bolts, which will already have been removed)**

a)  *Pilot bearing (in the rear end of the crankshaft)*
b)  *Driveshaft slip yoke*
c)  *Input shaft splines*
d)  *Release bearing bore*
e)  *Release bearing sliding surface*
f)  *Release fork ballstud*

27   After lubricating the above components, install the clutch components (see Chapter 8).
28   Raise the transmission into position and carefully slide it forward, engaging the input shaft with the clutch plate hub. Do not use excessive force to install the transmission - if the input shaft does not slide into place, readjust the angle of the transmission so it is level and/or turn the input shaft so the splines engage properly with the clutch.
29   Install the transmission-to-engine bolts and tighten them to the torque listed in this Chapter's Specifications.
**Caution:** *Don't use the bolts to draw the transmission to the engine. If the transmission doesn't slide forward easily and mate with the engine block, find out why before proceeding.*
30   Raise the transmission extension housing just high enough to clear the crossmember, install the crossmember and attach it to the frame rails. Install the transmission mount between the extension housing and the crossmember. Carefully lower the transmission extension housing onto the mount and the crossmember. When everything is properly aligned, tighten all nuts and bolts securely.
31   Remove the jacks supporting the transmission and the engine.
32   On 4WD models install the transfer case and shift linkage (see Chapter 7C).
33   Install the various components previously removed:

a)  *Clutch release cylinder (see Chapter 8)*
b)  *Driveshaft (see Chapter 8)*
c)  *Exhaust system components (see Chapter 4A)*

d)  *Starter motor (see Chapter 5)*

34   Install the Crankshaft Position (CKP) sensor (see Chapter 6).
35   Reconnect the electrical connector for the back-up light switch. Also reconnect any other wiring harness connectors that you might have disconnected. And make sure that any harnesses that were attached to clips or cable guides on the transmission housing are reattached.
36   Remove the jackstands and lower the vehicle.
37   Install the shift tower and shift lever assembly (see Section 3).
38   Fill the transmission to the correct level with the specified lubricant (see Chapter 1).
39   Reconnect the cable(s) to the negative battery terminal(s).
40   Road test the vehicle for proper operation and check for leakage.

## 7   Transmission overhaul - general information

1   Overhauling a manual transmission is a difficult job for the do-it-yourselfer. It involves the disassembly and reassembly of many small parts. Numerous clearances must be precisely measured and, if necessary, changed with select fit spacers and snap-rings. As a result, if transmission problems arise, it can be removed and installed by a competent do-it-yourselfer, but overhaul should be left to a transmission repair shop. Rebuilt transmissions might be available. Check with your dealer parts department and auto parts stores. At any rate, the time and money involved in an overhaul is almost sure to exceed the cost of a rebuilt unit.
2   Nevertheless, it's not impossible for an inexperienced mechanic to rebuild a transmission if the special tools are available and the job is done in a deliberate step-by-step manner so nothing is overlooked.
3   The tools necessary for an overhaul include internal and external snap-ring pliers, a bearing puller, a slide hammer, a set of pin punches, a dial indicator and possibly a hydraulic press. In addition, a large, sturdy workbench and a vise or transmission stand will be required.
4   During disassembly of the transmission, make careful notes of how each piece comes off, where it fits in relation to other pieces and what holds it in place. If you note how each part is installed before removing it, getting the transmission back together again will be much easier.
5   Before taking the transmission apart for repair, it will help if you have some idea what area of the transmission is malfunctioning. Certain problems can be closely tied to specific areas in the transmission, which can make component examination and replacement easier. Refer to the *Troubleshooting* Section at the front of this manual for information regarding possible sources of trouble.

mission jack (available at auto parts stores and at tool rental yards) or with a large heavy-duty floor jack. If you're going to use a floor jack to support the transmission, make sure that you use a transmission jack adapter head (also available at auto parts stores and at tool rental yards). These transmissions are very heavy, so it's a good idea to have someone help you lower the transmission to make sure that it doesn't fall off the jack.
18   Raise the transmission slightly, then disconnect and remove the transmission mount between the extension housing and the crossmember.
19   Remove the bolts and nuts attaching the crossmember to the frame rails, then remove the crossmember.
20   After the crossmember has been removed, lower the jack slightly so that the transmission is still supported but neither raised nor lowered by the jack.
21   Remove the bolts attaching the transmission to the engine (see illustrations).
**Note:** *Some models also use engine-to-transmission bolts (the bolts are installed from the engine side).*
22   Make a final inspection for any wiring harness or hoses that might still be connected to the transmission.
23   Keeping the transmission level, roll the jack toward the rear of the vehicle until the transmission input shaft clears the splined hub in the clutch disc.
24   Once the input shaft is clear, lower the transmission to the floor and remove it from under the vehicle.
25   While the transmission is removed, be sure to remove and inspect all clutch components (see Chapter 8). Always install new clutch components any time that you have to remove the transmission.

### Installation

26   Apply a light coat of high-temperature bearing grease (or a suitable equivalent) to the following components:

# Chapter 7 Part B
# Automatic transmission

## Contents

## Specifications

### General

| | |
|---|---|
| Transmission fluid type | See Chapter 1 |
| Torque converter bolt length | |
| 1994 | |
| 9.5-inch, 3-lug converter | 0.46-inch |
| 9.5-inch, 4-lug converter | 0.52-inch |
| 10.0-inch, 4-lug converter | 0.52-inch |
| 10.75-inch, 4-lug converter | 0.44-inch |
| 1995 and later | Specified in parts catalog only |

### Torque specifications

| | Ft-lbs |
|---|---|
| Adjustment swivel lockscrew | 90 in-lbs |
| Neutral start/backup light switch | 25 |
| Torque converter-to-driveplate bolts | |
| 1994 | |
| 9.5-inch, 3-lug converter | 40 |
| 9.5-inch, 4-lug converter | 55 |
| 10.0-inch, 4-lug converter | 55 |
| 10.75-inch, 4-lug converter | 23 |
| 1995 through 2001 models | |
| 10.75-inch converter | 23 |
| 12.2-inch converter | 35 |
| 2002 and later models | |
| 46RE and 48RE | N/A |
| 45RFE/545RFE | 23 |
| 47RE | 35 |
| Transmission-to-engine bolts | |
| 46RE and 48RE | N/A |
| 45RFE/545RFE/68RFE | 50 |
| All others | Not specified; tighten securely |

## 1  General Information

1    The vehicles covered in this manual are equipped with a five- or six-speed manual transmission or a three, four, or six-speed automatic transmission. Information on manual transmissions is in Part A of this Chapter. You'll also find extension housing oil seal replacement, which is a virtually identical procedure for both automatic and manual transmissions, in Part A. Information on automatic transmissions is included in this Part of Chapter 7. If you're looking for information on the transfer case, refer to Part C of this Chapter.

2    1994 models are equipped with a 32RH, 36RH or 37RH three-speed transmission. The 32RH is used with 3.9L and 5.2L engines; the 36RH is used for heavy-duty 5.2L and 5.9L engine applications; the 37RH is used with the V10 and with the Cummins Turbo Diesel.

3    1995 models are equipped with a 42RH, 46RH or 47RH four-speed transmission. The 42RH is used with 3.9L engines in 4X2 1500 models; the 46RH is used with 3.9L, 5.2L and 5.9L engines; the 47RH is used with V10 and Cummins Turbo Diesel applications.

4    1996 through 2001 models use a 42RE, 46RE or 47RE four-speed transmission with an electronic governor. Their applications are similar to those of 1995 models.

5    2002 and later models are equipped with a 45RFE or 545RFE, 46RE, 48RE four-speed automatic transmission or a 68RFE six-speed automatic transmission. All transmissions are equipped with a Torque Converter Clutch (TCC) system that engages in fourth gear, and in third gear when the overdrive switch is turned off. The TCC system provides a direct connection between the engine and the drive wheels, which improves fuel economy. The TCC system consists of a solenoid, controlled by the Powertrain Control Module (PCM), that locks the torque converter in fourth when the vehicle is cruising on level ground and the engine is fully warmed up.

6    All automatic transmissions covered in this chapter are equipped with an external air-to-oil transmission oil cooler, which is located in front of the radiator. All diesel engines are also equipped with a water-to-oil transmission cooler, which is located on the left side of the engine. On diesels, transmission fluid is routed through this water-to-oil transmission cooler first, then it's routed through the air-to-oil external cooler.

7    The air-to-oil coolers used on 5.9L V8 gasoline engines and on diesel engines are equipped with an internal thermostat that controls the flow of transmission fluid through the cooler. When the transmission fluid is below its operating temperature, it's routed through a cooler bypass. When the fluid reaches operating temperature, the thermostat closes the bypass, allowing transmission fluid to flow through the cooler. The thermostat can be serviced separately from the cooler (see Section 7). If you're going to back-flush the oil cooler, the thermostat MUST be removed.

8    All vehicles with an automatic transmission are equipped with a Brake Transmission Shift Interlock (BTSI) system that locks the shift lever in the Park position and prevents the driver from shifting out of Park unless the brake pedal is depressed. The BTSI system also prevents the ignition key from being turned to the Lock or Accessory position unless the shift lever is fully locked into the Park position.

9    Due to the complexity of the automatic transmissions covered in this manual and the need for specialized equipment to perform most service operations, this Chapter is limited to general diagnosis, routine maintenance, adjustments and removal and installation procedures.

10   If the transmission requires major repair work, leave it to a dealer service department or a transmission repair shop. However, even if a transmission shop does the repairs, you can save some money by removing and installing the transmission yourself.

## 2  Diagnosis - general

**Note:** *Automatic transmission malfunctions may be caused by five general conditions: poor engine performance, incorrect adjustments, hydraulic malfunctions, mechanical malfunctions or malfunctions in the computer or its signal network. Diagnosis of these problems should always begin with a check of the easily repaired items: fluid level and condition (see Chapter 1), shift cable adjustment and, if equipped, Throttle Valve (TV) cable adjustment. Next, perform a road test to determine if the problem has been corrected or if more diagnosis is necessary. If the problem persists after the preliminary tests and corrections are completed, additional diagnosis should be done by a dealer service department or transmission repair shop. Refer to the Troubleshooting section at the front of this manual for information on symptoms of transmission problems.*

### Preliminary checks

1    Drive the vehicle to warm up the transmission to its normal operating temperature.

2    Check the fluid level as described in Chapter 1 :

a) *If the fluid level is unusually low, add enough fluid to bring the level within the area between the high and low marks on the dipstick (see Chapter 1, Section 4), then check for external leaks (see below).*

b) *If the fluid level is abnormally high, it might have been overfilled. Drain off the excess. On models with diesel engines, which use a main water-to-oil cooler in addition to an auxiliary air-to-oil cooler,*

*the presence of engine coolant in the automatic transmission fluid could indicate a leak in the water-to-oil cooler, so check the drained fluid for coolant contamination. (Only diesel engines use a water-to-oil cooler in addition to the external air-to-oil cooler).*

c) *If the fluid is foaming, drain it and refill the transmission, then check for coolant in the fluid or a high fluid level.*

3    Check the engine idle speed.

**Note:** *If the engine is malfunctioning, do not proceed with the preliminary checks until it has been repaired and runs normally.*

4    Inspect the shift cable (see Section 3). Make sure it's properly adjusted and that it operates smoothly.

5    Check the throttle valve cable, if equipped, for freedom of movement. Adjust it if necessary (see Section 6).

**Note:** *The Throttle Valve (TV) cable might function correctly when the engine is shut off and cold, but it might not function correctly once the engine is hot. Always check the TV cable when the engine is cold and when it's at normal operating temperature.*

### Fluid leak diagnosis

6    Most fluid leaks are usually easy to locate because they leave a visible stain and/or wet spot. Most repairs are simply a matter of replacing a seal or gasket. If a leak is more difficult to find, the following procedure will help.

7    Identify the fluid. Make sure that it's transmission fluid, not engine oil or brake fluid. One way to positively identify Automatic Transmission Fluid (ATF) is by its deep red color.

8    Try to pinpoint the source of the leak. Drive the vehicle several miles, then park it over a large sheet of cardboard. After a minute or two, you should be able to locate the leak by determining the source of the fluid dripping onto the cardboard.

9    Make a careful visual inspection of the suspected component and the area immediately around it. Pay particular attention to gasket mating surfaces. A flashlight and mirror are often helpful for finding leaks in areas that are hard to see.

10   If you still can't find the leak, thoroughly clean the suspected area with a degreaser or solvent, then dry it off.

11   Drive the vehicle for several miles at normal operating temperature and varying speeds. After driving the vehicle, visually inspect the suspected component again.

12   Once you have located the leak, you must determine the source before you can repair it properly. For example, if you replace a pan gasket but the sealing flange is warped or bent, the new gasket won't stop the leak. The flange must first be straightened.

13   Before attempting to repair a leak verify that the following conditions are corrected or they might cause another leak.

**Note:** *Some of the following conditions cannot be fixed without highly specialized tools and expertise. Such problems must be referred to a transmission repair shop or a dealer service department.*

### Gasket leaks

14  Inspect the pan periodically. Make sure that the bolts are tight, that no bolts are missing, that the gasket is in good condition and that the pan is flat (dents in the pan might indicate damage to the valve body inside).

15  If the pan gasket is leaking, the fluid level or the fluid pressure might be too high, the vent might be plugged, the pan bolts might be too tight, the pan sealing flange might be warped, the sealing surface of the transmission housing might be damaged, the gasket might be damaged or the transmission casting might be cracked or porous. If sealant instead of gasket material has been used to form a seal between the pan and the transmission housing, it may be the wrong type sealant.

### Seal leaks

16  If a transmission seal is leaking, the fluid level or pressure might be too high, the vent might be plugged, the seal bore might be damaged, the seal itself might be damaged or incorrectly installed, the surface of the shaft protruding through the seal might be damaged or a loose bearing might be causing excessive shaft movement.

17  Make sure that the dipstick tube seal is in good condition and that the tube is correctly seated.

### Case leaks

18  If the case itself appears to be leaking, the casting is porous. A porous casting must be repaired or replaced.

19  Make sure that the oil cooler hose fittings are tight and in good condition.

### Fluid comes out vent pipe or fill tube

20  If this condition occurs, the transmission is overfilled, there is coolant in the fluid, the case is porous, the dipstick is incorrect, the vent is plugged or the drain-back holes are plugged.

---

**3   Shift linkage - check, adjustment and replacement**

## *Check*

1  Firmly apply the parking brake and try to momentarily operate the starter in each shift lever position. The starter should only operate when the shift lever is in the Park or Neutral positions. If the starter operates in any position other than Park or Neutral, adjust the shift linkage or cable (see below). If, after adjustment, the starter still operates in positions other than Park or Neutral, the Transmission Range (TR) sensor is defective (see Chapter 6).

## *Adjustment*

2  Place the shift lever in the Park position.

### Column shift linkage

3  Raise the front of the vehicle and support it securely on jackstands.

4  Before proceeding with the adjustment, inspect the condition of the linkage (see illustration). Note the condition of the shift rod,

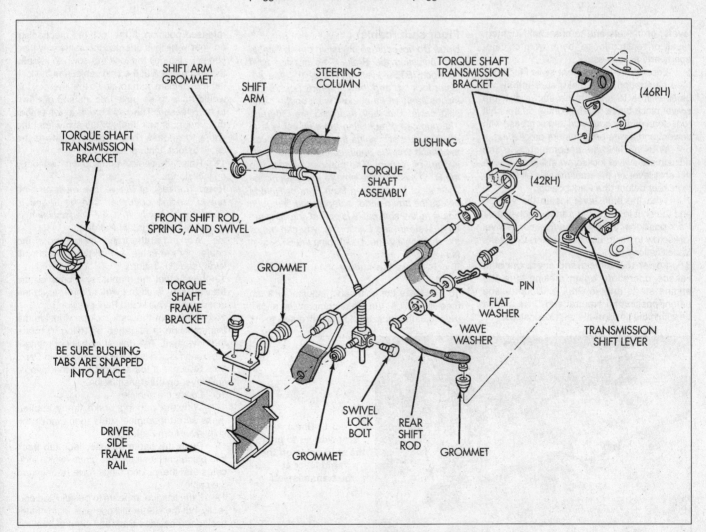

**3.4 An exploded view of the shift linkage assembly**

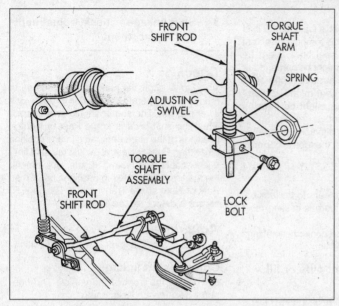

3.5 Shift linkage adjustment details

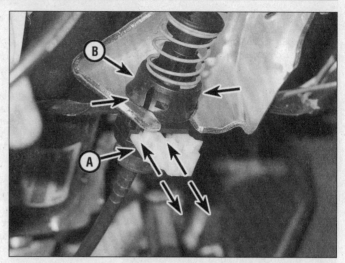

3.10 To release the shift cable adjuster lock tab (A), pull it away from the cable to its released position; to apply the lock tab, push it toward the cable until it snaps into place. To release the cable housing (B) from the cable bracket, depress the two tangs on the cable housing

levers, grommets and torque shaft. Tighten, repair or replace loose, bent, worn or damaged parts as necessary.

5    Loosen the adjustment swivel lock bolt (see illustration) and make sure the swivel block is free to turn on the shift rod. If the swivel block binds (even slightly) on the shift rod, clean off any corrosion, dirt or grease with solvent and a wire brush before proceeding.

6    With all linkage assembled and the adjustment swivel lockscrew still loose, move the shift lever on the transmission all the way to its rear detent (the Park position).

7    With the shift lever inside the vehicle and the shift lever on the transmission in their Park positions, tighten the adjustment swivel lockscrew to the torque listed in this Chapter's Specifications.

8    Lower the vehicle and check the shift linkage operation, again making sure the engine starts only in Park or Neutral. The detent position for Neutral and Drive should be within the limits of the shift lever stops.

### Floor shift (cable)

**Note:** *Do not confuse adjusting the shift cable with adjusting the Brake Transmission Shift Interlock (BTSI) system. The shift cable adjuster lock tab and the BTSI lock tab are just inches apart and they both work on the same shift cable. But their functions are different. The purpose of adjusting the shift cable is to make sure that it shifts the transmission correctly and that the engine can be started only in Park or Neutral. The purpose of adjusting the BTSI system is to ensure that the shift lever cannot be removed from Park or Neutral unless the brake pedal is depressed. Although adjusting the shift cable is part of adjusting the BTSI system (see Section 4), you can adjust the shift cable without disturbing the BTSI system.*

9    Remove the knee bolster (see Chapter 11).

10    Release the shift cable adjuster lock tab (see illustration). (In the accompanying photo, the adjuster lock tab is pulled down to its

released position. If the lock tab mechanism on your vehicle is oriented the same way then you will also pull the lock tab down to release the shift cable. But the shift cable, and the lock tab mechanism, can rotate so that the lock tab would have to be pulled up instead of down to be released. The key here is to remember that you must pull the lock tab away from the cable to release it, and push it toward the cable to lock it into place.)

11    Raise the vehicle and support it securely on jackstands.

**Note:** *The rear of the vehicle must also be raised, so the driveshaft can be turned in Step 13 (to verify that the transmission is completely engaged in Park).*

12    Working at the transmission end of the cable, pry the cable end off the manual shift lever (see illustration).

13    Verify that the manual shift lever on the transmission is all the way to the rear, in the last detent. (This is the Park position.)

14    Verify that the park lock pawl inside the transmission is engaged by trying to rotate the driveshaft. The driveshaft will not rotate if the transmission is correctly engaged in Park.

15    Reconnect the shift cable to the manual shift lever on the transmission.

16    Lower the vehicle.

17    With the parking brake firmly applied make sure the engine starts (don't move the shift lever from Park yet).

18    Push the cable adjuster lock tab back into place until it snaps into place (which indicates that the locking tangs have re-engaged the cable).

19    If the linkage appears to be adjusted correctly, but the starter still operates in any other position(s) besides Park and Neutral, replace the Transmission Range (TR) sensor (see Chapter 6).

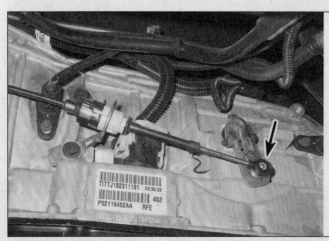

3.12 Use a screwdriver to pry the shift cable off the shift lever at the transmission

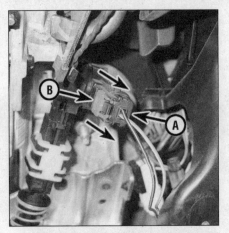

**3.26 To disconnect the electrical connector (A) from the Brake Transmission Shift Interlock (BTSI) solenoid, slide the sliding lock toward you, then depress the button (B) on the slide lock and pull off the connector**

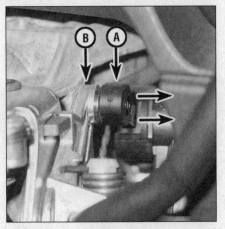

**3.27 To disconnect the shift cable (A) from the shift lever pin (B), insert a small, thin flat blade screwdriver between them and pry them apart**

**3.28 To disengage the shift cable from its mounting bracket, squeeze the two tangs on the cable housing together, then pull the cable straight down. To remove the cable, disengage the grommet (A) from the hole in the firewall, then pull the cable through the hole**

### Shift cable replacement

20   Make sure the shift lever is in the Park position.

21   Raise the vehicle and place it securely on jackstands.

22   Working at the transmission end of the cable, pry the cable end off the manual shift lever (see illustration 3.12).

23   Lower the vehicle.

24   Remove the knee bolster (see Chapter 11) and the steering column covers (see Chapter 11).

25   Remove the shift cable grommet (see illustration 3.28) from the firewall.

26   Disconnect the electrical connector from the Brake Transmission Shift Interlock (BTSI) solenoid (see illustration).

27   Pry the cable end off the lever on the steering column (see illustration).

28   To disengage the cable assembly from the lower steering column bracket, squeeze the two tangs on the cable housing together (see illustration 3.10), then pull the cable assembly straight down (see illustration).

29   Installation is the reverse of removal. When you're done, adjust the cable (see Steps 9 through 19).

---

**4    Brake Transmission Shift Interlock (BTSI) system (2002 and later 1500 models/2003 and later 2500 and 3500 models) - description, check and adjustment**

---

### Description

1    The Brake Transmission Shift Interlock (BTSI) system is a solenoid-operated device, located on the shift cable, that locks the shift lever into the Park position when the ignition key is in the Lock or Accessory position.

When the ignition key is in the Run position, a magnetic holding device, inline with the park lock cable, is energized. When the system is functioning correctly, the only way to unlock the shift lever and move it out of Park is to depress the brake pedal. The BTSI system also prevents the ignition key from being turned to the Lock or Accessory position unless the shift lever is fully locked into the Park position.

### Check

2    Verify that the ignition key can be removed only in the Park position.

3    When the shift lever is in the Park position and the shift lever Overdrive Off ("O/D Off") button is not activated, you should be able to rotate the ignition key from Off to Lock. But when the shift lever is in any gear position other than Park (including Neutral), you should not be able to rotate the ignition key to the Lock position.

4    You should not be able to move the shift lever out of the Park position when the ignition key is turned to the Off position.

5    You should not be able to move the shift lever out of the Park position when the ignition key is turned to the Run or Start position until you depress the brake pedal.

6    You should not be able to move the shift lever out of the Park position when the ignition key is turned to the ACC or Lock position.

7    Once in gear, with the ignition key in the Run position, you should be able to move the shift lever between gears, or put it into Neutral or Park, without depressing the brake pedal.

8    If the BTSI system doesn't operate as described, try adjusting it as follows.

### Adjustment

**Note:** *Do not confuse adjusting the shift cable with adjusting the Brake Transmission Shift Interlock (BTSI) system. The shift cable adjuster lock tab and the BTSI lock tab are just inches*

*apart and they both work on the same shift cable. But their functions are different. The purpose of adjusting the shift cable is to make sure that it shifts the transmission correctly and that the engine can be started only in Park or Neutral. The purpose of adjusting the BTSI system is to ensure that the shift lever cannot be moved from Park or Neutral unless the brake pedal is depressed. Although adjusting the shift cable is part of adjusting the BTSI system, you can adjust the shift cable without disturbing the BTSI system (see Section 3).*

9    Remove the knee bolster (see Chapter 11).

10   Put the shift lever in the Park position.

11   Release the BTSI lock tab (see illustration) and the shift cable adjuster lock tab (see illustration 3.10).

12   Make sure that the shift lever is in the Park position.

13   Raise the vehicle and place it securely

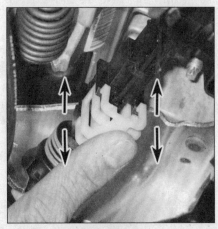

**4.11 To release the Brake Transmission Shift Interlock (BTSI) cable lock tab, pull it away from the cable; to apply the lock tab, push it toward the cable**

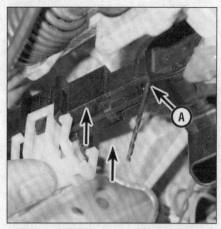

**4.17 Slide the BTSI assembly up or down the shift cable as necessary until you can insert a small drill bit into the alignment hole (A) and up through the assembly, then push the BTSI lock tab toward the cable until it snaps into place and remove the drill bit**

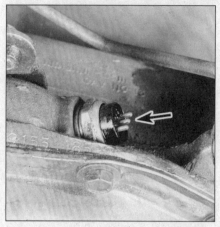

**5.3 Unplug the electrical connector from the Neutral start/backup light switch; the center terminal (arrow) is the ground terminal for the starter solenoid circuit when the transmission is in Neutral or Park**

on jackstands. (Make sure that the rear wheels are off the ground so that you can rotate the rear wheels or the driveshaft in the next step.)

14    Verify that the transmission park lock is positively engaged by trying to rotate the driveshaft (the driveshaft will not rotate when the park lock is correctly engaged).

15    Turn the ignition key to the Lock position. (Make sure that the ignition key is in the Lock position, because the cable cannot be correctly adjusted with the key in any other position.)

16    Make sure that the shift cable is free to self-adjust itself by pushing it to the rear and releasing it. Then push the shift cable lock tab (see illustration 3.10) toward the cable until it snaps into place (which indicates that the locking tangs have re-engaged the cable)

17    Locate the BTSI alignment hole (see illustration) on the underside of the BTSI mechanism, between the BTSI lock tab and the electrical terminal for the BTSI solenoid. Slide the BTSI assembly up or down on the shift cable until you can insert an appropri-

ate size drill bit into the alignment hole and through the mechanism.

18    Push the BTSI lock tab toward the shift cable (see illustration 4.17) until it snaps into place, then remove the drill bit.

19    Install the knee bolster (see Chapter 11).

## 5    Neutral start/backup light switch (2001 and earlier 1500 models/2002 and earlier 2500 and 3500 models) - check and replacement

1    The Neutral start/backup switch is threaded into the lower left front edge of the transmission case. The Neutral start and backup light switch functions are combined into one unit, with the center terminal of the switch grounding the starter solenoid circuit when the transmission is in Park or Neutral, allowing the engine to start. The outer terminals make up the backup light switch circuit.

### Check

2    Prior to checking the switch, make sure the shift linkage is properly adjusted (see Section 3). Raise the vehicle and support it securely on jackstands.

3    Unplug the connector and use an ohm-meter or self-powered test light to check for continuity between the center terminal and the transmission case (see illustration). Continuity should exist only when the transmission is in Park or Neutral.

4    Check for continuity between the two outer terminals. There should be continuity only when the transmission is in Reverse. There should be no continuity between either of the outer terminals and the transmission case.

### Replacement

5    Place a container under the transmission to catch the fluid which will be released, then use a six-point socket to remove the switch.

6    Move the shift lever from Park to Neutral. Make sure that the switch operating fingers are centered in the switch opening in the case (see illustration). If they aren't, the shift linkage is incorrectly adjusted or there is an internal problem with the transmission.

7    Install the new switch and O-ring (be sure to use a new O-ring, even if installing the original switch), tighten it to the torque listed in this Chapter's Specifications, then recheck the switch before plugging in the connector.

## 6    Throttle Valve (TV) cable - description, check, adjustment and replacement

**Note:** *The following procedure applies only to 46RE and 48RE automatic transmissions. The 45RFE and 545RFE transmissions, both of which are electronically controlled, do not use a Throttle Valve (TV) cable.*

### Description

1    The throttle lever on 42RH, 46RH, 47RH, 46RE and 48RE transmissions is cable-operated. Adjusting the Throttle Valve (TV) cable correctly is critical because the transmission won't operate properly with an incorrectly adjusted cable. How well the TV cable is adjusted determines how well - or poorly - the transmission works because the cable adjustment determines the position of the throttle valve on the transmission, which controls shift speed, shift quality and part-throttle downshift sensitivity. If the cable is correctly adjusted, the throttle lever on the transmission will move simultaneously with the throttle lever on the throttle body from idle to wide-open throttle. If the cable is too loose, the transmission will upshift too early and it might slip. If it's too tight, upshifts will be late, and downshifts during part-throttle operation will occur too soon. If the transmission on your vehicle has been exhibiting some of the above-described symptoms, check the adjustment of the TV cab. If it's out of adjustment, adjust it as described below.

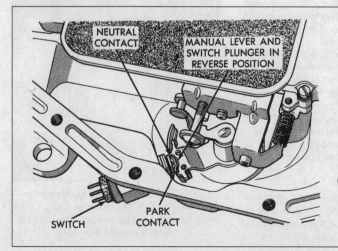

**5.6 Make sure that the switch operating fingers are centered in the opening; if they're not, the shift linkage is incorrectly adjusted or there's a problem inside the transmission (transmission oil pan removed for clarity)**

NEUTRAL CONTACT

MANUAL LEVER AND SWITCH PLUNGER IN REVERSE POSITION

SWITCH

PARK CONTACT

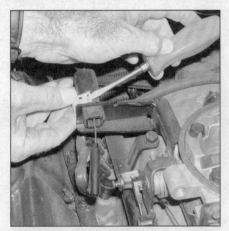

**6.16 On older models, pry off the TV cable retainer clip to adjust the cable; on newer models, simply pry up the TV cable lock (in the same spot) to adjust the cable**

**6.17 Slide the TV cable sheath forward or backward inside the adjuster mechanism to center the eyelet on the end of the cable with the stud on the throttle lever**

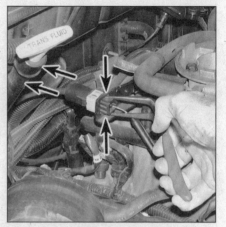

**6.22 To disengage the TV cable from the cable bracket, squeeze these tangs together and shove the cable housing through the bracket, toward the firewall**

2    The throttle valve on the transmission is operated by a cam on the throttle lever, which is operated by the TV cable. The TV cable, which is connected to an arm on the throttle lever shaft, is easy to adjust. Simply remove the retaining clip at the engine-end of the cable, make your adjustment, then install the clip on the TV cable to lock in the adjustment.

### Check

3    Remove the air intake duct and, if equipped, the resonator (see Chapter 4A).
4    Verify that the lever on the throttle body is at its curb-idle position (resting against its stop).
5    Raise the vehicle and place it securely on jackstands.
6    Verify that the throttle valve lever on the transmission is also at its idle position, i.e., in the fully forward position.
7    Disconnect the TV cable from the stud on the control lever at the throttle body: Rotate the lever to put some slack in the cable, hold the lever in this position, slide the plastic cable end forward, then pull it off the stud. Don't pry it off; just use your fingers.
8    Release the cable and compare the position of the cable end to the attachment stud on the throttle body lever (see illustration 5.17). The end of the cable and the attachment stud on the throttle lever should be aligned (or centered on one another) to within 1/32-inch in either direction.
9    If the end of the TV cable is within the specified distance from the throttle lever stud, reconnect the cable to the stud, then with the aid of a helper, note the movement of the throttle lever on the throttle body and the throttle lever on the transmission:

a)    *If both levers move simultaneously from idle to half-throttle and back to idle, the cable is correctly adjusted, and no further adjustment is necessary.*
b)    *If the transmission throttle lever moves ahead of or lags behind the throttle body lever, or if the throttle body lever prevents*

*the transmission lever from returning to its closed position, the TV cable must be adjusted (see below).*

10    If the end of the TV cable is not within the specified distance from the throttle lever stud, adjust the cable as follows.

### Adjustment

**Note:** *If you've just finished checking the TV cable adjustment, some of the following steps simply repeat the steps that you've already taken to check the cable. Disregard those steps.*

11    Turn the ignition key to the Off position.
12    Remove the air intake duct and, if equipped, the resonator (see Chapter 4A).
13    Disconnect the TV cable from the stud on the control lever at the throttle body: Rotate the lever to put some slack in the cable, hold the lever in this position, slide the plastic cable end forward, then pull it off the stud. Don't pry it off; just use your fingers.
14    Raise the vehicle and place it securely on jackstands.
15    Verify that the throttle valve lever on the transmission is in the fully closed position (in the fully forward position), then verify that the throttle lever on the throttle body is at the curb idle position, i.e., resting against its stop.
16    On earlier models, use a small screwdriver to pry the TV cable lock-retaining clip from the cable adjuster (see illustration) and remove it. On later models, there's a cable lock instead of a retaining clip; on these models, simply pry the cable lock up to unlock the cable for readjustment.
17    Slide the cable sheath forward or backward within the adjuster mechanism as necessary to center the eyelet on the end of the cable with the stud on the throttle lever (see illustration). Make sure that it's within 1/32-inch. Pulling the cable too tight will cause the TV lever on the transmission to move out of its idle position.
18    While holding the cable casing in this position, reinstall the retaining clip on the

adjuster mechanism, or push the TV cable lock down, to lock the TV cable in place.
19    Reconnect the eyelet on the end of the TV cable to the stud on the throttle lever.
20    Check the TV cable adjustment.

### Replacement

21    Remove the air intake duct and, if equipped, the resonator (see Chapter 4A).
22    Disconnect the end of the TV cable from the stud on the throttle lever on the throttle body (see Step 7), then squeeze the tangs on the cable retainer and slide the cable through the cable bracket (see illustration).
23    Raise the vehicle and support it securely on jackstands.
24    Disconnect the cable from the throttle lever on the transmission (see illustration), then disengage the cable from the cable bracket.

**6.24 To disconnect the TV cable from the stud on the throttle lever (A) at the transmission, carefully pry it loose with a small screwdriver. To disengage the cable from the cable bracket (B), squeeze the tangs on the cable housing together and slide the cable housing out of the bracket**

**7.4 To disconnect each transmission oil cooler line fitting (A), insert the special quick-connect release tool (B) into each fitting, push the tool into the fitting until it releases the locking fingers inside the fitting, then pull the two sides of the fitting apart. Once both fittings are disconnected, detach both lines from the clips (C) on the radiator side tank**

**7.6 To detach the transmission oil cooler on 3.7L V6, 4.7L V8 and Hemi models, remove the mounting bolt (1) and disengage the two locator tabs (2). On 5.9L V8 and on diesel models the oil cooler is retained by four mounting bolts, two on each side**

25    Trace the routing of the TV cable from the throttle body to the transmission throttle lever, note the routing to ensure correct installation, then disengage the cable from any clips which may be securing it.

26    Remove the TV cable.

27    Installation is the reverse of removal. Adjust the cable as described in Steps 11 through 19.

## 7    Transmission oil cooler - removal and installation

### *Air-to-oil cooler*

**Note:** *All vehicles with an automatic transmission are equipped with an external air-to-oil cooler as standard equipment. All coolers are mounted in front of the radiator in a similar fashion, although they vary in size and in the location and number of mounting bolts used.*

1    Disconnect the cable(s) from the negative battery terminal(s) (see Chapter 5).

2    Put a drain pan underneath the oil cooler line fittings to catch any spilled transmission fluid.

3    Raise the front of the vehicle and place it securely on jackstands.

4    Using a quick-connect release tool (available at most auto parts stores), disconnect the transmission oil cooler line fittings (see illustration). Plug the lines to prevent fluid spills.

5    Detach the transmission oil cooler lines from the radiator side tank (see illustration 6.4).

6    Remove the transmission oil cooler mounting bolts (see illustration) and remove the cooler. Be careful not to damage the oil cooler tubes or the radiator cooling fins.

7    On vehicles with a 5.2L, 5.9L V8 or a diesel engine, remove the oil cooler ther-

mostat (see below) from the cooler, clean it, inspect it, then install the old thermostat or a new unit.

8    If you removed the cooler in order to flush it after a transmission failure, have it flushed by a dealer service department or by a transmission shop. A number of special tools are needed to flush the cooler correctly.

9    Installation is the reverse of removal. When you're done, check the transmission fluid level and add some if necessary (see Chapter 1).

### *Thermostat*

**Note:** *The air-to-oil coolers on 5.2L, 5.9L V8 gasoline engines and on diesel engines are equipped with an internal thermostat that's serviceable. The thermostat is located inside a housing located at the upper left corner of the cooler, at the left end of the cooler bypass tube. Other engines are not equipped with this thermostat.*

10    Remove the transmission oil cooler (see Steps 1 through 6).

11    Remove the snap-ring that retains the thermostat end-plug.

12    Remove the end-plug, the thermostat and the spring from the thermostat housing.

13    Thoroughly clean out the thermostat bore in the housing and wash the end-plug, thermostat and spring in clean solvent. Inspect the parts for wear and damage. If anything is worn or damaged, replace it.

14    Installation is the reverse of removal.

### *Water-to-oil cooler*

**Warning:** *Wait until the engine is completely cool before beginning this procedure.*

**Note:** *Only diesel engines are equipped with this cooler.*

15    Disconnect the cables from the negative battery terminals.

16    Remove the starter motor (see Chapter 5).

17    Drain the cooling system (see Chapter 1).

18    Disconnect the coolant lines from the oil cooler. Be sure to use a back-up wrench on the transmission cooler boss to protect the cooler.

19    Disconnect the transmission fluid lines from the oil cooler. Plug the cooler lines to prevent dirt and moisture from entering the lines.

20    Remove the cooler mounting bracket-to-transmission adapter bolt.

21    Remove the two cooler mounting bracket-to-engine block bolts.

22    Remove the cooler assembly.

23    Installation is the reverse of removal. Check the transmission fluid level and add some if necessary (see Chapter 1).

## 8    Transmission mount - check and replacement

### *Check*

1    Raise the vehicle and support it securely on jackstands.

2    Insert a large screwdriver or prybar into the space between the transmission extension housing and the crossmember. Try to pry the transmission up slightly (see illustration).

3    The transmission should not move much at all and the rubber in the center of the mount should fully insulate the center of the mount from the mount bracket around it.

### *Replacement*

4    To replace the mount, remove the bolts or nuts attaching the mount to the crossmember and the bolts attaching the mount to the transmission.

**8.2 To check the transmission mount, insert a large screwdriver between the extension housing and the crossmember and try to lever the transmission up**

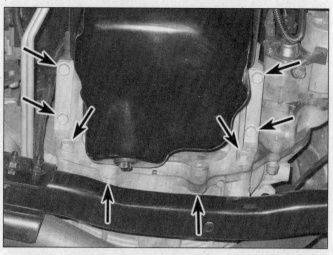

**9.10 To remove the transmission brace, remove these bolts (Hemi engine shown, other transmission braces similar)**

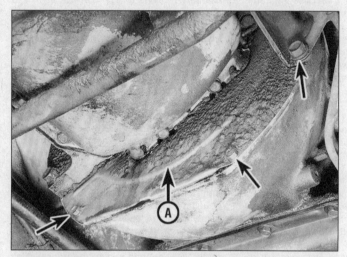

**9.11 To remove the torque converter access cover (A), remove all the retaining bolts and pull it off. The number and location of the cover bolts varies with the engine-transmission combination**

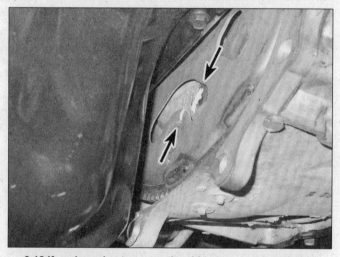

**9.12 If you're going to re-use the old torque converter, mark the relationship of the torque converter to the driveplate to ensure that their dynamic balance is preserved when the torque converter is reattached**

5   Raise the transmission slightly with a jack and remove the mount.

6   Installation is the reverse of the removal procedure. Be sure to tighten all fasteners securely.

## 9   Automatic transmission - removal and installation

### Removal

**Caution:** *The transmission and torque converter must be removed as a single assembly. If you try to leave the torque converter attached to the driveplate, the converter driveplate, pump bushing and oil seal will be damaged. The driveplate is not designed to support the load, so none of the weight of the transmission should be allowed to rest on the plate during removal.*

1   Disconnect the cable(s) from the negative battery terminal(s) (see Chapter 5).

2   Raise the vehicle and support it securely on jackstands.

3   Remove the skid plate, if equipped.

4   Remove all exhaust components that interfere with transmission removal (see Chapter 4A).

5   If the transmission is being removed for overhaul, remove the oil pan, drain the transmission fluid and reinstall the pan (see Chapter 1).

6   Remove the engine-to-transmission struts, if equipped.

7   Remove the starter motor (see Chapter 5).

8   Mark the yokes and remove the driveshaft (see Chapter 8). On 4WD models, remove both driveshafts.

9   On gasoline engines, remove the Crankshaft Position (CKP) sensor, which is located at the rear of the engine block near the driveplate (see Chapter 6).

10   Remove the transmission brace, if equipped (see illustration).

11   Remove the torque converter access cover, if equipped (see illustration).

12   Mark the relationship of the torque converter to the driveplate (see illustration) to ensure that their dynamic balance is maintained when the converter is reattached to the driveplate.

13   Remove the torque converter-to-drive-

**9.13 To remove the torque converter-to-driveplate bolts, turn the crankshaft to access each bolt**

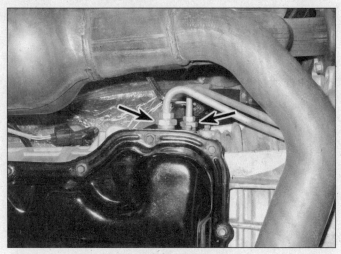

**9.22 To prevent damage to the lines, use a back-up wrench on the stationary fittings when unscrewing the transmission cooler line fittings**

plate bolts (see illustration). Turn the crankshaft for access to each bolt.

14   Disconnect all electrical connectors from the transmission. Generally speaking, the connectors to various electrical and/or electronic devices on the transmission are different in shape, color and the number of terminals, so there's little danger of accidentally reconnecting a connector to the wrong device. The wiring harness is also designed so that each connector will only reach the device to which it's supposed to be connected. However, if any of the connectors look identical or look like they could be accidentally reconnected to the wrong device, be sure to mark them to prevent mix-ups.

15   On transmissions with a shift cable, disconnect the shift cable from the transmission (see Section 3).

16   On transmissions with a Throttle Valve (TV) cable, disconnect the TV cable from the transmission (see Section 6).

17   On 4WD models, disconnect the shift rod from the transfer case shift lever (see Chapter 7C).

18   Support the rear end of the trans-

mission with a floor jack, then raise the transmission slightly to take the weight off the crossmember.

19   Unbolt the transmission mounting bracket from the transmission and from the crossmember and remove the bracket.

20   Unbolt and remove the transmission crossmember.

21   On 4WD models, remove the transfer case (see Chapter 7C).

**Note:** *If you are not planning to replace the transmission, but are removing it in order to gain access to other components such as the torque converter, it isn't really necessary to remove the transfer case. However, the two components are awkward and heavy when removed and installed as a single assembly. They're much easier to maneuver off and on as separate units. If you decide to leave the transfer case attached, disconnect the shift rod from the transfer case shift lever, or remove the shift lever from the transfer case and tie the rod and lever to the chassis (see Chapter 7C).*

**Warning:** *If you decide to remove the transfer case and transmission as a single assembly,*

*use safety chains to help stabilize them and to prevent them from falling off the jack head, which could cause serious damage to the transmission and/or transfer case and serious bodily injury to you.*

22   Using a flare-nut wrench, disconnect the transmission cooler lines from the transmission (see illustration). Plug the ends of the lines to prevent fluid from leaking out after you disconnect them.

23   Remove the oil filler tube bracket bolts and withdraw the tube from the transmission. Don't lose the filler tube seal (unless it's damaged, in which case you should replace it). On 4WD models, remove the bolt that attaches the transfer case vent tube to the converter housing (unless you already did so when removing the transfer case).

24   Support the transmission with a transmission jack (available at most equipment rental facilities) and secure the transmission to the jack with safety chains. Support the engine with a jack. Use a block of wood under the oil pan to spread the load.

25   Remove the bolts securing the transmission to the engine (see illustration). A long extension and a U-joint socket will greatly simplify this step.

**Note:** *The upper bolts are easier to remove after the transmission has been lowered (see the next Step). Also, on some models, you might have to remove the oil filter (see Chapter 1) before you can remove the lower right (passenger's side) bolt.*

26   Lower the engine and transmission slightly and clamp a pair of locking pliers onto the lower portion of the transmission case, just in front of the torque converter. The pliers will prevent the torque converter from falling out while you're removing the transmission.

27   Move the transmission to the rear to disengage it from the engine block dowel pins and make sure the torque converter is detached from the driveplate. Lower the transmission with the jack.

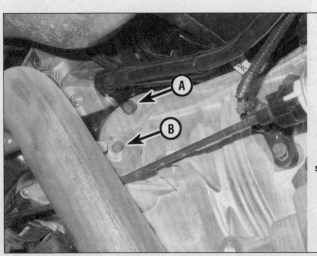

**9.25a To detach the transmission from the engine, remove all transmission-to-engine bolts (A) and engine-to-transmission bolts (B) (left side shown, right side similar; not all bolts visible in this photo)**

## Installation

28   Prior to installation, make sure the torque converter is securely engaged in the pump. If you've removed the converter, spread transmission fluid on the torque converter rear hub, where the transmission front seal rides. With the front of the transmission facing up, rotate the converter back and forth. It should drop down into the transmission front pump in stages. To make sure the converter is fully engaged, lay a straightedge across the transmission-to-engine mating surface and make sure the converter lugs are at least 1/2-inch below the straightedge. Reinstall the locking pliers to hold the converter in this position.

29   With the transmission secured to the jack, raise it into position. Connect the transmission fluid cooler lines.

30   Turn the torque converter to line up the holes with the holes in the driveplate. The marks on the torque converter and driveplate made during removal must line up.

31   Move the transmission forward carefully until the dowel pins and the transmission are engaged. Make sure the transmission mates with the engine with no gap. If there's a gap, make sure there are no wires or other objects pinched between the engine and transmission and also make sure the torque converter is completely engaged in the transmission front pump. Try to rotate the converter - if it doesn't rotate easily, it's probably not fully engaged in the pump. If necessary, lower the transmis-

sion and install the converter fully.

32   Install the transmission-to-engine bolts and tighten them to the torque listed in this Chapter's Specifications, if applicable (if there's no torque specification for the transmission that you're servicing, tighten the bolts securely). As you're tightening the bolts, make sure that the engine and transmission mate completely at all points. If not, find out why. Never try to force the engine and transmission together with the transmission-to-engine bolts or you'll break the transmission case!

33   Install the torque converter-to-driveplate bolts. Tighten them to the torque listed in this Chapter's Specifications, if applicable (if there's no torque specification for the transmission that you're servicing, tighten the bolts securely).

**Caution:** *Using the correct length bolts for bolting the converter to the driveplate is critical. A number of different converters are used on the vehicles covered by this manual. If the bolts are too long, they will damage the converter. If you're planning to use new bolts, make sure you obtain original equipment replacement bolts of the same length.*

**Note:** *Install all of the bolts before tightening any of them.*

34   If you're installing a 45RFE or 545RFE transmission, install the transmission brace and tighten the bolts to the torque listed in the Chapter Specifications 2A, in the sequence indicated in *Oil pan - removal and installation*

in Chapter 2A or Chapter 2B or Chapter 2C or Chapter 2D that covers the engine in your vehicle.

35   The remainder of installation is the reverse of removal.

36   When you're done, refill the transmission with the specified fluid (see Chapter 1), run the engine and check for fluid leaks.

## 10   Automatic transmission overhaul - general information

1   In the event of a fault occurring, it will be necessary to establish whether the fault is electrical, mechanical or hydraulic in nature, before repair work can be contemplated. Diagnosis requires detailed knowledge of the transmission's operation and construction, as well as access to specialized test equipment, and so is deemed to be beyond the scope of this manual. It is therefore essential that problems with the automatic transmission are referred to a dealer service department or other qualified repair facility for assessment.

2   Note that a faulty transmission should not be removed before the vehicle has been assessed by a knowledgeable technician equipped with the proper tools, as troubleshooting must be performed with the transmission installed in the vehicle.

# Notes

# Chapter 7 Part C
# Transfer case

## Contents

## Specifications

### Torque specifications

**Note:** *One foot-pound (ft-lb) of torque is equivalent to 12 inch-pounds (in-lbs) of torque. Torque values below approximately 15 ft-lbs are expressed in inch-pounds, because most foot-pound torque wrenches are not accurate at these smaller values.*

|  | **Ft-lbs** (unless otherwise indicated) |
|---|---|
| Electric shift motor mounting bolts | 12 to 18 |
| Shift-rod lock bolt | 90 in-lbs |
| Transfer case-to-transmission bolts/nuts |  |
| 5/16-inch studs/nuts | 20 to 30 |
| 3/8-inch studs/nuts | 30 to 35 |
| Companion flange nut |  |
| 2001 and earlier models | 130 to 200 |
| 2002 and later models | 190 to 230 |

## 1   General Information

1    The transfer case is a device which transmits power from the transmission to the front and rear driveshafts. The models covered by this manual may be equipped with any one of the following transfer cases, all of them manufactured by New Venture (NV):

a) *1994 models are equipped with an NP241 transfer case, which is a part-time unit with a low-range reduction gear system. The NP241 has three operating ranges and a Neutral position. The low-range (4L) position provides a gear*
reduction ratio of 2.72: 1 for increased low speed torque capability. The three operating ranges are 2-high, 4-high and 4-low.

b) *1995 models are equipped with either an NP231, NP241 or NP241HD (heavy-duty). The NP231 and NP241HD are similar in design and operation to the NP241 described above.*

c) *1996 through 2001 models are equipped with an NV231, NV241 or NV241HD. Aside from their different designations, these units are identical to the 1994 and 1995 transfer cases.*

d) *The NV241 LD and NV241 HD transfer cases*

e) *The NV241 GEN II and NV271 transfer cases*

f) *The NV244 GEN II transfer case*

g) *The NV243 and NV273 transfer cases*

2    We don't recommend trying to rebuild any of these transfer cases at home. They're difficult to overhaul without special tools, and rebuilt units may even be available (on an exchange basis) for less than it would cost to rebuild your own. However, there are a number of components that you can check, adjust and or replace - and those items are covered in this Chapter.

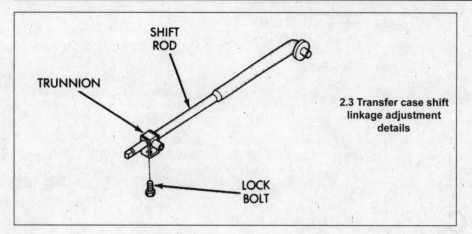

**SHIFT ROD**

**TRUNNION**

**LOCK BOLT**

**2.3 Transfer case shift linkage adjustment details**

## 2   Shift linkage adjustment (manual shift models)

1   Move the shift lever into the 2H position.
2   Raise the vehicle and support it securely on jackstands.
3   Loosen the shift-rod lock bolt at the trunnion (see illustration).
4   Check the fit of the shift rod in the trunnion. Make sure it doesn't bind in the trunnion.
5   Verify that the transfer case range lever is in the 2H position.
6   Align the adjustment locating hole on the lower shifter lever with the adjustment channel located on the shifter bracket assembly.
7   Insert a drill bit with the correct diameter through the adjustment channel and into the locating hole to lock the shifter in position.
8   Tighten the shift-rod lock bolt to the torque listed in this Chapter's Specifications.
9   Remove the jackstands and lower the vehicle.

## 3   Shift range selector switch (electric shift models) - replacement

1   Disconnect the cable(s) from the negative battery terminal(s) (see Chapter 5).
2   Raise the vehicle and support it securely on jackstands.
3   Remove the center instrument panel bezel (see Chapter 11, *Dashboard trim panels - removal and installation*).
4   Disconnect the switch assembly electrical connectors.
5   Separate the shift range selector switch from the panel bezel.
6   Installation is the reverse of the removal.

## 4   Electric shift motor (electric shift models) - replacement

**Note:** *New shift motors are packaged with the shift motor positioned in the 2WD/AWD mode. The transfer case must be selected for 2WD/AWD before the shift motor can be installed.*

1   Disconnect the cable(s) from the negative battery terminal(s) (see Chapter 5).
2   Raise the vehicle and support it securely on jackstands.
3   Disconnect the shift motor and the mode sensor connectors.
4   Remove the shift motor and mode sensor assembly mounting bolts and separate the unit from the transfer case.
5   Installation is the reverse of removal. Replace the shift sector O-ring with a new part. If the sector shaft does not align with the shift motor, manually shift the transfer case to the correct position.
6   Tighten the electric shift motor mounting bolts to the torque Specifications listed in this Chapter.

## 5   Oil seal - replacement

1   Disconnect the cable(s) from the negative battery terminal(s) (see Chapter 5, Section 1).
2   Raise the vehicle and support it securely on jackstands.
3   Remove the skid plate, if equipped.
4   Drain the transfer case lubricant (see Chapter 1).

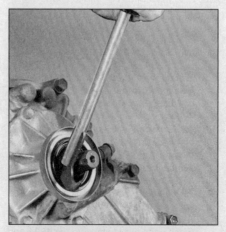

**5.9 Use a seal removal tool to pry the transfer case seal out of the housing**

### Front (output shaft) seal

5   Remove the front driveshaft (see Chapter 8).
6   On models equipped with a companion flange, remove the companion flange nut. Discard the nut; it's not reusable.
7   Tap the companion flange off the front output shaft with a brass or plastic hammer.
8   On models without a companion flange, remove the driveshaft seal boot from the seal slinger around the output shaft, then remove the seal slinger by bending its ears outward.
9   Carefully pry out the old seal with a screwdriver or a seal removal tool (see illustration). Make sure you don't scratch or gouge the seal bore.
10   Lubricate the lips and the outer diameter of the new seal with multi-purpose grease. Place the seal in position, square to the bore, making sure the garter spring faces toward the inside of the transfer case.
11   Use a seal driver or a suitable equivalent to drive the seal into place. A large deep socket (see illustration) with an outside circumference slightly smaller than the circumference of the new seal will work fine. Start the seal in the bore with light hammer taps. Continue tapping the seal into place until it is recessed the correct amount.
12   Install the seal slinger and driveshaft seal boot. Secure the boot with a new clamp.
13   Install the companion flange, if equipped, on the front output shaft, then install a NEW flange nut and tighten it to the torque listed in this Chapter's Specifications.
14   Install the front driveshaft (see Chapter 8).
15   Remove the jackstands and lower the vehicle.

### Extension housing seal

16   This procedure is identical to the extension housing seal replacement procedure for the transmission (see Chapter 7A).

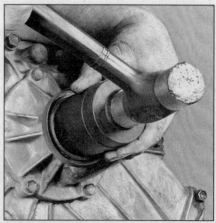

**5.11 The new seal can be driven into place using a seal installer tool or a large socket**

## 6    Transfer case - removal and installation

### Removal

1    Disconnect the cable(s) from the negative battery terminal(s) (see Chapter 5).
2    Raise the vehicle and support it securely on jackstands.
3    Remove the skid plate, if equipped.
4    Drain the transfer case lubricant (see Chapter 1).
5    Detach all vacuum/vent lines, if equipped, and electrical connectors from the transfer case.
6    On manual shift models, disconnect the shift lever rod from the grommet in the transfer case shift lever or from the shift lever arm on the floor, whichever provides easier access. Press the rod out of the grommet with adjustable pliers.
7    On electric shift models, disconnect the transfer case shift motor and transfer case sensor.
8    Remove the front and rear driveshafts (see Chapter 8).
9    On some 2002 heavy duty models (2500/3500), it may be necessary to remove the rear crossmember.
10    Support the transmission with a transmission jack.
11    Support the transfer case with a transmission jack. Secure the transfer case to the transmission jack with safety chains.
12    Remove the transfer case-to-transmission bolts/nuts (see illustration).
13    Make a final check that all wires and hoses have been disconnected from the transfer case, then move the transfer case and jack toward the rear of the vehicle until the transfer case is clear of the transmission. Keep the transfer case level as this is done.
14    Once the input shaft is clear, lower the transfer case and remove it from under the vehicle.

### Installation

15    Remove all gasket material from the rear of the transmission. Apply RTV sealant to both sides of the transfer-case-to-transmission gasket and position the gasket on the mating surface of the transmission.
16    With the transfer case secured to the jack as on removal, raise it into position behind the transmission and then carefully slide it forward, engaging the input shaft with the transmission output shaft. Do not use excessive force to install the transfer case - if the input shaft does not slide into place, readjust the angle so it is level and/or turn the input shaft

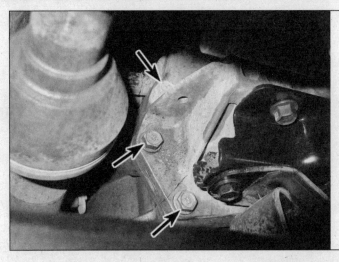

6.12 Remove the transfer case bolts/ nuts from the transmission - remaining bolts/nuts hidden from view

so the splines engage properly with the transmission.
17    Install the transfer case-to-transmission bolts/nuts, tightening them to the torque listed in this Chapter's Specifications.
18    Remove the safety chains and remove the jack supporting the transfer case.
19    Install the rear crossmember, if removed.
20    Remove the transmission jack from under the transmission.
21    Install the driveshafts (see Chapter 8).
22    Reattach all vacuum and/or vent lines. Plug in all electrical connectors.
23    On manual shift models, connect the shift rod to the transfer case shift lever or to the floor-mounted shift lever arm, and adjust the shift linkage (see Section 2).
24    On electric shift models, connect the transfer case shift motor and transfer case sensor electrical connectors.
25    Refill the transfer case with lubricant (see Chapter 1). If the vehicle has a manual transmission, this is also a good time to check the lubricant level for the transmission (see Chapter 1).
26    Install the skid plate, if equipped.
27    Remove the jackstands and lower the vehicle.
28    Connect the negative battery cable.
29    Road test the vehicle for proper operation and check for leakage.

## 7    Transfer case overhaul - general information

1    Overhauling a transfer case is a difficult job for the do-it-yourselfer. It involves the disassembly and reassembly of many small parts. Numerous clearances must be pre-cisely measured and, if necessary, changed with select fit spacers and snap-rings. As a result, if transfer case problems arise, it can be removed and installed by a competent do-it-yourselfer, but overhaul should be left to a transmission repair shop. Rebuilt transfer cases may be available - check with your dealer parts department and auto parts stores. At any rate, the time and money involved in an overhaul is almost sure to exceed the cost of a rebuilt unit.
2    Nevertheless, it's not impossible for an inexperienced mechanic to rebuild a transfer case if the special tools are available and the job is done in a deliberate step-by-step manner so nothing is overlooked.
3    The tools necessary for an overhaul include internal and external snap-ring pliers, a bearing puller, a slide hammer, a set of pin punches, a dial indicator and possibly a hydraulic press. In addition, a large, sturdy workbench and a vise or transmission stand will be required.
4    During disassembly of the transfer case, make careful notes of how each piece comes off, where it fits in relation to other pieces and what holds it in place. Note how parts are installed when you remove them; this will make it much easier to get the transfer case back together.
5    Before taking the transfer case apart for repair, it will help if you have some idea what area of the transfer case is malfunctioning. Certain problems can be closely tied to specific areas in the transfer case, which can make component examination and replacement easier. Refer to the Troubleshooting section in the introductory pages of this manual for information regarding possible sources of trouble.

# Notes

# Chapter 8
# Clutch and driveaxles

## Contents

## Specifications

### Torque specifications

**Ft-lbs (unless otherwise indicated)**

**Note:** *One foot-pound (ft-lb) of torque is equivalent to 12 inch-pounds (in-lbs) of torque. Torque values below approximately 15 ft-lbs are expressed in inch-pounds, since most foot-pound torque wrenches are not accurate at these smaller values.*

| | |
|---|---|
| Clutch housing-to-engine bolts (NV4500 transmission) (see illustration 4.21) | |
| A bolts | 30 to 50 in-lbs |
| B bolts | 20 to 40 |
| C bolts | 35 to 65 |
| Clutch master cylinder mounting nuts | 21 |
| Clutch release cylinder mounting nuts | 17 |
| Clutch pressure plate-to-flywheel bolts | |
| 2002 and earlier 2500/3500 models | |
| 5/16 inch diameter bolts | 17 |
| 3/8 inch diameter bolts | 30 |
| 2002 1500 models | 37 |
| 2003 and later models | |
| V6/V8 engines | 37 |
| V10 engines | 23 |
| Driveaxle hub/nut (independent front suspension) | 185 |
| Axle hub/nut (solid front axle) | |
| 2002 and earlier models | 175 |
| 2003 and later models | 263 |
| Driveshaft center bearing mounting bolts | |
| 2002 and earlier models | 50 |
| 2003 and later models | 40 |

## Torque specifications (continued)

**Ft-lbs (unless otherwise indicated)**

**Note:** *One foot-pound (ft-lb) of torque is equivalent to 12 inch-pounds (in-lbs) of torque. Torque values below approximately 15 ft-lbs are expressed in inch-pounds, since most foot-pound torque wrenches are not accurate at these smaller values.*

Driveshaft-to-front axle (4WD)
  2001 and earlier universal joint clamp bolts
    Front driveshaft
      Flange yoke bolts ............................................................ 65
      U-joint strap-to-axle yoke bolts........................................ 168 in-lbs
  2002 1500 models.................................................................. 80
  2002 2500/3500 models......................................................... 14
  2003 models (all).................................................................. 80
  2004 and later 1500 models.................................................... 85
  2004 and later 2500/3500 models............................................ 21

Driveshaft-to-rear axle
  2001 and earlier universal joint clamp bolts
    9-1/4 axle .......................................................................... 168 in-lbs
    Model 60/70/80 axle ........................................................... 22
  2002 (1500) models .............................................................. 85
  2002 (2500/3500) models ...................................................... 22
  2003 models.......................................................................... 85
  2004 and later (1500) models ................................................. 85
  2004 and later (2500/3500) models ......................................... 22

Driveshaft-to-transfer case (4WD)
  Front driveshaft
    2002 (2500/3500) models..................................................... 65
    2003 (2500/3500) models..................................................... 22
    2004 and later (2500/3500) models........................................ 65
Hub bearing-to-steering knuckle nuts (solid axle) ............................ 125
Rear axleshaft flange bolts............................................................. 95
Rear differential pinion mate shaft lock bolt...................................... 96 in-lbs
Wheel lug nuts.............................................................................. See Chapter 1
Differential cover bolts .................................................................. See Chapter 1
Companion flange-to-differential pinion nut
  Front axle
    Model 44 ............................................................................. 190 to 290
    Model 60 ............................................................................. 215 to 315
  Rear axle
    9-1/4 inch ........................................................................... 210 (minimum)
    Model 60 ............................................................................. 215 to 315
    Model 70 ............................................................................. 220 to 280
    Model 80 ............................................................................. 440 to 500
Rear axleshaft (Model 60/70/80)
  Flange bolts ......................................................................... 90
  Axleshaft locking nut ............................................................. 120 to 140
Pinion shaft lock bolt..................................................................... 96 in-lbs
Shift motor housing bolts................................................................ 96 in-lbs

### 1  General information

1    The information in this Chapter deals with the components from the rear of the engine to the rear wheels, except for the transmission (and transfer case, if equipped), which is dealt with in the previous Chapter. For the purposes of this Chapter, these components are grouped into three categories: clutch, driveshaft and axles. Separate Sections within this Chapter offer general descriptions and checking procedures for components in each of the three groups.

2    Since nearly all the procedures covered in this Chapter involve working under the vehicle, make sure it's securely supported on sturdy jackstands or on a hoist where the vehicle can be easily raised and lowered.

### 2  Clutch - description and check

1    All vehicles with a manual transmission have a single dry plate, diaphragm spring-type clutch. The clutch disc has a splined hub which allows it to slide along the splines of the transmission input shaft. A sleeve-type release bearing is operated by a release fork in the clutch housing. The fork pivots on a ballstud mounted inside the housing.

2    The clutch release system is operated by hydraulic pressure. The hydraulic release system consists of the clutch pedal, a master cylinder and fluid reservoir, the hydraulic line, a release cylinder, and a release fork mounted inside the clutch housing.

3    When pressure is applied to the clutch pedal to release the clutch, hydraulic pressure is exerted against the release fork by the release cylinder pushrod. When the release fork is moved, it pushes against the release bearing. The bearing pushes against the fingers of the diaphragm spring of the pressure plate assembly, which in turn releases the clutch plate.

4    Terminology can be a problem when discussing the clutch components because common names are in some cases different from those used by the manufacturer. For example, the driven plate is also called the clutch plate or disc, the clutch release bearing is sometimes called a throwout bearing, and the release cylinder is sometimes called the slave cylinder.

5    Unless you're replacing components with obvious damage, do these preliminary checks to diagnose clutch problems:

a)  *The first check should be of the fluid level in the master cylinder. If the fluid level is low, add fluid as necessary and inspect the hydraulic system for leaks.*

b)  *To check "clutch spin-down time," run the engine at normal idle speed with the transmission in Neutral (clutch pedal up - engaged). Disengage the clutch (pedal down), wait several seconds and shift the transmission into Reverse. No grinding noise should be heard. A grinding noise would most likely indicate a bad pressure plate or clutch disc.*

c)  *To check for complete clutch release, run the engine (with the parking brake applied to prevent vehicle movement) and hold the clutch pedal approximately 1/2-inch from the floor. Shift the transmission between 1st gear and Reverse several times. If the shift is rough, component failure is indicated.*

d)  *Visually inspect the pivot bushing at the top of the clutch pedal to make sure there's no binding or excessive play.*

### 3  Clutch hydraulic release system - removal and installation

#### *Removal*

**Note:** *The clutch hydraulic release system is serviced as an assembly. The components cannot be serviced separately. They're filled with fluid during manufacture, then sealed. They must not be disassembled or disconnected. If the system is leaking or has air in it, replace the entire assembly.*

1    Raise the vehicle and support it securely on jackstands.

2    On diesel models, remove the slave cylinder shield, if equipped.

3    Remove the fasteners attaching the release cylinder to the clutch housing (see illustration) then separate the release cylinder from the clutch housing.

4    Disengage the clutch hydraulic fluid line from the retaining clip from the stud on the firewall (see illustration).

5    Lower the vehicle.

6    Pry off the retainer clip from the pushrod-to-clutch pedal pin, then slide the pushrod off the pin. Remove the pin bushing and inspect it. If it's worn, replace it (see illustrations).

7    Unplug the electrical connector for the clutch pedal position switch, then remove the clutch master cylinder mounting fasteners.

8    To avoid spillage, make sure that the cap on the master cylinder's remote reservoir is tight, then remove the reservoir mounting fas-

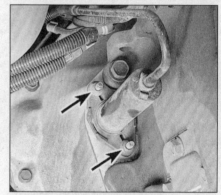

**3.3 To detach the clutch slave (release) cylinder from the clutch housing, remove these two nuts (arrows)**

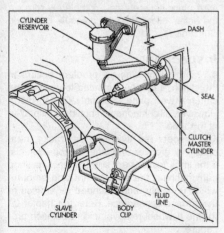

**3.4 Clutch hydraulic release system details**

**3.6a To disconnect the clutch master cylinder pushrod from the pivot pin at the top of the clutch pedal, pry off this retainer clip with a screwdriver - early models shown, later models similar**

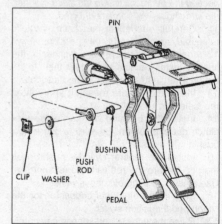

**3.6b Clutch master cylinder pushrod-to-pedal pivot pin installation details (some models may be equipped with two washers; one flat, one wave)**

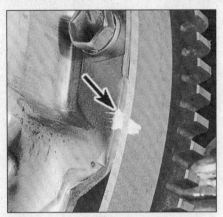

**4.7 Mark the relationship of the pressure plate to the flywheel (if you're planning to re-use the old pressure plate)**

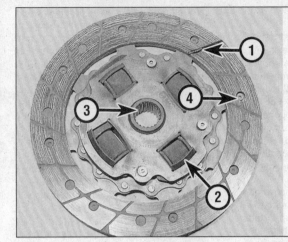

**4.11 The clutch disc**

1. *Lining - this will wear down in use*
2. *Springs or dampers - check for cracking and deformation*
3. *Splined hub - the splines must not be worn and should slide smoothly on the transmission input shaft splines*
4. *Rivets - these secure the lining and will damage the flywheel or pressure plate if allowed to contact the surfaces*

teners.

**Caution:** *Brake fluid will damage paint. If any is accidentally spilled, wash it off with water.*

9    On 2001 and earlier models, rotate the clutch master cylinder 45-degrees in a counterclockwise direction to unlock it, then remove it from the firewall. Do not attempt to disconnect the clutch fluid hydraulic line from the master cylinder or the slave cylinder. After removing the master cylinder, remove the rubber seal around the hole in the firewall. Inspect this seal for cracks and tears. If it's damaged or worn, replace it.

10    On 2002 and later models, detach the master cylinder from the firewall, then carefully lift the system from the vehicle.

## *Installation*

**Caution:** *If you're installing a new clutch hydraulic release system, you'll notice a shipping stop on the master cylinder pushrod. Do not remove this shipping stop until after the clutch release cylinder has been installed, but do remove it before the clutch is operated.*

**Note:** *The new clutch hydraulic system comes as two pieces to ease installation. After connecting the hydraulic line to the slave cylinder, the line should not be disconnected.*

11    Carefully maneuver the clutch hydraulic release system assembly into position.

12    Insert the clutch master cylinder in the firewall. Install the nuts and tighten them to the torque listed in this Chapter's Specifications.

13    Install the remote reservoir and tighten the fasteners securely.

14    Install the bushing on the pushrod-to-clutch pedal pivot pin. Be sure to use a new bushing, if necessary.

15    Install the master cylinder pushrod on the pin. Secure the rod with the retainer clip. Use a new clip if the old one is weak.

16    Plug in the electrical connector for the clutch pedal position switch.

17    Raise the vehicle and support it securely on jackstands.

18    Attach the clutch fluid hydraulic line to the retaining clip and stud on the firewall.

19    Install the release cylinder. Make sure the cap at the end of the cylinder rod is seated

properly in the release fork.

20    Install the release cylinder mounting fasteners and tighten them securely. If a new clutch hydraulic release system has been installed, connect the hydraulic line to the release cylinder.

21    Remove the jackstands and lower the vehicle.

22    If a new clutch hydraulic release system has been installed, remove the plastic shipping stop from the master cylinder pushrod before operating the clutch.

23    Test drive the vehicle and make sure the clutch hydraulic release system is operating properly.

## 4    Clutch components - removal, inspection and installation

**Warning:** *Dust produced by clutch wear and deposited on clutch components is hazardous to your health. Do not blow it out with compressed air and do not inhale it. Do not use gasoline or petroleum-based solvents to remove the dust. Brake system cleaner should be used to flush the dust into a drain pan. After the clutch components are wiped clean with a rag, dispose of the contaminated rags and cleaner in a covered, marked container.*

### *Removal*

1    Access to the clutch components is normally accomplished by removing the transmission and clutch housing, leaving the engine in the vehicle. If, of course, the engine is being removed for major overhaul, then check the clutch for wear and replace worn components as necessary. However, the relatively low cost of the clutch components compared to the time and trouble spent gaining access to them warrants their replacement anytime the engine or transmission is removed, unless they are new or in near-perfect condition. The following procedures are based on the assumption the engine will stay in place.

2    Raise the vehicle and support it securely on jackstands.

3    Detach the clutch release cylinder from

the clutch housing (see Section 3).

**Caution:** *Do not disconnect the clutch hydraulic fluid line from the release cylinder. The hydraulic release system cannot be bled if air is allowed to enter the system.*

4    Remove the transmission (see Chapter 7A).

**Note:** *On NV4500 transmissions, the clutch housing must be unbolted from the engine after the transmission has been removed to access the clutch pressure plate and disc.*

5    The clutch fork and release bearing can remain attached to the clutch housing for the time being.

6    To support the clutch disc during removal, install a clutch alignment tool through the clutch disc hub.

7    Carefully inspect the flywheel and pressure plate for indexing marks. The marks are usually an X, an O or a white letter. If they cannot be found, scribe marks yourself so the pressure plate and the flywheel will be in the same alignment during installation (see illustration).

8    Turning each bolt only 1/4-turn at a time, loosen the pressure plate-to-flywheel bolts. Work in a criss-cross pattern until all spring pressure is relieved. Then hold the pressure plate securely and completely remove the bolts, followed by the pressure plate and clutch disc.

### *Inspection*

9    Ordinarily, when a problem occurs in the clutch, it can be attributed to wear of the clutch driven plate assembly (clutch disc). However, all components should be inspected at this time.

10    Inspect the flywheel for cracks, heat checking, grooves and other obvious defects. If the imperfections are slight, a machine shop can machine the surface flat and smooth, which is highly recommended regardless of the surface appearance. Refer to Chapter 2A for the flywheel removal and installation procedure.

11    Inspect the lining on the clutch disc. There should be at least 1/16-inch of lining above the rivet heads. Check for loose rivets, distortion, cracks, broken springs and other obvious damage (see illustration). As men-

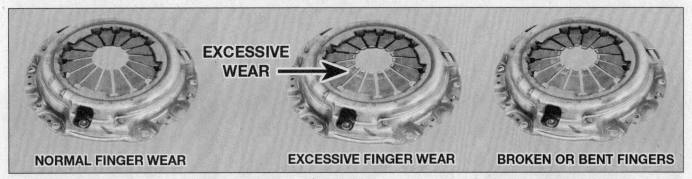

**NORMAL FINGER WEAR**     **EXCESSIVE FINGER WEAR**     **BROKEN OR BENT FINGERS**

**4.13a Replace the pressure plate if excessive wear or damage is noted**

tioned above, ordinarily the clutch disc is routinely replaced, so if in doubt about the condition, replace it with a new one.

12  The release bearing should also be replaced along with the clutch disc (see Section 5).

13  Check the machined surfaces and the diaphragm spring fingers of the pressure plate (see illustrations). If the surface is grooved or otherwise damaged, replace the pressure plate. Also check for obvious damage, distortion, cracking, etc. Light glazing can be removed with emery cloth or sandpaper. If a new pressure plate is required, new and remanufactured units are available.

14  Check the pilot bearing in the end of the crankshaft for excessive wear, scoring, dryness, roughness and any other obvious damage. If any of these conditions are noted, replace the bearing (see Section 6).

**Note:** *Considering the amount of work you've done to get to this point, it's a good idea to go ahead and replace the pilot bearing at this time.*

## Installation

15  Clean the machined surfaces with lacquer thinner or acetone. It's important that no oil or grease is on these surfaces or the lining of the clutch disc. Handle the parts only with clean hands. Install the flywheel (see Chapter 2A).

16  Position the clutch disc and pressure plate against the flywheel. If installing the original pressure plate, align the index marks. Hold the clutch in place with an alignment tool (see illustration). Make sure it's installed properly (most replacement clutch plates will be marked "flywheel side" or something similar - if it's not marked, install the clutch disc with the damper springs toward the transmission).

17  Tighten the pressure plate-to-flywheel bolts only finger-tight, working around the pressure plate.

18  Center the clutch disc by ensuring the alignment tool extends through the splined hub and into the pilot bearing in the crankshaft. Wiggle the tool up, down or from side-to-side as needed to bottom the tool in the pilot bearing. Tighten the pressure plate-to-flywheel bolts a little at a time, working in a criss-cross pattern, to prevent distorting the cover. After all the bolts are snug, tighten them to the torque listed in this Chapter's Specifica-

**4.13b Inspect the pressure plate surface for excessive score marks, cracks and signs of overheating**

tions. Remove the alignment tool.

19  Using high-temperature grease, lubricate the inner groove of the release bearing (see Section 5). Also place grease on the release lever contact areas and the transmission input shaft bearing retainer.

20  Install the clutch release bearing, if removed (see Section 5).

**4.16 Center the clutch disc in the pressure plate with an alignment tool before the bolts are tightened**

21  If equipped with an NV4500 transmission, install the clutch housing and tighten the bolts to the torque listed in this Chapter's Specifications (see illustration).

22  Install the transmission (see Chapter 7A) and all components removed previously.

23  Remove the jackstands and lower the vehicle.

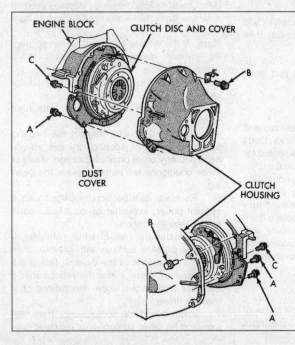

**4.21 Bolt torque guide for clutch housing-to-engine bolts and engine-to-clutch housing bolts (NV4500 transmission) (torque specifications for A, B and C bolts are listed in this Chapter's Specifications)**

**5.5 To check the clutch release bearing, hold the hub (the center) of the bearing and rotate the outer portion while applying pressure; if the bearing doesn't turn smoothly or if it's noisy or rough, replace it**

**6.5 To remove the pilot bearing, use a special puller designed for the job**

**6.6 Tap the bearing into place with a bearing driver or a socket slightly smaller than the outside diameter of the bearing**

## 5   Clutch release bearing - removal, inspection and installation

**Warning:** *Dust produced by clutch wear is hazardous to your health. Do not blow it out with compressed air and do not inhale it. Do not use gasoline or petroleum-based solvents to remove the dust. Brake system cleaner should be used to flush the dust into a drain pan. After the clutch components are wiped clean with a rag, dispose of the contaminated rags and cleaner in a covered, marked container.*

### Removal

1   Raise the vehicle and support it securely on jackstands.
2   Remove the transmission (see Chapter 7A).
**Note:** *On vehicles equipped with an NV4500 transmission, remove the clutch housing (see Section 4).*
3   Detach the clutch release lever from the ballstud and remove the bearing and lever from the input shaft.

### Inspection

4   Wipe off the bearing with a clean rag and inspect it for damage, wear and cracks. Don't immerse the bearing in solvent - it's sealed for life and immersion in solvent will ruin it.
5   Hold the center of the bearing and rotate the outer portion while applying pressure (see illustration). If the bearing doesn't turn smoothly or if it's noisy or rough, replace it.
**Note:** *Considering the difficulty involved with replacing the release bearing, we recommend replacing the release bearing whenever the clutch components are replaced.*

### Installation

6   Lightly lubricate the friction surfaces of the release bearing, ballstud and the input

shaft with high-temperature grease.
**Note:** *Make sure the spring clip is fully engaged with the release fork pivot ball stud and the release fork.*
7   Install the release lever and bearing onto the input shaft.
8   The remainder of installation is the reverse of removal.

## 6   Pilot bearing - inspection and replacement

1   The clutch pilot bearing is a needle roller type bearing which is pressed into the rear of the crankshaft. It's greased at the factory and does not require additional lubrication. Its primary purpose is to support the front of the transmission input shaft. The pilot bearing should be inspected whenever the clutch components are removed from the engine. Because of its inaccessibility, replace it with a new one if you have any doubt about its condition.
**Note:** *If the engine has been removed from the vehicle, disregard the following Steps which don't apply.*
2   Remove the transmission (see Chapter 7A).
3   Remove the clutch components (see Section 4).
4   Using a flashlight, inspect the bearing for excessive wear, scoring, dryness, roughness and any other obvious damage. If any of these conditions are noted, replace the bearing.
5   Removal can be accomplished with a special puller, available at most auto parts stores (see illustration).
6   To install the new bearing, lightly lubricate the outside surface with grease, then with the letter side of the bearing facing the transmission, drive it into the recess with a hammer and socket (see illustration) or a bushing driver.
7   Install the clutch components, transmission and all other components removed pre-

viously. Tighten all fasteners to the recommended torque.

## 7   Clutch pedal position switch - check and replacement

### Check

1   The clutch pedal position switch, which is part of the starter relay circuit, is mounted on the clutch master cylinder pushrod. The switch closes the starter relay circuit only when the clutch pedal is fully depressed. The switch is an integral part of the clutch master cylinder pushrod and cannot be serviced separately. If the switch must be replaced, so must the clutch hydraulic release system (see Section 3).
2   To test the switch, verify that the engine will not crank over when the clutch pedal is in the released position, and that it does crank over with the pedal depressed.
3   If the engine starts without depressing the clutch pedal, replace the switch.

### Replacement

4   Replace the clutch hydraulic release system (see Section 3).

## 8   Driveshaft(s) - general information

1   A driveshaft is a tube that transmits power between the transmission or transfer case and the differential(s). Universal joints are located at either end of the driveshaft and allow the driveshaft to operate at different angles as the suspension moves.
2   Three different types of universal joints are used: single-cardan, double-cardan and constant velocity.
3   Some models have a two-piece driveshaft. The two driveshafts are connected at a center support bearing.

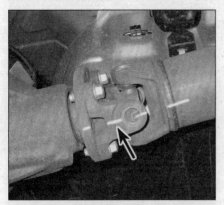

**9.2 Mark the relationship of the driveshaft to the pinion flange or yoke**

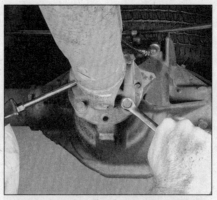

**9.3 Insert a large screwdriver or prybar through the driveshaft or pinion yoke as shown, to prevent the shaft from turning when you loosen the fasteners**

**9.19 Remove the dust boot clamp, then slide the end of the driveshaft out of the transfer case (4WD 1500 models)**

4    The rear driveshaft employs a splined yoke at the front, which slips into the extension housing of the transmission. The front driveshaft on 4WD models (and the rear half of the driveshaft on models with a two-piece driveshaft) incorporates a slip yoke as part of the shaft. This arrangement allows the driveshaft to alter its length during vehicle operation. On 2WD models the slip yoke is splined to the transmission output shaft. An oil seal prevents fluid from leaking out of the extension housing and keeps dirt from entering the transmission or transfer case. If leakage is evident at the front of the driveshaft, replace the extension housing oil seal (see Chapter 7A).

5    The driveshaft assembly requires very little service. Factory U-joints are lubricated for life and must be replaced if problems develop. The driveshaft must be removed from the vehicle for this procedure. (Some aftermarket universal joints have grease fittings to allow periodic lubrication.)

6    Since the driveshaft is a balanced unit, it's important that no undercoating, mud, etc., be allowed to accumulate on it. When the vehicle is raised for service it's a good idea to clean the driveshaft and inspect it for any obvious damage. Also, make sure the small weights used to originally balance the driveshaft are in place and securely attached. Whenever the driveshaft is removed it must be reinstalled in the same relative position to preserve the balance.

7    Problems with the driveshaft are usually indicated by a noise or vibration while driving the vehicle. A road test should verify if the problem is the driveshaft or another vehicle component. Refer to the *Troubleshooting* Section at the front of this manual. If you suspect trouble, inspect the driveline (see the next Section).

## 9    Driveshaft(s) - removal and installation

**Note:** *The manufacturer recommends replacing driveshaft fasteners with new ones when installing the driveshaft.*

### Rear driveshaft
#### Removal
**Note:** *Where a two-piece driveshaft is involved, the rear shaft must be removed before the front shaft.*

1    Raise the vehicle and support it securely on jackstands.

2    Use chalk or a scribe to "index" the relationship of the driveshaft to the differential axle assembly mating flange or yoke. This ensures correct alignment when the driveshaft is reinstalled (see illustration).

3    Remove the bolts securing the driveshaft flange or universal joint clamps to the differential pinion flange or yoke (see illustration). Turn the driveshaft (or wheels) as necessary to bring the bolts into the most accessible position.

4    Pry the universal joint away from its mating flange or yoke and remove the shaft from the flange. Be careful not to let the caps fall off of the universal joint (which would cause contamination and loss of the needle bearings).

5    Lower the rear of the driveshaft. If the driveshaft is a one-piece unit, slide the front end of the driveshaft out of the transmission extension housing; if it's a two-piece driveshaft, mark the relationship of the center support bearing to the support bracket, then unbolt the center support bearing and slide the front end of the front driveshaft out of the extension housing.

6    Wrap a plastic bag over the extension housing and hold it in place with a rubber band. This will prevent loss of fluid and protect against contamination while the driveshaft is out.

#### Installation
7    Remove the plastic bag from the transmission or transfer case extension housing and wipe the area clean. Inspect the oil seal carefully. If it's leaking, now is the time to replace it (see Chapter 7A).

8    Inspect the center support bearing, if equipped. If it's rough or noisy, replace it (see Section 10).

9    Insert the front end of the driveshaft

assembly into the transmission or transfer case extension housing.

10   If the driveshaft is a one-piece unit, raise the rear of the driveshaft into position, checking to be sure the marks are in alignment. If not, turn the pinion flange until the marks line up.

11   If the driveshaft is a two-piece unit, raise the center support bearing and bolt it loosely into place, raise the rear end of the rear shaft into position and make sure the alignment marks are in alignment. If not, turn the pinion flange until they do.

12   Remove the tape securing the bearing caps and install the clamps, if equipped, and fasteners. Tighten the fasteners center support bearing bolts to the torque listed in this Chapter's Specifications.

### Front (4WD)
#### Removal
13   Raise the vehicle and support it securely on jackstands.

14   If equipped, remove the skid plate.

15   If necessary, remove the exhaust crossover pipe.

16   Use chalk or a scribe to mark the relationship of the driveshaft to the differential axle assembly mating flange or yoke (see illustration 9.2). This ensures correct alignment when the driveshaft is reinstalled.

17   Remove the bolts and straps that secure the front end of the driveshaft to the differential mating flange or yoke.

18   On models equipped with a transfer case flange, make alignment marks on the driveshaft and transfer case flanges. Unbolt the flange that secures the driveshaft universal joint to the transfer case and differential, then remove the driveshaft.

19   On 1500 models, remove the dust boot clamp, then slide the end of the driveshaft out of the transfer case (see illustration).

#### Installation
20   Installation is the reverse of removal. If the shaft cannot be lined up due to the components of the differential or transfer case having been rotated, put the vehicle in Neutral

**12.2 A pair of needle-nose pliers can be used to remove the universal joint snap-rings**

**12.4 To press the universal joint out of the driveshaft yoke, set it up in a vise with the small socket pushing the joint and bearing cap into the large socket**

**12.9 If the snap-ring will not seat in the groove, strike the yoke with a brass hammer - this will relieve the tension that has set up in the yoke and slightly spring the yoke ears (this should also be done if the joint feels tight when assembled)**

or rotate one wheel to allow the original alignment to be achieved. Make sure the universal joint caps are properly placed in the flange seat. Tighten the fasteners to the torque listed in this Chapter's Specifications.

## 10  Driveshaft center support bearing - removal and installation

1    Raise the vehicle and support it securely on jackstands.
2    Remove the driveshaft assembly (see Section 9). Mark the relationship of the front portion of the driveshaft to the rear portion of the driveshaft.
3    Loosen the slip-joint boot clamp and pull back the boot on the front of the rear driveshaft.
4    Pull the rear driveshaft out of the center bearing.
5    Take the front driveshaft and center bearing to an automotive machine shop and have the old bearing pressed off and a new bearing pressed on.
6    Installation is the reverse of removal. Be sure the match marks line up so the driveshaft is properly "phased."

## 11  Universal joints - general information and check

1    Universal joints are mechanical couplings which connect two rotating components that meet each other at different angles.
2    These joints are composed of a yoke on each side connected by a crosspiece called a trunnion. Cups at each end of the trunnion contain needle bearings which provide smooth transfer of the torque load. Snap-rings, either inside or outside of the bearing cups, hold the assembly together.
3    Wear in the needle roller bearings is

characterized by vibration in the driveline, noise during acceleration, and in extreme cases of lack of lubrication, metallic squeaking and ultimately grating and shrieking sounds as the bearings disintegrate.
4    It is easy to check if the needle bearings are worn with the driveshaft in position, by trying to turn the shaft with one hand, the other hand holding the rear axle flange when the rear universal joint is being checked, and the front half coupling when the front universal joint is being checked. Any movement between the driveshaft and the front half couplings, and around the rear half couplings, is indicative of considerable wear. Another method of checking for universal joint wear is to use a prybar inserted into the gap between the universal joint and the driveshaft or flange. Leave the vehicle in gear and try to pry the joint both radially and axially. Any looseness should be apparent with this method. A final test for wear is to attempt to lift the shaft and note any movement between the yokes of the joints.
5    If any of the above conditions exist, replace the universal joints with new ones.

## 12  Universal joints - replacement

### Single-cardan U-joints
**Note:** *A press or large vise will be required for this procedure. It may be advisable to take the driveshaft to a local dealer service department, service station or machine shop where the universal joints can be replaced for you, normally at a reasonable charge.*
1    Remove the driveshaft as outlined in Section 9.
2    On U-joints with external snap-rings, use a small pair of pliers to remove the snap-rings from the spider (see illustration).
3    Supporting the driveshaft, place it in position on a workbench equipped with a vise.
4    Place a piece of pipe or a large socket,

having an inside diameter slightly larger than the outside diameter of the bearing caps, over one of the bearing caps. Position a socket with an outside diameter slightly smaller than that of the opposite bearing cap against the cap (see illustration) and use the vise or press to force the bearing cap out (inside the pipe or large socket). Use the vise or large pliers to work the bearing cap the rest of the way out.
5    Transfer the sockets to the other side and press the opposite bearing cap out in the same manner.
6    Pack the new universal joint bearings with grease. Ordinarily, specific instructions for lubrication will be included with the universal joint servicing kit and should be followed carefully.
7    Position the spider in the yoke and partially install one bearing cap in the yoke.
8    Start the spider into the bearing cap and then partially install the other cap. Align the spider and press the bearing caps into position, being careful not to damage the dust seals.
9    Install the snap-rings. If difficulty is encountered in seating the snap-rings, strike the driveshaft yoke sharply with a hammer. This will spring the yoke ears slightly and allow the snap-rings to seat in the groove (see illustration).
10    Install the grease fitting and fill the joint with grease. Be careful not to overfill the joint, as this could blow out the grease seals.
11    Install the driveshaft (see Section 9).

### Double-cardan U-joints
12    Use the above procedure, but note that it will have to be repeated because the double-cardan joint is made up of two single-cardan joints. Also pay attention to how the spring, centering ball and bearing are arranged.
**Note:** *Both U-joints in the double-cardan assembly must be replaced at the same time, even if only half of it is worn out.*

**14.6 Remove the snap-ring from the groove in the end of the axleshaft**

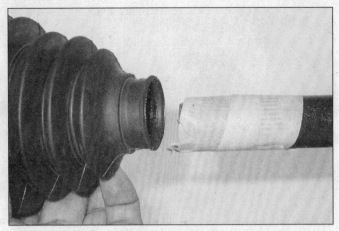

**14.12 Wrap the driveshaft splines with tape to prevent damaging the boot as it's slid onto the shaft**

### 13   Driveaxle (4WD models with independent front suspension) - removal and installation

1   Loosen the wheel lug nuts, raise the vehicle and support it securely on jackstands. Remove the wheel(s).
2   Remove the caliper and brake disc as outlined in Chapter 9, then disconnect the ABS sensor and secure the sensor and wire harness aside.
3   Remove the driveaxle/hub nut. Place a prybar between two of the wheel studs to prevent the hub from turning while loosening the nut.
4   Support the lower control arm with a floor jack, then slightly raise it to take the force of the spring off the upper control arm. Remove the shock absorber lower mounting bolt, then remove the upper control arm balljoint nut and separate the control arm from the steering knuckle (see Chapter 10).
5   Using a prybar or slide hammer with CV joint adapter, pry the inner CV joint assembly from the front differential. Be careful not to damage the front differential. Suspend the driveaxle with a piece of wire - don't let it hang, or damage to the outer CV joint may occur.
6   Pull the steering knuckle out and away from the outer CV joint of the driveaxle. If the driveaxle proves difficult to remove, tap the end of the driveaxle with a soft-faced hammer or a hammer and a brass-punch. If the driveaxle is stuck in the hub splines and won't move, it may be necessary to push it from the hub with a two-jaw puller.
7   Once the driveaxle is loose from the hub splines, pull out on the hub/knuckle assembly. Remove the support wire and guide the driveaxle out from under the vehicle.
8   Installation is the reverse of the removal procedure, noting the following points:

a)  *Thoroughly clean the splines and bearing shield on the outer CV joint. This is very important, as the bearing shield protects the wheel bearings from*
water and contamination. Also clean the wheel bearing area of the steering knuckle.
b)  *Thoroughly clean the splines and oil seal sealing surface on the inner tripod CV joint. Apply a film of multi-purpose grease around the oil seal contact surface of the inner CV joint.*
c)  *When installing the driveaxle, hold the driveaxle straight out, then push it in sharply to seat the set-ring on the splines of the inner CV joint. To make sure the set-ring is properly seated, attempt to pull the inner CV joint housing out of the differential by hand. If the set-ring is properly seated, the inner joint will not move out.*
d)  *Tighten the driveaxle/hub nut to the torque listed in this Chapter's Specifications.*
e)  *Install the wheel and lug nuts, lower the vehicle and tighten the lug nuts to the torque listed in the Chapter 1, Specifications.*
f)  *The upper balljoint-to-steering knuckle nut should not be reused. A new one should always be used. Be sure to tighten it to the torque listed in the Chapter 10, Specifications.*

### 14   Driveaxle boot (independent front suspension) - replacement

**Note:** *If the CV joints exhibit wear, indicating the need for an overhaul (usually due to torn boots), explore all options before beginning the job. Complete rebuilt driveaxles may be available on an exchange basis, which eliminates a lot of time and work. Whatever is decided, check on the cost and availability of parts before disassembling the joints.*

1   Loosen the wheel lug nuts. Raise the vehicle and support it securely on jackstands, then remove the wheel.
2   Remove the driveaxle (see Section 13).

### Inner CV joint
#### Disassembly
3   Mount the driveaxle in a bench vise with wood blocks to protect it.
**Caution:** *Do not overtighten the vise.*
4   Remove the boot retaining clamps and slide the inner boot back onto the shaft.
5   Pull the inner CV joint housing off the shaft and tripod.
6   Use a pair of snap-ring pliers and remove the snap-ring from the end of the shaft (see illustration).
7   Mark the end of the shaft and the tripod, then remove the tripod from the shaft.
8   Remove the boot from the shaft.
9   Clean the housing and the tripod with solvent.
10   Check the tripod components and the housing for excessive wear and/or damage.
11   If any components are worn or damaged, the entire joint must be replaced.

#### Assembly
12   Wrap the splines of the shaft with tape to prevent damage to the boot, then install the small boot clamp and boot onto the shaft (see illustration).
13   Install the tripod onto the end of the shaft, with the mark you made facing the end of the shaft (and aligned with the mark on the shaft).
14   Install the snap-ring, making sure it is completely seated in its groove.
15   Apply CV joint grease to the tripod and interior of the housing.
**Note:** *If grease was not included with the new boot, obtain some CV joint grease - don't use any other type of grease.*
16   Apply the remainder of the grease into the boot, then insert the shaft and tripod into the housing.
17   Position the large-diameter end of the boot over the edge of the housing and seat the lip of the boot into the locating groove at the edge of the housing. Insert the lip of the small-diameter end of the boot into the locating groove on the shaft.
18   Adjust the length of the joint by positioning it mid-way through its travel.

**14.19 After positioning the joint mid-way through its travel, equalize the pressure inside the boot by inserting a small, dull screwdriver between the boot and the CV joint housing**

**14.20 Depending on the type of clamps furnished with the replacement boot, you'll most likely need a special pair of clamp tightening pliers (most auto parts stores carry these)**

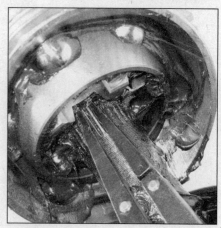

**14.23 After expanding the snap-ring, the outer joint assembly can be removed**

**14.27 Mark the bearing cage, inner race and housing relationship after removing the grease**

19   Insert a small screwdriver between the boot and the housing to equalize the pressure inside the boot (see illustration).
20   Tighten the boot clamps (see illustration).

## *Outer CV joint*
### Disassembly

21   Mount the axleshaft in a vise with wood blocks to protect it, remove the boot clamps and push the boot back.
22   Wipe the grease from the joint.
23   Using a pair of snap-ring pliers, expand the snap-ring retaining the outer joint to the shaft, then remove the joint (see illustration).
24   Slide the boot off the driveaxle.
25   Clean the axle spline area and inspect for wear, damage, corrosion and broken splines.
26   Clean the outer CV joint bearing assembly with a clean cloth to remove excess grease.

27   Mark the relative position of the bearing cage, inner race and housing (see illustration).
28   Mount the CV joint in the vise with wood blocks to protect the stub shaft. Push down one side of the cage and remove the ball bearing from the opposite side (see illustration). The balls may have to be pried out.
29   Repeat this procedure until all of the balls are removed. If the joint is tight, tap on the inner race (not the cage) with a hammer and brass drift.
30   Remove the bearing assembly from the housing by tilting it vertically and aligning two opposing cage windows in the area between the ball grooves (see illustration).
31   Turn the inner race 90-degrees to the cage and align one of the spherical lands with an elongated cage window. Raise the land into the window and swivel the inner race out of the cage (see illustration).
32   Clean all of the parts with solvent and dry them with compressed air (if available).

**14.28 With the cage and inner race tilted, the balls can be removed one at a time**

**14.30 Align one of the elongated windows in the cage with one of the lands on the housing (outer race), then rock the cage and inner race out of the housing**

**14.31 Tilt the inner race 90-degrees, align the race lands with the windows in the cage, then separate the two components**

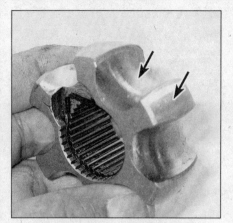

**14.34a Check the inner race lands and grooves for pitting and score marks**

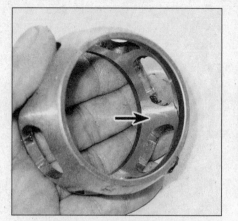

**14.34b Check the cage for cracks, pitting and score marks (shiny spots are normal and don't affect operation)**

**14.40 Apply grease through the splined hole, then insert a wooden dowel into the hole and push down - the dowel will force the grease into the joint**

33   Inspect the housing, splines, balls and races for damage, corrosion, wear and cracks.
34   Check the inner race for wear and scoring. If any of the components are not serviceable, the entire CV joint assembly must be replaced with a new one (see illustrations).

## Assembly

35   Apply a thin film of oil to all CV joint components before beginning reassembly.
36   Align the marks and install the inner race in the cage so one of the race lands fits into the elongated window (see illustration 14.31).
37   Rotate the inner race into position in the cage and install the assembly in the CV joint housing, again using the elongated window for clearance (see illustration 14.30).
38   Rotate the inner race into position in the housing. Be sure the large counterbore of the inner race faces out. The marks made during disassembly should face out and be aligned.
39   Pack the lubricant from the kit into the ball races and grooves.
40   Install the balls into the holes, one at a time, until they are all in position. Fill the joint with grease through the splined hole, then insert a wooden dowel into the splined hole to force the grease into the joint (see illustration).
41   Place the driveaxle in the vise and slide the inner clamp and boot over it (wrap the shaft splines with tape to prevent damaging the boot) (see illustration 14.12).
42   Place the CV joint housing in position on the axle, align the splines and push it into place. If necessary, tap it on with a soft-faced hammer. Make sure it is seated on the snapring by attempting to pull it from the shaft.
43   Make sure the boot is not distorted, then install and tighten the clamps (see illustration 14.20).

## 15   Rear axle - general information

1   The rear axle assembly consists of a straight, hollow housing enclosing a differen-tial assembly and axleshafts. These assemblies support the vehicle's "sprung" weight components through leaf springs attached between the axle housings and the vehicle's frame rails.
2   There are two different rear axle assemblies: 9-1/4 inch axles are a "semi-floating" design, in which the axle supports the weight of the vehicle on the axleshaft in addition to transmitting driving forces to the rear wheels.
3   Heavy duty models use a full-floating axle. A full floating axleshaft doesn't carry any of the vehicle's weight; this is supported on the axle housing itself by roller bearings. Full-floating axles can be identified by the large hub projecting from the center of the wheel. The axle flange is secured by bolts on the end of the hub.
4   Due to the need for special tools and equipment, it is recommended that operations on these models be limited to those described in this Chapter. Where repair or overhaul is required, remove the axle assembly and take it to a rebuilder, or exchange it for a new or reconditioned unit. Always make sure that an axle unit is exchanged for one of identical type and gear ratio.

## 16   Rear axle assembly - removal and installation

### Removal

1   Raise the rear of the vehicle and support it with jackstands placed under the frame rails.
2   Remove the rear wheels.
3   Disconnect the driveshaft from the rear axle (see Section 9).
4   Disconnect the ABS sensor.
5   Disconnect the parking brake cable from the parking brake lever (see Chapter 9).
6   Unscrew the vent hose fitting to detach the brake line junction block from the axle tube.
7   Disconnect the brake lines from the clips and brackets on the axle housing. Remove

the rear brake calipers (see Chapter 9).
**Caution:** *Tie the calipers up with wire to keep any strain off the flexible brake lines.*
8   Support the rear axle with a floor jack. If the rear differential is offset to one side, you'll have to use two jacks - one placed under each axle tube.
9   Remove the lower mounting bolts securing the rear shocks to the axle (see Chapter 10).
10   With the jack(s) supporting the axle, remove the nuts and U-bolts securing the axle to the springs (see illustration).
11   Lower the axle assembly and remove it from under the vehicle.

### Installation

12   Installation is the reverse of the removal procedure.
13   Tighten the U-bolt nuts to the torque listed in the Chapter 10, Specifications. Tighten the caliper mounting bolts to the torque listed in the Chapter 9, Specifications. If necessary, check and fill the axle with the specified lubricant (see Chapter 1).

**16.10 The rear axle is retained to each leaf spring by two U-bolts and four nuts**

17.3a Remove the pinion mate shaft lock bolt . . .

17.3b . . . then carefully remove the pinion mate shaft from the differential carrier (don't turn the wheels or the carrier after the shaft has been removed, or the pinion gears may fall out)

17.4 Push the axle flange in, then remove the C-lock from the inner end of the axleshaft

## 17   Rear axleshaft - removal and installation

### Semi-floating axleshaft

**Warning:** *The dust created by the brake system is harmful to your health. Never blow it out with compressed air and don't inhale any of it. An approved filtering mask should be worn when working on the brakes. Do not, under any circumstances, use petroleum-based solvents to clean brake parts. Use brake system cleaner only!*

1    The axleshaft is usually removed only when the bearing is worn or the seal is leaking. To check the bearing, raise the vehicle, support it securely on jackstands and remove the wheel and brake drum. Try to move the axle flange up and down. If the axleshaft moves up and down, bearing wear is excessive. Also check for differential lubricant leaking out from below the axleshaft - this indicates the seal is leaking.
2    Remove the cover from the differential carrier and allow the lubricant to drain into a

suitable container.
3    Remove the lock bolt from the differential pinion mate shaft and remove the shaft (see illustrations).
4    Push the outer (flanged) end of the axleshaft in and remove the C-lock from the inner end of the shaft (see illustration).
5    Withdraw the axleshaft, taking care not to damage the oil seal in the end of the axle housing as the splined end of the axleshaft passes through it.
6    Installation is the reverse of removal. Apply thread-locking compound to the threads and tighten the pinion shaft lock bolt to the torque listed in this Chapter's Specifications.
7    Always use a new cover gasket (or clean off the old RTV sealant and apply new sealant [see Chapter 1 ]) and tighten the cover bolts to the torque listed in the Chapter 1 Specifications.
8    Refill the axle with the correct quantity and grade of lubricant (see Chapter 1).

### Full-floating axleshaft

9    Loosen the rear wheel lug nuts, raise the rear of the vehicle and support it securely on

jackstands. Remove the wheel.
**Note:** *If you're just removing the axleshaft, it isn't necessary to remove the wheel or raise the rear of the vehicle. If you are going to replace the hub seals and/or bearings, the rear of the vehicle must be supported on jackstands and the wheel will have to be removed.*
10   Remove the axleshaft flange bolts (see illustration).
11   Pull out the axleshaft (see illustration). If the same axleshaft is going to be installed, clean the flange mating surface.
12   Clean the flange mating surface on the hub. While the axleshaft is removed, inspect and, if necessary, replace the hub and bearing seals and bearings (see Section 18). This is also a good time to inspect the rear brake assembly (see Chapter 9).
13   Slip a new gasket over the end of the axleshaft and slide the axleshaft into the axle housing.
14   Before engaging the axleshaft splines with the differential, apply RTV sealant to the gasket mating surface of the hub and place the new gasket in position (see illustrations). Push the axleshaft into the axle housing until

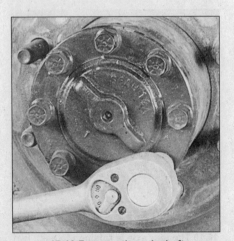

17.10 Remove the axleshaft flange bolts . . .

17.11 . . . and pull out the axleshaft

17.14a Apply a coat of RTV sealant to the mating surface of the hub . . .

**17.14b . . . then place the new gasket in position on the hub**

**19.2a Use a seal removal tool (shown) or a screwdriver to remove the old seal from the axle housing**

**19.2b You can even use the end of the axleshaft to pry out the old seal**

the axleshaft splines are fully engaged with the differential. If you have difficulty engaging the splines with the differential, have an assistant turn the other wheel slightly while you push on the axleshaft.

15    Install the flange bolts and tighten them to the torque listed in this Chapter's Specifications.

**Caution:** *The manufacturer recommends using new bolts, but the old bolts can be used if the threads are cleaned and a thread locking compound is used when they are installed.*

16    If the wheel was removed, install it and the lug nuts. Lower the vehicle and tighten the lug nuts to the torque listed in the Chapter 1 Specifications.

## 18   Rear wheel hub bearing and grease seal (full-floating axle) - removal, installation and adjustment

### Removal

1    Remove the axleshaft (see Section 17).
2    Remove the retaining ring and key from the end of the axle housing.
3    Remove the hub nut, using a special socket available at most auto parts stores.
4    Pull the hub and bearing assembly straight off the axle tube.
5    Remove and discard the oil seal from the back of the hub.
6    To further disassemble the hub, use a hammer and a long bar or drift punch to knock out the inner bearing, cup (race) and oil seal.
7    Remove the outer retaining ring, then knock the outer bearing and cup from the hub.
8    Clean the old sealing compound from the seal bore in the hub.
9    Use solvent to clean the bearings, hub and axle tube. A small brush may prove useful; make sure no bristles from the brush embed themselves in the bearing rollers. Now

spray the bearings with brake system cleaner, which will remove the solvent and allow the bearings to dry much more rapidly.

10    Carefully inspect the bearings for cracks, wear and damage. Check the axle tube flange, studs and hub splines for damage and corrosion. Check the bearing cups (races) for pitting or scoring. Worn or damaged components must be replaced with new ones.

11    Lubricate the bearings, races and the axle tube contact areas with wheel bearing grease. Work the grease completely into the bearings, forcing it between the rollers, cone and cage.

12    Reassemble the hub by reversing the disassembly procedure. Use only the proper size bearing driver when installing the new bearing cups (races), and make sure they are driven in straight and completely.

### Installation

13    Make sure the axle housing oil deflector is in position. Place the hub assembly on the axle tube, taking care not to damage the oil seals.

14    Install the hub nut and adjust the bearings as described below.

### Adjustment

15    Rotate the hub, making sure it turns freely.

16    While rotating the hub in the normal direction of rotation (forward), tighten the hub nut to 22 ft-lbs with a torque wrench. Again, this will require the special socket, which is available at most auto parts stores.

17    Back the nut off 1/4-turn, then tighten the nut hand-tight (just enough to remove the freeplay in the bearing with the special socket).

18    Turn the nut to align the closest slot in the nut with the keyway in the spindle, then install the key.

19    Install the retaining ring in the end of the spindle.

20    Try to wiggle the hub assembly; you shouldn't be able to detect any play, but the

hub should turn freely (there shouldn't be any preload on the bearings, but there shouldn't be any freeplay, either). If necessary, repeat the adjustment procedure.

21    Install the axleshaft (see Section 17).

## 19   Rear axleshaft oil seal (semi-floating axle) - replacement

1    Remove the axleshaft (see Section 17).
2    Pry the oil seal out of the end of the axle housing with a seal removal tool (see illustrations).
3    Apply a film of multi-purpose grease to the oil seal recess and tap the new seal evenly into place with a hammer and seal installation tool (see illustration), large socket or piece of pipe so the lips are facing in and the metal face is visible from the end of the axle housing. When correctly installed, the face of the oil seal should be flush with the end of the axle housing.
4    Install the axleshaft (see Section 17).

**19.3 Use a seal driver (shown) or a large socket to install the new seal**

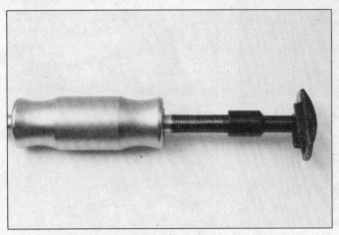

**20.2 A typical slide hammer and axleshaft bearing remover attachment**

**21.3 Use an inch-pound torque wrench to check the torque necessary to rotate the pinion shaft**

## 20   Rear axleshaft bearing (semi-floating axle) - replacement

1    Remove the axleshaft (see Section 19) and the oil seal (see Section 17).
2    A bearing puller which grips the bearing from behind will be required for this job (see illustration). Extract the bearing from the axle housing.
3    Clean out the bearing recess and drive in the new bearing with a bearing driver. Make sure the bearing is tapped in to the full depth of the recess.
4    Install a new oil seal (see Section 19), then install the axleshaft (see Section 17).

## 21   Pinion oil seal - replacement

**Note:** *This procedure applies to the front and rear pinion oil seals.*
1    Loosen the wheel lug nuts. Raise the front (for front differential) or rear (for rear differential) of the vehicle and support it securely on jackstands. Block the opposite set of wheels to keep the vehicle from rolling off the stands. Remove the wheels.
2    Disconnect the driveshaft from the differential pinion flange and support it out of the way with a piece of wire or rope (see Section 9).
3    Rotate the pinion a few times by hand. Use a beam-type or dial-type inch-pound torque wrench to check the torque required to rotate the pinion (see illustration). Record it for use later.
4    Mark the relationship of the pinion flange to the shaft, then count and write down the number of exposed threads on the shaft.
5    A special tool, available at most auto parts stores, can be used to keep the companion flange from moving while the self-locking pinion nut is loosened. A chain wrench can also be used to immobilize the flange (see illustration).
6    Remove the pinion nut.
7    Withdraw the flange. It may be necessary to use a two-jaw puller engaged behind the flange to draw it off. Do not attempt to pry or hammer behind the flange or hammer on the end of the pinion shaft.
8    Pry out the old seal and discard it (see illustration).

9    Lubricate the lips of the new seal and fill the space between the seal lips with wheel bearing grease, then tap it evenly into position with a seal installation tool or a large socket (see illustration). Make sure it enters the housing squarely and is tapped in to its full depth.
10    Install the pinion flange, lining up the marks made in Step 4. If necessary, tighten the pinion nut to draw the flange into place. Do not try to hammer the flange into position.
11    Apply a bead of RTV sealant to the ends of the splines visible in the center of the flange so oil will be sealed in.
12    Install the washer and a new pinion nut. Tighten the nut until the number of threads recorded in Step 4 are exposed.
13    Measure the torque required to rotate the pinion and tighten the nut in small increments (no more than 5 ft-lbs) until it matches the figure recorded in Step 3. To compensate for the drag of the new oil seal, the nut should be tightened a little more until the rotational torque of the pinion exceeds the earlier recording by 5 in-lbs.
14    Reinstall all components removed previously by reversing the removal Steps, tightening all fasteners to their specified torque values.

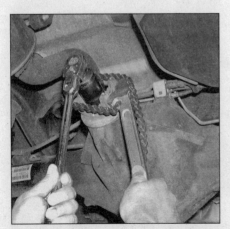

**21.5 A chain wrench can be used to hold the pinion flange while the nut is loosened**

**21.8 Use a seal removal tool or a large screwdriver to remove the pinion seal (be careful not to disturb the pinion while doing this)**

**21.9 A large socket with a diameter the same as that of the new seal can be used to drive the pinion seal into the differential housing**

## 22 Front axle assembly (4WD models) - removal and installation

### Independent front suspension

1 Raise the front of the vehicle and support it with jackstands placed under the frame rails.
2 Remove the front wheels.
3 Remove the driveaxles (see Section 13).
4 Remove the crossmember mounting bolts, then remove the crossmember (see illustration).
5 Remove the exhaust crossover pipe, if it will interfere with removal on your particular vehicle (see Chapter 4A).
6 Disconnect the driveshaft from the differential pinion flange and support it out of the way with a piece of wire or rope (see Section 9).
7 Support the axle assembly with a floor jack under the differential.
8 At the top of the differential housing, remove the two mounting bolts.
9 Remove the remaining mounting bolts for the axle assembly (see illustrations).
10 Lower the jack slowly, then remove the axle assembly from under the vehicle.
11 Installation is the reverse of removal.

### Solid axle

12 Loosen the front wheel lug nuts. Raise the vehicle and support it securely with jackstands positioned under the frame rails. Remove the front wheels.
13 Remove the brake calipers and discs (see Chapter 9) and ABS wheel speed sensors, if equipped.
14 Disconnect the vent hose.
15 Disconnect the driveshaft from the differential pinion flange and support it out of the way with a piece of wire or rope (see Section 9).
16 Disconnect the stabilizer bar link from the axle bracket.
17 Disconnect the shock absorbers from the axle brackets.
18 Disconnect the tie-rod and drag link from the steering knuckle (see Chapter 10). Support the axle assembly with two floor jacks, one positioned under the differential and one positioned under the long axle tube.

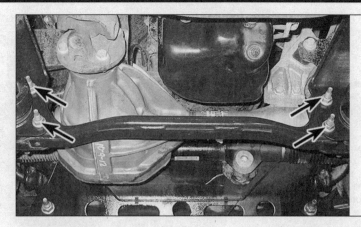

**22.4 Remove the crossmember mounting bolts**

19 Disconnect the track bar from the axle bracket (see Chapter 10).
20 Remove the coil springs (see Chapter 10).
21 Mark the relationship of the alignment cams to ensure proper reassembly, then remove the bolts and disconnect the lower suspension arms from the axle bracket.
22 Lower the jacks and remove the axle from under the vehicle.
23 Installation is the reverse of removal. Tighten all bolts to the torque listed in this Chapter's Specifications and in the Specifications in Chapters 9 and 10.

## 23 Front driveaxle oil seal (independent front suspension) - removal and installation

1 Remove the driveaxle (see Section 13).
2 Pry the oil seal out of the end of the axle housing with a seal removal tool.
3 Apply high-temperature grease to the oil seal recess and tap the new seal evenly into place with a hammer and seal driver, so the lips are facing in and the metal face is visible from the end of the axle housing. When correctly installed, the face of the oil seal should be flush with the end of the axle housing.

4 Lubricate the lips of the seal with multi-purpose grease, then install the driveaxle (see Section 13).
5 Check the front differential lubricant level, adding as necessary (see Chapter 1).

## 24 Front hub bearing assembly and axleshaft (solid axle) - removal and installation

### Removal

**Note:** If you're removing the axleshaft in order to replace the axleshaft seal or bearing, we recommend having the job done by a dealer service department or a qualified independent garage. Replacing either the seal or the bearing requires special tools.
1 Loosen the wheel lug nuts. Raise the vehicle and support it securely on jackstands. Remove the wheel.
2 Remove the brake caliper and support it out of the way with wire (see Chapter 9). Remove the brake disc.
3 Remove the cotter pin and axle hub nut.
**Note:** On some models, the axle hub nut on the driver's side has left-hand threads (turn clockwise to loosen).
4 Remove the hub-to-knuckle bolts (see illustration).

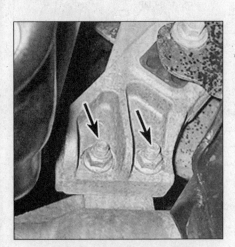

**22.9a Remove the axle tube mounting bolts . . .**

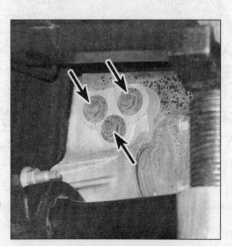

**22.9b . . . and the mounting bolts at the differential housing**

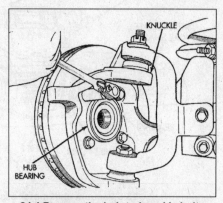

**24.4 Remove the hub-to-knuckle bolts from the back of the steering knuckle, then remove the hub bearing assembly from the steering knuckle and axleshaft (axleshaft already removed for clarity)**

5    Remove the hub bearing from the steering knuckle and axleshaft. If the axleshaft splines stick in the hub, a two-jaw puller may be required to push the axle out.
**Note:** *The hub bearing assembly may become rusted and seized to the steering knuckle depending on the severity of driving conditions (snow, rain, salt, etc.). In this event, have the hub bearing assembly removed by an automotive repair shop.*
6    Remove the brake dust shield from the steering knuckle.
7    Carefully pull the axleshaft from the axle housing. If the U-joint is worn out, it can be replaced using the procedure described in Section 12.

## Installation

8    Clean the axleshaft and apply a thin film of wheel bearing grease to the shaft splines, seal contact surface and hub bore. Install the axleshaft, engaging the splines with the differential side gears. Be very careful not to damage the axleshaft oil seals.
9    Install the dust shield.
10   Install the hub bearing. Install the hub bearing-to-steering knuckle bolts and tighten them to the torque listed in this Chapter's Specifications.
11   Install the axleshaft washer and nut, tighten the nut to the torque listed in this Chapter's Specifications. Line-up the nut with the next cotter pin hole and install a new cotter pin.
12   Install the brake disc and caliper (see Chapter 9).
13   Install the wheel and hand-tighten the wheel lug nuts.
14   Remove the jackstands, lower the vehicle and tighten the wheel lug nuts to the torque listed in the Chapter 1 Specifications.

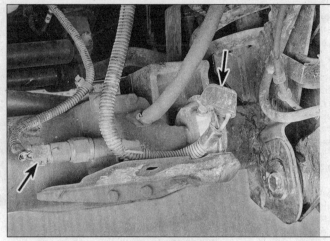

**25.2 Unplug the electrical connector (left arrow) from the indicator light switch (right arrow), then unscrew and remove the switch; detach the vent hose and the two vacuum lines from the vacuum shift motor**

## 25   Vacuum shift motor - removal and installation

### Removal

1    Raise the vehicle and support it securely on jackstands.
2    Unplug the electrical connector for the indicator light switch (see illustration).
3    Unscrew the indicator switch.
4    Detach the two vacuum lines from the vacuum shift motor. Detach the vent hose from the motor.
5    Remove the shift motor housing cover, gasket and shield from the housing (see illustration).
6    Remove the E-clips from the shift motor housing and shaft. Remove the shift motor and shift fork from the housing (see illustration).
7    Remove the O-ring seal from the shift motor shaft.
8    Clean and inspect all parts. If any part is worn or damaged, replace it.

### Installation

9    Install a new O-ring on the shift motor shaft.
10   Insert the shift motor shaft through the hole in the housing and shift fork. The offset portion of the shift fork must face toward the differential.
11   Install the E-clips on the shift motor shaft and housing.
12   Install the shift motor housing gasket and cover. Make sure the shift fork is correctly guided into the shift collar groove.
13   Install the shift motor housing shield and bolts. Tighten the bolts to the torque listed in this Chapter's Specifications.
14   Add five ounces of API grade GL 5 hypoid gear lubricant to the shift motor housing. Add lubricant through the indicator switch mounting hole.
15   Install the indicator switch.
16   Attach the vacuum line.
17   Plug in the electrical connector.

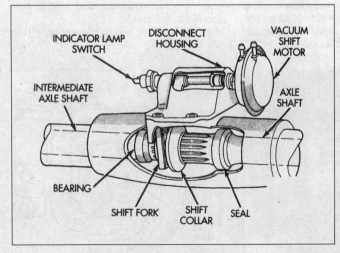

**25.5 Vacuum shift motor assembly**

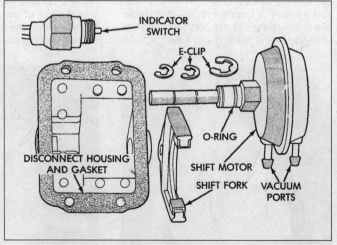

**25.6 An exploded view of the shift motor components**

# Chapter 9
# Brakes

## Contents

## Specifications

### General

| | |
|---|---|
| Brake fluid type | See Chapter 1 |

### Disc brakes

| | |
|---|---|
| Brake pad minimum thickness | See Chapter 1 |
| Disc lateral runout limit | 0.004 inch |
| Disc minimum thickness | Cast into disc |

### Drum brakes

| | |
|---|---|
| Minimum brake lining thickness | See Chapter 1 |
| Maximum drum diameter | Cast into drum |

### Torque specifications — Ft-lbs (unless otherwise indicated)

**Note:** *One foot-pound (ft-lb) of torque is equivalent to 12 inch-pounds (in-lbs) of torque. Torque values below approximately 15 ft-lbs are expressed in inch-pounds, since most foot-pound torque wrenches are not accurate at these smaller values.*

| | |
|---|---|
| Brake hose-to-caliper banjo bolt | |
| Front | |
| 1998 and earlier models | Not available |
| 1999 through 2001 models | 18 |
| 2002 and later models | 20 |
| Rear | |
| 1998 and earlier models | Not available |
| 1999 and 2000 models | 18 |
| 2001 models | 28 |
| 2002 models | |
| 1500 | 28 |
| 2500/3500 | 30 |
| 2003 and later models | 20 |

## Torque specifications (continued)                    Ft-lbs (unless otherwise indicated)

**Note:** *One foot-pound (ft-lb) of torque is equivalent to 12 inch-pounds (in-lbs) of torque. Torque values below approximately 15 ft-lbs are expressed in inch-pounds, since most foot-pound torque wrenches are not accurate at these smaller values.*

Caliper mounting bolts
  Front
    1999 and earlier models ................................................. 38
    2000 and later models .................................................... 24
  Rear
    2001 models ................................................................... 25
    2002 models
      1500 ......................................................................... 132 in-lbs
      2500 and 3500 .......................................................... 22
    2003 and later models ................................................... 22
Caliper mounting bracket bolts
  Front
    1500 .............................................................................. 130
  2500/3500
    2000 through 2002 models ............................................ 210
    2003 and 2004 models .................................................. 130
    2005 and later models ................................................... 250
  Rear
  1500
    2002 models ................................................................. 85
    2003 and later models ................................................... 100
  2500 and 3500 models .................................................... 145
Hydraulic booster mounting nuts .............................................. 21
Hydraulic booster pressure lines .............................................. 30
Master cylinder mounting nuts
  1999 and earlier models ...................................................... 21
  2000 and 2001 models ........................................................ 17
  2002 through 2004 models .................................................. 160 in-lbs
  2005 and later models ......................................................... 18
Power brake booster mounting nuts ......................................... 21
Rear brake disc-to-hub bolts .................................................... 95

## 1  General Information

1    The vehicles covered by this manual are equipped with hydraulically operated front and rear brake systems. The front brakes are disc type and the rear brakes are disc or drum type. Both the front and rear brakes are self adjusting. The disc brakes automatically compensate for pad wear, while the drum brakes incorporate an adjustment mechanism that is activated as the parking brake is applied.

### Hydraulic system

2    The hydraulic system consists of two separate circuits. The master cylinder has separate reservoir chambers for the two circuits, and, in the event of a leak or failure in one hydraulic circuit, the other circuit will remain operative. A dynamic proportioning valve, integral with the ABS hydraulic unit, provides brake balance to each individual wheel.

### Power brake booster and vacuum pump

3    The power brake booster, utilizing engine manifold vacuum, and atmospheric pressure to provide assistance to the hydraulically operated brakes, is mounted on the firewall in the engine compartment. An auxiliary vacuum pump, mounted below the power brake booster in the left side of the engine compartment, provides additional vacuum to the booster under certain operating conditions.

### Parking brake

4    The parking brake operates the rear brakes only, through cable actuation. It's activated by a lever mounted in the center console.

### Service

5    After completing any operation involving disassembly of any part of the brake system, always test drive the vehicle to check for proper braking performance before resuming normal driving. When testing the brakes, perform the tests on a clean, dry, flat surface. Conditions other than these can lead to inaccurate test results.

6    Test the brakes at various speeds with both light and heavy pedal pressure. The vehicle should stop evenly without pulling to one side or the other. Avoid locking the brakes, because this slides the tires and diminishes braking efficiency and control of the vehicle.

7    Tires, vehicle load and wheel alignment are factors which also affect braking performance.

### Precautions

8    There are some general cautions and warnings involving the brake system on this vehicle:

a)  *Use only brake fluid conforming to DOT 3 specifications.*

b)  *The brake pads and linings contain fibers that are hazardous to your health if inhaled. Whenever you work on brake system components, clean all parts with brake system cleaner. Do not allow the fine dust to become airborne. Also, wear an approved filtering mask.*

c)  *Safety should be paramount whenever any servicing of the brake components is performed. Do not use parts or fasteners that are not in perfect condition, and be sure that all clearances and torque specifications are adhered to. If you are at all unsure about a certain procedure, seek professional advice. Upon completion of any brake system work, test the brakes carefully in a controlled area before putting the vehicle into normal service. If a problem is suspected in the brake system, don't drive the vehicle until it's fixed.*

d)  *Used brake fluid is considered a hazardous waste and it must be disposed of in accordance with federal, state and local laws. DO NOT pour it down the sink, into septic tanks or storm drains, or on the ground. Clean up any spilled brake fluid immediately and then wash the area with large amounts of water. This is especially true for any finished or painted surfaces.*

## 2  Troubleshooting

| PROBABLE CAUSE | CORRECTIVE ACTION |
| --- | --- |
| **No brakes - pedal travels to floor** | |
| 1 Low fluid level<br>2 Air in system | 1 and 2 Low fluid level and air in the system are symptoms of another problem a leak somewhere in the hydraulic system. Locate and repair the leak |
| 3 Defective seals in master cylinder | 3 Replace master cylinder |
| 4 Fluid overheated and vaporized due to heavy braking | 4 Bleed hydraulic system (temporary fix). Replace brake fluid (proper fix) |
| **Brake pedal slowly travels to floor under braking or at a stop** | |
| 1 Defective seals in master cylinder | 1 Replace master cylinder |
| 2 Leak in a hose, line, caliper or wheel cylinder | 2 Locate and repair leak |
| 3 Air in hydraulic system | 3 Bleed the system, inspect system for a leak |
| **Brake pedal feels spongy when depressed** | |
| 1 Air in hydraulic system | 1 Bleed the system, inspect system for a leak |
| 2 Master cylinder or power booster loose | 2 Tighten fasteners |
| 3 Brake fluid overheated (beginning to boil) | 3 Bleed the system (temporary fix). Replace the brake fluid (proper fix) |
| 4 Deteriorated brake hoses (ballooning under pressure) | 4 Inspect hoses, replace as necessary (it's a good idea to replace all of them if one hose shows signs of deterioration) |

| PROBABLE CAUSE | CORRECTIVE ACTION |
|---|---|

### Brake pedal feels hard when depressed and/or excessive effort required to stop vehicle

| PROBABLE CAUSE | CORRECTIVE ACTION |
|---|---|
| 1 Power booster faulty | 1 Replace booster |
| 2 Engine not producing sufficient vacuum, or hose to booster clogged, collapsed or cracked | 2 Check vacuum to booster with a vacuum gauge. Replace hose if cracked or clogged, repair engine if vacuum is extremely low |
| 3 Brake linings contaminated by grease or brake fluid | 3 Locate and repair source of contamination, replace brake pads or shoes |
| 4 Brake linings glazed | 4 Replace brake pads or shoes, check discs and drums for glazing, service as necessary |
| 5 Caliper piston(s) or wheel cylinder(s) binding or frozen | 5 Replace calipers or wheel cylinders |
| 6 Brakes wet | 6 Apply pedal to boil-off water (this should only be a momentary problem) |
| 7 Kinked, clogged or internally split brake hose or line | 7 Inspect lines and hoses, replace as necessary |

### Excessive brake pedal travel (but will pump up)

| PROBABLE CAUSE | CORRECTIVE ACTION |
|---|---|
| 1 Drum brakes out of adjustment | 1 Adjust brakes |
| 2 Air in hydraulic system | 2 Bleed system, inspect system for a leak |

### Excessive brake pedal travel (but will not pump up)

| PROBABLE CAUSE | CORRECTIVE ACTION |
|---|---|
| 1 Master cylinder pushrod misadjusted | 1 Adjust pushrod |
| 2 Master cylinder seals defective | 2 Replace master cylinder |
| 3 Brake linings worn out | 3 Inspect brakes, replace pads and/or shoes |
| 4 Hydraulic system leak | 4 Locate and repair leak |

### Brake pedal doesn't return

| PROBABLE CAUSE | CORRECTIVE ACTION |
|---|---|
| 1 Brake pedal binding | 1 Inspect pivot bushing and pushrod, repair or lubricate |
| 2 Defective master cylinder | 2 Replace master cylinder |

### Brake pedal pulsates during brake application

| PROBABLE CAUSE | CORRECTIVE ACTION |
|---|---|
| 1 Brake drums out-of-round | 1 Have drums machined by an automotive machine shop |
| 2 Excessive brake disc runout or disc surfaces out-of-parallel | 2 Have discs machined by an automotive machine shop |
| 3 Loose or worn wheel bearings | 3 Adjust or replace wheel bearings |
| 4 Loose lug nuts | 4 Tighten lug nuts |

### Brakes slow to release

| PROBABLE CAUSE | CORRECTIVE ACTION |
|---|---|
| 1 Malfunctioning power booster | 1 Replace booster |
| 2 Pedal linkage binding | 2 Inspect pedal pivot bushing and pushrod, repair/lubricate |
| 3 Malfunctioning proportioning valve | 3 Replace proportioning valve |
| 4 Sticking caliper or wheel cylinder | 4 Repair or replace calipers or wheel cylinders |
| 5 Kinked or internally split brake hose | 5 Locate and replace faulty brake hose |

### Brakes grab (one or more wheels)

| PROBABLE CAUSE | CORRECTIVE ACTION |
|---|---|
| 1 Grease or brake fluid on brake lining | 1 Locate and repair cause of contamination, replace lining |
| 2 Brake lining glazed | 2 Replace lining, deglaze disc or drum |

**Troubleshooting (continued)**

| PROBABLE CAUSE | CORRECTIVE ACTION |
|---|---|

## Vehicle pulls to one side during braking

| PROBABLE CAUSE | CORRECTIVE ACTION |
|---|---|
| 1 Grease or brake fluid on brake lining | 1 Locate and repair cause of contamination, replace lining |
| 2 Brake lining glazed | 2 Deglaze or replace lining, deglaze disc or drum |
| 3 Restricted brake line or hose | 3 Repair line or replace hose |
| 4 Tire pressures incorrect | 4 Adjust tire pressures |
| 5 Caliper or wheel cylinder sticking | 5 Repair or replace calipers or wheel cylinders |
| 6 Wheels out of alignment | 6 Have wheels aligned |
| 7 Weak suspension spring | 7 Replace springs |
| 8 Weak or broken shock absorber | 8 Replace shock absorbers |

## Brakes drag (indicated by sluggish engine performance or wheels being very hot after driving)

| PROBABLE CAUSE | CORRECTIVE ACTION |
|---|---|
| 1 Brake pedal pushrod incorrectly adjusted | 1 Adjust pushrod |
| 2 Master cylinder pushrod (between booster and master cylinder) | 2 Adjust pushrod incorrectly adjusted |
| 3 Obstructed compensating port in master cylinder | 3 Replace master cylinder |
| 4 Master cylinder piston seized in bore | 4 Replace master cylinder |
| 5 Contaminated fluid causing swollen seals throughout system | 5 Flush system, replace all hydraulic components |
| 6 Clogged brake lines or internally split brake hose(s) | 6 Flush hydraulic system, replace defective hose(s) |
| 7 Sticking caliper(s) or wheel cylinder(s) | 7 Replace calipers or wheel cylinders |
| 8 Parking brake not releasing | 8 Inspect parking brake linkage and parking brake mechanism, repair as required |
| 9 Improper shoe-to-drum clearance | 9 Adjust brake shoes |
| 10 Faulty proportioning valve | 10 Replace proportioning valve |

## Brakes fade (due to excessive heat)

| PROBABLE CAUSE | CORRECTIVE ACTION |
|---|---|
| 1 Brake linings excessively worn or glazed | 1 Deglaze or replace brake pads and/or shoes |
| 2 Excessive use of brakes | 2 Downshift into a lower gear, maintain a constant slower speed (going down hills) |
| 3 Vehicle overloaded | 3 Reduce load |
| 4 Brake drums or discs worn too thin | 4 Measure drum diameter and disc thickness, replace drums or discs as required |
| 5 Contaminated brake fluid | 5 Flush system, replace fluid |
| 6 Brakes drag | 6 Repair cause of dragging brakes |
| 7 Driver resting left foot on brake pedal | 7 Don't ride the brakes |

## Brakes noisy (high-pitched squeal)

| PROBABLE CAUSE | CORRECTIVE ACTION |
|---|---|
| 1 Glazed lining | 1 Deglaze or replace lining |
| 2 Contaminated lining (brake fluid, grease, etc.) | 2 Repair source of contamination, replace linings |
| 3 Weak or broken brake shoe hold-down or return spring | 3 Replace springs |
| 4 Rivets securing lining to shoe or backing plate loose | 4 Replace shoes or pads |
| 5 Excessive dust buildup on brake linings | 5 Wash brakes off with brake system cleaner |
| 6 Brake drums worn too thin | 6 Measure diameter of drums, replace if necessary |
| 7 Wear indicator on disc brake pads contacting disc | 7 Replace brake pads |
| 8 Anti-squeal shims missing or installed improperly | 8 Install shims correctly |

| PROBABLE CAUSE | CORRECTIVE ACTION |
|---|---|

### Brakes noisy (scraping sound)

| | |
|---|---|
| 1 Brake pads or shoes worn out; rivets, backing plate or brake | 1 Replace linings, have discs and/or drums machined (or replace) shoe metal contacting disc or drum |

### Brakes chatter

| | |
|---|---|
| 1 Worn brake lining | 1 Inspect brakes, replace shoes or pads as necessary |
| 2 Glazed or scored discs or drums | 2 Deglaze discs or drums with sandpaper (if glazing is severe, machining will be required) |
| 3 Drums or discs heat checked | 3 Check discs and/or drums for hard spots, heat checking, etc. Have discs/drums machined or replace them |
| 4 Disc runout or drum out-of-round excessive | 4 Measure disc runout and/or drum out-of-round, have discs or drums machined or replace them |
| 5 Loose or worn wheel bearings | 5 Adjust or replace wheel bearings |
| 6 Loose or bent brake backing plate (drum brakes) | 6 Tighten or replace backing plate |
| 7 Grooves worn in discs or drums | 7 Have discs or drums machined, if within limits (if not, replace them) |
| 8 Brake linings contaminated (brake fluid, grease, etc.) | 8 Locate and repair source of contamination, replace pads or shoes |
| 9 Excessive dust buildup on linings | 9 Wash brakes with brake system cleaner |
| 10 Surface finish on discs or drums too rough after machining | 10 Have discs or drums properly machined (especially on vehicles with sliding calipers) |
| 11 Brake pads or shoes glazed | 11 Deglaze or replace brake pads or shoes |

### Brake pads or shoes click

| | |
|---|---|
| 1 Shoe support pads on brake backing plate grooved or | 1 Replace brake backing plate excessively worn |
| 2 Brake pads loose in caliper | 2 Loose pad retainers or anti-rattle clips |
| 3 Also see items listed under Brakes chatter | |

### Brakes make groaning noise at end of stop

| | |
|---|---|
| 1 Brake pads and/or shoes worn out | 1 Replace pads and/or shoes |
| 2 Brake linings contaminated (brake fluid, grease, etc.) | 2 Locate and repair cause of contamination, replace brake pads or shoes |
| 3 Brake linings glazed | 3 Deglaze or replace brake pads or shoes |
| 4 Excessive dust buildup on linings | 4 Wash brakes with brake system cleaner |
| 5 Scored or heat-checked discs or drums | 5 Inspect discs/drums, have machined if within limits (if not, replace discs or drums) |
| 6 Broken or missing brake shoe attaching hardware | 6 Inspect drum brakes, replace missing hardware |

### Rear brakes lock up under light brake application

| | |
|---|---|
| 1 Tire pressures too high | 1 Adjust tire pressures |
| 2 Tires excessively worn | 2 Replace tires |
| 3 Defective proportioning valve | 3 Replace proportioning valve |

### Brake warning light on instrument panel comes on (or stays on)

| | |
|---|---|
| 1 Low fluid level in master cylinder reservoir (reservoirs with fluid level sensor) | 1 Add fluid, inspect system for leak, check the thickness of the brake pads and shoes |
| 2 Failure in one half of the hydraulic system | 2 Inspect hydraulic system for a leak |
| 3 Piston in pressure differential warning valve not centered | 3 Center piston by bleeding one circuit or the other (close bleeder valve as soon as the light goes out) |

**Troubleshooting (continued)**

| PROBABLE CAUSE | CORRECTIVE ACTION |
|---|---|

### *Brake warning light on instrument panel comes on (or stays on) (continued)*

| | |
|---|---|
| 4 Defective pressure differential valve or warning switch | 4 Replace valve or switch |
| 5 Air in the hydraulic system | 5 Bleed the system, check for leaks |
| 6 Brake pads worn out (vehicles with electric wear sensors - small | 6 Replace brake pads (and sensors) probes that fit into the brake pads and ground out on the disc when the pads get thin) |

### *Brakes do not self adjust*

### *Disc brakes*

| | |
|---|---|
| 1 Defective caliper piston seals | 1 Replace calipers. Also, possible contaminated fluid causing soft or swollen seals (flush system and fill with new fluid if in doubt) |
| 2 Corroded caliper piston(s) | 2 Same as above |

### *Drum brakes*

| | |
|---|---|
| 1 Adjuster screw frozen | 1 Remove adjuster, disassemble, clean and lubricate with high-temperature grease |
| 2 Adjuster lever does not contact star wheel or is binding | 2 Inspect drum brakes, assemble correctly or clean or replace parts as required |
| 3 Adjusters mixed up (installed on wrong wheels after brake job) | 3 Reassemble correctly |
| 4 Adjuster cable broken or installed incorrectly (cable-type adjusters) | 4 Install new cable or assemble correctly |

### *Rapid brake lining wear*

| | |
|---|---|
| 1 Driver resting left foot on brake pedal | 1 Don't ride the brakes |
| 2 Surface finish on discs or drums too rough | 2 Have discs or drums properly machined |
| 3 Also see Brakes drag | |

---

**3   Anti-lock Brake System (ABS) - general information**

## *General information*

1    The anti-lock brake system is designed to maintain vehicle steerability, directional stability and optimum deceleration under severe braking conditions on most road surfaces. It does so by monitoring the rotational speed of each wheel and controlling the brake line pressure to each wheel during braking. This prevents the wheels from locking up.

2    The ABS system has three main components - the wheel speed sensors, the anti-lock brake control module and the hydraulic control unit (see illustration). Wheel speed sensors - one at each front wheel and another located on the rear differential - send a variable voltage signal to the control unit, which monitors these signals, compares them to its program and determines whether a wheel is about to lock up. When a wheel is about to lock up, the control unit signals the hydraulic unit to reduce hydraulic pressure (or not increase it further) at that wheel's brake caliper. Pressure modulation is handled by electrically operated solenoid valves.

3    If a problem develops within the system, an "ABS" warning light will glow on the dashboard. Sometimes, a visual inspection of the ABS system can help you locate the problem. Carefully inspect the ABS wiring harness. Pay particularly close attention to the harness and connections near each wheel. Look for signs of chafing and other damage caused by incorrectly routed wires. If a wheel sensor harness is damaged, the sensor must be replaced.

**Warning:** *Do not try to repair an ABS wiring harness. The ABS system is sensitive to even the smallest changes in resistance. Repairing the harness could alter resistance values and cause the system to malfunction. If the ABS wiring harness is damaged in any way, it must be replaced.*

**Caution:** *Make sure the ignition is turned off before unplugging or reattaching any electrical connections.*

4    If a dashboard warning light comes on

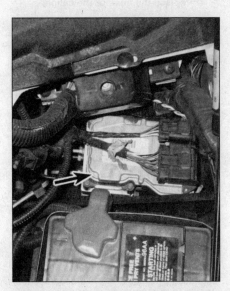

**3.2 The ABS hydraulic unit is mounted in the rear left corner of the engine compartment**

3.9a Front wheel speed sensor

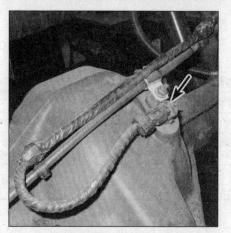

3.9b Rear wheel speed sensor

4.2a Before starting, wash down the brake disc and caliper assembly with brake cleaner

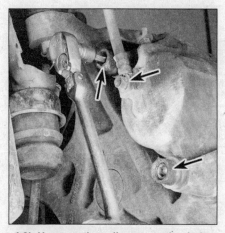

4.2b Unscrew the caliper mounting bolts (upper and lower arrows) and remove; don't remove the banjo bolt (center arrow) from the brake hose unless you plan to replace the hose or the caliper

4.2c Lift the caliper assembly off the brake disc

4.2d Support the caliper with a coat hanger or piece of wire - allowing it to hang by the brake hose can damage the hose

and stays on while the vehicle is in operation, the ABS system requires attention. Although special electronic ABS diagnostic testing tools are necessary to properly diagnose the system, you can perform a few preliminary checks before taking the vehicle to a dealer service department.

a) Check the brake fluid level in the reservoir.
b) Verify that the computer electrical connectors are securely connected.
c) Check the electrical connectors at the hydraulic control unit.
d) Check the fuses.
e) Follow the wiring harness to each wheel and verify that all connections are secure and that the wiring is undamaged.

5    If the above preliminary checks do not rectify the problem, the vehicle should be diagnosed by a dealer service department or other qualified repair shop. Due to the complex nature of this system, all actual repair work must be done by a qualified automotive technician.

### Wheel speed sensor - removal and installation

6    Loosen the wheel lug nuts, raise the vehicle and support it securely on jackstands. Remove the wheel.
7    Make sure the ignition key is turned to the Off position.
8    Trace the wiring back from the sensor, detaching all brackets and clips while noting its correct routing, then disconnect the electrical connector.
9    Remove the mounting fastener and carefully pull the sensor out from the knuckle or rear differential (see illustrations).
10    Installation is the reverse of the removal procedure. Tighten the mounting fastener securely.
11    Install the wheel and lug nuts, tightening them securely. Lower the vehicle and tighten the lug nuts to the torque listed in the Chapter 1 Specifications.

### 4    Disc brake pads - replacement

**Warning:** *Disc brake pads must be replaced on both front or rear wheels at the same time - never replace the pads on only one wheel. Also, the dust created by the brake system is harmful to your health. Never blow it out with compressed air and don't inhale any of it. An approved filtering mask should be worn when working on the brakes. Do not, under any circumstances, use petroleum-based solvents to clean brake parts. Use brake system cleaner only!*

### 1999 and earlier models

1    Refer to illustrations 4.2a through 4.2t
2    To replace the brake pads, follow the accompanying photo sequence, beginning with illustration 4.2a. Be sure to stay in order and read the caption under each illustration. Work on one brake assembly at a time so that you'll have something to refer to if you get in trouble.

4.2e Pry the ends of the retaining clip out of the holes in the caliper frame…

4.2f … and remove the outer pad

4.2g Pull the inner pad retaining clip loose from the piston and remove the pad

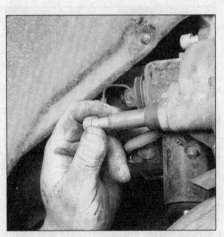

4.2h Remove the caliper mounting bolts

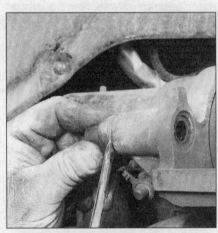

4.2i Pry off the caliper bolt dust boots and inspect them; if they're cracked or torn, replace them

4.2j Pry the seals out of the caliper bolt holes

4.2k Inspect the two small bushings inside each caliper bolt hole; if they're worn or damaged, replace them

4.2l Wipe off the seals, lubricate them with high-temperature brake grease and install them in the caliper bolt holes

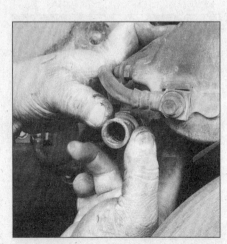

4.2m Install the caliper bolt dust boots

**4.2n Apply high-temperature brake grease to the upper sliding way of the caliper bracket . . .**

**4.2o . . . and to the lower way**

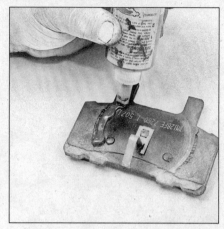

**4.2p Apply anti-squeal compound to the back of both pads and let it dry for a few minutes**

**4.2q When you install the new inner pad, make sure the retaining clip is fully seated in the piston**

**4.2r Pop the outer pad onto the caliper; make sure that the pad is pressed all the way down and the ends of the retaining clip are fully engaged with the caliper**

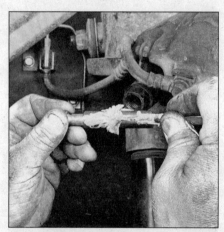

**4.2s Lubricate the caliper bolts with high-temperature brake grease . . .**

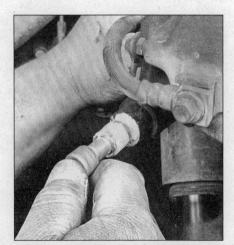

**4.2t . . . insert them into the caliper bolt holes, install the caliper and tighten both bolts to the torque listed in this Chapter's Specifications. Proceed to Step 10.**

3    While the pads are removed, inspect the caliper for brake fluid leaks and ruptures in the piston boot. Replace the caliper if necessary (see Section 5). Also inspect the brake disc carefully (see Section 6). If machining is necessary, follow the information in that Section to remove the disc.

### 2000 and later models

**Note:** *This procedure applies to the front and rear brake pads.*

4    Remove the cap from the brake fluid reservoir.

5    Loosen the wheel lug nuts, raise the end of the vehicle you're working on and support it securely on jackstands. Block the wheels at the opposite end.

6    Remove the wheels. Work on one brake assembly at a time, using the assembled brake for reference if necessary.

7    Inspect the brake disc carefully as outlined in Section 6. If machining is nec-

essary, follow the information in that Section to remove the disc, at which time the pads can be removed as well.

8    Push the piston back into its bore to provide room for the new brake pads. A C-clamp can be used to accomplish this (see illustration). As the piston is depressed to the bottom of the caliper bore, the fluid in the master cylinder will rise. Make sure that it doesn't overflow. If necessary, siphon off some of the fluid.

9    Follow the accompanying photos (illustrations 4.9a through 4.9n), for the actual pad replacement procedure. Be sure to stay in order and read the caption under each illustration.

10    After the job has been completed, firmly depress the brake pedal a few times to bring the pads into contact with the disc. Check the level of the brake fluid, adding some if necessary. Check the operation of the brakes carefully before placing the vehicle into normal service.

4.8 Before removing the caliper, be sure to depress the piston into the bottom of its bore in the caliper with a large C-clamp to make room for the new pads

4.9a Always wash the brakes with brake cleaner before disassembling anything

4.9b Remove the brake caliper mounting bolts (front caliper shown, rear caliper similar)

4.9c Remove the caliper . . .

4.9d . . . and use a piece of wire to tie it to the control arm - never let the caliper hang by the brake hose

4.9e Remove the inner pad . . .

4.9f . . . then remove the outer pad from the caliper mounting bracket

4.9g Remove the anti-rattle clips, paying close attention to how they're installed in the mounting bracket

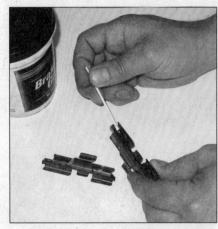

4.9h Lubricate the anti-rattle clips with high-temperature brake grease…

4.9i . . . then install the clips

4.9j Install the inner pad . . .

4.9k . . . and outer pad into the mounting
bracket - make sure both pads are
fully seated . . .

4.9l . . . then place the caliper
into position

4.9m Pull out both bushings and inspect
them for corrosion and wear; if either
bushing is damaged; replace it

4.9n Lubricate the bushings with high-
temperature brake grease, then install the
bushings and mounting bolts. Tighten the
bolts to the torque listed in this
Chapter's Specifications

5.2 To disconnect the brake hose, remove
the brake hose-to-caliper banjo bolt (rear
caliper shown, front caliper similar)

## 5   Disc brake caliper - removal and installation

**Warning:** *The dust created by the brake system is harmful to your health. Never blow it out with compressed air and don't inhale any of it. An approved filtering mask should be worn when working on the brakes. Do not, under any circumstances, use petroleum-based solvents to clean brake parts. Use brake system cleaner only!*
**Note:** *This procedure applies to the front and rear disc brake calipers.*

### Removal

1   Loosen the front or rear wheel lug nuts, raise the front or rear of the vehicle and place it securely on jackstands. Block the wheels at the opposite end. Remove the front or rear wheel.

2   Remove the brake hose-to-caliper banjo bolt and disconnect the brake hose from the caliper (see illustration). Discard the old sealing washers. Plug the brake hose immediately to keep contaminants and air out of the brake system and to prevent losing any more brake fluid than is necessary.
**Note:** *If you are simply removing the caliper for access to other components, leave the brake hose connected and suspend the caliper with a length of wire - don't let it hang by the hose see illustration 4.9d).*

3   Remove the caliper mounting bolts and detach the caliper from the mounting bracket (see illustration 4.9b).

### Installation

4   Installation is the reverse of removal. Don't forget to use new sealing washers on each side of the brake hose fitting and be sure to tighten the banjo bolt and the cali-

**6.2 The brake pads on this vehicle were obviously neglected - they wore down completely and cut deep grooves into the disc (wear this severe means the disc must be replaced)**

**6.3 Measure the brake disc runout with a dial indicator**

**6.4a The minimum (discard) thickness of the brake disc is cast into the disc**

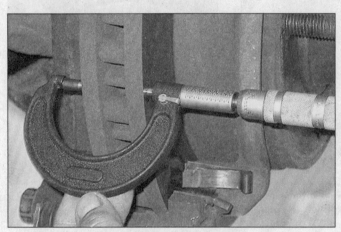

**6.4b Measure the brake disc thickness at several points with a micrometer**

**6.8 The caliper mounting bracket is retained by two bolts (rear shown, front similar)**

per mounting bolts to the torque listed in this Chapter's Specifications.

5    Bleed the brake system (see Section 12). **Note:** *If the brake hose was not disconnected, bleeding won't be required. Make sure there are no leaks from the hose connections. Test the brakes carefully before returning the vehicle to normal service.*

## 6    Brake disc - inspection, removal and installation

### *Inspection*

1    Loosen the wheel lug nuts, raise the vehicle and support it securely on jackstands. Apply the parking brake. Remove the wheels.
2    Visually inspect the disc surface for score marks and other damage (see illustration). Light scratches and shallow grooves are normal after use and won't affect brake operation. Deep grooves require disc removal and refinishing by an automotive machine shop. Be sure to check both sides of the disc.

3    To check disc runout, place a dial indicator at a point about 1/2-inch from the outer edge of the disc (see illustration). If you're checking a front disc, or rear disc on a vehicle with single rear wheels, install the lug nuts, with the flat sides facing in, and tighten them securely to hold the disc in place. Set the indicator to zero and turn the disc. The indicator reading should not exceed the runout limit listed in this Chapter's Specifications. If it does, the disc should be refinished by an automotive machine shop. If you elect not to have the discs resurfaced, deglaze them with sandpaper or emery cloth.
4    The disc must not be machined to a thickness less than the specified minimum thickness, which is cast into the disc (see illustration). The disc thickness can be checked with a micrometer (see illustration).

### *Removal and installation*

5    Remove the brake caliper (don't disconnect the brake hose) and hang them out of the way (see Section 5).

### 1999 and earlier models

6    If you're working on a two-wheel drive model, refer to Chapter 1, Section 26, Front wheel bearing check, repack and adjustment for the disc removal and installation procedure.
7    If you're working on a four-wheel drive model, refer to Chapter 8, Section 24, Hub bearing and front axleshaft (4WD models) - removal and installation, as the hub and disc must be removed as a unit. To separate the disc from the hub on these models, the wheel studs must be driven out with a brass mallet.

### *2000 and later models*

**Note:** *This procedure applies to both the front and rear disc brakes.*
8    Remove the caliper mounting bracket (see illustration).
9    If equipped, remove the hub extender from the hub.
10    Remove the lug nuts installed in Step 3 and pull the disc off the hub.

11 If you're working on a 3500 model, remove the nuts and detach the hub extension, then remove the disc. If you're removing a rear disc on a model with dual rear wheels, remove the axleshaft and the hub and bearing assembly (the disc will come with it) (see Chapter 8), then, from the backside of the disc, remove the hub-to-disc bolts and separate the disc from the hub/bearing assembly (see illustration).

12 Installation is the reverse of removal. On models so equipped, tighten the disc-to-hub bolts to the torque listed in this Chapter's Specifications.

13 Lower the vehicle and tighten the wheel lug nuts to the torque listed in the Chapter 1 Specifications.

## 7    Drum brake shoes - replacement

**Warning:** *Drum brake shoes must be replaced on both wheels at the same time - never replace the shoes on only one wheel. Also, the dust created by the brake system is harmful to your health. Never blow it out with compressed air and don't inhale any of it. An approved filtering mask should be worn when working on the brakes. Do not, under any circumstances, use petroleum-based solvents to clean brake parts. Use brake system cleaner only!*

**Caution:** *Whenever the brake shoes are replaced, the retractor and hold-down springs should also be replaced. Due to the continuous heating/cooling cycle that the springs are subjected to, they lose their tension over a period of time and may allow the shoes to drag* on the drum and wear at a much faster rate than normal.

1 There are two types of drum rear brakes on the vehicles covered by this manual; the 11-inch-diameter brakes used on 1500 models, and the 13-inch diameter brakes used on 2500 and 3500 models. The two systems are very similar in design, differing mainly in size and parking brake lever arrangement.

2 Loosen the wheel lug nuts, raise the rear of the vehicle and support it securely on jackstands. Block the front wheels to keep the vehicle from rolling and release the parking brake.

3 Remove the wheel.

**Note:** *All four rear brake shoes must be replaced at the same time, but to avoid mixing up parts, work on only one side at a time.*

4 Follow the accompanying illustrations for the inspection and removal of the brake

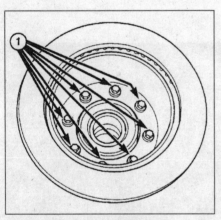

6.11 Remove the hub-to-disc bolts (1) from the back side of the disc (rear disc on 3500 models)

7.4a To remove the brake drum, simply pull it straight off

7.4b If you can't pull off the drum fairly easily, apply some penetrating oil at the hub-to-drum joint and allow it to soak in, lightly tap the drum to break it loose . . .

7.4c . . . then carefully tap around the outer edge of the drum to drive it off the studs - don't use excessive force!

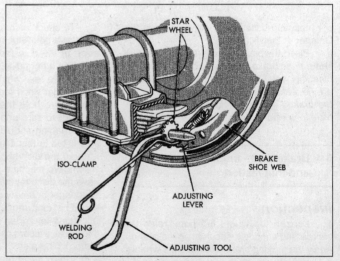

7.4d If the drum still can't be pulled off, the shoes have worn into the drum and will have to be retracted - this is done by inserting a screwdriver or piece of heavy wire into the slot in the backing plate to hold the adjusting lever away from the star wheel, then turning the star wheel with another screwdriver or a brake adjusting tool

shoes. Be sure to follow the photo sequence and read each caption (see illustrations).

**Note:** *If the brake drum cannot be easily pulled off the axle and shoe assembly, make sure that the parking brake is completely released, then apply some penetrating oil at the hub-to-drum joint. Allow the oil to soak in and try to pull the drum off. If the drum still cannot be pulled off, the brake shoes will have to be retracted. This is accomplished by first removing the plug from the backing plate. With the plug removed, pull the lever off the adjusting star wheel with one narrow screwdriver while turning the adjusting wheel with another narrow screwdriver, moving the shoes away from the drum (see illustration 7.4d). The drum should now come off.*

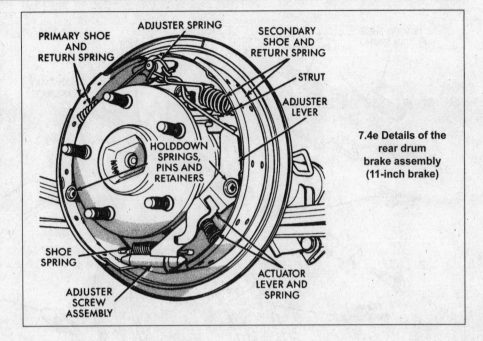

7.4e Details of the rear drum brake assembly (11-inch brake)

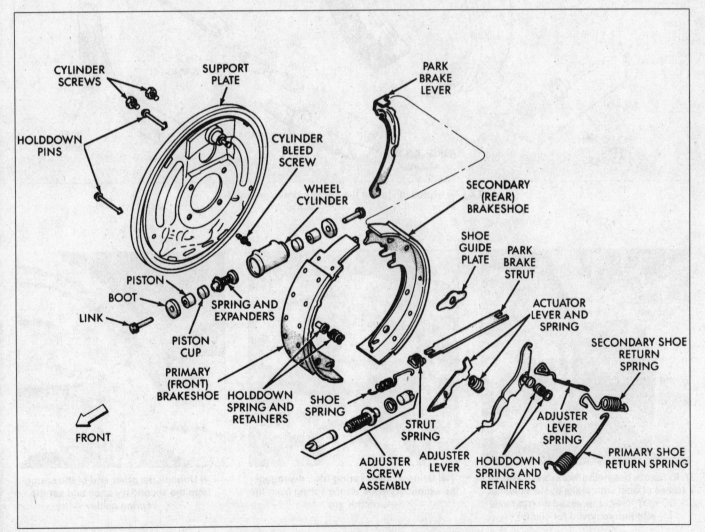

7.4f An exploded view of the 11-inch brake assembly

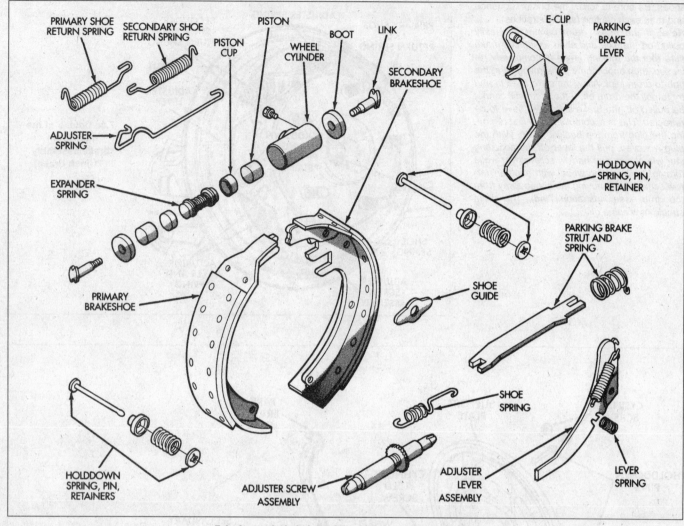

7.4g An exploded view of the 13-inch brake assembly

7.4h Before beginning work, wash away all traces of dust with brake system cleaner - DO NOT use compressed air (rear axle and hub removed for clarity)

7.4i Using a brake spring tool, disengage the secondary shoe return spring from the anchor pin

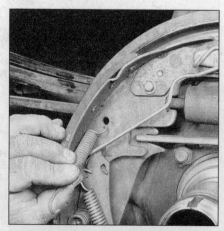

7.4j Unhook the other end of the spring from the secondary shoe and set the spring aside

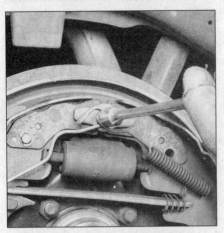

7.4k Using the brake spring tool, disengage the primary shoe return spring from the anchor pin

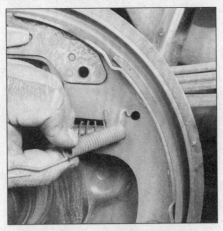

7.4l Unhook the other end of the spring from the primary shoe

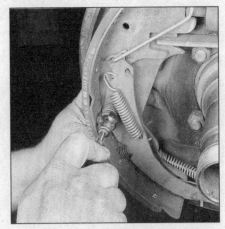

7.4m Using a hold-down spring tool, push in on the retainer and turn it 90-degrees . . .

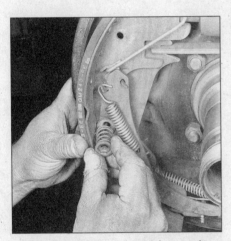

7.4n . . . and remove the retainer, spring and pin

7.4o Remove the spring from the parking brake lever

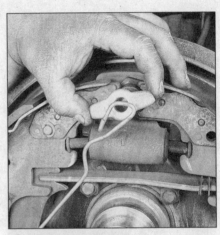

7.4p Remove the adjuster spring and the shoe guide

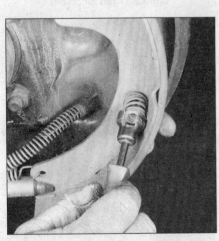

7.4q Using the hold-down spring tool, push in on the retainer and turn it 90-degrees . . .

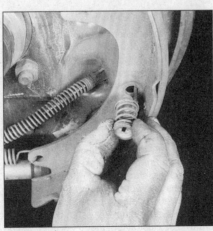

7.4r . . . and remove the retainer, spring and pin

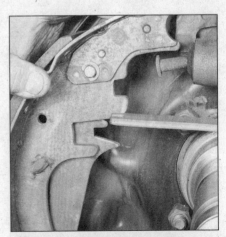

7.4s Disengage the parking brake strut from the secondary shoe . . .

7.4t . . . then disengage the parking brake strut from the primary shoe; don't lose the strut spring - and don't forget where it goes (on the end of the strut that engages the primary shoe)

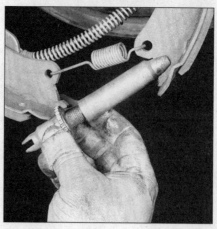

7.4u Remove the adjuster screw assembly

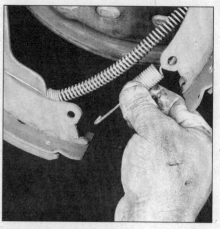

7.4v Unhook the lower shoe return spring from both shoes

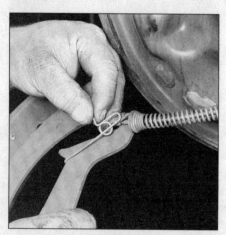

7.4w Move the parking brake cable retainer aside . . .

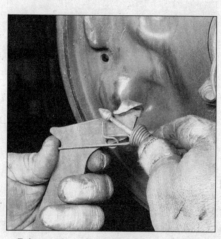

7.4x . . . then disengage the end of the parking brake cable from the parking brake lever

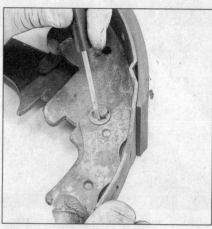

7.4y To separate the parking brake lever from the secondary shoe, remove this small E-clip retainer from the lever pivot pin (on 11-inch brakes the lever simply unhooks from the shoe)

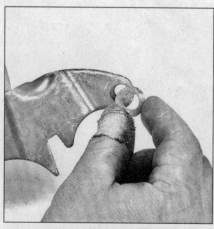

7.4z Note the washer that goes between the lever and the secondary shoe - don't forget to install this washer!

5    Follow the accompanying illustrations for the installation of the brake shoes. Be sure to follow the photo sequence and read each caption (see illustrations).

6    Before reinstalling the drum it should be checked for cracks, score marks, deep scratches and hard spots, which will appear as small discolored areas. If the hard spots cannot be removed with fine emery cloth or if any of the other conditions listed above exist, the drum must be taken to an automotive machine shop to have it resurfaced. If the drums are worn so much that they can't be resurfaced without exceeding the maximum allowable diameter (stamped into the drum) (see illustration), then new ones will be required. At the very least, if you elect not to have the drums resurfaced, remove the glaz-ing from the surface with emery cloth or sand-paper using a swirling motion.

7    Professionals recommend resurfacing the drums whenever a brake job is done. Resurfacing will eliminate the possibility of out-of-round drums.

8    Install the brake drum. Turn the brake adjuster until the shoes rub on the drum as the drum is turned, then back-off the adjuster until the shoes don't rub.

9    Mount the wheel, install the lug nuts, then lower the vehicle.

10    Make a number of forward and reverse stops to adjust the brakes until satisfactory pedal action is obtained.

11    Check brake operation before driving the vehicle in traffic.

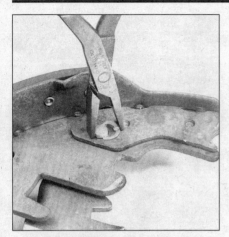

7.5a Clean off the parking brake lever
pivot pin, lube it with high temperature
grease, install the washer, install the lever
and pop the E-clip retainer into place with
a pair of pliers

7.5b Clean the backing plate, then
lubricate all the points on the plate that
support the shoes with a thin film of high-
temperature grease

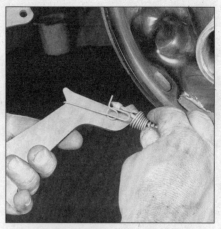

7.5c Reattach the parking brake cable to
the parking brake lever; make sure the
wire retainer is returned to its original
position to prevent the parking brake
cable from coming off

7.5d Install the secondary shoe and
parking brake lever as shown; make sure
that the crescent cutout in the shoe is
fully seated against the anchor and the
notch below it is engaged by the wheel
cylinder pushrod

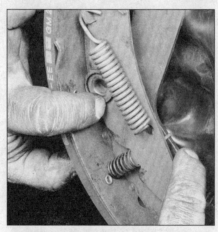

7.5e Place the small adjuster lever spring
in position between the lever and the
secondary shoe

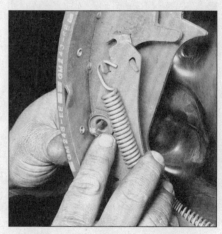

7.5f Insert the secondary hold-down
spring pin through the backing plate,
install the spring seat . . .

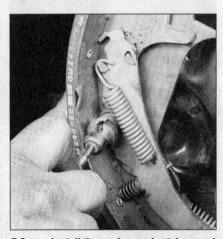

7.5g . . . install the spring and retainer and
twist the retainer to lock it into place

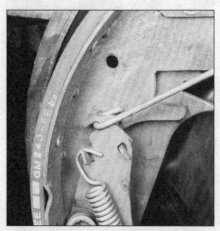

7.5h Engage the lower end of the adjuster
spring with the adjuster lever as shown

7.5i Install the shoe guide on the
anchor pin

7.5j Hook the upper end of the adjuster spring over the anchor pin

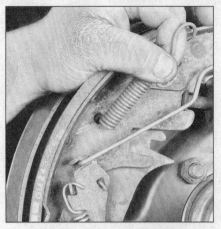

7.5k Engage the lower end of the secondary return spring with the secondary shoe

7.5l Using the brake spring tool, connect the upper end of the return spring with the adjuster spring

7.5m Place the parking brake strut in the slot in the parking brake lever

7.5n Place the primary shoe assembly into position; again, make sure the crescent cutout at the top of the shoe is fully seated against the anchor and the notch below is engaged with the wheel cylinder pushrod and, last but not least, that the parking brake strut and spring are properly engaged with the shoe

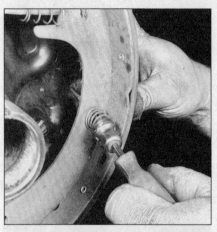

7.5o When everything is as it should be, insert the primary shoe hold-down spring pin through the backside of the backing plate, install the spring seat, the spring and the retainer, and give the retainer a twist with a hold-down spring tool

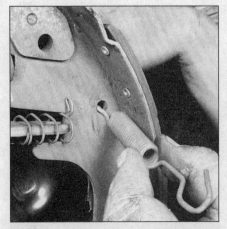

7.5p Engage the lower end of the primary return spring with the primary shoe . . .

7.5q . . . and hook the upper end of the spring over the anchor pin with a brake spring tool

7.5r This is how it should look; the return springs must be installed in this order - with the primary return spring on top of the secondary return spring

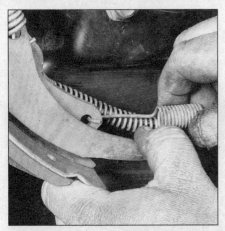

**7.5s Engage the long end of the lower return spring with the secondary shoe . . .**

**7.5t . . . and the short end of the spring with the primary shoe**

**7.5u Clean the adjuster screw, then lubricate the threads and the sliding surface of the button with high-temperature grease**

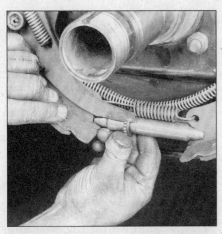

**7.5v Install the adjuster assembly between the lower ends of the shoes, then turn out the adjuster far enough to keep it in place (don't turn it out all the way or you won't be able to install the drum over the new shoes)**

**7.5w This is how it should look when you're done (right side shown)**

**7.6 The maximum allowable inside diameter is cast into the outer edge of the drum**

## 8   Wheel cylinder - removal and installation

### Removal

1   Remove the brake shoes (see Section 7).

2   Unscrew the brake line fitting from the rear of the wheel cylinder (see illustration). If available, use a flare-nut wrench to avoid rounding off the corners on the fitting. Don't pull the metal line out of the wheel cylinder - it could bend, making installation difficult.

3   Remove the two bolts securing the wheel cylinder to the brake backing plate.

4   Remove the wheel cylinder.

5   Plug the end of the brake line to prevent the loss of brake fluid and the entry of dirt.

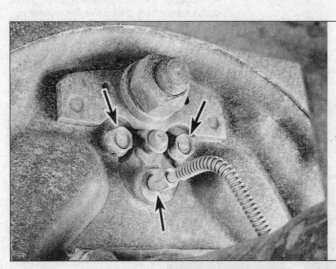

**8.2 Disconnect the brake line fitting (lower arrow) with a flare-nut wrench, then remove the mounting bolts (upper arrows)**

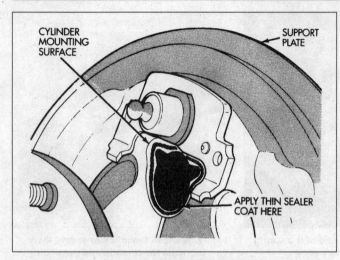

**8.6 Apply a thin coat of silicone sealant between the brake backing plate and the wheel cylinder to prevent water from entering the brake drum assembly**

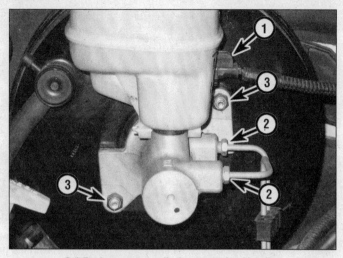

**9.4 Brake master cylinder mounting details:**

1  *Brake fluid switch electrical connector*
2  *Brake lines*
3  *Mounting nuts*

## Installation

6    It is recommended applying a thin coat of silicone sealant to the wheel cylinder mounting surface (see illustration) before installation. The sealant prevents road splash from entering the brake drum past the cylinder.

7    Installation is otherwise the reverse of removal. Attach the brake line to the wheel cylinder before installing the mounting bolts and tighten the line fitting after the wheel cylinder mountings bolts have been tightened. If available, use a flare-nut wrench to tighten the line fitting.

**Note:** *It is recommended, especially on 4WDs and vehicles driven in off-road conditions, to apply some RTV sealant around the opening in the backing plate before bolting in the wheel cylinder. This will keep out water and dust.*

8    Bleed the brakes (see Section 12). Don't drive the vehicle in traffic until the operation of the brakes has been thoroughly tested.

## 9    Master cylinder - removal and installation

### Removal

1    The master cylinder is located in the engine compartment, mounted to the power brake booster.

2    Remove as much fluid as you can from the reservoir with a syringe, such as an old turkey baster.

**Warning:** *If a baster is used, never again use it for the preparation of food.*

3    Place rags under the fluid fittings and prepare caps or plastic bags to cover the ends of the lines once they are disconnected.

**Caution:** *Brake fluid will damage paint. Cover all painted surfaces around the work area and be careful not to spill fluid during this procedure.*

4    Loosen the fittings at the ends of the brake lines where they enter the master cylinder (see illustration). To prevent rounding off

the corners on these nuts, the use of a flare-nut wrench, which wraps around the nut, is preferred. Pull the brake lines slightly away from the master cylinder and plug the ends to prevent contamination.

5    Disconnect the electrical connector at the brake fluid level, switch on the master cylinder reservoir, then remove the nuts attaching the master cylinder to the power booster. Pull the master cylinder off the studs and out of the engine compartment. Again, be careful not to spill the fluid as this is done.

6    If a new master cylinder is being installed, remove the fastener securing the reservoir to the master cylinder, then pull up on the reservoir to remove it from the master cylinder. Transfer the reservoir to the new master cylinder.

**Note:** *Be sure to install new seals when transferring the reservoir.*

## Installation

7    Bench bleed the new master cylinder before installing it. Mount the master cylinder in a vise, with the jaws of the vise clamping on the mounting flange.

8    Attach a pair of master cylinder bleeder tubes to the outlet ports of the master cylinder (see illustration).

9    Fill the reservoir with brake fluid of the recommended type (see Chapter 1).

10    Slowly push the pistons into the master cylinder (a large Phillips screwdriver can be used for this) - air will be expelled from the pressure chambers and into the reservoir. Because the tubes are submerged in fluid, air can't be drawn back into the master cylinder when you release the pistons.

11    Repeat the procedure until no more air bubbles are present.

12    Remove the bleed tubes, one at a time, and install plugs in the open ports to prevent fluid leakage and air from entering. Install the reservoir cap.

**9.8 The best way to bleed air from the master cylinder before installing it on the vehicle is with a pair of bleeder tubes that direct brake fluid into the reservoir during bleeding**

13   Install the master cylinder over the studs on the power brake booster and tighten the attaching nuts only finger-tight at this time.
**Note:** *Be sure to install a new O-ring onto the sleeve of the master cylinder.*

14   Thread the brake line fittings into the master cylinder. Since the master cylinder is still a bit loose, it can be moved slightly in order for the fittings to thread in easily. Do not strip the threads as the fittings are tightened.

15   Fully tighten the mounting nuts, then the brake line fittings. Tighten the nuts to the torque listed in this Chapter's Specifications.

16   Connect the brake fluid switch electrical connector.

17   Fill the master cylinder reservoir with fluid, then bleed the master cylinder and the brake system as described in Section 12. To bleed the cylinder on the vehicle, have an assistant depress the brake pedal and hold the pedal to the floor. Loosen the fitting to allow air and fluid to escape. Repeat this procedure on both fittings until the fluid is clear of air bubbles.
**Caution:** *Have plenty of rags on hand to catch the fluid - brake fluid will ruin painted surfaces. After the bleeding procedure is completed, rinse the area under the master cylinder with clean water.*

18   Test the operation of the brake system carefully before placing the vehicle into normal service.
**Warning:** *Do not operate the vehicle if you are in doubt about the effectiveness of the brake system. It is possible for air to become trapped in the anti-lock brake system hydraulic control unit, so, if the pedal continues to feel spongy after repeated bleedings or the Brake or Anti-lock light stays on, have the vehicle towed to a dealer service department or other qualified shop to be bled with the aid of a scan tool.*

### 10   Power brake booster (gasoline engine models) - check, removal and installation

1   The power brake booster unit requires no special maintenance apart from periodic inspection of the vacuum hose and the case.

2   Disassembly of the power unit requires special tools and is not ordinarily performed by the home mechanic. If a problem develops, it's recommended that a new or factory rebuilt unit be installed.

### Operating check

3   Depress the brake pedal several times with the engine off and make sure that there is no change in the pedal reserve distance.

4   Depress the pedal and start the engine. If the pedal goes down slightly, operation is normal.

### Airtightness check

5   Start the engine and turn it off after one or two minutes. Depress the brake pedal several times slowly. If the pedal goes down farther the first time but gradually rises after

**10.9 Remove the retaining clip, then detach the pushrod from the pedal**

the second or third depression, the booster is airtight.

6   Depress the brake pedal while the engine is running, then stop the engine with the pedal depressed. If there is no change in the pedal reserve travel after holding the pedal for 30 seconds, the booster is airtight.

### Removal

7   Remove the master cylinder (see Section 9).

8   Disconnect the vacuum hose from the power brake booster.

9   Working under the dash, disconnect the power brake pushrod from the top of the brake pedal by prying off the clip (see illustration).

10   Remove the nuts attaching the booster to the firewall (see illustration).

11   Carefully lift the booster unit away from the firewall and out of the engine compartment.

### Installation

12   To install the booster, place it into position and tighten the retaining nuts to the torque listed in this Chapter's Specifications.

13   Connect the booster pushrod to the brake pedal.

14   Install the master cylinder (see Section 9).

15   Connect the brake lines to the master cylinder and tighten all fitting nuts securely.

16   Connect the vacuum hose to the brake booster assembly.

17   Bleed the brake system (see Section 12).

18   Carefully test the operation of the brakes before placing the vehicle in normal operation.

### 11   Brake hoses and lines - inspection and replacement

### Inspection

1   Whenever the vehicle is raised and supported securely on jackstands, the rubber hoses which connect the steel brake lines with the front and rear brake assemblies

**10.10 Remove the brake booster mounting fasteners (one fastener not visible in photo)**

should be inspected for cracks, chafing of the outer cover, leaks, blisters and other damage. These are important and vulnerable parts of the brake system and inspection should be thorough. A light and mirror will be helpful for a complete check. If a hose exhibits any of the above conditions, replace it immediately.

### Flexible hose replacement

2   Clean all dirt away from the hose fittings.

3   Using a flare-nut wrench, disconnect the metal brake line from the hose fitting (see illustration). Be careful not to bend the frame bracket or line. If the threaded fitting is corroded, spray it with penetrating oil and allow it to soak in for about 10 minutes, then try again. If you try to break loose a fitting nut that's frozen, you will kink the metal line, which will then have to be replaced.

4   Disconnect the brake hose bracket from the frame. Immediately plug the metal line to prevent excessive leakage and contamination.

5   Unscrew the banjo bolt at the caliper and remove the hose, discarding the sealing washers on either side of the fitting.

6   Attach the new brake hose to the caliper.

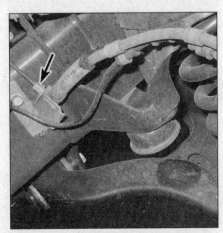

**11.3 Unscrew the line fitting with a flare-nut wrench**

**12.8 When bleeding the brakes, a hose is connected to the bleed screw at the caliper and submerged in brake fluid - air will be seen as bubbles in the tube and container (all air must be expelled before moving to the next wheel)**

7    When connecting a brake hose to a caliper, always use new sealing washers. Tighten the banjo bolt to the torque listed this Chapter's Specifications.
8    Connect the other end of the new hose making sure the hose isn't kinked or twisted. Then fit the metal line to the hose (or hose fitting), tighten the hose bracket and the brake tube fitting nut securely.
9    Carefully check to make sure the suspension or steering components don't make contact with the hose. Have an assistant push down on the vehicle while you watch to see whether the hose interferes with suspension operation. If you're replacing a front hose, have your assistant turn the steering wheel lock-to-lock while you make sure the hose doesn't interfere with the steering linkage or the steering knuckle.
10    After installation, bleed the brakes (see Section 12). Check the master cylinder fluid level and add fluid as necessary. Carefully test brake operation before returning the vehicle to normal service.

## Metal brake lines

11    When replacing brake lines, be sure to use the correct parts. Do not use copper tubing for any brake system components. Purchase steel brake lines from a dealer parts department or auto parts store.
12    Prefabricated brake line, with the tube ends already flared and fittings installed, is available at auto parts stores and dealer parts departments. If it is necessary to bend a line, use a tubing bender to prevent kinking the line.
13    When installing the new line make sure it's well supported in the brackets and has plenty of clearance between moving or hot components. Make sure you tighten the fittings securely.
14    After installation, check the master cylinder fluid level and add fluid as necessary.

Bleed the brakes (see Section 12). Carefully test brake operation before resuming normal operation.

## 12  Brake hydraulic system - bleeding

**Warning:** *The following procedure is a manual bleeding procedure. This is the only bleeding procedure which can be performed at home without special tools. However, if air has found its way into the hydraulic control unit, the entire system must be bled manually, then with a scan tool, then manually a second time. If the brake pedal feels "spongy" even after bleeding the brakes, or the ABS light on the instrument panel does not go off, or if you have any doubts whatsoever about the effectiveness of the brake system, have the vehicle towed to a dealer service department or other repair shop equipped with the necessary tools for bleeding the system.*
**Warning:** *Wear eye protection when bleeding the brake system. If the fluid comes in contact with your eyes, immediately rinse them with water and seek medical attention.*
**Note:** *Bleeding the hydraulic system is necessary to remove any air that manages to find its way into the system when it's been opened during removal and installation of a hydraulic component.*
1    It will be necessary to bleed the complete system if air has entered the system due to low fluid level, or if the brake lines have been disconnected at the master cylinder.
2    If a brake line was disconnected only at a wheel, then only that caliper must be bled.
3    If a brake line is disconnected at a fitting located between the master cylinder and any of the brakes, that part of the system served by the disconnected line must be bled. The following procedure describes bleeding the entire system, however.
4    Remove any residual vacuum (or hydraulic pressure) from the brake power booster by applying the brake several times with the engine off.
5    Remove the cap from the master cylinder reservoir and fill the reservoir with brake fluid. Reinstall the cap.
**Note:** *Check the fluid level often during the bleeding operation and add fluid as necessary to prevent the fluid level from falling low enough to allow air bubbles into the master cylinder.*
6    Have an assistant on hand, as well as a supply of new brake fluid, a clear container partially filled with clean brake fluid, a length of clear tubing to fit over the bleeder valve and a wrench to open and close the bleeder valve.
7    Beginning at the right rear wheel, loosen the bleeder screw slightly, then tighten it to a point where it's snug but can still be loosened quickly and easily.
8    Place one end of the tubing over the bleeder screw fitting and submerge the other end in brake fluid in the container (see illustra-

tion).
9    Have the assistant slowly depress the brake pedal and hold it in the depressed position.
10    While the pedal is held depressed, open the bleeder screw just enough to allow a flow of fluid to leave the valve. Watch for air bubbles to exit the submerged end of the tube. When the fluid flow slows after a couple of seconds, tighten the screw and have your assistant release the pedal.
11    Repeat Steps 9 and 10 until no more air is seen leaving the tube, then tighten the bleeder screw and proceed to the left rear wheel, the right front wheel and the front left wheel, in that order, and perform the same procedure. Be sure to check the fluid in the master cylinder reservoir frequently.
12    Never use old brake fluid. It contains moisture which can boil, rendering the brake system inoperative.
13    Refill the master cylinder with fluid at the end of the operation.
14    Check the operation of the brakes. The pedal should feel solid when depressed, with no sponginess. If necessary, repeat the entire process.
**Warning:** *Do not operate the vehicle if you are in doubt about the effectiveness of the brake system. It is possible for air to become trapped in the anti-lock brake system hydraulic control unit, so, if the pedal continues to feel spongy after repeated bleedings or the Brake or Anti-lock light stays on, have the vehicle towed to a dealer service department or other qualified shop to be bled with the aid of a scan tool.*

## 13  Parking brake shoes (disc brakes) - replacement

**Warning:** *Dust created by the brake system is harmful to your health. Never blow it out with compressed air and don't inhale any of it. An approved filtering mask should be worn when working on the brakes. Do not, under any circumstances, use petroleum-based solvents to clean brake parts. Use brake system cleaner only!*
**Note:** *Although the typical procedure illustrated here is shown with the axle still in place, it takes some dexterity to work behind the axle flange while replacing the parking brake shoes. If this proves difficult, you can remove the axle for better access (see Chapter 8).*
1    Loosen the wheel lug nuts, release the parking brake, raise the rear of the vehicle and support it securely on jackstands. Block the front wheels to keep the vehicle from rolling. Remove the rear wheels.
2    Remove the rear brake caliper (see Section 6) and hang it with a length of wire, then remove the caliper mounting bracket (see Section 5).
3    Remove the brake disc (see Section 6).
**Note:** *If the brake disc cannot be easily pulled off the axle and shoe assembly, make sure that the parking brake is completely released, then apply some penetrating oil at the hub-to-*

*disc joint. Allow the oil to soak in and try to pull the disc off. If the disc still cannot be pulled off, the parking brake shoes will have to be retracted. This is accomplished by first removing the plug from the backing plate. With the plug removed, turn the adjusting wheel with a narrow screwdriver or brake adjusting tool, moving the shoes away from the braking surface (see illustrations).The disc should now come off.*

4    Clean the parking brake shoe assembly with brake system cleaner, then follow the accompanying illustrations (10.4a through 10.4p) for the parking brake shoe replacement procedure. Be sure to stay in order and read the caption under each illustration.

**Note:** *All four parking brake shoes must be replaced at the same time, but to avoid mixing up parts, work on only one brake assembly at a time.*

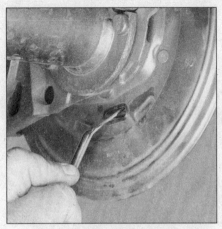

13.3a Remove the plug from the hole in the brake backing plate, insert a brake adjuster tool through the hole . . .

13.3b . . . position the tool at the top of the adjuster star wheel and rotate the wheel down (clockwise, as viewed from the rear of the vehicle, facing forward), moving the parking brake shoes away from the disc hub (which is already removed in this photo for the sake of clarity)

13.4a Pull down on the parking brake cable, then clamp a pair of locking pliers on the cable to retain slack . . .

13.4b . . . then release the cable from the lever behind the brake backing plate

13.4c Pushing on the pin from the backing plate side with your finger, pry the front hold-down clip loose, then pull the pin out

13.4d Remove the rear hold-down clip and pin the same way

13.4e Disengage the lower spring from the parking brake shoes

13.4f Remove the adjuster

13.4g Disengage the upper spring from the rear parking brake shoe

13.4h Remove both parking brake shoes

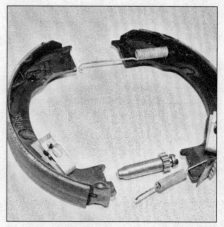

13.4i Here's how the shoes, springs and adjuster go together

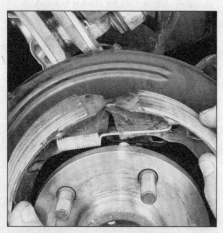

13.4j Holding them together with the upper spring, install the new shoes

13.4k Spread the upper ends of the shoes apart and engage them with the anchor

13.4l Install the adjuster

13.4m Make sure the adjuster is engaged with the shoes

13.4n Install the lower spring

13.4o Install the rear pin and hold-down clip as shown, with the head of the pin firmly seated into the lower, smaller part of the hole in the clip

**13.4p Install the front pin and hold-down clip the same way**

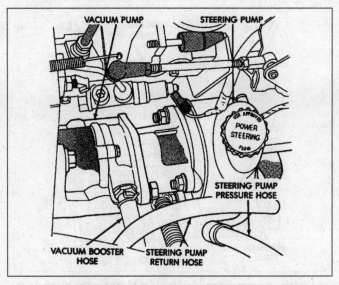

**14.2 Detach the vacuum hose from the vacuum pump**

5    Before reinstalling the disc, check the parking brake surfaces of the disc hub for cracks, score marks, deep scratches and hard spots, which will appear as small discolored areas. If hard spots or any of the other conditions listed above cannot be removed with sandpaper or emery cloth, the disc must be replaced.

6    Once all of the new parking brake shoes are in place, install the brake discs (see Section 5) and the brake calipers (see Section 6).

7    Remove the rubber plugs from the brake backing plates, insert a narrow screwdriver or brake adjusting tool through the adjustment hole and turn the star wheel until the shoes drag slightly as the disc is turned. Turn the star wheel in the opposite direction until the disc turns freely. Install the backing plate plugs.

8    Install the rear wheels and lug nuts, lower the vehicle and tighten the lug nuts to the torque listed in the Chapter 1 Specifications.

9    Operate the parking brake lever several times to release the lockout spring and adjust the cables.

10    Carefully check the operation of the brakes before placing the vehicle in normal service.

**14   Power brake vacuum pump (1996 and earlier diesel engine models) - removal and installation**

1    Disconnect the cables from the negative terminals of the battery (see Chapter 5).
**Note:** *If you're working on a 4WD model, it may be helpful to raise the vehicle, place it securely on jackstands, and work from below.*
2    Disconnect the vacuum hose from the vacuum pump (see illustration).
3    Disconnect the oil feed line from the vacuum pump (see illustration).
4    Loosen the two nuts that attach the vacuum pump to the power steering pump adapter (see illustration).

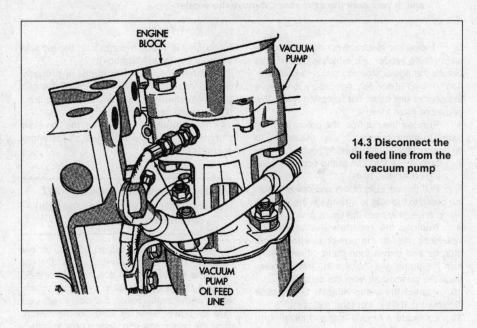

**14.3 Disconnect the oil feed line from the vacuum pump**

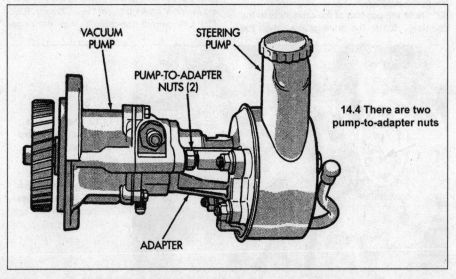

**14.4 There are two pump-to-adapter nuts**

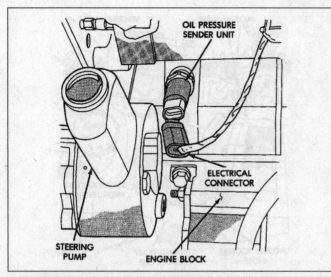

**14.5 The oil pressure sender unit is mounted in the block right behind the power steering pump; at least unplug the connector and, if you want the extra room, remove the sender**

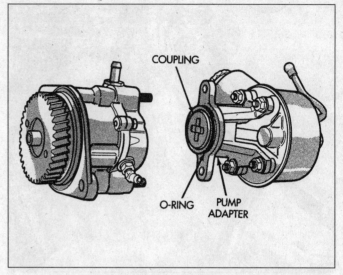

**14.10 Inspect the adapter O-ring and, if it's worn or damaged, replace it (be sure to lubricate the new O-ring lightly with clean engine oil)**

5    Unplug the electrical connector from the oil pressure sender unit, which is located right behind the power steering pump (see illustration). It isn't absolutely necessary to remove the sender unit itself, but removing it will give you more room to work.

6    Remove the nut from the power steering pump-to-block bracket. It isn't necessary to disconnect the power steering hoses.

7    Unbolt the vacuum pump from the gear housing cover (two bolts).

8    Pull the vacuum pump and power steering pump to the rear to disengage the vacuum pump drive gear from the timing gears.

9    Remove the two nuts that attach the vacuum pump to the power steering pump adapter and remove the pump. If necessary, turn the pump gear back and forth to disengage the pump shaft from the coupling.

10   Inspect the pump adapter O-ring (see illustration). If it's cut or torn, replace it.

11   Lubricate a new O-ring and install it on the pump adapter.

12   Note the position of the drive slots in the coupling. Rotate the drive gear to align the tangs on the vacuum pump with the slots in the coupling (see illustration).

13   Make sure that the pump is properly seated into the adapter, then install the two pump-to-adapter washers and nuts and tighten them securely.

14   Installation is otherwise the reverse of removal. Be sure to tighten all fasteners securely.

## 15   Hydraulic brake booster (1997 and later diesel engine models) - removal and installation

**Warning:** *The accumulator portion of the booster contains high-pressure gas. Do not carry the booster by the accumulator or drop the unit on the accumulator.*

**Note:** *If the brake booster is being replaced due to power steering fluid contamination, flush the power steering system prior to installing the new brake booster (see Chapter 10).*

1    Disconnect the cable(s) from the nega-

**14.12 These tangs on the vacuum pump must be aligned with the slots in the adapter coupling before tightening the pump-to-adapter nuts**

tive battery terminal(s) (see Chapter 5).

2    With the engine off, depress the brake pedal several times to discharge the accumulator.

3    Remove the master cylinder (see Section 9).

4    Remove the return hose and two pressure lines from the brake booster.

5    Working inside the vehicle, remove the clip and washer, then disengage the brake booster pushrod from the brake pedal (see illustration 10.9). Remove the brake booster mounting nuts (see illustration 10.10).

6    Working inside the engine compartment, remove the brake booster from the firewall.

7    Installation is the reverse of removal. Tighten the booster mounting nuts and the pressure lines to the torque listed in this Chapter's Specifications.

8    Bleed the brake hydraulic system (see Section 12), then bleed the power steering system (see Chapter 10).

## 16   Parking brake - adjustment

1    Raise the rear of the vehicle and support it securely on jackstands. Block the front wheels to prevent the vehicle from rolling.

2    Adjust the parking brake shoes as described in Section 13. Loosen the adjusting nut at the equalizer enough to create slack in the cables (see illustration).

3    Verify that the drums rotate freely without drag, then fully apply the parking brake.

4    Mark the tensioner rod about 1/4-inch from the tensioner.

5    Tighten the adjusting nut at the tensioner bracket until the mark on the tensioner rod moves into alignment with the tensioner.

**Caution:** *Do NOT loosen or tighten the tensioner adjusting nut after completing this adjustment.*

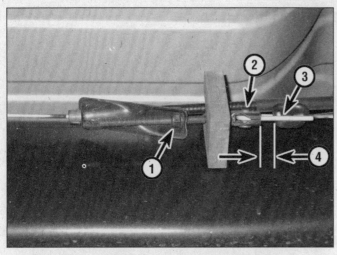

**16.2 Parking brake cable adjustment details:**

1 Adjuster nut
2 Tensioner

3 Tensioner rod
4 1/4 inch mark

**17.1 The brake light switch is attached to a bracket near the top of the brake pedal**

6    Release the parking brake pedal and verify that the rear wheels rotate freely without any drag.

7    Remove the jackstands and lower the vehicle.

8    Test the operation of the parking brake on an incline (be sure to remain in the vehicle for this check!).

## 17    Brake light switch - removal and installation

1    The brake light switch is mounted on a flange on the pedal support bracket. The switch is secured in the bracket by means of an integral retainer on the switch body (see illustration).

## Removal

2    Depress the brake pedal and hold it down.

3    Rotate the switch about 30-degrees in a counterclockwise direction to unlock the switch retainer, then pull the switch out of its bracket (see illustration).

4    Unplug the switch electrical connector and remove the switch.

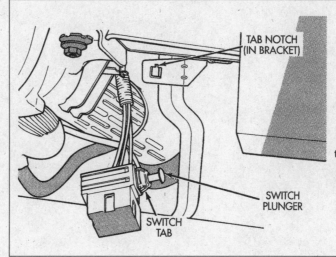

TAB NOTCH
(IN BRACKET)

SWITCH
PLUNGER

SWITCH
TAB

**17.3 To release the brake light switch locking tab from its notch in the switch mounting bracket, rotate the switch counterclockwise 30-degrees and pull out the switch; to install the switch, align the tab on the switch with the notch at the top of the hole, insert the plunger through the hole, and rotate the switch 30-degrees clockwise**

## Installation

5    Plug in the electrical connector to the new switch.

6    Press and hold the brake pedal in its fully applied position.

7    Align the tab on the switch with the notch in the switch bracket, then insert the switch in the bracket and turn it clockwise about 30-degrees to lock it into place.

8    Move the lever on the switch towards the support bracket (this will connect the contacts inside the switch).

9    Try the brakes and verify that the switch is operating properly.

# Notes

# Chapter 10
# Suspension and steering

## Contents

## Specifications

### Torque specifications

**Ft-lbs (unless otherwise indicated)**

**Note:** *One foot-pound (ft-lb) of torque is equivalent to 12 inch-pounds (in-lbs) of torque. Torque values below approximately 15 ft-lbs are expressed in inch-pounds, since most foot-pound torque wrenches are not accurate at these smaller values.*

### Front suspension

#### 2001 and earlier 1500/2002 and earlier 2500 and 3500 2WD models

Balljoints
  1994 through 1996
    Lower ballstud nut ............................................... 55
    Upper ballstud nut ............................................... 55
  1997 through 2001
    Lower ballstud nut
      Normal duty .................................................. 95
      Heavy duty ................................................... 110
    Upper ballstud nut ............................................. 60
Hub bearing/spindle nut
  2000 and 2001 1500 2WD models ........................... 185
  2000 through 2002 2500/3500 2WD models ............. 280
  Hub and bearing-to-steering knuckle bolts
    (2000 through 2002 3500 HD models) ..................... 122
Lower control arm bolts and nuts
  1994 and 1995 .................................................... 150
  1996
    Wax-coat frame* ................................................ 110
    E-coat frame* .................................................... 200
  1997 through 1999 ............................................... 145
  2000 and 2001 .................................................... 125
Shock absorbers
  Upper nut .......................................................... 30
  Lower bolt .......................................................... 100

**Note:** * *Refer to the 11th digit of the VIN number: If the 11th VIN digit is "J" (St. Louis), the frame uses an E-coat; if the 11th digit is an "S" (Dodge City), "G" (Saltillo, Mexico) or "M" (Lago Alberto, Mexico), the frame has a wax coat.*

## Torque specifications (continued)      Ft-lbs (unless otherwise indicated)

*Note: One foot-pound (ft-lb) of torque is equivalent to 12 inch-pounds (in-lbs) of torque. Torque values below approximately 15 ft-lbs are expressed in inch-pounds, since most foot-pound torque wrenches are not accurate at these smaller values.*

### Front suspension

#### 2001 and earlier 1500/2002 and earlier 2500 and 3500 2WD models (continued)

Stabilizer bar
  Link nut
    1994 through 1997................................................................. 25
    1998 through 2001................................................................. 27
  Stabilizer bushing clamp bolts
    1994 and 1995..................................................................... 35
    1996
      Wax-coat frame*................................................................ 35
      E-coat frame*.................................................................... 45
    1997 and later...................................................................... 40
Upper control arm bolts
  1994 and 1995......................................................................... 180
  1996
    Wax-coat frame*................................................................... 150
    E-coat frame*........................................................................ 200
  1997 through 1999................................................................... 150
  2000 and 2001......................................................................... 125

#### 2001 and earlier 1500/2002 and earlier 2500 and 3500 4WD models

Balljoints
  Model 44 axle
    Upper ballstud nut................................................................ 80
    Lower ballstud nut................................................................ 75
  Model 60 axle
    Step 1
      Lower ballstud nut............................................................ 35
      Upper ballstud nut........................................................... 70
    Step 2 (lower ballstud nut)................................................... 140 to 160
Shock absorber
  Bracket..................................................................................... 55
  Lower bolt................................................................................ 100
  Upper nut
    1994 through 1997................................................................ 30
    1998 through 2001................................................................ 35
Stabilizer bar
  Link lower nut
    1994.................................................................................... 70
    1995 and through 1997........................................................ 87
    1998.................................................................................... 50
    1999 through 2001............................................................... 35
  Link upper nut
    1994 through 1997............................................................... 27
    1998.................................................................................... 50
    1999 through 2001............................................................... 27
  Stabilizer bushing clamp bolts
    1994 and 1995..................................................................... 35
    1996
      Wax-coat frame*.............................................................. 35
      E-coat frame*.................................................................. 45
    1997 through 2001............................................................... 40
Track bar
  Ballstud nut
    1994 through 1996............................................................... 62
    1997 and later..................................................................... 70
  Track bar bolt ........................................................................... 130

**Note:** *\* Refer to the 11th digit of the VIN number: If the 11th VIN digit is "J" (St. Louis), the frame uses an E-coat; if the 11th digit is an "S" (Dodge City), "G" (Saltillo, Mexico) or "M" (Lago Alberto, Mexico), the frame has a wax coat.*

## Torque specifications (continued)                    Ft-lbs (unless otherwise indicated)

**Note:** *One foot-pound (ft-lb) of torque is equivalent to 12 inch-pounds (in-lbs) of torque. Torque values below approximately 15 ft-lbs are expressed in inch-pounds, since most foot-pound torque wrenches are not accurate at these smaller values.*

### 2001 and earlier 1500/2002 and earlier 2500 and 3500 4WD models

Upper suspension arms
  Arm-to-axle bracket nut
    1994 to 1999 ............................................................. 89
    2000 and 2001 ........................................................... 120
  Arm-to-frame nut
    1994 and 1995 ........................................................... 62
    1996
      Wax-coat frame* ..................................................... 62
      E-coat frame* ........................................................ 150
    1997 ........................................................................ 80
    1998 and 1999 ........................................................... 85
    2000 and 2001 ........................................................... 120
Lower suspension arms
  Arm-to-frame nut
    1994 and 1995 ........................................................... 88
    1996
      Wax-coat frame* ..................................................... 90
      E-coat frame* ........................................................ 150
    1997 ........................................................................ 125
    1998 and 1999 ........................................................... 130
    2000 and 2001 ........................................................... 140
  Arm-to-axle nut
    1994 ........................................................................ 170
    1995 and 1996 ........................................................... 110
    1997 through 1999 ...................................................... 95
    2000 and 2001 ........................................................... 140
Hub and bearing mounting bolts ............................................ 122

### 2002 and later 1500 models/2003 and later 2500 and 3500 models

Hub and bearing mounting bolts
  2WD models
    1500 ........................................................................ 120
    2500/3500 ................................................................ 130
  4WD models
    1500 ........................................................................ 120
    2500/35000 .............................................................. 149
Shock absorber
  Upper mounting nuts
    2WD models .............................................................. 40
    4WD models
      2002 through 2005 .................................................. 40
      2006 and later
        1500 .................................................................. 45
        2500/3500 ........................................................... 40
  Lower mounting bolts/nuts
    2WD models .............................................................. 25
    4WD models
      2002 through 2005 models ........................................ 100
      2006 and later models
        1500 .................................................................. 155
        2500/3500 ........................................................... 100
  Upper mounting bracket nuts (2500/3500 4WD models) ............ 55
Stabilizer bar - models without Electronic Stability Control
  Link nut
    Upper ...................................................................... 27
    Lower ...................................................................... 75
  Bracket bolts .............................................................. 45
Stabilizer bar - models with Electronic Stability Control
  Clamps-to-frame rail bolts .............................................. 45
  Link mounting nuts
    Upper ...................................................................... 110
    Lower ...................................................................... 110

**Note:** * *Refer to the 11th digit of the VIN number: If the 11th VIN digit is "J" (St. Louis), the frame uses an E-coat; if the 11th digit is an "S" (Dodge City), "G" (Saltillo, Mexico) or "M" (Lago Alberto, Mexico), the frame has a wax coat.*

## Torque specifications (continued)

**Ft-lbs (unless otherwise indicated)**

**Note:** *One foot-pound (ft-lb) of torque is equivalent to 12 inch-pounds (in-lbs) of torque. Torque values below approximately 15 ft-lbs are expressed in inch-pounds, since most foot-pound torque wrenches are not accurate at these smaller values.*

### Independent front suspension

Upper control arm
   Arm-to-frame pivot bolts
      1500
         2002 through 2005 models.................................................... 97
         2006 and later models........................................................ 130
      2500/3500 ........................................................................... 125
   Balljoint-to-steering knuckle nut
      2002 models
         1500 ................................................................................... 60
         2500/3500 .......................................................................... 110
      2003 and later models
         1500
            Step 1............................................................................ 40
            Step 2............................................................................ Tighten an additional 90-degrees (1/4-turn)
         2002 through 2005 models (2500/3500)..................................... 40
         2006 and later models (2500/3500)............................................ 50
Lower control arm
   Arm-to-frame pivot bolts
      2002 models
         1500 ................................................................................... 150
         2500/3500 .......................................................................... 125
      2003 and later 1500 models .................................................... 150
      2003 through 2005 2500/3500 models ..................................... 210
      2006 and later 2500/3500 models ........................................... 175
   Balljoint-to-steering knuckle nut
      2002 models
         1500 ................................................................................... 60
         2500/3500 .......................................................................... 110
      2003 and later models
         1500
            Step 1............................................................................ 40
            Step 2............................................................................ Tighten an additional 90-degrees (1/4-turn)
         2500/3500 .......................................................................... 100

### Link/coil suspension (4WD w/solid front axle)

Upper suspension arm-to-axle bracket nut
   2002 models........................................................................... 120
   2003 through 2005 models ....................................................... 110
   2006 and later models.............................................................. 120
Upper suspension arm-to-frame nut
   2002 models........................................................................... 120
   2003 through 2005 models ....................................................... 110
   2006 and later models.............................................................. 120
Lower suspension arm-to-axle bracket nut
   2002 models........................................................................... 140
   2003 through 2005 models ....................................................... 160
   2006 and later models.............................................................. 140
Lower suspension arm-to-frame nut
   2002 models........................................................................... 140
   2003 through 2005 models ....................................................... 160
   2006 and later models.............................................................. 170
Steering knuckle-to-upper balljoint stud nut ........................................... 70
Steering knuckle-to-lower balljoint stud nut
   Step 1 ................................................................................... 35
   Step 2* .................................................................................. 140 to 160

**Note:** *\*Tighten upper balljoint stud nut first, then Step 2 on the lower stud nut*

## Torque specifications (continued)                                    Ft-lbs (unless otherwise indicated)

**Note:** *One foot-pound (ft-lb) of torque is equivalent to 12 inch-pounds (in-lbs) of torque. Torque values below approximately 15 ft-lbs are expressed in inch-pounds, since most foot-pound torque wrenches are not accurate at these smaller values.*

### Rear suspension

#### 2001 and earlier 1500 models/2002 and earlier 2500 and 3500 models

| | |
|---|---|
| Shock absorber | |
| Lower nut | 100 |
| Upper nut | |
| 1994 and 1995 | 70 |
| 1997 through 2001 models | |
| Wax-coat frame* | 70 |
| E-coat frame* | 110 |
| Leaf springs | |
| U-bolt clamp nuts | |
| 6,010 to 10,500 GVW | 110 |
| 11,000 GVW cab-chassis | 120 |
| Front and rear eye nuts/bolts | |
| 6,010 to 7,500 GVW | |
| 1994 and 1995 | 100 |
| 1996 through 2001 models | 150 |
| 8,800 to 11,000 GVW | |
| 1994 and 1995 | 140 |
| 1996 through 2001 models | 210 |
| Stabilizer bar (1997 through 2001 models) | |
| Link-to-frame bolts and nuts | 70 |
| Bushing clamp nuts | 40 |

**Note:** *Refer to the 11th digit of the VIN number: If the 11th VIN digit is "J" (St. Louis), the frame uses an E-coat; if the 11th digit is an "S" (Dodge City), "G" (Saltillo, Mexico) or "M" (Lago Alberto, Mexico), the frame has a wax coat.*

#### 2002 and later 1500 models/2003 and later 2500 and 3500 models

| | |
|---|---|
| Rear shock absorber mounting bolts/nuts | 100 |
| Leaf spring-to-axle U-bolt nuts | |
| 1500/2500 | 110 |
| 3500 | |
| 2002 models | 120 |
| 2003 and later models | 110 |
| Leaf spring-to-front and rear spring hanger nut and bolt | |
| 2002 models | |
| 1500 | 120 |
| 2500/3500 | 130 |
| 2003 and later models | |
| 1500 | 120 |
| 2500/3500 | 170 |
| Rear shackle-to-frame bracket nut and bolt | |
| 2002 models | |
| 1500 | 120 |
| 2500/3500 | 130 |
| 2003 and later models | |
| 1500 | 120 |
| 2500/3500 | 170 |

### Steering

#### 2001 and earlier 1500 models/2002 and earlier 2500 and 3500 models

| | |
|---|---|
| Airbag module retaining nuts | 80 to 100 in-lbs |
| Drag link ballstud nuts (4WD) | 65 |
| Idler arm-to-frame bolts | |
| Regular bolts | 80 |
| Heavy-duty bolts | 200 |
| Power steering pump-to-adapter bracket nuts (diesel) | 18 |
| Steering wheel-to-steering shaft nut | 45 |

## Torque specifications (continued)     Ft-lbs (unless otherwise indicated)

**Note:** *One foot-pound (ft-lb) of torque is equivalent to 12 inch-pounds (in-lbs) of torque. Torque values below approximately 15 ft-lbs are expressed in inch-pounds, since most foot-pound torque wrenches are not accurate at these smaller values.*

### Steering

#### 2001 and earlier 1500 models/2002 and earlier 2500 and 3500 models (continued)

Steering damper
    Damper-to-center link nut (2WD).................................................... 50
    Damper-to-drag link nut (4WD)..................................................... 50
    Damper-to-frame nut
        1994 and 1995................................................................ 50
        1996 and later models
            Wax-coat frame*................................................... 50
            E-coat frame* ..................................................... 65
Steering coupler ............................................................................ 36
Steering gear mounting bolts.......................................................... 140
Pitman arm
    Pitman arm-to-steering gear nut .................................................. 185
    Pitman arm-to-center link nut ...................................................... 65
Tie rods
    Tie-rod ballstud nuts.................................................................... 65
    Tie-rod adjuster clamp nuts.......................................................... 40
Wheel lug nuts................................................................................ See Chapter 1

#### 2002 and later 1500 models/2003 and later 2500 and 3500 models

Airbag module-to-steering wheel screws.......................................... 120 in-lbs
Steering wheel bolt.......................................................................... 45
Steering column nuts....................................................................... 20
Intermediate shaft pinch bolts
    Upper (to steering column shaft).................................................. 45
    Coupler (to rack and pinion steering gear).................................... 36
    Coupler (to recirculating ball steering gear).................................. 36
Steering gear-to-crossmember mounting bolts (rack-and-pinion)
    1500 models................................................................................ 235
    2500/3500 2WD models................................................................ 185
Steering gear-to-frame mounting bolts (recirculating ball)..................... 145
Pitman arm nut
    2002 models................................................................................ 185
    2003 through 2005 models .......................................................... 225
    2006 and later models................................................................. 185
Drag link-to-Pitman arm nut
    2002 models................................................................................ 80
    2003 through 2005 models .......................................................... 65
    2006 and later models
        Step 1................................................................................ 40
        Step 2................................................................................ Tighten an additional 90 degrees
Steering damper-to-axle nut/bolt ..................................................... 75
Steering damper-to-tie-rod nut/bolt.................................................. 60
Tie-rod end adjuster clamp bolts ..................................................... 45
Tie-rod-to-steering knuckle nut
    1500 models
        2002................................................................................. 55
        2003 and later
            Step 1........................................................................ 45
            Step 2........................................................................ Tighten an additional 90-degrees
    2500/3500 models
        2002 (2WD)..................................................................... 80
        2002 (4WD)..................................................................... 80
        2003 and later (2WD)
            Step 1........................................................................ 45
            Step 2........................................................................ Tighten an additional 90-degrees
        2003 and later (4WD)
            Step 1........................................................................ 40
            Step 2........................................................................ Tighten an additional 90-degrees
Track bar mounting nuts/bolts .......................................................... 150
Wheel lug nuts................................................................................ See Chapter 1

**Note:** * *Refer to the 11th digit of the VIN number: If the 11th VIN digit is "J" (St. Louis), the frame uses an E-coat; if the 11th digit is an "S" (Dodge City), "G" (Saltillo, Mexico) or "M" (Lago Alberto, Mexico), the frame has a wax coat.*

**1.1a Front suspension - 2001 and earlier 1500/2002 and earlier 2500/3500 2WD models**

| | | |
|---|---|---|
| 1   Stabilizer bar | 6   Coil springs | 10   Idler arm |
| 2   Stabilizer bar bushing clamps | 7   Steering gear | 11   Inner tie rod |
| 3   Stabilizer bar links | 8   Pitman arm | 12   Tie-rod adjuster tube |
| 4   Stabilizer bar link-to control arm nuts | 9   Center link | 13   Tie-rod end |
| 5   Lower control arms | | |

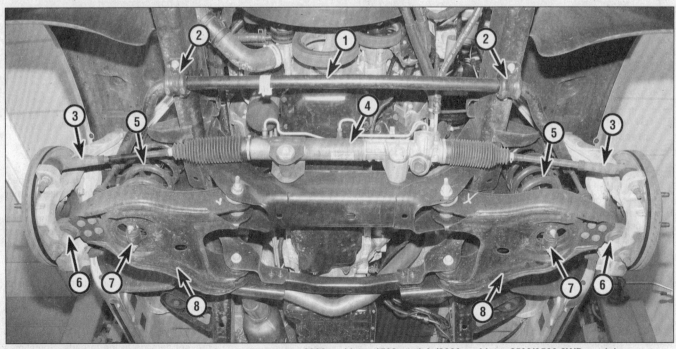

**1.1b Front suspension and steering components - 2002 and later 1500 models/2003 and later 2500/3500 2WD models**

| | | |
|---|---|---|
| 1   Stabilizer bar | 4   Rack-and-pinion steering gear | 7   Shock absorber |
| 2   Stabilizer bar bushing clamps | 5   Coil spring | 8   Lower control arm |
| 3   Tie-rod end | 6   Lower balljoint | |

**1.1c Front suspension and steering components (4WD models with a solid front axle)**

| | | | | | |
|---|---|---|---|---|---|
| 1 | Stabilizer bar | 5 | Pitman arm | 9 | Upper suspension arms |
| 2 | Stabilizer bar bushing clamps | 6 | Drag link | 10 | Lower suspension arms |
| 3 | Steering damper | 7 | Tie-rod | 11 | Tie-rod adjuster tube |
| 4 | Track bar | 8 | Coil springs | 12 | Drag-link adjuster tube |

## 1    General information and precautions

### Front suspension

1    2WD models and are equipped with an independent front suspension system with upper and lower control arms, coil springs and shock absorbers. A stabilizer bar controls body roll. Each steering knuckle is positioned by a pair of balljoints in the ends of the upper and lower control arms (see illustrations).

2    Light-duty 4WD models are equipped with an independent front suspension system with upper and lower control arms, torsion bars and shock absorbers. A stabilizer bar controls body roll. Each steering knuckle is positioned by a pair of balljoints in the ends of the upper and lower control arms.

3    Heavy-duty 4WD models utilize a solid front axle located by a pair of longitudinal suspension arms on either side. The front axle is suspended by a pair of coil springs and shock absorbers, and located laterally by a track bar.

### Rear suspension

4    The rear suspension consists of two shock absorbers and two leaf springs (see illustration). Some models are also equipped with a rear stabilizer bar.

### Steering

5    The steering system on heavy-duty 4WD models consists of a recirculating-ball steering gearbox, Pitman arm, drag link, tie-rod and a steering damper. When the steering wheel is turned, the gear rotates the Pitman arm which forces the drag link to one side. The drag link is connected to the right steering knuckle; the tie-rod is connected to the drag link and the left steering knuckle. The steering damper is attached to a bracket on the axle and to the tie-rod.

6    The steering system on other models consists of a rack-and-pinion steering gear and two adjustable tie-rods. Power assist is standard.

### Precautions

7    Frequently, when working on the suspension or steering system components, you may come across fasteners which seem impossible to loosen. These fasteners on the underside of the vehicle are continually subjected to water, road grime, mud, etc., and can become rusted or "frozen," making them extremely difficult to remove. In order to unscrew these stubborn fasteners without damaging them (or other components), be sure to use lots of penetrating oil and allow it to soak in for a while. Using a wire brush to clean exposed threads will also ease removal of the nut or bolt and prevent damage to the threads. Sometimes a sharp blow with a hammer and punch is effective in breaking the bond between a nut and bolt threads, but care must be taken to

**1.4 Rear suspension components**

| | | | | | |
|---|---|---|---|---|---|
| 1 | Leaf springs | 3 | Spring plates | 5 | Axle |
| 2 | Shock absorbers | 4 | Spring plate U-bolts | | |

prevent the punch from slipping off the fastener and ruining the threads. Heating the stuck fastener and surrounding area with a torch sometimes helps too, but isn't recommended because of the obvious dangers associated with fire. Long breaker bars and extension, or "cheater," pipes will increase leverage, but never use an extension pipe on a ratchet - the ratcheting mechanism could be damaged. Sometimes, turning the nut or bolt in the tightening (clockwise) direction first will help to break it loose. Fasteners that require drastic measures to unscrew should always be replaced with new ones.

8    Since most of the procedures that are dealt with in this Chapter involve jacking up the vehicle and working underneath it, a good pair of jackstands will be needed. A hydraulic floor jack is the preferred type of jack to lift the vehicle, and it can also be used to support certain components during various operations.

**Warning:** *Never, under any circumstances, rely on a jack to support the vehicle while working on it.*

9    Whenever any of the suspension or steering fasteners are loosened or removed they must be inspected and, if necessary, be replaced with new ones of the same part number or of original equipment quality and design. Torque specifications must be followed for proper reassembly and component retention. Never attempt to heat or straighten any suspension or steering components. Instead, replace any bent or damaged part with a new one.

## 2    Shock absorber (front) - removal and installation

1    On 4WD models with coil over type shock absorbers, loosen the driveaxle hub nut. Loosen the front wheel lug nuts. Raise the front of the vehicle and support it securely on jackstands, then remove the wheel.

2    Support the axle tube or the outer end of the lower control arm with a floor jack (the shock absorber serves as the down-stop for the suspension). The jack must remain in this position throughout the entire procedure.

### 2WD models

3    Using a back-up wrench on the stem, remove the shock absorber upper mounting nut (see illustration).

**Note:** *On 2007 and later models, a special tool is necessary to remove the shock absorber's upper mounting nut.*

4    Remove the retainer (metal washer) and grommet (rubber washer).

5    Working underneath the vehicle, remove the two nuts that attach the lower end of the shock absorber to the lower control arm (see illustrations) and pull the shock out from below.

**2.3a Hold the shock absorber stem (A) with a wrench to prevent it from turning when the upper mounting nut (B) is loosened (2WD model)**

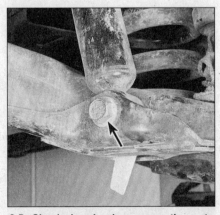

**2.5a Shock absorber lower mounting nuts (early 2WD model)**

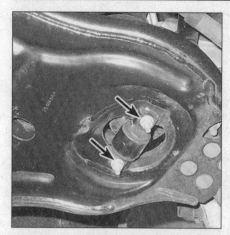

**2.5b Shock absorber lower mounting nuts (late 2WD model)**

6    Remove the lower grommet and retainer from the stem.
7    Installation is the reverse of removal. Before installing the shock absorber upper mounting nut, apply a thread locking compound to the threads of the shock absorber stud, then tighten the upper mounting nut and the lower mounting nuts to the torque listed in this Chapter's Specifications.

**3.2 Unscrew the stabilizer bar link nut while holding the link with a wrench**

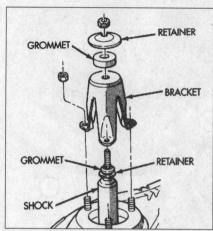

**2.11 An exploded view of the shock absorber upper mounting bracket**

### 4WD models (standard type)

8    Using a back-up wrench on the stem, remove the shock absorber upper mounting nut (see illustration 2.3). On 4WD models with a solid front axle, remove the three nuts and take off the shock absorber upper mounting bracket.
9    Remove the shock absorber lower

**2.12 Shock absorber lower mounting details**

**3.3 Remove the stabilizer bar bracket bolts**

mounting bolt.
10    Remove the shock absorber.

### 4WD models (coil over type)
#### 2001 and earlier models
11    Remove the upper mounting bracket (it's secured by three nuts) (see illustration).
12    Remove the lower mounting bolt and nut (see illustration), then pull the shock absorber up and out from the engine compartment. Remove the rubber grommets and washer from the top of the shock absorber.

#### 2002 and later models
13    Remove the three upper shock absorber mounting nuts.
14    Remove the lower shock absorber mounting fasteners.
15    Remove the brake caliper and disc (see Chapter 12).
16    Detach the wheel speed sensor from the steering knuckle and upper control arm (if equipped).
17    Detach the upper balljoint from the steering knuckle (see Section 7).
18    Detach the stabilizer link from the lower control arm (see Section 3).
19    Remove the shock absorber/coil spring assembly.
**Note:** *The manufacturer states that a special tool is necessary to compress the coil spring to remove it from the shock absorber. Because of this and the safety concerns involved with this procedure, we recommend that a professional repair shop remove the coil spring from the shock absorber and install it onto the replacement shock absorber.*

### All models
20    Installation is the reverse of removal. Tighten all fasteners to the torque listed in this Chapter's Specifications.
21    Install the wheels and lug nuts, lower the vehicle and tighten the lug nuts to the torque listed in the Chapter 1 Specifications,.

---

**3    Stabilizer bar and bushings (front) - removal and installation**

---

1    Raise the vehicle and support it securely on jackstands.
2    Remove the nuts from the link bolts and remove the link bolts (see illustration).
**Note:** *Be sure to keep the parts for the left and right sides separate.*
3    Remove the stabilizer bar bracket bolts and remove the brackets (see illustration).
4    Remove the stabilizer bar. Remove the rubber bushings from the stabilizer bar.
5    Inspect all rubber bushings for wear and damage. If any of the rubber parts are cracked, torn or generally deteriorated, replace them.
6    Installation is the reverse of removal. Be sure to tighten all the fasteners to the torque listed in this Chapter's Specifications. Tighten the wheel lug nuts to the torque listed in the Chapter 1 Specifications,.

**4.4 To detach a front suspension arm from the front axle, remove the nut(s) and knock out the bolt(s) with a punch**

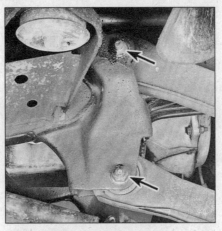

**4.5 To detach a front suspension arm from the frame bracket, remove the nut and knock out the pivot bolt**

**4.9 To disconnect the lower end of the track bar from the axle bracket, remove this bolt**

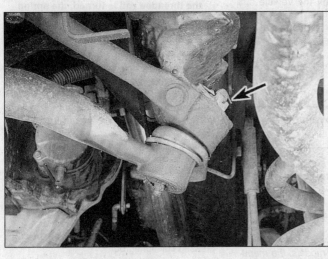

**4.10 To disconnect the upper end of the track bar from the frame bracket, remove the cotter pin, loosen the nut, install a small two-jaw puller and press the ballstud out of the bracket (you can also use a picklefork, but it will damage the boot)**

**5.2a Mark the relationship of the torsion bar to the lower control arm . . .**

## 4  Suspension arms (link/coil suspension) - removal and installation

**Note:** *This procedure applies to vehicles equipped with a solid front axle.*

### Upper and lower arms

1    Loosen the front wheel lug nuts. Raise the front of the vehicle and support it securely on jackstands. Remove the wheel.

2    If you're removing a lower suspension arm, paint or scribe alignment marks on the adjuster cams to ensure that the arm is installed correctly.

3    If you're removing an upper right side suspension arm, disconnect the exhaust system from the manifolds (see Chapter 4A).

4    Remove the suspension arm nut, cams and cam bolt from the axle (see illustration).

5    Remove the suspension arm nut and pivot bolt from the frame bracket (see illustration).

6    Installation is the reverse of removal. If you're installing a lower arm, align the marks you made in Step 2. Be sure to tighten all sus-

pension fasteners to the torque listed in this Chapter's Specifications after the vehicle is on the ground.

7    Have the front end alignment checked and, if necessary, adjusted.

### Track bar

8    Loosen the wheel lug nuts, raise the front of the vehicle and support it securely on jackstands placed under the frame rails. Remove the wheels and support the axle with a floor jack placed under the axle tube. Raise the axle enough to support its weight.

9    Disconnect the lower end of the track bar from the axle bracket (see illustration) on the right end of the axle.

10    To disconnect the upper end of the track bar (see illustration) from the frame bracket, loosen the nut, install a small two-jaw puller and separate the track bar ballstud from the bracket (a "picklefork" type balljoint separator will work too, but it will damage the boot).

11    Installation is the reverse of removal. Tighten the track bar mounting fasteners to the torque values listed in this Chapter's Specifications after the vehicle has been lowered.

## 5  Torsion bar - removal and installation

**Note:** *This procedure applies to 2002 and later 4WD models equipped with independent front suspension.*
**Note:** *The torsion bars are marked L for left and R for right; they aren't interchangeable.*
**Warning:** *Removing a torsion bar is potentially dangerous and utmost attention must be directed to the job, or serious injury may result. The following procedure requires the use of a tool specifically designed to unload the tension on the torsion bar. Carefully follow the instructions furnished with the tool.*

### Removal

1    Loosen the front wheel lug nuts, raise the vehicle and support it securely on jackstands placed under the frame rails. Remove the wheel.

2    Mark the relationship of the torsion bar to the lower control arm and to the torsion bar anchor (see illustrations).

5.2b . . . and to the torsion bar anchor

5.3 Torsion bar anchor adjustment bolt

6.3 A typical aftermarket internal spring compressor tool: the hooked arms grip the upper coils of the spring, the plate is inserted below the lower coil, and when the threaded rod is turned, the spring is compressed

3    Make a mark on the adjustment bolt where it goes into the nut that bears on the anchor (see illustration), or count the number of threads showing between the nut and the bolt head.

4    Install the special tool on the crossmember (a two-jaw puller can also be used); make sure the tool's center bolt is positioned on the dimple in the torsion bar anchor, then tighten the center bolt until the load is removed from the adjustment bolt and nut.

5    Unscrew the adjustment bolt and nut, then carefully unscrew the tool, allowing the torsion bar to unload.

6    Remove the anchor from the torsion bar. Pull the torsion bar out of the lower control arm and guide it through the crossmember.

## Installation

7    Installation is the reverse of removal. Be sure to clean out the hexagonal hole in the lower control arm and lube it with multi-purpose grease before inserting the torsion bar into the arm. Also apply some grease to the hex ends of the torsion bar, to the top of the anchor and to the adjustment bolt. Make sure that the marks you made on the rear end of the torsion bar and the crossmember and on the front end of the torsion bar and the control arm line up. And make sure that the torsion bar adjustment bolt is tightened until the same number of threads are showing between the bolt head and nut that were showing before removal.

8    Install the wheel, remove the jackstands and lower the vehicle.

9    Tighten the wheel lug nuts to the torque listed in the Chapter 1 Specifications.

## Adjustment

10    Drive the vehicle back-and-forth a few times to settle the suspension.

11    Make sure the tires are properly inflated and the vehicle is unloaded. Measure the vehicle's ride height on each side, from equal points on the frame to the ground. If the side that has been worked on is higher or lower than the other side, turn the torsion bar adjust-

ment bolt accordingly until the vehicle sits level. This may take a few tries, and it's important to roll the vehicle back and forth between adjustments, to settle the suspension and get an accurate reading.

12    Have the front end alignment checked, and if necessary, adjusted.

## 6    Coil spring - removal and installation

**Warning:** *Removing a coil spring is potentially dangerous and utmost attention must be directed to the job, or serious injury may result. Use only a high-quality spring compressor and carefully follow the manufacturer's instructions furnished with the tool.*

**Note:** *On coil over shock absorber assemblies, found on late model 4WD models, the manufacturer states that a special tool is necessary to compress the coil spring to remove it from the shock absorber (with the shock absorber assembly removed from the vehicle). Because of this and the safety concerns involved with this procedure, we recommend that a professional repair shop remove the coil spring from the shock absorber and install it onto the replacement shock absorber.*

## Models with independent front suspension

### Removal

1    Loosen the wheel lug nuts, raise the vehicle and support it securely on jackstands placed under the frame rails. Remove the wheel.

2    Support the outer end of the lower control arm with a floor jack. Remove the shock absorber (see Section 2).

3    Install a suitable internal-type spring compressor in accordance with the tool manufacturer's instructions (see illustration). Compress the spring sufficiently to relieve all pressure from the upper spring seat. This can be verified by wiggling the spring.

4    Disconnect the stabilizer bar from the

lower control arm (see Section 3).

5    Separate the lower control arm from the steering knuckle; loosen the lower balljoint nut a few turns (don't remove it), install a balljoint separator and break the balljoint loose from the knuckle. Now remove the nut.

**Note:** *If you don't have the proper balljoint removal tool, a "picklefork" type balljoint separator can be used, but keep in mind that this type of tool will probably destroy the balljoint boot.*

6    Lift the knuckle and hub assembly up, then place a block of wood between the upper control arm and the frame to support the assembly out of the way.

7    Lower the floor jack, then guide the compressed coil spring out.

### Installation

8    Place the insulator on top of the coil spring (the upper end of the spring is the end with the more tightly wound coils).

9    Install the top of the spring into the spring pocket and the bottom in the lower control arm.

10    Connect the lower control arm to the steering knuckle (see Section 8). Remove the spring compressor.

11    The remainder of installation is the reverse of removal. Tighten all fasteners to the proper torque values. Tighten the wheel lug nuts to the torque listed in the Chapter 1 Specifications.

12    Have the front end alignment checked and, if necessary, adjusted.

## Models with a solid front axle

13    Loosen the front wheel lug nuts, raise the front of the vehicle and support it securely on jackstands placed under the frame rails. Remove the wheels.

14    Support the end of the axle from which you're removing the spring with a floor jack.

15    Install a coil spring compressor on the coil spring and compress the spring slightly

**7.2 Back off the nut a few turns, then separate the balljoint from the steering knuckle (leaving the nut on the ballstud will prevent the balljoint from separating violently)**

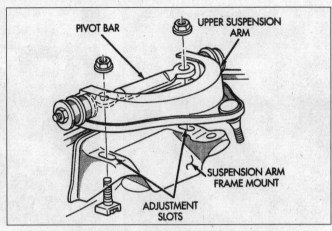

**7.4a To detach the upper control arm from the frame bracket, remove the nuts securing the pivot bar to the frame - 2001 and earlier 1500 models/2002 and earlier 2500 and 3500 models**

(this is to make sure it won't slip, fall off or fly out).

16   Remove the upper suspension arm and loosen the lower suspension arm nuts and pivot bolts (see Section 4).

17   Mark and disconnect the front driveshaft from the front axle (see Chapter 8).

18   Disconnect the track bar from the frame rail bracket.

19   Disconnect the drag link from the Pitman arm (see Section 17).

20   Disconnect the stabilizer bar link from the axle (see Section 3).

21   Disconnect the shock absorber from the axle (see Section 2).

22   Lower the axle until the coil spring is free and remove the spring.

23   Installation is the reverse of removal.

## 7   Upper control arm - removal and installation

**Note:** *This procedure applies to models equipped with independent front suspension.*

### Removal

1   Loosen the wheel lug nuts, raise the vehicle and support it securely on jackstands placed under the frame rails. Remove the wheel.

2   Loosen (but don't remove) the nut on the upper balljoint stud, then disconnect the balljoint from the steering knuckle with a balljoint removal tool (see illustration).

**Note:** *If you don't have the proper balljoint removal tool, a "picklefork" type balljoint separator can be used, but keep in mind that this type of tool will probably destroy the balljoint boot.*

3   On 2001 and earlier 1500 models/2002 and earlier 2500 and 3500 models, place a floor jack underneath the outer end of the lower control arm and raise the jack head until it touches the arm and moves it up slightly. The jack must remain in this position throughout the entire procedure.

4   Remove the nuts and pivot bolts that

attach the control arm to the frame (see illustrations). Pull the upper arm from its frame brackets.

### Installation

5   Installation is the reverse of removal. Be sure to tighten all fasteners to the torque values listed in this Chapter's Specifications. On 2002 and later 1500 models/2003 and later 2500 and 3500 models, don't tighten the pivot bolt nuts until the vehicle is sitting at normal ride height. If it's too hard to get to the nuts with the wheel on, normal ride height can be simulated by raising the outer end of the lower control arm with a floor jack.

6   Install the wheel and lug nuts. Lower the vehicle and tighten the lug nuts to the torque listed in the Chapter 1 Specifications. Have the front end alignment checked and, if necessary, adjusted.

## 8   Lower control arm - removal and installation

**Note:** *This procedure applies to models equipped with independent front suspension.*

### 2WD models

#### Removal

1   Loosen the wheel lug nuts, raise the vehicle and support it securely on jackstands placed under the frame rails. Remove the wheel.

2   Support the outer end of the lower control arm with a floor jack. Remove the shock absorber (see Section 2).

3   Install a suitable internal type spring compressor in accordance with the tool manufacturer's instructions (see illustration 6.3). Compress the spring sufficiently to relieve all pressure from the upper spring seat. This can be verified by wiggling the spring.

4   Loosen (but don't remove) the nut on the lower balljoint stud, then disconnect the balljoint from the steering knuckle with a

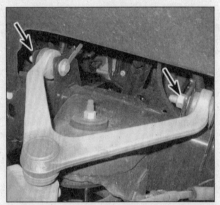

**7.4b Remove the nuts and the upper control arm pivot bolts (turn the nuts, not the bolts) - 2002 and later 1500 model shown (2003 and later 2500/3500 models similar)**

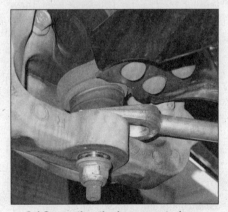

**8.4 Separating the lower control arm balljoint with a "picklefork" type balljoint separator**

balljoint removal tool (see illustration).

**Caution:** *A "picklefork" type balljoint separator can be used, but keep in mind that this type of tool will probably destroy the balljoint boot.*

5   Lift the knuckle and hub assembly up, then place a block of wood between the upper control arm and the frame to support the

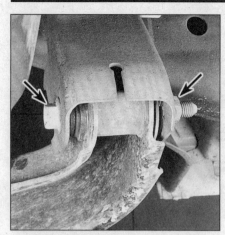

**8.7 To detach the lower control arm from the frame, remove the nuts and pivot bolts (arrows) (rear shown, front similar)**

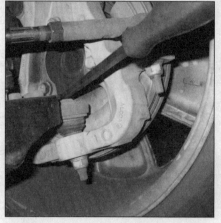

**9.10 Pry down on the balljoint to check for wear**

assembly out of the way.

6    Pull the lower control arm down, then guide the compressed coil spring out.

7    Remove the bolts that attach the control arm to the frame (see illustration). Pull the lower arm from its frame brackets.

### Installation

8    Installation is the reverse of removal. Be sure to tighten all fasteners to the torque values listed in this Chapter's Specifications, but don't tighten the pivot bolt nuts until the vehicle is sitting at normal ride height. If it's too hard to get to the nuts with the wheel on, normal ride height can be simulated by raising the outer end of the lower control arm with a floor jack.

9    Install the wheel and lug nuts. Lower the vehicle and tighten the lug nuts to the torque listed in the Chapter 1 Specifications. Have the front end alignment checked and, if necessary, adjusted.

### *4WD models*

#### Removal

10    Loosen the wheel lug nuts, raise the vehicle and support it securely on jackstands placed under the frame rails. Remove the wheel.

11    Remove the driveaxle (see Chapter 8), then reinstall the upper balljoint back into the steering knuckle and install the nut temporarily.

12    Disconnect the stabilizer bar from the lower control arm (see Section 3).

13    Remove the torsion bar (see Section 5).

14    Remove the shock absorber (see Section 2).

15    Loosen (but don't remove) the nut on the lower balljoint stud a few turns, then disconnect the balljoint from the steering knuckle arm with a balljoint removal tool. Now remove the nut.

**Note:** *If you don't have the proper balljoint removal tool, a "picklefork" type balljoint separator can be used, but keep in mind that this*

type of tool will probably destroy the balljoint boot *(see illustration 8.4).*

16    Remove the lower control arm pivot bolts and pull the lower arm from its frame brackets.

### Installation

17    Installation is the reverse of removal. Be sure to tighten all fasteners to the torque values listed in this Chapter's Specifications, but don't tighten the pivot bolt nuts until the vehicle is sitting at normal ride height. If it's too hard to get to the nuts with the wheel on, normal ride height can be simulated by raising the outer end of the lower control arm with a floor jack.

18    When installing the torsion bar, be sure to check and adjust the ride height (see Section 5). Have the front end alignment checked and, if necessary, adjusted.

---

## 9    Balljoints - replacement

1    Inspect the control arm balljoints for looseness anytime either of them is separated from the steering knuckle. See if you can turn the ballstud in its socket with your fingers. If the balljoint is loose, or if the ballstud can be turned, replace the balljoint. You can also check the balljoints with the suspension assembled as follows.

### *Upper balljoints*

#### Independent front suspension

2    Raise the lower control arm with a floor jack until the tire just barely touches the ground.

3    Using a large prybar inserted between the upper control arm and the steering knuckle, pry upwards on the upper control arm. The manufacturer specifies up to 0.020-inch movement is allowed; a dial indicator can be used to check for play. If you are unable to accurately measure balljoint play, have the balljoint checked at an automotive repair shop.

4    If replacement is indicated, replace the upper control arm (see Section 7); the balljoint cannot be replaced separately.

#### 4WD with solid axle

5    Raise the vehicle and support it securely on jackstands.

6    Grasp the top of the tire and "rock" the tire in-and-out. If there is significant movement at the balljoint, have the balljoint checked by an automotive repair shop.

7    If replacement is indicated, the balljoints on 4WD solid axle models are a press fit in the axle tube yoke, which necessitates the use of a special press tool and receiver cup to remove and install them. Equipment rental yards and some auto parts stores have these tools available for rent. If you don't have access to this tool, take the vehicle to an automotive machine shop or other qualified repair facility to have the balljoint replaced.

### *Lower balljoints*

#### Independent front suspension

8    Raise the vehicle and support it securely on jackstands.

9    Place a floor jack under the lower control arm, near the outer end, and raise it until the upper control arm lifts off its rebound bumper.

10    Now, insert the prybar between the top of the balljoint and the steering knuckle and pry down (see illustration). The manufacturer specifies up to 0.020-inch movement is allowed; a dial indicator can be used to check for play. If you are unable to accurately measure balljoint play, have the balljoint checked at an automotive repair shop.

11    If replacement is indicated, remove the lower control arm (see Section 8); the balljoint is press fit in the lower control arm, which necessitates the use of a special press tool and receiver cup to remove and install the balljoint. Equipment rental yards and some auto parts stores have these tools available for rent. If you don't have access to this tool, take the vehicle to an automotive machine shop or other qualified repair facility to have the balljoint replaced.

**Note:** *Some balljoint replacement tools are similar to a big, heavy-duty C-clamp. With this type of tool it is only necessary to separate the balljoint from the steering knuckle.*

**Note:** *The lower balljoints on some models are replaceable, but on others they're not. Check with your local auto parts store to check on the availability of replacement parts before disassembling your vehicle.*

#### 4WD with solid axle

12    Raise the vehicle and support it securely on jackstands.

13    Using a large prybar, pry upwards on the bottom of the steering knuckle, checking for significant movement at the balljoint. If there is significant movement at the balljoint, have the balljoint checked by an automotive repair shop.

14    If replacement is indicated, the balljoints on 4WD solid axle models are a press

fit in the axle tube yoke, which necessitates the use of a special press tool and receiver cup to remove and install them. Equipment rental yards and some auto parts stores have these tools available for rent. If you don't have access to this tool, take the vehicle to an automotive machine shop or other qualified repair facility to have the balljoint replaced.

## 10  Hub and bearing assembly - removal and installation

**Note:** *For front wheel bearing service on 1999 and earlier 2WD models, see Chapter 1, Section 26.*

### *2000 and 2001 1500 2WD models/2000 through 2002 2500 and 3500 2WD models*

1    Loosen the front wheel lug nuts, raise the vehicle and support it securely on jackstands. Remove the wheel.
2    Remove the brake caliper and hang it out of the way with a piece of wire (see Chapter 9). Remove the brake disc.
3    Disconnect the ABS wheel speed sensor electrical connector and free the harness from its clips.
4    On all except 3500 HD models, remove the hub and bearing nut from the spindle, then slide off the hub and bearing assembly off the spindle. Discard the nut - a new one must be used for reassembly.
5    On 3500 HD models, remove the hub and bearing nut from the spindle, then slide the spindle shaft inwards and unbolt the hub and bearing assembly from the steering knuckle.
6    Installation is the reverse of the removal procedure. Be sure to use a new spindle nut and tighten all fasteners to the specified torque values.

### *2002 and later 1500 models/2003 and later 2500 and 3500 models*

#### Independent front suspension models

**Note:** *This procedure applies to both 2WD and 4WD models.*
**Warning:** *The dust created by the brake system is harmful to your health. Never blow it out with compressed air and don't inhale any of it. Do not, under any circumstances, use petroleum-based solvents to clean brake parts. Use brake system cleaner only.*
**Note:** *The hub and bearing assembly is sealed-for-life. If worn or damaged, it must be replaced as a unit.*
7    Loosen the front wheel lug nuts, raise the vehicle and support it securely on jackstands. Remove the wheel.
8    If you're working on a 4WD model, remove the driveaxle (see Chapter 8).
9    Remove the brake caliper and hang it out

of the way with a piece of wire, then remove the caliper mounting bracket (see Chapter 9). Pull the disc off the hub.
10    On models equipped with ABS, remove the wheel speed sensor from the hub.
11    Working from the back side of the steering knuckle, remove the hub retaining bolts from the steering knuckle (see illustration).
12    Remove the hub from the steering knuckle. Remove the disc shield.

#### Installation

13    Clean the mating surfaces on the steering knuckle, bearing flange and knuckle bore.
14    Position the disc shield, insert the hub and bearing assembly into the steering knuckle and install the bolts, tightening them to the torque listed in this Chapter's Specifications.
15    Installation is the reverse of removal, noting the following points:
   a)  *If you're working on a 4WD model, tighten the driveaxle/hub nut to the torque listed in the Chapter 8 Specifications.*
   b)  *Tighten the brake caliper mounting bracket and brake caliper mounting bolts to the torque listed in the Chapter 9 Specifications.*
   c)  *Install the wheel, lower the vehicle and tighten the lug nuts to the torque listed in the Chapter 1 Specifications.*

#### Solid front axle models

16    See Chapter 8, Section 24 for the hub and bearing assembly replacement procedure.

## 11  Steering knuckle - removal and installation

### *Independent front suspension*

1    Loosen the wheel lug nuts, raise the vehicle and support it securely on jackstands. Remove the wheel.
2    If you're working on a 4WD model, unscrew the driveaxle/hub nut with a socket and large breaker bar (see Chapter 8). Brace a large prybar across two of the wheel studs or insert a large screwdriver through the center of the brake caliper and into the disc cooling vanes to prevent the hub from turning as the nut is loosened.
3    Remove the disc brake caliper and disc (see Chapter 9). If equipped, disconnect the electrical connector from the ABS sensor and remove the sensor.
4    Disconnect the tie-rod from the steering knuckle (see Section 17).
5    Support the lower control arm with a floor jack. The jack must remain in this position throughout the entire procedure.
6    Separate the lower control arm from the steering knuckle (see Section 8).
7    Separate the upper control arm from the steering knuckle (see Section 7).
8    Carefully inspect the steering knuckle for cracks, especially around the steering arm

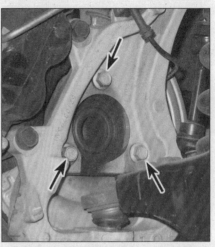

**10.11 To detach the hub from the steering knuckle, remove these bolts (2000 and later 2WD shown, 4WD similar)**

and spindle mounting area. Also inspect the balljoint stud holes. If they're elongated, or if you find any cracks in the knuckle, replace the steering knuckle.
9    Installation is the reverse of removal. Be sure to tighten all suspension fasteners to the torque listed in this Chapter's Specifications.

### *Link/coil suspension*

**Note:** *This procedure applies to vehicles equipped with a solid front axle.*
10    Loosen the wheel lug nuts, raise the vehicle and support it securely on jackstands. Remove the wheel.
11    Remove the disc brake caliper and disc (see Chapter 9). If equipped, remove the ABS sensor wire and bracket from the steering knuckle.
12    Remove the hub bearing and axle shaft (see Chapter 8).
13    Disconnect the tie-rod end or drag link from the steering knuckle (see Section 17).
14    Remove the cotter pin from the steering knuckle upper ballstud nut and loosen both the upper and lower ballstud nuts.
15    Separate the steering knuckle from the axle housing yoke. Use a brass hammer to knock it loose if necessary.
16    Installation is the reverse of removal. Be sure to tighten all suspension fasteners to the torque listed in this Chapter's Specifications after the vehicle has been lowered to the ground.

## 12  Shock absorber (rear) - removal and installation

1    Raise the rear of the vehicle and support it securely on jackstands placed under the frame rails. Support the rear axle with a floor jack placed under the axle tube on the side being worked on. Don't raise the axle - just support its weight.

**12.2 To detach a rear shock absorber from the frame, remove this nut and bolt**

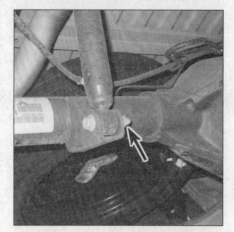

**12.3 To detach a rear shock from the axle, remove this nut and bolt**

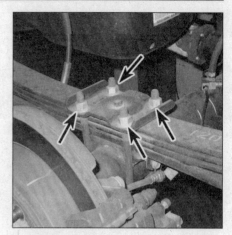

**13.2 To remove the spring plate and U-bolts, remove these four nuts**

2    Remove the nut and bolt that attach the upper end of the shock absorber to the frame (see illustration). If the nut won't loosen because of rust, apply some penetrating oil and allow it to soak in for awhile.

3    Remove the nut and bolt that attach the lower end of the shock to the axle bracket (see illustration). Again, if the nut is frozen, apply some penetrating oil, wait awhile and try again.

4    Extend the new shock absorber as far as possible. Install new rubber grommets into the shock absorber eyes (if they are not already present).

5    Installation is the reverse of removal. Be sure to tighten the shock absorber mounting fasteners to the torque listed in this Chapter's Specifications.

### 13  Leaf spring - removal and installation

## Removal

1    Loosen the wheel lug nuts, raise the rear of the vehicle and support it securely on jackstands placed under the frame rails. Remove the wheel and support the rear axle with a floor jack placed under the axle tube. Don't raise the axle - just support its weight.

2    Remove the nuts, U-bolts, spring plate, and spring seat that clamp the leaf spring to the axle (see illustration).

3    Remove the leaf spring shackle bolts and the shackle (see illustration).

4    Unscrew the front bolt (see illustration); remove the leaf spring from the vehicle.

## Installation

5    To install the leaf spring, position the spring on the axle tube so that the spring center bolt enters the locating hole on the axle tube.

6    Line up the spring front eye with the mounting bracket and install the front bolt and nut.

7    Install the rear shackle assembly.

8    Tighten the shackle bolt and the front bolt until all slack is taken up.

9    Install the U-bolts and nuts. Tighten the nuts until they force the spring plate against

the axle, but don't torque them yet.

10    Be sure the auxiliary spring, if equipped, aligns with the main spring.

11    Install the wheel and lug nuts. Tighten the lug nuts to the torque listed in the Chapter 1 Specifications. Remove the jackstands and lower the vehicle.

12    Tighten the U-bolt nuts, front bolt/nut and shackle bolts/nuts to the torque listed in this Chapter's Specifications.

### 14  Stabilizer bar and bushings (rear) - removal and installation (1997 through 2001 models)

1    Apply the parking brake. Raise the rear of the vehicle and support it securely on jackstands.

2    Remove the nuts from links at the stabilizer bar.

3    Carefully separate the link from the stabilizer bar with a two-jaw puller.

4    Remove the nuts and retainers from the rear axle brackets.

5    Remove the stabilizer bar from the vehicle.

6    If it's necessary, remove the link assembly's bolts and nuts and remove from the frame brackets.

7    Pull the bushings off the stabilizer bar and inspect them for cracks, hardness and other signs of deterioration. Inspect the bushings in the lower ends of the links. Replace all damaged bushings.

8    Installation is the reverse of removal. Position the bar and center it on the rear axle with equal spacing on each side. Do not torque any fasteners until the vehicle has been lowered to the ground. After lowering the vehicle, tighten all fasteners to the torque listed in this Chapter's Specifications.

**13.3 To detach the rear end of the leaf spring, remove the shackle nuts and bolts**

**13.4 To detach the front end of the leaf spring from the forward bracket, remove this nut and bolt**

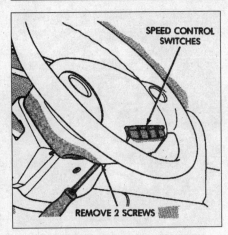

15.3a To detach the speed control switches on 2001 and earlier models (if equipped), remove two screws from the backside of the steering wheel . . .

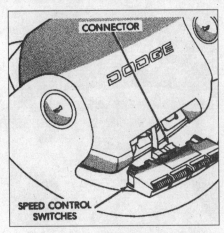

15.3b . . . then, pull the speed control switches out from the steering wheel and unplug the electrical connector

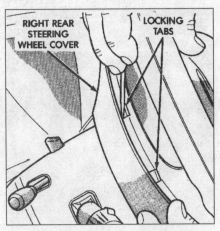

15.4 Pry off the right rear steering cover with a screwdriver, if equipped (2001 and earlier models)

## 15  Steering wheel - removal and installation

**Warning:** *These models are equipped with airbags. Always disable the airbag system whenever working in the vicinity of any airbag system component to avoid the possibility of accidental airbag deployment, which could cause personal injury (see Chapter 12).*

### *Steering wheel*

#### Removal

1    Park the vehicle with the front wheels in the straight-ahead position.

**Warning:** *Do NOT turn the steering shaft before, during or after steering wheel removal. If the shaft is turned while the steering wheel is removed, a mechanism known as the clockspring can be damaged. The clockspring, which maintains a continuous electrical circuit between the wiring harness and the airbag module, consists of a flat, ribbon-like electrically conductive tape which winds and unwinds as the steering wheel is turned.*

2    Disconnect the cable(s) from the negative battery terminal(s), (see Chapter 5).

3    On 2001 and earlier 1500 models/2002 and earlier 2500 and 3500 models equipped with speed control, remove the speed control switch retaining screws (see illustration). Pull off the switches and unplug the electrical connector (see illustration).

4    On 2001 and earlier 1500 models/2002 and earlier 2500 and 3500 models, remove the right rear steering wheel cover using a small screwdriver (see illustration), if equipped.

5    On 2001 and earlier 1500 models/2002 and earlier 2500 and 3500 models, remove the four nuts attaching the airbag module (see illustration). It will probably be necessary to turn the steering wheel to gain access to the nuts; just be sure to center the wheel after the nuts have been removed.

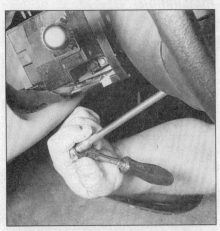

15.5 Remove the four airbag module retaining nuts

6    On 2002 and later 1500 models/2003 and later 2500 and 3500 models, remove the two airbag module retaining screws (see illustrations) and lift off the airbag module.

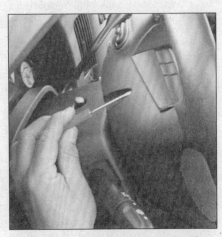

15.6a Remove the screws securing the speed control switches, then detach the switches from the steering wheel (2003 model shown)

**Warning:** *Carry the airbag module with the trim cover (upholstered side) facing away from you, and set the airbag module in a safe location with the trim cover facing up.*

15.6b Remove the airbag module retaining screws (2003 model shown - on later models, the retaining screws are removed from the back of the steering wheel)

**15.7 Lift the airbag off the steering wheel and unplug the electrical connectors for the horn and for the airbag**

**15.9 After removing the bolt, mark the relationship of the wheel to the shaft**

**15.10 Remove the steering wheel with a steering wheel puller**

7    On all models, unplug the electrical connectors for the airbag and horn (see illustration).

8    Remove the steering wheel nut or bolt, as applicable.

9    Mark the relationship of the steering wheel to the steering shaft (see illustration).

10   Use a puller and remove the steering wheel (see illustration).

**Caution:** *Any attempt to remove the steering wheel without using a puller can damage the steering column.*

11   If it is necessary to remove the clockspring, unplug the electrical connector for the clockspring, then disengage the plastic latches (2001 and earlier 1500 models/2002 and earlier 2500 and 3500 models) or remove the screws (2002 and later 1500 models/2003 and later 2500 and 3500 models) and lift the clockspring from the steering column (see illustration).

## Installation

12   When installing the clockspring, make absolutely sure that the airbag clockspring is centered with the arrows on the clockspring rotor and case line up. This shouldn't be a problem as long as you have not turned the steering shaft while the wheel was removed. If for some reason the shaft was turned, center the clockspring as follows:

a)  Rotate the clockspring clockwise until it stops (don't apply too much force). On 2001 and earlier 1500 models/2002 and earlier 2500 and 3500 models, depress the two plastic auto-locking tabs on the clockspring hub while doing this (see illustration).

b)  Rotate the clockspring counterclockwise about 2-1/2 turns until the arrows on the clockspring rotor and case line up.

**Caution:** *Make sure the front wheels are pointing straight ahead when installing the clockspring and steering wheel.*

13   Installation is the reverse of removal, noting the following points:

a)  *Make sure the airbag clockspring is centered before installing the steering wheel.*

b)  *When installing the steering wheel, align the marks on the shaft and the steering wheel hub.*

c)  *Install a NEW steering wheel bolt (2001 and later 1500/2002 and later 2500 and 3500 models). Tighten the steering wheel nut or bolt to the torque listed in this Chapter's Specifications.*

d)  *Install the airbag module on the steering wheel and tighten the mounting screws to the torque listed in this Chapter's Specifications.*

e)  *Enable the airbag system (see Chapter 12).*

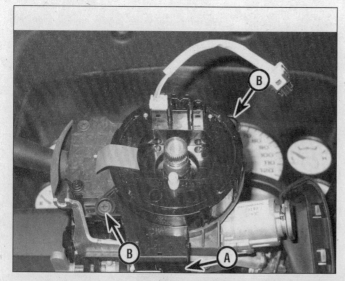

**15.11 Disconnect the clockspring electrical connector (A), then remove the mounting screws (B) (2002 and later 1500 models/2003 and later 2500 and 3500 models)**

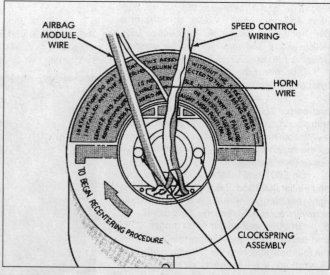

**15.12 Clockspring details**

**16.7 Remove the steering shaft coupler bolt**

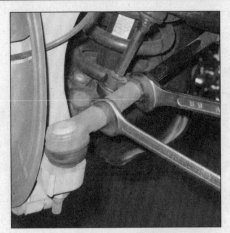

**17.2 Hold the tie-rod end with a wrench while loosening the jam nut**

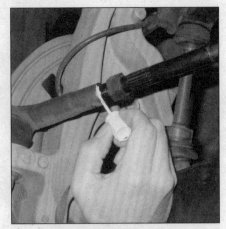

**17.3 Mark the position of the tie-rod end in relation to the threads**

## 16  Steering column - removal and installation

**Warning:** *These models are equipped with airbags. Always disable the airbag system whenever working in the vicinity of any airbag system component to avoid the possibility of accidental airbag deployment, which could cause personal injury (see Chapter 12).*

### Removal

1    Park the vehicle with the wheels pointing straight ahead. Disconnect the cable(s) from the negative battery terminal(s), (see Chapter 5). Wait at least two minutes before proceeding (to allow the backup power supply for the airbag system to become depleted.
2    Remove the steering wheel (see Section 14), then turn the ignition key to the Lock position to prevent the steering shaft from turning.
**Caution:** *If this is not done, the airbag clockspring could be damaged.*
**Note:** *Some automatic transmission models may not be equipped with an internal locking shaft. Remove the airbag clockspring to prevent accidental damage (see Section 15).*
3    Remove the knee bolster (see Chapter 11).
4    Remove the steering column covers (see Chapter 11).
5    On models with a column-mounted shifter, detach the shift cable from the shift lever on the column. Also detach the electrical connector (see Chapter 7B).
6    Remove the screw and detach the electrical connector from the multi-function switch (see Chapter 12). Unplug any other electrical connectors that would interfere with column removal.
7    Remove the shaft coupler bolt (securing the steering shaft to the intermediate shaft) (see illustration). Separate the intermediate shaft from the steering shaft.
8    Remove the steering column mounting nuts, lower the column and pull it to the rear, making sure nothing is still connected.

### Installation

9    Guide the steering column into position and install the mounting nuts, but don't tighten them yet.
10   Connect the intermediate shaft to the steering column. Install a new coupler bolt, then tighten the nut to the torque listed in this Chapter's Specifications.
11   Tighten the column mounting nuts to the torque listed in this Chapter's Specifications.
12   The remainder of installation is the reverse of removal. Adjust the shift cable following the procedures described in Chapter 7B.

## 17  Steering linkage - removal and installation

### Independent front suspension

#### Tie-rod end

**Removal**

1    Loosen the wheel lug nuts, raise the vehicle and support it securely on jackstands. Apply the parking brake. Remove the wheel.
2    Loosen the tie-rod end jam nut (see illustration).
3    Mark the relationship of the tie-rod end to the threaded portion of the tie-rod. This will ensure the toe-in setting is restored when reassembled (see illustration).
4    Loosen (but don't remove) the nut on the tie-rod end ballstud and disconnect the tie-rod end from the steering knuckle arm with a puller (see illustrations).
5    If you're replacing the tie-rod end, then unscrew the tie-rod end from the tie-rod, then thread the new tie-rod end onto the tie-rod to the marked position.

**Installation**

6    Connect the tie-rod end to the steering knuckle arm. Install the nut on the ballstud and tighten it to the torque listed in this Chapter's Specifications. Install the wheel. Lower

**17.4a If the ballstud turns while attempting to loosen the nut, hold it stationary with a wrench**

**17.4b Back-off the ballstud nut a few turns, then separate the tie-rod end from the steering knuckle with a puller (leaving the nut on the ballstud will prevent the tie-rod end from separating violently)**

**17.25 To replace the idler arm on 2WD models, remove the two mounting bolts and loosen the ballstud nut, then use a small puller to separate the idler arm ballstud from the center link**

the vehicle and tighten the lug nuts to the torque listed in the Chapter 1 Specifications.

7    Have the front end alignment checked and, if necessary, adjusted.

### Link/coil suspension

#### Tie-rod end

**Removal**

8    Loosen the wheel lug nuts, raise the vehicle and support it securely on jackstands. Apply the parking brake. Remove the wheel.

9    Measure the distance between the adjuster tube and the center line of the ballstud. This will ensure the toe-in setting is restored when reassembled.

10    Loosen (but don't remove) the nut on the tie-rod end ballstud and disconnect the tie-rod end from the steering knuckle arm with a puller.

11    If you're replacing the tie-rod end, lubricate the threaded portion of the tie-rod end with chassis grease. Screw the new tie-rod end into the adjuster tube and adjust the distance from the tube to the ballstud by threading the tie-rod end into the adjuster tube until the same number of threads are showing as before. Or use the measurement you made before removing the tie-rod end. Don't tighten the adjuster tube clamps yet.

**Installation**

12    Insert the tie-rod ballstud into the steering knuckle. Make sure the ballstud is fully seated. Install the nut and tighten it to the torque listed in this Chapter's Specifications. If the ballstud spins when attempting to tighten the nut, hold it stationary with a small wrench.

13    Tighten the tie-rod adjuster clamp bolts to the torque listed in this Chapter's Specifications. Have the front end alignment checked and, if necessary, adjusted.

#### Drag link

**Removal**

14    Loosen the wheel lug nuts, raise the vehicle and support it securely on jackstands. Apply the parking brake. Remove the wheels.

15    Remove the nut from the drag link ballstud.

16    Using a puller, separate the drag link

from the Pitman arm.

17    Loosen (but don't remove) the nuts on the tie-rod end ballstuds and disconnect the tie-rod ends from the steering knuckle and drag link with a puller.

**Installation**

18    Installation is the reverse of the removal procedure. Be sure to tighten all of the fasteners to the torque listed in this Chapter's Specifications.

19    Have the front end alignment checked and, if necessary, adjusted.

#### Pitman arm

**Removal**

20    Loosen the wheel lug nuts, raise the vehicle and support it securely on jackstands. Apply the parking brake. Remove the right wheel.

21    Remove the drag link nut from the Pitman arm ballstud.

22    Working at the right side steering knuckle, loosen (but don't remove) the nut on the end of the drag link ballstud, then disconnect the end of the drag link from the steering knuckle arm with a puller.

23    Remove the Pitman arm nut and washer. Mark the Pitman arm and the steering gear shaft to ensure proper alignment at reassembly time (only if the same Pitman arm is going to be used).

**Installation**

24    Installation is the reverse of the removal procedure. Be sure to tighten all of the fasteners to the torque listed in this Chapter's Specifications. Have the front end alignment checked and, if necessary, adjusted.

#### Idler arm (2WD models)

25    Remove the cotter pin and loosen the idler arm ballstud nut. Unbolt the idler arm from the frame (see illustration).

26    Separate the idler arm from the center link with a small two-jaw puller.

27    Installation is the reverse of removal. Be sure to tighten the fasteners to the torque listed in this Chapter's Specifications.

#### Steering damper

28    Inspect the steering damper for fluid leakage. A slight film of fluid near the shaft seal is normal, but if there's excessive fluid present and it's obviously coming from the steering damper, replace the damper.

29    Inspect the steering damper bushing for excessive wear. If it's in bad shape, replace the damper.

30    To test the damper itself, disconnect it from the tie-rod. Using as much travel as possible, extend and compress the damper. The resistance should be smooth and constant for each stroke. If any binding, dead spots or unusual noises are present, replace the damper.

31    Remove the damper-to-tie-rod mounting bolt and nut. Separate the damper from the tie-rod.

32    Remove the damper-to-axle mounting bolt and nut. Separate the damper from the axle.

33    Installation is the reverse of removal. Tighten the fasteners to the torque values listed in this Chapter's Specifications.

### 18   Steering gear boots - replacement

**Note:** *This procedure applies to models with independent front suspension with rack-and-pinion steering only.*

1    Loosen the wheel lug nuts, raise the vehicle and support it securely on jackstands. Remove the wheel.

2    Remove the tie-rod end and jam nut (see Section 17).

3    Remove the steering gear boot clamps and slide the boot off.

**Note:** *Check for the presence of power steering fluid in the boot. If there is a substantial amount, it means the rack seals are leaking and the power steering gear should be replaced with a new or rebuilt unit.*

4    Before installing the new boot, wrap the threads and serrations on the end of the steering rod with a layer of tape so the small end of the new boot isn't damaged.

5    Slide the new boot into position on the steering gear until it seats in the grooves, then install new clamps.

6    Remove the tape and install the tie-rod end (see Section 17).

7    Install the wheel and lug nuts. Lower the vehicle and tighten the lug nuts to the torque listed in the Chapter 1 Specifications.

8    Have the front end alignment checked and, if necessary, adjusted.

### 19   Steering gear - removal and installation

**Warning:** *DO NOT allow the steering column shaft to rotate with the steering gear removed or damage to the airbag system could occur.*

19.3 Remove the pinch bolt from the lower end of the intermediate shaft coupler (A), then unscrew the pressure and return line fittings from the power steering gear (B)

19.5 Location of the rack-and-pinion steering gear mounting bolts

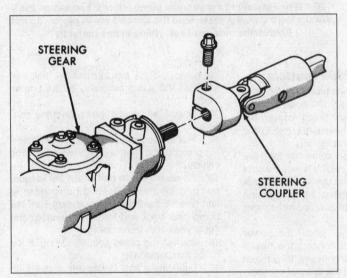

19.9 Mark the relationship of the steering coupler to the steering gear input shaft, then remove the pinch bolt

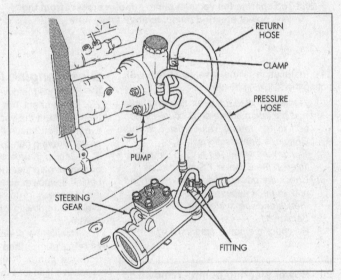

19.10 Typical power steering hose assembly (diesel shown, gasoline engines similar)

## Models with rack-and-pinion steering gear

1    Loosen the front wheel lug nuts, raise the front of the vehicle and support it securely on jackstands. Apply the parking brake. Remove the wheels.

2    Remove the skid plate bolts and the skid plate, if equipped.

3    Mark the relationship of the intermediate shaft coupler to the steering gear input shaft and remove the pinch bolt. Position a drain pan under the steering gear. Using a flare-nut wrench, if available, unscrew the power steering pressure and return lines from the steering gear (see illustration). Cap the lines to prevent leakage.

4    Detach the tie-rod ends from the steering knuckles (see Section 17).

5    Unscrew the mounting bolts, then lower the steering gear from the vehicle (see illustration).

6    Installation is the reverse of removal, noting the following points:

a)   *Tighten the steering gear mounting bolts and the intermediate shaft coupler pinch bolt to the torque values listed in this Chapter's Specifications.*

b)   *Tighten the wheel lug nuts to the torque listed in the Chapter 1 Specifications.*

c)   *Check the power steering fluid level and add some, if necessary (see Chapter 1), then bleed the system as described in Section 21.*

d)   *Re-check the power steering fluid level.*

## Models with recirculating ball steering gear

7    Raise the front of the vehicle and support it securely on jackstands. Apply the parking brake.

8    Remove the skid plate bolts and the skid plate, if equipped.

9    Mark the relationship of the intermediate shaft coupler to the steering gear input shaft, then remove the pinch bolt from the coupler (see illustration).

10    Position a drain pan under the steering gear, then unscrew the power steering lines from the steering gear (see illustration). Cap the lines to prevent leakage.

11    Separate the drag link from the Pitman arm (see Section 17).

12    Remove the steering gear retaining bolts from the frame rail, then detach the steering gear from the frame and remove it.

13    If you're installing a new steering gear or a new Pitman arm, remove the Pitman arm from the steering gear sector shaft (see Section 17).

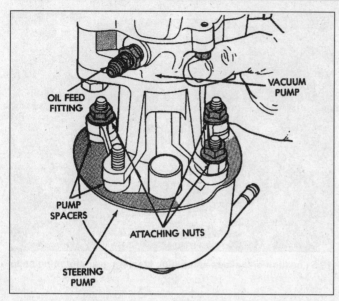

**20.3 To separate the vacuum pump adapter bracket from the power steering pump, remove these nuts**

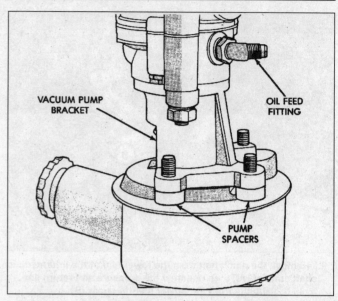

**20.4 When installing the vacuum pump adapter bracket on the power steering pump, make sure the spacers are in place - do not tighten the nuts until everything mates perfectly**

14   Installation is the reverse of removal, noting the following points:
a) *Tighten the steering gear mounting bolts and the intermediate shaft coupler pinch bolt to the torque values listed in this Chapter's Specifications.*
b) *Tighten the wheel lug nuts to the torque listed in the Chapter 1 Specifications.*
c) *Check the power steering fluid level and add some, if necessary (see Chapter 1), then bleed the system as described in Section 21.*
d) *Re-check the power steering fluid.*

## 20   Power steering pump - removal and installation

1   Disconnect the cable(s) from the negative battery terminal(s), (see Chapter 5).

### Diesel engine (1996 and earlier models)

2   Refer to Chapter 9, Section 14 (*Power brake vacuum pump - removal and installation*) and remove the vacuum pump and power steering pump as an assembly.
3   After separating the vacuum pump and power steering pump as described in Chapter 9, remove the adapter from the power steering pump (see illustration).
4   Install the adapter on the new power steering pump (don't forget the spacers) and tighten the nuts to the torque listed in Chapter 9 Specifications. Make sure the pump spacers and power steering pump mate perfectly with the vacuum pump adapter bracket (see illustration).
5   The remainder of installation is the reverse of removal (see Chapter 9, Section 14).

### Diesel engine (2002 models)

6   Remove the drivebelt (see Chapter 1).
7   Disconnect the vacuum hose and oil feed line from the vacuum pump. Loosen the two nuts that attach the vacuum pump to the power steering pump adapter.
8   Unplug the electrical connector from the oil pressure sender unit, which is located right behind the power steering pump. It isn't absolutely necessary to remove the sender unit itself, but removing it will give you more room to work.
9   Position a drain pan under the power steering pump, then disconnect the hoses from the pump. Plug the hoses to prevent excessive fluid loss and the entry of contaminants.
10   Remove the nut from the power steer-

**20.16 These tangs on the vacuum pump must be aligned with the slots in the adapter coupling before tightening the pump-to-adapter nuts**

ing pump-to-block bracket and the bolt that attaches the pump assembly to the engine block.
11   Unbolt the vacuum pump from the gear housing cover (one bolt).
12   Pull the vacuum pump and power steering pump to the rear and remove it from the vehicle.
13   Remove the nuts that attach the vacuum pump to the power steering pump adapter and remove the pump. If necessary, turn the pump gear back and forth to disengage the pump shaft from the coupling.
14   Inspect the pump adapter O-ring. If it's cut or torn, replace it.
15   Lubricate a new O-ring and install it on the pump adapter.
16   Note the position of the drive slots in the coupling. Rotate the drive gear to align the tangs on the vacuum pump with the slots in the coupling (see illustration).
17   Make sure that the pump is properly seated into the adapter, then install the pump-to-adapter spacers and nuts and tighten them securely.
18   Installation is the reverse of removal. Be sure to tighten all fasteners securely. Fill the power steering reservoir with the recommended fluid (see Chapter 21) and bleed the system following the procedure described in Section 1. Re-check the power steering fluid level.

### Diesel engine (2003 and later models)

19   Remove the drivebelt (see Chapter 1).
20   Using a large syringe or suction gun, suck as much fluid as possible out of the power steering fluid reservoir. Position a drain pan under the power steering pump, then disconnect the hoses from the pump. Plug the

hoses to prevent excessive fluid loss and the entry of contaminants.

21    Remove the intake air heater manifold (see Chapter 4B, Section 10).

22    Remove the left-side intercooler duct (see Chapter 4B, Section 16).

23    Remove the pump mounting bolts. The bolts can be accessed through the holes in the power steering pump pulley.

24    Lift the pump from the engine compartment, being careful not to let any power steering fluid drip on the vehicle's paint.

25    Installation is the reverse of removal. Be sure to tighten all fasteners securely. Fill the power steering reservoir with the recommended fluid (see Chapter 1) and bleed the system following the procedure described in Section 21. Re-check the power steering fluid level.

## Gasoline engines

26    Remove the drivebelt (see Chapter 1).

27    Using a large syringe or suction gun, suck as much fluid out of the power steering fluid reservoir. Position a drain pan under the power steering pump, then disconnect the hoses from the pump (see illustration). Plug the hoses to prevent excessive fluid loss and the entry of contaminants.

28    Remove the pump mounting bolts. The bolts can be accessed through the holes in the power steering pump pulley.

29    Lift the pump from the engine compartment, being careful not to let any power steering fluid drip on the vehicle's paint.

30    Installation is the reverse of removal. Be sure to tighten all fasteners securely. Fill the power steering reservoir with the recommended fluid (see Chapter 1) and bleed the system following the procedure described in Section 21. Re-check the power steering fluid level.

## 21   Power steering system - bleeding

1    The power steering system must be bled whenever a line is disconnected. Bubbles can be seen in power steering fluid that has air in it and the fluid will often have a milky appearance. Low fluid level can cause air to mix with the fluid, resulting in a noisy pump as well as foaming of the fluid.

2    Open the hood and check the fluid level in the reservoir, adding the specified fluid necessary to bring it up to the proper level (see Chapter 1).

3    Start the engine and slowly turn the steering wheel several times from left-to-right and back again. Do not turn the wheel completely from lock-to-lock. Check the fluid level, topping it up as necessary until it remains steady and no more bubbles are visible.

**20.27 Detach the pressure (A) and return (B) lines from the power steering pump (Hemi model shown)**

## 22   Wheels and tires - general information

1    Most models covered by this manual are equipped with radial tires (see illustration), or inch-pattern light truck tires. Use of other size or type of tires may affect the ride and handling of the vehicle. Don't mix different types of tires, such as radials and bias belted tires, on the same vehicle - handling may be seriously affected. It's recommended that tires be replaced in pairs on the same axle, but if only one tire is being replaced, be sure it's the same size, structure and tread design as the other tire on the same axle.

2    Because tire pressure has a substantial effect on handling and wear, the pressure of all tires should be checked at least once a month or before any extended trips are taken (see Chapter 1).

3    Wheels must be replaced if they are bent, dented, leak air, have elongated bolt holes, are heavily rusted, out of vertical symmetry or if the lug nuts won't stay tight. Wheel repairs that use welding or peening are not recommended.

4    Tire and wheel balance are important to the overall handling, braking and performance of the vehicle. Unbalanced wheels can adversely affect handling and ride characteristics as well as tire life. Whenever a tire is installed on a wheel, the tire and wheel should be balanced by a shop with the proper equipment and expertise.

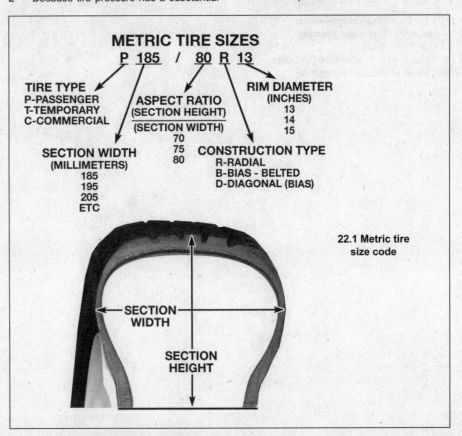

**METRIC TIRE SIZES**

**P 185 / 80 R 13**

TIRE TYPE
P-PASSENGER
T-TEMPORARY
C-COMMERCIAL

ASPECT RATIO
(SECTION HEIGHT)
(SECTION WIDTH)
70
75
80

RIM DIAMETER
(INCHES)
13
14
15

SECTION WIDTH
(MILLIMETERS)
185
195
205
ETC

CONSTRUCTION TYPE
R-RADIAL
B-BIAS - BELTED
D-DIAGONAL (BIAS)

SECTION WIDTH

SECTION HEIGHT

**22.1 Metric tire size code**

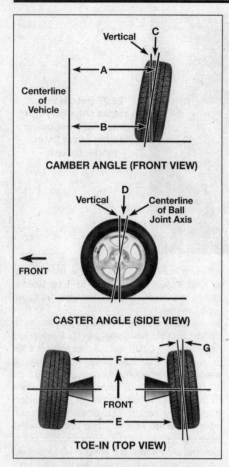

**CAMBER ANGLE (FRONT VIEW)**

**CASTER ANGLE (SIDE VIEW)**

**TOE-IN (TOP VIEW)**

**23.1 Front wheel alignment details**

G = toe-in (expressed in degrees)
A minus B = C (degrees camber)
D = degrees caster
E minus F = toe-in (measured in inches)
G = toe-in (expressed in degrees)

## 23  Wheel alignment - general information

**Note:** *Since wheel alignment requires special equipment and techniques it is beyond the scope of this manual. This section is intended only to familiarize the reader with the basic terms used and procedures followed during a typical wheel alignment.*

1    The three basic checks made when aligning a vehicle's front wheels are camber, caster and toe-in (see illustration).

2    Camber and caster are the angles at which the wheels and suspension are inclined in relation to a vertical centerline. Camber is the angle of the wheel in the lateral, or side-to-side plane, while caster is the tilt between the steering axis and the vertical plane, as viewed from the side. Camber angle affects the amount of tire tread which contacts the road and compensates for changes in suspension geometry as the vehicle travels around curves and over bumps. Caster angle affects the self-centering action of the steering, which governs straight-line stability.

3    Toe-in is the amount the front wheels are angled in relationship to the center line of the vehicle. For example, in a vehicle with zero toe-in, the distance measured between the front edges of the wheels and the distance measured between the rear edges of the wheels are the same. In other words, the wheels are running parallel with the centerline of the vehicle. Toe-in is adjusted by lengthening or shortening the tie-rods. Incorrect toe-in will cause the tires to wear improperly by allowing them to "scrub" against the road surface.

4    Proper wheel alignment is essential for safe steering and even tire wear. Symptoms of alignment problems are pulling of the steering to one side or the other and uneven tire wear. If these symptoms are present, check for the following before having the alignment adjusted:

a) *Loose steering gear mounting bolts*
b) *Damaged or worn steering gear mounts*
c) *Worn or damaged wheel bearings*
d) *Bent tie-rods*
e) *Worn balljoints*
f) *Improper tire pressures*
g) *Mixing tires of different construction*

5    Front wheel alignment should be left to an alignment shop with the proper equipment and experienced personnel.

# Chapter 11
# Body

## Contents

## 1 General Information

**Warning:** *The models covered by this manual are equipped with Supplemental Restraint Systems (SRS), more commonly known as airbags. Always disable the airbag system before working in the vicinity of any airbag system components to avoid the possibility of accidental deployment of the airbags, which could cause personal injury (see Chapter 12).*

1 Certain body components are particularly vulnerable to accident damage and can be unbolted and repaired or replaced. Among these parts are the hood, doors, tailgate, liftgate, bumpers and front fenders.

2 Only general body maintenance practices and body panel repair procedures within the scope of the do-it-yourselfer are included in this Chapter.

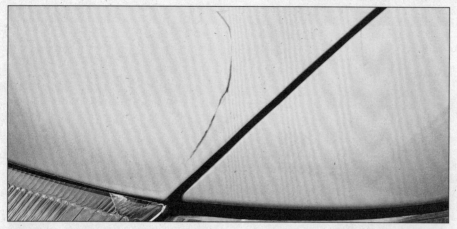

Make sure the damaged area is perfectly clean and rust free. If the touch-up kit has a wire brush, use it to clean the scratch or chip. Or use fine steel wool wrapped around the end of a pencil. Clean the scratched or chipped surface only, not the good paint surrounding it. Rinse the area with water and allow it to dry thoroughly

Thoroughly mix the paint, then apply a small amount with the touch-up kit brush or a very fine artist's brush. Brush in one direction as you fill the scratch area. Do not build up the paint higher than the surrounding paint

## 2    Repairing minor paint scratches

1    No matter how hard you try to keep your vehicle looking like new, it will inevitably be scratched, chipped or dented at some point. If the metal is actually dented, seek the advice of a professional. But you can fix minor scratches and chips yourself. Buy a touch-up paint kit from a dealer service department or an auto parts store. To ensure that you get the right color, you'll need to have the specific make, model and year of your vehicle and, ideally, the paint code, which is located on a special metal plate under the hood or in the door jamb.

## 3    Body repair - minor damage

### *Plastic body panels*

1    The following repair procedures are for minor scratches and gouges. Repair of more serious damage should be left to a dealer service department or qualified auto body shop. Below is a list of the equipment and materials necessary to perform the following repair procedures on plastic body panels.

*Wax, grease and silicone removing solvent*
*Cloth-backed body tape*
*Sanding discs*
*Drill motor with three-inch disc holder*
*Hand sanding block*
*Rubber squeegees*
*Sandpaper*
*Non-porous mixing palette*
*Wood paddle or putty knife*
*Wood paddle or putty knife*
*Curved-tooth body file*
*Flexible parts repair material*

### Flexible panels (bumper trim)

2    Remove the damaged panel, if necessary or desirable. In most cases, repairs can be carried out with the panel installed.
3    Clean the area(s) to be repaired with a

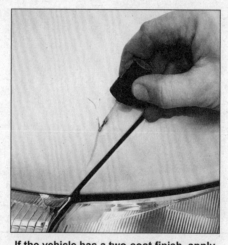

If the vehicle has a two-coat finish, apply the clear coat after the color coat has dried

wax, grease and silicone removing solvent applied with a water-dampened cloth.
4    If the damage is structural, that is, if it extends through the panel, clean the backside of the panel area to be repaired as well. Wipe dry.
5    Sand the rear surface about 1-1/2 inches beyond the break.
6    Cut two pieces of fiberglass cloth large enough to overlap the break by about 1-1/2 inches. Cut only to the required length.
7    Mix the adhesive from the repair kit according to the instructions included with the kit, and apply a layer of the mixture approximately 1/8-inch thick on the backside of the panel. Overlap the break by at least 1-1/2 inches.
8    Apply one piece of fiberglass cloth to the adhesive and cover the cloth with additional adhesive. Apply a second piece of fiberglass cloth to the adhesive and immediately cover the cloth with additional adhesive in sufficient quantity to fill the weave.
9    Allow the repair to cure for 20 to 30 min-

Wait a few days for the paint to dry thoroughly, then rub out the repainted area with a polishing compound to blend the new paint with the surrounding area. When you're happy with your work, wash and polish the area

utes at 60-degrees to 80-degrees F.
10    If necessary, trim the excess repair material at the edge.
11    Remove all of the paint film over and around the area(s) to be repaired. The repair material should not overlap the painted surface.
12    With a drill motor and a sanding disc (or a rotary file), cut a "V" along the break line approximately 1/2-inch wide. Remove all dust and loose particles from the repair area.
13    Mix and apply the repair material. Apply a light coat first over the damaged area; then continue applying material until it reaches a level slightly higher than the surrounding finish.
14    Cure the mixture for 20 to 30 minutes at 60-degrees to 80-degrees F.
15    Roughly establish the contour of the area being repaired with a body file. If low areas or

pits remain, mix and apply additional adhesive.

16    Block sand the damaged area with sandpaper to establish the actual contour of the surrounding surface.

17    If desired, the repaired area can be temporarily protected with several light coats of primer. Because of the special paints and techniques required for flexible body panels, it is recommended that the vehicle be taken to a paint shop for completion of the body repair.

## Steel body panels

### Repairing simple dents

18    When repairing dents, the first job is to pull the dent out until the affected area is as close as possible to its original shape. There is no point in trying to restore the original shape completely as the metal in the damaged area will have stretched on impact and cannot be restored to its original contours. It is better to bring the level of the dent up to a point that is about 1/8-inch below the level of the surrounding metal. In cases where the dent is very shallow, it is not worth trying to pull it out at all.

19    If the backside of the dent is accessible, it can be hammered out gently from behind using a soft-face hammer. While doing this, hold a block of wood firmly against the opposite side of the metal to absorb the hammer blows and prevent the metal from being stretched.

20    If the dent is in a section of the body which has double layers, or some other factor makes it inaccessible from behind, a different technique is required. Drill several small holes through the metal inside the damaged area, particularly in the deeper sections. Screw long, self-tapping screws into the holes just enough for them to get a good grip in the metal. Now pulling on the protruding heads of the screws with locking pliers can pull out the dent.

21    The next stage of repair is the removal of paint from the damaged area and from an inch or so of the surrounding metal. This is easily done with a wire brush or sanding disk in a drill motor, although it can be done just as effectively by hand with sandpaper. To complete the preparation for filling, score the surface of the bare metal with a screwdriver or the tang of a file or drill small holes in the affected area. This will provide a good grip for the filler material. To complete the repair, see the Section on filling and painting.

### Repair of rust holes or gashes

22    Remove all paint from the affected area and from an inch or so of the surrounding metal using a sanding disk or wire brush mounted in a drill motor. If these are not available, a few sheets of sandpaper will do the job just as effectively.

23    With the paint removed, you will be able to determine the severity of the corrosion and decide whether to replace the whole panel, if possible, or repair the affected area. New body panels are not as expensive as most people think and it is often quicker to install a new panel than to repair large areas of rust.

24    Remove all trim pieces from the affected area except those which will act as a guide to the original shape of the damaged body, such as headlight shells, etc. Using metal snips or a hacksaw blade, remove all loose metal and any other metal that is badly affected by rust. Hammer the edges of the hole in to create a slight depression for the filler material.

25    Wire-brush the affected area to remove the powdery rust from the surface of the metal. If the back of the rusted area is accessible, treat it with rust inhibiting paint.

26    Before filling is done, block the hole in some way. This can be done with sheet metal riveted or screwed into place, or by stuffing the hole with wire mesh.

27    Once the hole is blocked off, the affected area can be filled and painted. See the following subsection on filling and painting.

### Filling and painting

28    Many types of body fillers are available, but generally speaking, body repair kits which contain filler paste and a tube of resin hardener are best for this type of repair work. A wide, flexible plastic or nylon applicator will be necessary for imparting a smooth and contoured finish to the surface of the filler material. Mix up a small amount of filler on a clean piece of wood or cardboard (use the hardener sparingly). Follow the manufacturer's instructions on the package, otherwise the filler will set incorrectly.

29    Using the applicator, apply the filler paste to the prepared area. Draw the applicator across the surface of the filler to achieve the desired contour and to level the filler surface. As soon as a contour that approximates the original one is achieved, stop working the paste. If you continue, the paste will begin to stick to the applicator. Continue to add thin layers of paste at 20-minute intervals until the level of the filler is just above the surrounding metal.

30    Once the filler has hardened, the excess can be removed with a body file. From then on, progressively finer grades of sandpaper should be used, starting with a 180-grit paper and finishing with 600-grit wet-or-dry paper. Always wrap the sandpaper around a flat rubber or wooden block, otherwise the surface of the filler will not be completely flat. During the sanding of the filler surface, the wet-or-dry paper should be periodically rinsed in water. This will ensure that a very smooth finish is produced in the final stage.

31    At this point, the repair area should be surrounded by a ring of bare metal, which in turn should be encircled by the finely feathered edge of good paint. Rinse the repair area with clean water until all of the dust produced by the sanding operation is gone.

32    Spray the entire area with a light coat of primer. This will reveal any imperfections in the surface of the filler. Repair the imperfections with fresh filler paste or glaze filler and once more smooth the surface with sandpaper. Repeat this spray-and-repair procedure until you are satisfied that the surface of the filler and the feathered edge of the paint are perfect. Rinse the area with clean water and allow it to dry completely.

33    The repair area is now ready for painting. Spray painting must be carried out in a warm, dry, windless and dust free atmosphere. These conditions can be created if you have access to a large indoor work area, but if you are forced to work in the open, you will have to pick the day very carefully. If you are working indoors, dousing the floor in the work area with water will help settle the dust that would otherwise be in the air. If the repair area is confined to one body panel, mask off the surrounding panels. This will help minimize the effects of a slight mismatch in paint color. Trim pieces such as chrome strips, door handles, etc., will also need to be masked off or removed. Use masking tape and several thickness of newspaper for the masking operations.

34    Before spraying, shake the paint can thoroughly, then spray a test area until the spray painting technique is mastered. Cover the repair area with a thick coat of primer. The thickness should be built up using several thin layers of primer rather than one thick one. Using 600-grit wet-or-dry sandpaper, rub down the surface of the primer until it is very smooth. While doing this, the work area should be thoroughly rinsed with water and the wet-or-dry sandpaper periodically rinsed as well. Allow the primer to dry before spraying additional coats.

35    Spray on the top coat, again building up the thickness by using several thin layers of paint. Begin spraying in the center of the repair area and then, using a circular motion, work out until the whole repair area and about two inches of the surrounding original paint is covered. Remove all masking material 10 to 15 minutes after spraying on the final coat of paint. Allow the new paint at least two weeks to harden, then use a very fine rubbing compound to blend the edges of the new paint into the existing paint. Finally, apply a coat of wax

## 4    Body repair - major damage

1    Major damage must be repaired by an auto body shop specifically equipped to perform body and frame repairs. These shops have the specialized equipment required to do the job properly.

2    If the damage is extensive, the frame must be checked for proper alignment or the vehicle's handling characteristics may be adversely affected and other components may wear at an accelerated rate.

3    Due to the fact that all of the major body components (hood, fenders, etc.) are separate and replaceable units, any seriously damaged components should be replaced rather than repaired. Sometimes the components can be found in a wrecking yard that specializes in used vehicle components, often at considerable savings over the cost of new parts.

These photos illustrate a method of repairing simple dents. They are intended to supplement *Body repair - minor damage* in this Chapter and should not be used as the sole instructions for body repair on these vehicles.

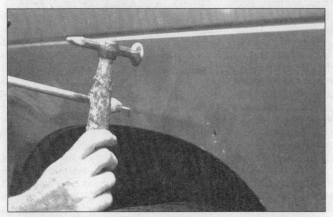

1  If you can't access the backside of the body panel to hammer out the dent, pull it out with a slide-hammer-type dent puller. Tap with a hammer near the edge of the dent to help 'pop' the metal back to its original shape, about 1/8-inch below the surface of the surrounding metal

2  Using coarse-grit sandpaper, remove the paint down to the bare metal. Clean the repair area with wax/silicone remover.

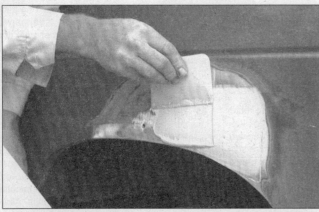

3  Following label instructions, mix up a batch of plastic filler and hardener, then quickly press it into the metal with a plastic applicator. Work the filler until it matches the original contour and is slightly above the surrounding metal

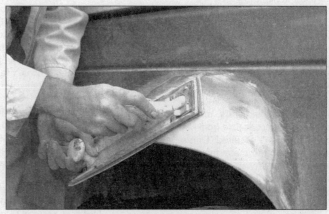

4  Let the filler harden until you can just dent it with your fingernail. File, then sand the filler down until it's smooth and even. Work down to finer grits of sandpaper - always using a board or block - ending up with 360 or 400 grit

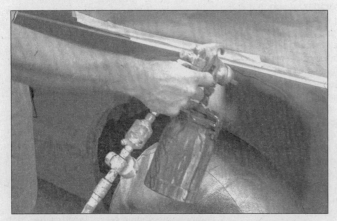

5  When the area is smooth to the touch, clean the area and mask around it. Apply several layers of primer to the area. A professional-type spray gun is being used here, but aerosol spray primer works fine

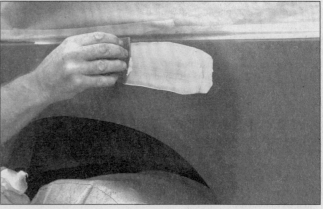

6  Fill imperfections or scratches with glazing compound. Sand with 360 or 400-grit and re-spray. Finish sand the primer with 600 grit, clean thoroughly, then apply the finish coat. Don't attempt to rub out or wax the repair area until the paint has dried completely (at least two weeks)

## 5   Fastener and trim removal

1   There is a variety of plastic fasteners used to hold trim panels, splash shields and other parts in place in addition to typical screws, nuts and bolts. Once you are familiar with them, they can usually be removed without too much difficulty.

2   The proper tools and approach can prevent added time and expense to a project by minimizing the number of broken fasteners and/or parts.

3   The following illustration shows various types of fasteners that are typically used on most vehicles and how to remove and install them (see illustration). Replacement fasteners are commonly found at most auto parts stores, if necessary.

4   Trim panels are typically made of plastic and their flexibility can help during removal. The key to their removal is to use a tool to pry the panel near its retainers to release it without damaging surrounding areas or breaking-off any retainers. The retainers will usually snap out of their designated slot or hole after force is applied to them. Stiff plastic tools designed for prying on trim panels are available at most auto parts stores (see illustration). Tools that are tapered and wrapped in protective tape, such as a screwdriver or small pry tool, are also very effective when used with care.

## 6   Upholstery, carpets and vinyl trim - maintenance

### *Upholstery and carpets*

1   Every three months remove the floormats and clean the interior of the vehicle (more frequently if necessary). Use a stiff whiskbroom to brush the carpeting and loosen dirt and dust, then vacuum the upholstery and carpets thoroughly, especially along seams and crevices.

2   Dirt and stains can be removed from carpeting with basic household or automotive carpet shampoos available in spray cans. Follow the directions and vacuum again, then

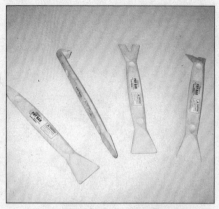

**5.4 These small plastic pry tools are ideal for prying off trim panels**

use a stiff brush to bring back the "nap" of the carpet.

3   Most interiors have cloth or vinyl upholstery, either of which can be cleaned and maintained with a number of material-specific cleaners or shampoos available in

# Fasteners

This tool is designed to remove special fasteners. A small pry tool used for removing nails will also work well in place of this tool

A Phillips head screwdriver can be used to release the center portion, but light pressure must be used because the plastic is easily damaged. Once the center is up, the fastener can easily be pried from its hole

Here is a view with the center portion fully released. Install the fastener as shown, then press the center in to set it

This fastener is used for exterior panels and shields. The center portion must be pried up to release the fastener. Install the fastener with the center up, then press the center in to set it

This type of fastener is used commonly for interior panels. Use a small blunt tool to press the small pin at the center in to release it . . .

. . . the pin will stay with the fastener in the released position

Reset the fastener for installation by moving the pin out. Install the fastener, then press the pin flush with the fastener to set it

This fastener is used for exterior and interior panels. It has no moving parts. Simply pry the fastener from its hole like the claw of a hammer removes a nail. Without a tool that can get under the top of the fastener, it can be very difficult to remove

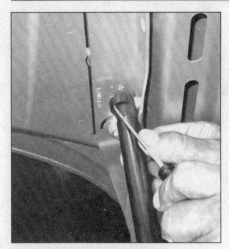

**7.2 Use a small screwdriver to pry the clips out, then detach the ends of the strut from the locating studs**

**8.2 Before removing the hood, draw a mark around the hinge plate**

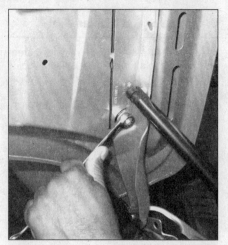

**8.4 Remove the hinge-to-hood retaining nuts and lift off the hood with the help of an assistant**

auto supply stores. Follow the directions on the product for usage, and always spot-test any upholstery cleaner on an inconspicuous area (bottom edge of a backseat cushion) to ensure that it doesn't cause a color shift in the material.

4     After cleaning, vinyl upholstery should be treated with a protectant.

**Note:** *Make sure the protectant container indicates the product can be used on seats - some products may make a seat too slippery.*

**Caution:** *Do not use protectant on vinyl-covered steering wheels.*

5     Leather upholstery requires special care. It should be cleaned regularly with saddle-soap or leather cleaner. Never use alcohol, gasoline, nail polish remover or thinner to clean leather upholstery.

6     After cleaning, regularly treat leather upholstery with a leather conditioner, rubbed in with a soft cotton cloth. Never use car wax on leather upholstery.

**8.10 Make a mark around the latch to use as a reference point. To adjust the hood latch, loosen the retaining bolts, move the latch and retighten bolts, then close the hood to check the fit**

7     In areas where the interior of the vehicle is subject to bright sunlight, cover leather seating areas of the seats with a sheet if the vehicle is to be left out for any length of time.

### Vinyl trim

8     Don't clean vinyl trim with detergents, caustic soap or petroleum-based cleaners. Plain soap and water works just fine, with a soft brush to clean dirt that may be ingrained. Wash the vinyl as frequently as the rest of the vehicle.

9     After cleaning, application of a high-quality rubber and vinyl protectant will help prevent oxidation and cracks. The protectant can also be applied to weather-stripping, vacuum lines and rubber hoses, which often fail as a result of chemical degradation, and to the tires.

---

**7    Hood support struts (2002 and later 1500/2003 and later 2500 and 3500 models) - removal and installation**

---

1     Open the hood and support it securely.

2     Using a small screwdriver, detach the retaining clips at both ends of the support strut. Then pry or pull sharply to detach it from the vehicle (see illustration).

3     Installation is the reverse of removal.

---

**8    Hood - removal, installation and adjustment**

---

**Note:** *The hood is heavy and somewhat awkward to remove and install - at least two people should perform this procedure.*

### Removal and installation

1     Use blankets or pads to cover the cowl area of the body and fenders. This will protect

the body and paint as the hood is lifted off.

2     Make marks or scribe a line around the hood hinge to ensure proper alignment during installation (see illustration).

3     Disconnect any cables or wires that will interfere with removal.

4     Have an assistant support one side of the hood while you support the other. Simultaneously remove the hinge-to-hood nuts (see illustration).

5     Lift off the hood.

6     Installation is the reverse of removal.

### Adjustment

7     Fore-and-aft and side-to-side adjustment of the hood is done by moving the hinge plate slot after loosening the bolts or nuts.

8     Mark around each hinge plate so you can determine the amount of movement (see illustration 8.2).

9     Loosen the bolts or nuts and move the hood into correct alignment. Move it only a little at a time. Tighten the hinge bolts and carefully lower the hood to check the position.

10    If necessary after installation, the hood latch can be adjusted up-and-down as well as from side-to-side on the radiator support so the hood closes securely and flush with the fenders. To make the adjustment, scribe a line or mark around the hood latch mounting bolts to provide a reference point, then loosen them and reposition the latch, as necessary (see illustration). Following adjustment, retighten the mounting bolts.

11    Finally, adjust the hood bumpers on the radiator support so the hood, when closed, is flush with the fenders (see illustration).

**Note:** *On 2001 and earlier 1500/2002 and earlier 2500 and 3500 models, the hood bumpers are adjusted using a Phillips-head screwdriver.*

12    The hood latch assembly, as well as the hinges, should be periodically lubricated with white, lithium-base grease to prevent binding and wear.

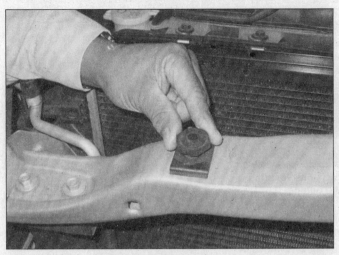

**8.11 Adjust the hood closing height by turning the hood bumpers in or out**

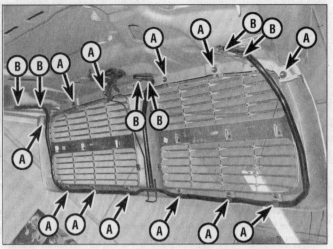

**10.2 Remove the grille mounting fasteners and detach the grille (A), then remove the fasteners attaching the bracket (B) and remove the bracket - 2002 and later 1500/2003 and later 2500 and 3500 models shown, earlier models similar**

## 9  Hood latch and release cable - removal and installation

### *Latch*

1    Scribe a line around the latch to aid alignment when reinstalling the latch assembly.

2    Remove the latch retaining bolts securing the latch to the radiator support (see illustration 8.10) and remove the latch.

3    Disconnect the hood release cable by disengaging the cable from the back of the latch assembly.

4    Installation is the reverse of the removal procedure.

**Note:** *Adjust the latch so the hood engages securely when closed and the hood bumpers are slightly compressed.*

### *Cable*

5    Remove the hood latch as described earlier in this Section, then detach the cable from the latch. On 2002 and later 1500/2003 and later 2500 and 3500 models, remove the battery tray (see Chapter 5).

6    Attach a length of wire to the end of the cable (in the engine compartment). This will be used to pull the new cable back into the engine compartment.

7    Working in the engine compartment, detach the cable from all of its retaining clips. It may be necessary to cut some of the clips to free the cable.

8    Working under the instrument panel, remove the screws and detach the hood release handle. Dislodge the grommet and pull the cable through the firewall and into the cab.

9    Detach the wire from the old cable, then attach it to the end of the new cable.

**Note:** *Make sure the new cable is equipped with a grommet.*

10   Pull the new cable through the firewall and into the engine compartment. Seat the grommet in the firewall.

11   The remainder of installation is the reverse of removal.

## 10  Radiator grille - removal and installation

1    Open the hood.

2    Remove the mounting screws and nuts, then detach the grille assembly from the assembly bracket (see illustration).

3    Remove the screws attaching the support bracket to the hood and detach it from the hood.

4    Installation is the reverse of removal.

## 11  Bumpers - removal and installation

### *Front bumper*

#### **2001 and earlier 1500/2002 and earlier 2500 and 3500 models**

1    Support the bumper with a jack or jackstand.

2    With an assistant supporting the bumper, remove the bolts, nuts and stud plates retaining the bumper to the frame (see illustration).

3    Disconnect any wiring harnesses or any other components that would interfere with bumper removal and detach the bumper.

4    Installation is the reverse of removal. Tighten the retaining bolts/nuts securely.

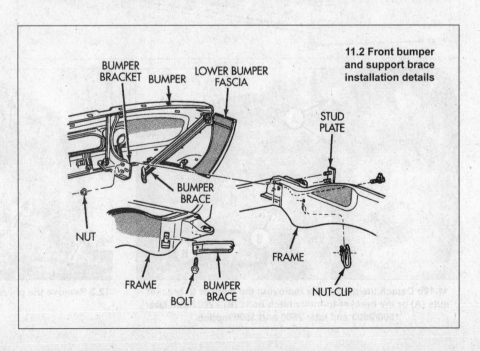

**11.2 Front bumper and support brace installation details**

BUMPER BRACKET   BUMPER   LOWER BUMPER FASCIA

STUD PLATE

BUMPER BRACE

NUT

FRAME

FRAME

BOLT   BUMPER BRACE

NUT-CLIP

**11.7 The bumper can either be detached from the mounting brackets, or the mounting brackets can be removed along with the bumper by detaching the brackets from the frame**

1   *Bumper-to-bracket nuts (fourth nut not visible in this photo)*
2   *Bumper bracket-to-frame nuts/bolts*

**11.11 Remove these two bolts securing the center of the bumper**

### 2002 and later 1500/2003 and later 2500 and 3500 models

5   Front bumpers on all models are composed of a plastic fascia, or exterior skin, and a structural beam.

6   Mark the position of the bumper brackets to the frame rail, or the bumper-to-bracket nuts. Unplug the electrical connectors to the fog lights, if equipped.

7   With an assistant supporting the bumper, remove the nuts/bolts retaining the bumper to the frame rails, or the nuts retaining the bumper to the brackets (see illustration).

8   Detach the bumper from the frame rails or brackets.

9   Installation is the reverse of removal.

### Rear bumper

10   Unplug any electrical connectors which would interfere with bumper removal.

11   On 2002 and later 1500/2003 and later 2500 and 3500 models, remove the bolts retaining the center of the bumper to the trailer hitch or crossmember (see illustration).

12   With an assistant supporting the bumper, remove the bolts retaining the bumper to the trailer hitch or frame rails, or the nuts retaining the bumper to the brackets (see illustrations).

13   Installation is the reverse of removal.

---

## 12   Front fender - removal and installation

1   Raise the vehicle and support it securely on jackstands and remove the front wheel.

2   Remove the fasteners retaining the fender inner splash shield (see illustration).

3   Remove the headlight housing (see Chapter 12).

### 2001 and earlier 1500/2002 and earlier 2500 and 3500 models

4   Remove the front bumper (see Section 11).

5   Disconnect the antenna and all lighting system electrical connectors and other components that would interfere with fender removal (see illustration).

6   Remove the fender mounting bolts (see illustrations).

### 2002 and later 1500/2003 and later 2500 and 3500 models

7   Remove the fender-to-rocker panel bolt

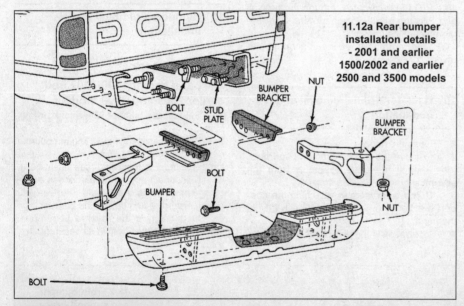

**11.12a Rear bumper installation details - 2001 and earlier 1500/2002 and earlier 2500 and 3500 models**

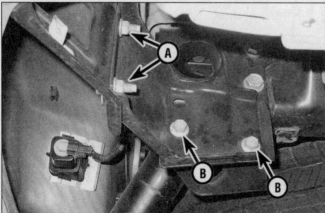

**11.12b Detach the bumper by removing the bumper to bracket nuts (A) or the bracket-to-trailer hitch bolts (B) - 2002 and later 1500/2003 and later 2500 and 3500 models**

**12.2 Remove the pin retainers from the inner fender splash shield**

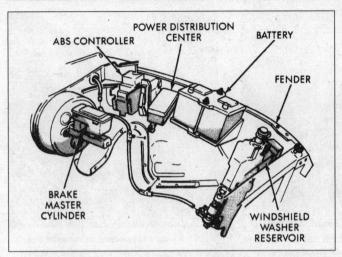

12.5 Remove the bolts and detach components such as the ABS controller, power distribution center and battery from the fender

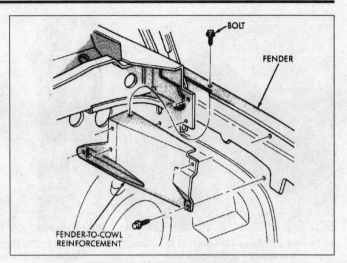

12.6a Cowl reinforcement-to-fender installation details

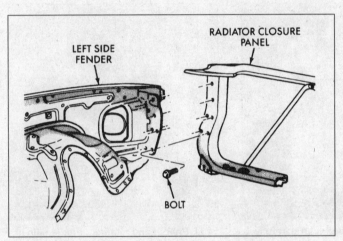

12.6b Fender-to-radiator panel installation details

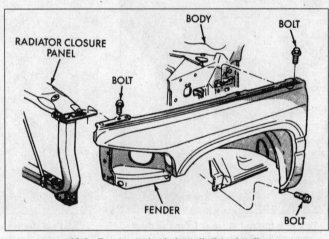

12.6c Fender-to-body installation details

and the fender-to-door pillar bolt (see illustration).
8  Remove the bolts retaining the fender to the headlight housing opening (see illustration).
9  If removing the left fender, or the right fender on a model equipped with a diesel engine, remove the battery and battery tray

(see Chapter 5).
10  Remove the remaining fender mounting bolts (see illustration).

### All models

11  Detach the fender. It's a good idea to have an assistant support the fender while it's

being moved away from the vehicle to prevent damage to the surrounding body panels. If you're removing the right-side fender, disconnect the antenna (see Chapter 12).
12  Installation is the reverse of removal.
13  Tighten all nuts, bolts and screws securely.

12.7 Open the door and remove the fender-to-door pillar and the fender-to-rocker panel bolts

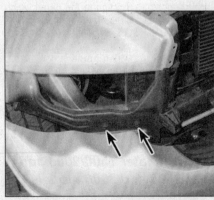

12.8 Remove the fender fasteners in the headlight housing opening

12.10 Fender upper mounting bolts

**13.1a Use a Phillips screwdriver to remove the screws in the door pull**

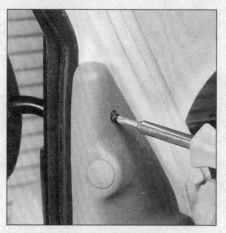

**13.1b One of the door trim panel screws is located at the upper front corner**

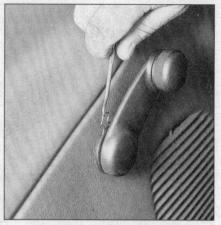

**13.2 Use a hook-tool to remove the retaining clip, then detach the window crank handle**

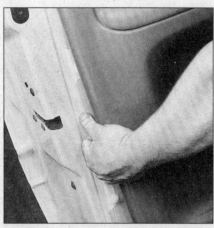

**13.4 Pull the panel away from the door and unplug the electrical connectors**

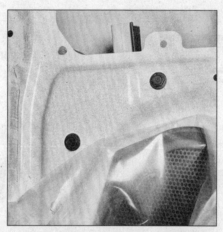

**13.5 Peel the water deflector carefully away from the door, taking care not to tear it**

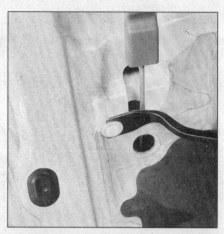

**13.6 Pry out any retainers that remain in the door and install them in the trim panel before installation**

## 13  Door trim panels - removal and installation

### 2001 and earlier 1500/2002 and earlier 2500 and 3500 models

1    Remove all door trim panel retaining screws and door pull/armrest assemblies (see illustrations). If equipped with power mirrors, remove the switch knob by pulling it straight back and remove the switch retaining nut.

2    On manual window models, remove the window crank (see illustration). On power window models, reach through the door pull opening and depress the switch tab and gently pull the rear of the switch up and remove the switch. Disconnect the electrical connectors from the switch.

3    Insert a putty knife between the trim panel and the door and disengage the retaining clips. Work around the outer edge until the panel is free.

4    Once all of the clips are disengaged, detach the trim panel, disconnect any wiring harness connectors and remove the trim panel from the vehicle (see illustration).

5    For access to the inner door, carefully peel back the plastic watershield (see illustration).

6    Prior to installation of the door panel, be sure to reinstall any clips in the panel which may have come out during the removal procedure and remain in the door itself (see illustration).

7    Connect the wiring harness connectors and place the panel in position in the door. Press the trim panel into place until the clips are seated.

8    Install the armrest/door pulls and the window crank. Connect the negative battery cable.

### 2002 and later 1500/2003 and later 2500 and 3500 models

9    On manual window models, remove the window crank (see illustration 13.2).

10   Remove the door handle, then remove all door trim panel retaining screws (see illustration).

11   Pull upward to release the door panel hooks from the door.

12   Once all of the hooks are disengaged, raise the trim panel up and off the door. Disconnect any wiring harness connectors and remove the trim panel from the vehicle.

13   For access to the inner door, carefully peel back the plastic watershield (see illustration).

14   Prior to installation of the door panel, be sure to reinstall any clips in the panel which may have come out during the removal procedure and remain in the door itself.

15   Connect the wiring harness connectors and place the panel in position on the door. Press the trim panel straight against the door until the clips on the trim panel align with all the holes in the door, then push down on the panel until the clips are seated.

16   The remainder of installation is the reverse of removal.

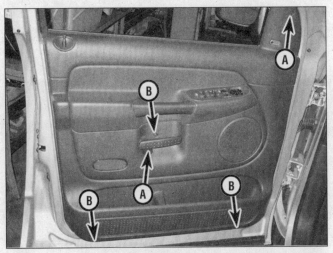

13.10 Lift the handle and remove the handle retaining screw (A),
then remove the handle - remove the remaining fasteners (B)

13.13 Peel the plastic watershield carefully away from the door,
taking care not to tear it

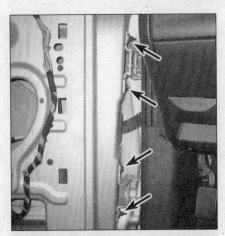

14.3 Mark their locations, then remove the
door retaining bolt and nut at each hinge

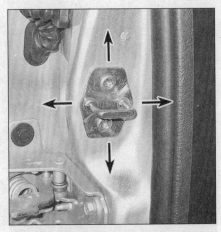

14.5 The latch striker on the door jamb
can be adjusted slightly up/down or in/out

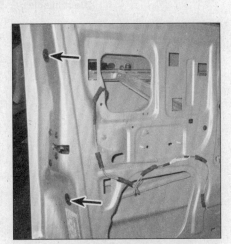

15.2 Remove the rear glass run channel
mounting bolts, then move the channel
for more working room (2002 and later
1500/2003 and later 2500 and
3500 models)

## 14   Door - removal, installation and adjustment

1   Remove the door trim panel (see Section 13). Disconnect any electrical connectors and push them through the door opening so they won't interfere with door removal. Leave the wiring harness boot attached to the body but disconnected from the door.

2   Place a jack under the door or have an assistant on hand to support it when the hinge bolts are removed.

**Note:** *If a jack is used, place a few rags between it and the door to protect the door's painted surfaces.*

3   Scribe around the mounting bolt/nut heads and hinges with a marking pen, remove the fasteners and carefully lift off the door (see illustration).

4   Installation is the reverse of removal, making sure to align the hinge with the marks made during removal before tightening the bolts.

5   Following installation of the door, check the alignment and adjust the hinges, if neces-

sary. Adjust the door lock striker, centering it in the door latch (see illustration).

## 15   Door latch, lock cylinder and handle - removal and installation

### *Latch*

1   Raise the window completely and remove the door trim panel and watershield (see Section 13).

2   On 2002 and later 1500/2003 and later 2500 and 3500 models, remove the bolts at the rear glass run channel and move the channel away from the latch (see illustration). This provides a little extra working room in the latch area inside the door.

3   Rotate the plastic retaining clips off the rods, then detach the latch links. Disconnect the electrical connector.

4   Remove the three mounting screws (it may be necessary to use an impact-type screwdriver to loosen them), then remove the latch from the door (see illustration).

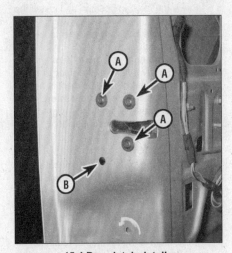

15.4 Door latch details

A   *Mounting screws*
B   *Adjustment screw*

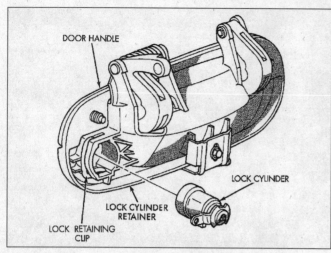

**15.8a On 2001 and earlier model door latches, remove the retaining clip and detach the lock cylinder from the outside door handle**

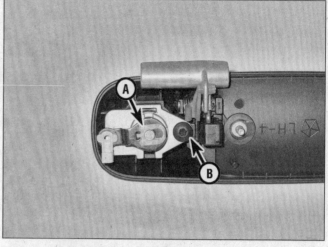

**15.8b 2002 and later door lock cylinder details**

A   *Lock cylinder lever retaining clip*
B   *Lock cylinder mounting screw*

**15.10 Disconnect the link rods, then remove the handle mounting nuts**

**16.3 Pull up on the weather seal and remove it from the door glass opening**

**16.4 On 2002 and later 1500/2003 and later 2500 and 3500 models, remove these bolts and remove the front glass run channel**

5   Place the latch in position and install the screws. Tighten the screws securely.
6   Connect the link rods and electrical connector to the latch.
7   The remainder of installation is the reverse of removal. Check the door to make sure it closes properly. If adjustment is necessary, loosen the latch adjustment screw, operate the handle several times, then tighten the adjustment screw (see illustration 15.4).

### Lock cylinder

8   Remove the outside door handle (see below). Disconnect the link, use a pair of pliers to pull the key lock cylinder clip or lever retainer off, then remove the mounting screw and withdraw the lock cylinder from the door handle (see illustrations).
9   Installation is the reverse of removal.

### Outside handle

10   Remove the door trim panel (see Sec-

tion 13). Disconnect the link rods from the outside handle, remove the mounting nuts and carefully detach the handle from the door (see illustration).
11   Place the handle in position, attach the link and install the nuts. Tighten the nuts securely.

---

## 16   Door window glass - removal and installation

---

### Front

1   Remove the door trim panel and watershield (see Section 13).
2   Lower the window.
3   Pry the inner weather seal out of the door glass opening (see illustration).
4   On 2002 and later 1500/2003 and later 2500 and 3500 models, remove the two bolts securing the front glass run channel (see illustration).

5   Raise the window for access to the glass retaining nuts, then remove the two nuts (see illustration).
6   Remove the window by tilting it forward, then lifting it out of the door.
7   To install, lower the glass into the door, slide it into position and install the nuts.
8   The remainder of installation is the reverse of removal.

### Rear

9   Follow Steps 1 through 3 as above for the front door glass.
10   Remove both the front and rear glass channels.
11   Raise the window for access to the glass retaining nuts, then remove the two nuts.
12   Remove the window.
13   Installation is the reverse of the removal procedure.

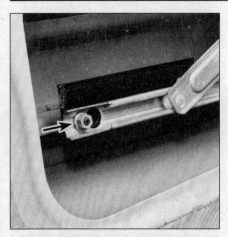

**16.5a On 2001 and earlier 1500/2002 and earlier 2500 and 3500 models, loosen the nut located at each end of the window regulator track (arrow), then slide the glass off the track and lift the glass out of the door**

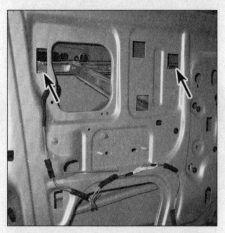

**16.5b On 2002 and later models, align the window so that the nuts can be removed from the glass track**

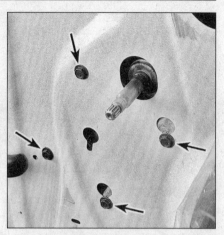

**17.3a Window regulator mounting bolt locations - 2001 and earlier 1500/2002 and earlier 2500 and 3500 models**

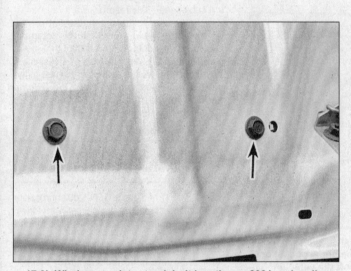

**17.3b Window regulator track bolt locations - 2001 and earlier 1500/2002 and earlier 2500 and 3500 models**

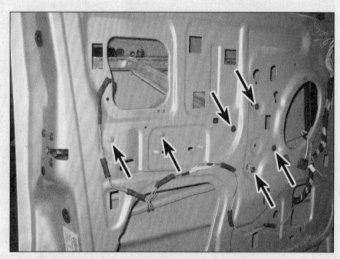

**17.3c Window regulator mounting bolt locations (front door shown, rear door similar) - 2002 and later 1500/2003 and later 2500 and 3500 models**

## 17  Door window glass regulator - removal and installation

1    Remove the door trim panel and water-shield.
2    Unbolt the window glass from the regulator (see Section 16). Push the glass all the way up and tape it to the door frame.
3    Remove the window regulator-to-door and track mounting fasteners (see illustrations).
4    On power window equipped models, unplug the electrical connector.
5    Remove the regulator from the door.
6    Installation is the reverse of removal.

## 18  Mirrors - removal and installation

### *Outside mirrors*

1    Remove the door trim panel (see Section 13).
2    On power mirrors, unplug the electrical connector.
3    Remove the nuts and detach the mirror from the door (see illustration).
4    Installation is the reverse of removal.

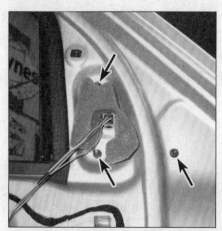

**18.3 Remove the nuts and detach the mirror from the door**

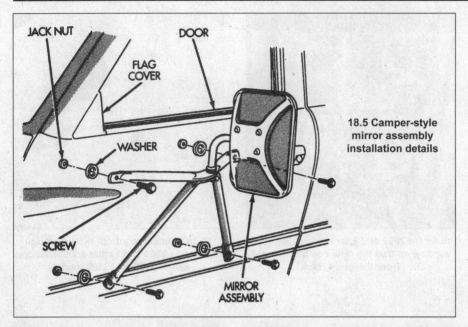

18.5 Camper-style mirror assembly installation details

## Camper-style outside mirror (early models)

5    Remove the bolts and detach the mirror assembly from the door (see illustration).
6    Installation is the reverse of removal.

## Inside mirror

7    Remove the setscrew, then slide the mirror up off the support base on the windshield. On models with optional automatic day/night mirror, disconnect the electrical connector.
8    Installation is the reverse of removal.
9    If the support base for the mirror has come off the windshield, it can be reattached with a special mirror adhesive kit available at auto parts stores. Clean the glass and support base thoroughly and follow the directions on the adhesive package.

## 19  Tailgate - removal and installation

1    Open the tailgate and detach the retaining cables (see illustration).
2    Lower the tailgate until the flat on the right side hinge-pin aligns with the slot in the hinge pocket. Lift the tailgate out of the pocket (see illustration). With the help of an assistant to support the weight, withdraw the left hinge pin from the body and remove the tailgate from the vehicle.
3    Installation is the reverse of removal.

## 20  Tailgate latch and handle - removal and installation

1    On 2001 and earlier 1500/2002 and earlier 2500 and 3500 models, use a small screwdriver to pry off the handle escutcheon (see illustrations). Be very careful not to chip the paint.
2    On 2002 and later 1500/2003 and later 2500 and 3500 models, lower the tailgate and remove the tailgate access cover (see illustration).

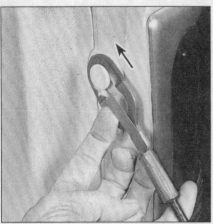

19.1 Lift the spring retainer up and slide the cable end off the pin

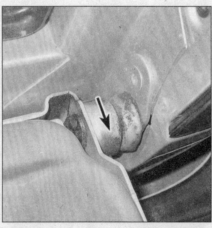

19.2 Align the flat on the right-side hinge pin with the slot in the hinge pocket and lift the tailgate off the vehicle

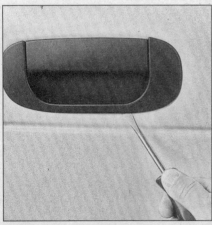

20.1a Use a small screwdriver to detach the escutcheon...

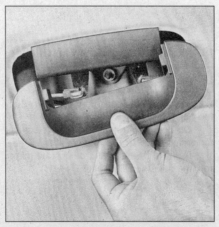

20.1b ... then lift the escutcheon out of the opening - 2001 and earlier 1500/2002 and earlier 2500 and 3500 models

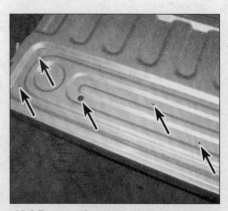

20.2 Remove the cover screws to access the inside of the tailgate (left side shown, right side similar). If the vehicle is equipped with a plastic bedliner, these screws will also secure the plastic panel to the tailgate - 2002 and later 1500/2003 and later 2500 and 3500 models

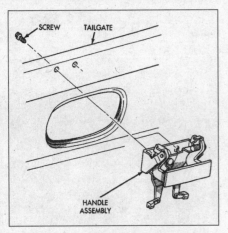

20.3 Remove the screws, pull the latch assembly off the tailgate and detach the control rod

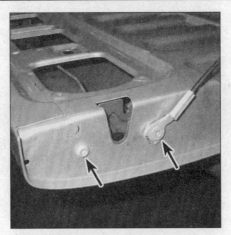

20.4 Remove the tailgate latch retaining screws

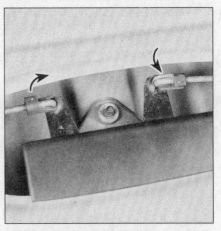

20.7 Rotate the plastic retaining clips off the control rods and detach the rods from the handle - 2001 and earlier 1500/2002 and earlier 2500 and 3500 models

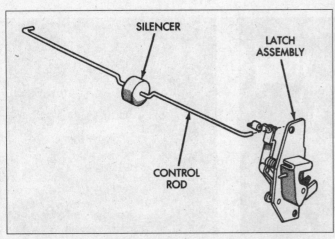

20.8 Remove the screws, pull the latch assembly off the tailgate and detach the control rod - 2001 and earlier 1500/2002 and earlier 2500 and 3500 models

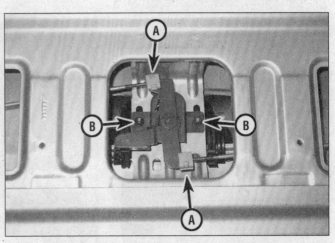

20.9 Disengage the handle-to-latch rods (A) and remove the handle retaining nuts (B) - 2002 and later 1500/2003 and later 2500 and 3500 models

## Latch

3    On 2001 and earlier 1500/2002 and earlier 2500 and 3500 models, remove the screws and withdraw the latch assembly from the end of the tailgate (see illustration).

4    On 2002 and later 1500/2003 and later 2500 and 3500 models, remove the latch mounting fasteners (see illustration). It may be necessary to use an impact-driver to loosen them.

5    Disconnect the control rods from the latch and remove the latch from the door.

6    Installation is the reverse of removal.

## Handle

7    On 2001 and earlier 1500/2002 and earlier 2500 and 3500 models, rotate the plastic retaining clips off the control rods and detach the rods from the handle (see illustration).

**Note:** *On some models it may be necessary to remove the hinge pocket mounting bolts.*

8    Remove the retaining screws and detach the handle from the tailgate (see illustration).

9    On 2002 and later 1500/2003 and later 2500 and 3500 models, disconnect the control rods (see illustration).

10    Detach the retaining nuts and remove the handle assembly from the tailgate.

11    Installation is the reverse of removal.

21.3 Grasp the cluster bezel securely and pull out sharply to detach the clips

## 21    Dashboard trim panels - removal and installation

**Warning:** *The models covered by this manual are equipped with a Supplemental Restraint System (SRS), more commonly known as airbags. Always disable the airbag system before working in the vicinity of any airbag system component to avoid the possibility of accidental deployment of the airbags, which could cause personal injury (see Chapter 12).*

1    Disconnect the cable(s) from the negative battery terminal(s) (see Chapter 5).

### Instrument cluster bezel

**2001 and earlier 1500/2002 and earlier 2500 and 3500 models**

2    Remove the cup holder (see Steps 30 and 31) and ashtray (see Steps 38 and 39).

3    Grasp the bezel securely and pull out sharply to detach the retaining clips from the instrument panel (see illustration).

21.8 Remove the two screws above the instrument cluster

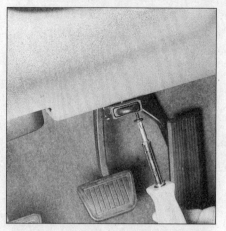

21.11 Remove the two screws and detach the anti-theft plug from the instrument panel

21.12 Remove the knee bolster mounting screws - 2003 model shown, all other models similar

21.15 Carefully release all of the retaining clips

21.18 Use a trim stick to release the retaining clips

21.21 Pull sharply to detach the airbag control module cover retaining clips

4　Disconnect the electrical connector from the cigar lighter and auxiliary power outlet.

5　Installation is the reverse of removal.

### 2002 and later 1500/2003 and later 2500 and 3500 models

6　Remove the headlight switch bezel (see Step 18).

7　Remove the center instrument panel bezel (see Steps 14 through 16).

8　On models with automatic transmission and column shift, apply the parking brake and put the shift lever in the Low position. If equipped with a tilt steering column, lower the column. Remove the screws above the instrument cluster (see illustration).

9　Grasp the bezel securely and pull out sharply to detach the retaining clips from the instrument panel.

10　Installation is the reverse of removal.

## Knee bolster

11　On 2001 and earlier 1500/2002 and earlier 2500 and 3500 models, remove the

screws and detach the anti-theft plug (if equipped) (see illustration).

12　Remove the screws at the bottom of the driver's knee bolster, then use a dull, flat-bladed tool around the top of the panel to release it from the clips at the top (see illustration).

13　Installation is the reverse of removal.

### Center instrument panel bezel - 2002 and later 1500/2003 and later 2500 and 3500 models

14　Pull the ashtray and cup holder out to gain access to the center instrument panel retaining screw.

15　Use a trim stick to carefully pry around the complete edge of the instrument panel bezel and detach it from the instrument panel (see illustration).

16　Pull the panel out far enough to disconnect all electrical connectors.

17　Installation is the reverse of removal.

### Headlight switch bezel - 2002 and later 1500/2003 and later 2500 and 3500 models

18　Use a trim stick to carefully pry around the edge of the headlight switch bezel (see illustration).

19　Pull the panel out far enough to disconnect all electrical connectors.

20　Installation is the reverse of removal.

### Airbag control module cover - 2002 and later 1500/2003 and later 2500 and 3500 models

21　Grasp the cover securely and pull sharply to detach the retaining clips from the instrument panel (see illustration).

22　Installation is the reverse of removal.

### Instrument panel top cover

23　Carefully pry around the complete edge of the top cover to release the clips (see illustration).

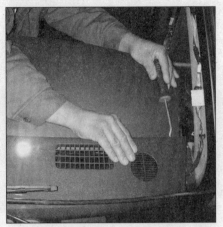

21.23 Remove the top cover using a trim stick or panel removal tool

21.27 Push on the rear of the glove box until the stop clears the instrument panel

21.31 Remove the two cup holder retaining screws

21.34 Fold the inner panel down, then remove the screws

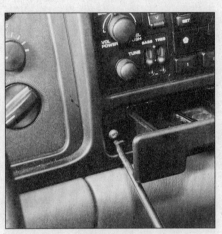

21.39 Remove the two ash tray retaining screws

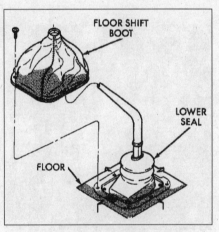

21.43 Floor shift boot installation details

24    Remove the panel.
25    Installation is the reverse of removal.

## Glove box

26    Open the glove box door.
27    Press down the two sides of the glove compartment bin together and pull the door down until the bumpers on the bin have cleared the stops (see illustration).
28    Lower the glove box door all the way down, then lift it away from the instrument panel until the hinge clips on the glove box door clear the pins in the instrument panel.
29    Installation is the reverse of removal.

## Cup holder

### 2001 and earlier 1500/2002 and earlier 2500 and 3500 models

30    Pull the cup holder out for access to the retaining screws.
31    Remove the two screws and detach the cup holder (see illustration).
32    Installation is the reverse of removal.

### 2002 and later 1500/2003 and later 2500 and 3500 models

33    Remove the center instrument panel bezel (see Steps 9 through 11).
34    Pull the cup holder open and fold down the inner panel, then remove the two screws (see illustration).
35    Remove the airbag module cover (see Step 21), then remove the cup holder lower mounting screws.
36    Remove the remaining screws from the cup holder. Remove the cup holder.
37    Installation is the reverse of removal.

### Ashtray - 2001 and earlier 1500/2002 and earlier 2500 and 3500 models

38    Pull the ashtray out for access to the retaining screws.
39    Remove the two screws and detach the ashtray (see illustration).
40    Installation is the reverse of removal.

## Floor shift lever boot

41    Unscrew the shift knob from the lever.
42    Pull up the edge of the carpeting for access to the boot retaining screws.
43    Remove the screws, detach the boot and lift it up over the shift lever (see illustration).
44    Installation is the reverse of removal.

### 22    Instrument panel - removal and installation

**Warning:** *The models covered by this manual are equipped with a Supplemental Restraint System (SRS), more commonly known as airbags. Always disable the airbag system before working in the vicinity of any airbag system component to avoid the possibility of accidental deployment of the airbags, which could cause personal injury (see Chapter 12).*

1    Disconnect the cable(s) from the negative battery terminal(s) (see Chapter 5). Turn the front wheels to the straight-ahead position

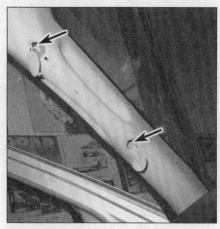

**22.2 The A-pillar trim is secured by two screws (left side shown, right side similar)**

**22.5 Disconnect the airbag control module electrical connector - later models shown, earlier models similar**

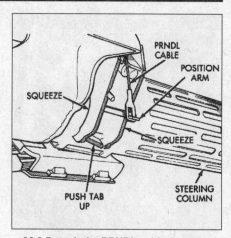

**22.8 Detach the PRNDL cable from the position arm, push the cable retainer tab up, squeeze the sides together and remove the retainer - 2001 and earlier models**

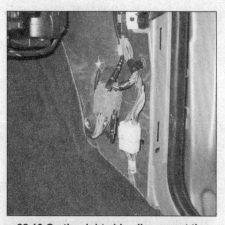

**22.10 On the right side, disconnect the antenna and harness connectors**

**22.12 Use a trim panel tool to remove the instrument panel end caps**

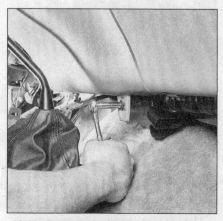

**22.16a Remove the bolts along the lower edge of the instrument panel**

and lock the steering column.

2     Remove the trim from the A-pillars (see illustration). Disconnect the headliner wiring harness at the A-pillar.

**22.16b Use a socket and extension to reach the bolts along the top edge of the instrument panel**

3     Remove instrument cluster bezel (see Section 21). Remove the instrument cluster (see Chapter 12).

4     Remove the knee bolster, cup holder, glove box, ashtray and airbag control module cover, if equipped (see Section 21).

5     Disconnect the electrical connector from the airbag control module (see illustration).

6     On 2001 and earlier models, remove air bag control module mounting screws, then remove the module from the vehicle and store it in a safe place.

7     Remove steering column covers (see Section 24).

8     On column shift models, pull the shift selector indicator (PRNDL) cable down and detach it from the position arm (see illustration). Remove the cable retainer.

9     Refer to Chapter 10 and lower the steering column. Lower the column and allow it to rest on the floor.

10     Remove the right and left side kick panels. Disconnect the antenna and electrical connectors (see illustration).

11     Remove the screws and detach hood

release and parking brake handles from the instrument panel.

12     On 2012 and later models, remove the instrument panel end caps (see illustration).

13     Under the driver's side of the instrument panel, disconnect the large electrical bulkhead connector (by removing the screw in the center).

14     While working under that side of the instrument panel, tag and disconnect all other electrical connectors connected to the instrument panel.

**Note:** *Watch for ground straps bolted to the cowl or the area behind the kick panels.*

15     Remove the instrument panel top cover (see Section 21).

### 2001 and earlier 1500/2002 and earlier 2500 and 3500 models

16     Remove the bolts along the bottom and top edges of the instrument panel (see illustrations).

17     Loosen the pivot bolts at each end, then rotate the instrument panel back and lift it off

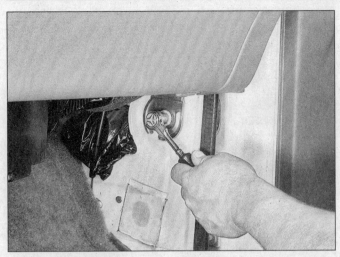

**22.17a Loosen the hinge bolts at each end of the instrument panel**

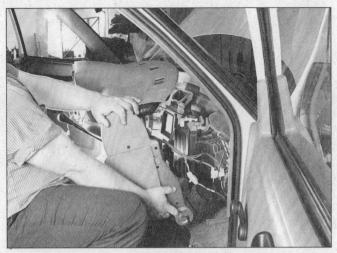

**22.17b Rotate the instrument panel back and lift it off the hinge bolts**

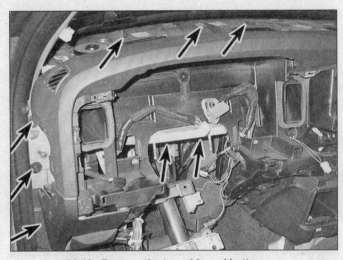

**22.19a Remove the top, side and bottom . . .**

**22.19b . . . fasteners securing the instrument panel**

the pivot bolts (see illustrations).

18    Disconnect any remaining electrical connectors. Disconnect the heater/air conditioning vacuum harness from the control panel and disconnect the temperature control cable from the heater core housing.

### *2002 and later 1500/2003 and later 2500 and 3500 models*

19    Disconnect any remaining electrical connectors, then remove the instrument panel retaining fasteners (see illustrations).

### *All models*

20    Remove the instrument panel from the vehicle.

21    Installation is the reverse of removal.

**23    Center console (2001 and earlier 1500/2002 and earlier 2500 and 3500 models) - removal and installation**

**Warning:** *If vehicle is equipped with airbags, refer to Chapter 12 to disarm the airbag system prior to performing any work described below.*

### *Center console and seat cushion*

1    Working under the seat cushion, remove the mounting bolts from the seat brackets (see illustration).

2    Detach the console and lift it up.

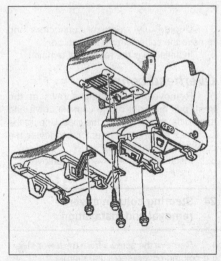

**23.1 Center console installation details**

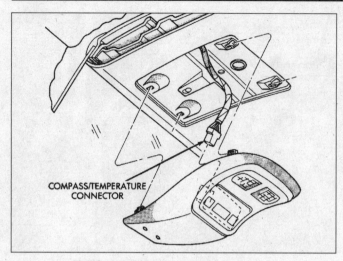

23.5 Overhead console installation details

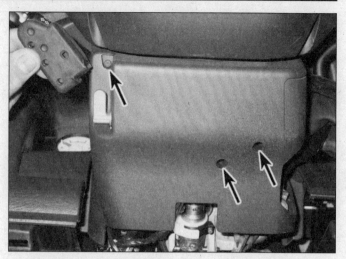

24.1 Detach the tilt lever handle, then remove the column cover fasteners

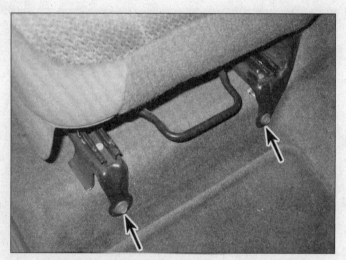

25.3a Remove the front bolts from the front seat . . .

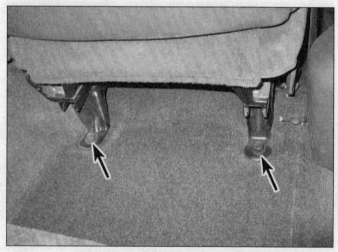

25.3b . . . then remove the rear bolts

3    Unplug any electrical connectors and remove the console from the vehicle.
4    Installation is the reverse of removal.

## Overhead console

5    Remove the retaining screws at the front, pull the front of the console down and toward the rear to detach the clips. Unplug the compass electrical connector and lower the console (see illustration).
6    Installation is the reverse of removal.

## 24   Steering column covers - removal and installation

1    Remove the screws from the lower steering column cover (see illustration).
**Note:** *Early models use a Torx head screw to*

secure he lower cover.
2    Separate the cover halves and detach them from the steering column.
3    Installation is the reverse of removal.

## 25   Seats - removal and installation

**Warning:** *The manufacturer states that whenever the seat fasteners are removed, they must be replaced with new ones of the same part number.*

## Front seat

1    On 2001 and earlier 1500/2002 and earlier 2500 and 3500 models, remove the center console and seat cushion (see Section 23), if equipped.
2    Position the seat all the way forward and all the way to the rear to access the front seat

retaining bolts.
3    Detach any bolt trim covers and remove the retaining bolts (see illustrations).
4    Tilt the seats upward to access the underneath, then disconnect any electrical connectors.
5    Remove the fasteners securing the center seat to the passenger's and driver's seats (see illustrations).
6    Separate the seats and remove them from the vehicle.
7    Installation is the reverse of removal.

## Rear seat

8    Remove the seat-to-floor mounting bolts, then lift the seat to disengage the seat back from the hooks on the back of the cab and lift it out of the vehicle (see illustration).
9    Installation is the reverse of removal.

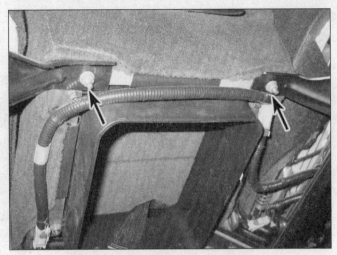

25.5a Remove the fasteners at the front . . .

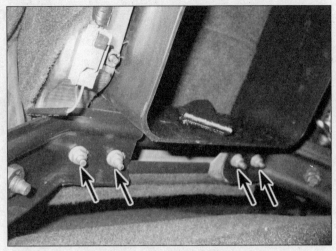

25.5b . . . and at the rear of the center seat

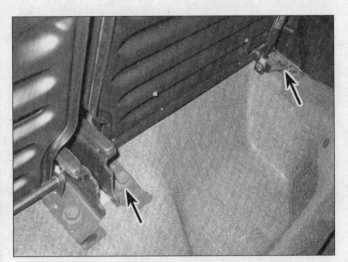

25.8 Remove the rear seat retaining bolts - left side shown, right side similar (two rear bolts not visible in picture)

26.3a Using a trim panel clip removal tool, pry off the plastic cowl grille fasteners

## 26   Cowl cover - removal and installation

1    Mark the position of the windshield wiper blades on the windshield with a wax marking pencil.

2    Remove the wiper arms (see Chapter 1).

3    Remove the screws and pushpins securing the left and right side cowl covers, then disconnect the windshield washer hoses and detach the cowl grille from the vehicle (see illustrations).

4    Installation is the reverse of removal. Make sure to align the wiper blades with the marks made during removal.

26.3b Detach the washer hose from the cowl grille

# Notes

# Chapter 12
# Chassis electrical system

## Contents

## 1   General Information

1   The electrical system is a 12-volt, negative ground type. Power for the lights and all electrical accessories is supplied by a lead/acid battery, which is charged by the alternator.

2   This Chapter covers repair and service procedures for the various electrical components not associated with the engine. Information on the battery, alternator and starter motor can be found in Chapter 5.

3   It should be noted that when portions of the electrical system are serviced, the negative battery cable should be disconnected from the battery to prevent electrical shorts and/or fires.

## 2   Electrical troubleshooting - general information

1   A typical electrical circuit consists of an electrical component, any switches, relays, motors, fuses, fusible links or circuit breakers related to that component and the wiring and connectors that link the component to both the battery and the chassis. To help you pinpoint an electrical circuit problem, wiring diagrams are included at the end of this Chapter.

2   Before tackling any troublesome electrical circuit, first study the appropriate wiring diagrams to get a complete understanding of what makes up that individual circuit. Trouble spots, for instance, can often be narrowed down by noting if other components related to the circuit are operating properly. If several components or circuits fail at one time, chances are the problem is in a fuse or ground connection, because several circuits are often routed through the same fuse and ground connections.

3   Electrical problems usually stem from simple causes, such as loose or corroded connections, a blown fuse, a melted fusible link or a failed relay. Visually inspect the condition of all fuses, wires and connections in a problem circuit before troubleshooting the circuit.

4   If test equipment and instruments are going to be utilized, use the diagrams to plan ahead of time where you will make the necessary connections in order to accurately pinpoint the trouble spot.

5    The basic tools needed for electrical troubleshooting include a circuit tester or voltmeter (a 12-volt bulb with a set of test leads can also be used), a continuity tester, which includes a bulb, battery and set of test leads, and a jumper wire, preferably with a circuit breaker incorporated, which can be used to bypass electrical components (see illustrations). Before attempting to locate a problem with test instruments, use the wiring diagram(s) to decide where to make the connections.

## Voltage checks

6    Voltage checks should be performed if a circuit is not functioning properly. Connect one lead of a circuit tester to either the negative battery terminal or a known good ground. Connect the other lead to a connector in the circuit being tested, preferably nearest to the battery or fuse (see illustration). If the bulb of the tester lights, voltage is present, which means that the part of the circuit between the connector and the battery is problem free. Continue checking the rest of the circuit in the same fashion. When you reach a point at which no voltage is present, the problem lies between that point and the last test point with voltage. Most of the time the problem can be traced to a loose connection. Note: Keep in mind that some circuits receive voltage only when the ignition key is in the Accessory or Run position.

## Finding a short

7    One method of finding shorts in a circuit is to remove the fuse and connect a test light or voltmeter in place of the fuse terminals. There should be no voltage present in the circuit. Move the wiring harness from side-to-side while watching the test light. If the bulb goes on, there is a short to ground somewhere in that area, probably where the insulation has rubbed through. The same test can be performed on each component in the circuit, even a switch.

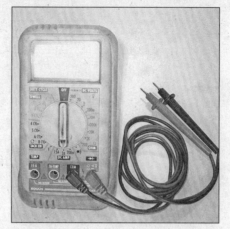

**2.5a The most useful tool for electrical troubleshooting is a digital multimeter that can check volts, amps, and test continuity**

## Ground check

8    Perform a ground test to check whether a component is properly grounded. Disconnect the battery and connect one lead of a continuity tester or multimeter (set to the ohms scale), to a known good ground. Connect the other lead to the wire or ground connection being tested. If the resistance is low (less than 5 ohms), the ground is good. If the bulb on a self-powered test light does not go on, the ground is not good.

## Continuity check

9    A continuity check is done to determine if there are any breaks in a circuit - if it is passing electricity properly. With the circuit off (no power in the circuit), a self-powered continuity tester or multimeter can be used to check the circuit. Connect the test leads to both ends of the circuit (or to the power end and a good ground), and if the test light comes on the circuit is passing current properly (see illustration). If the resistance is low

**2.5b A simple test light is a very handy tool for testing voltage**

(less than 5 ohms), there is continuity; if the reading is 10,000 ohms or higher, there is a break somewhere in the circuit. The same procedure can be used to test a switch, by connecting the continuity tester to the switch terminals. With the switch turned On, the test light should come on (or low resistance should be indicated on a meter).

## Finding an open circuit

10    When diagnosing for possible open circuits, it is often difficult to locate them by sight because the connectors hide oxidation or terminal misalignment. Merely wiggling a connector on a sensor or in the wiring harness may correct the open circuit condition. Remember this when an open circuit is indicated when troubleshooting a circuit. Intermittent problems may also be caused by oxidized or loose connections.

11    Electrical troubleshooting is simple if you keep in mind that all electrical circuits are basically electricity running from the battery, through the wires, switches, relays, fuses

**2.6 In use, a basic test light's lead is clipped to a known good ground, then the pointed probe can test connectors, wires or electrical sockets - if the bulb lights, the circuit being tested has battery voltage**

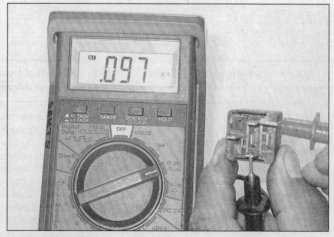

**2.9 With a multimeter set to the ohm scale, resistance can be checked across two terminals - when checking for continuity, a low reading indicates continuity, a high reading or infinity indicates high resistance or lack of continuity**

**2.15 To backprobe a connector, insert a small, sharp probe (such as a straight-pin) into the back of the connector alongside the desired wire until it contacts the metal terminal inside; connect your meter leads to the probes - this allows you to test a functioning circuit**

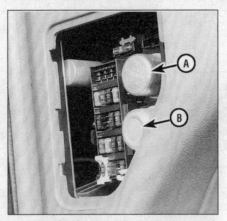

**3.1a On 2001 and earlier 1500/2002 and earlier 2500 and 3500 models models, the fuse block is located in the left end of the instrument panel under a cover - it also contains the hazard (A) and turn signal (B) flasher units (early models may also have an engine compartment-mounted fuse/relay box [see illustration 3.1b])**

**3.1b On 2002 and later 1500/2003 and later 2500 and 3500 models, the fuse and relay box is located at the left-front corner of the engine compartment. To locate a fuse or relay, refer to the fuse and relay guide imprinted on the underside of the lid**

and fusible links to each electrical component (light bulb, motor, etc.) and to ground, from which it is passed back to the battery. Any electrical problem is an interruption in the flow of electricity to and from the battery.

### Connectors

12   Most electrical connections on these vehicles are made with multi-wire plastic connectors. The mating halves of many connectors are secured with locking clips molded into the plastic connector shells. The mating halves of large connectors, such as some of those under the instrument panel, are held together by a bolt through the center of the connector.

13   To separate a connector with locking clips, use a small screwdriver to pry the clips apart carefully, then separate the connector halves. Pull only on the shell, never pull on the wiring harness as you may damage the individual wires and terminals inside the connectors. Look at the connector closely before trying to separate the halves. Often the locking clips are engaged in a way that is not immediately clear. Additionally, many connectors have more than one set of clips.

14   Each pair of connector terminals has a male half and a female half. When you look at the end view of a connector in a diagram, be sure to understand whether the view shows the harness side or the component side of the connector. Connector halves are mirror images of each other, and a terminal shown on the right side end-view of one half will be on the left side end view of the other half.

15   It is often necessary to take circuit voltage measurements with a connector connected. Whenever possible, carefully insert a small straight pin (not your meter probe) into the rear of the connector shell to contact the terminal inside, then clip your meter lead to the pin. This kind of connection is called

"backprobing" (see illustration). When inserting a test probe into a male terminal, be careful not to distort the terminal opening. Doing so can lead to a poor connection and corrosion at that terminal later. Using the small straight pin instead of a meter probe results in less chance of deforming the terminal connector.

---

### 3   Fuses - general information

### Fuses

1   The electrical circuits of the vehicle are protected by a combination of fuses and circuit breakers. The fuse and relay box is located on the left side of the engine compartment on all models (see illustrations) as well as under the instrument panel on 2001 and earlier 1500/2002 and earlier 2500 and 3500 models. Some later models may also have auxiliary fuse and relay box located near the main engine compartment box. (At a dealer parts department you might hear the phrase "Power Distribution Center" or "Integrated Power Module." These are just fancy Dodge terms for the fuse and relay box. In this manual, we simply use the term "fuse and relay box.")

2   Each of the fuses is designed to protect a specific circuit, and the various circuits are identified on the fuse panel itself.

3   Different sizes of fuses are employed in the fuse blocks. There are "mini" and "maxi" sizes, with the larger located in the fuse and relay box. The maxi fuses can be removed with your fingers (most of the time), but the mini fuses require the use of pliers or the small plastic fuse-puller tool found in most fuse boxes. If an electrical component fails, always check the fuse first. The best way to check the fuses is with a test light. Check for

power at the exposed terminal tips of each fuse. If power is present at one side of the fuse but not the other, the fuse is blown. A blown fuse can also be identified by visually inspecting it (see illustration).

4   Be sure to replace blown fuses with the correct type. Fuses of different ratings are physically interchangeable, but only fuses of the proper rating should be used. Replacing a fuse with one of a higher or lower value than specified is not recommended. Each electrical circuit needs a specific amount of protection. The amperage rating of each fuse is molded into the fuse body.

5   If the replacement fuse immediately fails, don't replace it again until the cause of the problem is isolated and corrected. In most cases, the cause will be a short circuit in the wiring caused by a broken or deteriorated wire or a failed component.

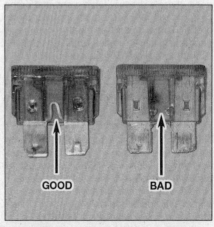

**3.3 When a fuse blows, the element between the terminals melts - the fuse on the right is blown, the one on the left is good**

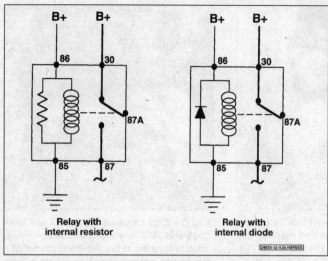

**5.5a Typical ISO relay designs, terminal numbering and circuit connections**

**5.5b Most relays are marked on the outside to easily identify the control circuit and power circuits - this one is of the four-terminal type**

## 4  Circuit breakers - general information

1  Circuit breakers protect certain heavy-load circuits (such as the power seat system, if equipped). Depending on the vehicle's accessories, there may be one to three circuit breakers located in the main fuse panel and also in the fuse and relay box.

2  Because the circuit breakers reset automatically, an electrical overload in a circuit-breaker-protected system will cause the circuit to fail momentarily, then come back on. If the circuit does not come back on, check it immediately.

3  For a basic check, pull the circuit breaker up out of its socket on the fuse panel, but just far enough to probe with a voltmeter. The breaker should still contact the sockets.

4  With the voltmeter negative lead on a good chassis ground, touch each end prong of the circuit breaker with the positive meter probe. There should be battery voltage at each end. If there is battery voltage only at one end, the circuit breaker must be replaced.

## 5  Relays - general information and testing

**Note:** *On 2006 and later models, there are many relays that are not replaceable except for the intake air heater relays (diesel engines), and the starter relay, to name a couple. The remaining relays are an integral part of the underhood fuse/relay box (Totally Integrated Power Module, or TIPM). Have the malfunctioning TIPM relay circuit diagnosed using a scan tool at a dealer service department or other qualified repair shop.*

1  Many electrical accessories in the vehicle utilize relays to transmit current to the compo-

nent. If the relay is defective, the component won't operate properly.

2  Most relays are located in the engine compartment fuse and relay box (see illustration 3.1b).

3  Some relays are located in other parts of the vehicle, primarily in various wiring harnesses underneath the instrument panel.

4  If a faulty relay is suspected, it can be removed and tested using the procedure below or by a dealer service department or a repair shop. Defective relays must be replaced as a unit.

### Testing

5  Most of the relays used in these vehicles are of a type often called "ISO" relays, which refers to the International Standards Organization. The terminals of ISO relays are numbered to indicate their usual circuit connections and functions. There are two basic layouts of terminals on the relays used in the vehicles covered by this manual (see illustrations).

6  Refer to the wiring diagram for the circuit to determine the proper connections for the relay you're testing. If you can't determine the correct connection from the wiring diagrams, however, you may be able to determine the test connections from the information that follows.

7  Two of the terminals are the relay control circuit and connect to the relay coil. The other relay terminals are the power circuit. When the relay is energized, the coil creates a magnetic field that closes the larger contacts of the power circuit to provide power to the circuit loads.

8  Terminals 85 and 86 are normally the control circuit. If the relay contains a diode, terminal 86 must be connected to battery positive (B+) voltage and terminal 85 to ground. If the relay contains a resistor, terminals 85 and

86 can be connected in either direction with respect to B+ and ground.

9  Terminal 30 is normally connected to the battery voltage (B+) source for the circuit loads. Terminal 87 is connected to the ground side of the circuit, either directly or through a load. If the relay has several alternate terminals for load or ground connections, they usually are numbered 87A, 87B, 87C, and so on.

10  Use an ohmmeter to check continuity through the relay control coil.

a) *Connect the meter according to the polarity shown in the illustration for one check; then reverse the ohmmeter leads and check continuity in the other direction.*

b) *If the relay contains a resistor, resistance will be indicated on the meter, and should be the same value with the ohmmeter in either direction.*

c) *If the relay contains a diode, resistance should be higher with the ohmmeter in the forward polarity direction than with the meter leads reversed.*

d) *If the ohmmeter shows infinite resistance in both directions, replace the relay.*

11  Remove the relay from the vehicle and use the ohmmeter to check for continuity between the relay power circuit terminals. There should be no continuity between terminal 30 and 87 with the relay de-energized.

12  Connect a fused jumper wire to terminal 86 and the positive battery terminal. Connect another jumper wire between terminal 85 and ground. When the connections are made, the relay should click.

13  With the jumper wires connected, check for continuity between the power circuit terminals. Now there should be continuity between terminals 30 and 87.

14  If the relay fails any of the above tests, replace it.

## 6 Electrical connectors - general information

1 Most electrical connections on these vehicles are made with multiwire plastic connectors. The mating halves of many connectors are secured with locking clips molded into the plastic connector shells. The mating halves of some large connectors, such as some of those under the instrument panel, are held together by a bolt through the center of the connector.

2 To separate a connector with locking clips, use a small screwdriver to pry the clips apart carefully, then separate the connector halves. Pull only on the shell, never pull on the wiring harness, as you may damage the individual wires and terminals inside the connectors. Look at the connector closely before trying to separate the halves. Often the locking clips are engaged in a way that is not immediately clear. Additionally, many connectors have more than one set of clips.

3 Each pair of connector terminals has a male half and a female half. When you look at the end view of a connector in a diagram, be sure to understand whether the view shows the harness side or the component side of the connector. Connector halves are mirror images of each other, and a terminal shown on the right side end-view of one half will be on the left side end-view of the other half.

4 It is often necessary to take circuit voltage measurements with a connector connected. Whenever possible, carefully insert a small straight pin (not your meter probe) into the rear of the connector shell to contact the terminal inside, then clip your meter lead to the pin. This kind of connection is called "backprobing." When inserting a test probe into a terminal, be careful not to distort the terminal opening. Doing so can lead to a poor connection and corrosion at that terminal later. Using the small straight pin instead of a meter probe results in less chance of deforming the terminal connector.

# Electrical connectors

Most electrical connectors have a single release tab that you depress to release the connector

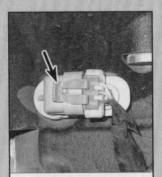

Some electrical connectors have a retaining tab which must be pried up to free the connector

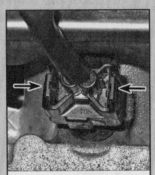

Some connectors have two release tabs that you must squeeze to release the connector

Some connectors use wire retainers that you squeeze to release the connector

Critical connectors often employ a sliding lock (1) that you must pull out before you can depress the release tab (2)

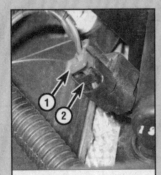

Here's another sliding-lock style connector, with the lock (1) and the release tab (2) on the side of the connector

On some connectors the lock (1) must be pulled out to the side and removed before you can lift the release tab (2)

Some critical connectors, like the multi-pin connectors at the Powertrain Control Module employ pivoting locks that must be flipped open

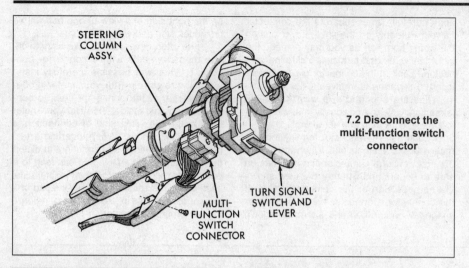

**7.2 Disconnect the multi-function switch connector**

## 7   Multi-function switch

**Warning:** *The models covered by this manual are equipped with a Supplemental Restraint System (SRS), more commonly known as airbags. Always disarm the airbag system before working in the vicinity of any airbag system component to avoid the possibility of accidental deployment of the airbag, which could cause personal injury (see Section 27). Do not use a memory-saving device to preserve the PCM's memory when working on or near airbag system components. After the battery is disconnected, wait at least 2 minutes before beginning work (the system has a back-up ca-*pacitor that must fully discharge).

### *2001 and earlier 1500 models, 2002 and earlier 2500/3500 models - check and replacement*

1   The multi-function switch is located on the left side of the steering column. It incorporates the turn signal, headlight dimmer and windshield wiper/washer functions into one switch.

#### Check

2   Remove the steering column covers and the knee blocker for access (see Chapter 11).

Disconnect the multi-function switch connector (see illustration).

3   Use an ohmmeter or self-powered test light and the accompanying diagrams (see illustrations) to check for continuity between the switch terminals with the switch in each position.

#### Replacement

4   Remove the multi-function switch bolts (this will require a special anti-theft Torx head tool), then detach the switch from the steering column (see illustration).

5   Installation is the reverse of removal.

### *2002 and later 1500 models, 2003 and later 2500/3500 models - replacement*

6   The multi-function switch is located on the steering column. One stalk is on the left of the column and controls the lighting functions such as the headlights and the turn signal lights. The other stalk, on the right of the column, controls the windshield wiper and washer systems. A button on top of the multi-function switch activates the hazard flasher system.

7   Disconnect the cable(s) from the negative battery terminal(s) (see Chapter 5, Section 1).

8   Remove the steering wheel (see Chapter 10).

9   Remove the steering column covers (see Chapter 11).

10   Disconnect the electrical connector from

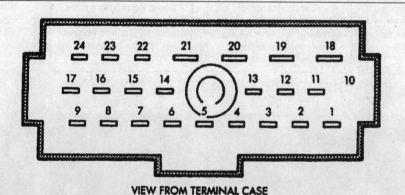

**VIEW FROM TERMINAL CASE**

| SWITCH POSITIONS | | |
|---|---|---|
| **TURN SIGNAL** | **HAZARD WARNING** | **CONTINUITY BETWEEN** |
| NEUTRAL | OFF | 12 AND 14 AND 15 |
| LEFT | OFF | 15 AND 16 AND 17 |
| LEFT | OFF | 12 AND 14 |
| LEFT | OFF | 22 AND 23 WITH OPTIONAL CORNER LAMPS |
| RIGHT | OFF | 11 AND 12 AND 17 |
| RIGHT | OFF | 14 AND 15 |
| RIGHT | OFF | 23 AND 24 WITH OPTIONAL CORNER LAMPS |
| NEUTRAL | ON | 11 AND 12 AND 13 AND 15 AND 16 |

**7.3a Turn signal and hazard flasher terminal guide and continuity chart**

the multi-function switch and remove the upper switch mounting screw (see illustration).

11  Disconnect the electrical connectors from the clockspring and remove the lower multi-function switch mounting screw (see illustration).

12  If you're going to replace the multi-function switch or the clockspring assembly, you'll need to separate the clockspring from the multi-function switch. Remove the screws that attach the clockspring to the multi-function switch (see illustration 6.5), remove the clockspring and install it on the new multi-function switch (or install the new clockspring on the old multi-function switch). (See Chapter 10, Section 15 for the clockspring installation procedure.)

13  Installation is the reverse of the removal procedure.

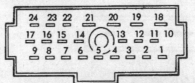

MULTIFUNCTION SWITCH PINS

| SWITCH POSITION | CONTINUITY BETWEEN |
|---|---|
| OFF | PIN 6 AND PIN 7 |
| DELAY | PIN 8 AND PIN 9<br>PIN 2 AND PIN 4<br>PIN 1 AND PIN 2<br>PIN 1 AND PIN 4 |
| LOW | PIN 4 AND PIN 6 |
| HIGH | PIN 4 AND PIN 5 |
| WASH | PIN 3 AND PIN 4 |

*RESISTANCE AT MAXIMUM DELAY POSITION SHOULD BE BETWEEN 270,000 OHMS AND 330,000 OHMS.

*RESISTANCE AT MINIMUM DELAY POSITION SHOULD BE ZERO WITH OHMMETER SET ON HIGH OHM SCALE.

**7.3b Windshield wiper/washer terminal guide and continuity chart**

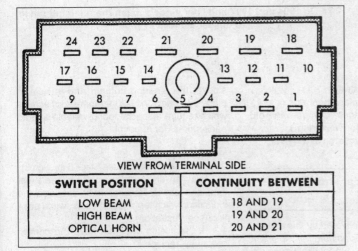

VIEW FROM TERMINAL SIDE

| SWITCH POSITION | CONTINUITY BETWEEN |
|---|---|
| LOW BEAM | 18 AND 19 |
| HIGH BEAM | 19 AND 20 |
| OPTICAL HORN | 20 AND 21 |

**7.3c Headlight dimmer switch terminal guide and continuity chart**

**7.4 Disconnect the multi-function switch electrical connector (A), remove the three Torx-head tamper-proof screws (B) and detach the switch**

**7.10 Multi-function switch details**

1  Electrical connector
2  Upper mounting screw
3  Clockspring mounting screws
4  Locator pin

**7.11 View of the multi-function switch from underneath - 2002 and later models shown, 2001 and earlier similar**

1  Electrical connectors
2  Lower mounting screw

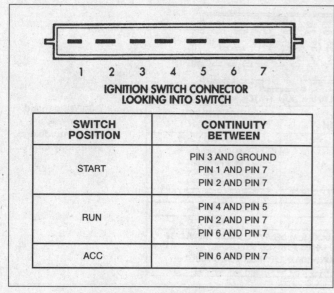

IGNITION SWITCH CONNECTOR
LOOKING INTO SWITCH

| SWITCH POSITION | CONTINUITY BETWEEN |
|---|---|
| START | PIN 3 AND GROUND<br>PIN 1 AND PIN 7<br>PIN 2 AND PIN 7 |
| RUN | PIN 4 AND PIN 5<br>PIN 2 AND PIN 7<br>PIN 6 AND PIN 7 |
| ACC | PIN 6 AND PIN 7 |

9.3 Ignition switch terminal guide and continuity chart

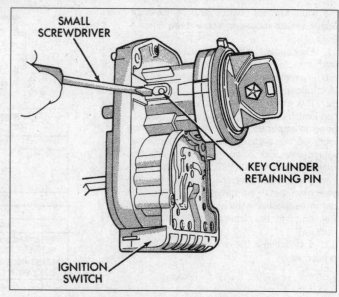

9.7a On 1994 and 1997 and later models, push the retaining pin in to unseat the lock cylinder

## 8   Turn signal and hazard flashers (2001 and earlier 1500 models, 2002 and earlier 2500/3500 models) - check and replacement

### Turn signal flasher

1   The turn signal flasher, a small canister-shaped unit located in the fuse block, flashes the turn signals (see illustration 3.1a).
2   When the flasher unit is functioning properly, an audible click can be heard during its operation. If the turn signals fail on one side or the other and the flasher unit does not make its characteristic clicking sound, a faulty turn signal bulb is indicated.
3   If both turn signals fail to blink, the problem may be due to a blown fuse, a faulty flasher unit, a broken switch or a loose or open connection. If a quick check of the fuse box indicates that the turn signal fuse has blown, check the wiring for a short before installing a new fuse.
4   To remove the flasher, simply pull it out of the fuse block.
5   Make sure that the replacement unit is identical to the original. Compare the old one to the new one before installing it.
6   Installation is the reverse of removal.

### Hazard flasher

7   The hazard flasher, a small canister-shaped unit located in the fuse block, flashes all four turn signals simultaneously when activated.
8   The hazard flasher is checked in a fashion similar to the turn signal flasher (see Steps 2 and 3).
9   To replace the hazard flasher, pull it from

the fuse block (see illustration 3.1a).
10   Make sure the replacement unit is identical to the one it replaces. Compare the old one to the new one before installing it.
11   Installation is the reverse of removal.

## 9   Key lock cylinder and ignition switch

**Warning:** *The models covered by this manual are equipped with a Supplemental Restraint System (SRS), more commonly known as airbags. Always disarm the airbag system before working in the vicinity of any airbag system component to avoid the possibility of accidental deployment of the airbag, which could cause personal injury (see Section 27). Do not use a memory-saving device to preserve the PCM's memory when working on or near airbag system components. To prevent accidental deployment (and possible injury), disconnect the negative battery cable(s) whenever working near airbag components. After the battery is disconnected, wait at least 2 minutes before beginning work (the system has a back-up capacitor that must fully discharge).*
**Note:** *If the key is difficult to turn, the problem might not be in the ignition switch or the key lock cylinder. On automatic transmission vehicles, the shift cable might be out of adjustment (see Chapter 7B).*

### Ignition switch/key lock cylinder (2001 and earlier 1500 models, 2002 and earlier 2500/3500 models) - check and replacement

1   The ignition switch is located on the right

side of the steering column and is held in place by three Torx T-20 tamper-proof screws which require a special tool (available at auto parts stores) for removal.

### Check

2   Remove the switch (see Steps 5 through 8).
3   Use an ohmmeter or self-powered test light and check for continuity between the indicated switch terminals in each switch position (see illustration).
4   If the switch does not have the correct continuity, replace it.

### Replacement

5   Disconnect the negative battery cable(s) (see Chapter 5).
6   Remove the steering column covers (see Chapter 11). Remove the steering column tilt lever (if equipped) by unscrewing it and, if equipped with an automatic transmission, place the transmission shift lever in Park.
7   Remove the key lock cylinder to access the ignition switch:

a)   *On 1994 through 1996 models, insert the ignition key and turn it to the LOCK position. Use a small screwdriver to depress the lock cylinder retaining pin on 1994 models (see illustration 9.7a). Use a Torx bit to remove the lock cylinder retaining screw on 1995 and 1996 models (see illustration 9.7b). Turn the ignition key to the OFF position which will unseat the key lock cylinder slightly. With the cylinder unseated, rotate the ignition key counterclockwise to the LOCK position (see illustration 9.7c), remove the key then remove the lock cylinder from the ignition switch (see illustration 9.7d).*

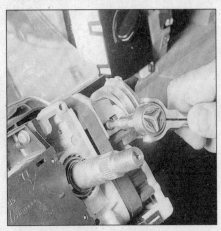

9.7b On 1995 and 1996 models, remove the tamper-proof screw

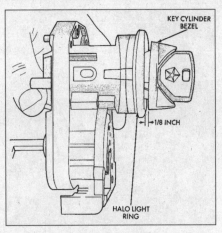

9.7c The lock cylinder will protrude about 1/8-inch from the switch once it's unseated - don't try to remove it until you rotate it to the Lock position and remove the key

9.7d With the lock cylinder in the Lock position, it will pull out easily

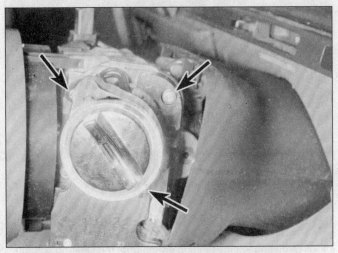

9.8 The ignition switch is held in place by three Torx-head tamper-proof screws (the lower screw is located under the cover)

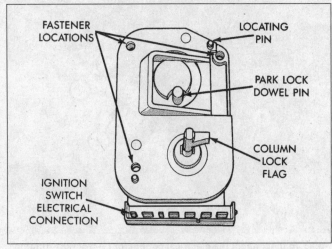

9.9 Make sure the switch column lock flag is parallel with the electrical connection before installation

b)  On 1997 and later models (through 2001/2002), insert the ignition key and turn it to the RUN position. Use a small screwdriver to depress the lock cylinder retaining pin (see illustration 9.7a) while removing the lock cylinder from the ignition switch.

8    Remove the tamper-proof screws and detach the switch from the steering column. Disconnect the electrical connector and remove the switch (see illustration).

9    Mount the ignition switch to the steering column:

a)  On 1994 through 1996 models, the park lock dowel pin must engage with the column park lock slider linkage. Make sure the ignition switch is in the LOCK position by locating the column lock flag parallel with the ignition switch termi-

nals (see illustration). Be sure the pin is inserted into the park lock link contour slot. Tighten the Torx screws securely.

b)  On 1997 and later models (through 2001/2002), make sure the ignition switch is in the RUN position by rotating the column lock flag to the 5 o'clock position in relation to the ignition switch terminals. Do not install the ignition switch. Proceed to Step 10.

10   Insert the key lock cylinder into the ignition switch:

a)  On 1994 through 1996 models, with the ignition switch in the LOCK position, insert the key lock cylinder until it bottoms. While pushing the lock cylinder in, insert the key and turn it clockwise to the RUN position. Be sure to insert the theft

proof retaining screw on the 1995 and 1996 model ignition switches.

b)  On 1997 and later models (through 2001/2002), with the ignition switch in the RUN position and the ignition key inserted in the lock cylinder and the retaining pin depressed, align the retaining pin with the slot in the ignition switch until the retaining pin engages. Rotate the ignition key to OFF or LOCK. The park lock dowel pin must be indexed with the park lock linkage and the column lock flag must be aligned properly with the steering wheel lock lever (automatic transmission models). Apply a light coat of grease and install the ignition switch into the steering column. Tighten the screws securely.

11   The remainder of installation is the reverse of removal.

9.15 To remove the key lock cylinder, turn the ignition key to the RUN position, insert a small drill bit or screwdriver into this hole and depress the retaining pin, then pull the lock cylinder out of the steering column

9.16 When installing the key lock cylinder into the steering column, be sure to align the end of the cylinder with these two flats inside the small receptacle in the floor of the lock cylinder mounting bore

9.22 To access the upper tilt lever mounting screw, remove the electrical connectors (1) from the clockspring, then remove the tilt lever mounting screws (2)

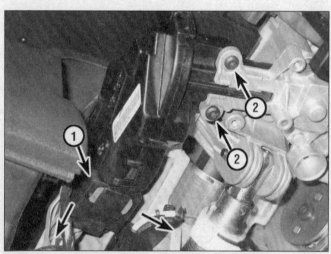

9.23 To disconnect the electrical connector (1) from the ignition switch, push the red sliding lock toward the steering column, then pull the connector toward the front of the vehicle. To detach the ignition switch from the steering column, remove these two mounting screws (2)

9.25 To disengage the ignition switch from the steering column, pry this locking tab away from the column, then pull off the switch

## 2002 and later 1500 models, 2003 and later 2500/3500 models - replacement

### Key lock cylinder

12   Disconnect the cable(s) from the negative battery terminal(s) (see Chapter 5).

13   Remove the upper and lower steering column covers (see Chapter 11).

14   Insert the ignition key into the key lock cylinder and, if the vehicle is equipped with an automatic transmission, put the shift lever in the PARK position.

15   Turn the ignition key to the RUN position, then insert a small punch or a Phillips screwdriver into the hole for the key lock cylinder retaining pin (see illustration), depress the retaining pin and pull the key lock cylinder out of the steering column.

16   Before installing the key lock cylinder, make sure that the ignition key is still in the RUN position. Then align the inner end of the key lock cylinder with the flats (see illustration) in the receptacle at the inner end of the lock cylinder bore and push the lock cylinder into the ignition switch until it clicks into place.

17   Installation is otherwise the reverse of removal.

### Ignition switch

18   Disconnect the cable(s) from the negative battery terminal(s) (see Chapter 5).

19   Disable the airbag system (see Section 27).

20   Remove the upper and lower steering column covers (see Chapter 11).

21   Remove the ignition key lock cylinder (see Steps 13 through 15).

22   On models equipped with a tilt steering column, disconnect the electrical connectors from the clockspring, then remove the tilt lever mounting screws (see illustration). On steering columns without tilt, remove the small bracket located in the same spot as the tilt lever (directly underneath the ignition switch mounting screws).

23   Disconnect the electrical connector from the forward end of the ignition switch (see illustration).

24   Remove the ignition switch mounting screws.

25   To disengage the ignition switch from the steering column, carefully pry the small locking tab away from the steering column (see illustration). Remove the ignition switch from the steering column.

26   Installation is the reverse of removal. Refer to Step 16 when installing the lock cylinder.

**10.3a Remove the headlight switch retaining screws**

**10.3b Disconnect the electrical connector**

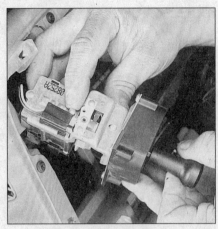

**10.4 Depress the release button on the bottom of the switch, then withdraw the knob and shaft**

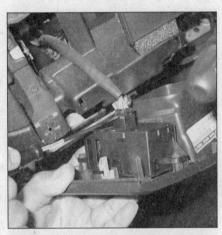

**10.6 After removing the headlight switch bezel, disconnect the electrical connector from the backside of the headlight switch**

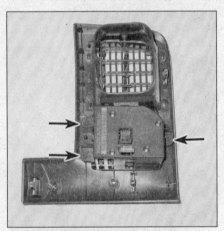

**10.7 To detach the headlight switch from the switch bezel (trim panel), remove these three screws**

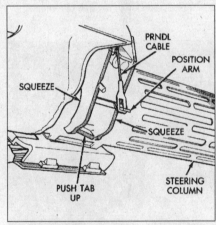

**11.3 Disconnect the gear indicator (PRNDL) cable and retainer from the steering column**

## 10  Headlight switch - replacement

1    Disconnect the cable(s) from the negative battery terminal(s) (see Chapter 5).
2    Carefully pry the headlight switch bezel (trim panel) loose from the dash, disconnecting any electrical connectors.

### 2001 and earlier 1500/2002 and earlier 2500 and 3500 models

3    Remove the retaining screws, pull the switch out and disconnect the electrical connector (see illustrations).
4    Press the release button on the bottom of the switch and withdraw the knob and shaft (see illustration).
5    Installation is the reverse of removal.

### 2002 and later 1500/2003 and later 2500 and 3500 models

6    Disconnect the electrical connector from the headlight switch (see illustration), then remove the headlight switch bezel and place it on a clean working surface.
7    To detach the headlight switch from the switch bezel, remove the switch mounting screws (see illustration).
8    Installation is the reverse of removal.

## 11  Instrument cluster - removal and installation

1    Disconnect the cable(s) from the negative battery terminal(s) (see Chapter 5).

2    On 2001 and earlier 1500 models/2002 and earlier 2500 and 3500 models, remove the instrument cluster bezel and the knee bolster (see Chapter 11, Section 21).
3    On 2001 and earlier 1500 models/2002 and earlier 2500 and 3500 models, remove the gear indicator cable from the position arm, push the release tab on the retainer up, squeeze the sides together and remove the retainer from the steering column (see illustration).
4    On 2002 and later 1500 models/2003 and later 2500 and 3500 models, remove the headlight switch bezel (see Section 10).
5    On 2002 and later 1500 models/2003 and later 2500 and 3500 models, remove the center instrument panel bezel and instrument cluster bezel (see Chapter 11, Section 21).

11.6a To remove the instrument cluster from the instrument panel, remove these mounting screws . . .

2    Bend each wiper arm at its hinge point (to relieve spring tension on the wiper arm-to-wiper pivot shaft connection), then pull out the latch on the pivot end of each wiper arm and remove the pivoting end of the wiper arm from the pivot shaft (see illustrations). It's not necessary to mark the relationship of the windshield wiper arms to their shafts because a locking tab fits into the keyway on the side of each shaft. When you install the arms again, make sure that the locking tab is aligned with this keyway.

3    Remove the cowl cover (see Chapter 11).

4    Disconnect the electrical connector from the windshield wiper motor. Remove the windshield wiper motor mounting bolts and the wiper linkage arm mounting bolts (see illustration).

5    Remove the windshield wiper motor and linkage as a single assembly.

6    If you're going to replace the windshield wiper motor or the windshield wiper arm linkage, remove the nut and detach the crank arm from the shaft (see illustration), then remove the motor mounting bolts and detach

6    Remove the four instrument cluster mounting screws, pull out the cluster and disconnect the electrical connectors from the backside of the cluster (see illustrations).

7    Installation is the reverse of removal.

## 12  Windshield wiper motor - replacement

1    Disconnect the cable(s) from the negative battery terminal(s) (see Chapter 5).

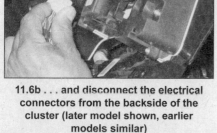

11.6b . . . and disconnect the electrical connectors from the backside of the cluster (later model shown, earlier models similar)

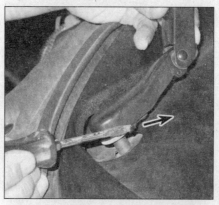

12.2a To remove each windshield wiper arm from its shaft, pry the latch away from the arm (toward the windshield) . . .

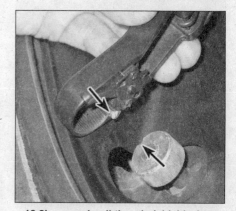

12.2b . . . and pull the windshield wiper arm assembly off the shaft - note how the keyway must be aligned with the locking tab for the pivot end of the wiper arm to fit onto the splined shaft

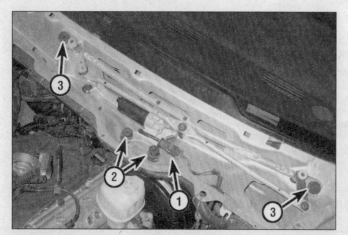

12.4 To detach the windshield wiper motor and linkage assembly from the vehicle, disconnect the electrical connector (1), remove the motor mounting bolts (2) and remove the wiper linkage arm mounting bolts (3) - later models shown, earlier models similar

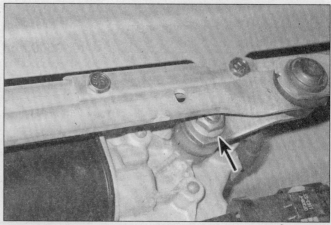

12.6 To detach the crank arm from the wiper motor shaft, remove this nut. Be sure to mark the alignment of the arm to the shaft before removing the arm

the motor. Before detaching the crank arm from the motor shaft, be sure to make alignment marks on the arm and on the shaft to ensure correct alignment when installing the crank arm on the shaft.

7    Installation is the reverse of removal.

### 13  Radio and speakers - removal and installation

**Warning:** *These models are equipped with an airbag. The airbag is armed and can deploy (inflate) anytime the battery is connected. To prevent accidental deployment (and possible injury), disconnect the negative battery cable whenever working near airbag components. After the battery is disconnected, wait at least 2 minutes before beginning work (the system has a back-up capacitor that must fully discharge). For more information see Section 27.*

### *Radio*

1    Disconnect the cable(s) from the negative battery terminal(s) (see Chapter 5).

2    Remove the center instrument panel bezel (see Chapter 11).

3    Remove the radio mounting screws (see illustration) and pull the radio out of the dash.

4    Disconnect the electrical connectors and the antenna from the radio (see illustration).

5    Installation is the reverse of removal.

### *Speakers*

#### Front door speakers

6    Disconnect the cable(s) from the negative battery terminal(s) (see Chapter 5).

7    Remove the door trim panel (see Chapter 11).

8    Remove the four speaker mounting screws (see illustration).

9    Pull out the speaker and disconnect the electrical connector.

10    Installation is the reverse of removal.

#### Instrument panel center speaker and end speakers

11    Disconnect the cable(s) from the nega-

tive battery terminal(s) (see Chapter 5).

12    Remove the instrument panel top cover (see Chapter 11).

13    Remove the speaker mounting screws (see illustration).

14    Pull out the speaker and disconnect the electrical connector.

15    Installation is the reverse of removal.

#### Rear cab side speakers or rear door speakers

**Note:** *Once the B-pillar lower trim or the rear door trim panel have been removed, removing and installing one of these speakers is virtually identical to the procedure for removing and installing a front door speaker, except that the amount of mounting bolts used may vary.*

16    Disconnect the cable(s) from the negative battery terminal(s) (see Chapter 5).

17    Disconnect the B-pillar lower trim or the rear door trim panel (see Chapter 11).

18    Remove the speaker mounting screws.

19    Pull out the speaker and disconnect the electrical connector.

20    Installation is the reverse of removal.

**13.3 To detach the radio from the dash, remove these four mounting screws - later models shown, earlier models similar**

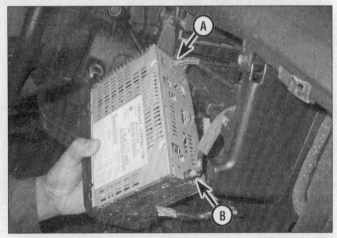

**13.4 Pull the radio out of the dash and disconnect the electrical connectors (A) and the antenna cable (B)**

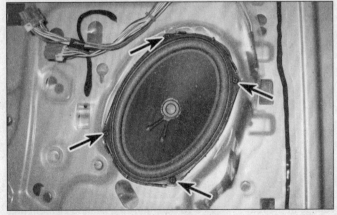

**13.8 To detach a front door speaker from a front door, remove these four mounting screws**

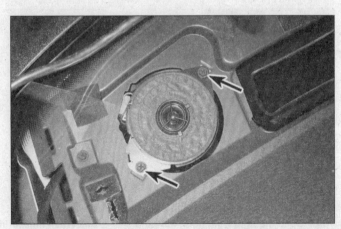

**13.13 To detach an instrument panel end speaker or center speaker, simply remove these two mounting screws, pull out the speaker and disconnect the electrical connector (left end speaker shown, other two speakers identical)**

## 14   Antenna and cable - replacement

1    Disconnect the cable(s) from the negative battery terminal(s) (see Chapter 5).

2    Remove the right-side kick panel.

3    Disconnect the antenna cable's coaxial connector, which is located in the right kick panel area (see illustration).

4    Tie an appropriate length of string to the antenna cable near the upper end of the cable, as close to the antenna body as possible. (You're going to use this string to pull the new cable into position, so make sure that the string is tied securely to the old cable; if it comes off while removing the old cable, you'll have to re-route the new cable yourself.)

5    Remove the antenna from its mounting base (see illustration).

6    Using an antenna wrench (available at auto parts stores), unscrew the nut from the antenna mounting base (see illustration) and remove the base.

7    Open the right front door, pull the antenna body out of its mounting hole in the fender, then work the antenna cable out through the grommet in the body (see illustration).

8    Untie the string from the old antenna cable, tie it to the new cable, then pull the new cable back through the grommet.

9    The remainder of installation is the reverse of removal.

## 15   Rear window defogger - check and repair

1    The rear window defogger consists of a number of horizontal heating elements baked onto the inside surface of the glass. Power is supplied through a relay and fuse from the interior fuse/relay box. A defogger switch on the instrument panel controls the defogger grid.

2    Small breaks in the element can be repaired without removing the rear window.

### *Check*

3    Turn the ignition and defogger switches to the On position.

4    Using a voltmeter, place the positive probe against the defogger grid positive side and the negative probe against the ground side. If battery voltage is not indicated, check that the ignition switch is On and that the feed and ground wires are properly connected. Check the two fuses, defogger switch, defogger relay and related wiring. The dealer can scan the body control module if necessary. If voltage is indicated, but all or part of the defogger doesn't heat, proceed with the following tests.

5    When measuring voltage during the next two tests, wrap a piece of aluminum foil around the tip of the voltmeter positive probe and press the foil against the heating element with your finger (see illustration). Place the negative probe on the defogger grid ground terminal.

6    Check the voltage at the center of each heating element (see illustration). If the voltage is 5 to 6 volts, the element is okay (there is no break). If the voltage is 0 volts, the element is broken between the center of the ele-

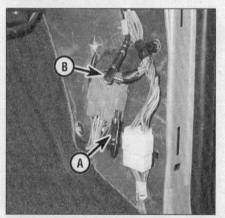

**14.3 Working in the right kick panel area, disconnect the antenna side of the cable (A) from the radio side of the cable (B)**

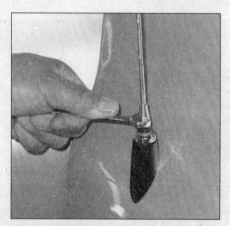

**14.5 Using a small wrench of the appropriate size, unscrew the antenna from its mounting base**

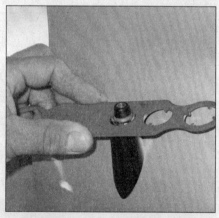

**14.6 Using an antenna wrench (available at auto parts stores) or needle nose pliers, unscrew the nut from the antenna mounting base, then remove the base by pulling it straight up**

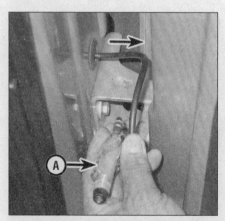

**14.7 Open the right front door, work the antenna body (A) out of its mounting hole in the fender, then pull the antenna cable out through the grommet in the body**

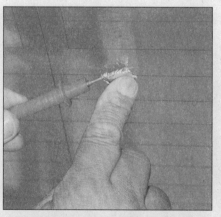

**15.5 When measuring voltage at the rear window defogger grid, wrap a piece of aluminum foil around the positive probe of the voltmeter and press the foil against the wire with your finger**

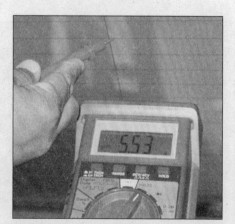

**15.6 To determine if a heating element has broken, check the voltage at the center of each element - if the voltage is 6 volts, the element is unbroken**

ment and the positive end. If the voltage is 10 to 12 volts, the element is broken between the center of the element and the ground side. Check each heating element.

7    If none of the elements are broken, connect the negative probe to a good chassis ground. The voltage reading should stay the same. If it doesn't, the ground connection is bad.

8    To find the break, place the voltmeter negative probe against the defogger ground terminal. Place the voltmeter positive probe with the foil strip against the heating element at the positive side and slide it toward the negative side. The point at which the voltmeter deflects from several volts to zero is the point where the heating element is broken (see illustration).

### Repair

9    Repair the break in the element using a repair kit specifically for this purpose, such as Dupont paste No. 4817 (or equivalent). The kit includes conductive plastic epoxy.

10    Before repairing a break, turn off the system and allow it to cool for a few minutes.

11    Lightly buff the element area with fine steel wool; then clean it thoroughly with rubbing alcohol.

12    Use masking tape to mask off the area being repaired.

13    Thoroughly mix the epoxy, following the kit instructions.

14    Apply the epoxy material to the slit in the masking tape, overlapping the undamaged area about 3/4-inch on either end (see illustration).

15    Allow the repair to cure for 24 hours before removing the tape and using the system.

### 16   Headlight bulb - replacement

**Warning:** *Halogen bulbs are gas-filled and under pressure and they can shatter if the surface is scratched or the bulb is dropped. Wear eye protection and handle the bulbs carefully, grasping only the base whenever possible. Don't touch the surface of the bulb with your fingers because the oil from your skin could cause it to overheat and fail prematurely. If you do touch the bulb surface, clean it with rubbing alcohol.*

1    If it is difficult to reach behind the headlight housing to remove the desired headlight bulb, remove the headlight housing (see Section 17).

2    Rotate the lock ring counterclockwise and remove the headlight bulb holder from the headlight housing (see illustrations).

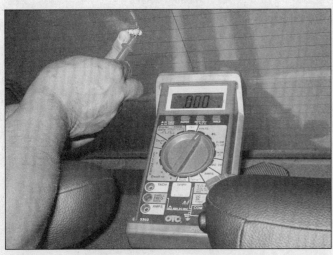

15.8 To find the break, place the voltmeter negative lead against the defogger ground terminal, place the voltmeter positive lead with the foil strip against the heat wire at the positive terminal end and slide it toward the negative terminal end. The point at which the voltmeter deflects from several volts to zero volts is the point at which the wire is broken

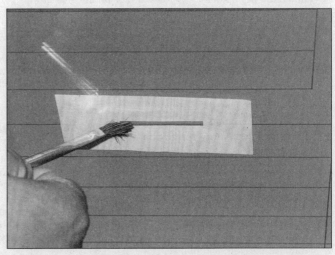

15.14 To use a defogger repair kit, apply masking to the inside of the window at the damaged area, then brush on the special conductive coating

16.2a To remove the headlight bulb from the headlight housing, rotate the lock ring counterclockwise . . .

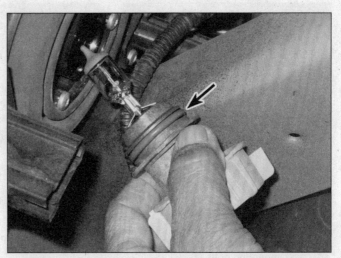

16.2b . . . then pull out the bulb holder. If the new bulb doesn't come with its own dedicated bulb holder, examine the condition of the bulb holder's O-ring and replace it if necessary

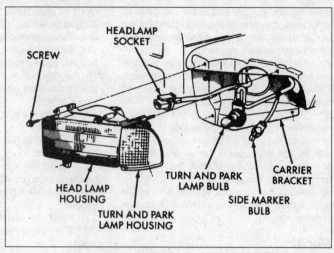

**16.3 To separate the headlight bulb holder from the electrical connector, pry open the two release tabs on the side of the connector with a screwdriver and pull off the bulb holder (on most models, no further disassembly is necessary - the new bulb should come with its own bulb holder)**

**17.3 2001 (1500) / 2002 (2500/3500) and earlier models - headlight housing details**

3    Disconnect the headlight bulb holder from the electrical connector (see illustration).
4    Installation is the reverse of removal.

## 17    Headlight housing - removal and installation

### 2001 and earlier 1500 models/2002 and earlier 2500 and 3500 models

1    Open the hood.
2    Remove the park and turn signal lamp (see Section 19).
3    Remove the retaining screws, pull the housing out and disconnect the electrical connector (see illustration).
4    Installation is the reverse of removal.

After you're done, check the headlight adjustment (see Section 18).

### 2002 and later 1500 models/2003 and later 2500 and 3500 models

5    Remove the push-pin screw that attaches the headlight seal to the fender, then remove the headlight mounting bolts (see illustrations).
6    Pull out the headlight housing far enough to remove the bulb holders for the headlight bulb and for the turn signal bulb (see Section 19 and Section 16).
7    Remove the headlight housing from the vehicle.
8    Installation is the reverse of removal. After you're done, check the headlight adjustment (see Section 18).

## 18    Headlights - adjustment

**Warning:** *The headlights must be aimed correctly. If adjusted incorrectly, they could temporarily blind the driver of an oncoming vehicle and cause an accident or seriously reduce your ability to see the road. The headlights should be checked for proper aim every 12 months and any time a new headlight is installed or front-end bodywork is performed. The following procedure is only intended to provide temporary adjustment until you can have the headlights professionally adjusted by a dealer service department.*

### Headlights

1    Each headlight has an adjusting screw for horizontal adjustments and a screw for vertical adjustments (see illustrations).
2    There are several methods of adjusting the headlights. The simplest method requires an open area with a blank wall and a level floor (see illustration).
3    Position masking tape vertically on the wall in reference to the vehicle centerline and the centerlines of both headlights.
4    Position a horizontal tape line in reference to the centerline of the headlights.
**Note:** *It might be easier to position the tape on the wall with the vehicle parked only a few inches away.*
5    Adjustment should be made with the vehicle parked 25 feet from the wall, sitting level, the gas tank full and no unusually heavy load in the vehicle.
6    The high intensity zone should be vertically centered with the exact center, about three inches below the horizontal line.
7    Have the headlights adjusted by a qualified technician at the earliest opportunity.

**17.5a To remove the headlight housing, remove the push-pin (1) and inner mounting bolts (2) . . .**

**17.5b . . . then remove the outer mounting bolt (3) (2002 through 2005 1500/2003 through 2005 2500 and 3500 models). On 2006 and later models, the outer mounting fastener is accessed from behind, through a hole in the fender splash shield**

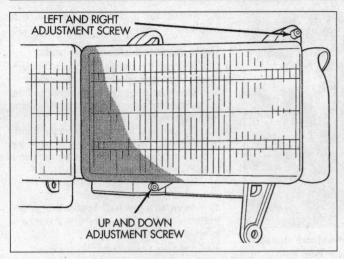

**18.1a Headlight adjustment screws - early models**

LEFT AND RIGHT ADJUSTMENT SCREW

UP AND DOWN ADJUSTMENT SCREW

**18.1b Headlight adjustment screws - later models**

*A Horizontal adjuster screw*     *B Vertical adjuster screw*

### Fog lights

8    Fog lights are optional on these vehicles.

9    Park the vehicle 25 feet from the wall.

10    Tape a horizontal line on the wall that represents the height of the fog lights and tape another line four inches below that line.

11    Using the adjusting screw on each fog light, adjust the pattern on the wall so that the top of the fog light beam meets the lower line on the wall.

### Light bar

12    The roof-mounted light bar is optional equipment.

13    Park the vehicle 25 feet from the wall.

14    Attach a horizontal piece of tape to the wall at seven feet, nine inches from the ground.

15    Cover three of the four lights and aim the fourth using the adjustment screw in the rear. The center of its high intensity zone should be on the tape line.

16    Repeat the procedure for the other three lights.

**18.2 Headlight adjustment screen details**

High-Intensity Area

Floor to Center of Headlamp Lens

Center of Vehicle to Center of Headlamp Lens

Vehicle Centerline

25 FT

Front of Headlamp

---

### 19    Bulb replacement

### Exterior lights

#### Front turn signal/parking light/ sidemarker lights

**2001 and earlier 1500 models, 2002 and earlier 2500/3500 models**

1    Remove the screw that secures the turn signal/parking light housing, then rotate the housing out for access to the bulb holders (see illustration).

2    Turn the bulb holder counterclockwise to remove it from the housing, then pull the bulb straight out of the holder (see illustrations 19.4 and 19.5 for examples).

3    Installation is the reverse of removal.

**19.1 Remove the Phillips head screw and detach the turn signal light housing**

**19.4 To remove bulb holder for the front turn signal/parking light/sidemarker light bulb from the headlight housing, rotate the holder counterclockwise and pull it out of the housing**

**2002 and later 1500 models, 2003 and later 2500/3500 models**

4    Remove the headlight housing (see Section 17) and remove the bulb holder for the front turn signal/parking light/sidemarker light bulb (see illustration).

**19.5 To remove the front turn signal/parking light/sidemarker light bulb from its bulb holder, simply pull it straight out of the holder**

5    Remove the turn signal/parking light/sidemarker light bulb from its bulb holder by simply pulling it straight out of the holder (see illustration).
6    Install the new bulb by pushing it straight into the bulb holder until it's fully seated.

7    Installation is otherwise the reverse of removal.

### High-mounted brake light bulbs

8    Remove the screws that attach the high-mount brake light housing (see illustration).
9    Disconnect the electrical connector from the center high-mounted brake light housing (see illustration).
10    To remove a bulb holder from the center high-mounted brake light housing, rotate the bulb holder counterclockwise, then remove it from the housing (see illustration).
11    To replace an old bulb, simply pull it straight out of the bulb holder.
12    To install a new bulb, push it straight into the bulb holder. Make sure that the bulb is fully seated in the holder.
13    Installation is the reverse of removal.

### License plate light bulbs

**2001 and earlier 1500 models, 2002 and earlier 2500/3500 models**

14    Remove the Torx-head screws, detach the bulb cover, then pull the bulb straight out of the holder (see illustration).
15    Installation is the reverse of removal.

**19.8 To detach the high-mounted brake light housing from the cab, remove these two screws - 2002 and later model shown, earlier models similar**

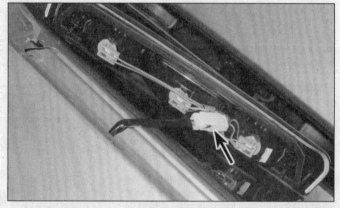

**19.9 Disconnect the electrical connector for the center high-mounted brake light housing**

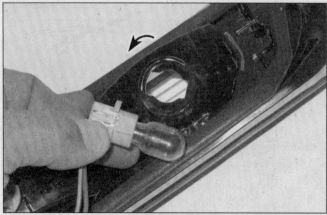

**19.10 To replace one of the three bulbs in the center high-mounted brake light housing, rotate the bulb holder counterclockwise and pull out the housing**

**19.14 Remove the screws and detach the license bulb cover for access to the lamp bulbs**

**2002 and later 1500 models,
2003 and later 2500/3500 models**

16   The license plate light bulbs are located on either side of the license plate. To change a bulb, get underneath the rear bumper cover and locate the bulb holder for the bulb that you want to replace (see illustration).

17   To install a new bulb in its holder, push it straight into the holder until it's fully seated.

18   Installation is the reverse of removal.

**Rear turn signal/brake light/back-up light bulbs**

19   Open the tailgate, then remove the taillight housing mounting screws (see illustration). Disconnect the electrical connectors from the housing assembly (see illustration) and remove the taillight housing.

20   On early models, rotate the bulb holder counterclockwise and remove it from the back of the housing (see illustration). Squeeze the tabs and pull the bulb from the holder.

21   On later models, remove the bulb back-

ing plate from the taillight housing (see illustrations).

22   Remove the bulb that you want to replace from its socket (see illustration).

23   To install a new bulb into the socket, insert it into the socket and push it in until it snaps into place.

24   Installation is otherwise the reverse of removal.

## Interior lights

**Warning:** *The models covered by this manual are equipped with a Supplemental Restraint System (SRS), more commonly known as airbags. Always disarm the airbag system before working in the vicinity of any airbag system component to avoid the possibility of accidental deployment of the airbag, which could cause personal injury (see Section 27). Do not use a memory-saving device to preserve the PCM's memory when working on or near airbag system components.*

**19.16 To replace a license plate light bulb, rotate the bulb holder counterclockwise and pull out the holder, then pull the bulb straight out of the holder**

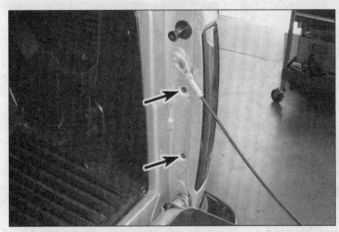

**19.19a To detach the taillight housing from the rear fender, remove these two mounting screws . . .**

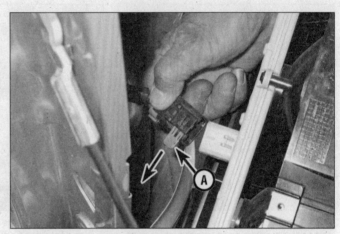

**19.19b . . . then pull out the housing, push the sliding lock to its released position and disconnect the electrical connector**

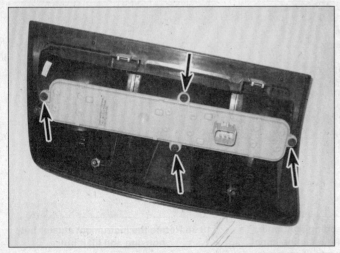

**19.21a To detach the bulb backing plate from the taillight housing, remove these four screws . . .**

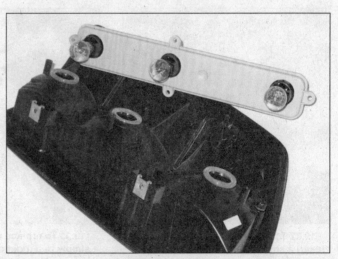

**19.21b . . . then carefully lift the backing plate straight up for access to the bulbs**

**19.22 To remove a bulb from its socket, spread the two small locking tangs apart slightly and pull out the bulb. To install a new bulb in the socket, push it into the socket until it snaps into place**

### Dome light

25  Using a small flat-bladed screwdriver, carefully pry down the dome light lens (see illustration), swing down the lens and allow it to hang.

26  Remove the dome light bulb from the dome light housing (see illustration).

27  Insert a new dome light bulb into its socket in the dome light housing until it's fully seated.

28  Installation is otherwise the reverse of removal.

### Glove box light bulb

29  Open the glove box door and locate the glove box light bulb at the right front corner.

30  To remove the glove box light bulb, simply pull it straight out toward the front of the vehicle (see illustration).

31  To install a new glove box light bulb, simply push it straight into its socket until it's fully seated.

### Reading light bulbs

32  There are two reading lights. Find one of the slots along the edge of the lens for the bulb that you're replacing, carefully insert the blade of a small screwdriver into the slot (see illustration) and pry off the lens.

33  Remove the reading light bulb from its terminals (see illustration).

34  Installation is the reverse of removal.

### Instrument cluster lights (early models)

35  To gain access to the instrument cluster illumination lights, the instrument cluster will have to be removed (see Section 11). The bulbs can then be removed and replaced from the rear of the cluster.

36  Rotate the bulb counterclockwise to remove it (see illustration).

37  Installation is the reverse of removal.

**19.25 To access the dome light bulb on 2004 and earlier models, pry down the left side of the dome light lens with a small screwdriver (on 2005 and later models, pry between the notch in the lens and the housing)**

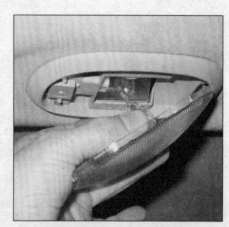

**19.26 To remove the dome light bulb from the dome light housing, simply pull it straight out**

**19.30 The glove box light bulb is located at the right front corner of the glove box. To remove it, simply pull it straight out (forward, toward the front of the vehicle)**

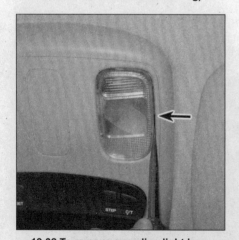

**19.32 To remove a reading light lens, insert a small flat-blade screwdriver into one of the slots along the edge of the lens and carefully pry off the lens**

**19.33 To replace a reading light bulb, simply pull it out of the retaining clips/ connectors at both ends (if prying is necessary, pry only on the metal ends). To install a new bulb, push it into the clips/ connectors until it pops into place**

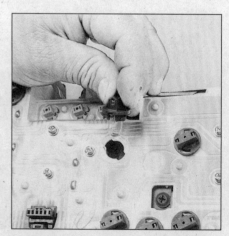

**19.36 Rotate the instrument cluster bulb housing and lift it out**

## Side identification lamp (early models)

**Note:** *The side identification lamp must be replaced as a unit.*

38   Use a small screwdriver detach the housing, then disconnect the electrical connector (see illustration).

39   Installation is the reverse of removal.

## 20   Horn - replacement

1   On 2001 and earlier 1500 models/2002 and earlier 2500 and 3500 models, the horns are located behind the front bumper. On 2002 and later 1500 models/2003 and later 2500 and 3500 models, the horns are located under the engine compartment fuse and relay box. To access the horns, remove the fuse and relay box mounting bolts (Chapter 5, Section 3), disengage the box from the battery tray and slide it toward the engine to provide some room to work. If this doesn't give you enough room to work, loosen the left front wheel lug nuts, raise the front of the vehicle, remove the left front wheel and remove the inner fender splash shield (see Chapter 11, Section 12).

2   Disconnect the electrical connector from the horns (see illustrations).

3   Installation is the reverse of removal.

## 21   Electric side-view mirrors - general information

1   The electric side-view mirrors can be adjusted up-and-down and left-to-right by a driver's side switch located on the left door trim panel. On models with factory-installed dual power mirrors, each mirror is also equipped with a heater grid behind the mirror glass to clear the mirror surface of fog, ice or snow. On these models, the mirror heater grid is an integral component of each mirror. If a heater grid fails, replace the mirror (see Chapter 3). The heater grid switches and the heated mirror system indicator light are integral components of the heater/air conditioning control panel on the dash. If one of these components fails, replace the heater/air conditioning control assembly (see Chapter 3). The heated mirror relay is located in the engine compartment fuse and relay box (see Section 11).

2   The mirror control switch has a Left-Right selector switch that allows you to send voltage to the side-view mirror that you want to adjust. With the ignition switch in the ACC position, roll down the windows and operate the mirror control switch through all functions (left-right and up-down) for both the left and right side-view mirrors.

3   Listen carefully for the sound of the electric motors running in the mirrors.

4   If you can hear the motors but the mirror glass doesn't move, the problem is probably a defective drive mechanism inside the mirror, which will necessitate replacement of the mirror.

5   If the mirrors don't operate and no sound comes from the mirrors, check the fuse in the engine compartment fuse and relay box (see Section 3).

6   If the fuse is OK, refer to Chapter 11 and remove the door panel for access to the back of the mirror control switch, without disconnecting the wires attached to it. Turn the ignition On and check for voltage at the switch. There should be voltage at one terminal. If there's no voltage at the switch, check for an open in the wiring between the fuse panel and the switch.

7   If there's voltage at the switch, disconnect it. Check the switch for continuity in all its operating positions. If the switch does not have continuity, replace it.

8   Reconnect the switch. Locate the wire going from the switch to ground. Leaving the switch connected, connect a jumper wire between this wire and ground. If the mirror

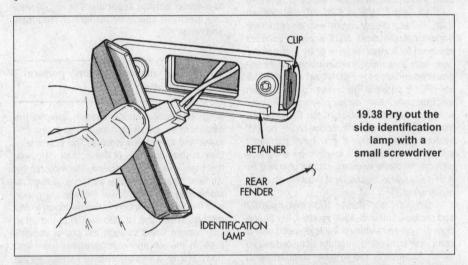

**19.38 Pry out the side identification lamp with a small screwdriver**

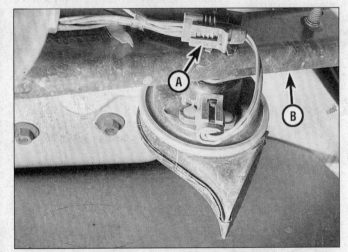

**20.2a On early models - disconnect the horn connector (A) and remove the retaining bolt (B)**

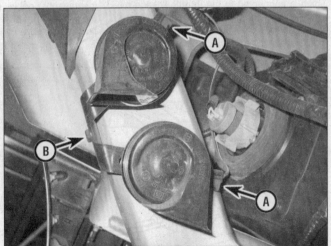

**20.2b On later models - to replace either horn, disconnect the electrical connectors (A) from both horns, remove the horn mounting bracket bolt (B), remove the horns and mounting bracket as a single assembly, then detach the horn that you're replacing by removing the retaining nut (not shown) for that horn**

works normally with this wire in place, repair the faulty ground connection.

9   If the mirror still doesn't work, remove the mirror and check the wires at the mirror for voltage. Check with the ignition key turned to On and the mirror selector switch on the appropriate side. Operate the mirror switch in all its positions. There should be voltage at one of the switch-to-mirror wires in each switch position, except the Neutral (Off) position.

10   If voltage is not present in each switch position, check the wiring between the mirror and control switch for opens and shorts.

11   If there's voltage, remove the mirror and test it off the vehicle with jumper wires. Replace the mirror if it fails this test.

## 22   Cruise control system - general information

**Note:** *The following general information applies to vehicles equipped with a 3.7L V6, a 3.9L V6, a 4.7L V8, a 5.2L V8, 5.9L V8, an 8.0L V10 or a diesel engine with an automatic transmission. It does NOT apply to vehicles powered by a Hemi engine or by a diesel engine with a manual transmission. On Hemi-powered vehicles the Powertrain Control Module (PCM) controls the cruise control system electronically. On diesel-powered vehicles with a manual transmission, the Engine Control Module (ECM) controls the cruise control system electronically. If you have problems with the cruise control system on a vehicle with one of these engines, have it checked by a dealer service department or other qualified repair shop.*

1   On 2001 and earlier 1500 models/2002 and earlier 2500 and 3500 models, the cruise control system maintains vehicle speed with a computer-controlled vacuum actuated servo motor located in the engine compartment, which is connected to the throttle linkage by a cable (see illustration). Listed below are some general procedures that may be used to locate common problems.

2   On 2002 and later 1500 models/2003 and later 2500 and 3500 models, the cruise control system maintains vehicle speed with a servo motor connected to the throttle linkage by a cable. The system consists of the servo motor, brake switch, clutch switch (only on vehicles with a manual transmission), the control switches (on the steering wheel on all vehicles) and the wiring and vacuum hoses connecting all of these components. Some features of the system require the use of a scan tool and diagnostic procedures that are beyond the scope of the home mechanic. Listed below are some general procedures that may be used to locate common problems.

3   Locate and check the fuse (see Section 3).

4   Visually inspect the vacuum hose connected to the servo and check the control linkage between the cruise control servo and the throttle linkage and replace as necessary.

5   Test-drive the vehicle to determine if the cruise control is now working. If it isn't, take it to a dealer service department or an automotive electrical specialist for further diagnosis and repair.

## 23   Power window system - general information

1   The power window system controls the electric motors, mounted inside the doors, that lower and raise the windows. The power window system consists of the control switches, the fuse, the circuit breaker, the motors, the window "regulators" (the scissor-like mechanisms that raise and lower the window glass) and the wiring connecting the switches to the motors. When the ignition switch is turned to On, current flows through the power window fuse in the engine compartment fuse and relay box to a circuit breaker located in the instrument panel wiring harness (located near the parking brake pedal). From there, current flows to the power window switches.

2   The power windows are wired so that

they can be lowered and raised from the master control switch by the driver or by passengers using remote switches located at each passenger window. Each window has a separate motor that is reversible. The position of the control switch determines the polarity and therefore the direction of operation.

3   The power window system will only operate when the ignition switch is turned to On. In addition, a window lockout switch at the master control switch can, when activated, disable the power window switches on the other doors. Always check these items before troubleshooting a window problem.

4   These procedures are general in nature, so if you can't find the problem using them, take the vehicle to a dealer service department.

5   If the power windows don't work at all, check the fuse or circuit breaker.

6   If only the rear windows are inoperative, or if the windows only operate from the master control switch, check the window lockout switch for continuity in the unlocked position. If it doesn't have continuity, replace it.

7   Check the wiring between the switches and the fuse for continuity. Repair the wiring, if necessary.

8   If only one window is inoperative from the master control switch, try the control switch at the window that doesn't work. **Note:** *This doesn't apply to the driver's door window.*

9   If the same window works from one switch, but not the other, check the switch for continuity.

10   If the switch tests OK, check for a short or open in the wiring between the affected switch and the window motor.

11   If one window is inoperative from both switches, remove the trim panel from the affected door (see Chapter 11), then check for voltage at the switch and at the motor while operating the switch. First check for voltage at the electrical connectors for the circuit. With the ignition key turned to On and the connectors all connected, backprobe at the designated wire (see the wiring diagrams at the end of this Chapter) with a grounded test light. Pushing the driver's window switch to

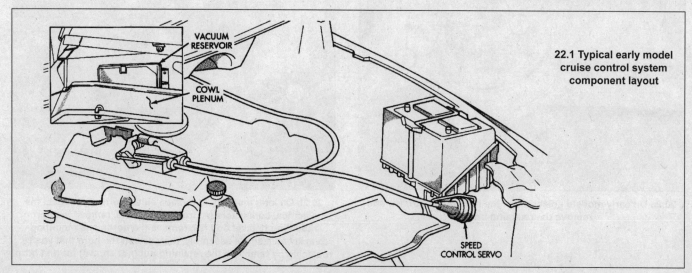

**22.1 Typical early model cruise control system component layout**

the Down position, there should be voltage at one terminal. Pushing the same switch to the Up position, there should be voltage at another terminal. If these voltage checks are OK, disconnect the electrical connector at the driver's motor, and check it for voltage when the switch is operated.

12    If voltage is reaching the motor and the switch is OK, disconnect the door glass from its regulator (see Chapter 11). Move the window up and down by hand while checking for binding and damage. Also check for binding and damage to the regulator. If the regulator is not damaged and the window moves up and down smoothly, replace the motor. If there's binding or damage, lubricate, repair or replace parts, as necessary.

13    If voltage isn't reaching the motor, check the wiring in the circuit for continuity between the switches and motors (see the wiring diagram at the end of this Chapter).

14    If you have to replace the main power window switch, pry it out of the door trim panel, then disconnect the electrical connector(s) from the switch.

15    When you're done, test the windows to confirm that the window system is functioning correctly.

## 24    Power door lock system - general information

1    The power door lock system operates the power door motors, which are integral components of the door latch units in each door. The system consists of a fuse (in the engine compartment fuse and relay box), the instrument cluster, the control switches (in each of the front doors), the power door motors and the electrical wiring harnesses connecting all of these components.

2    The lock mechanisms in the door latch units are actuated by a reversible electric motor in each door. When you push the door lock switch to Lock, the motor operates one way and locks the latch mechanism. When you push the door lock switch the other way, to the Unlock position, the motor operates in the other direction, unlocking the latch mechanism. Because the motors and lock mechanisms are an integral part of the door latch units, they cannot be repaired. If a door lock motor or lock mechanism fails, replace the door latch unit (see Chapter 11).

3    Even if you don't manually lock the doors or press the door lock switch to the Lock position before driving, the instrument cluster automatically locks the doors when the vehicle speed exceeds 15 mph, as long as all the doors are closed and the accelerator pedal is depressed. (You can turn off this feature if you don't want the doors to lock automatically. Refer to your owner's manual.)

4    Some vehicles have an optional Remote Keyless Entry (RKE) system that allows you to lock and unlock the doors from outside the vehicle. The RKE system consists of the transmitter (the electronic push-button "key")

and a receiver located on the instrument cluster. The RKE receiver, which operates all the time, is protected by a fuse in the engine compartment fuse and relay box. Vehicles are shipped from the factory with two RKE transmitters but, if you want to purchase extra units, the RKE receiver can actually handle up to four vehicle access codes.

5    Some features of the door lock system on these vehicles rely on resources that they share with other electronic modules through the Programmable Communications Interface (PCI) data bus network. Professional diagnosis of these modules and the PCI data bus network requires the use of a DRB III, (proprietary factory) scan tool and factory diagnostic information. At-home repairs are therefore limited to inspecting the wiring for bad connections and for minor faults that can be easily repaired. If you are unable to locate the trouble using the following general steps, consult your dealer service department.

6    Always check the circuit fuses (in the engine compartment fuse and relay box) first.

7    When depressed, each power door lock switch locks or unlocks all of the doors. The easiest way to verify that each door lock switch is operating correctly is to watch the door lock button in each door as you operate the switch. The door lock buttons should all go down when you push the door lock switch to the Lock position, and go up when you push the door lock switch to the Unlock position. Also, with the engine turned off so that you can hear better, operate the door lock switches in both directions and listen for the faint click of the motors locking and unlocking the latch mechanisms.

8    If there's no click, check for voltage at the switches. If no voltage is present, check the wiring between the fuse and the switches for shorts and opens (see the wiring diagrams at the end of this chapter).

9    If voltage is present, but no clicking sound is apparent, remove the switch from the door trim panel (see Chapter 11) and test it for continuity. If there is no continuity in either direction, replace the switch.

10    If the switch has continuity but the latch mechanism doesn't click, check the wiring between the switch and the motor in the latch mechanism for continuity. If the circuit is open between the switch and the motor, repair the wiring.

11    If all but one motor is operating, remove the trim panel from the affected door (see Chapter 11) and check for voltage at the motor while operating the lock switch. One of the wires should have voltage in the Lock position; the other should have voltage in the Unlock position.

12    If the inoperative motor is receiving voltage, replace the latch mechanism.

13    If the inoperative motor isn't receiving voltage, check for an open or short in the circuit between the switch and the motor.

**Note:** *It's common for wires to break in the harness between the body and the door because repeatedly opening and closing the door fatigues and eventually breaks the wires.*

## 25    Power seats - general information

**Warning:** *The models covered by this manual are equipped with a Supplemental Restraint System (SRS), more commonly known as airbags. Additionally, some models are equipped with seat belt pre-tensioners, which are explosive devices. Always disarm the airbag/restraint system before working in the vicinity of any airbag/restraint system component to avoid the possibility of accidental deployment of the airbag/seat belt pre-tensioners, which could cause personal injury (see Section 27). Do not use a memory-saving device to preserve the PCM's memory when working on or near airbag system components.*

1    Some models feature an optional eight-way power seat system that allows the driver and passenger to adjust the front seats up, down, front up, front down, rear up, rear down, forward and rearward. The system consists of the driver's power seat switch, the passenger's power seat switch, the driver's power seat track, the passenger's power seat track and, on some models, the optional power lumbar adjusters.

2    The power seat switches are located on the outboard side of the seat cushions, on the seat cushion side panels. If the vehicle is equipped with the optional power lumbar adjusters, the lumbar switches are located on the power seat switch assemblies. Each switch assembly is attached to the seat side panel by two Torx screws. Refer to your owner's manual for instructions regarding switch functions. Individual switches in the power seat switch assemblies cannot be repaired or replaced separately. If one of the switches in a power seat switch assembly fails, replace the entire switch assembly.

3    The seats are powered by three reversible motors that are attached to the upper half of the power seat track assembly. These motors are controlled by the power seat switches on the sides of the seats. Each switch changes the direction of seat travel by reversing polarity to the drive motor. The motors are an integral part of the power seat track assembly and cannot be repaired or replaced separately. If a motor fails, replace the power seat track assembly.

4    The optional power lumbar adjuster and motor are located on the back of the seat, under the seat trim cover and padding, where they're attached to a molded plastic back panel and to the seat back frame. The power lumbar adjuster and motor cannot be repaired or replaced separately from the seat back frame. If either the adjuster or the motor fails, replace the entire seat back frame unit.

5    Diagnosis is usually a simple matter, using the following procedures.

6    Look under the seat for any object which may be preventing the seat from moving.

7    If the seat won't work at all, check the fuse, which is located in the engine compartment fuse and relay box.

8    With the engine off to reduce the noise

level, operate the seat controls in all directions and listen for sound coming from the seat motors.

9    If the motor doesn't work or make noise, check for voltage at the motor while an assistant operates the switch.

10   If the motor is getting voltage but doesn't run, test it off the vehicle with jumper wires. If it still doesn't work, replace it. The individual components are not available separately. The whole power-seat track must be purchased as an assembly.

11   If the motor isn't getting voltage, remove the seat side panel to access the switch and check for voltage. If there's no voltage at the switch, check the wiring between the fuse and the switch. If there's voltage at the switch, check for a short or open in the wiring between the switch and the motor. If that circuit is okay, replace the switch. No further testing is recommended. If the power seat system is still malfunctioning at this point, have the system checked out by a dealer service department.

## 26   Daytime Running Lights (DRL) - general information

1    Canadian models are equipped with Daytime Running Lights (DRL). The DRL system illuminates the headlights whenever the engine is running and the parking brake is disengaged. The DRL system provides reduced power to the headlights so that they won't be too bright for daytime use and it prolongs the headlight bulbs' service life. It does this by modulating the pulse-width of the power to the headlights. The duration and interval of these power pulses is programmed into the Front Control Module (FCM), which is located on the instrument cluster. If you want to alter the pulse-width, you must have it done by a dealer service department.

## 27   Airbag system - general information

1    These models are equipped with a Supplemental Restraint System (SRS), more commonly called airbags. There are at least two airbags, one for the driver and one for the front seat passenger, on all models. The SRS system is designed to protect the driver and passenger from serious injury in the event of a head-on or frontal collision. The airbag control module is located on the transmission tunnel, right below the center of the instrument panel. Some models are also equipped with optional side curtain airbags. Vehicles with this option can be identified by the "SRS - AIRBAG" logo printed on the headliner above the B-pillar.

### *Airbag modules*

2    The airbag module houses the airbag and the inflator unit. The inflator unit is mounted on the back of the housing over a hole through which gas is expelled, inflating

the bag almost instantaneously when an electrical signal is received from the airbag control module. On the driver's airbag, the specially wound wire that carries this signal to the module is called a "clockspring." The clockspring is a flat, ribbon-like electrically conductive tape that winds and unwinds as the steering wheel is turned so it can transmit an electrical signal regardless of wheel position. The procedure for removing the driver's airbag is part of Steering wheel - removal and installation in Chapter 10.

3    The passenger's airbag is located in the top of the dashboard, above the glove box. There's also a passenger's airbag On/Off switch located at the lower right corner of the center instrument panel bezel. This switch allows you to deactivate the passenger's airbag if you're transporting an infant or a young child in a child safety seat. We don't recommend removing the passenger's airbag because there is no reason to do so unless it has been activated during an accident and needs to be replaced afterward. Although the electrical connector for the passenger's airbag must be disconnected when removing the instrument panel (see *Instrument panel - removal and installation* in Chapter 11), the airbag module itself does not need to be removed.

4    Optional side-curtain airbags, if equipped, are located on each roof side rail, above the headliner, and they extend from the A-pillar to the C-pillar on quad cab models. Again, we don't recommend trying to remove the side-curtain airbags because there is no reason to do so unless they've been deployed in an accident and must be replaced.

### *Airbag Control Module (ACM) and Side Impact Airbag Control Modules (SIACMs)*

5    The Airbag Control Module (ACM) is the microprocessor that monitors and operates the airbag system. The ACM checks the system every time the vehicle is started. When you start the car, an Airbag indicator light comes on for about six seconds, then goes off, if the system is operating properly. If there is a fault in the system, the ACM stores a Diagnostic Trouble Code (DTC) and illuminates the Airbag indicator light, which remains on until the problem is repaired and the ACM memory is cleared of any DTCs. If the Airbag indicator light comes on at any time other than the bulb test and remains on, or doesn't come on at all, there's a problem in the system. A DRBIII scan tool is the only means by which the system can be diagnosed. Take the vehicle to your dealer immediately and have the system professionally diagnosed and repaired.

6    The ACM controls the operation of the standard driver's and passenger's airbags. Vehicles with optional side-curtain airbags are also equipped with Side Impact Airbag Control Modules (SIACMs). There are two SIACMs, one for each side-curtain airbag. The SIACMs are located behind the B-pillar trim, above the outboard front seat belt retractor inside each B-pillar.

### *Servicing components near the SRS system*

7    There are times when you need to remove the steering wheel, the instrument cluster, the radio, the heater/air conditioning control assembly or other components on or near the dashboard. At these times you'll be working around components and wire harnesses for the SRS system. Do not use electrical test equipment on airbag system wires; it could cause the airbag(s) to deploy. ALWAYS DISABLE THE SRS SYSTEM BEFORE WORKING NEAR THE SRS SYSTEM COMPONENTS OR RELATED WIRING.

### *Disabling the system*

8    Whenever working in the vicinity of the steering wheel, steering column, floor console or near other components of the airbag system, the system should be disarmed. To do this perform the following steps:

a)  *Turn the ignition switch to the Off position.*

b)  *Disconnect the cable(s) from the negative battery terminal(s) (see Chapter 5).*

c)  *Wait for at least two minutes before beginning work (during this two-minute interval the capacitor that provides emergency back-up power to the system loses its charge).*

### *Enabling the system*

9    To enable the airbag system, perform the following steps:

a)  *Turn the ignition switch to the Off position.*

b)  *Connect the cable(s) to the negative battery terminal(s).*

c)  *Without putting your body in front of either airbag, turn the ignition switch to the On position. Note whether the airbag indicator light glows for six seconds, then goes out. If it does, this indicates that the system is functioning properly.*

## 28   Wiring diagrams - general information

1    Since it isn't possible to include all wiring diagrams for every year covered by this manual, the following diagrams are those that are typical and most commonly needed.

2    Prior to troubleshooting any circuits, check the fuse and circuit breakers (if equipped) to make sure they are in good condition. Make sure the battery is properly charged and has clean, tight cable connections (see Chapter 1).

3    When checking the wiring system, make sure that all electrical connectors are clean, with no broken or loose pins. When disconnecting an electrical connector, do not pull on the wires, only on the connector housings.

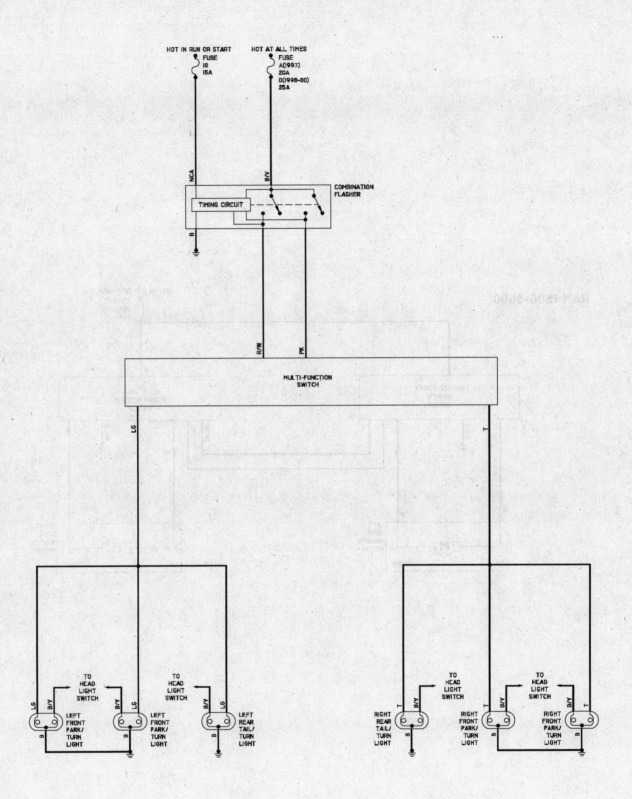

**1997-98 Ram 1500-3500 Chassis Schematics**

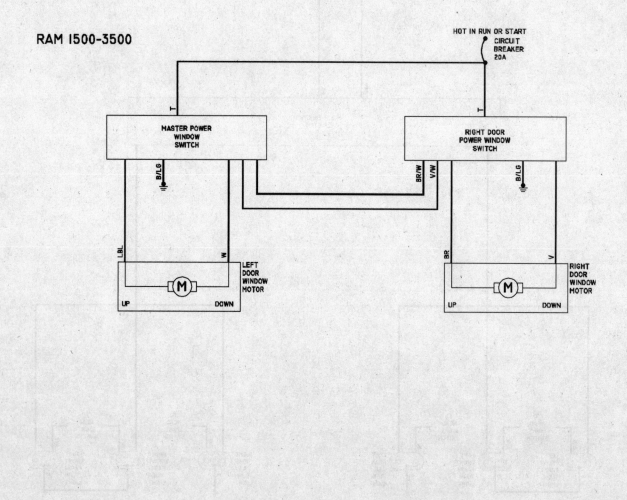

RAM 1500-3500

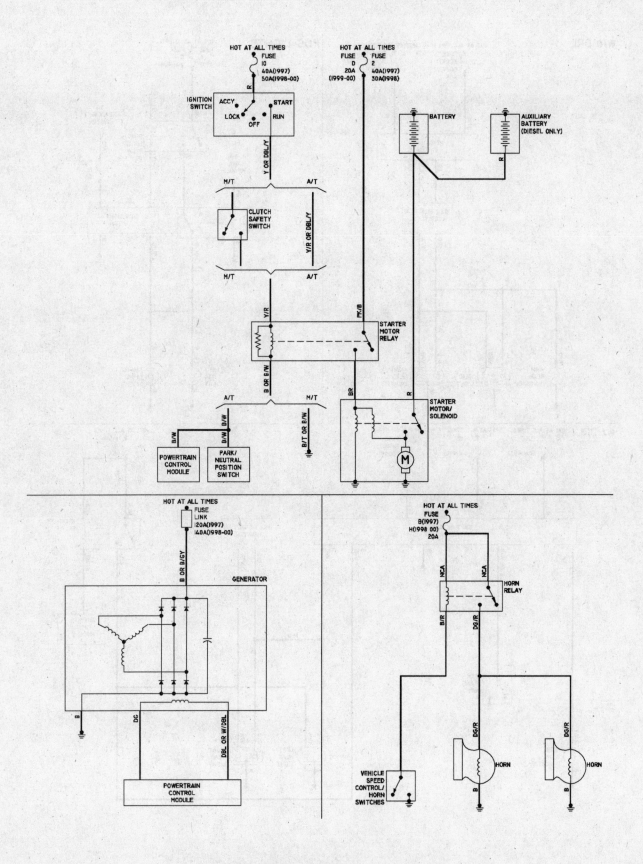

**1997-01 Ram 1500-3500 Chassis Schematics**

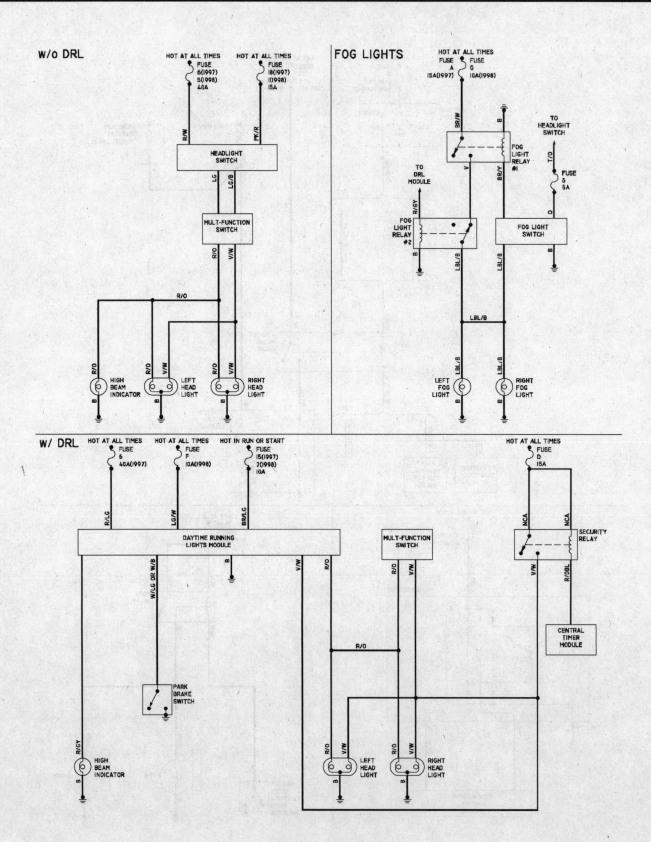

**1997-98 Ram 1500-3500 Chassis Schematics**

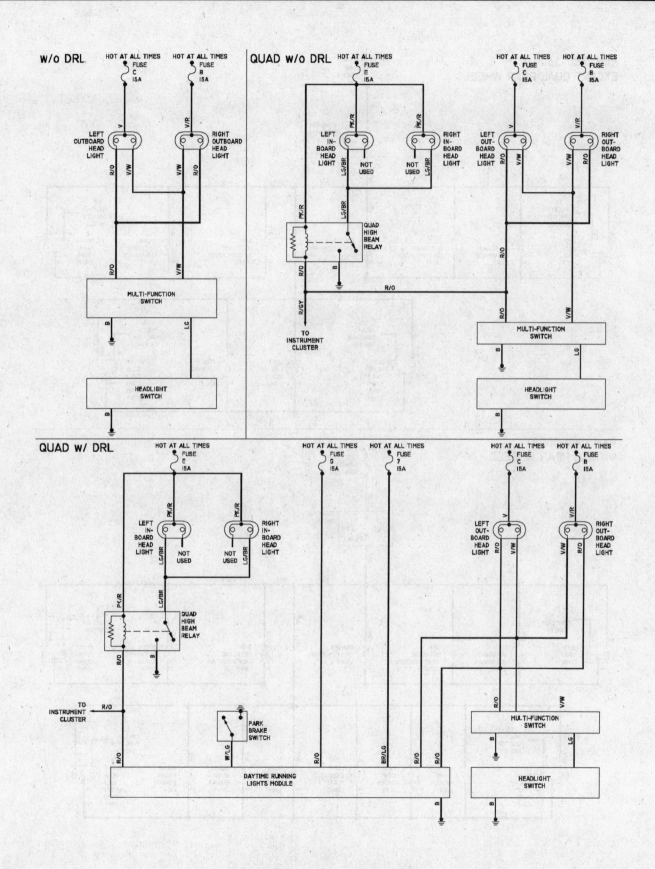

**1999-01 Ram 1500-3500 Chassis Schematics**

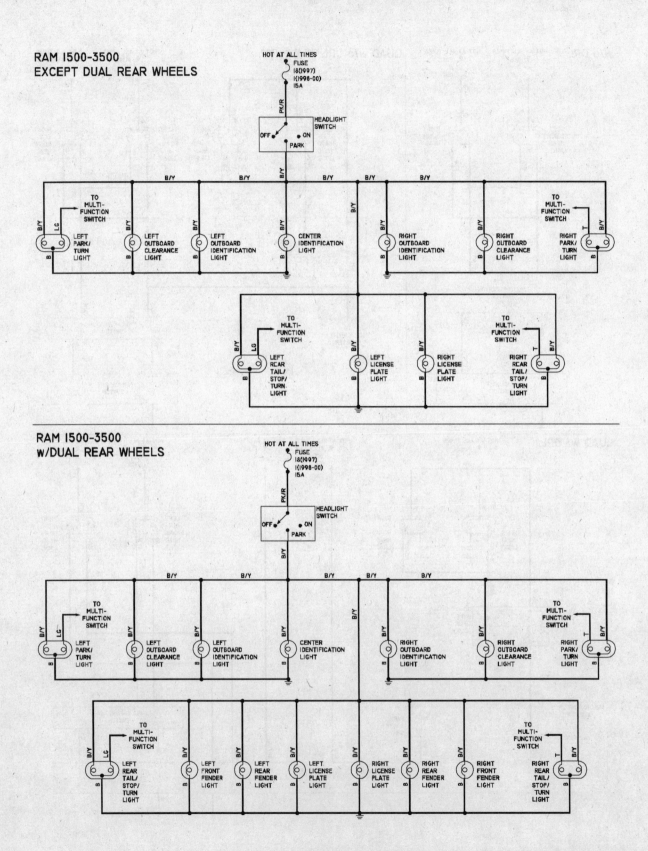

**1997-01 Ram 1500-3500 Chassis Schematics**

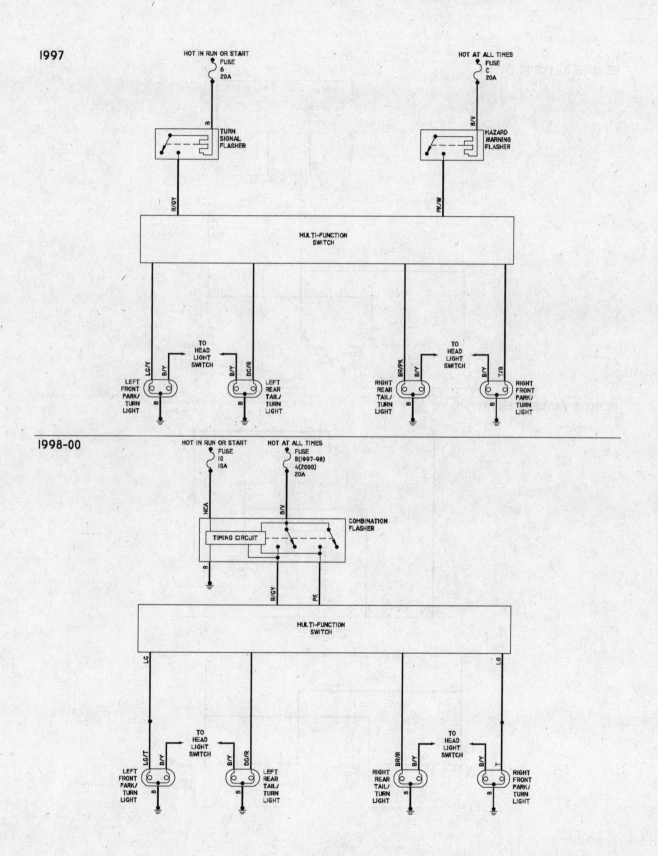

**1997-01 Ram 1500-3500 Chassis Schematics**

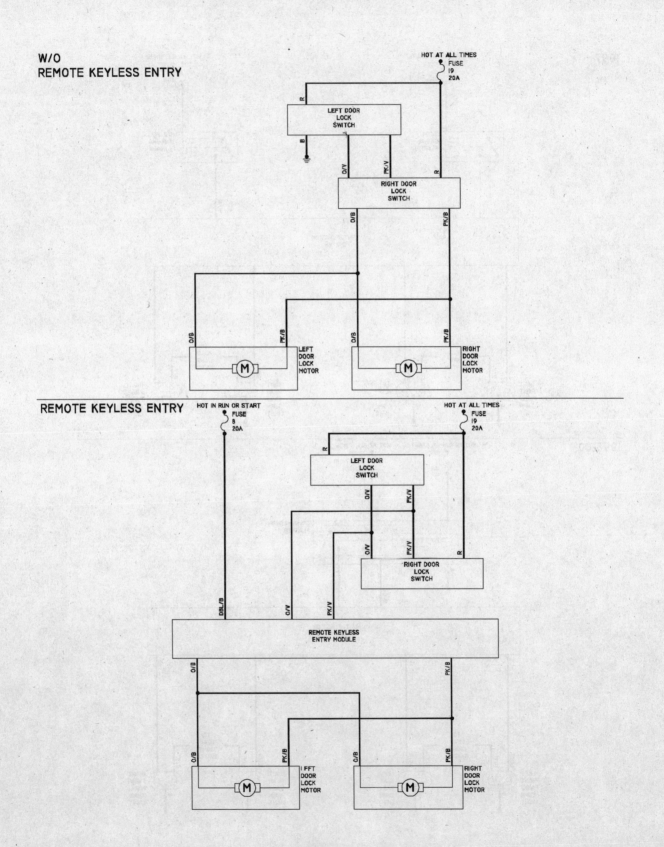

**1997 Ram 1500-3500 Chassis Schematics**

INTEGRATED
ELECTRONIC
MODULE

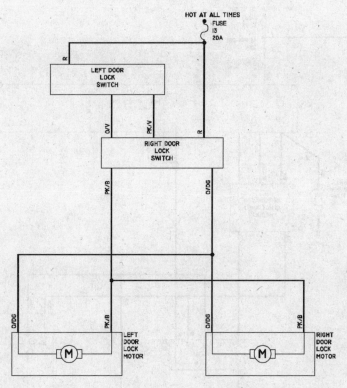

CENTRAL TIMER MODULE

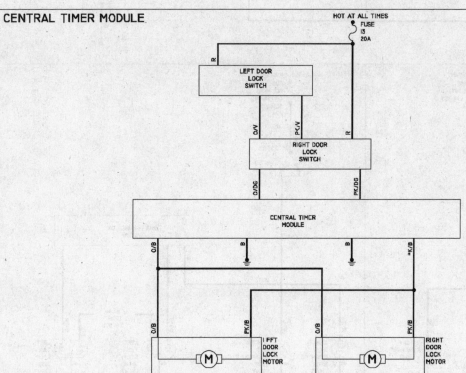

**1998-01 Ram 1500-3500 Chassis Schematics**

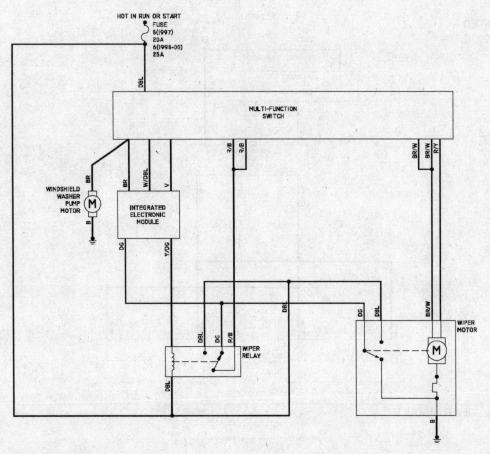

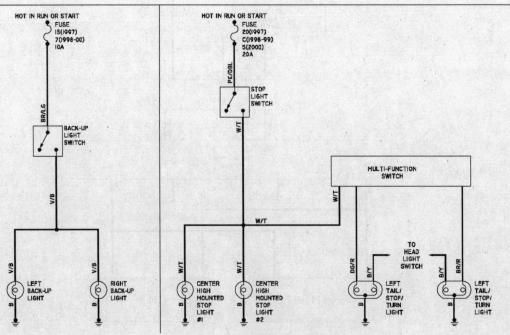

**1997-01 Ram 1500-3500 Chassis Schematics**

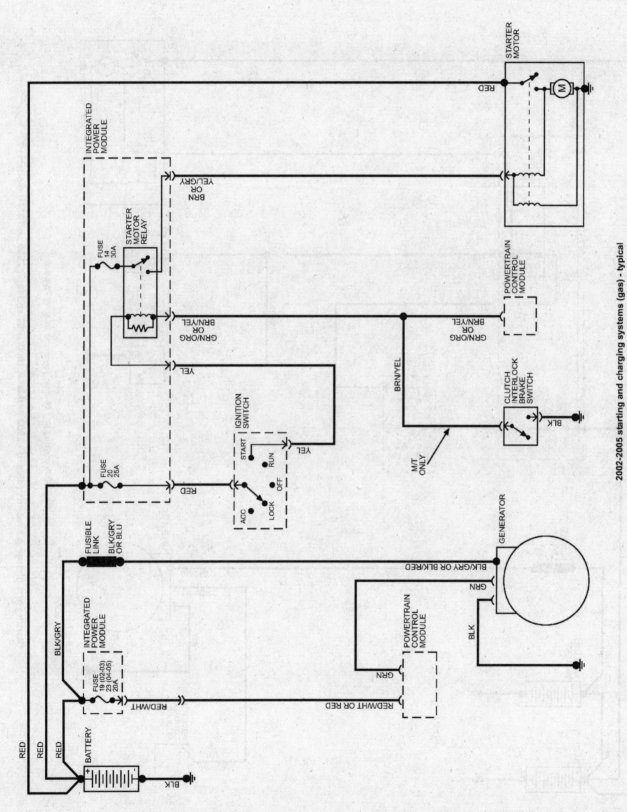

Starting and charging systems (gas) - 2002 and later 1500/2003 and later 2500 and 3500 models

2002-2005 starting and charging systems (gas) - typical

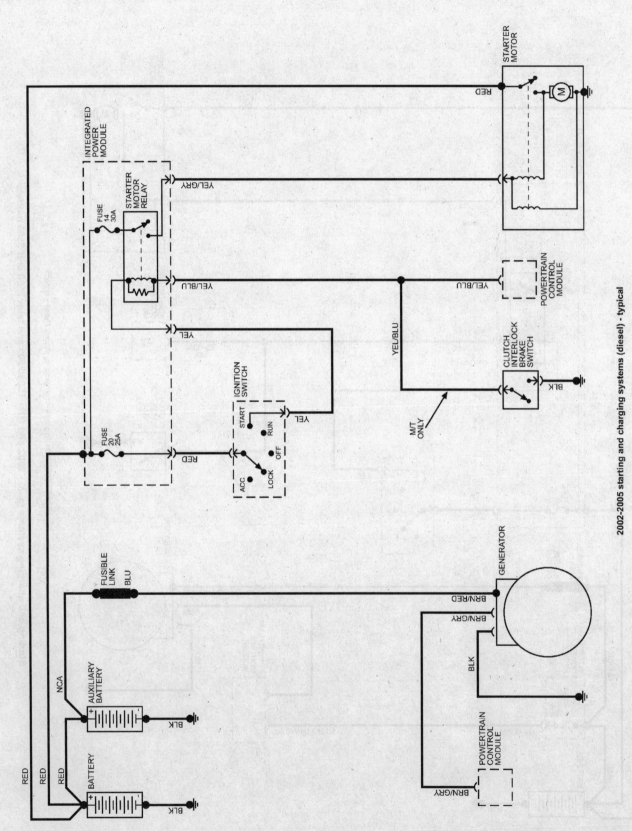

**Starting and charging systems (diesel) - 2002 and later 1500/2003 and later 2500 and 3500 models**

**2002-2005 starting and charging systems (diesel) - typical**

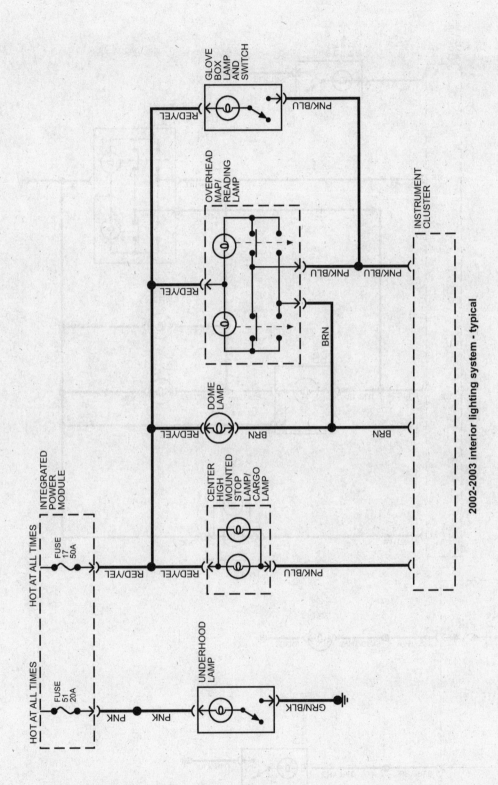

Interior lighting system - 2002 and 2003 1500/2003 2500 and 3500 models (1 of 2)

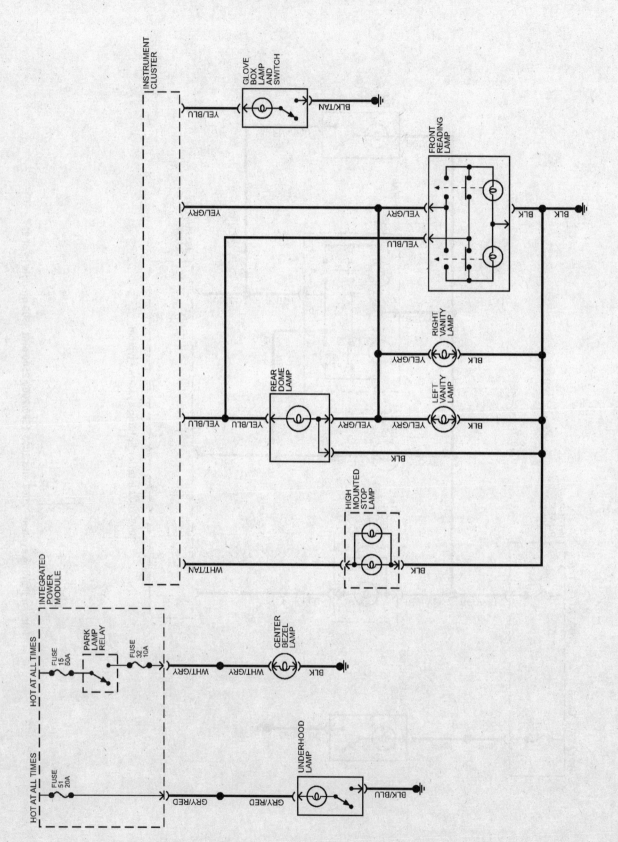

Interior lighting system - 2002 and later 1500/2003 and later 2500 and 3500 models (2 of 2)

2004-2005 interior lighting system - typical

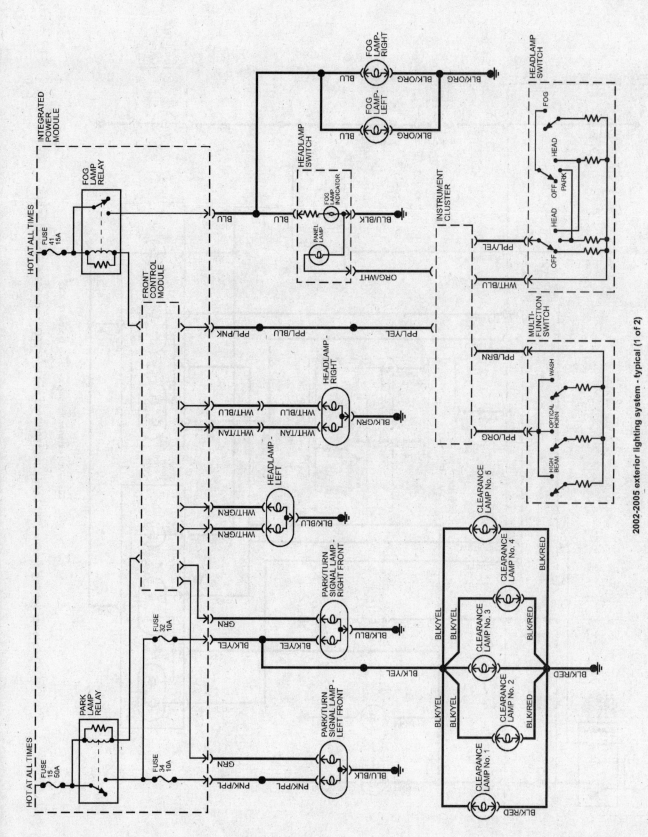

Exterior lighting system - 2002 and later 1500/2003 and later 2500 and 3500 models (1 of 2)

2002-2005 exterior lighting system - typical (1 of 2)

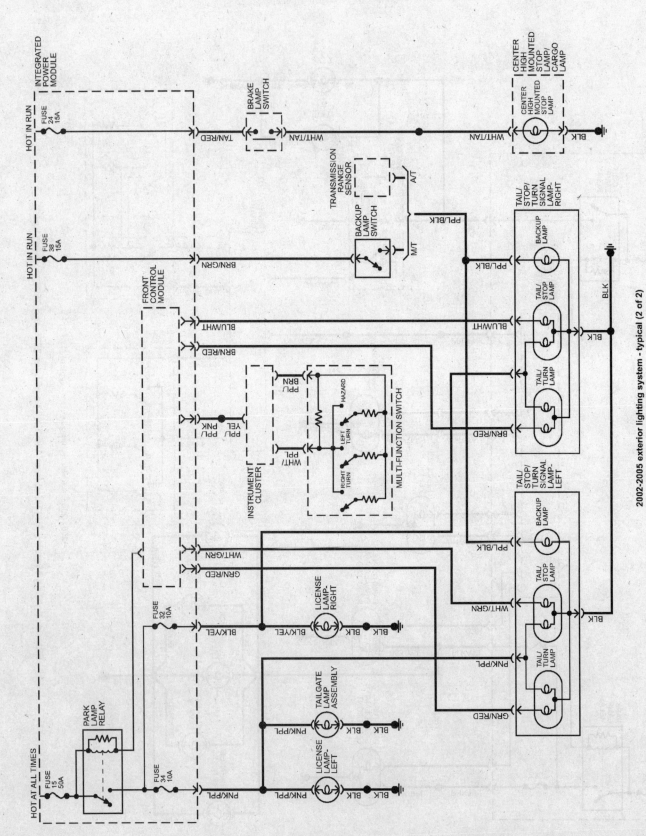

**Exterior lighting system - 2002 and later 1500/2003 and later 2500 and 3500 models (2 of 2)**

2002-2005 exterior lighting system - typical (2 of 2)

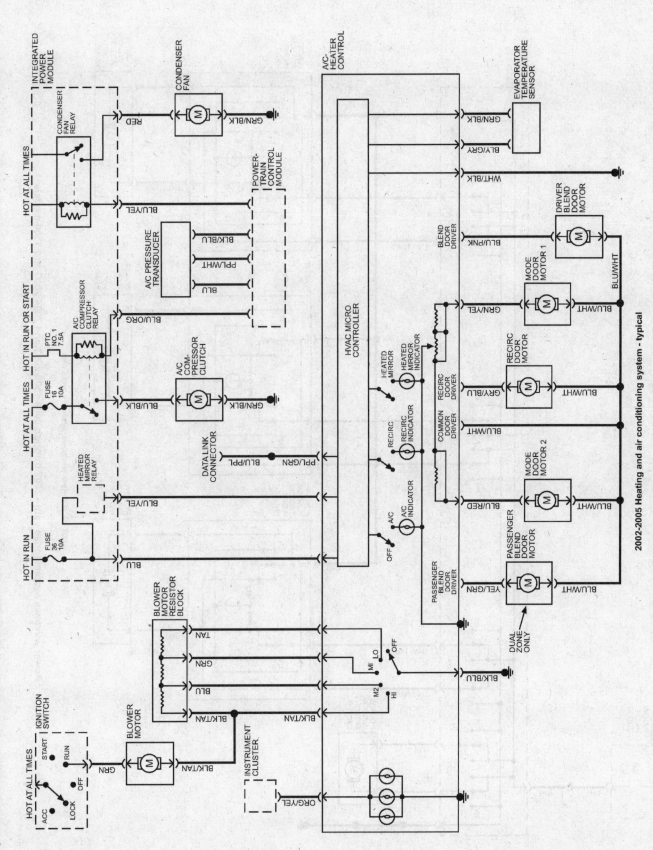

Heating and air conditioning system - 2002 and later 1500/2003 and later 2500 and 3500 models

2002-2005 Heating and air conditioning system - typical

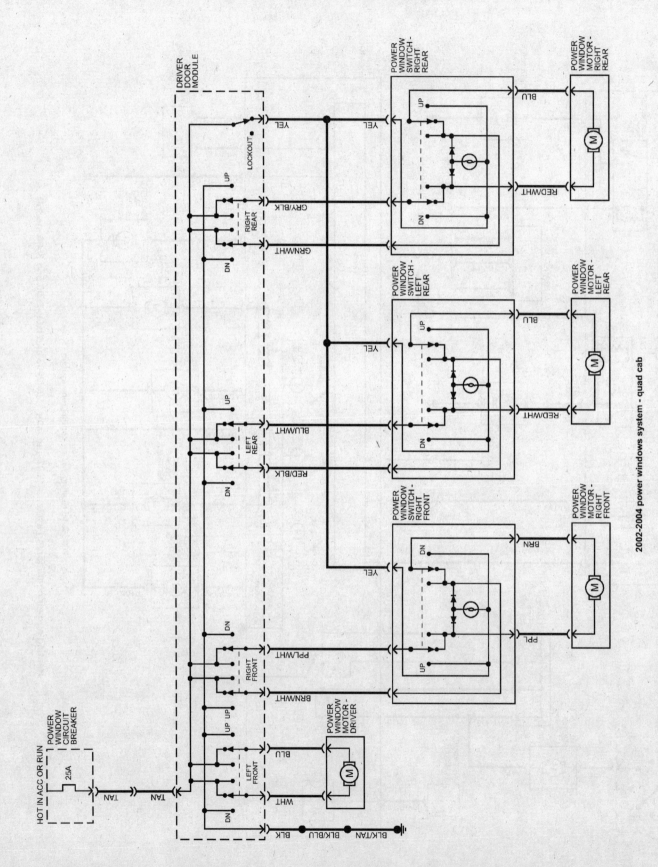

**Power windows system (quad cab) - 2002 through 2004 1500/2003 and 2004 2500 and 3500 models**

2002-2004 power windows system - quad cab

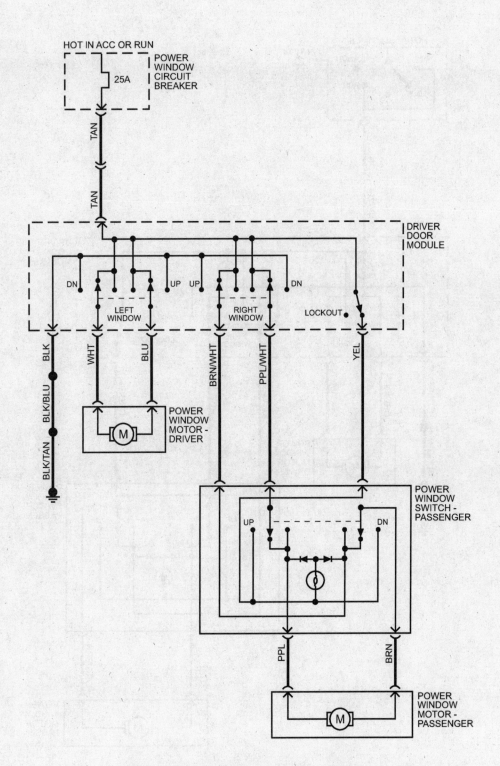

**2002-2004 power windows system - standard cab**

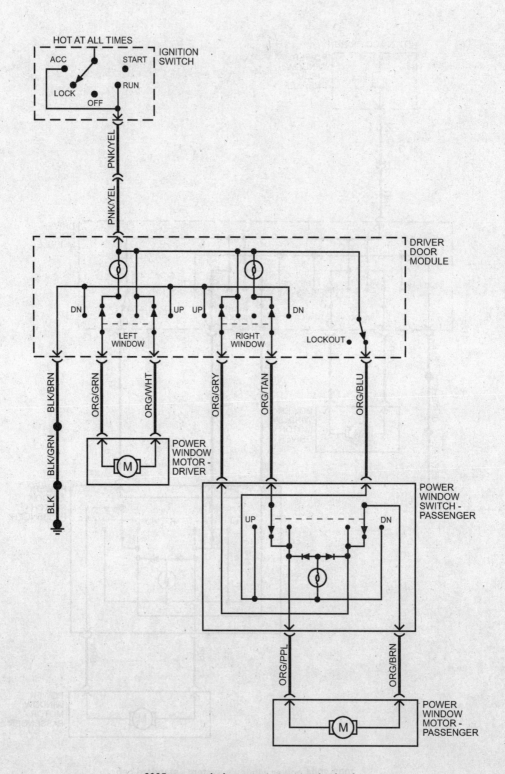

**2005 power windows system - standard cab**

**Power windows system (standard cab) - 2005 and later models**

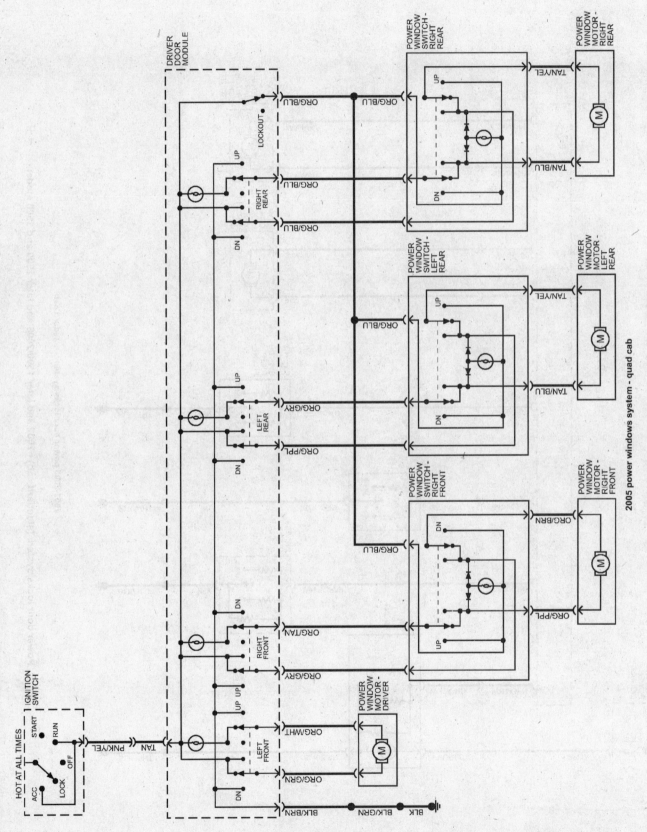

Power windows system (quad cab) - 2005 and later models

2005 power windows system - quad cab

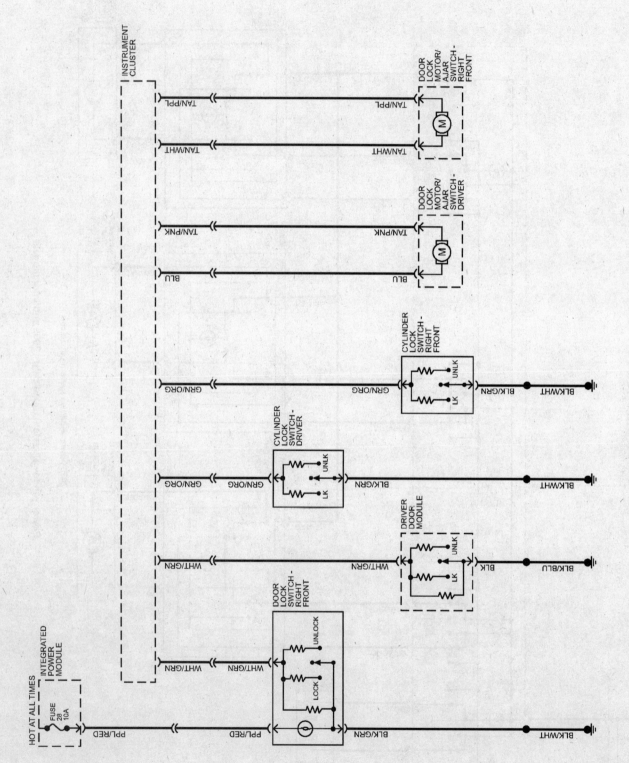

**2002-2005 power door locks system - standard cab**

Power door locks system (standard cab) - 2002 and later 1500/2003 and later 2500 and 3500 models

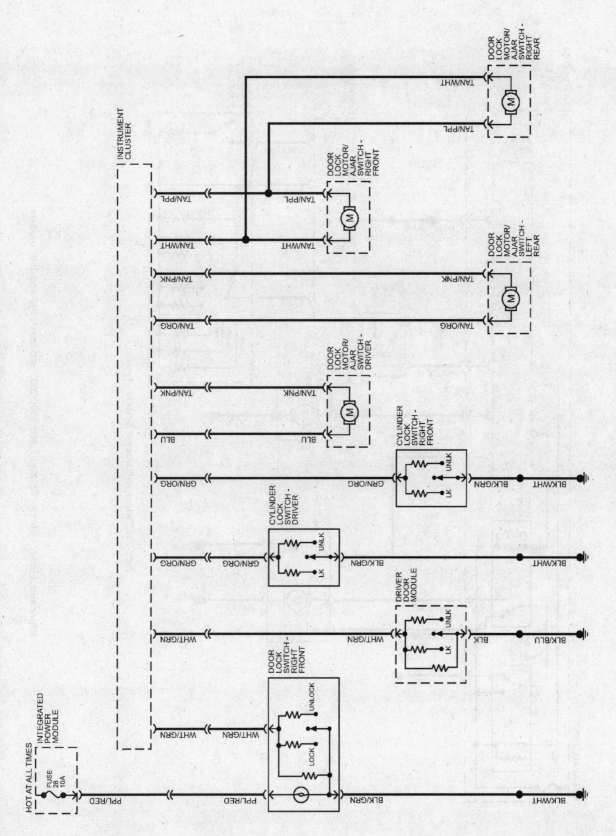

2002-2005 power door locks system - quad cab

Power door locks system (quad cab) - 2002 and later 1500/2003 and later 2500 and 3500 models

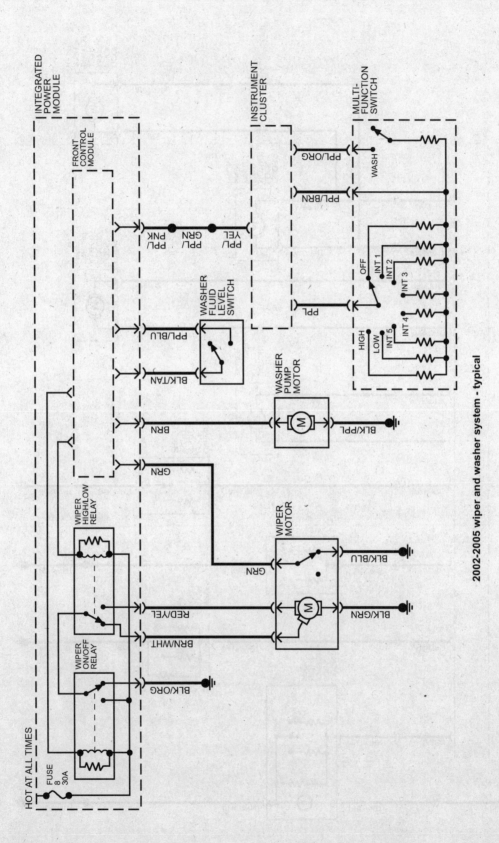

**2002-2005 wiper and washer system - typical**

**Wiper and washer system - 2002 and later 1500/2003 and later 2500 and 3500 models**

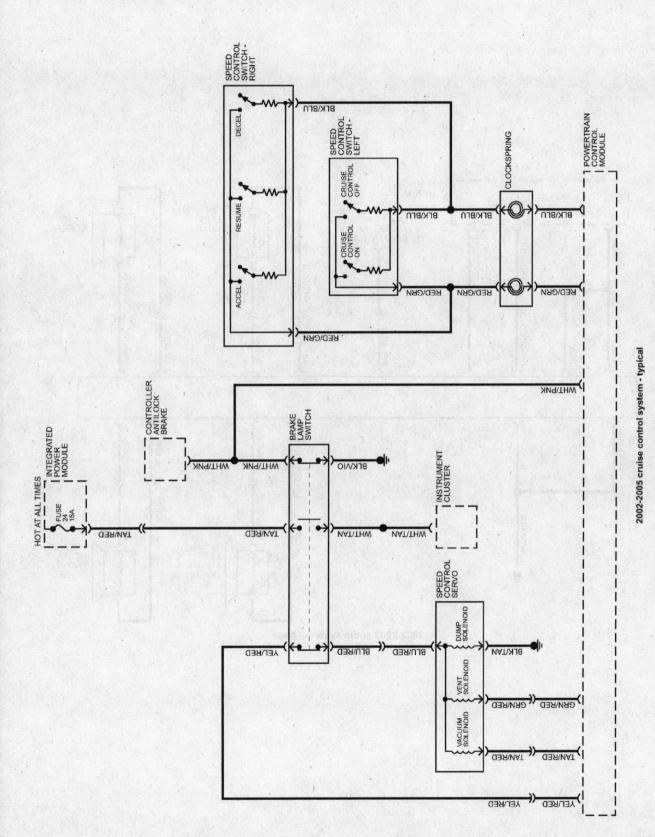

Cruise control system - 2002 and later 1500/2003 and later 2500 and 3500 models

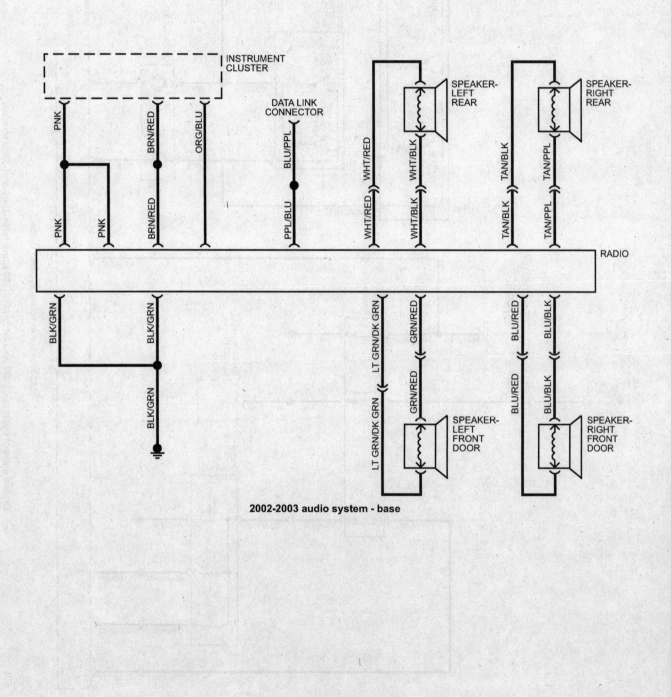

**2002-2003 audio system - base**

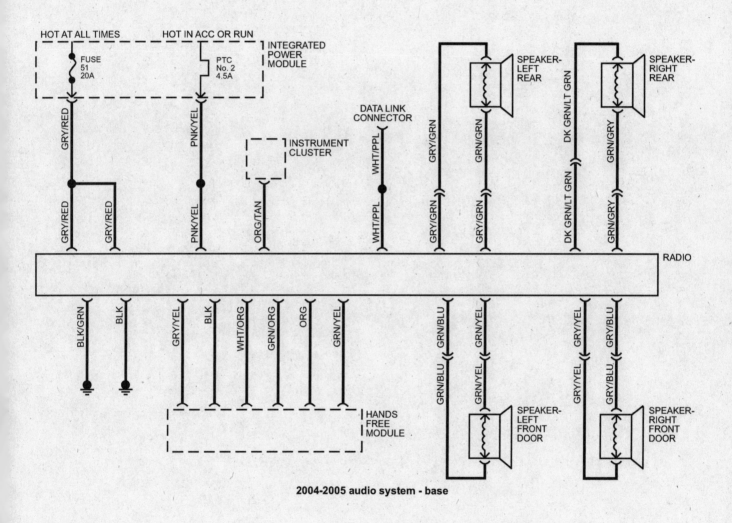

**2004-2005 audio system - base**

# Notes

# Index

## A

# Haynes Automotive Manuals

## ACURA
- **12020** Integra '86 thru '89 & Legend '86 thru '90
- **12021** Integra '90 thru '93 & Legend '91 thru '95
  Integra '94 thru '00 - see HONDA Civic (42025)
  MDX '01 thru '07 - see HONDA Pilot (42037)
- **12050** Acura TL all models '99 thru '08

## AMC
- **14020** Mid-size models '70 thru '83
- **14025** (Renault) Alliance & Encore '83 thru '87

## AUDI
- **15020** 4000 all models '80 thru '87
- **15025** 5000 all models '77 thru '83
- **15026** 5000 all models '84 thru '88
  Audi A4 '96 thru '01 - see VW Passat (96023)
- **15030** Audi A4 '02 thru '08

## AUSTIN-HEALEY
Sprite - see MG Midget (66015)

## BMW
- **18020** 3/5 Series '82 thru '92
- **18021** 3-Series incl. Z3 models '92 thru '98
- **18022** 3-Series incl. Z4 models '99 thru '05
- **18023** 3-Series '06 thru '14
- **18025** 320i all 4-cylinder models '75 thru '83
- **18050** 1500 thru 2002 except Turbo '59 thru '77

## BUICK
- **19010** Buick Century '97 thru '05
  Century (front-wheel drive) - see GM (38005)
- **19020** Buick, Oldsmobile & Pontiac Full-size (Front-wheel drive) '85 thru '05
  Buick Electra, LeSabre and Park Avenue; Oldsmobile Delta 88 Royale, Ninety Eight and Regency; Pontiac Bonneville
- **19025** Buick, Oldsmobile & Pontiac Full-size (Rear wheel drive) '70 thru '90
  Buick Estate, Electra, LeSabre, Limited, Oldsmobile Custom Cruiser, Delta 88, Ninety-eight, Pontiac Bonneville, Catalina, Grandville, Parisienne
- **19027** Buick LaCrosse '05 thru '13
  Enclave - see GENERAL MOTORS (38001)
  Rainier - see CHEVROLET (24072)
  Regal - see GENERAL MOTORS (38010)
  Riviera - see GENERAL MOTORS (38030, 38031)
  Roadmaster - see CHEVROLET (24046)
  Skyhawk - see GENERAL MOTORS (38015)
  Skylark - see GENERAL MOTORS (38020, 38025)
  Somerset - see GENERAL MOTORS (38025)

## CADILLAC
- **21015** CTS & CTS-V '03 thru '14
- **21030** Cadillac Rear Wheel Drive '70 thru '93
  Cimarron - see GENERAL MOTORS (38015)
  DeVille - see GENERAL MOTORS (38031 & 38032)
  Eldorado - see GENERAL MOTORS (38030)
  Fleetwood - see GENERAL MOTORS (38031)
  Seville - see GM (38030, 38031 & 38032)

## CHEVROLET
- **10305** Chevrolet Engine Overhaul Manual
- **24010** Astro & GMC Safari Mini-vans '85 thru '05
- **24013** Aveo '04 thru '11
- **24015** Camaro V8 all models '70 thru '81
- **24016** Camaro all models '82 thru '92
- **24017** Camaro & Firebird '93 thru '02
  Cavalier - see GENERAL MOTORS (38016)
  Celebrity - see GENERAL MOTORS (38005)
- **24018** Camaro '10 thru '15
- **24020** Chevelle, Malibu & El Camino '69 thru '87
  Cobalt - see GENERAL MOTORS (38017)
- **24024** Chevette & Pontiac T1000 '76 thru '87
  Citation - see GENERAL MOTORS (38020)
- **24027** Colorado & GMC Canyon '04 thru '12
- **24032** Corsica & Beretta all models '87 thru '96
- **24040** Corvette all V8 models '68 thru '82
- **24041** Corvette all models '84 thru '96
- **24042** Corvette all models '97 thru '13
- **24044** Cruze '11 thru '19
- **24045** Full-size Sedans Caprice, Impala, Biscayne, Bel Air & Wagons '69 thru '90
- **24046** Impala SS & Caprice and Buick Roadmaster '91 thru '96
  Impala '00 thru '05 - see LUMINA (24048)
- **24047** Impala & Monte Carlo all models '06 thru '11
  Lumina '90 thru '94 - see GM (38010)
- **24048** Lumina & Monte Carlo '95 thru '05
  Lumina APV - see GM (38035)
- **24050** Luv Pick-up all 2WD & 4WD '72 thru '82
- **24051** Malibu '13 thru '19
- **24055** Monte Carlo all models '70 thru '88
  Monte Carlo '95 thru '01 - see LUMINA (24048)
- **24059** Nova all V8 models '69 thru '79
- **24060** Nova and Geo Prizm '85 thru '92
- **24064** Pick-ups '67 thru '87 - Chevrolet & GMC
- **24065** Pick-ups '88 thru '98 - Chevrolet & GMC
- **24066** Pick-ups '99 thru '06 - Chevrolet & GMC
- **24067** Chevrolet Silverado & GMC Sierra '07 thru '14
- **24068** Chevrolet Silverado & GMC Sierra '14 thru '19
- **24070** S-10 & S-15 Pick-ups '82 thru '93, Blazer & Jimmy '83 thru '94,
- **24071** S-10 & Sonoma Pick-ups '94 thru '04, including Blazer, Jimmy & Hombre
- **24072** Chevrolet TrailBlazer, GMC Envoy & Oldsmobile Bravada '02 thru '09
- **24075** Sprint '85 thru '88 & Geo Metro '89 thru '01
- **24080** Vans - Chevrolet & GMC '68 thru '96
- **24081** Chevrolet Express & GMC Savana Full-size Vans '96 thru '19

## CHRYSLER
- **10310** Chrysler Engine Overhaul Manual
- **25015** Chrysler Cirrus, Dodge Stratus, Plymouth Breeze '95 thru '00
- **25020** Full-size Front-Wheel Drive '88 thru '93
  K-Cars - see DODGE Aries (30008)
  Laser - see DODGE Daytona (30030)
- **25025** Chrysler LHS, Concorde, New Yorker, Dodge Intrepid, Eagle Vision, '93 thru '97
- **25026** Chrysler LHS, Concorde, 300M, Dodge Intrepid, '98 thru '04
- **25027** Chrysler 300 '05 thru '18, Dodge Charger '06 thru '18, Magnum '05 thru '08 & Challenger '08 thru '18
- **25030** Chrysler & Plymouth Mid-size front wheel drive '82 thru '95
  Rear-wheel Drive - see Dodge (30050)
- **25035** PT Cruiser all models '01 thru '10
- **25040** Chrysler Sebring '95 thru '06, Dodge Stratus '01 thru '06 & Dodge Avenger '95 thru '00
- **25041** Chrysler Sebring '07 thru '10, 200 '11 thru '17 Dodge Avenger '08 thru '14

## DATSUN
- **28005** 200SX all models '80 thru '83
- **28012** 240Z, 260Z & 280Z Coupe '70 thru '78
- **28014** 280ZX Coupe & 2+2 '79 thru '83
  300ZX - see NISSAN (72010)
- **28018** 510 & PL521 Pick-up '68 thru '73
- **28020** 510 all models '78 thru '81
- **28022** 620 Series Pick-up all models '73 thru '79
  720 Series Pick-up - see NISSAN (72030)

## DODGE
- 400 & 600 - see CHRYSLER (25030)
- **30008** Aries & Plymouth Reliant '81 thru '89
- **30010** Caravan & Plymouth Voyager '84 thru '95
- **30011** Caravan & Plymouth Voyager '96 thru '02
- **30012** Challenger & Plymouth Sapporro '78 thru '83
- **30013** Caravan, Chrysler Voyager & Town & Country '03 thru '07
- **30014** Grand Caravan & Chrysler Town & Country '08 thru '18
- **30016** Colt & Plymouth Champ '78 thru '87
- **30020** Dakota Pick-ups all models '87 thru '96
- **30021** Durango '98 & '99 & Dakota '97 thru '99
- **30022** Durango '00 thru '03 & Dakota '00 thru '04
- **30023** Durango '04 thru '09 & Dakota '05 thru '11
- **30025** Dart, Demon, Plymouth Barracuda, Duster & Valiant 6-cylinder models '67 thru '76
- **30030** Daytona & Chrysler Laser '84 thru '89
  Intrepid - see CHRYSLER (25025, 25026)
- **30034** Neon all models '95 thru '99
- **30035** Omni & Plymouth Horizon '78 thru '90
- **30036** Dodge & Plymouth Neon '00 thru '05
- **30040** Pick-ups full-size models '74 thru '93
- **30042** Pick-ups full-size models '94 thru '08
- **30043** Pick-ups full-size models '09 thru '18
- **30045** Ram 50/D50 Pick-ups & Raider and Plymouth Arrow Pick-ups '79 thru '93
- **30050** Dodge/Plymouth/Chrysler RWD '71 thru '89
- **30055** Shadow & Plymouth Sundance '87 thru '94
- **30060** Spirit & Plymouth Acclaim '89 thru '95
- **30065** Vans - Dodge & Plymouth '71 thru '03

## EAGLE
Talon - see MITSUBISHI (68030, 68031)
Vision - see CHRYSLER (25025)

## FIAT
- **34010** 124 Sport Coupe & Spider '68 thru '78
- **34025** X1/9 all models '74 thru '80

## FORD
- **10320** Ford Engine Overhaul Manual
- **10355** Ford Automatic Transmission Overhaul
- **11500** Mustang '64-1/2 thru '70 Restoration Guide
- **36004** Aerostar Mini-vans all models '86 thru '97
- **36006** Contour & Mercury Mystique '95 thru '00
- **36008** Courier Pick-up all models '72 thru '82
- **36012** Crown Victoria & Mercury Grand Marquis '88 thru '11
- **36014** Edge '07 thru '19 & Lincoln MKX '07 thru '18
- **36016** Escort & Mercury Lynx all models '81 thru '90
- **36020** Escort & Mercury Tracer '91 thru '02
- **36022** Escape '01 thru '17, Mazda Tribute '01 thru '11, & Mercury Mariner '05 thru '11
- **36024** Explorer & Mazda Navajo '91 thru '01
- **36025** Explorer & Mercury Mountaineer '02 thru '10
- **36026** Explorer '11 thru '17
- **36028** Fairmont & Mercury Zephyr '78 thru '83
- **36030** Festiva & Aspire '88 thru '97
- **36032** Fiesta all models '77 thru '80
- **36034** Focus all models '00 thru '11
- **36035** Focus '12 thru '14
- **36045** Fusion '06 thru '14 & Mercury Milan '06 thru '11
- **36048** Mustang V8 all models '64-1/2 thru '73
- **36049** Mustang II 4-cylinder, V6 & V8 models '74 thru '78
- **36050** Mustang & Mercury Capri '79 thru '93
- **36051** Mustang all models '94 thru '04
- **36052** Mustang '05 thru '14
- **36054** Pick-ups & Bronco '73 thru '79
- **36058** Pick-ups & Bronco '80 thru '96
- **36059** F-150 '97 thru '03, Expedition '97 thru '17, F-250 '97 thru '99, F-150 Heritage '04 & Lincoln Navigator '98 thru '17
- **36060** Super Duty Pick-ups & Excursion '99 thru '10
- **36061** F-150 full-size '04 thru '14
- **36062** Pinto & Mercury Bobcat '75 thru '80
- **36063** F-150 full-size '15 thru '17
- **36064** Super Duty Pick-ups '11 thru '16
- **36066** Probe all models '89 thru '92
  Probe '93 thru '97 - see MAZDA 626 (61042)
- **36070** Ranger & Bronco II gas models '83 thru '92
- **36071** Ranger '93 thru '11 & Mazda Pick-ups '94 thru '09
- **36074** Taurus & Mercury Sable '86 thru '95
- **36075** Taurus & Mercury Sable '96 thru '07
- **36076** Taurus '08 thru '14, Five Hundred '05 thru '07, Mercury Montego '05 thru '07 & Sable '08 thru '09
- **36078** Tempo & Mercury Topaz '84 thru '94
- **36082** Thunderbird & Mercury Cougar '83 thru '88
- **36086** Thunderbird & Mercury Cougar '89 thru '97
- **36090** Vans all V8 Econoline models '69 thru '91
- **36094** Vans full size '92 thru '14
- **36097** Windstar '95 thru '03, Freestar & Mercury Monterey Mini-van '04 thru '07

## GENERAL MOTORS
- **10360** GM Automatic Transmission Overhaul
- **38001** GMC Acadia '07 thru '16, Buick Enclave '08 thru '17, Saturn Outlook '07 thru '10 & Chevrolet Traverse '09 thru '17
- **38005** Buick Century, Chevrolet Celebrity, Oldsmobile Cutlass Ciera & Pontiac 6000 all models '82 thru '96
- **38010** Buick Regal '88 thru '04, Chevrolet Lumina '88 thru '04, Oldsmobile Cutlass Supreme '88 thru '97 & Pontiac Grand Prix '88 thru '07
- **38015** Buick Skyhawk, Cadillac Cimarron, Chevrolet Cavalier, Oldsmobile Firenza, Pontiac J-2000 & Sunbird '82 thru '94
- **38016** Chevrolet Cavalier & Pontiac Sunfire '95 thru '05
- **38017** Chevrolet Cobalt '05 thru '10, HHR '06 thru '11, Pontiac G5 '07 thru '09, Pursuit '05 thru '06 & Saturn ION '03 thru '07
- **38020** Buick Skylark, Chevrolet Citation, Oldsmobile Omega, Pontiac Phoenix '80 thru '85
- **38025** Buick Skylark '86 thru '98, Somerset '85 thru '87, Oldsmobile Achieva '92 thru '98, Calais '85 thru '91, & Pontiac Grand Am all models '85 thru '98
- **38026** Chevrolet Malibu '97 thru '03, Classic '04 thru '05, Oldsmobile Alero '99 thru '03, Cutlass '97 thru '00, & Pontiac Grand Am '99 thru '03
- **38027** Chevrolet Malibu '04 thru '12, Pontiac G6 '05 thru '10 & Saturn Aura '07 thru '10
- **38030** Cadillac Eldorado, Seville, Oldsmobile Toronado & Buick Riviera '71 thru '85
- **38031** Cadillac Eldorado, Seville, DeVille, Fleetwood, Oldsmobile Toronado & Buick Riviera '86 thru '93
- **38032** Cadillac DeVille '94 thru '05, Seville '92 thru '04 & Cadillac DTS '06 thru '10
- **38035** Chevrolet Lumina APV, Oldsmobile Silhouette & Pontiac Trans Sport all models '90 thru '96
- **38036** Chevrolet Venture '97 thru '05, Oldsmobile Silhouette '97 thru '04, Pontiac Trans Sport '97 thru '98 & Montana '99 thru '05
- **38040** Chevrolet Equinox '05 thru '17, GMC Terrain '10 thru '17 & Pontiac Torrent '06 thru '09

## GEO
Metro - see CHEVROLET Sprint (24075)
Prizm - '85 thru '92 see CHEVY (24060), '93 thru '02 see TOYOTA Corolla (92036)
- **40030** Storm all models '90 thru '93
Tracker - see SUZUKI Samurai (90010)

*(Continued on other side)*

# Haynes Automotive Manuals (continued)

NOTE: If you do not see a listing for your vehicle, please visit **haynes.com** for the latest product information and check out our **Online Manuals!**

## GMC

Acadia - see GENERAL MOTORS (38001)
Pick-ups - see CHEVROLET (24027, 24068)
Vans - see CHEVROLET (24081)

## HONDA

42010 Accord CVCC all models '76 thru '83
42011 Accord all models '84 thru '89
42012 Accord all models '90 thru '93
42013 Accord all models '94 thru '97
42014 Accord all models '98 thru '02
42015 Accord '03 thru '12 & Crosstour '10 thru '14
42016 Accord '13 thru '17
42020 Civic 1200 all models '73 thru '79
42021 Civic 1300 & 1500 CVCC '80 thru '83
42022 Civic 1500 CVCC all models '75 thru '79
42023 Civic all models '84 thru '91
42024 Civic & del Sol '92 thru '95
42025 Civic '96 thru '00, CR-V '97 thru '01 & Acura Integra '94 thru '00
42026 Civic '01 thru '11 & CR-V '02 thru '11
42027 Civic '12 thru '15 & CR-V '12 thru '16
42030 Fit '07 thru '13
42035 Odyssey all models '99 thru '10
Passport - see ISUZU Rodeo (47017)
42037 Honda Pilot '03 thru '08, Ridgeline '06 thru '14 & Acura MDX '01 thru '07
42040 Prelude CVCC all models '79 thru '89

## HYUNDAI

43010 Elantra all models '96 thru '19
43015 Excel & Accent all models '86 thru '13
43050 Santa Fe all models '01 thru '12
43055 Sonata all models '99 thru '14

## INFINITI

G35 '03 thru '08 - see NISSAN 350Z (72011)

## ISUZU

Hombre - see CHEVROLET S-10 (24071)
47017 Rodeo '91 thru '02, Amigo '89 thru '94 & '98 thru '02 & Honda Passport '95 thru '02
47020 Trooper '84 thru '91 & Pick-up '81 thru '93

## JAGUAR

49010 XJ6 all 6-cylinder models '68 thru '86
49011 XJ6 all models '88 thru '94
49015 XJ12 & XJS all 12-cylinder models '72 thru '85

## JEEP

50010 Cherokee, Comanche & Wagoneer Limited all models '84 thru '01
50011 Cherokee '14 thru '19
50020 CJ all models '49 thru '86
50025 Grand Cherokee all models '93 thru '04
50026 Grand Cherokee '05 thru '19 & Dodge Durango '11 thru '19
50029 Grand Wagoneer & Pick-up '72 thru '91
Grand Wagoneer '84 thru '91, Cherokee & Wagoneer '72 thru '83, Pick-up '72 thru '88
50030 Wrangler all models '87 thru '17
50035 Liberty '02 thru '12 & Dodge Nitro '07 thru '11
50050 Patriot & Compass '07 thru '17

## KIA

54050 Optima '01 thru '10
54060 Sedona '02 thru '14
54070 Sephia '94 thru '01, Spectra '00 thru '09, Sportage '05 thru '20
54077 Sorento '03 thru '13

## LEXUS

ES 300/330 - see TOYOTA Camry (92007, 92008)
ES 350 - see TOYOTA Camry (92009)
RX 300/330/350 - see TOYOTA Highlander (92095)

## LINCOLN

MKX - see FORD (36014)
Navigator - see FORD Pick-up (36059)
59010 Rear-Wheel Drive Continental '70 thru '87, Mark Series '70 thru '92 & Town Car '81 thru '10

## MAZDA

61010 GLC (rear-wheel drive) '77 thru '83
61011 GLC (front-wheel drive) '81 thru '85
61012 Mazda3 '04 thru '11
61015 323 & Protegé '90 thru '03
61016 MX-5 Miata '90 thru '14
61020 MPV all models '89 thru '98
Navajo - see Ford Explorer (36024)
61030 Pick-ups '72 thru '93
Pick-ups '94 thru '09 - see Ford Ranger (36071)
61035 RX-7 all models '79 thru '85
61036 RX-7 all models '86 thru '91
61040 626 (rear-wheel drive) all models '79 thru '82
61041 626 & MX-6 (front-wheel drive) '83 thru '92
61042 626 '93 thru '01 & MX-6/Ford Probe '93 thru '02
61043 Mazda6 '03 thru '13

## MERCEDES-BENZ

63012 123 Series Diesel '76 thru '85
63015 190 Series 4-cylinder gas models '84 thru '88
63020 230/250/280 6-cylinder SOHC models '68 thru '72
63025 280 123 Series gas models '77 thru '81
63030 350 & 450 all models '71 thru '80
63040 C-Class: C230/C240/C280/C320/C350 '01 thru '07

## MERCURY

64200 Villager & Nissan Quest '93 thru '01
All other titles, see FORD Listing.

## MG

66010 MGB Roadster & GT Coupe '62 thru '80
66015 MG Midget, Austin Healey Sprite '58 thru '80

## MINI

67020 Mini '02 thru '13

## MITSUBISHI

68020 Cordia, Tredia, Galant, Precis & Mirage '83 thru '93
68030 Eclipse, Eagle Talon & Plymouth Laser '90 thru '94
68031 Eclipse '95 thru '05 & Eagle Talon '95 thru '98
68035 Galant '94 thru '12
68040 Pick-up '83 thru '96 & Montero '83 thru '93

## NISSAN

72010 300ZX all models including Turbo '84 thru '89
72011 350Z & Infiniti G35 all models '03 thru '08
72015 Altima all models '93 thru '06
72016 Altima '07 thru '12
72020 Maxima all models '85 thru '92
72021 Maxima all models '93 thru '08
72025 Murano '03 thru '14
72030 Pick-ups '80 thru '97 & Pathfinder '87 thru '95
72031 Frontier '98 thru '04, Xterra '00 thru '04, & Pathfinder '96 thru '04
72032 Frontier & Xterra '05 thru '14
72037 Pathfinder '05 thru '14
72040 Pulsar all models '83 thru '86
72042 Roque all models '08 thru '20
72050 Sentra all models '82 thru '94
72051 Sentra & 200SX all models '95 thru '06
72060 Stanza all models '82 thru '90
72070 Titan pick-ups '04 thru '10, Armada '05 thru '10 & Pathfinder Armada '04
72080 Versa all models '07 thru '19

## OLDSMOBILE

73015 Cutlass V6 & V8 gas models '74 thru '88
For other OLDSMOBILE titles, see BUICK, CHEVROLET or GENERAL MOTORS listings.

## PLYMOUTH

For PLYMOUTH titles, see DODGE listing.

## PONTIAC

79008 Fiero all models '84 thru '88
79018 Firebird V8 models except Turbo '70 thru '81
79019 Firebird all models '82 thru '92
79025 G6 all models '05 thru '09
79040 Mid-size Rear-wheel Drive '70 thru '87
Vibe '03 thru '10 - see TOYOTA Corolla (92037)
For other PONTIAC titles, see BUICK, CHEVROLET or GENERAL MOTORS listings.

## PORSCHE

80020 911 Coupe & Targa models '65 thru '89
80025 914 all 4-cylinder models '69 thru '76
80030 924 all models including Turbo '76 thru '82
80035 944 all models including Turbo '83 thru '89

## RENAULT

Alliance & Encore - see AMC (14025)

## SAAB

84010 900 all models including Turbo '79 thru '88

## SATURN

87010 Saturn all S-series models '91 thru '02
Saturn Ion '03 thru '07- see GM (38017)
Saturn Outlook - see GM (38001)
87020 Saturn L-series all models '00 thru '04
87040 Saturn VUE '02 thru '09

## SUBARU

89002 1100, 1300, 1400 & 1600 '71 thru '79
89003 1600 & 1800 2WD & 4WD '80 thru '94
89080 Impreza '02 thru '11, WRX '02 thru '14, & WRX STI '04 thru '14
89100 Legacy all models '90 thru '99
89101 Legacy & Forester '00 thru '09
89102 Legacy '10 thru '16 & Forester '12 thru '16

## SUZUKI

90010 Samurai/Sidekick & Geo Tracker '86 thru '01

## TOYOTA

92005 Camry all models '83 thru '91
92006 Camry '92 thru '96 & Avalon '95 thru '96
92007 Camry, Avalon, Solara, Lexus ES 300 '97 thru '01

92008 Camry, Avalon, Lexus ES 300/330 '02 thru '06 & Solara '02 thru '08
92009 Camry, Avalon & Lexus ES 350 '07 thru '17
92015 Celica Rear-wheel Drive '71 thru '85
92020 Celica Front-wheel Drive '86 thru '99
92025 Celica Supra all models '79 thru '92
92030 Corolla all models '75 thru '79
92032 Corolla all rear-wheel drive models '80 thru '87
92035 Corolla all front-wheel drive models '84 thru '92
92036 Corolla & Geo/Chevrolet Prizm '93 thru '02
92037 Corolla '03 thru '19, Matrix '03 thru '14, & Pontiac Vibe '03 thru '10
92040 Corolla Tercel all models '80 thru '82
92045 Corona all models '74 thru '82
92050 Cressida all models '78 thru '82
92055 Land Cruiser FJ40, 43, 45, 55 '68 thru '82
92056 Land Cruiser FJ60, 62, 80, FZJ80 '80 thru '96
92060 Matrix '03 thru '11 & Pontiac Vibe '03 thru '10
92065 MR2 all models '85 thru '87
92070 Pick-up all models '69 thru '78
92075 Pick-up all models '79 thru '95
92076 Tacoma '95 thru '04, 4Runner '96 thru '02 & T100 '93 thru '08
92077 Tacoma all models '05 thru '18
92078 Tundra '00 thru '06 & Sequoia '01 thru '07
92079 4Runner all models '03 thru '09
92080 Previa all models '91 thru '95
92081 Prius all models '01 thru '12
92082 RAV4 all models '96 thru '12
92085 Tercel all models '87 thru '94
92090 Sienna all models '98 thru '10
92095 Highlander '01 thru '19 & Lexus RX330/330/350 '99 thru '19
92179 Tundra '07 thru '19 & Sequoia '08 thru '19

## TRIUMPH

94007 Spitfire all models '62 thru '81
94010 TR7 all models '75 thru '81

## VW

96008 Beetle & Karmann Ghia '54 thru '79
96009 New Beetle '98 thru '10
96016 Rabbit, Jetta, Scirocco & Pick-up gas models '75 thru '92 & Convertible '80 thru '92
96017 Golf, GTI & Jetta '93 thru '98, Cabrio '95 thru '02
96018 Golf, GTI, Jetta '99 thru '05
96019 Jetta, Rabbit, GLI, GTI & Golf '05 thru '11
96020 Rabbit, Jetta & Pick-up diesel '77 thru '84
96021 Jetta '11 thru '18 & Golf '15 thru '19
96023 Passat '98 thru '05 & Audi A4 '96 thru '01
96030 Transporter 1600 all models '68 thru '79
96035 Transporter 1700, 1800 & 2000 '72 thru '79
96040 Type 3 1500 & 1600 all models '63 thru '73
96045 Vanagon Air-Cooled all models '80 thru '83

## VOLVO

97010 120, 130 Series & 1800 Sports '61 thru '73
97015 140 Series all models '66 thru '74
97020 240 Series all models '76 thru '93
97040 740 & 760 Series all models '82 thru '88
97050 850 Series all models '93 thru '97

## TECHBOOK MANUALS

10205 Automotive Computer Codes
10206 OBD-II & Electronic Engine Management
10210 Automotive Emissions Control Manual
10215 Fuel Injection Manual '78 thru '85
10225 Holley Carburetor Manual
10230 Rochester Carburetor Manual
10305 Chevrolet Engine Overhaul Manual
10320 Ford Engine Overhaul Manual
10330 GM and Ford Diesel Engine Repair Manual
10331 Duramax Diesel Engines '01 thru '19
10332 Cummins Diesel Engine Performance Manual
10333 GM, Ford & Chrysler Engine Performance Manual
10334 GM Engine Performance Manual
10340 Small Engine Repair Manual, 5 HP & Less
10341 Small Engine Repair Manual, 5.5 HP 20 HP
10345 Suspension, Steering & Driveline Manual
10355 Ford Automatic Transmission Overhaul
10360 GM Automatic Transmission Overhaul
10405 Automotive Body Repair & Painting
10410 Automotive Brake Manual
10411 Automotive Anti-lock Brake (ABS) Systems
10420 Automotive Electrical Manual
10425 Automotive Heating & Air Conditioning
10435 Automotive Tools Manual
10445 Welding Manual
10450 ATV Basics

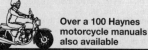

Over a 100 Haynes motorcycle manuals also available

10/22

**Haynes North America, Inc. • (805) 498-6703 • www.haynes.com**